Case Studies in Drowning Forensics

Case Studies in Drowning Forensics

by
Kevin Gannon
D. Lee Gilbertson

with Contributions by
Anthony Duarte

CRC Press
Taylor & Francis Group
Boca Raton London New York

CRC Press is an imprint of the
Taylor & Francis Group, an **informa** business

CRC Press
Taylor & Francis Group
6000 Broken Sound Parkway NW, Suite 300
Boca Raton, FL 33487-2742

First issued in paperback 2020

ISBN-13: 978-1-4398-7664-0 (hbk)
ISBN-13: 978-0-367-65593-8 (pbk)

Library of Congress Cataloging-in-Publication Data

Gannon, Kevin.
Studies in drowning forensics / Kevin Gannon and D. Lee Gilbertson.
pages cm
Includes bibliographical references and index.
ISBN 978-1-4665-3993-8 (alk. paper)
1. Drowning--Case studies. 2. Forensic pathology--Case studies. I. Gilbertson, D. Lee. II. Title.

RA1076.G36 2013
617.1'8--dc23 2013032170

Visit the Taylor & Francis Web site at
http://www.taylorandfrancis.com

and the CRC Press Web site at
http://www.crcpress.com

Dedication

First and foremost, this book is dedicated to a very special group of persons. It is dedicated to those young men whose lives were erased from this earth and whose deaths were not fully, or properly in some cases, investigated by those in authority. This includes the men whose stories appear in this text as well as the hundreds of others that we know about, and the untold number that we may not know.

Second, this book is dedicated to the parents of those young men. We extend our most sincere and heartfelt understanding to the moms and dads. Losing a loved one is difficult, but it does not compare to losing a child. We have seen and heard mothers and fathers respond in different ways, silent withdrawal, lashing out in anger, or releasing their pain with a gut-wrenching primeval scream. There are many more families out there whom we personally know who have been touched by mysterious drowning deaths than the few presented herein. We pray for all of you throughout the year. We apologize if your son's story was not presented within the pages of this work. We could only present a few of the cases without composing a document that could easily become too large and unmanageable. In some cases, we did not have the documentation that we would need to properly evaluate your son's death.

Our hope is that this book will increase recognition of all of these young men's stories, fostering a greater interest among those persons in authority to act upon them. We thank all of the mothers and fathers for believing in our integrity, professionalism, compassion, and fairness. You knew that we would continue to ethically and correctly work on your sons' cases no matter how long it took. We have tried to physically get to as many as possible, and to provide each family with the same measure of care and investigatory skill. But, there were only so many hours in a year. We thank you for understanding how busy we were, especially when we didn't call you back right away.

Finally, this book is dedicated to those men and women who have sworn to serve and protect – the Thin Blue Line. It is our desire as authors, a detective supervisor and a criminal justice professor, that this document will educate those who perform death investigations and autopsies so they can do their jobs even better in the interest of justice for victims and families.

Kevin Gannon
D. Lee Gilbertson

Contents

Foreword

This book written by Kevin Gannon and Dr. D. Lee Gilbertson is compiled from case studies after years of working, actually physically responding to, and investigating the suspicious drowning deaths of young men all across the United States and Canada. I was fortunate to have been a part of this enormous, complicated, and very expensive expedition. The information obtained during our quest for the truth is subsequently encompassed here in this text.

Kevin Gannon and Lee Gilbertson have produced an exceptionally detailed book on ways and methods to differentiate homicide and water-related deaths for the field investigator. Their explanation of the various procedures that could be adopted to identify homicide is extensive and based on considerable investigative experience. I believe that this book and subsequent books will stand for many years as the international standard and definitive source of information on investigative techniques on the forensics of drowning.

I am, of course, biased, as I happened to observe firsthand the tedious reading and examining (over and over again) of documentation and photographs of victims and onsite locations. More importantly, I witnessed the on-scene investigations into the suspicious nature of these drownings, as well as the collection, deciphering, and analyzing of the material related to the victims and potential suspects who were responsible for these heinous acts.

I provided the role of the skeptic throughout all of this. I, like the police and medical examiners, was the "doubting Thomas" who had to be shown every piece of evidence along the way to substantiate the fact that murder was in fact being committed, much less by an organized group of individuals across North America.

The first thing these two (Gannon and Gilbertson) realized was that they needed to prove all of the victims were murdered and not just a couple of young men, which the authorities have agreed with in the cases of Patrick McNeil and Christopher Jenkins. Then, what was needed was that the cases were definitely connected; especially, after all the disbelief from skeptics such as the police, medical examiners, criminal profilers, and the FBI. They also wanted to prove their initial claim that not only were these young men being abducted, drugged, and murdered, but that they were actually being held for a period of time before they were being placed into the water. This I felt was unnecessary and was a significantly more difficult process than just proving murder. To then prove the cases were connected along with having to identify those who were responsible for these horrific crimes were more than what was their responsibility. This was the role of law enforcement.

The amazing thing throughout this whole investigation was that they both were right. Yes, the victims were murdered. Yes, in most cases, the victims were drugged before being abducted. I would have been content to stop right there. Unfortunately, they had to prove more. Yes, there was an organized group or organization that was responsible for this behavior. Many people thought they were crazy when they claimed that this organization's sick behavior also involved the holding and possible torturing (physically and mentally) of the victims before their actual murder. But, they also proved that to be true as well.

Unfortunately, for the public in general, for the families specifically, and for law enforcement and the medical community as a whole, the facts to substantiate their claim in many cases were right there in the official reports and were missed by everyone. This isn't something that they made up, but something that is recognized forensically by experts in the field of medical pathology. These are things that will not hold water unless they are substantiated by physical and forensic fact(s) and evidence (as they are in this text) and not by supposition, conjecture, or speculation.

In their search for the truth, which is contained within these pages, you will read the amazing case studies of 13 vibrant young men whose lives were violently taken not only from them and their families but also from all of us as these were the future leaders of our nation. You now get a glimpse into not only the mind(s) of a serial killer(s) but also into the inner workings of the most complicated investigation in the annals of American or criminal law enforcement. I say this as this movement has now apparently spread and has been recently recognized in Europe.

I sincerely congratulate the authors on their tremendous effort to produce this comprehensive invaluable text on drowning forensics. I would like to strongly recommend it to the whole cross section of professionals, researchers, and academics who deal with the examination and evaluation of drowning deaths. I am thankful to have actually been a part of this investigation and to have been associated with these two brilliant investigators.

Anthony Duarte
U.S. Department of Homeland Security
Transportation Security Manager
Expert Behavior Detection Officer
NYPD Detective 2nd Grade (Retired)

Preface

On a Friday night in April 2011, I was watching the Public Broadcasting Station (PBS) channel and caught a newly released documentary entitled "Post Mortem: Death Investigation in America." It was based on a cooperative investigation conducted by ProPublica, National Public Radio (NPR), and the Investigative Reporting Program at the University of California – Berkeley. In that documentary, investigator reporter Lowell Bergman (previously of *60 Minutes*) examined the state of affairs of forensic pathology and the coroner system in this country. Bergman presented video clips from his interviews with some of the most well-respected forensic pathologists in the United States: Dr. Vincent DiMaio, former Chief Medical Examiner, San Antonio, Texas; Dr. Marcella Fierro, former Chief Medical Examiner, Virginia; and Dr. Ross Zumwalt, Chief Medical Investigator, New Mexico. Each of these experts suggested that the state of affairs of forensic pathology in this country is in shambles.

Unbeknownst to me was the fact that a lot of small counties where it is extremely hot (especially in the rural south) didn't even have the proper facilities with air conditioning, must less refrigerated containers to hold and preserve bodies requiring autopsy. The autopsies were sometimes done in a garage or shack and without refrigeration along with poor lighting, thus complicating the diagnosis of the decedent as to whether or not there was any foul play, along with identifying any physical or trace evidence. This was even when the autopsy was done right away. If the body was held for any period of time, then all parts of decomposition, insects and so forth, have already contaminated the autopsy process.

What was really disturbing was that I always assumed that a forensic pathologist was almost infallible when it came to a medical diagnosis. Of course, after reviewing numerous autopsies and examinations over the years, I have found much to my dismay that this isn't correct. Having a good autopsy depends on the pathologist you have, like having a thorough investigation from the police depends on what type of investigator you have who is working your or your family's case. The documentary covered the fact that coroners (some with little or no medical or scientific background) in over 1,300 counties across America are often in charge of autopsies and investigations into possibly suspicious deaths. Some coroners can be medical doctors who are gynecologists or foot doctors and have no business doing any type of autopsy to begin with, much less one in a criminal or suspicious investigation. One segment told about a coroner in New Orleans who shipped out bodies to forensic pathologists for autopsy. He had a history of assessing cases and filing official reports that sometimes conflicted with pathologists' findings and were based specifically on what the police wanted the final scenario to be. In the documentary, pathologists who had no business being forensic pathologists, or worse, presiding over death investigations, were shuffled from agency to agency (mostly in California) making mistake after mistake.

In the documentary, Dr. DiMaio stated: "You could run a dead person for coroner and he'd probably get elected." He also stated that there are approximately 500 forensic pathologists in the country, which is about half of what we should have as a nation. If the country is already 50% short on the number of forensic pathologists needed to properly investigate crimes in this country and a portion of them – small as it may be – are incompetent to say the least, then it really shows the deep problems that exists in handling any type of suspicious death in our country. A California coroner (Los Angeles County) postulated that, in any given year, he would be unable to autopsy the body in 2/3rds (40,000 or 66%) of the 60,000 cases he received. Chief Coroner Investigator Craig Harvey stated, "If you see only 1 in 3 cases, a large amount of homicides will be missed." The decedents in a lot of suspicious, violent-death cases (gunshot, stabbing, etc.) would be denied a proper investigation into their deaths. Even when a case was clearly a homicide, this meant that if an arrest wasn't immediately affected regarding a decedent's death, then the possibility of an arrest ever being effected without a confession was null and void. This also meant that 2/3rds of the murderers in that county were essentially going to go free. Marcella Fierro (M.D., forensic pathology) stated, "You call a death an accident or miss a homicide altogether, a murderer goes free. Lots of very bad things happen if death investigation is not carried out completely."

If this is the case with regard to forensic pathology in our country, how could I or anyone (especially the distraught families of the victims) expect that police officers or medical examiners would spend a moment examining drowning cases, which are the most difficult cases to solve. Even though the police should have been alerted to the suspicious nature of a lot of these cases, the medical examiners (especially once finding alcohol in these young men) classified the cases as accidental. In cases where the medical examiners made the case "undetermined," the police followed their normal routine, which was to close the case pending further information. They labeled these cases as tragic accidents fueled by alcohol and risky behavior that had been engaged in by young men, and then quickly moved on to the next case.

This happens because many police officers tend to assume drownings are accidents. We all know what happens when people assume things. In fact, Ronald F. Becker, J.D. (2000, p. 4) spoke about this in his article in the *FBI Law Enforcement Bulletin* ("Myths of Underwater Recovery Operations") in the section entitled, "ACCIDENT ASSUMPTIONS."

> *Myth: All drownings are presumed accidents.* Experienced homicide investigators generally presume that all unattended deaths are murders until proven otherwise, except when they occur in water. . . . By correctly processing the bodies of drowning victims, investigators can obtain a variety of forensic evidence. For example, divers should place bodies in body bags to avoid losing transient evidence, such as hairs and fibers. . . .*

In fact, medical examiners even fail to test the liquid in a victim's lungs and stomach to see whether it matches the body of water that the victim was recovered in. It would not only seem incumbent upon them to do this, but would be a prudent step in confirming the case as a accident or homicide. Yet, unfortunately, this is never done as the medical examiners assume that they are the same water or liquid. One of the reasons for this occurring

* Becker, R. F. (2000, September). Myths of Underwater Recovery Operations. *FBI Law Enforcement Bulletin*, *69*(9), 1–5.

according to Dr. Ross Zumwalt (who co-authored the National Academy of Sciences study *Strengthening Forensic Science in the United States: A Path Forward*) is because there is no national standard, inspection or accreditation between the states. Everything else is accredited; hospitals are accredited, barbers are accredited, you would think a medico-legal death investigation system would have to go through a periodic inspection and accreditation.

Considering the state of affairs of forensic pathology and the rights of all Americans to have their loved ones' deaths properly investigated – especially if suspicious, we need to increase the amount of resources needed to hire more pathologists. During the *FRONTLINE* interview, Dr. DiMaio said that the price of a good medical examiner's office at this time is roughly "going to cost you about $2.25 to $2.50 a person in your community per year, which is probably less than what you pay for a Coca-Cola in a movie theater," which would put in place the proper safeguards necessary to thoroughly investigate deaths. This doesn't seem important at first unless you have been involved every year with the thousands of people who lost loved ones and are looking for just an answer to what may have happened to their loved ones. This does not even include those who have been viciously murdered. Vincent DiMaio went on to say, "You have a family who looks at this official decision typed on this neat piece of paper with this official seal and the family thinks, I guess they must know what they are doing." We also need to properly train medical examiners, coroners, and police officers, specifically with regard to drowning investigations.

After examining hundreds of drowning cases over the past decade, I can now understand why these drowning cases are so difficult for both the police and the medical community to reach a consensus on. To begin with, drowning cases offer very little in actually proving that the decedent drowned even if the victim is recovered with water in the lungs. Water in the lungs could come from effusion (passing of fluids into the organs) from being submersed in water. No water in the lungs could be caused by a spasm of the larynx (contracting of the muscles) before death in an attempt to keep the water from entering the body during the drowning process. All this complicates drownings as a cause of death. These cases offer very little to determine an actual entry point of the deceased, and as such, an actual potential crime scene. The amount of decomposition on a body is not always consistent with each case, being dependent on the specific elements of the victim's size (e.g., weight, body fat, and body mass index), water temperature, amount of time in the water, clothing, and such. Although drowning cases are difficult to investigate, both for the criminal investigator and the medical examiner, these cases are not beyond the realm of being solved. They are, however, difficult and require the utmost attention to detail and observation from both parties.

For the police investigator, this means doing things right the first time and realizing when things don't quite seem to fit or make sense. In the words of my mentor, Lieutenant Commander Vernon Geberth at NYPD Bronx Homicide (who wrote the book entitled *Practical Homicide Investigation*), this means to use your knowledge as a criminal investigator, enhanced with experience, flexibility and common sense, to know when something is wrong and doesn't make sense. For a medical examiner, this means to be more diligent with the autopsy; that is, to look for, and try to explain, things that don't quite fit with a body (like rigor mortis or lividity) instead of just documenting them. Medical examiners and especially forensic pathologists know or should know when things aren't quite right with a body, even in drowning cases. Rigor mortis on a body in warm water (over 60 degrees) after 5-plus days – when it should have subsided within 2 to 3 days maximum – is or should be a sign that something isn't quite right.

Although medical examiners and forensic pathologists may not know the exact Cause of Death (e.g., drowning, suffocation, alcohol poisoning or the inhalation of drugs) and may be inclined to declare the Manner of Death as "unknown" or as "undetermined," it shouldn't preclude them from having the moxie or moral courage to make a proper determination as to the Manner of Death (e.g., homicide, accident, suicide, natural, or undetermined). In most of these cases, the consensus was always to label them as "undetermined." This is a catch-all for law enforcement. This means to the police that the medical examiner can't determine whether it was an accident or a homicide, and so the police can just close the case as a tragic accident and move on. No police department wants to carry a case that is an open homicide with very few clues, especially in situations when there may be more cases, thus making it serial crime, as in La Crosse, Wisconsin. Serial anything (three or more) is something police departments dread, and "Serial Homicide" are the two most dreaded words in the English language next to the words "Task Force," which are almost certain to follow homicide.

In one case in Pennsylvania, the medical examiner did one of the best jobs I've ever seen done on an autopsy and admitted to us that he didn't know the cause of death because of contributing circumstances. He was 99% sure it was a homicide, considering the body was brought back and placed into the water 12 to 13 days later, with footprints and drag marks to substantiate this. Yet, although he believed the case should be handled as a homicide by the police, he wouldn't make the manner of death a homicide because he didn't know exactly what caused the victim's death. This is semantics! He also told us it was a very political town. And, since the police had initially requested our help and then later refused to follow up when he (the Medical Examiner) had personally substantiated our initial findings of months earlier, who knows how politics played into this investigation. All I know is that this case was quickly "put to bed" by the police department that had informed us that they were more concerned about how to answer questions related to our serial homicide investigation than they were about actually trying to solve the case.

To solve these cases, both the police and medical community need to work hand-in-hand as the medical examiner's investigation is directly dependant on the observation of the investigating detective unless he or she personally responds to the scene. Therefore, as police officers (first responders) or detectives (criminal investigators), we need to be more diligent in our observation and reporting, and do things right the first time, and not rush to find answers quickly so we can move on to the next case, especially in a death investigation. Dr. Cyril Wecht (a leading forensic pathologist) always said that you should handle all deaths as a homicide and work backwards until proven otherwise. This is because if you do everything right and it proves to be a tragic accident, then you did your job correctly. If you assume it to be an accident and you didn't do your job correctly, and it turns out to be a homicide as in these cases, then you missed critical and crucial pieces of evidence that may have led you to those who were responsible for these murders. You then failed the victim, the family and the community you were sworn to protect. You failed as an investigator.

Last but not least, the medical community must remember to always be a separate investigating body, free from the grasp of the law enforcement community or the political community. We've seen too many times when it appears as though the medical examiner and the police were working hand-in-hand to not investigate freely, but to put forth a finding that was more favorable or conducive to the police or the universities and what they wanted to project, rather than to the victim, family or public in general. This cannot occur at any time! My mentor Vernon Geberth said, "Death investigation constitutes a heavy responsibility, and as such, let no person deter you from the truth and your own personal commitment to see that justice is done, not only for the deceased, but for the surviving family as well." He presents this *Oath of Practical Homicide Investigation* in his book, which is considered the bible for homicide investigators. It would be something were every investigator to be given this homicide oath just as doctors are given the Hippocratic oath when they receive their medical licenses. It would be good for all investigators to remember this when they handle any death investigation, especially the difficult ones as these cases are. We should never forget that these could be our sons or daughters who are being murdered out there. Who speaks for them if we don't?

Kevin Gannon

Acknowledgments

I wish to extend my deepest gratitude to the following individuals:

My parents for their direction in raising me to always try to "do the right thing" even in the midst of tremendous odds. My mother for her work with the poor and disenfranchised people of all races, colors, and religions. My father for saving my life and for being my best friend and the greatest police officer/detective ever. He taught me to stand up and question authority and to prove things investigatively with facts. He always said, "Don't believe anything you hear and only half of what you see."

Detective Michael Donovan for being the best cop, partner, and friend anyone could ever have. Mike, "Ace," you're the best!

Lieutenant Ralph Manente, Lieutenant Tom Duno, Detective Joe DeEttore, and Detective Mike Donovan for helping to make our plainclothes unit a force to be reckoned with in the Bronx.

Sergeant Thomas Mistretta for being the best "boss" (supervisor) ever. I struggled every day attempting to be the kind of leader you were. Tom, thank you for taking a few snot-nosed kids and entrusting them with your plainclothes unit and possibly your career. You made the aforementioned individuals and me everything we became.

Police Officer Gene DiSilvio for being the first cop to acknowledge me in the precinct and allowing me to become accepted as one of the guys. Gino, thanks for your 30-plus years of beautiful friendship.

Police Officer Gary Jessamy for all your years of friendship. To your whole family for being the best family on the block while growing up, according to my dad. Thanks also for pushing me in everything you did. You never gave less than 110% and expected the same from everyone around you. You as much as anyone were responsible for making me realize what I was capable of achieving in my life. Your inspiration is what enabled me to believe that I could survive cancer. Thanks for everything!!!

Detective Derrick Nash, Detective John Muniz, Sergeant Donald Martin, Detective James Tafurri, Detective William Simion, Lieutenant Kevin Moroney, Police Officer Edward Santiago, and Sergeant Rose Negron for your dedication to service and excellence in work, which helped to propel my career as a supervisor. I had very little to do in supervising you and more to do with just attempting to keep up with you guys. Over 500 robbery and 250 criminal possession of a weapon (gun) arrests in 5 years. You were truly the best!

Police Officer Donald Hoyle (police delegate) for taking a rookie sergeant under his wings and keeping him from shooting himself in the foot on many occasions. I owe you more than I could ever repay. Thanks Donny for everything!

Captain Terrence Tunnock who was one of the best men I've ever met and the greatest boss the NYPD has ever had. Thank you for your friendship, for your years of service, and for your respect for the simple cop. The job owes you more than we could ever repay!!!

Lieutenant Commander Vernon J. Geberth (author of *Practical Homicide Investigation*) for taking a rookie police officer under your wings and imparting some of your amazing knowledge and wisdom on handling criminal investigations, specifically homicides. Also, for your "Oath of the Homicide Investigator," which is the reason I'm still pursuing justice today.

Detective 1st Grade Victor "Vic" Cipullo, vice president, the Detective Endowment Association (DEA), for your friendship and mentoring of a rookie who was attempting to be the kind of cop and investigator that you were. Vic, you were the best!

Detective 1st Grade, Gerald "Jerry" Carley for your friendship, leadership, and assistance in helping me to succeed as a supervisor in an investigative capacity. Jerry, there is no better detective or funnier man alive.

Lieutenant Thomas Richardson for your friendship and belief in us (Anthony, Mike, and myself) to entrust the security of so many dignitaries (including President Clinton) into our hands during the United Nations General Assembly (UNGA) Millennium Celebration. Tom, there is no nicer man alive.

Detective John O'Malley, "Bronx Homicide Task Force" (now investigator for the U.S. Attorney's Office, Southern District of New York), for your 25 years of friendship and for recommending me for entrance into the Detective Bureau. There is no greater homicide investigator. Johny O, thanks for sticking your neck out for me.

Detective Michael Diaz, NYPD/FBI Joint Robbery Apprehension Team (JRAT) and captain of the football team, for your friendship and for helping to secure my entrance into the Detective Bureau. Mike, you were the best detective and athlete ever.

Captain Stephen Finnegan (Emergency Services Unit, ESU#3) for being not only one of my dearest friends but also one of the bravest and most honorable individuals I've been fortunate enough to have met. One Medal of Valor with the NYPD and three tours of duty in Iraq. Steve, when I grow up, I want to be half the man you are.

Sergeant James Shaw, Bronx Homicide Nightwatch, for recommending me to replace him and convincing me to take this position. Jim, thanks for your help and your continued friendship over the years.

Chief John Hodges (Westchester County Police) for your continued friendship and support over the years. John, you're a great boss, friend, and a true gentleman.

Dr. Cyril Wecht, one of the leading forensic pathologists in the nation, for your time and energy in repeatedly assisting us with forensic aspects of our analyses. Thanks Doc for all your time and genuine concern in helping us to get these cases reinvestigated. You are a true gentleman.

Walter "Butch" Hendricks, and Andrea Zafares of LifeGuard System, Inc. (New York) for your assistance in initially helping Anthony and me to confirm that we were on the right track. Thank you also for providing your network of water professionals to assist us at other scenes. You guys are the true leaders in water rescue and investigation.

Herb Meyers and his crew of water experts for their assistance in searching the Wisconsin River for forensic evidence at their own expense.

Gary Huber for inviting us into your home and imparting your knowledge of forensic application of death investigations to us.

Dr. Michael Baden, a leading forensic pathologist in the country, for sharing your valuable time with us to review some of the case material in pursuit of true investigations and justice. Thanks for everything, Doc.

Police Academy Instructors and Police Officers William Freeley, Maryanne Highland, and Hank Meyers, for the knowledge, wisdom, and friendship you imparted to me helping me to do the best job I could in every endeavor.

Sergeant Robert Ganley, vice president, Sergeants Benevolent Association for your friendship in entrusting us with the security of both President Clinton and Vice President Al Gore during the Millennium Celebration. More importantly, for assisting me in your current position with my health issues (in 2003) related to my cancer and for helping to save my life. Bob, I can't thank you enough.

Nicole Weismann Eagan of *People Magazine* for your assistance in initially telling the story of the Smiley Face Murders and for your constant support in helping us in attempting to get these cases investigated. Also, for your journalistic integrity being the only journalist we entrusted with the knowledge of who was responsible for these heinous crimes, and yet preserving the integrity of the investigation for the good of all concerned. Thank you, Nicky. You're the best!

Detective Andrea Campbell, who when we last spoke about my removal from the McNeil and Andrews cases along with my insistence of their murders, said only one thing to me, "Kevin, do what you do best and be Spiderman and solve these cases." Those words have stayed with me. Andrea, thank you!

Investigator John P. O'Neil (FBI Counterterrorist Unit) who lost his life in the collapse of the World Trade Center. Thank you for your dedication combating terrorism and attempting to prevent the impending and horrific events of 9/11 despite the outside influences of those around you who were unaware of your keen insight. I had so deeply longed to have worked for and with you. You were a true hero! You were truly the "Man Who Knew!"

Attorney Robert F. Stein. Bob, thanks for all your assistance in helping me along the way in attempting to bring this story to the public and law enforcement. Your time and friendship have been something I have truly cherished. We can only hope that it will finally see the light of day regarding a true investigation. Bob, you're the best!

My neighbor Andy for always asking about the investigation and taking the time to listen and to read the material on the investigation and supply his corporate insights into how to help bring this information forward. Thanks, Andy.

Trinka Porrata at *Project GHB* (projectghb.org), retired Los Angeles Police Detective (rape unit), for your assistance and information related to the danger and effects of the many analogs of the drug GHB. Thank you so much for your time and assistance.

Vance Holmes at *Drowning in Coincidence* (www.vanceholmes.com/court/trial_missing.html) for being the first website devoted to the initial drownings occurring in the Mid-West. You helped to make me aware of the scope and depth of this investigation. Thank you.

Lisa R. at *Footprints at the River's Edge* (footprintsattheriversedge.blogspot.com) for putting together the most comprehensive and thorough website dedicated to presenting the true information available about what happened to our victims. Thank you for not engaging in uninformed rhetoric and not promoting a certain hypothesis, a specific agenda, or yourself.

Adam Carlson (doctoral student) for your intellectual insight into many different topics related to this investigation. Your investigative instincts along with your critical thinking are something to be marveled. You are the perfect example of why education is so important. Along with your two masters degrees, you could be one of the leaders in the field of forensic investigations. Now, finish your PhD! Thanks, Adam, for all your assistance.

Last but not least, my partners (Anthony Duarte and D. Lee Gilbertson) for their assistance in this endeavor and for their altruistic efforts to bring to light the largest number of serial killings in the history of criminal investigations. Your dedication to seeing justice for the victims, at your own expense, with no timetable in sight, is a tribute to your integrity and class. I am deeply honored to have been fortunate enough to have been involved with two of the finest individuals I've ever met, who also happened to be the best investigators I've ever encountered. You guys are truly the best!!!

Kevin Gannon

This book presents our findings for 14 cases that were considered by most law enforcement officers and the public to be accidental deaths. It is the product of intensive field investigation and archival research. It is about the deaths of 13 young men and 1 survivor over the past decade and a half. We have faced many challenges along the way. We (Gannon, Duarte, Carlson, and I) have met with some very important individuals since 2006 when we first formed the team. We pleaded with them for action, only to leave and to see nothing to ever become of our efforts. Investigating so many deaths (there are 322 cases in my database), especially under these circumstances, had the potential to be incredibly depressing.

As a man of faith, I thank my God for giving us the physical and psychological strength to continue our work of helping families to better understand what happened to their sons, and to see this book through to publication. There are so many people who should be recognized for being by my side and bringing me to the place in life that I am today. I thank my loved ones, friends, past and current work associates, and students for being patient with me each time I thought out loud or discussed the cases. I must have sounded like a scratched record. I also thank them for being so understanding when I had to be gone or could not go somewhere because we were working on a case. Their support of our work and this book is highly valued and is most sincerely appreciated. I would like to thank the staff at Taylor & Francis for believing in this book and for understanding how important it is to the families and victims, and for helping us to get the word out about the cases.

Although we encountered several law enforcement officers with closed minds who thought we were not in touch with the facts, there were a few who either sought out our counsel or listened to us with open minds. Those law enforcement officers who openly discussed their cases with us, and allowed us to critically examine their cases, demonstrated real strength of character and good professional ethics. Thank you.

Specifically, I want to thank Anthony Duarte and Adam Carlson for their part in this story and for providing balance in the team. Their encouragement recharged our efforts as we traveled side-by-side with them for hours, or when the team hit another snag in an investigation, or when we (Kevin and I) became despondent in the face of possibly never seeing justice for families. They kept our analyses honest and unbiased by playing the role of skeptics while we examined page after page of law enforcement and autopsy reports and photographs, and tossed around ideas and theories about what things meant or how they may have occurred. Their skill as investigators in the field is impressive, but most importantly, they give me real friendship.

The most significant acknowledgment has to go to Kevin, my friend and colleague. Up to this point in my life, I have never met a person who so thoroughly and faithfully persisted in a task to keep a promise despite the repeated setbacks and nonbelievers. He is truly a man of his word with sincere integrity. We spent hours together, in the field and on the phone, examining case reports and analyzing every possibility. He taught me so much about homicide investigation, specifically how to work a case from every angle. Thank you for being so patient with this professor.

D. Lee Gilbertson

Authors

Kevin Gannon retired as a Sergeant in the Detective Bureau from the New York City Police Department (NYPD) after 20 years of service, which included more than 14 years as a supervisor. He has diversified training and experience in personal and physical security, investigation and surveillance, and disaster response. Gannon's background includes leadership positions responsible for the personal protection of numerous international dignitaries and personalities. As a member of Operation I.C.E. (Mayor Giuliani's 1997 task force to respond to any major chemical disaster or attack), he received Department of Defense training in nuclear, biological, and chemical warfare. Gannon has supervised plainclothes personnel in anticrime, narcotics, and robbery units, and was second in charge of the NYPD's Missing Persons Squad. He was in charge of the Bronx Homicide Task Force/Nightwatch from 1999 until his retirement in 2001. Gannon has made over 1000 felony apprehensions for crimes involving narcotics, burglaries, robberies, and homicides. During his distinguished career, Gannon was awarded almost 100 medals for bravery. He was the most decorated member of the Special Investigation Division of the Detective Bureau and one of the most highly decorated Sergeants in the NYPD before his retirement. He received the Medal of Valor twice (1994 and 1996) from Mayor Giuliani for heroism in the line of duty. For his investigative work on gang crime, Gannon received the Frederic Milton Thrasher Award (2008) from the National Gang Crime Research Center. This is his first book. It is the culmination of investigative work that started in 1997 and has continued until this day.

D. Lee Gilbertson holds a doctorate (PhD) in sociology (2002; with a concentration in gangs and substance abuse) and a Master of Science in criminal justice (1996; focusing on criminology and victimology). His background includes 16 years of exemplary military service (infantry and signals intelligence) from 1976 to 1992. In addition to his regular duties, he also received training in and served as the unit Alcohol and Drug Coordination Officer (responsible for substance abuse prevention training and supervising urinalysis collections), and as the unit Nuclear, Biological, and Chemical Warfare Defense Officer. He currently teaches at Saint Cloud State University and has consulted with law enforcement and provided training in the areas of forensic victimology, crime analysis, and gangs. He has studied gangs, militias, and extremist groups since 1995 and is a certified gang specialist. Gilbertson has presented and taught at numerous national and international conferences and academic institutions. He is a European polyglot. He is a staff member of the National Gang Crime Research Center and has participated in every iteration of its International Gang Specialist Training Conference. Gilbertson is a three-time recipient of the Frederic Milton Thrasher Award (2002, 2005, and 2008), and is an executive editor for the *Journal of Gang Research*.

Anthony Duarte currently works for the U.S. Department of Homeland Security as a Transportation Security Administration (TSA) Transportation Security Manager. He supervises airport screening checkpoints, monitors operations using various performance metrics, and coordinates crisis management and incident response protocols. Previously, he was a TSA Expert Behavior Detection Officer and was trained to detect individuals exhibiting behaviors that indicate they may be a threat to aviation and/or transportation security. He is a retired Detective 2nd Grade with the NYPD, and holds a Bachelor of Arts degree from John Jay College of Criminal Justice. His background includes almost 21 years in law enforcement, honing his skills investigating homicide, robbery, burglary, and other high-profile crimes. He served on two major federal task forces involving organized crime, receiving two awards from the U.S. Attorney's Office, Southern District of New York. Duarte is proficient in using state-of-the-art computer technology for data research, and in employing electronic audio-video recording devices. Because of his demonstrated investigative capability, as well as the quality and results of his casework, he received ten Excellence in Police Duty Awards and five Commendations for Meritorious Service. Duarte was a recipient of the Frederic Milton Thrasher Award (2008) from the National Gang Crime Research Center for his work in gang crime investigation.

Introduction

1

Gannon: Doc, now that you've read the autopsy report and looked at the photos, what do you think?
Gilbertson: I've got problems with it right from the get-go.
Gannon: Let me guess, the body condition.
Gilbertson: Yup, you too I take it. He's in rigor, no putrefaction, no maceration....
Gannon: That's right professor, there's no way this kid could be in the water that long and look this good.
Gilbertson: I know. Once again, the length of time he was missing is not the same as the length of time he was actually dead and in the water.
Gannon: Exactly!! He's probably only been dead for 48 hours and in the water for no more than 24 to 36 at the most – so, where was he the rest of the time?

The Beginning

It all began on a crisp February evening in 1997, two days after Valentine's Day, when 19-year-old Patrick McNeil went out drinking with some of his friends from Fordham University. They made their way down to an Upper East Side pub in Manhattan called The Dapper Dog. Patrick was a tall, good-looking and strapping young man. His parents, Pat and Jackie, had done right by him, raising him to be of sound morals, good work ethic, and a real gentleman. Patrick went outside for some fresh air – and that was the last time any of his family or friends ever saw him alive again. Four days later on February 20th, the task of finding Patrick was assigned to Detective Sergeant Kevin Gannon on the Missing Persons Squad in the Special Investigation Division of the Detective Bureau (Figure 1.1). Family and friends could not have asked for a more qualified law enforcement officer to work this case. From the average person who knew him during his days of walking a beat on the streets of New York City, to his peers in uniform, and to his bosses, Gannon was held in high regard. He was exceptionally trained and experienced, as well as highly decorated (to include 2 Medals of Valor for saving lives at the risk of his own), New York Police Department (NYPD) officer, who came from a long family tradition of NYPD policemen. That day, Gannon's life changed.

Gannon continued his search. Some 50 days later on April 7th, Patrick was found floating face-up in the Upper New York Bay 12 miles south of where he was last seen. Patrick's death was ruled an accident despite evidence that Gannon and his partner had uncovered, which suggested that Patrick had been drugged and his body dumped near a Brooklyn pier. Gannon's superiors thwarted every effort made by him to further investigate Patrick's death. Against their advice, Gannon persisted in investigating Patrick's case. Two other surprisingly similar cases (i.e., Lawrence Andrews, Jr., and Joshua Bender) heightened his interest – both had been recovered from the river far from where they were last seen. In

Figure 1.1 A moment of thought and reflection at the riverside for Gannon.

fact, Lawrence was found 9 miles south of where he was last seen and in the same spot as Patrick near Owls Head Water Pollution Control Plant in Brooklyn. Over the next few years, Gannon became convinced that these young men and a host of others across the country had been abducted, murdered, and dumped. His promise to Pat and Jackie McNeil became his driving force.

Intersecting Lives

During Spring Semester 2006, a tragic event happened at Saint Cloud State University in Minnesota. A young male student, Scott Radel, went downtown to party and had too much to drink. He became separated from his friends and disoriented. He was at one bar and was supposed go back east to meet his friends at another. He talked to them on his cell phone and described his location, which seemed to suggest that he had gone in a westerly direction. They told him to turn around. Yet, his next phone call suggested that he had gone even further to the west. Scott was later found drowned in the Mississippi River several blocks back to the east and north of his last described location. He was reported to be the victim of circumstances that involved excessive drinking, hypothermia, and eventually water – so the official story goes.

Gilbertson was an Assistant Professor of Criminal Justice at Saint Cloud State University at that time. He began teaching there in August 2000 and his primary teaching responsibilities were criminological theory and research methods. He has consulted with law enforcement in the areas of forensic victimology, crime mapping and analysis, and racial profiling. He has studied gangs, militias, and extremist groups since 1995, and is a published author who has presented at numerous national and international conferences. Gilbertson is part of the National Gang Crime Research Center staff and an executive editor for the *Journal of Gang Research*. His background includes a doctorate in sociology, masters in criminal justice, and 16 years of exemplary military service (infantry and signals intelligence).

He became interested in Scott Radel's case. Since there was no local television station, he went online to see whether any additional information could be found using "missing student" and "drowned" as a query string. He was surprised when hundreds of websites popped up referencing other, similar tragic cases. He also learned about the urban legend of the I-94 Serial Killer. Due to his background as an intelligence analyst in the U. S. Army, Gilbertson quickly recognized that patterns possibly existed among the data related to those other cases. He constructed a spreadsheet, recorded some initial data, did some quick analysis, and concluded he might be correct. He then assigned the task of a deeper analysis to two graduate students in his "Spatio-Temporal Crime Analysis" (CJS 596) course. Guiding them with additional analytical modeling, he oversaw their work and the presentation of their findings in May 2006 to the Saint Cloud Police Department's Chief of Police, Intelligence Crime Analyst, and a reporter from KMSP Fox 9 News in the Twin Cities. It was aired on May 19, 2006. At that time, Gilbertson felt that he had addressed the issue and that interest in it had waned.

Back in October 2002, Gannon became aware of numerous missing persons in the Midwest who had all gone missing within 10 days of each other. He phoned and spoke with the different police departments in Minnesota and Wisconsin in an attempt to ascertain the circumstances of the cases and to relay to them the specifics of his investigations from 5 years earlier (i.e., McNeil, Andrews, and Bender). Eventually, all the Midwest missing persons were found drowned and the official police reports stated that there were no signs of foul play. Although Gannon had never read any of the autopsy reports, he was not convinced that the cases were accidents. Then in 2005, after a year and a half of battling cancer, Gannon was astonished to find out that there were approximately 25 of these "accidental" drowning deaths in the Midwest (i.e., stretching through Minnesota, Iowa, Wisconsin, Illinois, Michigan and Indiana).

That was when he phoned Anthony Duarte, his old friend and co-worker since the police academy in 1981. Duarte was an excellent cop and a highly skilled investigator, a fact that was evidenced by the numerous awards he received for the quality of his work and which included 5 Commendations for Meritorious Service. He had extensive experience working homicide investigations and sex crimes, as well as dignitary and executive protection (e.g., Russian President Putin, Israeli Prime Minister Barak, and Vice President Gore). Duarte was promoted to the rank of Detective 3rd Grade for his attention to detail in handling some very important and sensitive cases for the NYPD. He worked on two federal task forces regarding organized crime and was again promoted to the rank of Detective 2nd Grade before retiring in 2001.

In April 2006, Gannon and Duarte decided to travel to the Midwest for the express purpose of examining the cases first-hand. They traveled to Minnesota and Wisconsin and met with a few of the families to examine the case materials as well as the scenes where the victims had gone missing and where they were eventually recovered. In October 2006, while they were preparing for another trip, Gannon learned of Gilbertson and his students' findings via the Internet. He told Duarte, "We gotta talk to this guy!" So, the two retired NYPD detectives set out for Minnesota to "hit him cold and see what he's got" and sought out Gilbertson at his office on the campus of Saint Cloud State University (Figure 1.2). The discussion that followed over the course of the next hours was a mutual epiphany. The work that Gannon and Duarte had done filled in the blanks for Gilbertson, and vice versa. That momentous meeting led to the formation of Nationwide Investigations, which was comprised of four people with complementing areas of knowledge and experience that would become vital to the investigation (Figure 1.3).

Figure 1.2 Gannon, Gilbertson, and Duarte at the 2006 meeting.

Figure 1.3 The Team (left to right): Duarte, Carlson, Gannon, and Gilbertson.

Protocols and Models

Having been presented with new information by each other, the team concluded that the only correct way to conduct an investigation of this magnitude was to examine this phenomenon in its natural setting (a field research method) and to pour over every available document (an archival research method). The team set out to determine the truth at its own financial expense. The findings and conclusions were reached after thousands of hours of pouring over law enforcement incident reports and records, autopsy reports and photos, on-site visits, telephonic and in-person field interviews, database and map analysis. Gannon has been investigating these cases since 1997, and the team as a whole since late-2006. Since January 2007, the team has physically revisited many of the sites on multiple occasions, to include where the young men were last seen, where they lived or were to return to that night, where evidence was discovered, and where the bodies were recovered. Photographs and geodecimal GPS coordinates were taken at those sites (Figure 1.4). The team has also re-interviewed persons who were previously interviewed by law enforcement, as well as those who were not, and spoken with several parents or family members of victims.

Figure 1.4 Gannon and Gilbertson determining the body recovery location from police reports and photographs.

Many law enforcement criminal profilers and officers, media reporters, Internet website authors and bloggers have all commented on the events that have become known as the "Smiley Face Killers" and have referred to them as "serial" crimes. Any proclamation that these may be serial crimes is incorrect. Any analysis based on this presumption is errant. Although some of the murders may have been committed by the same individuals within the same criminal elements, these crimes are neither serial, spree or mass homicides when one adheres to strict definitions established by the Federal Bureau of Investigation. These cases should be properly referred to as the "Linked Smiley Face Homicides." An analysis of any set of events in order to determine whether or not they may be linked crimes cannot begin until after an investigator first identifies which events were actually crimes – whether they be homicides, assaults, burglaries, robberies, forcible rapes, or whatever. Although members of the media repeatedly pressured us to publicly announce which cases were linked, we never did. We have consistently asserted that it does no good to attempt to link events when some may and some may not be actual crimes. This has always been our stance.

From the beginning, the team's investigative approach has been a two-step process. Step one involved examining the individual cases in order to determine which ones were actually crimes. Then, step two used criminological and victimological variables, and not supposed commonalities as proposed by others, to identify which cases were potentially linked crimes or separate crimes. This book demonstrates step one and its 7 aspects (as follows).

1. *Human and canine searches:* The team would review all human and canine searches, whether ground-based, airborne or waterborne. What assets were used? Did the supervisors or search team members have experience? Had the dogs proven themselves in previous searches? What routes or paths were used? What time of day and for how long? What were the results? How did this all map out? Was there any evidence of a potential for bias of auspices or conflict of interest (Figure 1.5)?
2. *Status and location of personal property:* The team would identify what items of personal property (i.e., clothing, head gear, wallet, keys, cell phones, and vehicle or bicycle) were present on or with the victim when he went missing, and compare that with when he was recovered. What were they and what was their

Figure 1.5 Searching everywhere for clues.

description? Were they appropriate for that individual – were they his? When and where were they recovered, and how did they get there?

3. *Scenario and events timeline:* In order to go forward while conducting any investigation, you must first go backwards – especially homicide. The team would attempt to identify every person who had encountered the victim within a 48-hour period prior to his disappearance, or who may have had pertinent knowledge of the victim's state of mind. Who were they relative to the victim and society? Where were they and what were they doing? Are their statements to police consistent with each other and congruent within themselves? What happened during the week before the victim's disappearance and specifically within the 24 hours prior? When interviewed separately, what does each person say happened that night?
4. *Location of the body:* The team was interested in several locations relative to physical description and geodecimal GPS coordinates (Figure 1.6). Where was the victim last seen before his disappearance, or where did he say he was located

Figure 1.6 Team members (Carlson, Duarte, and Gilbertson) discussing the relationship of GPS coordinates for a body recovery site with those taken earlier at the last seen location.

and can it be verified? To where was he supposed to go next? To where was he to return at the end of the evening (e.g., a home, apartment, hotel room, friend's home, and so forth)? Where is his residence? Where is his hometown? Where was he recovered? In which direction does the water current flow and how did this relate to where the victim was last seen and recovered? Can a possible water entry point be identified?

5. *Condition of the body:* The team would carefully read through all autopsy reports and interview medical examiners where possible (given they would agree to speak with us as many refused) to identify the condition of the victim's body regarding rigidity (*rigor mortis*), lividity (*livor mortis*), Washerwoman's Hands (*Wauschaut*), decomposition and discoloration, skin slippage and sloughing, marbling (putrefaction and maceration), physical trauma and bruising, and insects. How did the medical examiner and or coroner describe these? What were the official manner and cause of death? What were the environmental conditions during the time that the victim was missing and presumed to be in the water (i.e., air and water temperature, precipitation and water shed)? Were these forensic indicators consistent with the length of time that the victim was surmised to have been in the water and the environmental conditions? If not, then how could they be explained? These terms will be discussed and defined throughout this work for readers.
6. *Position of the body:* The team would specifically center on lividity and its relationship to the victim's head position, body position upon recovery, and the potential for posing of the victim.
7. *Toxicology:* The team looked for references to any preliminary or final laboratory results regarding all forms of alcohol and drug testing. This proved to be one of the more persistently inconsistent areas of postmortem examination among the cases.

You Decide

The purpose of this book was twofold. First, our underlying objective of this work was to increase the general knowledge base of forensic evidence that exists within the academic literature and the discipline of forensic pathology, specifically that which is related to drowning cases. We intended that this work could be used in conjunction with other academic texts during the instruction of forensic evidence as it relates to determining manner of death. There are 14 case studies, one for each week of a semester minus midterm break and finals week, which can be used as analytical essay assignments. A primary goal was to increase readers' understanding of the forensic evidence in these cases so they can make up their own minds about them.

The team has been on local, regional, and national television and radio stations trying to inspire discussions of specific cases and to bring forth forensic evidence that would prove homicide. We have contacted several United States Senators and Congressmen. We have reached out to national nonprofit organizations. We have had private meetings with high-level federal law enforcement and prosecution officials. Our focus has been to first prove which cases were homicides, and to then talk about linkages among the cases. However, everyone around us – from the media, to Internet bloggers, to academics, to law enforcement – has been more interested in the hype of the linkages and the "Smiley Face Killers."

Thus, with this book, we seek to reinvigorate our original approach to these cases – that has always been to prove the homicides first. Herein, we explain what each piece of forensic evidence was, how to interpret it for yourself, and then we present the specific evidence from that case. It will be your task to take notes, to analyze the evidence for yourself, and to draw your own conclusions. What was the manner of death: undetermined, natural, accident, suicide, or homicide? Were these merely accidental drownings as authorities would proclaim, or were they homicides? Did law enforcement do all it could to investigate each case? Was there justice? Was evidence missed, or was it ignored? You decide.

Note: Please see the Appendices for "Suggested Discussion Questions" and other learning aids.

Patrick James McNeil*

2

Background

This is the case that got Gannon started. Gannon was assigned to Pat McNeil's case, since at the time he was a Detective Supervisor with the Missing Persons Squad, Special Investigations Division, NYPD Headquarters. However, the case became the responsibility of the Brooklyn precinct where Pat's body was recovered and Gannon was taken off the case. He made a promise to the parents, Patrick (Pat) and Jacqueline (Jackie) McNeil, that he would find out what had happened to Pat and that he would try to bring in those who had done this to him. In his final 6-page autopsy report (dated April 8, 1997), the New York City Medical Examiner recorded that the body was found in the water with the manner of death listed as undetermined. He assessed the cause of death as drowning. Pat was recovered on April 7, 1997, and the autopsy was conducted the next morning on April 8, 1997. It took more than a decade for Pat and Jackie McNeil to receive a complete package (i.e., autopsy report, photographs, and toxicology report) from the Office of Chief Medical Examiner, City of New York. Pat and Jackie did not receive that package until almost 12 years later on December 29, 2008. Jackie shared the information in that package with us on February 15, 2009. Just over a month later on March 19, 2009, Gannon and Duarte met with the NYPD Chief of the Special Investigations Division to share our findings.

All on-site photographs in this report were taken by members of our team. Pat and Jackie McNeil (Figure 2.1) gave us permission to use and show discreetly excerpted photos from their son's autopsy. In fact, they encouraged us to do so since they wanted the truth to be shown. However, even though the Office of Chief Medical Examiner finally accommodated the McNeil family's Freedom of Information Act (FOIA) letter of request for documents and photographs (after 11 years 8 months), it declined Gilbertson's official

* Photo courtesy of the McNeil family.

Figure 2.1 Pat (center) with his parents Pat and Jackie McNeil (left and right). (Photo courtesy of the McNeil family.)

written request for permission to cite those documents and to show selected pictures in accordance with the McNeils' wishes. Therefore, this chapter was compiled using Gannon's notes and memory of the original 1997 investigation, as well as our notes taken during personal observation of case photos and while reading official documents.

Circumstances

Last Seen

Patrick James McNeil ("Pat") was a White male, 20 years old, 6 feet 1 inch, 185 pounds (Body Mass Index: 24.41), brown hair and brown eyes. He resided at D-82, Martyr's Court, a dormitory on the Rose Hill Campus of Fordham University in the Bronx. Pat was last seen about 00:30 hours (12:30 a.m.) on Monday, February 17, 1997. He was in the Dapper Dog bar, which is now The Big Easy (Figure 2.2) located at 1768 2nd Avenue (Manhattan), New York City. He was drinking with friends and was seen in the bathroom of the bar

Figure 2.2 The site of the Dapper Dog (1997) is now The Big Easy (2007). Gilbertson took GPS coordinates at the last location where Pat McNeil was seen on the night he disappeared.

Figure 2.3 To the left of the Owls Head Water Pollution Control Plant entry gate was the spot in the Upper New York Bay where Pat McNeil was recovered on April 7, 1997.

throwing up right before getting ready to leave. Pat was then observed by witnesses outside the bar in a highly unstable and disoriented state, reminiscent of someone who was on a type of debilitating narcotic drug. Witnesses reported seeing him stumbling, falling against parked vehicles, and vomiting. Pat started walking south on 2nd Avenue from 92nd Street. Witnesses observed a double-parked vehicle outside the bar, occupied by a man and a woman, that followed Pat south on 2nd Avenue. Pat fell to the ground a short distance later, and the vehicle that was following him stopped and waited. When Pat started walking south again, the vehicle started to follow him. Pat was last observed turning left onto 90th Street, heading in the direction of the East River with the vehicle still following him.

Recovery

Pat was found drowned in the Upper New York Bay almost two months later (50 days) on Monday, April 7, 1997. He was recovered in the Bay Ridge section of Brooklyn at Owls Head Water Pollution Control Plant at the 69th Street Pier at about 6700 Shore Road (Brooklyn), New York City (Figure 2.3). He was found over 12 miles away from where he was last observed in Manhattan (Figure 2.4, *Turquoise Dot* & *Red-X Dot*).

Analysis of Evidence

Recovery Location

Further investigation revealed that Pat's body should never have been recovered where it had been considering information obtained by Gannon about the water currents for the East River and the Upper New York Bay from the NYPD Harbor Unit that patrols the river daily. Pat had to have been abducted (probably by the couple who were following him in the car), driven to that location, and deposited there, for him to have been recovered at that location.

Vehicle Plate Number

Gannon had a partial vehicle plate number. The Missing Persons supervisor would not pay for a "lawman search" (i.e., a search of all number-letter combinations) in order to identify a plate number for the vehicle that was following Pat and described by witnesses at

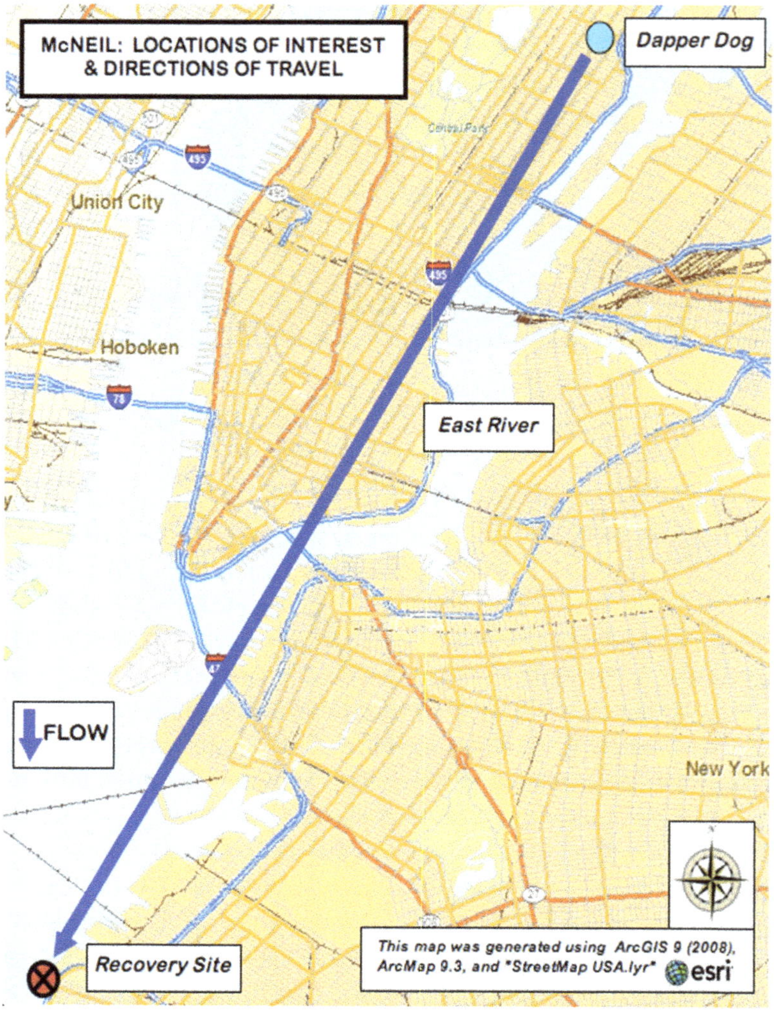

Figure 2.4 Pat McNeil was recovered at Owls Head Water Pollution Control Plant (*Red-X Dot*) 12 miles from the Dapper Dog (*Turquoise Dot*) where he was last seen.

the scene. Authorities said it was too expensive ($1,200 at that time). This information was critical and would have led to the identity of those in question who were in that vehicle that evening and were certainly "Persons of Interest" regarding Pat's disappearance.

Clothing

The New York City Medical Examiner reported that Pat was recovered in only his white socks, boxers, and button-fly blue jeans. The removal of clothing is characteristic of persons who experience hypothermia. We found it hard to believe that Pat took off most of his clothing and shoes, and then jumped into the cold waters of New York City's East River in February, especially since the Medical Examiner did not describe any physical indicators of hypothermia in the autopsy report. We also found it difficult to accept the idea that the river current pulled off all his upper-body clothing without disturbing the positioning of his socks, boxers, and pants.

Relative Concentration of Alcohol at Equilibrium

Specimen	Concentration
Urine (ureteral)	1.30
Plasma or serum	1.12–1.20
Spinal fluid	1.10–1.27
Whole blood	1.00
Brain tissue	0.85
Liver tissue	0.85
Alveolar air	1/2100

Figure 2.5 Blood Alcohol Concentration (BAC) naturally varies within a body. (Modified from Spitz, W., & Spitz, D. (Eds.) 2006. *Spitz and Fisher's Medicolegal Investigation of Death* (4th ed.), Table XXIII, p. 1222. Springfield, IL: Charles C. Thomas.)

Toxicology

It is common for Blood Alcohol Concentration (BAC) test results to differ among specimens taken from various locations in a body (Figure 2.5; Spitz & Spitz, 2006). Test results can be confounded by the diffusion of alcohol among the organs after death, as well as the production of various alcohols as part of the human decomposition process (Gilliland & Bost, 1993; Heatley & Crane, 1990). An accurate determination of BAC is important in unraveling whether a death was an accident, homicide, or suicide. Researchers suggest that multiple samples should be taken and compared in order to produce more robust findings (Ionescu, Janssen, & Omalu, 2005). Recommended sites include femoral muscle blood, heart blood, urine, and vitreous humor.

Pat was recovered with a 0.16 BAC. More precisely, the level of ethyl alcohol (ethanol) in his blood was at 0.16, in some unidentified decomposition fluid at 0.18, and in his brain it was at 0.23. The autopsy report did not state from which part of his body the blood and fluid samples were collected. Since human bodies naturally produce alcohol postmortem (after death) as a part of decomposition, and considering that Pat was supposed to have been in the water for almost two months (50 days), his BAC should have increased by about 0.03 due to postmortem alcohol production. This means that his BAC upon entering the water was probably more like 0.13 or around 6 drinks. This was not that drunk for a healthy, 6 foot, 185 pound, young man. It was also inconsistent with the kind of behavior he exhibited in the bar's bathroom and outside the bar right after that. If this (0.13) were his true BAC upon leaving the bar, then something else made Pat sick that night. Clearly, Pat was messed up on something, and it was not just alcohol.

Gastrointestinal System

The assertion that Pat must have been drugged was tested by examining the contents of the gallbladder and stomach. Both were empty according to the autopsy report. The liver produces a digestive juice known as "bile" that is stored in the gallbladder between meals (NIDDK, 2008). An average human gallbladder holds about 10.7 milliliters (mL) of bile before a meal. It initially dumps some of the bile shortly after ingestion marking the first low (*early nadir*), then refills (*early peak*) and begins to empty again very slowly to a second low (*late nadir*) at 146 minutes post-ingestion, plus or minus 33 minutes (Howard, Murphy, & Dowling, 1991). The gallbladder will refill in about 42 to 50 minutes (Mesgarzadeh, Krishnamurthy, Bobba, & Langrell, 1983).

Relative to the digestive system, very little emptying takes place during the first 20 to 30 minutes in the stomach, small intestine, and colon. The rate at which emptying occurs is dependent upon the makeup of the food (i.e., liquid or solid), the volume of the meal, and extent of muscle action in the stomach and small intestine (Bowen, 2005; NIDDK, 2008). The transit time of food through the digestive system may even be influenced by psychological stress, biological sex, and whether or not a person is pregnant (Bowen, 2006). Liquids leave more quickly than solid foods. About 50 percent of the stomach contents will be emptied in 2.5 to 3 hours post-ingestion, with total emptying in 4 to 5 hours (Bowen, 2006); some researchers suggest as long as 6 hours. This means that once a person starts to eat, then logically we should not see both an empty gallbladder and an empty stomach under normal conditions (Figure 2.6).

An empty gallbladder suggested that Pat had eaten (solid food or liquid) and that there should have been something in his stomach. However, his stomach was also empty. We know that Pat vomited in the bathroom of the Dapper Dog. We concluded that his BAC was insufficient to cause nausea-induced vomiting and that this was most likely engendered by the presence of some undetected drug in his system (e.g., one of the side effects of date rape drugs is nausea). This may have helped to explain his empty stomach, but it did not explain his empty gallbladder. The digestion process began that night when Pat ate his evening meal and continued throughout his drinking session. His gallbladder would have been emptying and refilling all night. As soon as Pat stopped drinking beer and left the bar, his gallbladder would have started to refill and would have refilled within 42 to 50 minutes. The only way to have an empty gallbladder and an empty stomach at the same time was for Pat to (1) reach *late nadir*, (2) vomit, and then (3) die within only a few minutes of leaving the bar, which would have stopped the digestion process before his gallbladder could even begin to refill.

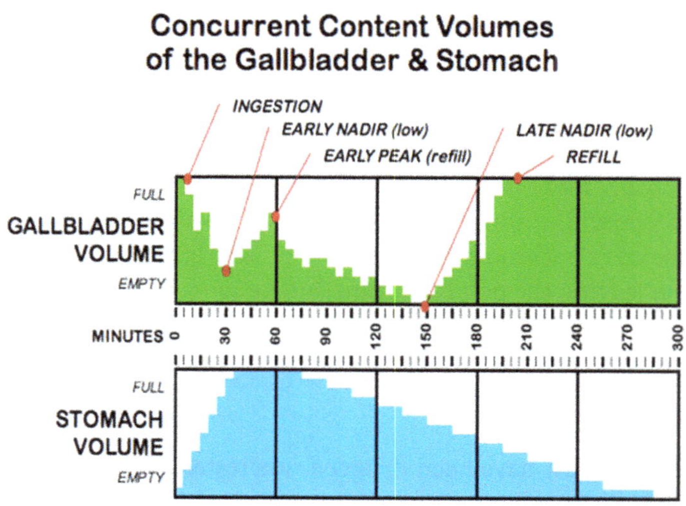

Figure 2.6 The gallbladder dumps sufficient bile into the stomach during the first 2.5 hours post-ingestion to carry it through the 4 to 6 hour digestive process. At the point where the gallbladder reaches *late nadir,* the stomach has emptied only about 50 percent of its contents.

Skeptics will say that this scenario was not only possible, but that it occurred. Recall that witnesses reported having observed Pat that night. They claimed that they saw him stumbling, falling against parked vehicles, and vomiting. Analysis of their statements suggested that Pat started walking south on 2nd Avenue from 92nd Street, at which point he turned toward the East River. As the lead investigating officer, Gannon personally walked and searched 92nd Street, as well as all east-west streets from 90th up to 96th Street to the bank of the East River. He also walked north from 96th Street all the way up to the Willis Avenue Bridge, and south from 96th Street all the way down to 42nd Street along the shoreline, except for the area where the Franklin D. Roosevelt East River Drive is inaccessible on foot because it runs right along the river. He did not find any vomitus anywhere. When was Pat's last meal and what was it? Did police attempt to discover this while interviewing witnesses? Were there any partially digested food particles in his small intestine or colon?

Body Position and Lividity

Pat was recovered supine (face-up), which was extremely unusual for drowning cases, especially for someone of his height and body weight (Hendrick, Zaferes, & Nelson, 2003). Most drowning victims are found floating prone (face-down). Exceptions occur when a victim is obese or the water is that of a raging-type river that is capable of flipping a body from its normal prone position. Pat's body position was inconsistent with normal drowning cases. Lividity (*livor mortis*) is the postmortem discoloration due to the gravitation of blood into the dependent capillaries and veins (DiMaio & DiMaio, 2001); basically, it is the pooling and settling of the blood that starts within 30 minutes after death (Figure 2.7). The fixing of lividity starts around 8 hours postmortem. Fixed means that the blood has settled to one side of the body and will resist displacement to a different part of the body as time passes; it is completely fixed by 10 to 12 hours (DiMaio & DiMaio, 2001; Shkrum & Ramsay, 2007).

Examination of Pat's autopsy report and photographs disclosed additional problems with body position and lividity. When a body is found supine, then lividity is normally posterior (toward or at the rear). When it is found prone, then lividity is anterior (toward or at the front). Pat was discovered supine and lividity did not match. The Medical Examiner wrote in the autopsy report that he could not determine any kind of lividity. The autopsy photographs clearly showed that Pat's body was clear enough of decomposition that the Medical Examiner should have been able to determine lividity if it was there. In fact, Pat's waist area, front and back, was nearly clear of decomposition and no discernible indication of lividity was present.

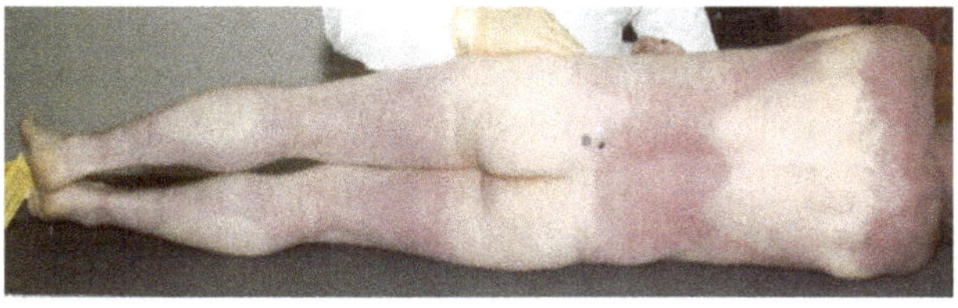

Figure 2.7 Lividity (*livor mortis*), the settling of blood, presents as dark areas at the lowest points of the body; points of contact with the ground or an object appear as light areas. (From Armstrong, E., & Erskine, K. 2011. *Water-Related Death Investigation: Practical Methods and Forensic Applications*. Boca Raton, FL: CRC Press.)

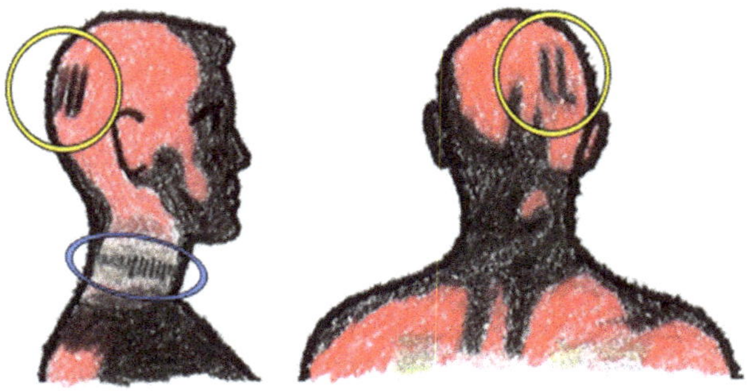

Figure 2.8 The Medical Examiner called Pat McNeil's death a drowning despite the fact that he had personally identified and described a possible ligature mark around the neck (*Blue Ellipse*). He also wrote that Pat's skull was unremarkable even though it had a clear 1/2 inch deep, 11.7 square inches, indentation (*Yellow Circles*).

Ligature Mark

In the autopsy report, the New York City Medical Examiner described a patterned mark that ran all the way around Pat's neck (i.e., 1/16 inch lines that were spaced 1/16 inch apart, and appeared to be about 1 inch in height). He even suggested that the mark resembled some kind of ligature (Figure 2.8, *Blue Ellipse*).

Injuries

The Medical Examiner suggested that the loss of hair was due to decomposition processes. He described the scalp as presenting nothing out of the ordinary. He also specifically remarked that there was no damage to Pat's skull. However, damage was clearly visible to the upper-right rear area of Pat's skull. There were 2 side-by-side indentations. Utilizing the autopsy scale that was visible in the photograph, Gilbertson measured each of these indentations at about 1-1/4 inch in width by 3-1/8 inches in height, and 1/2 inch in depth at the middle. They were separated in the middle by a ridge (undamaged skull) of equal proportion. Thus, the damaged area was about 3-3/4 inches by 3-1/8 inches (Figure 2.8, *Yellow Circles*). What caused this damage? Why was it not described? Was this damage missed, or ignored?

Flecks and Fibers

Close examination of the autopsy photographs turned up small blue flecks on Pat's left arm and face, as well as unidentified fine yellow fibers on his left arm and right midriff. These items were not described, analyzed, sampled, or collected and preserved by anyone. Were they related to some procedure done during the autopsy (e.g., dental impression)? Were they originally present and missed by the Medical Examiner?

Burning and Charring

Our team adamantly disagreed with the Medical Examiner's opinion that the severe blackening of Pat's head and upper torso, and the condition of his body, were the result of exposure to the elements and advanced decomposition. Our examination of the autopsy photographs concluded that Pat had been burned to charring from his head to mid-torso, with 2nd and 3rd degree burns around his belly and sides. A spot on his right elbow and his right ear looked like plasticized or melting flesh. Furthermore, the condition of Pat's face suggested that he had turned his face to the right, away from the flame that was burning him (perhaps, a type of broad-tipped blow torch was used). This caused charring to the left side of his face, while only burning his right side. Pat's attempted act of withdrawal and self-preservation was futile since he was tied with a 1 inch wide ligature about his neck to a high-back chair. Pat's burns and death were no accident; but, were clearly an act of torture and intentional murder.

One argument that we heard was that the mark around Pat's neck was not produced by a ligature, rather by the collar band of his undershirt. We recognize the scientific fact that clothing will protect and preserve surface skin tissue, particularly on bodies in the water. Unfortunately for those who peddled that myth and still cling to it, Pat was recovered not wearing a shirt. The area where the ligature mark was located and preserved did not look like the rest of Pat's face and chest. This meant that whatever caused him to appear blackened and leathery happened while the ligature was still secured around his neck. If it had been caused by the preserving affect of his T-shirt while decomposing, then he would have had to have been found still wearing it. These facts clearly pointed to injuries that happened antemortem (before death).

A closer look at the autopsy photographs supported a conclusion that Pat's back was protected from these injuries, except slightly around the midriff region. This information showed that Pat was most likely bound around his neck to a chair or some type of object that held his back flush with it, which subsequently protected his upper back while allowing part of the fire or flame to move around his lower waist to partially burn that area (but not to the point of charring). Our finding was consistent with the research literature on burn patterns (Bohnert, 2004; Moritz & Henriques, 1947a; Moritz & Henriques, 1947b). An additional fact that helped to convince us that Pat had been burned was the presence of hair. Recall that the Medical Examiner suggested that Pat had lost the hair on his head due to decomposition processes. We disagreed with that assessment. Yes, Pat was missing all of his head hair and eyebrows. However, he maintained the small hairs on the back of his neck and legs, and on the protected and undamaged areas of his arms and chest. Had he been deceased and in the water for 50 days, and decomposed to the advanced stage that the Medical Examiner may have wished readers to believe, then all of his hair should have been missing. Instead, the hair on Pat's body was consistent with the picture of torture that we just described.

Using the "Rule of 9s," we estimated that Pat had sustained burns on about 32 percent of his body. They ranged from 1st degree burns to 4th degree burns. It takes over a 6 hour period to cause a burn at 111.2 °Fahrenheit (44 °Celsius). On the other hand, 158.0 °Fahrenheit (70 °Celsius) can cause a burn in less than 1 second (Cooper, 2006, p. 218). Gases burn at different temperatures and burn even hotter when mixed with oxygen for industrial purposes; for example, propane and air – about 3,630 °Fahrenheit (2,000 °Celsius), propane and oxygen – about 4,530 °Fahrenheit (2,500 °Celsius), and acetylene and oxygen – about 6,330 °Fahrenheit (3,500 °Celsius). Whatever method or device was used to burn Pat, it had to have produced a broad area of extreme dry heat, which was targeted at his face. At one point, Gannon even posited that a blow torch may have been used. The Medical Examiner reported no anomalies in the bronchial tree except that it contained an unidentified red-black liquid. If it was blood mixed with soot, then our assumption about Pat being burned was once again supported by the existing research literature. In one study that involved the use of blow torches in bunkers, the researchers found that the low heat capacity of dry air causes the superheated air to cool quickly and that it did not burn the lower respiratory tree (Phillips, Tanner, & Cope, 1963, p. 799). Therefore, Pat's bronchial tree was not damaged, but it contained a small amount of bloody soot.

After having viewed Pat's autopsy photographs, Dr. Cyril Wecht concurred with our finding that Pat McNeil was bound and burned. Cyril Wecht, M.D. and J.D. (forensic pathologist & attorney), is one of the world's leading medical-legal consultants. He has performed over 14,000 autopsies during his career as coroner and medical examiner in Allegheny County and Pittsburgh. He has held professor positions at the University of Pittsburgh and adjunct appointments at Duquesne University. During a telephone discussion with Gannon on March 12, 2009, Dr. Wecht agreed that these were antemortem thermal injuries caused by some type of fire or burning while Pat was secured to an object by a ligature about his neck. He reaffirmed his conclusion during an interview on the *Larry King Live* program on March 27, 2009.

Fly Eggs

Additional review of the autopsy photographs discovered that there were multiple fly eggs in the pubic hairs of Pat's groin area. They were in an arrested state of development. First, if the blackened portion of Pat's face and upper torso had been due to normal decomposition in water, then it would have been moist and attractive to flies and they would have laid their eggs there. Instead, this area was burnt to the point of charring (hard and dry) which made it unsuitable to flies as a location to lay eggs. Subsequently, they laid their eggs in the most desirable and exposed location that they could find, his groin area. Second, had Pat actually fallen into the East River where he then died, then his groin area would have been underneath his boxers and immersed in water. Simply put, the flies could not have gotten there once Pat was in the water. Third, flies do not lay eggs on a deceased human body in temperatures under 50 °Fahrenheit, especially in the moving water of New York City's East River or the Upper New York Bay at night with temperatures in the 40s (like when Pat went missing). The suspicious location of the fly eggs (i.e., in Pat's groin area underneath his boxers and immersed in water) should have been a red flag.

This brought into question how the fly eggs could have been disregarded without any further investigation. An entomologist should have been brought in to assist in the investigation. Not only would this have helped with identification of the involved species, but also with determining the time element based on the maturation of the larvae, which is pretty consistent for each given species. Fly eggs are normally deposited within hours after death. The Bluebottle or Blowfly (*Calliphora erythrocephala*; see Figure 2.9), Greenbottles (*Lucilia caesar*), and Sheep Maggot flies (*Lucilia sericata*) are the most common types of fly recovered on victims outdoors (Geberth, 2006). Many insects, especially the adult female Common Housefly (*Musca domestica*), lay eggs in moist areas of a deceased body, that is, the eyes, nostrils, mouth, or open wounds when they are present.

The team concluded that Pat had to have been dead on land for a period of time in order for flies to lay their eggs on him before he was placed into the water. Gannon conferred with the following experts: Dr. Cyril Wecht (Forensic Pathologist), Dr. Richard Jantz (Forensic Pathologist from the "Body Farm" in Tennessee), Dr. Bradley Adams (Forensic

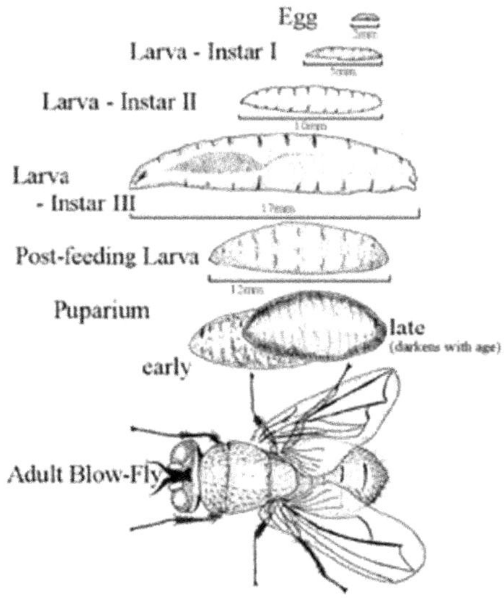

Figure 2.9 Illustration depicting the life cycle of the blowfly. The time interval between each stage is dependent upon ambient temperature and is species specific. (From Swift, B. 2006. The timing of death. In G. Rutty (Ed.), *Essentials of Autopsy Practice: Current Methods and Modern Trends* (pp. 189–214). London, UK: Springer-Verlag London Ltd.)

Anthropologist, Office of the Chief Medical Examiner, NYC), and Dr. Lou Sorkin (Entomologist, American Museum of Natural History). No one would go on record and commit to a public statement regarding any particular explanation for the presence of the fly eggs without having performed a physical examination themselves. However, they agreed that flies should not have been able to lay eggs on a decedent who was outdoors, at night, in temperatures under 50 °Fahrenheit, and floating in the East River. Pat had to have been dead indoors, in a environment warm enough for flies to survive and to be active during a New York winter, for a sufficient period of time for the flies to lay their eggs (usually about 24 hours), which ceased their development upon entering the frigid water.

Respiratory System

Both of Pat's lungs were above normal weight according to the autopsy report. There was no discussion of whether or not this was caused by the presence of river water as a result of drowning. In fact, no attempt (e.g., chemical test) was made to identify the contents of his lungs. However, assuming that the increased lung weight was caused by some sort of fluid, one cannot presume that it was river water. In a study of 239 admissions to a hospital burn unit (Witten, Quan, Sobonya, & Lemen, 1988, p. 34), 76 (32%) developed pulmonary edema and 57 (75%) of those patients died. The researchers reported that the greatest risk for developing pulmonary edema was for patients whose bodies had been 50 percent burned.

Additionally, they (Witten, Quan, Sobonya, & Lemen, 1988, p. 34) examined burn patients at the time of their admission for the presence of inhalation injury and measured extravascular lung water volume. They discovered that the extravascular lung water volume had increased by 10.1 mL plus or minus 3.4 mL per kilogram (kg) of body weight for those patients with parenchymal inhalation injury. The data for water are

1 liter (1,000 mL) = 1 kg (1,000 grams (gm)) = 2.204 pounds (lbs), or 1 cubic centimeter (cc) = 1 mL = 1 gm = 0.002204 lbs.

The Medical Examiner described Pat's parenchyma as red-black. Assuming that this was a description of inhalation injury and using Pat's normal weight of 185 lbs (or 83.914 kg), then Pat's lungs could have filled with extravascular fluid: 847.5 mL plus or minus 285.3 mL (range = 562.2 mL to 1,132.8 mL). Thus, each lung could have filled with fluid and increased in weight by as much as 281.1 to 566.4 gm. This could account for the increased lung weight (right at 640 gm and left at 610 gm) and the fact that his pleural cavities contained a lot of fluid (right at 250 cc and left at 300 cc).

Decomposition and Maceration

Pat's body at autopsy presented a graduated destruction and decomposition pattern. That is, its condition at one end did not match that of the other end. Pat's body at autopsy presented what appeared to be 8 distinct regions (Figure 2.10): (1) Anterior Head and Upper Torso, (2) Posterior Head and Shoulders, (3) Anterior Midriff, (4) Posterior Midriff, (5) Waistline and Buttocks, (6) Anterior Legs, (7) Posterior Legs, and (8) Feet.

Our examination of Pat's autopsy photographs disclosed the following for each region. The blackened skin of the anterior head and upper torso had contracted or shrunk (a tight leathery appearance). It had not swollen and become mushy in appearance as normally seen in a bloating body of a drowning victim. This portion of the body had been burned to charring. The posterior head and shoulders showed a deep red (or cherry red) color. Skin slippage was not as extensive as reported and we assessed the color in this region to be the

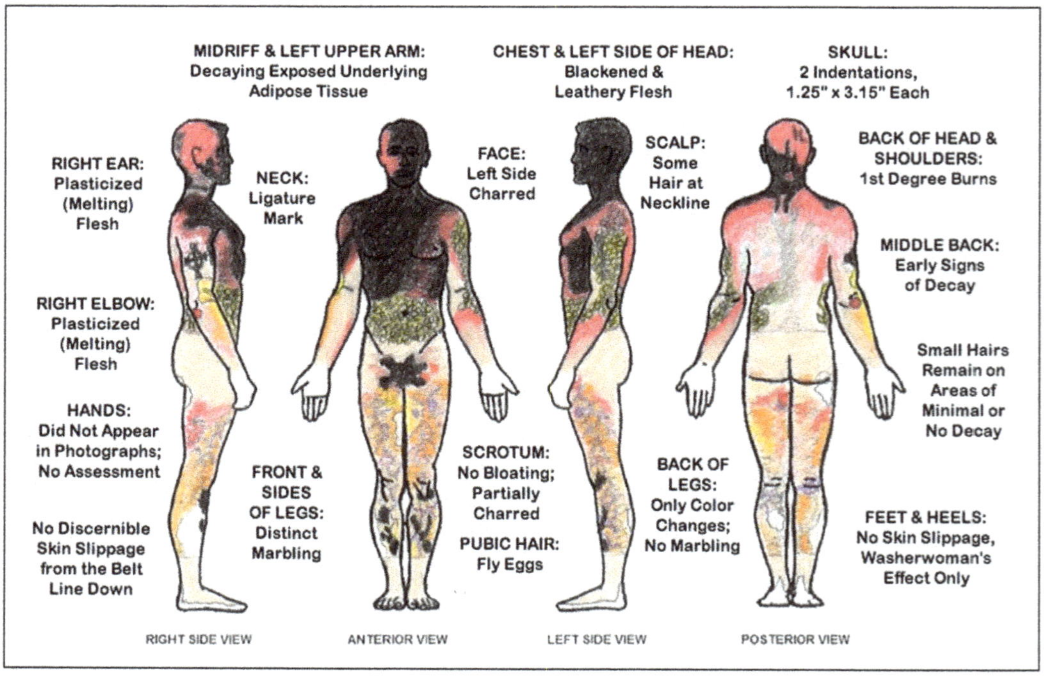

Figure 2.10 Patrick McNeil's body at autopsy; artist rendition from observations of autopsy photographs.

result of 1st degree burns and early decomposition. The middle of the posterior torso presented with areas of blue-green and gray-green. Again, we attributed this to early decomposition. This stage of postmortem decomposition requires only 3 days to occur on land and 6 days in the water. However, keeping in mind that the lungs may have filled with fluid due to inhalation injury, the colors in this region (cherry red, blue-green and gray-green) may have been associated with those injuries, carbon monoxyhemoglobin, and cyanosis (Phillips, Tanner, & Cope, 1963).

Inconsistencies in decomposition were also observed upon moving down to the anterior midriff, posterior midriff, waistline and buttocks. The anterior midriff clearly resembled exposed and burnt underlying fatty tissue (yellowish-black) that had started to decay. The body about his waist, however, showed evidence of "Red Line," which is an effect caused by the protection of clothing and demarks protected from unprotected skin during exposure to a heat source. In Pat's case, the Red Line appeared at the top of his blue jeans. This marked the point where his unprotected anterior and posterior midriff met his clothing-protected waistline and buttocks. This, in our mind, was the only thing that could account for the distinct areas of light burning (seen as marbled redness), the protected area that showed almost no decomposition, and areas of accelerated decomposition (seen as yellowish-green). Pat's legs showed established marbling, but only on the anterior side.

Here is where the contradiction rested. Pat's body was not consistent from front to rear, it was not consistent from left to right, and was not consistent from head to toe. His chest was blackened and his back was cherry red and shades of green. His left shoulder and bicep showed exposed adipose tissue, while the right shoulder was pretty much intact. There was little decomposition around his waistline. The front and sides of his thighs and calves were clearly marbled, but there were spots (about 3 inches to 4 inches wide) on the front that were free of decay. The back of his legs was similar in color to the front (yellowish-orange), but lacked distinctive marbling. There were no autopsy pictures that showed his hands or palms, so we could not assess the description of extensive skin loss on the palms of the hands. Pat's feet, however, did not present any extent of skin slippage that would be consistent with having been submerged in water for 50 days. In fact, the absence of any skin slippage suggested to us that his feet had been in the water for no more than a few days.

Since the extent of decomposition among the regions was inconsistent with 50 days in the water, we looked for other possible explanations. We discovered that a special form of morphological change resulting from the heat of 2nd degree burns can occur that mimics Washerwoman's Hands (*Wauschaut*) and degloving (Bohnert, 2004). Thus, the Medical Examiner cannot have it both ways. He cannot have advanced decomposition due to environmental exposure on one side and end of a body, while having very little to none on the other side and end of the body.

Conclusion

Given all of this, we posit that Pat's death was not an accidental drowning. He was stalked, drugged, abducted, held for an extended period of time, murdered, and disposed. After his torture and burning, he remained on land for a short period of time in order for the flies to lay eggs in his groin area. During this time, decomposition started, and became visible on his legs. He was then transported to Owls Head pier and placed into the East River. Whereon, he was discovered and recovered within 24 hours, which explains the absence of skin slippage on his feet. Since Pat's murder and disposal only involved 3 to 4 days of the total 50 days that he was missing, then one must ask, "Where was Pat for the other 46 to 47 days?"

Bodies that are dead before being placed in the water usually do not sink (Armstrong & Erskine, 2011). The evidence was consistent with this premise and also explained why Pat was found floating. It usually takes weeks for a body in water to decompose enough for gases to form, especially in cold water, and for the body to rise to the surface. If Pat was only in the water for a day or two at the most, then how is it that he was found floating in the Upper New York Bay? There are two ways a body may be found on the surface of cold water after only a day or two, or may stay on the surface without ever sinking. A body may stay at the surface when killed in another location, allowed to decompose and to produce gases, and then dumped into a waterway. Another way a body does not sink and stays afloat is when an individual has been killed prior to water submersion, and air trapped within the lungs contributes to floating (Armstrong & Erskine, 2011).

Therefore, we assert that the idea that Pat was murdered was not only correct, but the assumption that the murder took place indoors was also correct. After examining the photos and considering all the evidence related to this case, Dr. Cyril Wecht concurred with us on March 12, 2009, that Pat McNeil was definitely murdered and the case should be classified as a homicide. As previously stated, on March 19, 2009, Gannon and Duarte presented this evidence to the NYPD Chief of the Special Investigations Division who was going to confer with the current NYC Chief Medical Examiner and get back to us. To this date, we have received no official or unofficial reply.

3 Lawrence Robert Andrews, Jr.*

February 25, 1976–February 12, 1998

Background

The problem with drowning cases across the country is that they do not fit the criteria for entry into the Violent Criminal Apprehension Program (ViCAP) system. The ViCAP system was formed to collect, collate and analyze all aspects of an investigation using the latest computer and communications technology. The idea for a system to identify serial offenders came from Pierce Brooks, a retired Chief of Police (Lakewood, Colorado) and former homicide detective with the Los Angeles Police Department. He introduced the idea to the Federal Bureau of Investigation in the early 1980s and it became a reality in 1985. Many drownings are witnessed. However, a large portion of them is not witnessed by anyone or they are suspicious in nature because of the circumstances (e.g., occurred during winter months, alone or unaccompanied, low levels of alcohol, drugs in the system, condition or position of the body inconsistent with a normal drowning, or decomposition inconsistent with the victim's supposed time in the water). None of these reasons fit the criteria for entry into the ViCAP system. This is why there is a need for a new entry criterion in the ViCAP system to help chart similar suspicious drowning deaths across the country.

Larry Andrews was the second in a series of 3 young men who were found suspiciously drowned in New York City during a 15-month period from February 17, 1997, to May 13, 1998. Gannon is confident that the only drowning case in the ViCAP system that is not classified as a homicide is Pat McNeil. As the supervisor in charge of McNeil's investigation, Gannon convinced his boss that there was enough evidence to point to homicide.

* Photo courtesy of the Andrews family.

Figure 3.1 Larry (left) with his parents Susan and Lawrence Andrews (center), and sister Jennifer (right). (Photo courtesy of the Andrews family.)

He was allowed to have McNeil's case put into the ViCAP system by the detective assigned to the case with him. Gannon knows for a fact that no other investigators have accessed the ViCAP system to either put in one of their drowning cases or to check to see whether there were any others that matched their specific drowning case. If any other detective had accessed the ViCAP system to research suspicious drowning deaths, then he or she would have gotten information on McNeil and would have had to contact Gannon to see why he thought there was reasonable evidence to feel that his case was a homicide. No one has ever contacted Gannon in the past 16 plus years since McNeil's case was entered. When Gannon subsequently attempted to do the same with the case of Larry Andrews, his bosses quickly shot him down.

The Andrews family had never received a complete package (i.e., autopsy report, photographs, and toxicology report) from the medical examiner's office. After Jackie McNeil received her son's autopsy photos 11 years after his case was closed, the Andrews family attempted to also obtain photographs of their son's autopsy more than 10 years after the fact. The NYC Office of Chief Medical Examiner finally turned over 27 autopsy photographs. As in the McNeil case, the Medical Examiner's office denied our request for permission to show excerpts from the reports and photographs that were approved by the Andrews family (Figure 3.1). Therefore, this chapter on Larry's death was derived from Gannon's memory and notes of the case, as well as the team's analysis of the autopsy and toxicology reports, 27 autopsy photographs, and our repeated visits to locations associated with this case.

Circumstances

Last Seen

Lawrence Robert Andrews, Jr. ("Larry"), was a White male, 22 years old, 6 feet 3 inches, 185 pounds (Body Mass Index: 23.12), with brown hair and brown eyes. He was last seen on the evening of December 31, 1997. The evening started out with some partying and drinking at a friend's home in Brewster, New York. The group, which included Larry, then

Figure 3.2 Larry Andrews arrived with his friends at Grand Central Terminal on New Year's Eve; witnesses claimed to have seen him back in the terminal at a bar after midnight.

Figure 3.3 Like all of the cases in this book, we retraced the footsteps of victims for the nights that they disappeared. The team (Gilbertson pictured) started its walk down 42nd Street from inside the Grand Central Terminal just like Larry Andrews did.

continued to drink while traveling by train and arrived at Grand Central Terminal about 22:30 hours (Figure 3.2). They stopped for a couple more drinks as they made their way along 42nd Street (Figures 3.3 and 3.4). The group was together at Houlihan's just prior to entering the streets to join the celebration. According to personal accounts, Larry became separated from this group just after the ball dropped at midnight signaling the New Year. Larry was last seen about 00:30 hours on Thursday, January 1, 1998, by the friends who came with him to New York City. However, a different group of Brewster residents reported talking with him around 01:00 hours in a bar inside Grand Central Terminal. Two other Brewster residents reported seeing Larry headed west on 42nd Street sometime between 02:00 hours and 02:30 hours (Figure 3.5).

Recovery

Larry was found drowned in the Upper New York Bay just over 6 weeks later (42 days 5 hours 30 minutes) on February 12, 1998. He was recovered in the Bay Ridge section of

Figure 3.4 The view down 42nd Street looking back toward the East River while standing outside the Grand Central Terminal at the intersection with Park Avenue.

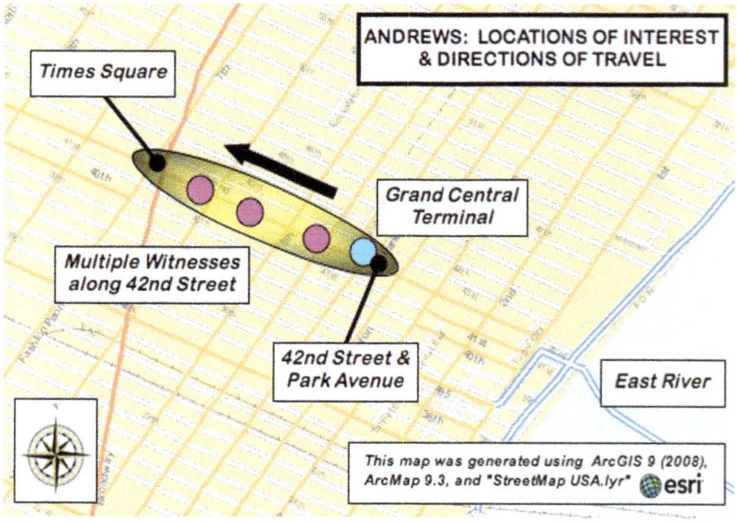

Figure 3.5 Larry Andrews arrived at Grand Central Terminal (*Turquoise Dot*) and spent New Year's Eve walking along 42nd Street (*Yellow Ellipse*) drinking with his friends. Multiple Brewster residents sighted him at various times (*Purple Dots*). The last sightings suggested that he was headed in a westerly direction (*Black Arrows*) away from the East River.

Brooklyn at Owls Head Water Pollution Control Plant at the 69th Street Pier on Shore Road (Figure 3.6); he was over 9 miles away from where he was last observed in Manhattan. Larry was no longer a missing person; he was now a recovered body and deceased person. At that point, the Andrews case no longer belonged to NYPD's Missing Persons Unit (specifically, Detective Sergeant Gannon) and became the jurisdiction of investigators in the Detectives Bureau of the 68th Precinct in Brooklyn.

Figure 3.6 The area in which Larry Andrews was recovered on February 12, 1998, was just to the left of the entry gate to Owls Head Water Pollution Control Plant. This was the same location where Pat McNeil had been recovered almost a year earlier on April 7, 1997.

Analysis of Evidence

Recovery Location

Larry was recovered within yards of the location where Pat McNeil had been recovered less than a year earlier on April 7, 1997 (Figure 3.7). Further investigation revealed that Larry's body should have never been recovered where it was considering information about the water currents for the East River and the Upper New York Bay that was obtained from the NYPD Harbor Unit that patrols the river daily. Gannon reviewed many other cases and discovered that people's bodies had been routinely recovered within a football field's distance from where they had fallen into the East River near Manhattan. The bodies of persons falling into the Hudson River (on the west side of Manhattan Island) would normally stay in the Hudson River. The more he learned from harbor personnel, the greater Gannon found it difficult to believe that Larry could float the 9 miles of open water. How could Larry not receive any distinctive postmortem injury as a result of being struck by one of the many commercial ships? How could Larry not become entangled with one of the numerous bridges, piers, and buoys? The only possible answer was that Larry had to have been abducted, driven to that location, and deposited there, in order for him to have been recovered at that location.

Clothing

Larry was prepared and dressed for being outdoors on a cold night. Although some statements given by witnesses claimed that Larry was not wearing all of his clothing, he was recovered wearing the following: black/blue jacket, black turtleneck thermal shirt, gray long-sleeved shirt, black thermal shirt, short green pants, black full-length pants, two pairs of socks, and black boots.

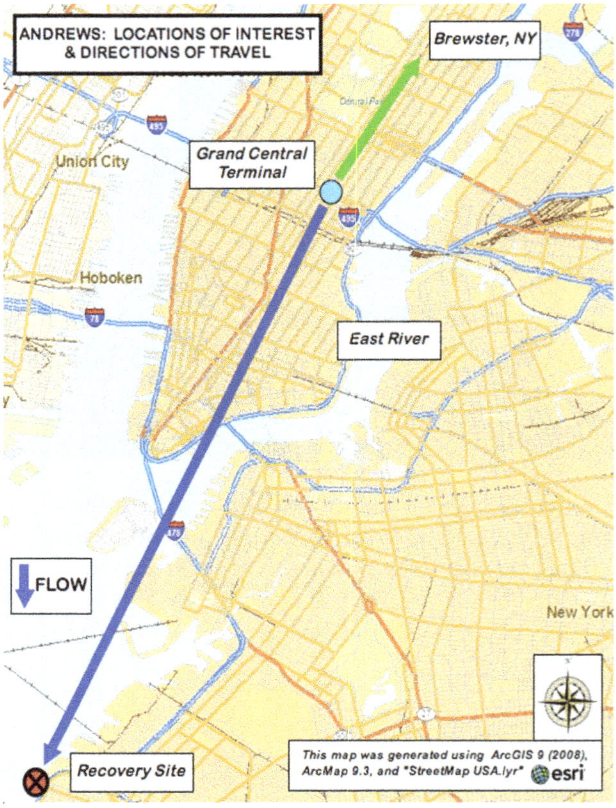

Figure 3.7 Larry was last seen in the vicinity of the Grand Central Terminal (*Turquoise Dot*), and he was supposed to return to Brewster with his friends (*Green Arrow*). Instead, his body was recovered at Owls Head Water Pollution Control Plant in Brooklyn (*Red-X Dot*).

Toxicology

Larry was recovered with a 0.19 BAC (Blood Alcohol Concentration). Human bodies naturally produce alcohol postmortem (after death) as a part of decomposition (Dix & Graham, 1999). Considering that he was supposed to have been in the water for about 6 weeks (42 days 5 hours 30 minutes), his BAC should have increased by about 0.03 due to postmortem alcohol production. This meant that his actual BAC upon entering the water was probably more like 0.16 or around 8 drinks. This was not that drunk for a young, 6 foot 3 inch, 190 pound man. Once again, as in the McNeil case, the toxicology tests demonstrated different levels of ethanol BAC in the blood (0.19), brain (0.21), and urine (0.30) (Spitz & Spitz, 2006).

The toxicology screening tested for the normal array of street drugs: opiates, benzoylecgonine (a cocaine metabolite), phencyclidine (PCP), cannabinoids (a group of substances that are structurally related to tetrahydrocannabinol (THC)), methadone (synthetic opioid), salicylates, phenothiazines (the largest of the five main classes of neuroleptic antipsychotic drugs), barbiturates, amphetamines, and acetaminophen. They did not test for the date rape drugs of ketamine, Rohypnol, or gamma-hydroxybutyrate (GHB). All tests came back "not detected" except one; the toxicology report indicated that diphenhydramine had been "detected." No actual amount was determined or recorded. Diphenhydramine can be prescribed to treat hay fever, allergies, common cold symptoms, insomnia, motion sickness, or early-stage Parkinsonian syndrome. Potential side effects include dry mouth, nose, and throat; drowsiness; dizziness; nausea; vomiting; loss of appetite; constipation; increased chest congestion; headache; muscle weakness; excitement (especially in children); nervousness; vision problems; and difficulty urinating or painful urination.

Larry had a cold and he was taking medication. But, he had told his sister that he was not going to take the medication that night since he knew he would be drinking. This clearly demonstrated his maturity and extent of forethought regarding his personal well-being. Since the amount of diphenhydramine found in Larry's system was not reported, we could not determine whether it was a trace amount from medication he had voluntarily taken the previous day, whether he continued to take the medication, or whether it was involuntarily given to him at some point that night.

Body Position and Lividity

Gannon knew that this was very peculiar right from the start. Most drowning victims are found floating prone (face-down) (Hendrick, Zaferes, & Nelson, 2003). Exceptions occur when a victim is obese or the water is similar to that of a raging river and is capable of flipping a body from its normal prone position. Larry's body position was inconsistent with normal drowning cases; he was recovered supine (face-up). Not only was this extremely unusual for drowning cases, especially one of an individual with Larry's height and body weight, but this was also the same position in which Pat McNeil had been found in this same location.

Lividity (*livor mortis*) is the postmortem discoloration due to the gravitation of blood into the dependent capillaries and veins; basically, it is the pooling and settling of the blood that starts within 30 minutes after death (Geberth, 2006). On dry land, fixed lividity can usually be seen by about 10 to 12 hours after death. Fixed means the blood has settled in one position and can no longer be significantly shifted by changing the position of the body (Shkrum & Ramsay, 2007).

Examination of Larry's autopsy report and photographs disclosed additional problems with body position. The Medical Examiner clearly mentioned in the autopsy report that lividity was fixed on Larry's anterior (front side). This was inconsistent with having been found floating in a supine position (on his back). Furthermore, we could not determine any evidence of lividity below Larry's rib cage. If lividity was anterior as stated in the autopsy report, then it should have been detectable on his midriff, groin area, or legs – it was not. Strangely, it could not even be identified as anterior or posterior below the rib cage. It seemed to be slightly anterior and above the rib cage.

Decomposition and Maceration

The autopsy report (i.e., Report of Autopsy, Final Diagnoses) from the Chief Medical Examiner's Office described discoloration, marbling and skin slippage across Larry's body. Specifically, the report stated that Larry's forehead presented marbling. The Medical Examiner suggested that there was skin slippage on Larry's face, lower forearms, legs, and back. She professionally opined that the nasal structure was intact and that the color of Larry's nose was the result of *ecchymoses* related to decomposition that extended up into his eyes. Ecchymosis (ecchymoses, plural) is the medical term for a hemorrhagic spot or bruise. One may surmise that as a medical doctor she would know and be able to visually discern the difference between ecchymoses and "Tardieu spots." As the Postmortem Interval (PMI) lengthens, Tardieu spots develop and appear as petechiae and purpuric hemorrhages in areas of lividity as decomposing capillaries rupture. The Medical Examiner did know the difference, she knew that there was bruising, and she described it as such (i.e., ecchymoses). Although it seemed that the Medical Examiner had clearly described the "blacks eyes" that one might get after being punched and having his nose broken, no attempt was ever made to explain the cause of the bruising on Larry's nose and eyes.

However, our examination of the autopsy photographs came away with significantly different conclusions. We determined that color changes due to early decomposition were only easily visible in the upper chest, somewhat visible in the lower back, and barely visible in the mid to upper back. The only discernible marbling was a slight presence in his shoulders. Skin slippage had only occurred in a spotty pattern and was present on the front and back of his legs, and along the midline of his chest. Contrary to what the Medical Examiner had said, Larry's lower forearms and back were clear of any skin slippage. The Medical Examiner also suggested that the first layers of skin on Larry's face showed signs of sloughing. The skin on his face was becoming white from prolonged immersion, but it was not sloughing.

The presence of Washerwoman's Hands (*Wauschaut*) on the hands and feet is a good indicator of immersion in a body of water, and can help to estimate the approximate amount of time that was spent submerged in said water (Figure 3.8). Degloving is when the top layer of skin (epidermis) separates from the second layer of skin (dermis) (Figure 3.9). It presents like a loose glove lifting and pulling away from the hands. On the feet, it begins to deglove at the heel. Given the amount of time that he had been in the water, Larry's hands and the feet should not only have presented with a *Wauschaut* effect, they should have also completely degloved – they had not. Instead, the skin on Larry's hands was just starting to come off his fingers.

As for the color and anatomical integrity of Larry's nose and eyes, it became evident upon comparing the different autopsy pictures of Larry's face that when his head was turned to the left, then his nose hung downward to the left. When his head was turned to the right, then his nose hung downward to the right. The nose was broken, dark red-purple in color, and subsequently bruised a dark red up into the eyes. We concurred that the

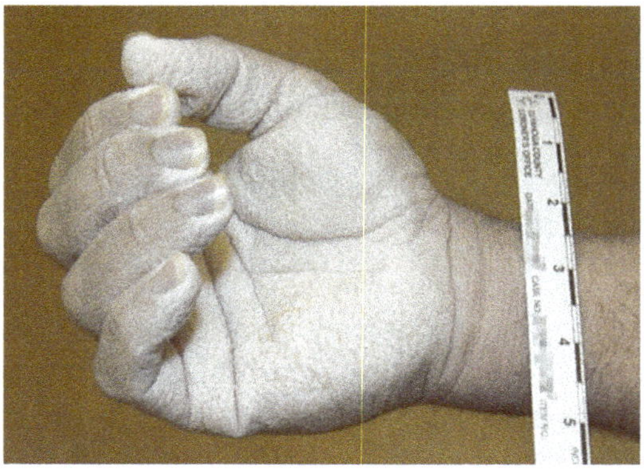

Figure 3.8 Washerwoman's Hands (*Wauschaut*) occurs when the hands are exposed to moisture or submerged in a liquid for a prolonged period of time. This hand was submerged for less than a day. (From Armstrong, E., & Erskine, K. 2011. *Water-Related Death Investigation: Practical Methods and Forensic Applications*. Boca Raton, FL: CRC Press.)

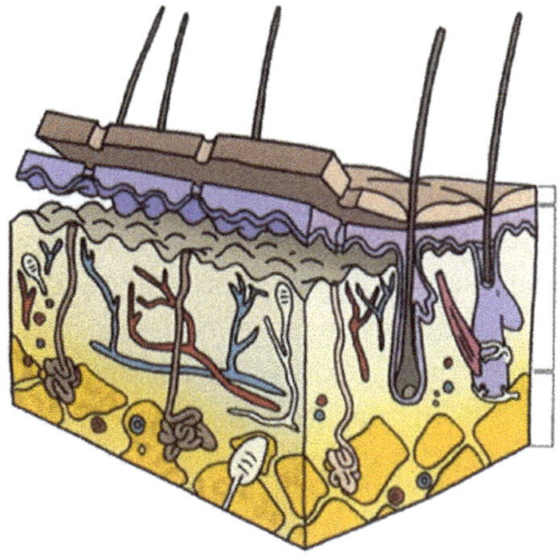

Figure 3.9 "Degloving" of the hands and feet occurs during decomposition when the epidermis separates from the dermis. (From Armstrong, E., & Erskine, K. 2011. *Water-Related Death Investigation: Practical Methods and Forensic Applications*. Boca Raton, FL: CRC Press.)

Medical Examiner had described the nose and eyes correctly, but only within the context that she had used the medical term *ecchymoses* – the nose was in fact severely bruised as a result of trauma to the underlying tissues and vessels. The bruising process requires a living being and sufficient time following injury for the heart to pump blood to the damaged area in order to produce a bruise. Sometimes, damage to a forehead or face can result from traveling in the water and bouncing off rocks or the bottom during refloat (a.k.a., travel abrasions). This kind of postmortem injury may appear as scuffs, scratches, scrapes, and cuts (Hendrick, Zaferes, & Nelson, 2003). But, it will not have concurrent bruising. Clear bruising indicates antemortem injury. Furthermore, there was a distinct mark or bruise on Larry's right cheek just below his eye. There was absolutely no identifiable marbling on Larry's forehead; rather, there was some physical damage with light bruising.

The appearance of Larry's body at the time of autopsy was inconsistent with established scientific knowledge concerning the general condition of a decaying human body that had purportedly been in water for 42 days (6 weeks). The extent of putrefaction and maceration characteristics resembled more like that of someone who had been in the water for only a couple of weeks at most, and not the 42 days that Larry had been missing. On the other hand, we were convinced that Larry had not been in the water for even a week. Rather than relying on the description of the body in the autopsy report, we concluded that the extent of decomposition and skin slippage actually presented in the autopsy photographs more closely reflected a body that had probably been in the water for only 4 days. This conclusion was reached, in part, by taking into account that the effect of 1 day of decomposition on land is roughly equivalent to 2 days in the water.

Hemolysis and hydrogen sulfide gas production cause the blue-green to dark green discoloration that shows up as part of decomposition. Green discoloration starts in the Right Lower Quadrant (RLQ) and then spreads to the entire body in approximately 48 hours in water (Shkrum & Ramsay, 2007). In Larry's case, this blue-green to dark green discoloration was only distinctive in his upper chest and neck, and somewhat identifiable in his lower back area. The autopsy report stated that Larry's head was still covered by thick dark brown hair. After 42 days in the water, Larry's hair should have been falling out, if not gone – autopsy photographs confirmed that it was not. Additionally, the scrotum should have been bloating with decomposition gases within 72 to 96 hours after death. However, the autopsy photographs confirmed that the scrotum was not visibly bloating.

We received all associated autopsy photographs for these cases from either family members or as a result of Freedom of Information Act (FOIA) letters of request that we filed. However, we did not receive written permission from some of the agencies to publish them in this book. Why would they not give us permission to show the pictures? In some cases, state law prohibited the release of autopsy photographs to persons who were not members of the immediate family. We were given permission so long as a victim's family granted it. In other cases, state law precluded the release and presentation of photographs of deceased victims. A sticking point was that we intended to name our victims and to associate specific photos with them. In a typical forensics textbook, photographs are presented anonymously and victims' names are never disclosed. This is why it was so disheartening for us that we could not show to readers the discrete recovery and autopsy photographs that the families approved for many of these cases. Instead, we have had to settle with creating our own "artist's rendition" in some cases (Figure 3.10).

However, in some cases, no state statute disallowed the release and use of autopsy photographs. So, returning to the original question, why would some agencies not give us permission to show the pictures? This is why it is so important to take numerous photographs during body recoveries and autopsies. A picture truly is worth a thousand words. It can either support or refute the story told in the autopsy report. In so many of the cases that we have examined, it was the forensic photographs that helped us to discern what had happened and how to accurately interpret the autopsy results. Without the existence of several forensic photographs, medical examiners, coroners, water rescue teams, and law enforcement investigators can write whatever they want into their reports. We know of an agency

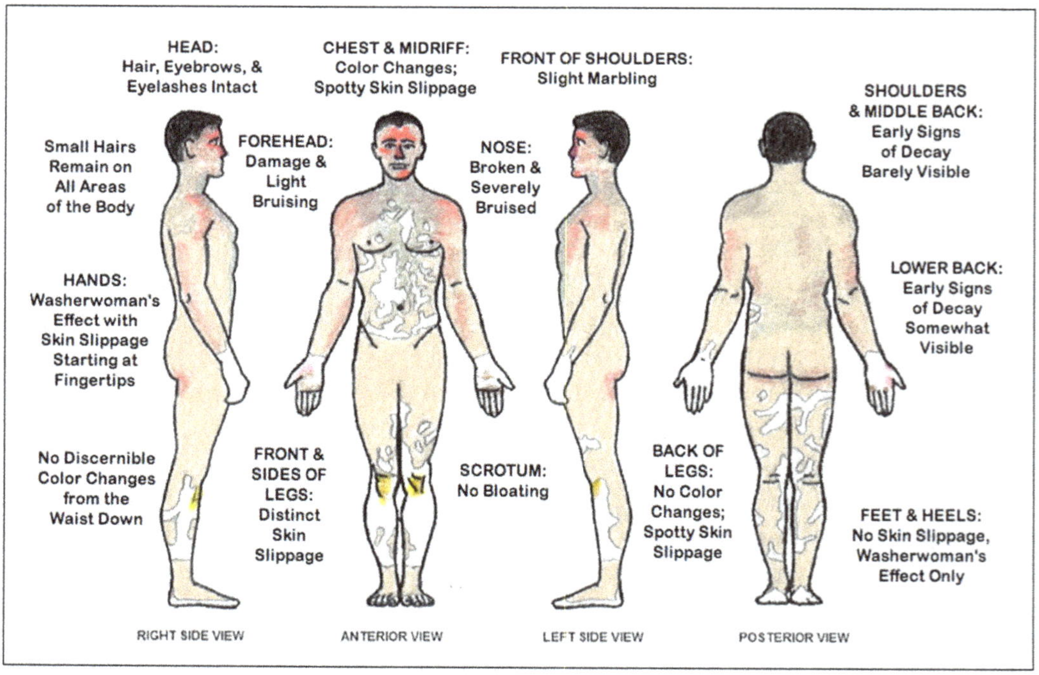

Figure 3.10 Lawrence Andrews's body at autopsy; artist rendition from observations of autopsy photographs.

that provided us with only one autopsy photograph of the victim's face. When we inquired regarding the remaining pictures, we were told that they only take one "identification" photograph in accordance with standard practices. Needless to say, that one forensic photograph did not match the rest of the report.

Empty Systems

The presence of empty systems told us that Larry's death may not have been a drowning. Not all victims of drowning aspirate water and not all bodies vacate their bowels upon death. Typically, people refer to an older study which reported that 10 to 15 percent of all cases are dry drownings (Lunetta, Modell, & Sajantila, 2004; Lunetta, Penttilla, & Sajantila, 2002). That statistic has been challenged by a more recent study that found that as few as 2 percent of cases are actually dry drownings (Armstrong & Erskine, 2011). A drowning is referred to by this term when there is no water present in the lungs (Armstrong & Erskine, 2011). This can happen due to a laryngeal spasm; a pinkish foam may be present in the throat and airway as a result of broken blood vessels. Larry's right lung weighed 500 grams and his left lung weighed 400 grams (approximate normal weights for human adult lungs). The Medical Examiner described the bronchi as unremarkable and suggested that normal-appearing mucosa lined the esophagus. This suggested to us that Larry was either alive and did not aspirate water upon submersion, or that he was not breathing for some reason upon entry into the water. Additionally, about 50 cubic centimeters (approximately 1.7 fluid ounces) of a thick, gray-brown mucus was discovered in his stomach, and his bladder contained 300 cubic centimeters (about 10.2 fluid ounces) of urine. His small and large intestines showed only autolyzed mucosa. Under normal circumstances, depending on the type and volume of food, a stomach empties its contents no more than 4 to 6 hours after a meal. If the small intestine is empty, then death probably occurred at least 12 or more hours after the last meal. When, where, and what was Larry's last meal?

Flecks and Fibers

After having received the autopsy photographs, close examination disclosed small fluorescent orange flecks on Larry's coat, as well as unidentified white fibers that resembled Alaskan Husky hairs. These items were not described, analyzed, sampled, or collected and preserved by the Medical Examiner or law enforcement officers. Were these items important or were they unrelated to Larry's death? Had they been picked up in the water? Did they hold any evidentiary value? Do not forget this seemingly "insignificant" evidence, because it will show up again later on in this book.

Conclusion

Two extremely similar young men, who disappeared in Manhattan within 10 months of each other, started their evenings out about 3 miles apart and then ended up in the same location. Pat McNeil was last seen near the intersection of 2nd Avenue and 90th Street. Larry Andrews, Jr., was last seen on 42nd Street and Park Avenue near the Grand Central Terminal. Both were recovered in the Bay Ridge section of Brooklyn at Owls Head Water Pollution Control Plant at the 69th Street Pier on Shore Road. Besides this geographic commonality, they demonstrated many other similar demographics. Our investigation has convinced us that this was not a coincidence.

	Pat McNeil	Larry Andrews, Jr.
Date of Birth	*February 24, 1976*	*February 25, 1976*
Age	*20*[a]	*21*
Last Seen	*February 17, 1997*	*January 1, 1998*
Recovered	*April 7, 1997*	*February 12, 1998*
Missing	*50 days*	*42 days*
Race	*White*	*White*
Height	*73 inches*	*72 inches*
Weight	*185 lbs.*	*185 lbs.*
Hair Color	*Brown*	*Brown*
Eye Color	*Brown*	*Brown*

[a] Pat was abducted on February 17th, one week before his 21st birthday.

Official reports and newspaper articles always quoted the police spokespersons and the Medical Examiners as suggesting that there were "no signs of foul play" in all but one of the cases in this book. However, Larry's autopsy photographs clearly displayed that he had sustained antemortem injuries; he had a scuff on his chin and his nose had been broken. In fact, Larry's nose was so severely damaged that it hung to whatever side his head was turned. According to his sister, Larry was a fighter and would not have gone down without some sort of resistance. The photographs suggested that he had most likely been beaten up while physically restrained since he did not have any defensive injuries to his hands or forearms.

The facts of the case screamed that something was not right. Larry was the same physical size and age as Pat McNeil. Both young men had fallen into the water during the same time of the season. Both had fallen into the same body of water 3 miles apart, but were then recovered in the same location within yards of each other. Since Larry was missing for only 6 days less than Pat, we assert that the condition of his body upon recovery should have looked a lot like Pat's. How does a person explain the presence of skin slippage and no discoloration due to decomposition on Larry's abdomen, buttocks, or legs? Perhaps, Larry did not drown. Maybe, he died as a result of gas-related asphyxia. The subsequent color of lividity will change in association with the responsible poisonous gas when different gases are inhaled and contribute to death (Armstrong & Erskine, 2011; Shkrum & Ramsay, 2007).

More commonly known as "sewer gas," hydrogen sulfide is a flammable, colorless gas, that smells like rotten eggs. According to the Agency for Toxic Substances and Disease Registry (ATSDR, 2006), it can be found in natural gas, crude petroleum and refineries, hot springs and volcanoes, food processing, coke ovens, paper mills, and tanneries. Human and animal wastes, as well as bacterial decomposition of organic matter, also produce hydrogen sulfide gas. Exposure to higher-than-normal levels of hydrogen sulfide may be experienced by people in the general public who live near a "wastewater treatment plant, a gas and oil drilling operation, a farm with manure storage or livestock confinement facilities, or a landfill" (ATSDR, 2006, p. 3). Loss of consciousness and possible death can result from even brief exposure to high concentrations of hydrogen sulfide (i.e., greater than 500 parts per million). There are ways to test for exposure to hydrogen sulfide. Exhaled air can be tested, but must be done within 2 hours of exposure. Another way is to test the urine for levels of thiosulfate within 12 hours of exposure (ATSDR, 2006). Hydrogen sulfide (H_2S) poisoning will cause lividity to appear green (Armstrong & Erskine, 2011; Shkrum & Ramsay, 2007).

We also know that colors associated with decomposition can mask signs of lividity, and lividity colors from gas-related asphyxia can be mistaken for decomposition colors. If Larry had been placed in a *Trendelenburg* position (a supine, head-down position on a pivoting bed), then the blood in his body would have settled into his upper torso. He would have looked like the autopsy pictures that we saw (see above, Figure 3.10). Had he succumbed to hydrogen sulfide poisoning through inhalation, then his lividity would have appeared blue-green to dark green and may have been confused by the Medical Examiner for the signs of decomposition. We have not claimed that this is the scenario by which Larry died. Rather, we offer it as a possible explanation that could be explored and discussed.

Given all of this, we posit that Larry's death was not an accidental drowning. He was abducted on 42nd Street, beaten and held for a period of time, murdered, and then transported to Owls Head Water Pollution Control Plant where he was placed into the water to create the appearance of an accidental drowning. Larry Andrews, Jr., was placed in the same location as Pat McNeil as a taunt of local law enforcement. He was intentionally taken from one borough (Manhattan) and placed in another (Brooklyn) in order to confound investigative efforts related to jurisdiction. The manner of death was entered as undetermined. The cause of death was listed as drowning even though there was no evidence to indicate a drowning had occurred – except that he was found deceased in water. Until only recently, the NYC Chief Medical Examiner's Office withheld Larry's autopsy photographs from his family and our team's scrutiny.

Adam Michael Falcon*

4

Background

Adam Falcon was an accomplished soccer player at the prestigious school of Saint Lawrence University in Canton, New York (Figure 4.1). At first glance, he was a handsome young man with an athletic build. However, Adam was not just another campus jock, he was a philosophy major with a 3.4 GPA. Adam was also civically and socially minded, and coached kids' summer camps. Adam had plans for the evening of Friday, November 12, 2004, with "J.M." and other friends. He was scheduled for an early morning wake up for the teams' championship soccer game the following day. Because he was injured, Adam was assisting the coaching staff.

Adam's father, Michael (Mike) Falcon, shared information with us that suggested that the university had a strict policy against drinking games on campus, and that the university's public safety department was closely watching the Dean Eaton dormitory due to some crime tips that had been received. In addition to the party at the Dean Eaton dormitory, there were three other large parties going on that night: (a) the Glass Onion restaurant (near the Tick Tock Inn) served as the location for a hockey party, (b) the local Knights of Columbus Hall hosted a dance that night, and (c) there was a large student party on Minor Street close to the Knights of Columbus. As such, law enforcement activity was high that night with at least 1 sheriff's vehicle, 2 United States Border Patrol vehicles, and 1 Canton police vehicle.

On Saturday, May 19, 2007, at 09:00 hours, the team met with Mike Falcon in upstate New York. After breakfast, we visited the sites in Canton that were associated with Adam's case. All on-site photographs in this report were taken that day by members of our team.

* Photo courtesy of the Falcon family.

Figure 4.1 Adam Falcon thoroughly enjoyed playing soccer. (Photo courtesy of the Falcon family.)

Mike gave us permission to use whatever we needed to get his son's story out. This chapter was compiled using notes that we took during the on-site visit, from interviews with key personnel, from personal observations of body recovery and autopsy photographs, and while reading official documents.

Circumstances

Last Seen

Adam Michael Falcon was a White male, 20 years old, 5 feet 9 inches, 180 pounds (Body Mass Index: 26.58), with brown hair and brown eyes. The night of Friday, November 12, 2004, involved a lot of activity and movement on the part of Adam and his friends. Adam started out by eating two plates of spaghetti around 18:00 hours. Then, he and "J.M." headed out about 19:00 hours for a Saint Lawrence University hockey game. When the hockey game was over about 21:15 hours, they left to attend a party at Dean Eaton dormitory where the theme for the night was a drinking game called "Around the World." About 30 kids (many of whom were under the legal drinking age) were at the party, which included 3 dormitory rooms. Adam and his friends left the party at Dean Eaton dormitory about 22:00 hours and relocated to the Coffee House to hear some live music; they stayed there for about 1/2 hour and no drinking occurred. Adam and 2 of his friends then walked to the Hoot Owl Bar around 23:00 hours, but Adam was denied entrance since the bouncer picked up on his fake identification card. Since Adam could not get in, they walked back to the party at the dormitory (security disclosed that his pass card was used to access a dormitory door at 23:30 hours). It may have been at this time that Adam ate pizza with meat and some corn.

Adam and "J.M." left the party about 00:30 hours and walked back downtown to the Tick Tock Inn (Figure 4.2). Adam approached the bar at the "Over 21" door and was allowed access using his fake identification card. "J.M." entered the bar at the "Underage" door. Adam and "J.M." were both served alcohol while in the bar. Witnesses suggested that Adam left the Tick Tock Inn via the back door about 01:38 hours on Saturday morning, November 13, 2004. According to information gathered by Adam's dad, there were about

Figure 4.2 The Tick Tock Inn – the last place Adam Falcon was seen alive.

200 to 300 people at the Tick Tock Inn that night. Witnesses claimed that they saw Adam go out the back door of the bar about 01:38 hours on Saturday, November 13th, walk down the stairs, and step into the parking lot. Minutes later, the bar was emptied of its patrons at about 01:45 hours; employees locked up and departed at about 02:15 hours. Adam was never seen alive again.

Thus, once the hockey game ended, Adam spent a great deal of his time that night walking back and forth from location (downtown) to location (campus) and from activity to activity. In fact, a total of 4 hours 13 minutes existed between the time he left the hockey game at Appleton Arena and the time he went out the back door at the Tick Tock Inn (Figure 4.3). Estimated travel data were calculated for Adam's walking that night. He spent a total of about 53 minutes that night walking around 2.7 miles. Since Adam was walking, we subtracted the time he spent walking from his total available time. That left 3 hours 23 minutes of actual available drinking time for Adam that night. From what we learned about Adam as a person, we surmised that he would not walk back-and-forth all night in public while drinking a beer (or any alcoholic drink) and run the risk of losing his athletic eligibility were he caught by police or campus security.

Falcon: Estimated Timeline Based on Interview Information

DEPARTURE		ARRIVAL		TRAVEL	
TIME	LOCATION	TIME	LOCATION	MILES	MINS.
18:00	*Jencks Hall*	NA	*Ate Spaghetti*	*0.0*	*0*
19:00	*Jencks Hall*	19:15	*Appleton Arena*	*0.8*	*15*
21:15	*Appleton Arena*	21:25	*Dean Eaton Residence*	*0.5*	*10*
22:00	*Dean Eaton Residence*	22:05	*Coffee House*	*0.3*	*5*
23:00	*Coffee House*	23:05	*Hoot Owl Bar*	*0.2*	*5*
23:20	*Hoot Owl Bar*	23:30	*Dean Eaton Residence*	*0.5*	*10*
00:30	*Dean Eaton Residence*	00:38	*Tick Tock Inn*	*0.4*	*8*
01:38	*Tick Tock Inn*	NA	*?*	*0.0*	*0*
				2.7	
			Estimated Minutes Spent Walking		*53*

Figure 4.3 Adam Falcon spent 26% of his time that night walking between locations.

Recovery

Adam was recovered in the afternoon at approximately 15:00 hours on Thursday, November 18, 2004, from a 7 feet deep sink hole in the Grasse River in Canton after having been missing for a period of approximately 5 days. Authorities were about to call off search efforts for the day when he was discovered.

Analysis of Evidence

Recovery Location

The spot where Adam was recovered was absolutely illogical and contradicted evidence trails on land. It was behind the Knights of Columbus Hall where a dance was held that night. Did Adam walk over there after leaving the Tick Tock Inn in order to check out what was going on there? His friends had been walking and partying with him all night. Did any of his friends go with him to the Knights of Columbus Hall? No one reported walking over there that night, much less walking over there with Adam. He had not shown an interest all night in the dance being held over there. Why would he go there at bar closing instead of going home? Whether he had gone there voluntarily or not that night, with all the people there for the dance, then someone should have seen what transpired to cause him to end up in the Grasse River. No one has come forward with any such information.

An examination of Adam's route of travel that night disclosed some troubling findings. First, the map clearly demonstrated his awareness of directions, his knowledge of the city's streets, and his ability to successfully navigate them – all despite the fact that he was drinking (Figure 4.4). Second, it showed that Adam had been walking back-and-forth all night long in the general direction of his university residence (Jencks Hall) without becoming disoriented. Somehow, on the last trip of the night, we are supposed to believe that Adam became confused and walked 85 degrees in the wrong direction, only to end up in the Grasse River. Lastly, physical evidence associated with Adam (i.e., his baseball cap and cell phone) was found in the opposite direction of his body recovery site (by about 135 degrees), without leaving any scent for a tracking dog to follow.

Evidence Trails

Adam's case was weird right from the start. What made all of this extremely suspicious was the fact that personal property associated with Adam kept turning up within areas that had been previously searched by law enforcement, trained search specialists with tracking dogs, numerous volunteers, and family members. Full-scale searching for Adam and or evidence began on the second day that he had been missing (Sunday, November 14th). That morning, Adam's hat (a baseball cap) was found by a Canton Village police officer at about 09:20 hours across a small parking lot, up by a house between two buildings, and behind a low wire fence (Figure 4.5). It was less than a block from the bar heading north in a direction away from the Tick Tock Inn, away from the dormitory, and away from his recovery location in the Grasse River. In other words, the location where the hat was found suggested that Adam went in a completely different and new direction other than that which he had traveled back-and-forth along all night long. How did the hat get there without Adam leaving a scent trail?

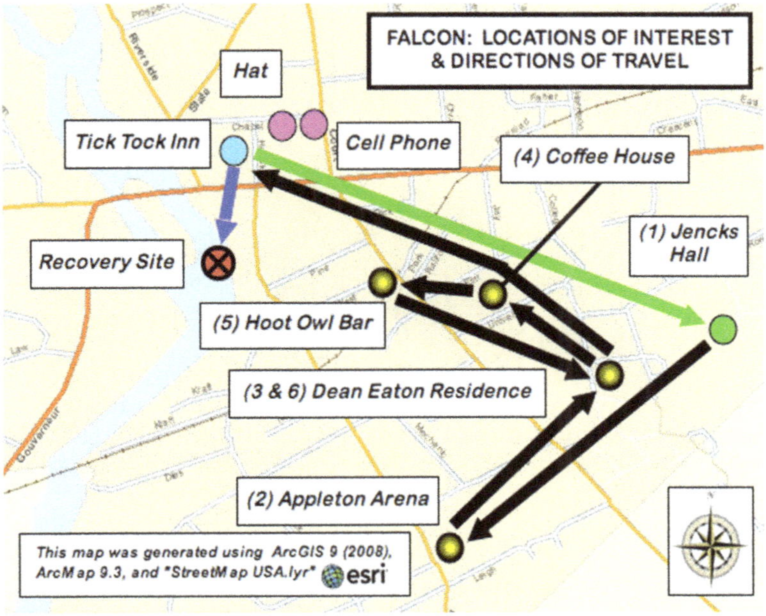

Figure 4.4 Adam Falcon's route that night (*Yellow Dots* and *Black Arrows*) demonstrated his ability to navigate the city. However, we were supposed to believe that instead of leaving the Tick Tock Inn (*Blue Dot*) and going back to his dorm (*Green Dot* and *Green Arrow*) on his last trip, he went the wrong direction and ended up in the Grasse River (*Red-X Dot* and *Blue Arrow*). Physical evidence was discovered in a completely different direction; hat and cell phone (*Purple Dots*).

Adam held on to his girlfriend's cellular telephone the evening he went missing (November 13th). After the hat's mysterious appearance and discovery on November 14th, family members and volunteers conducted another search of the entire area the next day (Monday, November 15th). That search included the porch of a nearby church rectory and found nothing. Adam's uncle had actually gone under the front porch and rectory steps looking for additional property of Adam's or clues into his disappearance with negative results. The cell phone was recovered the following day (Tuesday, November 16th) about

Figure 4.5 Adam Falcon's hat was found behind this wire fence between two buildings.

Figure 4.6 Adam Falcon's father (Mike) took our team to the church rectory porch, where he used his own cell phone and a handful of leaves to recreate what it looked like the day that the cell phone was discovered.

a block away from where Adam's hat was recovered. It was recovered by a Canton police officer on top of the porch of the church rectory house that had been searched the day before, face-down in the corner, on top of some leaves, as though someone had put it there for others to find (Figure 4.6).

It appeared as though someone was watching the search process and reintroducing evidence into the scene (which was characteristic of many of these drowning cases). Again, the direction where Adam's hat and his girlfriend's cellular telephone were found was in a northeasterly direction away from the dormitory, and more importantly, away from the water and in an area that had been searched twice before (Figure 4.7). The three directions of interest were inconsistent with each other: the direction to return to his dormitory, the direction of recovered personal property as an evidence trail, and the direction of Adam's final body recovery.

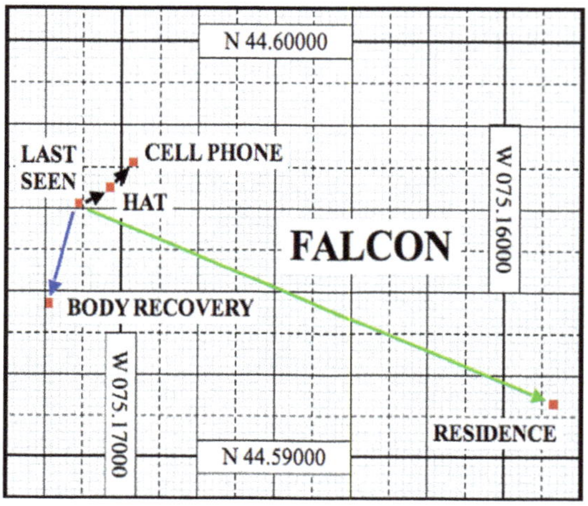

Figure 4.7 Three directions of interest for Adam Falcon: his route to return to his dorm (*Green Arrow*), an evidence trail along which personal property was recovered (*Black Arrow*), and the direction in which his body was recovered (*Blue Arrow*).

Dog Searches

Several search dogs were brought in right away by the New York State Police and they scented Adam coming out of the back door of the Tick Tock Inn, down a flight of stairs into the rear parking lot, and then lost the scent as though Adam got into a vehicle. The dogs found no scent of Adam leading up to any of the locations where his personal property was discovered. It was as though someone else had put his property at these locations after Adam went missing or was abducted. The Federation of New York State Search and Rescue teams were contacted on Tuesday, November 16th, but because of miscommunication, they were not given the go-ahead to start their search until two days later on Thursday, November 18th. The Chairman of the Federation sent roughly 24 to 26 people and 4 dogs to the scene that day even though they were told by local authorities that their dogs were not needed.

Four Teams responded:

1. Cayuga County Highland Search and Rescue
2. Oswego County Pioneer Search and Rescue
3. Western New York Search Dogs
4. Massasauga Search and Rescue

The Executive Coordinator for the Cayuga County Highland Search and Rescue mentioned that she was consistently told by authorities that they had already searched the area above the bridge on several occasions and that they had already brought dogs down to the water. Those same authorities were adamant that the dogs did not get anything down near the water and that Adam was not at that location. At 09:30 hours on Thursday, November 18th, a Massasauga Search and Rescue tracking dog got a "hit" (picked up a scent) on the island in the middle of the river on the bank opposite of where Adam was eventually recovered. He reported his findings to the Forest Rangers in charge of the scene, but they gave this information very little credence and the hit was ignored.

Water Searches

The area where Adam was recovered had only been "officially" searched on Monday, November 15th, by boat (Ogdensburg Fire Department) and by helicopter on one occasion.

However, a witness who lived in the neighborhood and within sight of the recovery location reported having observed local officials in a small boat searching the 7 feet deep sink hole with poles on Tuesday, November 16th, with negative results. This was two days prior to his actual recovery. That neighborhood witness commented that to him it looked like they were searching the bottom of the hole with poles very diligently for several hours (personal communication; source wished to remain anonymous). This waterborne search was never officially recorded or reported anywhere.

Shoe Tracks

In actuality, no one had physically searched the shoreline until Thursday, November 18th, when the additional search and rescue teams arrived. Against all advice that he was getting from authorities, experience told the leader of the regional rescue diver team (hereafter, "Marv") that he needed to search the area behind the Knights of Columbus Hall anyway, particularly, the 7 feet deep sink hole. On November 18th, he acted against the consensus of opinion to not search this area and informed Police Chief Mulkin of his intentions. While walking along the shoreline, he found 5 shoe tracks in the water starting about 12 inches from the shoreline and leading directly to the sink hole. Marv observed that the scene seemed to be undisturbed. In his opinion, there had not been any search in the area on foot because his team did not come across any other foot or shoe tracks either on shore or in the shallow water along either shoreline. The only tracks that were found were the ones leading to Adam's body (Figure 4.8).

A Cayuga County Highland Search and Rescue handler (hereafter, "Kristi") and her dog were called to the scene along with "Julie" after Marv found the shoe tracks. Kristi's cadaver dog (tracks the scent of deceased humans) picked up a strong scent indicating that in all likelihood someone was in the water. Upon viewing the shoe tracks, Kristi mentioned to Julie that she was amazed at how clear the impressions were since they were in the water. She stated they were definitely shoe tracks as she could see them very clearly from the shoreline. A total of 6 witnesses (i.e., Marv, Kristi, Julie, "Dan," "Jack," and "Pat") saw the shoe tracks that led directly to Adam's body. All stated that the tracks were not made by sneakers (like Adam was wearing), rather apparently by someone wearing a pair of shoes (Figure 4.9). Marv broke a stick off a nearby tree and used it to measure the impression in order to get an approximate size. He then gave the stick to Julie, who sketched an outline drawing of one of the shoe tracks onto a piece of paper using the stick as a scale to present the actual size of the impression as closely as possible. Julie gave her drawing on the paper to a Forest Ranger – and it was never seen again.

The police said that anyone could have made those shoe tracks – which was correct. They also said that no one knew when the shoe tracks were made – which was also correct. They should have at least been concerned about the shoe tracks since they led directly to where Adam's body was eventually recovered. It would have seemed reasonable for the police to say that the shoe tracks were Adam's since there were no return tracks from the water's edge. However, the tracks had obviously not been there as long as Adam had been

Figure 4.8 The leader of the local water recovery and dive team (blue hat) described what happened during the body recovery on November 18th to our team members (Carlson and Gannon, left) and Mike Falcon (Adam's dad; right).

Figure 4.9 The local water recovery and dive team leader identified this sole as being the same as the shoe prints he and 5 others had seen in the Grasse River near Adam Falcon's body recovery site. The sole can be found on a popular brand of Oxford shoes.

missing. If they had been there the whole time, then the flowing water would have erased them. Considering that 6 witnesses described the shoe tracks as not looking anything like the shoes that Adam was wearing that night, then the police should have wanted to know more about the shoes. Preservation measures should have been taken. As is standard operating procedure in a suspicious missing person case, the police usually make some effort to preserve prints and impressions made by feet or footwear (photographs, artist's rendering, or casts/molds) even if they eventually turn out to be the victim's. Questions should have been asked. What brand name and size were they? Why were there no return shoe tracks? Which direction did the person wearing the shoes go after entering the water? Did the individual who made the shoe tracks continue to walk across the Grasse River and come out on the other side? Would that account for the tracking dog's "hit" on the island in the middle of the river? Did he slip into the river and float away downstream where he came out and either did not make any additional impressions or they were not discovered by the search teams? The shoe tracks were never considered by the police.

Smokeless Tobacco Can

Marv also found a smokeless tobacco container on the shoreline near the entry point for the shoe prints. The can was found to the right of a tree and was marked by Julie with a blue tag as something that needed to be looked into by the authorities. Marv asked whether Adam used smokeless tobacco products, to which the reply was in the negative. Marv described the can as being blue in color and a well-known national brand. It did not appear to him to have been there very long. Two other witnesses noticed the can as well. Julie agreed with Marv regarding the color, perceived age of the can, and length of time it had been there. A third searcher, "Joe," also remembered the new smokeless tobacco can described by Marv and Julie. However, in his opinion, he felt that the color of the can was dark green. "Loraine," of the Canton Village Police, said that the can which she saw was green.

Although they reported two different colors, all 4 witnesses referred to it by the same brand name, which comes in both its traditional green can and a newer blue can. Marv noticed that the can was still there at 21:30 hours on November 18th (the day Adam was recovered), but it was gone the next morning when he returned. Photograph number 40 from the body recovery effort confirmed that the can was blue and was present the night of the 18th. This confirmed Marv's statement that the can was blue and demonstrated his accuracy as an eyewitness. It also showed the extent to which he (as the leader of the body recovery dive team) exercised conscientious attention to detail with respect to investigating Adam's death. There was no mention of whether or not the police ever attempted to fingerprint the can, or to check for DNA on the can, in order to identify its owner.

Clothing

Adam was found on November 18th with all his clothes on (brown work style coat with, green long-sleeved sweatshirt with a hood under the coat, white T-shirt, a pair of plaid boxer shorts, white socks and black sneakers) except for his jeans, which mysteriously came off without disturbing his boxers and sneakers. The next day, Marv went back to the scene to attempt to recover Adam's pants (jeans), but was told by State law enforcement authorities who were now on-scene that they were taking over the investigation. They told him that one of the organizations was already in possession of Adam's pants, cell phone, wallet and keys. Information pertaining to exactly where this property was recovered was not released to the family per Police Chief Mulkin's orders. However, we have learned that the jeans were recovered that day (Friday, November 19th) on the riverbank in shallow weeds and in 2 feet of water a slight distance (50 to 80 feet) downstream from where the body was recovered. How is it that these jeans were missed by all investigators and search personnel the previous day, only to be discovered nearby the subsequent day? Much like the baseball cap and cell phone, were the jeans re-entered into the scene after the area had already been searched?

Position Relationships

Much like the inconsistency among the locations and directions of travel for Adam's baseball cap and cell phone found on land, similar problems existed among the relationships of evidence found in the water. The current in the Grasse River was about 2 to 3 miles per hour. Adam's body was found lying on the bottom of the 7 feet deep sink hole with his head facing downstream, he was lying on his side with his right arm raised above his head and his left arm was down at his side. Adam pants (jeans) were reportedly recovered 50 to 80 feet downstream. Adam's wallet was found upstream within several feet of his body. In our opinion, the current was not strong enough to remove Adam's jeans. Even if it were, then why did it not also remove other articles of clothing, or move the wallet further downstream? Second, if it were strong enough to remove his jeans after he had fallen into the water, then he should have been found facing upstream. He was not. Therefore, given the position of the body, the jeans had to have been removed before entering the water. The presence of searchers on November 18th during the body recovery and their failure to see the jeans, suggests that the jeans were placed at the site during the late evening hours of November 18th after everyone left the scene.

Witnesses

Two other witnesses, a Canton couple out late one evening, stated that they remembered seeing a light-colored vehicle approach a person fitting Adam's description on Chapel Street. They said that the person whom they observed continued to walk east on Chapel

Street and was approached again on Court Street, where the person then got into the back seat of the vehicle. It should be noted that the church rectory house where the cell phone was found is at the corner of Chapel and Court Streets.

Hypothermia

The Medical Examiner (Dr. Sikirica) who performed the autopsy suggested that hypothermia contributed to Adam's demise that night. It was extremely cold during the night that Adam went missing. The temperature was about 30°Fahrenheit early that evening (November 12th) and dropped to about 17°Fahrenheit by 07:00 hours the next morning (November 13th). Despite the fact that Adam was appropriately dressed for the cold weather, the Medical Examiner (a forensic pathologist from Albany, NY) said he believed that Adam had fallen asleep outside somewhere after leaving the bar and had become hypothermic. Adam's father, Mike Falcon, asked Dr. Sikirica how Adam wound up in the water since most hypothermic individuals never regain consciousness after falling asleep. He was told that Adam must have awakened at some point during the night and then wandered into the Grasse River.

We disagree with the official explanation for the cause of death and description of the body in the autopsy report. The Medical Examiner suggested a cause-and-effect model that started with hypothermia on land, which then linked to freshwater drowning that brought about asphyxia. Furthermore, he described the color of the body as being consistent with hypothermia. Hypothermia occurs when an individual comes into contact with a medium (e.g., air, snow, or water) that is cooler than the average human body temperature and remains in contact long enough for the loss of sufficient body heat, thus slowing brain function that affects internal organ processes, motor functions, and cognition. Even in 44°Fahrenheit water (as was the temperature reported by the recovery dive team), Adam would have become exhausted and drowned prior to succumbing to hypothermia in the water (Ohio Department of Natural Resources, 2011). Hypothermia in water could only occur when an individual is conscious long enough to swim, tread water, or struggle until the deleterious affects of hypothermia takeover. The suggestion that Adam had experienced hypothermia on land prior to entering the water was absurd. As hypothermia would have taken over Adam's brain functions, his body core temperature would have dropped along with his blood pressure, respiration rate, and heart rate. He would have slipped into a deep sleep and would not have awakened on his own to walk into the Grasse River.

Furthermore, if Dr. Sikirica was correct in suggesting that Adam had succumbed to hypothermia, then he should have been able to see and describe at least one of the characteristic injuries associated with deaths that are due wholly or in part to hypothermia related to cold-water submersion (Armstrong & Erskine, 2011). These injuries could have been found in the stomach, lungs, and pancreas. However, he did not. Regarding the lining of Adam's stomach, there was no mention of small superficial erosions (a.k.a., *Wischnewski's Ulcers*; Figure 4.10). Also, he did not report the presence of small hemorrhages within the lungs. Specific to the pancreas, no comment was made that related to finding hemorrhages in the pancreas or focal acute pancreatitis with fat necrosis (i.e., the localized death of tissues). The autopsy report stated that there was no evidence of injury or natural disease. In fact, the Medical Examiner specifically stated that there was no evidence of any kind of hemorrhage or necrosis. In other words, no physical proof was presented that supported the theory that hypothermia had played any role in Adam's death.

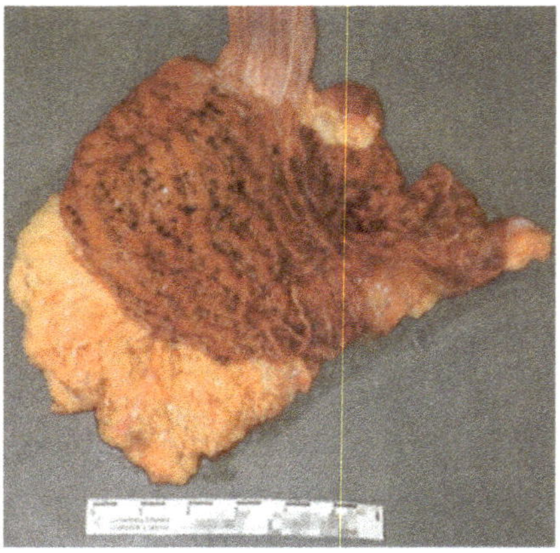

Figure 4.10 Superficial gastric erosions (a.k.a., *Wischnewski's Ulcers*) are one example of the injuries associated with hypothermia. (From Armstrong, E., & Erskine, K. 2011. *Water-Related Death Investigation: Practical Methods and Forensic Applications*. Boca Raton, FL: CRC Press.)

Rigidity

Rigidity (*rigor mortis*) is the postmortem stiffening of the muscles and joints as a result of the disappearance of adenosine triphosphate (ATP) from muscle tissue (Geberth, 2006). Rigidity becomes discernible within 2 to 4 hours after death. Rigor begins to disappear within 24 to 36 hours after death on land, and is completely gone in the average individual within 48 to 60 hours, but may take up to 72 hours in cold weather or water. Adam's body was described in the Final Autopsy Report as being in a moderate, but full, state of rigor mortis. Adam had been missing since November 13th at approximately 01:38 hours (Figure 4.11, *Red Triangle*). He was recovered on November 18th at 15:00 hours (*Yellow Triangle*). Therefore, the maximum amount of time that he could have been in the water was 5 days, 13 hours, 22 minutes, or about 133.4 hours (*Blue Bar*). However, the autopsy was not conducted until 22 hours 15 minutes later (*Green Bar*) on November 19th at 13:15 hours (*Black Triangle*). This meant that Adam had been theoretically deceased for a total of about 6 days, 11 hours, 37 minutes, or about 155.6 hours (*Blue & Green Bars*).

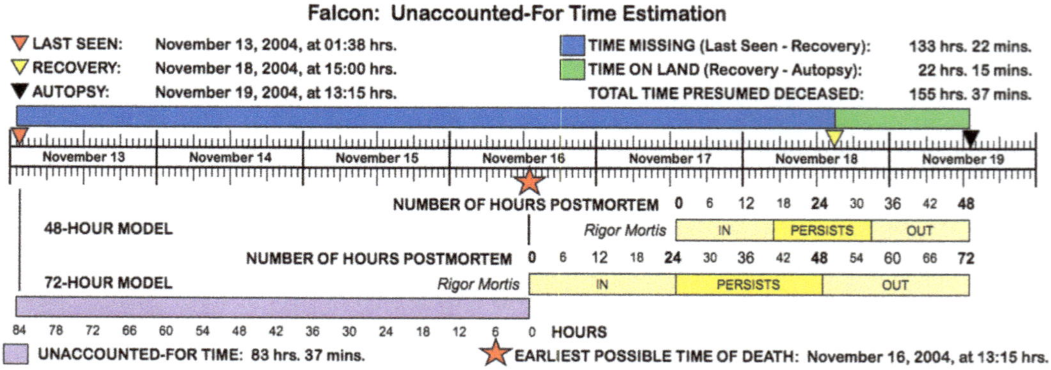

Figure 4.11 The presence of *rigor mortis* in Adam Falcon's body at autopsy (155.6 hours after he went missing) meant that he did not drown and die 6 days earlier. Adam had to have died sometime after 13:15 hours on November 16th in order to still be in rigor at autopsy.

We acknowledge that cold temperatures could prolong postmortem processes. However, since rigor is usually gone within the average sized and shaped individual (like Adam) within 48 to 72 hours in colder water, then why was Adam still in full rigor at autopsy some 150 plus hours after he presumably died? The only reasonable explanation for this was that Adam could not have entered the water during the early morning hours of November 13th. Had he actually drowned on November 13th, then rigor should have relented on either November 15th or 16th.

When we worked the timeline backwards and subtracted the amount of time required for rigor to relent in a cold environment (i.e., 48 to 72 hours; Figure 4.11, *Yellow Bars*), then we were left with 83 hours 37 minutes of unaccounted-for time (*Purple Bar*). Even if we were to double the time requirement for rigor to relent in water to 144 hours, then we would still be left with 11.6 hours of unaccounted-for time. No matter how we did the math, Adam could not have been dead the full 155.6 hours, still been in full rigor, and looked as good as he did at autopsy. This analysis suggested that in all likelihood Adam had probably died sometime after 13:15 hours on November 16th (Figure 4.11, *Red Star*), and raised a whole set of questions related to the offender's or offenders' motive and *modus operandi* (method of operation).

Body Position and Lividity

Lividity (*livor mortis*) is the postmortem discoloration due to gravitation of the blood into the dependent capillaries and veins (Dix & Graham, 1999). Lividity begins within about 30 minutes after death and becomes "fixed" within 10 to 12 hours. Fixed means that the lividity has settled in one position and can no longer be significantly shifted by changing the position of the body (DiMaio & DiMaio, 2001). In the Final Autopsy Report, the Medical Examiner described Adam's body as presenting lividity that was barely detectable and predominantly anterior (toward the front).

Two distinct problems concerning lividity should have been identified by the Medical Examiner and were not. Since lividity is completely fixed within 12 hours and bodies generally float face-down when they drown, then the lividity should be fixed anteriorly. At first glance then, the Medical Examiner's autopsy description of lividity seemed to fit with a freshwater drowning since he referenced anterior lividity. However, upon examination of the autopsy photographs, the first problem was that lividity was not exclusively anterior as one would expect in a drowning and it was present in other parts of Adam's body. The only way to have lividity in other parts of the body was that Adam's body had to be in at least one other position after death, or it had to have been repeatedly moved in order for the blood to not settle in one location. Given the Grasse River's 2 to 3 miles per hour current, and the fact that Adam's body was protected in a 7 feet deep sink hole, one cannot explain-away the diffuseness of lividity on account of being rolled by the current.

The second problem associated with lividity was simple and should have been caught by the trained eyes of both the Medical Examiner and the law enforcement investigator. Adam was found lying on his side in the 7 feet deep sink hole, supposedly for 5 days. Therefore, lividity should have been fixed and should have presented on his side – not diffusely and anteriorly. Furthermore, considering that lividity was only on Adam's face and not his whole body (i.e., chest, abdomen, legs or side) suggested that he may have been held somewhere in a somewhat upside-down position for all the blood to rush only to his upper facial area.

Decomposition and Maceration

Putrefaction is the decomposition of soft tissues by bacteria and fermentation and enzymes. After death, the bacterial flora of the gastrointestinal tract invades the vascular system, spreading throughout the body, producing putrefaction (Shkrum & Ramsay, 2007). As the decomposition process progresses and the micro-organisms continue to grow, the body will begin to swell from the gases that they produce and body tissues will become discolored (Spitz & Spitz, 2006). The extent of decomposition relative to time varies depending on the environmental temperature, amount of clothing worn by the deceased, the proportion of fatty tissue relative to the size of the body, and so forth (Geberth, 2006).

There was no mention of putrefaction or maceration on Adam's body by the Medical Examiner. It is almost always mentioned even when a drowning victim is immediately recovered. Even though Adam was purportedly in the water for only 5-1/2 days and the water temperature was 44 °Fahrenheit, there would still have been the beginnings of decomposition on the body. The stomach should have begun to swell and the discoloration should have turned greenish. The scrotum should have shown signs of swelling with gases. The skin on the hands should have started to slip or deglove. However, not one of those expected characteristics of decomposition was present. Adam's stomach was completely firm, flat and clean in color. His scrotum appeared normal. His hands presented with early indications of Washerwoman's Hands (*Wauschaut*) and absolutely no indication of skin slippage or degloving (consistent with short-term immersion in water). This was another reason besides rigidity and lividity that proved to us that Adam was not in the water for the 5-plus days he was missing; rather, only for a fraction of that time (Figure 4.12).

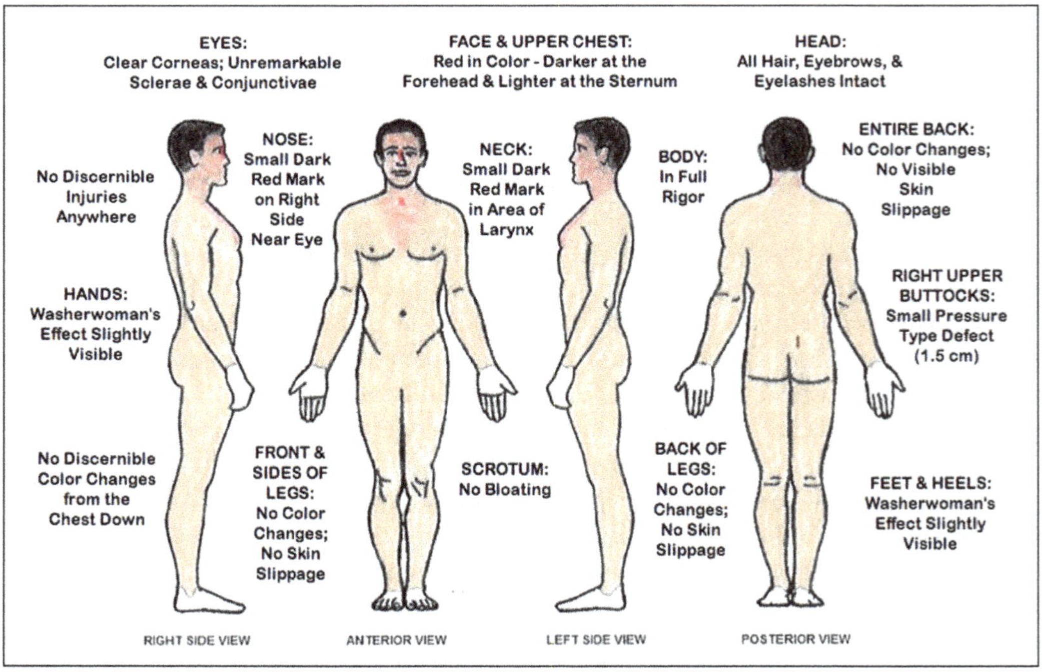

Figure 4.12 Adam Falcon's body at autopsy; artist rendition from observations of autopsy photographs.

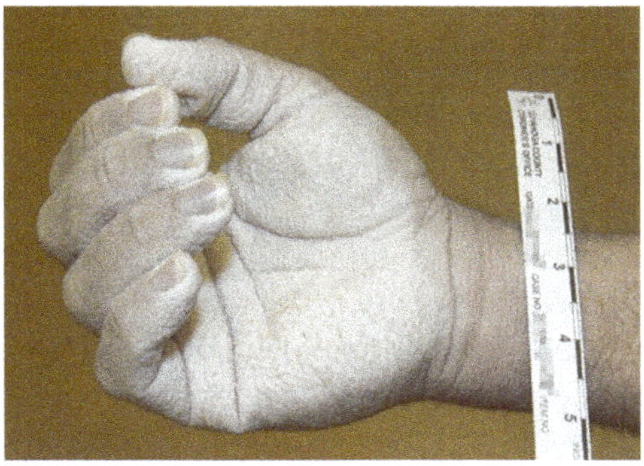

Figure 4.13 Washerwoman's Hands (*Wauschaut Effect*): this hand was submerged for less than 24 hours. This is not Adam Falcon's hand, but it resembles what it looked like at autopsy. (From Armstrong, E., & Erskine, K. 2011. *Water-Related Death Investigation: Practical Methods and Forensic Applications.* Boca Raton, FL: CRC Press, Color Figure 9.1.)

Since Adam could not be in such pristine condition after being in the water 133.4 hours, he had to have been (a) held somewhere alive for a couple days, killed, and then placed into the water, or (b) abducted, killed, preserved in a freezer, and then placed into the water a couple days later. In case anyone doubts this assertion, Adam appeared in slightly better condition than Thomas Booth (a January 2008 case in Pennsylvania), who was proven by that local Medical Examiner's own expanded investigation to have only been in the 44° Fahrenheit water anywhere from a few hours to no more than 2 days. Therefore, Adam could not have been in the water for a full 5-1/2 days. In fact, he was probably in the water less than 2 days (Figure 4.13).

Facial Hair

The Medical Examiner described Adam as being clean-shaven. There was no record of him having shaved before going out that night. Since Adam's face was clean-shaven and forensic evidence suggested that he had only been immersed in the water for approximately 2 days at most, then only a couple possibilities existed: (a) Adam was held alive for about 3 days and then required to shave before being killed and subsequently placed into the river, (b) Adam was killed soon after abduction and his condition was preserved by means of refrigeration, or (c) Adam did not grow facial hair very quickly and did not need to shave every day.

Injuries

The Medical Examiner reported that there were no injuries to the face or scalp. However, examination by the funeral director from Jarmuze-Cotton funeral home stated that Adam had a slight abrasion starting under his scalp and running down his forehead, down the bridge of the nose and a little bit on his chin. The funeral director noticed these injuries while he was applying makeup to Adam's body for the viewing. Adam looked so good that he had an open casket that was viewed by everyone. This would not have happened were he in the water for 5-plus days. We do not understand why there was no mention of these injuries at all in the autopsy report. Typically, these injuries are described and medical examiners will attempt to explain them. The injuries could have occurred while Adam was being dragged on the bottom of the river by the current; an unlikely possibility given the slow current and the fact that travel abrasion only occur during the refloating process. Once a body sinks, it stays on the bottom until gases in the body form and the body starts to refloat (Hendrick, Zaferes & Nelson, 2003). Since Adam was recovered on the bottom of the 7 feet deep sink hole, this process did not occur.

Additionally, there is the issue of "significant injury" and whether it is assessed objectively or subjectively by medical examiners. Does the term significant refer to the extent of damage or trauma as can be measured by the length of a laceration or the severity of a bone break? Or, does it refer to the extent of importance of an injury such as a cut on the hand of a butcher as compared with a cut over the eyebrow of an asserted assault victim? Whether or not the injury was antemortem or postmortem is another question.

The Medical Examiner recorded an absence of significant, before-death injury. We felt that this was strange for an active soccer player. There was no mention of any injury to Adam's leg anywhere in the autopsy report or in any law enforcement report. Yet, several individuals recalled seeing a mark on Adam's leg. His father, Mike Falcon, stated that there was a small imprint on his leg. During a meeting on January 27, 2005, the Medical Examiner and 2 law enforcement investigators mentioned that they remembered seeing a mark on Adam's leg. They suggested that he had been laying on a rock in the water. They agreed that he had probably fallen into that position and had not moved from that spot. However, Marv (leader of the dive team) said that Adam was not laying on anything at the bottom of the 7 feet deep sink hole in the Grasse River.

Neck Exam

Medical examiners routinely examine the neck and throat region for signs of hemorrhage, ligature, manual strangulation, or other factors contributing to death. The muscles that form the neck are examined for bruising. They will describe the condition and appearance of objects as remarkable or unremarkable. Objects that are usually assessed are the thyroid, carotid arteries and jugular veins, the musculature and soft tissue. The thyroid cartilage of the larynx forms the Adam's Apple. In Adam's case, the Medical Examiner described the thyroid as unremarkable, and even suggested that the absence of Adam's right superior coroner was congenital. The hyoid bone is a small U-shaped bone at the base of the tongue. This is almost always mentioned by medical examiners in autopsy reports to show whether strangulation may or may not have occurred. The hyoid bone often ruptures when a person is strangled. There was no mention of the hyoid bone at all in the autopsy report.

Foreign Matter

According to the autopsy report, Adam had some kind of muddy or slimy dirty material on the front of his thighs. Medical examiners are supposed to analyze any foreign material (e.g., mud, grass, vegetation, etc.) to see whether it matches with where the victim was recovered. Microbiological comparisons, in addition to mineral comparisons, can also be made. The color of the soil, minerals and bacterial profiles can be distinctive (Geberth, 2006). This is to determine the true location where the victim may have entered the water and to determine whether it was truly an accident or not. If the location differs from where the victim was recovered, then one might not only have a murder instead of an accident, one might also have a different entry point and potential crime scene with the possibilities of additional forensic evidence relating to the crime. This was not done in this case. The Medical Examiner never checked whether the mud on Adam's thighs matched the mud from the 7 feet deep sink hole from which Adam was recovered or whether it came from somewhere else in the river.

The material on the front of Adam's thighs was not the only piece of organic foreign matter on his body at recovery that was ignored. The recovery photographs disclosed that some kind of thistle was snarled up in the shoelaces on Adam's right sneaker. This was confirmed by the Medical Examiner who described them as burdocks (similar in appearance to cockleburs). However, no record existed of any effort to locate them in the environment. Adam had been walking around in buildings and on streets all night. Where did he pick up the thistles: in a backyard or along the river? Did any exist in town? We will never know now. In these situations, medical examiners should seek the assistance of competent forensic geologists and forensic botanists.

Gastrointestinal System and Vomitus

Two extremely important facts were not followed up by all involved authorities: stomach and gallbladder contents, and their relationship with known meals. The Medical Examiner described the stomach as containing about 400 cubic centimeters (about 13.5 fluid ounces) of some nondescript brown fluid with chewed-up corn kernels, a doughy-like substance, and small fragments of meat. Additionally, Dr. Sikirica reported that the gallbladder was intact and contained 20 cubic centimeters (0.68 fluid ounces) of bile. In most people, food leaves the stomach in about 4 to 6 hours depending on its substance and what liquids are taken with it. Milk may prolong the digestive process and beef steak takes longer than ground hamburger to digest. Thus, stomach contents and their condition coupled with the volume of bile in the gallbladder can help to estimate a possible time of death relative to the intake of one's last meal and the digestive process.

Adam started out his evening by eating two plates of spaghetti with his friend "J.M." at about 18:00 hours. The matter found in Adam's stomach could be partially digested spaghetti with a meat sauce; it could also be pizza with hamburger or sausage. Adam had been walking around all night from one place to another and was reported to have left out the back door of the bar at about 01:38 hours on Saturday morning, November 13, 2004. Had Adam only eaten the spaghetti that night and completed his meal by 19:00 hours, then one could logically calculate that it would have cleared his stomach by 01:00 hours. Given that we know that he ate two plates of spaghetti, but do not know the volume, then the contents of his stomach may have been spaghetti and could have taken until 03:00 hours to leave the stomach. Regardless of any point of argument, the fact remains that the Medical Examiner had a very specific and clearly identifiable matter in Adam's stomach – the partially digested kernels of corn. What else was eaten and drunk with the spaghetti meal? Were any other meals eaten throughout the night, and if so, then what and when were they? What and when was the origin of the corn? To the best of our knowledge and research, this evidence was not followed up.

On the second day that Adam was missing (November 14th), Mike Falcon (Adam's father) took photos of vomitus behind the Tick Tock Inn (where Adam was last seen). It was located on the east side of the walkway, around to the left of the building as one was walking towards the front of the bar. Using the presence and location of this vomitus, the police attempted to disprove the dog searches by suggesting that Adam took this route to the front of the bar. If this were the scenario that the police wanted the family and public to believe, then would not it have been obvious to them that they needed to take a sample of the vomitus for testing to see whether it really belonged to Adam, thus substantiating their claim. This is standard operating procedure in a suspicious case.

Toxicology

In a toxicology report (dated December 9, 2004), Adam was recovered with a blood alcohol concentration (BAC) of 0.21 for ethanol, his vitreous ethanol level was 0.21, and his urine ethanol level was 0.29. The toxicology report (dated December 6, 2004) showed that two tests were ordered that are not normally requested. Generally speaking, medical examiners do not look for date rape drugs among male victims, much less drowning victims. The first test was a urine screening test for gamma-hydroxybutyric acid (GHB), which suggested further testing was required. This was appropriately followed up by using a full confirmation test for GHB that used urine with a reporting limit of 2.0 micrograms per milliliter. The test reported that no GHB was detected. This really meant that if any GHB was present it had not reached the reporting limit. It did not mean that no GHB was present. A more accurate test would have been the assay that included GHB and gamma-butyrolactone (GBL). One of the problems with date rape drugs like GHB is that they have a short half-life. They can be gone in 0.03 to 1.0 hours (18 to 60 minutes) depending on dosage and victim size. If a victim is held for a period of time before death occurs (e.g., like Adam), then the GHB could be completely out of his system in 3 to 5 hours; or have dropped below the amount needed for detection at the reporting limit.

A Father's Story

Mike Falcon shared the following story with us. On January 27, 2005 (about 2 months after his son's death), he met with the Medical Examiner, a Forensic Identification Unit investigator (NY State Police); the Canton Police Chief, and the District Attorney. This narration was recorded by Mike immediately following the meeting, and stands as an example of how authorities in many of these cases spoke to and treated the parents of the deceased, and how they handled evidence. This story is also indicative of one of the biggest problems today regarding police investigations of bodies found in water, that is, operating under a preconceived opinion that a body in water must be an accident or suicide and not a homicide. Presented here is a summary of the stated "facts" that were proposed in agreement during that meeting by everyone except Mike Falcon.

1. Adam's death was an accidental drowning contributed to by hypothermia.
2. Adam left the bar and passed out immediately, possibly for a couple of hours somewhere near the water. Adam then woke up in a daze several hours later and staggered to where he lost his hat.
3. The shoe tracks in the water leading toward Adam's body were entirely discounted because they could have come from or been made by anyone.
4. Adam's pants were removed by the water current.
5. Adam may have had a disease called Long QT Syndrome. The LQT Syndrome is a condition that impairs the electrical system of the heart; a person may go into

cardiac arrest when faced with a physical struggle. Its symptoms include fainting, seizures, abnormal heartbeats, and even death. It is usually a hereditary condition, but can occur under emotional stress, or when engaged in vigorous physical activities. It is extremely rare.

6. They could not determine whether Adam had experienced coronary arrest.

Mike Falcon said, "I wanted to slap the entire group. They insulted my intelligence with very little factual information. This meeting was, in my opinion, a lot of hot air and theory with an underlying theme: Let's close this case as quickly as possible." Adam's case was closed the next day (January 28, 2005).

Additional Autopsy Evaluations

Mike Falcon showed the autopsy report and photos to two other forensic pathologists. One pathologist (from New York) stated that it was inconclusive; his reaction seemed to be that bodies found in water ultimately drowned. The second pathologist (from Massachusetts) reviewed the autopsy and stated that in no way did he feel that Adam had drowned. He admitted that his findings were not an exact science. He did say he felt that Adam was alive when he entered the water, but admitted that Adam could have been put into the water in an unconscious state. To put this another way, the Massachusetts pathologist told Mike Falcon that Adam died after being submerged in water, but he did not drown. But then, he wrote down in his report that his assessment for cause of death was drowning. That does not make sense. Any way you slice it, Adam would have been alive (conscious or not) when he entered the water, and therefore, would have drowned. Yet, in attempting to clarify the fact that Adam was murdered by drowning and did not accidentally drown, the Massachusetts pathologist did nothing to help Mike Falcon to understand his son's death. This is another example of a medical examiner not being able to clarify his finding, or to make a clear finding.

Conclusion

We believe that Adam Falcon was abducted and murdered. Considering the primary facts of the investigation (i.e., the presence of rigidity, inconsistent lividity, shoe tracks leading to the body that would have been erased by the water within two days, the body showing up in a location that had already been searched two days earlier), Adam could not have been deceased and in the water for the 5-1/2 days that he was missing. Only a couple scenarios were possible given the forensic evidence: (a) he was alive somewhere for a couple days, died, and was placed in the water the next day, or (b) he died during that first 24 hour period, was preserved in an extremely cold environment for a few days, then placed into the water. The forensic evidence suggested that hypothermia had not occurred and therefore did not play a role in Adam's death.

We assert that testing blood or heart tissue specimens for the genetic LQT Syndrome markers would have aided in determining whether or not it contributed to Adam's death. Mike told us that no one in his family history was known to have LQT Syndrome. Additionally, testing the blood would have identified any signs of cardiac arrest. We believe that Adam was drowned since froth and foam are good indicators of drowning. Lack of froth and foam does not mean that a person did not drown (as there are other factors), but having them is a sure indicator that he did ingest water while alive. Whether it was in the Grasse River or not, we cannot say since no testing was done on the contents of the fluid in either his stomach or lungs. He could have drowned indoors with tap water or in another body of water and placed into Grasse River. We can categorically say that Adam Falcon did not die from hypothermia. He was, however, drowned and placed into the water several days after he went missing. If that does not constitute an investigation into his disappearance and death as a homicide, then we do not know what does. The father (Mike Falcon) was told from the very beginning, even before Adam's body had been recovered, that this was probably just a tragic accident. It seemed to us that the investigation was conducted in accordance with a predetermined conclusion that this was an accidental death. This is not and should not be the role of medical examiners and law enforcement officials.

Gerald Lee Smith* 5

Background

Jerry Smith was last seen during the early morning hours of May 1, 2009, and was recovered from the Wabash River 7 days later on May 8, 2009. He grew up in the town of Avon, Indiana. His parents (Robin and Billy Hill) and his girlfriend of 2.5 years (hereafter, "Erika") would tell you that Jerry was a very kind and social individual, who had several friends, and was well liked by everyone who met him (Figure 5.1). He attended Indiana State University in Terre Haute, where he majored in Insurance and Risk Management within the College of Business. According to one of his professors, Jerry was a leader, an excellent student, and someone with a promising future. In fact, things were looking pretty good for him to secure a position after graduation with an independent insurance agency in Wabash. By all accounts, everyone who hung out with Jerry knew that something was seriously wrong when he went missing since this was so out of character for him. They were all pretty shocked by his death.

An autopsy was conducted at the Department of Pathology, Terre Haute Regional Hospital, on May 9, 2009. The Medical Examiner, Dr. Roland Kohr (a forensic pathologist), classified the cause of death as drowning and recorded the manner of death as an accident. His autopsy report consisted of 4.5 pages. Although our team had received all of the case materials from Jerry's mother (Robin Hill) in 2009, Indiana state law precluded the Medical Examiner from granting permission to cite those materials (autopsy reports and photographs). On the other hand, we acknowledge the openness of the Indiana State University Police Department (ISUPD), which gave us permission to use and cite its reports and all associated photographs (dated May 17, 2011). We respect the ISUPD, which demonstrated professionalism and integrity in sharing its case documents while knowing that

* Photo courtesy of his mother, Robin Hill.

Figure 5.1 Robin Hill with her son, Jerry Smith. (Photo courtesy of his mother, Robin Hill.)

they would be laid bare for scrutiny. We have maintained close contact with Robin Hill since May 2009 and have personally visited Terre Haute and Vincennes (Figure 5.1).

Circumstances

Last Seen

Gerald Lee Smith ("Jerry") was a White male, 22 years old, 5 feet 7 inches, 160 pounds (Body Mass Index: 25.06), brown hair and brown eyes. On the night of April 30, 2009 (Thursday), Jerry attended an end of year party at the Ballyhoo Tavern and Ballyhoo Pizza King building with faculty and classmates from a business course (Figure 5.2). They were celebrating the successful completion of a capstone business project. The party was to run from 18:30 hours until 22:00 hours. Some of those in attendance were professors (hereafter, Daniel and Allen), and several classmates (hereafter, Rita, Alice, Cal, Walt, Tom, Ben, and Bert) (ISUPD, 2009, p. 8). Jerry was drinking heavily, which was something he rarely or never did according to witnesses (ISUPD, 2009, p. 8).

Alice said that she talked to Jerry about 00:20 hours and that she saw Jerry being escorted out the front door about 00:40 hours by two guys she thought were off-duty

Figure 5.2 Jerry Smith was celebrating at the Ballyhoo Tavern on the night of April 30, 2009. He was last seen alive just across the street chatting with a professor and another student.

police officers. She heard that Jerry had been asked to leave because he vomited in the bar (ISUPD, 2009, p. 5). This timeline was confirmed by Detective Denzil Lewis, a Terre Haute Police Department (THPD) officer who was working off-duty at the Ballyhoo Tavern. He stated that he ordered Jerry to leave the bar at approximately 00:20 hours on Friday, May 1, 2009. Jerry was very polite and cooperative according to the detective (ISUPD, 2009). Matt Cardin was the other officer working the bar that evening. After being walked out of the bar, Jerry was seen walking across Chestnut Street and 9th Street, and was stopped by one of his professors and a student who had also attended the party (respectively, Allen and Rita). The professor attempted to get Jerry to take a cab back to campus, but he refused and said he was able to walk to his dorm (ISUPD, 2009, p. 8). He was never seen alive again.

Recovery

The weather that evening was partly cloudy and about 75 °Fahrenheit, and no precipitation was falling. At about 19:00 hours on Friday, May 8, 2009, four local residents from Vincennes were at Kimmell Park that ran along the Wabash River on the northwest side of the City of Vincennes, Knox County, Indiana. A husband and wife were sitting in their vehicle checking out the river at flood stage, while two men were inside a nearby building (the Vincennes Boat Club). All four noticed a body floating prone (face-down) in the river and watched it slowly collide with a floating boat dock out in front of them (Figure 5.3, *Red-X Dot*). The body spun around and became trapped up against the dock and entangled among some typical flood debris (i.e., tree branches and such). Both parties immediately dialed 911 and reported what they had witnessed. Vincennes Detective Lieutenant Dustin Luking was dispatched to the scene at 19:20 hours. Upon arrival at 19:40 hours, he secured the location as though it were a possible crime scene. Personnel from several other agencies were also at the scene that night: Vincennes Fire Department (4 employees), Vincennes Township Fire Department (1 employee), Knox County Sheriff's

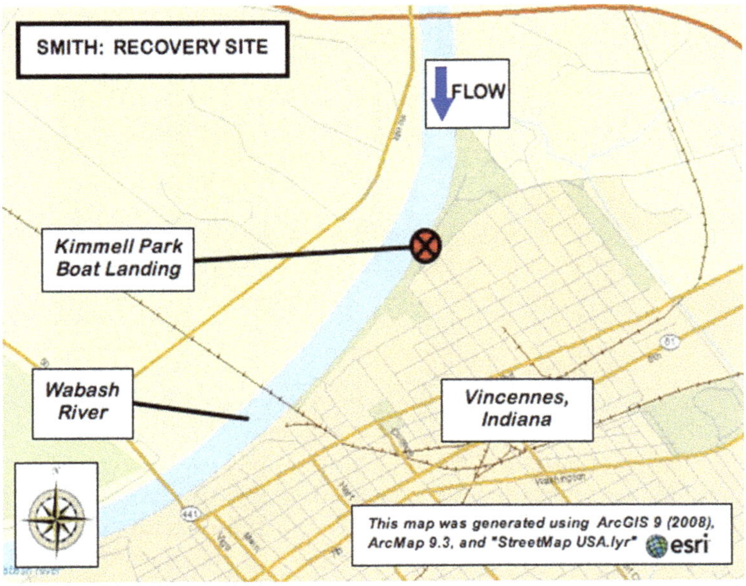

Figure 5.3 Jerry Smith was recovered (*Red-X Dot*) near the boat landing at Kimmell Park in the city of Vincennes, Indiana, at approximately 20:40 hours on the evening of May 8, 2009.

Department (2 employees), the Knox County Coroner (1 employee), and an Indiana State Conservation Officer. Jerry was removed from the water at approximately 20:40 hours on the evening of May 8, 2009.

Analysis of Evidence

Search Efforts

Search efforts were perhaps some of the best we have seen. They were exhaustive and conducted on all shifts, day and night, on foot, horseback, ATV, boat, and vehicle (ISUPD, 2009, pp. 11, 21) (Figure 5.4). Aircraft searches were planned for Saturday (May 9th), but became unnecessary after Jerry's discovery and recovery on Friday evening (May 8th). A West Lafayette company (3 View Search Services) volunteered to conduct aerial searches of the riverbanks and railroad corridors surrounding the university using heat detecting cameras and to canvass the riverbanks and railroad corridors surrounding the university. The ground searches covered large open areas, along the river, inside campus facilities and buildings, on rooftops, under bridges and overpasses, along train tracks, at restaurants, and local businesses (ISUPD, 2009, pp. 7, 10, 13, 16, 20, 28, 30). Police officers scoured the Hilton Garden Inn parking lot and the lower level of the Terre Haute Transit Authority's Multi-Modal Parking Garage, as well as inside the National Guard Armory (ISUPD, 2009, pp. 15, 18). They looked in such areas as the on-campus tunnel system, elevators,

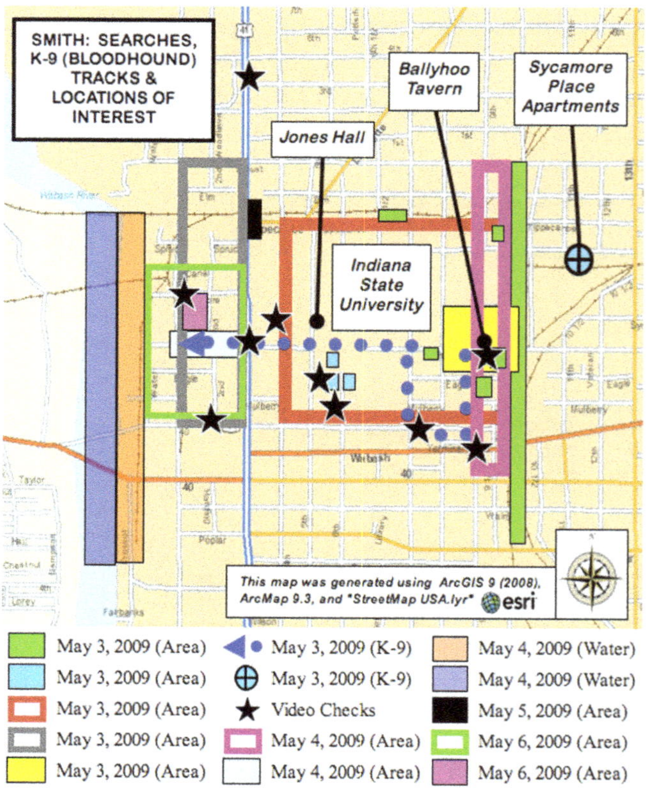

Figure 5.4 Search locations as described in the ISUPD Supplemental Case Reports.

and electrical buildings, landfills, manholes, and sewer entrances, storm drains and inside dumpsters, abandoned buildings and inside semitrailers at Yellow Freight (ISUPD, 2009, pp. 11, 14, 23, 25, 27, 32, 35). Officers checked every bar that was open that night (ISUPD, 2009, pp. 7, 15, 19). Many of these areas were searched daily or multiple times due to the overlapping search patterns. Just in case Jerry had already been picked up by a nearby law enforcement agency or brought into a hospital, officers from the ISUPD contacted the Clay County Jail, Saint Vincent Clay Hospital, Sullivan County Jail, Sullivan County Hospital, Green County Jail, Green County General Hospital, Vermillion County Jail, Vermillion County Hospital, and Parke County Jail (ISUPD, 2009, p. 6).

It should be noted that all search efforts were oriented along an east-west axis, from the Ballyhoo Tavern toward Jerry's residence (Jones Hall) and the Wabash River beyond it. No distinctive evidence was ever located in this area to explain his whereabouts. No efforts were made to search in a northerly or southerly direction. Why? Was a presumption made that he had to have gone toward his residence and the river?

Video Recordings

When it comes to video evidence, investigators should look for two kinds of video-recorded evidence: what happened inside the bar, and what happened outside the bar. They should be concerned with the entire time period that the missing person was reported to have been on the premises. Next, they should shift to finding public and private video recordings throughout the city and surrounding area of what transpired outside the bar, beginning at least an hour before the person entered the bar and continuously through at least an hour after the person left the bar. They should search in all directions, because a finding of no appearance of the missing person on a video-recording is a finding that the person did not go in that direction. We have seen cases where a person is seen on camera going in one direction and then vanishes before reaching the next possible camera; he did not return to the previous camera either. That same kind of evidence trail occurred here too.

The ISUPD reports indicated that officers canvassed the area looking for video recordings and contacted nearly every business (ISUPD, 2009, pp. 3, 23). Numerous video cameras were found and hours of tape watched for any sign of Jerry, each with negative results (Figure 5.4, *Black Stars* indicate the areas in which videos were sought and not individual cameras). However, the reports did not always indicate the extent to which follow-ups were conducted when mangers were not present in order to access recorders. Essentially, no video evidence existed to describe Jerry's path out of the vicinity of the Ballyhoo Tavern. When the Bloodhound track on May 3rd (Figure 5.4, *Blue Dotted Arrow*) suggested that Jerry's path had taken him through a parking ramp at 8th Street and Cherry Street (i.e., the Terre Haute Transit Authority's Multi-Modal Parking Garage), no evidence of his presence was discovered upon watching the facility's security system video recording from 00:00 to 06:45 hours (ISUPD, 2009, p. 33). No combined video and Bloodhound evidence existed to explain how Jerry may have gotten to the river.

Another kind of video phenomenon seems to exist among many of these cases: video-recorder malfunctioning or blank spots on the videotape. In many of these cases, police found that either the on-premises Closed Circuit Television (CCTV) recorder was not working that night at all, or it strangely did not record during the period of time that the missing person was in the bar. The recorder was working, stopped for an hour or so, and then started back up. At least, that is what appeared to have happened when viewing the copy of the surveillance video that was provided to police. The Ballyhoo Tavern's CCTV cameras recorded all occurrences in the bar during the evening that Jerry went missing. That is, it recorded all except for the time period of 00:00 hours to 01:00 hours, which would have captured specific activity that was related to Jerry's level of intoxication and his removal from the bar. Did the police receive the original or an altered copy?

Dog Searches

The only solid Bloodhound track resulted in a lost scent at the intersection of North 1st Street and Chestnut Street (ISUPD, 2009, p. 12) (Figure 5.4, *Blue Dotted Arrow*). Deputy O'Hare scented his K-9 with one of Jerry's pillow cases and a T-shirt from his dorm room (ISUPD, 2009, p. 15). They started at the Ballyhoo Tavern on May 3rd, headed south down 9th Street and then tracked west in the alley behind the Terminal Bar and Grill. They then continued to the parking lot of the Hilton Garden Inn. Once there, the K-9 tracked north and continued through the lower level of the Terre Haute Transit Authority's Multi-Modal Parking Garage. The K-9 continued north to Chestnut Street, then turned west continuing to 1st Street. Jerry's scent was lost upon reaching 1st Street. Was there something special about this location that contributed to the lost scent, or was Jerry picked up in a vehicle at that point?

However, there were other K-9 scent hits for Jerry elsewhere outside the vicinity of the Ballyhoo Tavern. Vigo County Sheriff's Department Search and Rescue member Deputy Jim O'Hare and his K-9 found Jerry's scent on May 3rd at the Sycamore Place Apartments on Spruce Street (ISUPD, 2009, p. 15). The K-9 was rescented upon arrival at the apartment complex and promptly tracked across the parking lot at Spruce Street to a stairway in the southwest corner of the building (Figure 5.4, *Blue-X Dot*). The K-9 tracked up the stairs to the door for the apartment complex's laundry room and gave a positive indication by scratching on the door. The K-9 then came back down the stairway and went directly to an apartment, whereon, it indicated a positive hit by scratching on the door several times. The resident of that apartment opened the door before the officers knocked. He was there with his parents and granted the officers request for a voluntary search without a warrant (ISUPD, 2009, p. 11). Vigo County Deputy O'Hare and his K-9 searched the apartment, but nothing was discovered therein. The investigating officers stated that they did not know what had contributed to the K-9's positive hit on the apartment. They concluded that it could have possibly been a residual or transfer scent on a young lady with whom Jerry had interacted inside the bar (hereafter referenced by the alias "Karen"). She had visited the apartment after she left the Ballyhoo Tavern on the night Jerry disappeared (ISUPD, 2009, p. 11).

We agreed that transfer scents can occur and linger for great periods of time. However, we did not believe that this was an acceptable explanation in this case. First, had Karen's visit to the apartment that night left a residual scent at the front door, then it should have also left a residual scent inside the apartment. It did not. Second, no explanation was offered for the positive K-9 hit at the laundry room door. No mention could be found as to whether the investigating officers entered the laundry room with the K-9 or even went in themselves to look around. Was Jerry's scent present inside the laundry room? Why did the scent go from the middle of the parking lot to the laundry room door, and then only to the front door of the apartment? Did someone return by vehicle to the rental complex early that morning with Jerry's scent, go to the laundry room, strip down to underwear, walk barefooted to the apartment and leave a scent on the door while opening it, and then proceed to shower?

At that time, the apartment was rented by Karen's boyfriend. During the party at the Ballyhoo Tavern, Jerry had placed his arm around Karen's shoulder in a friendly manner. That action made her boyfriend jealous and he verbally confronted Jerry. The boyfriend later stormed out of the Ballyhoo Tavern followed by his 3 friends. Karen did not think that her boyfriend could do anything to physically harm Jerry. Yet, she wanted police to know anyway that he was upset about seeing Jerry with his arm on her shoulder. A source told us that Karen was said to have reported to police that her boyfriend had thought about committing suicide after Jerry went missing.

Side Scan Sonar

An Indiana Department of Natural Resources Conservation Officer used side scan sonar to search the river for Jerry on May 5, 2009. In the end, negative results were obtained. But, that is not how it started out. At approximately 10:01 hours on May 5th, officers thought that they may have located a body in the water at a depth of 20.1 feet. The water temperature was 60.8 °Fahrenheit and the speed of the river was 2.7 miles per hour at the time. The sonar reading located the object at 39 degrees 28.304 minutes North latitude by 87 degrees 25.204 minutes West longitude (geodecimal coordinates 39.472, −087.420). Those coordinates placed the object on the river bottom about 200 feet south of the train trestle that is nearest to Sycamore Street. However, no divers were sent down that day to identify or recover the object. The police reported that they went back to this location the following day (Thursday, May 6th) to try and identify the object – but by that time it was gone. Although not completely sure whether or not it was Jerry's body that they had observed on the sonar the previous day, investigators suggested that it may have just been a sand bar on the river bottom that had washed away overnight.

Reported Sightings

On the night he went missing, Jerry was wearing a very distinctive red Hawaiian shirt. However, this was complicated by two facts. First, the video camera for the Ballyhoo Tavern recorded other individuals who were also wearing red Hawaiian-type shirts on the night that Jerry went missing. Second, for some undeclared reason, the Ballyhoo Tavern's video cameras were working for most of the night except for the period of time between 00:00 hours (midnight) and 01:00 hours. We found this recording gap to be very odd since this was the time period in question when Jerry's behavior had prompted the off-duty police officers to remove him from the premises.

During an interview with ISUPD officers on the night of May 5th–6th, a local Circle K night clerk at 380 North 3rd Street reported seeing Jerry between 01:00 and 01:30 hours on Thursday when he stopped in and made a purchase (ISUPD, 2009, p. 31). She suggested that another night clerk had seen Jerry out by the storage and dumpsters on Friday (Figure 5.5, *Red-K Dot*). She also stated that they have video and that the manager has access to it. The manager was supposed to come in at 08:00 hours later that morning. ISUPD officers went back to the Circle K at 09:45 hours, spoke with the manager, and obtained the video (ISUPD, 2009, p. 34). They watched the video for the period of time related to the reported sighting of Jerry (00:58 to 03:15 hours) and found no indication of his presence within the

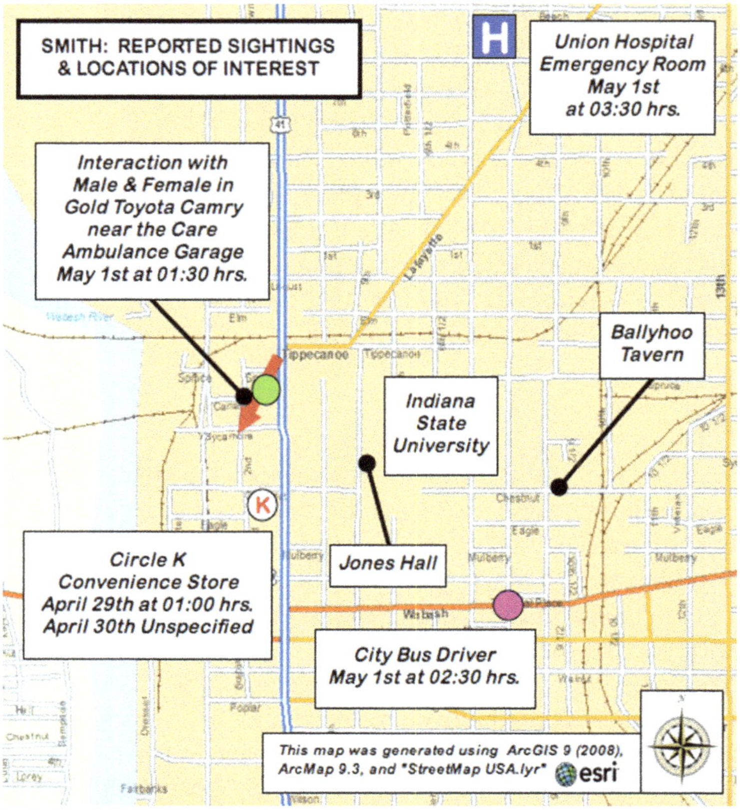

Figure 5.5 Jerry Smith was last known to be seen at the Ballyhoo Tavern (00:40 hours). Reported sightings placed him near the Care Ambulance garage (01:30 to 01:45 hours), near a bus stop at 8th and Wabash (02:30 hours), and lastly at Union Hospital's Emergency Room lobby (03:30 hours).

convenience store. We found no report of whether a Bloodhound was ever brought in to look for Jerry's scent on the premises.

A witness who was standing on the west side of the Care Ambulance garage at about 01:30 hours on May 1, 2009 (Figure 5.5, *Green Dot*), reported that he saw a person fitting Jerry's physical description and attire in the vicinity of the intersection of Canal Street and North 2nd Street (ISUPD, 2009, p. 29). This is a rather isolated part of town that sits between the train tracks to the north and south, the Wabash River to the west, and North 3rd Street to the east. Some of the buildings in the area at that time included the Care Ambulance garage, a business related to vacuum cleaners, a fenced storage facility, a fuel access card facility, a window and door company, and a truck repair service company. Jerry was approximately 40 to 50 yards away from the witness. The witness observed Jerry walking slowly and staggering through this area in a southwesterly direction for approximately 15 minutes, from about 01:30 to 01:45 hours (Figure 5.5, *Red Arrow*). During that time, Jerry was stopped by a man and a woman in a gold Toyota Camry. Their conversation lasted approximately 2 to 4 minutes and the occupants drove away in their vehicle. This location was about 3 blocks west of Jerry's dormitory (i.e., Jones Hall). University police ran a check on all gold Toyota Camry motor vehicle registrations, and did call several of the owners to ask where they were on the night that Jerry went missing. However, police records do not indicate that any follow-up was ever made to verify vehicle owners' alibis. We were left wondering what these two people were doing in a remote part of town at that time of the morning. The police never brought a Bloodhound out there to validate the sighting.

Another witness, a Terre Haute city bus driver, said she saw a picture of Jerry on a missing person poster and said it resembled a person who attempted to board her bus around 02:30 hours on Friday, May 1, 2009 (ISUPD, 2009, pp. 10, 11). She stated that the man was accompanied by another white male, both of whom she estimated to be of college age. She could not give them a ride because she was off-duty at the time. She said the man resembled Jerry, but without the glasses. This incident occurred in the area of 8th Street and Wabash Avenue (Figure 5.5, *Purple Dot*).

Approximately 2 hours after the last reported sighting, the next witness put Jerry 6 blocks east and 11 blocks north in the vicinity of North 7th Street and 8th Avenue (ISUPD, 2009, p. 25). A security officer at Union Hospital's Emergency Room lobby said that a young man showed up at 03:30 hours on May 1st (Figure 5.5, *Blue Square*). The young man stated that he had walked from the Ballyhoo Tavern to the hospital because he "believed" that his girlfriend was en route to the emergency room via ambulance. A receptionist checked with the emergency room staff and stated that there were no ambulances en route. The young man promptly departed Union Hospital upon hearing the security officer's suggestion that the girlfriend could have been transported to Regional Hospital.

Was it or was it not Jerry at the hospital that night? In the police supplemental report, the officer referred to this young man as "Mr. Smith" (ISUPD, 2009, p. 25). How did the police officer know or verify that this was in fact Jerry Smith? The hospital security officer had not asked the young man for identification or even for his name. There was no record of having asked the security officer to identify him from a photograph or to describe him as he appeared that night. Why did the police not bring a Bloodhound up to the hospital and check for Jerry's scent? The security cameras were not functioning properly during the time frame that the young man was supposed to be at the hospital. So, he could not have been identified that way. If the young man was Jerry, then this begged several questions. The security officer quoted the young man as saying that he "believed" his girlfriend was en route to the hospital. Upon what did he base that belief? What had Jerry been told and by whom? Was this ploy the bait to get him out on the streets alone that night focused on his girlfriend's well-being rather than his own safety?

Old Photographs

During the early morning hours of Saturday, May 2, 2009, Officer Cummings examined Jerry's *facebook* page and found numerous pictures along the railroad tracks that paralleled Tippecanoe Street (ISUPD, 2009, p. 13). From east to west (Figure 5.6), they showed Jerry underneath the North 3rd Street bridge that passed over the tracks, walking to the west along the tracks (inset upper left-hand corner), on the train trestle over the Wabash River, and down by the river (inset lower left-hand corner). Officer Cummings and Sergeant Smith determined that the *facebook* photographs had been taken in September 2006. To what extent did this discovery shape the investigators' thinking? Did law enforcement investigators come to their conclusion that Jerry's death was a tragic accident based on photos that were taken over 2.5 years earlier?

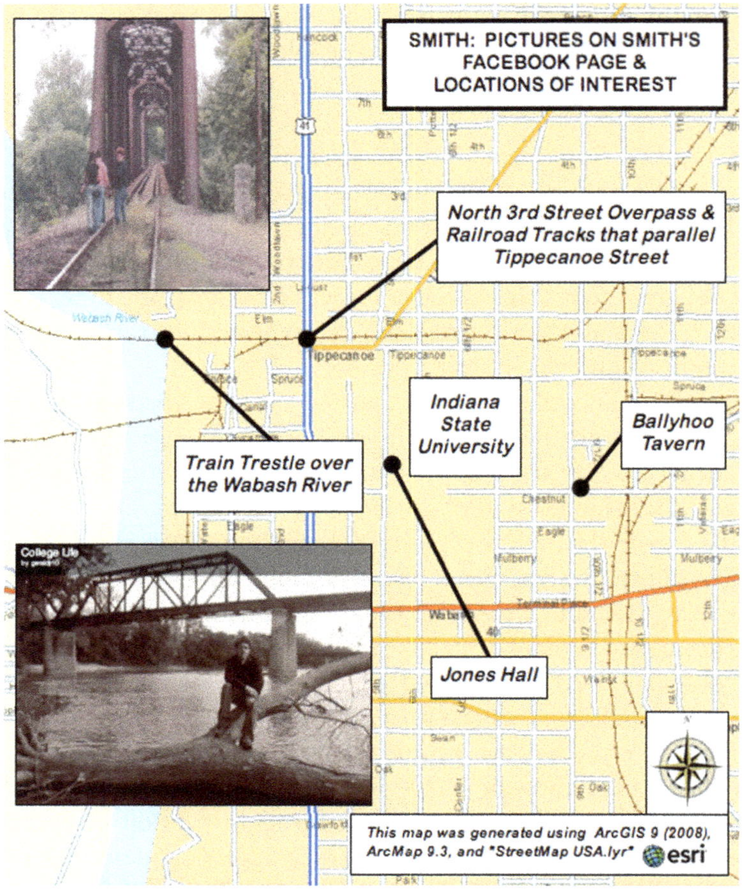

Figure 5.6 Several digital photographs were found on Jerry Smith's *facebook* page, which showed him on the railroad tracks and trestle. One of those pictures showed Jerry sitting on a tree that had fallen into the Wabash River just south of the trestle.

Other Important Incidents

Four unusual incidents were reported to police during the weeks just prior to and after Jerry's disappearance. They involved a female presenting herself as a police officer, two assaults on a homeless man, and a strange drive-off. A date and time for the first incident could not be pinned down. Police reports specified the event as having happened "the other night" and "a couple of weeks ago" (respectively, ISUPD, 2009, p. 60). Gilbertson called the phone number listed in the police report in order to get more details; it was no longer in service. He then, to no avail, attempted to track-down the female who reported the incident that was experienced by her son.

According to the report, the young man was stopped for a traffic light at the intersection of 13th Street and Lafayette in the Twelve Points area of north Terre Haute (Figure 5.7, *Light Blue Dot*). A Toyota Camry pulled up behind him with its emergency flashers going. The female driver exited the vehicle and approached his car. She was not in uniform, but identified herself as police officer and asked for his driver's license. He asked her to show him a law enforcement badge. Whereon, she informed him that she did not have to show him her badge, and insisted once more that he produce a driver's license. He refused to

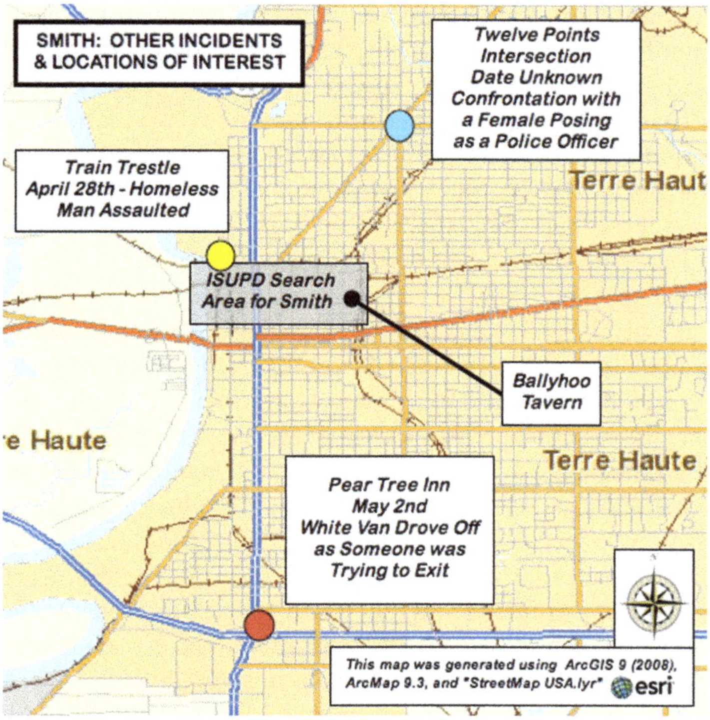

Figure 5.7 Law enforcement knew about 3 other incidents that occurred around the time that Jerry Smith went missing and died. Was there a connection?

comply. She wanted him to pull into the parking lot at a nearby CVS pharmacy. He did not comply. Rather, he departed the area in his vehicle and she did not pursue him. Now, keep in mind that the sighting of a person talking to two people in a gold Toyota Camry was not publicized in the media. When the mother called police to report the incident, she described it as a gold Camry. Her son later told police that it was a dark-colored Camry, possibly blue or black. Even though the son's description of the vehicle matched the make and model of the sighting (i.e., a Toyota Camry), the police did not follow up on any possible connection between the two incidents because the son's memory of the vehicle's color did not match the color from the possible sighting.

The next incident occurred on Tuesday, April 28th, between 15:00 and 16:00 hours – just 2 days before Jerry vanished. Police recorded an assault on a homeless man (hereafter, Bob) who was living under the train trestle near the 600 block of North Water Street (Figure 5.7, *Yellow Dot*). Police interviewed Bob, who stated that he did not see anything since he had been attacked from behind. However, his three friends (i.e., Tom, Dick, and Harry) had witnessed the assault. An ISUPD officer contacted those friends and recorded a statement from Tom (ISUPD, 2009, p. 60). Tom stated that he observed a large white male chasing Bob along the train tracks in a westerly direction heading back toward the trestle and the river. Tom hollered at the unidentified male and asked him what he was doing, which interrupted and ended the chase. The unidentified male answered Tom, declaring that he had seen Bob and thought that he was trying to hurt himself, and that his actions were intended as intervention. The police report did not specify whether or not the unidentified assailant had offered any further explanation regarding what behavior he had seen that might indicate potential self-inflicted harm. Tom also reported that the suspect drove a white Pontiac Grand Am. The police did not follow up on any possible connection because it was "not the type of vehicle that we have been looking for" (ISUPD, 2009, p. 60).

The April 28th assault on Bob along the train tracks near North Water Street was a potentially significant piece of intelligence information for two reasons. First, it occurred in the same location known to have been frequented by Jerry and his friends in the past – that is, the train trestle near North Water Street under which Bob lived and the tracks between North 1st Street and the Wabash River. Second, it was in the vicinity of the possible sighting of Jerry and the incident with the gold Toyota Camry – that is, the intersection of North 2nd Street and Canal Street, which was three blocks south and 1 block east. And lastly, it was only 1 block west and 1 block north of another assault. A gentleman who lived in the 600 block of North Water Street reported having witnessed an assault on Tuesday, May 5th (ISUPD, 2009, p. 53). This was 4 days after Jerry went missing. The assault occurred near the intersection of North 1st Street and Tippecanoe Street. The man believed the victim to be a homeless man whom he knew by the name of Bob. We considered the possibility that this was just a clerical error resulting from looking at the wrong calendar, and that the officer who received the report wrote down Tuesday, May 5th, when in fact it was the same assault as reported earlier and occurring on Tuesday, April 28th. We discerned that there was no confusion and that it was a separate incident due to the number of involved persons: Incident #1 = 1 victim, 1 assailant, and 3 friends on-scene (5 people total); and Incident #2 = 1 victim, 2 assailants (3 people total).

The last unusual incident of potential importance was recorded on May 2nd – just 1 day after Jerry vanished (ISUPD, 2009, p. 58). A reliable eyewitness, an employee of the law enforcement crime lab in Indianapolis, reported that she had seen an older model, white van with tinted windows parked near the Pear Tree Inn at the intersection of 3rd Street and Margret Avenue in Terre Haute (Figure 5.7, *Red Dot*). She observed the arm of a presumed Caucasian ("a white arm") reach out of the van door only to be abruptly withdrawn as the door closed and the vehicle drove off. She was unable to obtain a vehicle license plate number. Absolutely no record existed of whether or not this incident was followed up by local law enforcement.

Recovery Location

On Friday evening, May 8, 2009, 4 people in 2 pairs witnessed Jerry's body floating down the Wabash River and coming to rest amongst debris next to a dock (ISUPD, 2009). He was recovered in front of the Vincennes Boat Club in Kimmell Park just off Oliphant Avenue in Vincennes (Figure 5.3). After performing an external examination, the Medical Examiner reported that Jerry had no significant injuries and that his skin required no comment. Although we agreed with the Medical Examiner's physical description of Jerry, we challenged the hypothesis asserted by ISUPD investigators and the Medical Examiner that Jerry traveled the full distance down the river from Terre Haute to Vincennes. This assertion was put forth as an empirical fact (i.e., observable and measurable), but when tested proved to be no more than an axiom (i.e., something believed to be true without proof).

In order to believe that this was an accidental drowning, one would have to accept four variables and relationships amongst them: (1) the distance was not too great, (2) the path was not too adverse, (3) there was enough time for everything to happen, and (4) environmental conditions were favorable for all events to occur. First, one would have to believe that Jerry's body traveled that distance at a sufficient speed within the known time period (i.e., within about 7.8 days). Second, one would have to believe that Jerry's body traveled the length of the Wabash River all the way from Terre Haute without becoming hung up somewhere upstream of Vincennes. And last, the weather and water conditions had to favor decomposition and bloating in less than 1 week.

We have heard that the distance from Terre Haute to Vincennes by river was about 96 miles. Gilbertson estimated the distance at greater than 84.6 miles by using maps.google.com to measure a vehicle route nearest to the Wabash River (Figure 5.8). Jerry was last seen at about 00:40 hours on May 1st and his body was removed from the water at about 20:40 hours on May 8th (approximately 188 hours or 7.8 days). If Jerry traveled the 90 miles of river in 188 hours, then he would have traveled at about 0.48 miles per hour. An easily accomplished task since the river was reported to be flowing at 2.7 miles per hour during the side scan sonar search near Terre Haute on May 5th.

However, 188 hours were not available in this scenario. In accordance with the hypothesis that this was an accidental drowning, Jerry had to have entered the water during the early morning hours of May 1st, drowned and sank to the bottom, bloated from decomposition gases and resurfaced, and then floated down to Vincennes by the evening of May 8th. The Wabash River was reported to be at 60.8 °Fahrenheit during the side scan sonar search. Detective Lieutenant Luking, the Vincennes Police Department officer on-scene for the body recovery, reported the outside air temperature at 76 °Fahrenheit. Thus, the

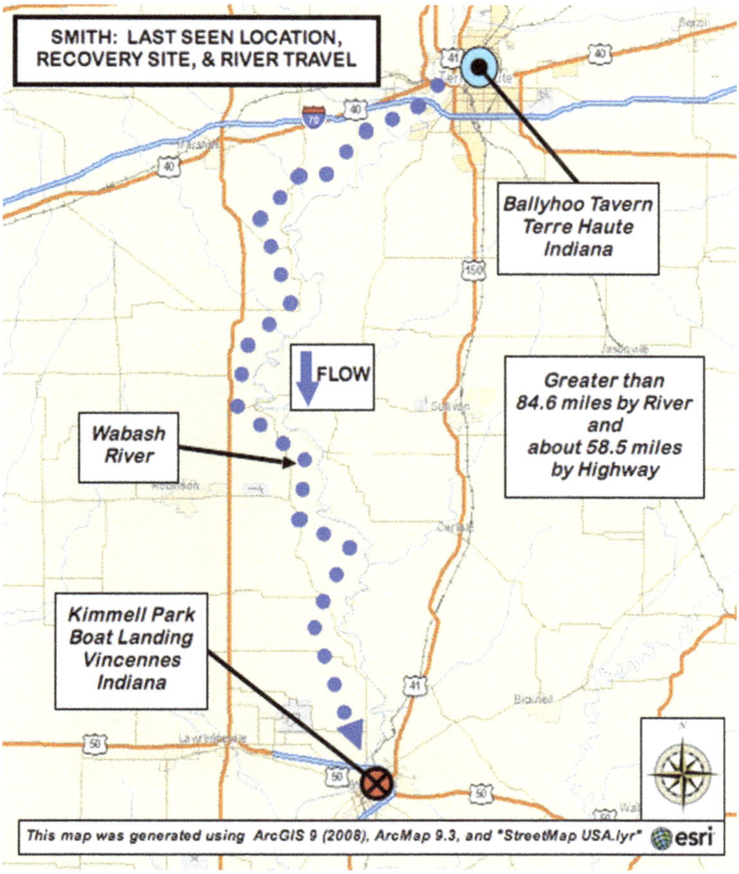

Figure 5.8 Investigators purported that Jerry Smith traveled more than 84.6 miles down the Wabash River during flood stage without receiving one postmortem injury to his body.

water and air environmental conditions were favorable to steady decomposition. Bloating from decomposition gases in a temperate environment (68 to 75 °Fahrenheit) on dry land begins about 36 hours postmortem. This process is delayed by a factor of 2 in water, and would have therefore taken 72 hours in this scenario. The amount of time afforded to float from Terre Haute to Vincennes was reduced to 116 hours (188 total hours minus 72 hours to sink, bloat from gases, and then resurface).

As a result of the reduction to elapsed time, Jerry would have had to have floated at a greater speed than previously calculated (62.5% faster). Rather than 0.48 miles per hour as thought earlier, Jerry needed to travel at about 0.78 miles per hour in order to travel the 90 miles in 116 hours (about 18.6 miles per day). It seemed that Jerry's body was not moving all that quickly even though the Wabash River was still at flood stage and crested at 18 feet; 10 feet over a normal height of 8 feet. In fact, the individuals within each pair of witnesses had time to verbally interact and comment on what they were seeing while Jerry's body came to rest against the floating dock. As can be seen in the photograph (Figure 5.9), no waves existed out in the open water and no wake or ripples were created along the shore where the water ran against objects such as the dock. An average person can walk at 2 miles per hour fairly easily – that is 1/2 mile per fifteen minutes. If the calculations were correct, then Jerry may have traveled at 0.78 miles per hour. That sounded like a really slow rate of movement, slower than a steady walking pace. In reality, it was still a fairly fast rate of movement and equated to 1029.6 feet every 15 minutes, or 3.43 football fields in 15 minutes. Moving at that pace on land and walking into a tree, bushes, or a solid structure would probably cause some kind of injury to a live human body. Should it not cause some kind of injury to a deceased body softened by exposure to water (e.g., cuts, scrapes, scratches, abrasions, contusions, and/or broken bones)?

All of these speed calculations could be wrong anyway. Recall that the side scan sonar reported the river to be flowing at 2.7 miles per hour on May 5th. At that speed, Jerry would have traveled the 90 miles in 33.4 hours. Also recall that the decomposition and bloating process would have taken about 72 hours. In accordance with the hypothesis that this was

Figure 5.9 After floating nearly 90 miles in the Wabash River and avoiding such obstacles, Jerry Smith's body was finally trapped by a boat dock in front of the Vincennes Boat Club in Kimmell Park just off Oliphant Avenue in Vincennes during the evening of May 8, 2009. (*Special note:* Use of this photograph was approved by Robin Hill. All yellow graphics were added by Gilbertson.) (From Indiana State University Police Department, 2009.)

Figure 5.10 Four witnesses watched as Jerry Smith's body floated downstream, bounced off a tree, and then came to rest against this over-turned floating dock amongst other flood-water debris. (*Special note:* Use of this photograph was approved by Robin Hill. All yellow graphics were added by Gilbertson.) (From Indiana State University Police Department, 2009.)

an accidental drowning, Jerry had to have entered the water during the early morning hours of May 1st, drowned and sank to the bottom, bloated from decomposition gases and resurfaced (72 hours), and then floated down to Vincennes (33.4 hours), and arrived at the Kimmell Park boat dock on May 5th sometime around 11:00 hours (105.4 hours later). However, he did not arrive in Vincennes until the evening of May 8th. This simple exercise in mathematics and logic told us that something unusual happened here.

Although the travel speed would have been easily achieved in the river at flood stage, the travel route was not conducive to passage across the whole distance. One person even remarked to newspaper reporters how surprised he was that Jerry's body had made it all the way down to Vincennes from Terre Haute. The Wabash River generally forms the border between Illinois and Indiana (Figure 5.8). It meanders back and forth while flowing from north to south, often changing its heading from east to west, then west to east. There are few straight sections greater than a couple miles. If one defines a "curve in the river" as any change in direction less than 90 degrees, and a "bend in the river" as any change in direction greater than 90 degrees (a 180 degree change in direction counted as 2 "bends"), then a body floating down the Wabash River between Terre Haute and Vincennes would have encountered a nearly impassable route. Along this stretch of the river (Figure 5.8), there were 15 right-hand and 13 left-hand curves, and 31 right-hand and 34 left-hand bends in the river. Not counting the first train trestle in Terre Haute, there were the cutwaters and abutments of 2 additional trestles and 5 bridges that crossed the river, plus innumerable boat docks and fallen trees. In other words, there were 93 twists and turns in the river, with 90 miles of obstacles along its banks, each with a potential to snag a floating body or to cause damage due to collision (Figure 5.10).

Recovered Property

Jerry's Pontiac Grand Prix was found parked in Indiana State University Lot #24 right where he had left it (ISUPD, 2009, pp. 9, 14). It was booted for security purposes and watched. An inspection of the vehicle produced nothing to indicate what may have become of Jerry. The

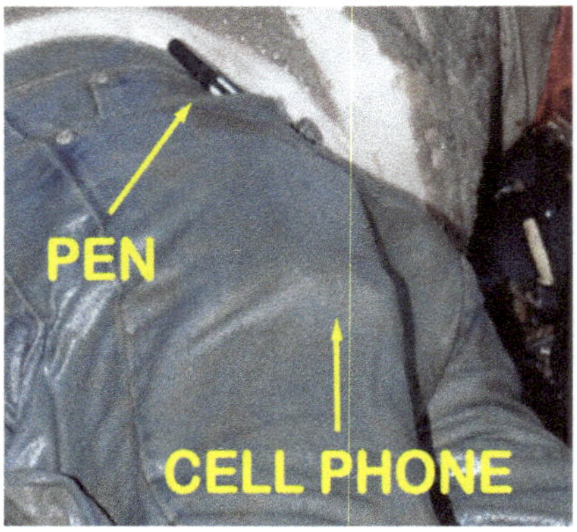

Figure 5.11 Among the property recovered on Jerry Smith's body was a ballpoint pen and his cell phone. How did the pen stay in his pocket during the nearly 90 mile trip down the river? (*Special note:* Use of this photograph was approved by Robin Hill. All yellow graphics were added by Gilbertson.) (From Indiana State University Police Department, 2009.)

parking lot was 1/2 block north and 1 block west of Jerry's on-campus residence in Jones Hall, or approximately 700 feet from west door to mid-lot by sidewalk. Interestingly, Lot #24 is physically halfway between, and along a straight line from, Jones Hall and the Care Ambulance company building on Canal Street where Jerry was reportedly sighted talking to the couple in the gold Toyota Camry.

According to the official property inventory recorded during the autopsy, Jerry was recovered wearing brown loafer-style work shoes, blue jeans, a red short-sleeve Hawaiian print shirt, white T-shirt, white socks, and white boxer briefs. Valuables included a wallet with personal effects, identification cards, a set of keys, a cell phone (iPhone), a ballpoint pen, $43 in cash, and 76 cents in loose change (Figure 5.11). The autopsy stated that Jerry was wearing loafer-style work shoes. However, this was incorrect. As can be seen in the police department's recovery photographs (i.e., Figure 5.12), Jerry was wearing lace-up

Figure 5.12 Jerry Smith was presumed deceased and in the water for more than 7 days (188 hours) by the time his body was recovered. This picture, taken at recovery, clearly showed his arms in an elevated position up off his body – he was still in rigor. (*Special note:* Use of this photograph was approved by Robin Hill.) (From Indiana State University Police Department, 2009.)

work boots that went up past his ankles. It might seem like a small thing, but Robin Hill told us that when police gave her Jerry's property, she received a lead pencil instead of a ball point pen. Did the medical examiner give her property from another victim or did he just misclassify the property recovered from Jerry's person? This also begged the question of how did he float almost 90 miles without the pen falling out of his pocket? This information along with the other information from the autopsy told us that Jerry was probably already dead before his entry into the Wabash River, and that he was entered into the river much closer to the recovery location since he was still in possession of his pen.

External Assessment

The Medical Examiner's findings while performing the external examination were described in the autopsy report. He stated that there was no evidence of injury and that Jerry's ears were not pierced. However, Gilbertson noticed that Jerry was clearly wearing a posted earring through a hole in his left earlobe in numerous pictures. Jerry's mother (Robin Hill) confirmed that he did have a pierced left earlobe. In fact, when she first became aware of this small detail as reported by Dr. Kohr, Robin thought that the body may not be her son's.

Medical Examiners routinely check under fingernails for foreign material and often take fingernail clippings and samples (Armstrong & Erskine, 2011). Victims who struggle with their assailants often end up with the suspect's DNA material under their fingernails. Drowning victims often end up with dirt from the river or lake bottom under their fingernails. This usually occurs during the drowning process when the victim becomes disoriented, reaches out and grabs for anything to survive, including at times even the river bottom. Jerry's fingernails were described as closely trimmed with no underlying dirt, debris, hair or tissue. There was no dirt under Jerry's fingernails even though his whole body was covered with mud.

Ocular Changes

Medical examiners always comment on the eyes (i.e., the color of the irides, clearness or cloudiness of the conjunctiva, the general color of the sclera, and any petechial hemorrhaging if present). In this autopsy report, there was no mention of the condition of Jerry's eyes whatsoever. This was a key forensic fact that was missed. An accurate description of the eyes would have told us whether or not Jerry was deceased on land with his eyes open or closed before entry into the water. Words that one should normally see in an autopsy report in association with the eyes are film, cloudiness, opacity, or tache noire. None of them were there.

Rigidity

Rigidity (*rigor mortis*) is the stiffening of the muscles that begins shortly after death and is detectable within 2 to 4 hours on land. It usually subsides within 24 to 36 hours on land depending on the temperature of the body and the environment, and the extent of muscle mass in the body (Geberth, 2006). In temperatures of 58 °Fahrenheit, rigor usually subsides or relents within 36 hours as it has in other cases we have investigated. We know that the water temperature was about 60 °Fahrenheit when Jerry went missing and that the air temperature was about 75 °Fahrenheit when he was recovered from the river. We also know that postmortem processes are extended by a factor of 2 in water as compared to on land (2 days in water = 1 day on land; Hendrick, Zaferes, & Nelson, 2003). Thus, Jerry could have taken as long as 72 hours (3 days) to go into, persist, and then come out of rigor. We also knew that 188 hours (7.8 days) had elapsed between the time when Jerry went missing and his recovery, plus an additional 11 hours 20 minutes until autopsy, for a total possible postmortem period of 199 hours 20 minutes. Something was wrong – the numbers did not add up.

We could clearly see in the recovery photographs (Figure 5.12) that Jerry's arms were still in full rigor at that time. Approximately 11 hours 20 minutes later at autopsy, the Medical Examiner stated that rigor was present in Jerry's body. He provided no other clear descriptor of rigor or any assessment of whether it was in on-set (going in), persisting, or relenting (going out). Medical Examiners will often comment on the extent of rigor in the jaw and arms. This one did not. Rigor sets first in smaller muscles and then proceeds to larger muscles beginning in the jaw and going to the legs (DiMaio & DiMaio, 2001). As rigor relents, the smaller muscles will become relaxed first followed by the larger muscles. This flaccidity may cause widening of the anal and vaginal orifices that can be confused with sexual assault. Careful examination is required. In this case, the Medical Examiner was most likely focusing on whether or not he could exclude sexual assault when he described the anus as not being dilated. This, however, told us that the small muscles of the anal orifice were not relaxed and that Jerry was still in full rigor at autopsy. Thus, it seemed that he was not even beginning to relent after having been missing and presumed deceased for nearly 200 hours. In fact, he was probably no more than 48 hours into the 72-hour rigor process by the time he reached autopsy.

Body Position and Lividity

The Medical Examiner also stated that lividity (*livor mortis*) was indistinct. Livor is the pooling of the blood after death (Shkrum & Ramsay, 2007). The Medical Examiner never mentioned whether the lividity was even fixed anywhere on the body, which usually takes 10 to 12 hours to become fixed in one position. After 12 hours, lividity will not displace with any amount of movement and it will not blanch under any amount of pressure. Since Jerry was recovered in the normal drowning position of face-down, then lividity should have been fixed permanently and anteriorly (on his front) because he was supposedly in the water in this position for 188 hours. We concluded that there were only two ways to account for an absence of identifiable lividity. First, Jerry had not been dead that long and had been moved often enough on land to preclude livor from fixing prior to being placed in the river. Second, had he hypothetically rolled around in the water for 7 days, constantly flipping from front to back, then this may have prevented livor from fixing. But, it would have also likely caused him to lose some of his personal property like his wallet, shirt, and pen (none of which he lost).

Decomposition and Maceration

Postmortem artifacts related to decomposition (bacterial putrefaction and enzymatic autolysis) and maceration (the softening and breakdown of tissues) become evident around 12 hours on land and 24 hours in the water (Shkrum & Ramsay, 2007). Discoloration of the Right Lower Quadrant may be detectable as early as 24 hours in the water. The blue-green color of decomposition will spread to the entire body by 48 hours, gradually turning darker and darker until marbling is present. A body will then begin to purge around 96 hours in the water (fluids seeping from facial orifices would be the earliest signs). Washerwoman's hands (*Wauschaut*) begins almost immediately, so it is difficult to estimate time using only this artifact. However, skin slippage and degloving of the hands that is associated with immersion in water are relatively good estimators of time. The skin will begin to come loose from a body at about 48 to 96 hours (2 to 4 days) and is easily discerned by 96 to 168 hours (4 to 7 days). The skin on exposed hands will begin to deglove around 72 to 96 hours (3 to 4 days) and be completed by 144 to 168 hours (6 to 7 days).

The Medical Examiner described Jerry's appearance as presenting with early skin slippage (which reflects 2 to 3 days), a distended abdomen bloated with foul smelling gases (consist with 3 to 4 days), and Washerwoman's wrinkling of the fingers (characteristic of 2 to 3 days). We could discern from the recovery and autopsy photographs that Jerry had changed color to blue-green across his back and that some marbling was just starting to show. This indicated that he was at about 72 hours postmortem. He looked to be slightly bloated, which was consistent with 72 hours in water after death. He had not begun to purge, which meant that he had most likely been deceased and in the water for less than 96 hours. We could see no sign of extensive skin slippage. This suggested to us that he had not been in the water more than 96 hours. The skin on his hands was firmly intact at the wrists, which indicated that degloving would not occur for several days. At the time that the Medical Examiner recorded his description and the autopsy photographs were taken, Jerry had been presumed deceased for about 199 hours 20 minutes. The Medical Examiner's description and our assessment of Jerry's condition were consistent with each other. The postmortem artifacts collectively suggested that Jerry had not been deceased for almost 200 hours as presumed by authorities, rather he had died sometime between 60 and 80 hours before autopsy, or 50 to 70 hours before recovery.

Gastrointestinal System

The Medical Examiner reported that Jerry's stomach contained 50 milliliters (1.7 fluid ounces) of food particulate and that no smell of alcohol was present. The partially digested food matter was not identified to see whether it was consistent with his last meal. It was not tested to see whether it matched the beverages that he had been drinking, the water in the river, or city tap water. No odor of alcohol in the stomach was inconsistent with someone who was drinking heavily that evening.

Toxicology

There exists much debate out in the field among coroners, medical examiners, forensic pathologists, and law enforcement investigators as to whether or not postmortem alcohol production actually occurs. However, the forensic research literature is full of articles that support an assertion of postmortem alcohol production (Canfield, Kupiec, & Huffine, 1993). The sugars and bacteria in a body literally ferment and produce alcohol during putrefaction. Postmortem alcohol production is usually more active in organs than in the blood and will produce higher values. Additionally, alcohol concentration values will be higher in blood than in muscle tissue (Athanaselis, Stefanidou, & Koutselinis, 2005).

When speaking of testing for alcohol, it is important to note that this includes ethanol (found in beer, wine, and liquor) and other C3 alcohols, as well as other volatiles such as methanol, isopropanol, n-propanol, acetaldehyde, 2-propanol, acetone, isobutanol, t-butanol, n-butanol and sec-butanol. Generally speaking, n-propanol and n-butanol can help to distinguish between antemortem alcohol ingestion and postmortem alcohol production, especially in bodies that have been underwater for long periods of time (Armstrong & Erskine, 2011). The detection of small amounts of alcohols such as n-propanol, n-butanol, and isobutyric acid is an indicator of postmortem ethanol production (Garriott, 1996; Kugelberg & Jones, 2007; Moriya & Hashimoto, 2004).

A study done by Johnson, Lewis, Angier, and Vu (2004) reported on two specific temperatures and the preserving affect of sodium fluoride: 77 °Fahrenheit (25 °Celsius) and 39.2 °Fahrenheit (4 °Celsius). Relative to the states that the cases in this book are from (i.e., Minnesota, Wisconsin, Illinois, Michigan, Indiana, and New York), 77.0 °Fahrenheit could be considered the equivalent of "temperate" outdoor weather. Whereas, 32.9 °Fahrenheit may be considered reflective of moderate winter weather, or a medical examiner's storage cooler. The researchers found that autopsy specimens with no preservative stored at 77 °Fahrenheit showed an average 1,432 percent increase in the ethanol concentration after just 48 hours (2 days); ranging from 109 to 6,100 percent. Specimens with no preservative stored at 39.2 °Fahrenheit demonstrated, on average, a 1,470 percent increase in the ethanol concentration after 96 hours (4 days); ranging from 107 to 7,500 percent. In other words, half the temperature required twice as long to produce about the same amount of change.

77.0 °Fahrenheit for 48 hrs. = 1,432% of Change
39.2 °Fahrenheit for 96 hrs. = 1,470% of Change

This clearly demonstrated the affect of cooler or colder temperatures on the decomposition process. It also supported our use of 72 hour and 96 hour models in estimating the postmortem intervals for bodies in cooler environments such as water.

A similar debate exists regarding the postmortem production of γ-hydroxybutyric acid or gamma-hydroxybutyrate (GHB). Again, the forensic research literature demonstrates an overall conclusion that the postmortem production of GHB has been confirmed (Nishimura, Moriya, & Hashimoto, 2009). This whole issue is confounded by the fact that GHB is an endogenous compound (i.e., naturally occurring) and can be found in the central nervous system and peripheral tissue of mammals (National Highway Traffic Safety Administration, 2012). It is also found in the brain, cerebrospinal fluid, vitreous humor, liver, and kidney. GHB is a metabolite and precursor of the neurotransmitter γ-aminobutyric acid (GABA). It generally becomes undetectable in plasma or blood after 6 to 8 hours. Like most things in forensics, we found no agreement on GHB when it came to cut-off values for postmortem production levels. However, as a general rule, the level of GHB concentration that can be found naturally occurring in living humans was typically below 1 milligram per liter (mg/L) (which equals 1 microgram per milliliter, or 1 mcg/mL) (National Highway Traffic Safety Administration, 2012), and ranged from 0.9 to 3.5 mg/L (Wang, Giang, Lu, & Kuo, 2006).

Samples taken at autopsy (i.e., blood, urine, tissues and vitreous humor) for toxicological testing are routinely sent out to specialized facilities. These laboratories maintain the specimens in appropriate storage for a period of one year from the date that they are received. In this case, Jerry's autopsy specimens were sent to the American Institute of Toxicology (AIT) Laboratories in Indianapolis. They were received on May 14, 2009, and scheduled for destruction on May 14, 2010. Jerry's blood alcohol concentration (BAC) was initially determined using chest cavity blood and reported at 0.149 mcg/mL. Each drink is approximately 0.02 milliliters (mL), which meant that Jerry's BAC was equivalent to just under 7-1/2 drinks for a 180-pound male. However, Jerry only weighed 160 pounds. Therefore, this equated to just under 6-1/2 drinks. Considering the amount of alcohol in Jerry's system and the fact that he supposedly vomited in the bar, we argued early on that there was a distinct possibility that he was drugged in the bar. His behavior, which reflected high intoxication and was incongruent with the BAC, was similar to numerous other drowning cases that we have examined. Therefore, we decided to take a closer look at the toxicology results.

First, the toxicology report indicated the presence of caffeine. However, the ISUPD reports made no mention of how the caffeine got into Jerry's bloodstream. No one reported having seen him consume any food product or drink any beverage that contained caffeine. No one reported that Jerry had consumed caffeine "alertness" tablets. They all only reported that he was drinking alcohol the whole evening and that he was quite intoxicated. So, how did the caffeine get into Jerry's blood?

Second, we have always asserted that additional toxicology tests might yield more information in many of these cases. Faced with the reality that the destruction date was quickly approaching for Jerry's autopsy specimens (May 14, 2010), we paid AIT Laboratories to have the specimens preserved for an additional year (until May 14, 2011). The initial toxicology report (Figure 5.13, SET 1, dated May 27, 2009) listed a *Comprehensive Drug Panel, Blood* (test code 70510) using chest cavity blood, as well as two other tests using chest cavity blood and liver tissue that came back inconclusive (test code 49900). No test for GHB had been done during the initial drug screening. On April 29, 2011, we ordered and paid for additional toxicology tests with AIT Laboratories (Figure 5.13, SET 2, dated May 31, 2011), and paid to have the samples preserved for yet another year (until May 14, 2012). Using body cavity blood, Gilbertson ordered a repeat of the *Comprehensive Drug Panel, Blood* (test code 70510) and an *Alcohol Panel* (test code 45620) with *Isopropanol QN2* (code IPA-F). A test for *Gamma-Hydroxybutyrate* (test code 44590) was also requested using a liver tissue sample.

We set up an experimental design. In simplest terms, an experiment is where you take things or people (i.e., objects of interest) and do something to them (the treatment), in order to see what happens. In our experiment, the blood and tissue specimens were our "objects of interest" and the "treatment" was cold storage for 2 years (2009 to 2011). In order to see whether a treatment has any affect on objects of interest, one must measure them before and after the treatment. For example, if a researcher is interested in how much weight is gained or lost as a result of increased exercise, then the objects' weights must be determined before (pretest measure) and after (posttest measure) the period of exercise (the treatment) and then compared. The results from SET 1 (which served as our pretest measure) were compared with the results from SET 2 (which served as our posttest measure). Specifically, we compared the *Comprehensive Drug Panel, Blood* (test code 70510) results from the initial and follow-up tests. This afforded a baseline understanding of the specimens that were tested in 2009 and again in 2011. It demonstrated whether or not any of the specific drugs or drug types that were identified by the initial 2009 test had changed or were no longer identifiable in the 2011 test, or whether any values for those drugs had changed. It also identified the extent of continued decomposition that may have occurred in cold storage during the two years between testing. In other words, it told us whether or not cold storage had done its job and stopped all further decomposition of the specimens and any postmortem production of chemicals. A second and alcohol specific test (*Alcohol Panel*, test code 45620, with *Isopropanol QN2*, code IPA-F) served as a cross-check on

Smith: Toxicology Test Results

DONE BY	SPECI.	TEST NO. & NAME	ANALYTE OF INTEREST	SET 1 5/27/2009	SET 2 5/31/2011	SET 3 6/6/2012
AIT	Blood, CAVITY	70510 Comprehensive Drug Panel, Blood	Methanol	Negative	Negative	Negative
			Ethanol	0.149	0.149	0.149
			Acetone	Negative	Negative	Negative
			Isopropanol	Negative	Negative	Negative
			Caffeine	Positive	Positive	Positive
AIT	Blood, CAVITY	45620 Alcohol Panel, IPA-F Isopropanol QN2	Methanol		Negative	Negative
			Ethanol		0.162	0.162
			Acetone		Negative	Negative
			Isopropanol		Unsuitable	Unsuitable
AIT	Blood, CAVITY	45650 Alcohol Panel	Methanol			Negative
			Ethanol			0.162
			Acetone			Negative
			Isopropanol			Negative
MED TOX	Blood, CAVITY	45070 Nicotine and Metabolite (Forensic)	Nicotine			10 ng/mL
			Cotinine			<10 ng/mL
NMS	Blood, CAVITY	70500 Sexual Assault Panel, Blood	Ethanol			0.163
			Caffeine			Positive
			Flunitrazepam			Negative
			GHB			Negative
AIT	Tissue, LIVER	44590 Gamma Hydroxybutyrate	GHB		<100 mcg/g *	<100 mcg/g *
NMS	Tissue, LIVER	16620 Gamma-Hydroxybutyric Acid, Tissue	GHB			100 mcg/g †

* Unable to quantitate due to interference.

† The value reported for GHB includes its lactone (GBL) in the specimen.

Figure 5.13 Three sets of toxicology tests (2009, 2011, & 2012) demonstrated stability in the preservation of the specimens. They also raised questions about the presence of caffeine, nicotine, cotinine, and GHB in Jerry Smith's body.

postmortem alcohol production. As such, we could propose with certainty that any drugs currently in the specimens in 2011 had been present at the time of Jerry's death in 2009.

Both the 2009 and 2011 *Comprehensive Drug Panels* 70510 returned the same results for all substances (Figure 5.13, SET 1 and SET 2). Specifically, both tests disclosed findings of (a) Ethanol Alcohol – Positive 0.149, and (b) Caffeine – Positive. The *Alcohol Panel* 45620 reported ethanol alcohol slightly higher at 0.162, which was attributed to the greater level of accuracy and specificity of the test. We were confident in this judgment since no other alcohols had been produced and had not started to break down into acetone. The results were (a) Methanol – Negative, (b) Acetone – Negative, and (c) Isopropanol – Unsuitable. These collective findings convinced us that no further degradation or decomposition of the samples had occurred and that storage conditions had maintained the specimens.

Since no postmortem alcohol production had occurred, we surmised that no postmortem GHB production had occurred. Therefore, any GHB that was present could most likely be attributed to antemortem ingestion in 2009 and was not related to postmortem production during storage from 2009 to 2011. Since concentration levels are higher in liver tissue than in blood specimens, we used a liver tissue sample to test for the presence of GHB. The *Gamma-Hydroxybutyrate* test using a liver tissue sample (test code 44590) returned a "Positive" finding with a nonspecific concentration of less than 100 micrograms per gram (mcg/gm, which equals mcg/mL). Unfortunately, the test was unable to precisely quantitate the specimen due to interference. Thus, GHB had been present all along in Jerry, but not identified during the initial toxicology testing in 2009. Was this evidence that Jerry had been drugged with GHB back in 2009?

Initially, we had decided to do the toxicology tests in 2011 in order to scientifically examine assertions made by some skeptics of our work. Most of the victims whose cases we have investigated were not tested for GHB at autopsy, including several in this book. Our critics purported that the GHB which had been found in many of the victims during later toxicological testing was a result of postmortem production. They insisted that the GHB was endogenous and had been produced either during the long period that the young man was in the water and decomposing, or during the long period that his specimens were in storage. We sought to reject or accept that null hypothesis by testing Jerry's specimens after 2 years of cold storage. A secondary benefit of the tests would be to discern whether or not he had any GHB in his system. Since the tests showed that no postmortem production of alcohol had occurred, we extrapolated that finding to postmortem GHB production. We considered the toxicology tests to be fruitful because GHB had been found, even though it could not be quantitated due to interference. We were somewhat perplexed by the finding that isopropanol was present but unsuitable.

Prior to the 2011 tests, we had decided to extend the experiment into 2012 and had paid AIT Laboratories to maintain Jerry's specimens for another year. On May 1, 2012, via e-mail, Gilbertson officially requested another round of testing for Jerry's specimens. He repeated the *Comprehensive Drug Panel, Blood* (test code 70510), and *Alcohol Panel* with *Isopropanol QN2* (test code 45620 & IPA-F), as well the liver tissue test for *Gamma-Hydroxybutyrate* (test code 44590) to double-check and verify once more that no changes had occurred in the past year due to postmortem production. The 3 tests returned identical results as previous years (Figure 5.13, SET 3, dated June 6, 2012). So, we lost nothing, but we also did not gain any new knowledge.

Fortunately, during the course of early-2012 discussions, we had decided to run 4 additional tests in May 2012. We decided on 2 redundant tests for quality control. One was performed at AIT Laboratories and the other at National Medical Services (NMS) in Willow Grove, Pennsylvania. We had AIT Laboratories add the *Alcohol Panel* (test code 45650) to cross-check the other two alcohol tests. We also knew that these agencies offered different testing procedures for some substances. So, we decided to have blood and liver tissue specimens sent to NMS in order to get, as it were, a "second opinion" on the alcohols and GHB. As a result, NMS performed 2 tests: *Sexual Assault Panel, Blood* (test code 70500), and *Gamma-Hydroxybutyric Acid, Tissue* (test code 16620).

The NMS blood test confirmed the presence and level of ethanol, and the presence of caffeine. However, it returned negative findings for flunitrazepam (Rohypnol or "roofies") and GHB. This seemed to contradict an earlier AIT Laboratories' finding that showed the presence of GHB. However, all it meant was that the NMS measurement of GHB in the specimen had not reached the minimum level required by NMS reporting criteria for that test. In other words, not enough GHB was found to be noteworthy of reporting. This was clarified by the NMS liver tissue test that returned a finding of 100 mcg/gm. So, there we had it. AIT

Laboratories had found GHB at less than 100 mcg/gm and NMS found it at precisely 100 mcg/gm. What had made the difference? Was it postmortem production during the past year?

The research literature informed us that gamma-butyrolactone (GBL) breaks down into GHB in the body (NHTSA, 2012). It is an industrial solvent that is used in making cleaners, paint removers, and engine degreasers. It is also sold in some health stores, gyms, and on the Internet as a supplement. Some body builders use GHB as a substitute for anabolic steroids to stimulate muscle growth (Porrata, 2011). Since GBL converts quickly to GHB in the body as it metabolizes, it too can be used in this manner. We also learned that isopropanol is sometimes used to thin or "cut" substances like GBL. Furthermore, alcohol enhances the affects of GHB and GBL on behavior, sedation, and toxicity.

Additional conversation with the Forensic Business Unit at AIT Laboratories confirmed our thoughts. The different quantitations of GHB had resulted due to different testing procedures. The AIT Laboratories GHB test used chemical derivatization followed by gas chromatography-mass spectrometry (GC-MS), whereas the NMS test did not. Although there are several reasons for using chemical derivatization, what is important to know is that GHB is converted to GBL during the chemical derivatization process (Lin, Wang, Wu, Chen, & Liu, 2008; Wang, Giang, Lu, & Kuo, 2006). Therefore, the NMS test took into account both GHB and GBL. Whereas, the AIT Laboratories test only accounted for GHB. We posited that the interference reported by the AIT Laboratories' results was caused by the presence of GBL in Jerry's system that had not yet converted to GHB. Once a test was used that looked at both GHB and GBL, then the confusion disappeared. The NMS result may also have helped to explain the interference with isopropanol that caused the "unsuitable" report.

In the final analysis, then, we were confident that all toxicology tests had shown that no postmortem production of alcohol or GHB had occurred from 2009 when the specimens were collected to the tests in 2011 and 2012. Additionally, we were confident that all toxicology tests had shown that 100 mcg/gm of GHB and GBL were present in Jerry's body at the time of his death. Furthermore, the GHB in Jerry's body could have been twice as high just 18 minutes to 1 hour earlier (200 mcg), and as much as 4 times higher (400 mcg) 36 minutes to 2 hours before his death.

Smoking Gun

One additional toxicological issue came up during our examination of Jerry's death. A female who personally knew Jerry, and who was one of the central witnesses in this case (one of the three friends who left the bar with Kathy's boyfriend), told police in her written statement that Jerry had asked for a cigarette and she gave him one. Thus, we knew that Jerry had smoked at least one cigarette on the night of April 30th sometime after 23:30 and before 00:00 hours on May 1st. So, was there nicotine and cotinine in Jerry's system? It had not been reported in the initial toxicology test in 2009.

Cotinine is an alkaloid and metabolite of nicotine (Wall, Johnson, Jacob, & Benowitz, 1988). It normally shows up in the blood work of smokers during toxicology tests and has even be used in research studies to demonstrate exposure to second-hand tobacco smoke in nonsmokers (Gallo et al., 2010). Nicotine is metabolized in the liver into cotinine. Many variables affect the rate at which people convert nicotine to cotinine such as age, biological sex, and race (Hukkanen, Jacob, & Benowitz, 2005). Cotinine levels are normally higher in the blood of smokers than are nicotine levels. Typically, nicotine clears an individual's body at a rate of 17.2 milliliters per minute per kilogram of body weight, and cotinine clears a body at about 12.1 milliliters per minute per kilogram of body weight (Benowitz & Jacob, 1997). The research literature studied by Gilbertson indicated various half-lives with a general consensus at about 2 hours for nicotine and 20 hours for cotinine. The affect of the half-lives was not linear, rather log linear. This means that it is not a one-for-one reduction process (e.g., the same amount of nicotine is metabolized every minute). Instead, more is metabolized at first, and as time goes on, less and less is metabolized during each minute. The studies indicated that cotinine is completely eliminated from the bloodstream by day 5 after smoking cessation (Feyerabend, Bryant, Jarvis, & Russell, 1986; Jarvis, Russell, Benowitz, & Feyerabend, 1988; Sepkovic, Haley, & Hoffman, 1986).

Pollutants within the environment in which we conduct our daily lives cause our bodies to present a "background" level of cotinine during testing. The workplace environment has gotten better for some Indiana workers due to changes in the law restricting smoking. However, to this day, bars that do not allow entrance or service to persons under the age of 21 years old remain exempt under Indiana law. As such, Jerry was most likely exposed to second-hand smoke and should have presented with some extent of cotinine during testing. A study of 32,252 adults was conducted between 1994 and 1996 (Jarvis, Feyerabend, Bryant, Hedges, & Primatesta, 2001). Researchers found a geometric mean cotinine concentration of 0.41 nanograms per milliliter (ng/mL) among confirmed nonsmokers. Another study suggested that exposure to unventilated, smoke-filled rooms could increase the carboxyhaemoglobin levels in nonsmokers to that which was an equivalent of having smoked one middle-tar cigarette (Jarvis, Russell, & Feyerabend, 1983). In that study, measurements taken before exposure and at the end of 2 hours of exposure showed plasma nicotine levels rose from 0.76 to 2.49 ng/mL, and plasma cotinine levels rose from 1.07 to 7.33 ng/mL.

Research suggests that approximately 70 to 80 percent of nicotine is converted to cotinine (Benowitz & Jacob, 1994). A statistical average of 1 milligram (mg) of nicotine is absorbed into a person's body while smoking (Benowitz & Jacob, 1984; Gori & Lynch, 1985). Analysis of one study's graphed findings disclosed that nicotine and cotinine levels rose sharply, and at about the same rate demonstrating covariance (Murphy, Villalta, Ho, & von Weymarn, 2007). The line for nicotine on the graph started to rise right away. The line for cotinine started to rise later in time and eventually rose higher. In that study, peak plasma nicotine concentration was reached at 25 minutes after smoking began and peak plasma cotinine concentrations at 120 to 150 minutes.

Smoking one cigarette can generate venous blood nicotine concentrations from 5 to 30 ng/mL depending on how it is smoked (Hukkanen, Jacob, & Benowitz, 2005). In one study (Russell, Jarvis, Feyerabend, & Fernö, 1983), subjects smoked a middle-tar cigarette (with 1.4 milligrams of nicotine) for 6 minutes taking a puff every 40 seconds. Blood samples were collected before smoking and 1.5 minutes after smoking ended (i.e., 7.5 minutes apart). The average plasma nicotine concentration peak was 25.7 ng/mL at about 7 minutes, which dropped to about 17.6 ng/mL at 10 minutes, 10.4 ng/mL at 30 minutes, and 7.0 ng/mL at 60 minutes. Another study that focused on cotinine reported an average plasma level of 80 ng/mL among occasional smokers (16 cigarettes per week) (Williams, Eng, Botvin, Hill, & Wynder, 1979). However, cotinine could not be detected in those individuals who self-reported only smoking 1 cigarette per week unless that cigarette had been smoke within 48 hours of specimen collection.

So, the question was, how much nicotine and cotinine should have been in Jerry's bloodstream at the time of his death? Using the data from the aforementioned studies and his weight (160 pounds or 72.6 kilograms), Jerry's body would have theoretically cleared nicotine at about 1,248 mL per minute and cotinine at about 878 mL per minute. We knew that he smoked at least 1 cigarette that night between 23:30 and 00:00 hours, so we used 23:45 hours as the "mark" time. The smoke-filled environment of the bar which he was in for more than four hours, plus the 1 cigarette that we knew he had smoked, could have raised his nicotine level to a peak of 32.5 ng/mL within 7 to 25 minutes. Splitting the difference, we set 00:00 hours (midnight) as the time that nicotine peaked in his blood. Since we knew that he did not leave the bar until 00:40 hours, his nicotine level would have started to drop and the level of cotinine would have still been rising. Both would have likely been above 25 ng/mL at that point in time.

Discounting all of the possible, unsubstantiated sightings of Jerry that were reported to police, and estimating that he walked directly to the river without delay, fell in, and drowned, then that would have added at least another 15 minutes to his time. This would have set the timetable to approximately 70 minutes since he smoked the cigarette and 55 minutes since nicotine reached its peak in his blood. By that time, the level of nicotine could have then been down around 20 ng/mL while his cotinine level was still increasing and probably at or above 30 ng/mL. On the other hand, if one included all of the sightings (i.e., Circle K, Care Ambulance garage, city bus stop, & Union Hospital emergency room entrance), then the timetable would have been extended to 03:30 hours and an additional 155 minutes. This would have brought the total time since smoking the cigarette to about 225 minutes (23:45 to 03:30 hours). He would have still needed about another 15 minutes to get back to the river. Thus the total time in this scenario would have been 240 minutes. Had he died at that moment and taking into account the 2-hour half-life of nicotine, then the level of nicotine in Jerry's blood could have been reduced to about 8 ng/mL. The level of cotinine in his blood could have still been well above 25 ng/mL.

Herein, laid the problem. The toxicology tests that Gilbertson ordered from AIT Laboratories on May 1, 2012, included a specific test for nicotine and cotinine. They sent a chest cavity blood specimen to MEDTOX Laboratories in Saint Paul, Minnesota. The *Nicotine and Metabolite (Forensics)* (test code 45070) test showed that, at the moment of death, Jerry had 10 ng/mL of nicotine in him and less than 10 ng/mL of cotinine. The values were completely against logic and upside-down. The only way for him to have a nicotine level higher than a cotinine level would have been for him to die shortly after having started to smoke a cigarette and before hardly any nicotine could be metabolized into cotinine. The only way for him to have the nicotine and cotinine values that he did was to have died before the nicotine peaked in his blood and any cotinine appeared. In other words, Jerry would have had to have died within 1/2 hour of beginning to smoke the cigarette. But, nearly an hour had already passed between when he smoked the cigarette (23:45 hours) and when he left the bar (00:40 hours). Since residual cotinine would have remained in his blood from the cigarette he had smoked in the Ballyhoo Tavern, this meant that the cotinine in Jerry's bloodstream from the night he disappeared had to entirely clear his system and then the process restarted. So, where was Jerry for 4 to 5 days while the cotinine left his system? Where was he when he smoked that last cigarette within minutes of dying? And, who gave him that last cigarette?

Cell Phone Records

The ISUPD attempted to get Jerry's cell phone data right away. They contacted the AT&T National Compliance Center on May 1, 2009 (ISUPD, 2009, p. 3), and started to receive phone record information the next day via fax. Two documents were faxed on May 2nd and each ended with a 1 minute incoming call on Jerry's phone at 19:06:01 hours on April 30th. The number remains unidentified. However, the records indicated that the call was transmitted via the cell tower near 913 Crawford Street (Geodecimal Coordinates 39.45917, −87.40361). The phone records also listed 6 text messages on April 30th at 21:11, 21:42, 22:35, 23:05, and 23:36 hours, followed by another on May 1st at 01:14 hours.

Jerry's cell phone was recovered with his body. It was sent for forensic examination to a company in Oak Park, Illinois. They recovered and confirmed all of the same phone calls. They also reported Jerry's other activity on his phone such as checking his voicemail, opening both his private and school e-mail accounts, sending and receiving text messages, using apps (such as music software applications), and utilizing media software to take and transmit a photograph. Their data recovery efforts were generally successful considering the phone had been underwater. One of the many files that they were able to recovery was "call_history.db" that recorded the last 100 calls. Gilbertson received a copy of the recovered files on compact disc and a hardcopy of the final report produced by the forensics company. Everything checked out. Their report was perfect relative to the recovered files. However, when he compared the report, the recovered files, and the phone records that had been received from the phone company, discrepancies existed.

Gilbertson was only able to correlate incoming and outgoing phone calls listed on the AT&T phone record with those listed in the last 100 calls (call_history.db) up to and including the 1 minute call at 19:06:01 hours on April 30th. As stated earlier, there was no record of any phone call activity on any of the AT&T documents after that incoming call, except for 6 text messages. However, 8 additional phone calls were listed in the last 100 calls (calls_history.db) after 19:06:01 hours. Furthermore, the memory in Jerry's phone recorded activity outside the physical proximity of where he was supposed to be that night. By all accounts, Jerry was at the Ballyhoo Tavern for the party from 18:30 to 22:00 hours. One of his professors reported in an e-mail to ISUPD Director Mercier that he (the professor) had briefly left the Ballyhoo and recalled seeing Jerry when he (the professor) returned to the bar at about 21:20 hours. One young woman reported speaking to him at 00:20 hours and observed him being escorted out of the bar at 00:40 hours. Jerry should have been in the Ballyhoo between 21:00 and 22:00 hours that night.

However, it appeared that his phone was not there with him. Someone used the phone to take a photograph ("IMG_0253.THM") at 21:51:17 hours in the vicinity of 65–69 South 19th Street (Geodecimal Coordinates 39.46706, −87.38849). Then at 22:04:56 hours, the files "cell-local.plist" and "cells.plist" were modified and GPS stamped with the same geodecimal coordinates (Figure 5.14, *Light Blue Star*). The Ballyhoo Tavern sits at the corner of Chestnut Street and North 9th Street. It is a straight shot east down Chestnut Street to South 19th Street, and then 2 blocks south to the address in question. One way on foot is 1.1 miles. Did Jerry leave the Ballyhoo, travel across town to take the picture, and then return to the bar? Or, did someone borrow his phone, leave the bar, come back, and return Jerry's phone to him? Although we pointed out this information, to our knowledge it was never followed up by anyone with subpoena power.

Conclusion

Considering all the forensic information available to us in the Jerry Smith drowning investigation, we believe sufficient evidence existed that clearly pointed to Jerry being abducted,

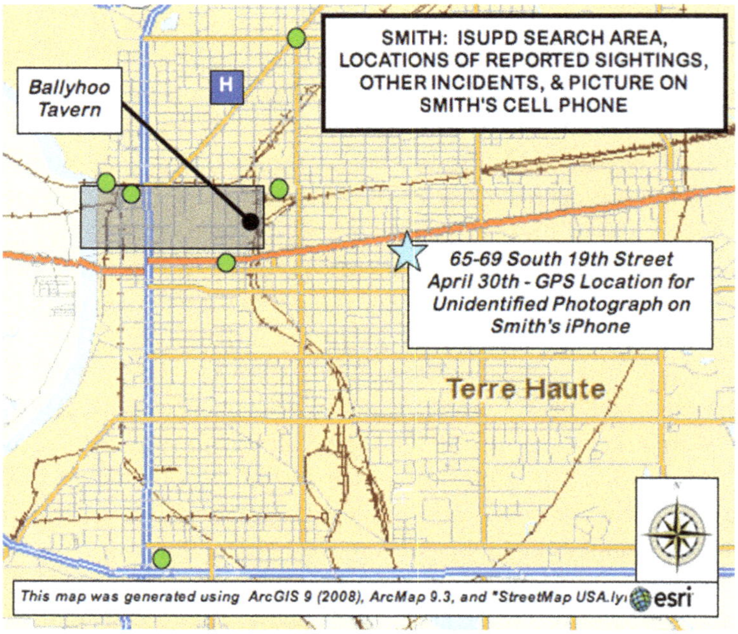

Figure 5.14 Forensic analysis of the metadata on Jerry Smith's recovered cell phone revealed that a photograph had been taken during the time that he was supposed to be in the Ballyhoo Tavern. Its location did not fit when compared with all other locations of interest (*Green Dots*). GPS coordinates placed the photo near 65–69 South 19th Street (*Light Blue Star*) far to the east.

held for several days, and then murdered. There were solid forensic artifacts that pointed directly to this conclusion. There were also numerous pieces of investigatory evidence that influenced our decision. Some of the things we learned about the case made us upset with the manner in which the case was resolved. It is extremely important that readers always remember that we do not condemn entire agencies or career fields. Rather, we take issue with the laziness and poor attitudes of some individuals within the criminal justice system.

If this were truly an accident, then Jerry would have had to have walked all the way from the Ballyhoo Tavern to the train trestle. He would have walked past countless video cameras: ATMs and banks, business night security systems, convenience store CCTVs, and parking ramp recorders. Somehow, Jerry did not exist that night or was invisible to cameras. He miraculously made it from the interior of the Ballyhoo Tavern to the Wabash River without showing up on any recorded video. He should have been on the Ballyhoo's recorder – he was not. Somehow, the Ballyhoo's own CCTV stopped working during the most important hour of the night when Jerry's behavior and direction of travel were in question.

The ground search efforts were exemplarily performed. The one thing their search proved was that Jerry was not inside the box. The ISUPD looked everywhere, everywhere except outside the box to the north, to the south, and to the east. The idea that Jerry had gone to the train trestle that night so influenced their thinking that they focused on the area between the Ballyhoo Tavern and the Wabash River. The one Bloodhound trail abruptly ended. Why did they not take the dogs for a walk to see whether the scent could be picked up nearby? Although an explanation was offered for Jerry's scent at the apartment entrance, one was never offered for why his scent was not inside the apartment. Why was it at the laundry room? Did they think to check the young woman's garment for Jerry's scent to determine whether or not a transfer scent was even possible? No. Why did they not follow up the several possible sightings of Jerry with a localized Bloodhound search to confirm his presence? Furthermore, if those sightings were actually of Jerry, then he would have left a scent trail back and forth across the city that night before going to the river. Why did the Bloodhounds not find Jerry's scent all over the city? Was he snatched off the street shortly after he left the Ballyhoo Tavern?

Speaking of being snatched off the street, what about the strange incident with the van and what appeared to be a passenger trying to flee the vehicle as it drove off? We do not know whether or not it was related to Jerry's disappearance. In fact, since the incident was treated like just another anecdote, we do not know anything beyond what was written in the complaint when the incident was reported to police. Then, there was also the incident with the woman posing as a police officer. One would think – related to Jerry's disappearance or not – that it would have garnered more attention than it did. If nothing else, then the criminal impersonation of a police officer should have been investigated. And, what about the two assaults on Bob that occurred by the very train trestle that the police believed was the location Jerry had accidentally fallen from into the river? Were they ever followed up or simply dropped because they happened to a homeless man? The side scan sonar picked up an image on the river bottom south of the train trestle. The police were right and the image they received probably was just a sand bar and not a body. However, considering the importance of the discovery and the time of day at which it occurred (early in the morning), as well as its proximity to the train trestle, it would have seemed logical for the police to do everything possible to confirm or deny the existence of the image on the sonar. They did not.

There existed a general lack of attention to detail on the part of some individuals. The property record stated Jerry had a pen, but the mother was given a pencil. He was not described with an earring. Perhaps, he was not wearing one that night or it had fallen out when his ear wrinkled in the water. We can excuse the Medical Examiner for this one. Although it is a common feature found in nearly every autopsy report except this one, why was there no description of the condition of Jerry's eyes? Why was there no description of decomposition discoloration? With no test to prove drowning, Dr. Kohr said he had to eliminate other possibilities. He ruled out a struggle because there were no injuries (specifically, lacerations, bruises, or fractures). He ruled out robbery because Jerry's wallet was in his pocket. The doctor could probably rule out robbery as a motive since Jerry's wallet was on his person, but without absolutely knowing the exact amount of money in a victim's wallet, who can still say that he was not robbed? He fervently argued that Jerry had walked in a drunken state to his old haunt, the train trestle, and fallen into the Wabash River, where he drowned. To him, this made a lot more sense than any other scenario because he could not imagine what a supposed assailant's motive might be for killing Jerry. It is not a medical examiner's responsibility to determine motive, rather he is to determine cause of death and manner of death. The manner of death can be *natural*, *accidental*, *suicide*, or *homicide*, and when he does not know how it happened, then it is *undetermined*.

The trip that Jerry's body would have had to have taken in order to get from Terre Haute to Vincennes presented us with several difficulties. There were 93 twists and turns in the river, with 90 miles of obstacles along its banks, each with a potential to snag a floating body or to cause damage due to collision. First, Jerry had no sign of postmortem trauma to his body. Second, we would have had to believe that he actually floated the whole distance without becoming snagged somewhere upstream of Vincennes. We found it absurd to believe that Jerry sustained no postmortem injuries to his body considering he was supposed to have fallen off a train trestle, floated at least 90 miles, and been witnessed striking at least one tree and a dock near the Vincennes Boat Club (Figures 5.9 and 5.10). He did not even have something as minor as a laceration or abrasion. Furthermore, we found it difficult to understand how he could make the aforementioned journey without losing the pen sticking out of his pocket (Figure 5.11).

Third, the timing of events just did not add up when you set things in motion the way the Medical Examiner wanted them to have happened. As we pointed out earlier in this chapter, Jerry's body would have required some time to sink to the bottom in Terre Haute, decompose, bloat and resurface, and then float to Vincennes. We calculated all the times and determined that he would have needed to travel at about 0.78 miles per hour in order to travel the 90 miles in 116 hours (about 18.6 miles per day). We agreed that this speed was possible. The Medical Examiner who performed Jerry's autopsy repeatedly asserted that he believed Jerry had drowned in the Wabash River near Terre Haute on the night he went missing. For the sake of argument, let us start by accepting the Medical Examiner's hypothesis that Jerry went into the river that night. It would have taken no less than 72 hours to decompose and bloat; let us round it up and use 80 hours to give the hypothesis the benefit of a doubt. So, 80 hours postmortem, Jerry would have resurfaced and started to float downstream toward Vincennes at 2.7 miles per hour as reported by the side scan sonar device. Jerry would have arrived in Vincennes about 33 hours 20 minutes later on May 5th. This would have contradicted reality since Jerry actually arrived at the Vincennes Boat Club on the evening of May 8th (3 days later than the hypothetical accounting).

All of this (i.e., no injuries, too great of a distance, too many obstacles, and the timing was off), coupled with the fact that no one saw his body floating in the river for over 33 hours and 90 miles, led us to conclude that Jerry had been transported closer to the Vincennes Boat Club and placed into the Wabash River at a location somewhere just upstream within a short period of time before he was spotted by the four witnesses. However, as in the past, some individuals will still criticize our logic even in the face of such evidence. An example of this involved an academic in La Crosse (Wisconsin). She challenged our assertion that some of the cases were homicides and clung to the myth that they were accidents. By means of an analogy, she stated that when you hear hoof beats behind you, you expect to turn around and see horses not zebras. That kind of thinking demonstrates the imposition of one's paradigm on a situation without considering the context and speaking as an "expert" without knowledge of all the facts. Like calling Jerry Smith's death an accidental drowning before knowing all the facts. If it were Africa, then one would expect zebras, or maybe even wildebeest. In other words, if one sees a vulture flying overhead, then that is an interesting event – even in Minnesota. If one sees 4 vultures flying overhead in a circle, then something nearby is dead or dying – no matter where you are. It is a sign from above. Literally. All of the trip factors in this case (i.e., no injuries, too great of a distance, too many obstacles, and the timing was off) circled one common truth – Jerry did not enter the Wabash River near Terre Haute on May 1st. No one saw him floating because he was not in the water for 33 hours and 90 miles.

The empirical fact that his body was still in full rigor after being missing for 7.8 days, and that lividity was indistinct, screamed that this was inconsistent with an accidental drowning. This evidence pointed to someone who was not only abducted, but who was either held for a period of time before he was murdered or who was murdered and then preserved in a cold environment (e.g., a freezer) to prevent the body from going through the processes of rigor mortis, putrefaction, and maceration. The indistinct lividity showed that the body was not in the recovery position (face-down) the whole time, rather it was in other positions for a period of time. Since lividity was not fixed on any part of the body, which required the body to be in one position for 10 to 12 hours, also meant that the body was probably placed into the water only hours before its eventual recovery. If the body had been in the water for the 7 plus days, regardless of whether it was face-down or not, then there should still have been fixed lividity in whatever position it was most likely in. Since it was recovered face-down, then lividity should have been fixed anteriorly (front). Also, since the body was observed by people floating into Kimmell Park at dusk, then the possibility of it not being spotted floating down the Wabash River somewhere else earlier in that day or the day before was very unlikely. We, therefore, concluded that Jerry was placed into the water somewhere very close to the actual recovery site, and that the shoreline immediately upstream should have been checked for evidence (e.g., vehicle tracks, footprints, broken branches, contact marks, pieces of clothing or fibers) to substantiate this occurrence.

Returning to the matter of rigor, it was impossible for Jerry to drown on the morning of May 1st and to be in full rigor on the morning of May 9th at autopsy, much less on the evening of May 8th at recovery. Given the environmental conditions (i.e., the air and water temperatures) during the time of Jerry's disappearance, he should have been completely out of rigor long before he was recovered on May 8th. Gannon had a telephone conversation with leading forensic pathologist Dr. Cyril Wecht. Gannon mentioned that Jerry had been missing for almost 8 days (7 days 20 hours), that the water temperature was about 60 °Fahrenheit, and that Jerry was recovered in rigor. Wecht asked Gannon whether he was sure that the autopsy report did not state "3 days" and that he was not misreading it. He even suggested that the "8" was possibly a typo for the number "3." When Gannon confirmed the exact dates for Jerry being missing (i.e., May 1st through May 8th), Dr. Wecht only said, "Even without looking at the autopsy, I'd say he's [the Medical Examiner] got a real problem with this one."

The only way for him to be in full rigor at recovery and autopsy was to have died somewhere around 08:00 hours on May 7, 2009. We also know that he was smoking and should have had a considerable amount of cotinine (a nicotine metabolite) in his bloodstream had he actually died on May 1st. Since he did not, that meant that he had been kept alive for about 5 days without smoking or without exposure to other smokers. Accounting for 5 days for the cotinine to clear his bloodstream before his murder also accounts for his being in full rigor at autopsy (Figure 5.15).

We assert that Jerry Smith was abducted and held for a period of at least 5 days. At that point in time, he was given a concoction of alcohol and GBL. Whether he took the beverages voluntarily or forcefully is unknown. After a couple hours of drinking, his abductor(s) offered him a cigarette – sort of like a last smoke before execution. The GBL had converted to GHB in Jerry's body and had finally taken affect. The GHB (at 100 mcg/mL) and alcohol (BAC at 0.149) made Jerry drowsy, compliant and easy to manipulate. Only about 20 minutes had passed since he lit the cigarette, so nicotine was on its way up (10 ng/mL) and cotinine was just starting to be produced in the liver (less than 10 ng/mL). Jerry was then easily murdered by hypoxia or asphyxia. He was not deceased long enough for sufficient decomposition to occur. Thus, he did not float due to bloating. Rather, the reason he floated was because he was dead before he was placed into the water (Armstrong & Erskine, 2011). We posited that Jerry was placed into the Wabash River very close to the actual spot of his recovery. We might agree with the Medical Examiner that Jerry drowned, but whether it occurred in the Wabash River or another body of water at another location, or in a bath tub,

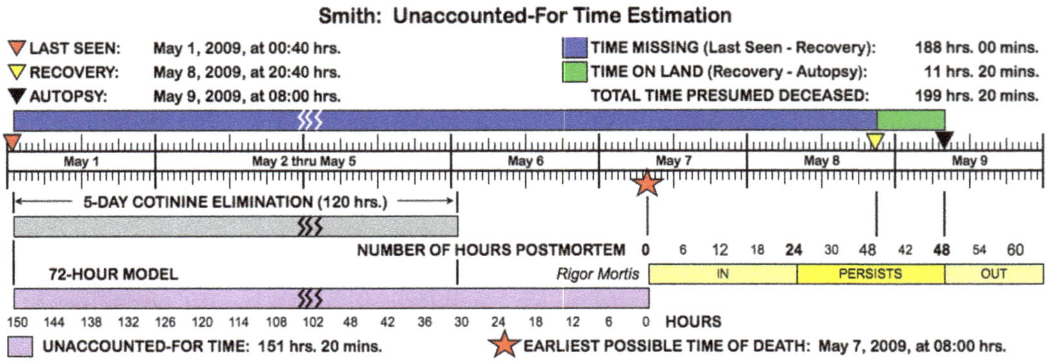

Figure 5.15 Jerry Smith had to have been abducted on May 1st and held for at least 5 days before he was murdered. Since he was in full rigor at autopsy, that meant that 151 hours 20 minutes of unaccounted for time existed. This helped to explain how cotinine had cleared his bloodstream before toxicology tests were done at autopsy.

cannot now be tested. As a result of our experimental testing, we also know that his body contained GHB and that its presence cannot be attributed to postmortem production. We propose that Jerry's murder was not the first and will not be the last in the Terre Haute area. In May 2002, Scott Javins went missing and was later found drowned. Physically, the two young men were quite similar. Both men were declared accidental drownings.

Jerry Smith – 67 inches, 160 pounds, brown hair, brown eyes.
Scott Javins – 68 inches, 150 pounds, brown hair, brown eyes.

Scott was last seen leaving a keg party on the east side of town near 22nd Street and 1st Avenue. That location was in between two other important sites. It was north of the location where the last photograph on Jerry's phone was taken (65-69 South 19th Street) and east of the location where the woman was reported to have falsely identified herself as a police officer (the 12 Points area). It is our opinion that the Medical Examiner and police detectives should have known that this case was clearly a homicide based on the forensic evidence, and that this case should now be classified as a homicide and an investigation conducted.

Brian Richard Welzien*

6

March 16, 1978–March 17, 2000

Background

Brian Welzien was a junior and finance major at Northern Illinois University (NIU) with a 3.8 Grade Point Average. He was athletic and well liked by everyone who met him. Brian took college, soccer, and his health seriously. This was evidenced by the fact that he was on the Dean's list, and that he did not use drugs and rarely drank. On Friday, December 31, 1999, Brian went out to celebrate New Year's Eve in the Wrightwood Neighbors area of Chicago. He was with a group of five males: two of his own friends (hereafter, Neil and Mark) and three acquaintances (hereafter, Ryan and two unidentified individuals). That was the last time Brian was ever seen alive again. He was found 76.6 days later (March 17, 2000), washed up on a remote beach about 40 miles away by road in Gary, Indiana.

Brian's case was investigated by detectives from the Youth Division in Area 3 of the Chicago Police Department. The investigation concluded quickly with the assumption that Brian had too much to drink and wandered away from his friends and drowned in Lake Michigan near the 1300 Block of North Lake Shore Drive, and then floated over 30 miles across Lake Michigan to Gary, Indiana. Stephany Welzien (Figure 6.1), Brian's mother, called us during the summer of 2008 after the team's television interviews had aired. In September 2008, Chief Deputy Medical Examiner Jeff Wells in Indiana stated that he would need a letter of formal request from Mrs. Welzien in order for her to receive the autopsy report and photographs. Gannon drafted the letter for her and it was sent to the Medical Examiner's office. After receiving the materials, Stephany sent all of the documents that she had and put us in contact with the private investigator whom she had hired, who was a family friend and has also investigated the suspicious disappearance and death of Jay Pohill in downtown

* Photo courtesy of his mother, Stephany Welzien.

Figure 6.1 Brian Welzien (left) with his parents, Richard and Stephany Welzien. (Photo courtesy of his mother, Stephany Welzien.)

Chicago in 2010 (which was later changed to a homicide). Gannon has maintained contact with Stephany over the years and received permission to share Brian's story (Figure 6.1).

Circumstances

Last Seen

Brian Richard Welzien was a White male, 21 years old at the time of his disappearance, 5 feet 9 inches, 145 pounds (Body Mass Index: 21.41), brown hair and brown eyes. Brian and his two friends (Neil and Mark) drove to Chicago where they planned to stay in a room at the Ambassador East Hotel with an acquaintance (Ryan) who had also been an NIU student, and two of his friends (names unknown, hereafter referred to as PERS-1 and PERS-2). Although the hotel's address was listed as 1301 North State Parkway, the main entrance actually sat on the southwest corner of the block facing East Goethe Street that ran west-east toward Lake Michigan. On the night of December 31, 1999, Brian, Neil, Mark, Ryan, PERS-1 and PERS-2 all went to a couple of bars to ring in the new millennium with a special Y2K New Year's Eve celebration. All six of them started the evening out at a New Year's Eve party on Lake Shore Drive where one of Ryan's friends was a disc jockey. At about 23:15 hours, they arrived at the "Irish Eyes" pub at 2519 North Lincoln Avenue. The bouncer and his wife both remembered quite clearly that Brian only had 2 drinks and left the bar around 02:00-02:15 hours on January 1st. In their opinion, Brian seemed pretty coherent compared to the average guest.

Upon leaving the Irish Eyes pub, Brian expressed that he was ready to return to the hotel. His friends (Neil and Mark) decided to head over to another bar that stayed open until 04:00 hours. Ryan and his two friends agreed that they were ready to go back to the hotel. So, Ryan drove his Nissan Maxima with the small group (PERS-1, PERS-2, and Brian) to the Ambassador East Hotel (Figure 6.2). When they arrived at the front door of the hotel, Ryan's two friends exited the vehicle and proceeded directly upstairs to the hotel room. Brian remained in the car because he had fallen asleep. Upon being awakened

Figure 6.2 The main entrance to the Ambassador East Hotel and Pump Room restaurant where Brian Welzien was last seen alive on January 1, 2000.

by Ryan, Brian vomited twice inside the vehicle, seemingly sick from drinking too much. Upset, Ryan told Brian to get out of the car so he could go park it. Ryan did not see Brian near the front door to the hotel when he returned after parking his car. A couple employees from the hotel (i.e., the doorman and the bartender) reported having observed Brian getting sick by the hotel entrance. The upscale restaurant in the hotel was called the Pump Room. A man had parked his car on East Goethe Street near the entrance to the hotel and the restaurant, and was waiting for his girlfriend to get off work as a waitress in the restaurant. Brian leaned on the man's parked vehicle around 03:30 hours and vomited again.

The last time anyone reported having seen Brian was in front of the Ambassador East Hotel during the early morning hours of January 1, 2000. The doorman recalled seeing someone who matched Brian's description vomiting by the curb across the street at about 03:45 hours. Neil and Mark returned to the hotel shortly thereafter at about 04:00 hours. They found the other three sleeping soundly when they got to the room, but Brian was missing. At that time, Neil and Mark immediately went back out to look for Brian. Even though they were only about 15 minutes behind him, they did not catch up to him or see him anywhere. They searched up and down the streets and alleys for about 2 hours. They returned to the Ambassador East Hotel around 06:00 hours and went to bed, thinking that Brian would show up on his own. They awoke about noon and there was still no sign of Brian. As they were checking out, they stopped at the concierge's desk and used the telephone to call 911 and to report Brian missing.

Recovery

Brian was recovered on Friday, March 17, 2000 (about 77 days after he went missing). He was discovered on a less-frequented, almost remote, stretch of sand that was often referred to as Lake Street Beach in Gary, Indiana (Figure 6.3). This beach ran from Marquette Park to Ogden Dunes. When we went there, we noticed that the beach presented a gentle approach into the water. It is more for strolling than for sunbathing since it is often pounded by heavy surf and winds coming off Lake Michigan and is surrounded by the scenery of American industry. On clear days, the Chicago skyline can be seen by the naked eye far off in the

Figure 6.3 The stretch of beach where Brian Welzien was recovered on March 17, 2000.

distance to the Northwest. Brian was discovered by someone who was just walking the beach that evening. Brian's body (i.e., face, hair and clothing) was covered with sand from the beach.

Once they had identified the body, the Gary Police Department (Indiana) eventually notified the Chicago Police Department (Illinois) since Brian was missing from one of their hotels. The Gary Police Department conducted a cursory initial investigation and then handed the case over to the Chicago Police Department, which sent officers from the Youth Division in Area 3 to investigate the recovery site. Gannon called the Chicago Police Department in September 2008 and was told that officers from the Violent Crime Unit in Area 3 were sent to Brian's dorm room to look for a suicide note or any signs of depression regarding his disappearance. No such indicators were discovered by those officers. During the course of his conversation with the investigator, Gannon also learned that officers from the Violent Crime Unit were sent due to personnel shortages even though it did not routinely handle these type of cases.

Gannon maintained a running dialogue with investigators from the Chicago Police Department over an 8-month period (from May 2008 to January 2009). He spoke with numerous detectives from Chicago, including those who worked the case and those who stated that they would look for information pertaining to Brian's investigation (e.g., Detective John DeBartolo, Sergeant Robert Battalini, Lieutenant Edmund Beazley, and Sergeant Bill McDermott). Based on those conversations, we were led to conclude that very little was ever really done by any police department regarding Brian's death. Yet, a Chicago Tribune reporter (Kaiser, 2000) wrote that DeBartolo, for his part in the investigation, started by attempting to track down Brian's electronic footprint on the grid by calling banks and credit card companies. He then went to Brian's off-campus apartment in DeKalb and interviewed his roommates there. While there, he looked in the refrigerator and found no alcohol. This supported the comments made by others that Brian was not a drinker. DeBartolo was said to have sat for hours watching recorded CCTV video in search of Brian (Kaiser, 2000). He did not see him. Other newspaper articles reported that divers from the Chicago Police Marine Unit searched Lake Michigan near Division Street (Staff Writer, 2000), and that police had chopped holes in the ice in various locations and used dogs to search for Brian's scent.

When Gannon asked them about forwarding the missing person file to him, they said they would have to find it. Gannon spoke with Detective Steven Tyler numerous times during the month of January 2009. Tyler attempted to assist, but eventually informed Gannon that he could not find anything regarding the case. Gannon was then switched over to the detective's partner, who told him to call the Gary Police Department as they (the Chicago Police Department) only made a closing report on the case after Brian was recovered in March 2000. That detective then stated that all files were destroyed after 7 years. Gannon then asked, "If all the files were destroyed after a period of 7 years, then why did you guys have me call back for the past 8 months while you were supposedly looking for the files?" They did not answer the question. In other words, if the files created for Brian's case in March 2000 had been destroyed in March 2007, then why did the detectives give Gannon the run-around for 5 months from September 2008 to January 2009? Were they telling the truth, then logically they would have told Gannon right away that they could not find the report because it had actually been written, maintained for 7 years, and then destroyed according to standard operating procedures. Even if the case files were destroyed, then did they honestly not have any notes regarding this investigation at all, or did they not want him to read them?

It seemed that everyone involved in Brian's investigation was hoping that Gannon would become disheartened and go away empty-handed. In a Chicago Tribune article published in February 2000 (Kaiser, 2000), the reporter started out the piece by telling a story of Detective DeBartolo who was replacing the common manila folder that held Brian's case with a larger folder marked "File No. F001135." However, after an 5-month period of phone conversations, another detective told Gannon that his unit did not create a file in this kind of investigation. Gannon asked the detective, "If you never even did this report as part of protocol, why didn't you just tell me this 5 months ago instead of having me call back numerous times while you said you were attempting to locate the paper work?" This question was never answered either. Why did they not tell him right away that they had not done the report as a matter of procedure. It seemed that they had the report all along and just did not want Gannon to read it. Perhaps, they were hoping that Gannon would wear down under all the stalling and just go away. Once they realized that was not going to happen, then it appeared that they had to come up with another scenario about never doing this type of report.

Gannon then called the Gary Police Department, which recovered the body, and spoke with Sergeant Bill Fazekas who remembered the case and said that his detective (Bruce Troxol) thought the case was suspicious. He said the body was fully clothed, but was missing a shoe. He could not remember which one. Once they discerned that the body was that of a missing young man, they informed the Chicago Police Department. Chicago came out and basically did a recovery form and nothing else. He said the coroner came out and took pictures.

According to a Chicago Tribune article (Kaiser, 2000), Chicago police investigators tried to wear down the young men who were with Brian on the night he disappeared by questioning them for hours. Supervisor Battalini was reported to have expressed the opinion that the young men who were with Brian that night had nothing to do with his being missing. Instead, Battalini told a newspaper reporter that, at that point in time, it was his professional conclusion that Brian was the victim of a violent crime that had been perpetrated by someone unknown to him (Kaiser, 2000). The fact that law enforcement investigators held this opinion early in the investigation was confirmed in another article (Wilson & Donato, 2000). However, opinions sometimes change, especially in these drowning cases. The Indiana Coroner listed the official manner of death as undetermined with the cause of death as asphyxia due to drowning. Part of the investigative dilemma in Brian's case was created by issues related to cross-jurisdictional and multiunit communication and cooperation (i.e., between Indiana and Illinois, and amongst investigators from Missing Persons, the Youth Division, and the Violent Crime Unit). Even though the Chicago Police Department's Missing Persons Unit referred to this case as one of the strangest and most challenging it had ever dealt with, Brian's case was quickly closed.

Analysis of Evidence

Recovery Location

The importance of the recovery site was amplified by the significance of the purported water entry location. Brian had returned to the Ambassador East Hotel where he had rented a room. He was last seen vomiting in front of the hotel by four witnesses (Ryan, the doorman, the bartender, and the guy sitting in a parked car). Law enforcement investigators presumed that Brian had left that location and walked to the beach on Lake Michigan. Considering distance alone, it is not that far and a drunk could crawl it. But, it was not your average midnight jaunt down a sidewalk. The trip would have started with an easy 4 block walk along the sidewalk to reach North Lake Shore Drive. At that point, the obstacle course began (Figure 6.4). Brian would have had to cross about 50 feet of 4-lane traffic on North Lake Shore Drive (2 north-bound and 2 southbound), which would have then placed him on a narrow median standing next to a waist-high chain-link fence along a guardrail. Having climbed over that, he then had to cross another 50 feet of 4-lane traffic on southbound U.S. Route 41, whereon, he would have encountered another median and a pair of guardrails. After catching his breath, Brian would have then had to cross another 75 feet of 4-lane traffic and a merge lane on northbound U.S. Route 41, yet another guardrail and chain-link fence, then 22 feet of lakefront trail and 85 feet of concrete apron. As impossible as this may seem, this is another commonality among a handful of these cases, that is, some victims will cross unbelievable obstacles (e.g., fences, ditches, walls, dense brush, and security systems) without assistance in order to get to the water.

Was there another path to the beach? We found the assertion that Brian walked directly to the beach to be absolutely preposterous. So, we began looking for ways to the beach that did not involve mastering an obstacle course. We discovered that two pedestrian tunnels

Figure 6.4 The obstacle course of traffic lanes, fences, and guardrails that Brian Welzien would have had to negotiate on the night he disappeared.

existed, one about 1900 feet to the north at 1580 North Lake Shore Drive, and one about 640 feet to the south at the intersection with East Division Street (Figure 6.5). Within the context of the police's theory that this was an accidental death, we opined that Brian's intent was to walk off his intoxication and may have desired to go to the beach in order to accomplish that task. Upon encountering the obstacle in front of him presented by all the traffic lanes and fences, he may have changed his mind and decided to continue his walk south along North Lake Shore Drive. Brian may have resumed his initial goal of going to the beach when he came upon the pedestrian tunnel at East Division Street. During our search of the area, we noted that appropriate graffiti related to these cases were present within the pedestrian tunnel and on the sidewalks nearby (which included the smiley face and other symbols). However, that did not indicate or convince us that Brian took this route, rather, that those persons responsible for his murder normally hung out in that area. We surmised that Brian's goal was not the beach, rather it was just to walk off whatever had made him sick, and that he was abducted and taken from the area in a vehicle while he was out walking about.

As previously stated, the importance of the recovery site was amplified by the significance of the purported water entry location. Historically, a pattern existed between the location where a live human was presumed to have entered Lake Michigan and the known location where his body was recovered. Brian's case was incongruent with this knowledge. Albert Papandreou, Glen Leadley, and Trevor Boehm were all found near the site of their presumed entry into Lake Michigan. The intersection of East Goethe Street and North Lake Shore Drive where Brian supposedly entered the water is at about the 1300 block. Albert Papandreou was recovered near the 1200 block (Figure 6.6, *Yellow Triangle*). Glen Leadley was last seen near the 1400 block (*Red Triangle*) and was recovered a few blocks north of that location near the intersection with Fullerton Parkway. Trevor Boehm was last seen near the 4500 block of North Simonds Drive and was recovered a couple blocks south in Montrose Harbor. Whether they only wandered a short distance on foot before entering the water and drowning or floated a short distance after drowning, the fact remained that

Figure 6.5 While Gannon and Duarte looked around for clues, and Carlson took photographs to document the scene, Gilbertson took GPS coordinates at the entrance to the pedestrian tunnel at East Division Street and North Lake Shore Drive for later analysis.

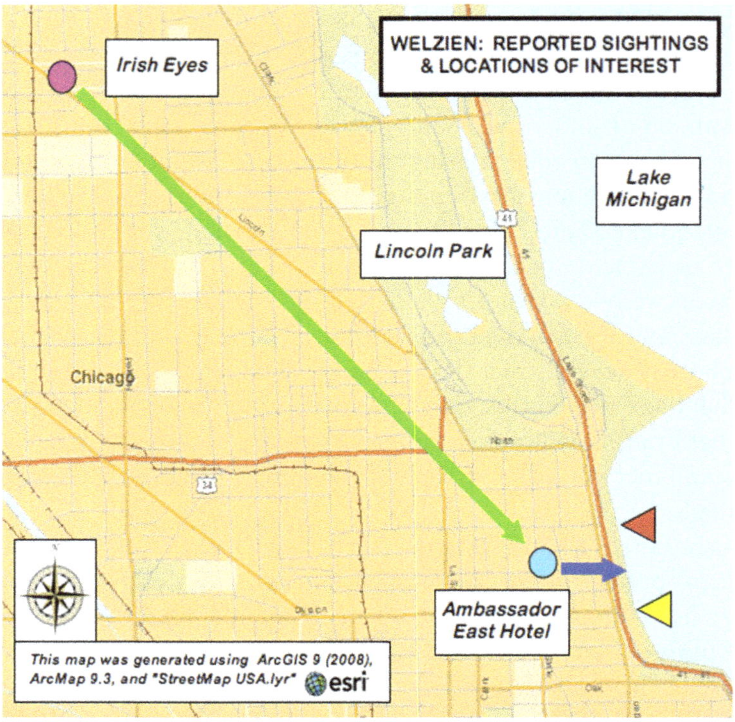

Figure 6.6 Brian Welzien left the Irish Eyes pub (*Purple Dot*) and was last seen in front of the Ambassador East Hotel (*Light Blue Dot*). He supposedly entered the water at about the 1300 block of North Lake Shore Drive (*Blue Arrow*). Glen Leadley was last seen at the 1400 block (*Red Triangle*) and Albert Papandreou was recovered at about the 1200 block (*Yellow Triangle*).

they were all recovered within a short distance of their last known locations; that is, all except for Brian Welzien who ended up 30 miles across Lake Michigan.

Brian was recovered on a remote beach in Gary, Indiana. A strange place for a body to be recovered. It was in a secluded stretch of beach with sand dunes next to the belching smokestacks of American industry. The recovery location was about 28 miles by water, and about 40 miles by road, from his last reported location (Figure 6.7). Although it is possible for bodies to float a long distance in water before being recovered, especially with strong winds, the likelihood that Brian floated to this exact spot on the beach was more suspicious to us than his floating the extreme distance. When one couples that with the lack of alcohol in his body and the appearance of drugs in his system (which probably caused his vomiting), it appeared that Brian may well have been drugged and driven to the proximity of this location, drowned, and then placed into the water. If the Coroner wanted to confirm that Brian actually did drown in Lake Michigan in Chicago and not in Indiana, then he could have done one simple test to prove his hypothesis. He could have examined Brian for diatoms.

Diatoms and Chemicals

Diatoms (*Bacillariophyta*) are both living organisms and part of the fossil record. They are a form of algae and make up the most common types of phytoplankton. Basically, diatoms are single-celled organisms (unicellular) inside silica-based shells called frustules (they quite literally live in glass houses). Some researchers suggest that more than 200 types of

Figure 6.7 According to the "accidental drowning" theory held by local investigators, Brian Welzien's deceased body had to have traveled about 28 miles across Lake Michigan.

living diatoms exist, while about 100,000 different kinds of species may have existed in the fossil record back to the Jurassic period (Canter-Lund & Lund, 1995; Round, Crawford, & Mann, 1990). Diatoms live in wet or moist environments; they can live in damp air, soil, and all types of water. They are abundant in plankton and the sediments of saltwater and freshwater ecosystems, and serve as a major food source for aquatic fauna. Although they present great diversity, every genus will not be found in every location. They tend to be specific in type and concentration by locale. The kinds and numbers of diatoms found in a river at one spot may not be the same 5 miles downstream in the same river.

The extent to which diatoms can be used forensically to determine the location of a potential drowning remains controversial. On the one hand, it is a given that the variety (qualitative characteristics) and population density (quantitative characteristics) of species of diatoms will differ from location to location. Thus, making each location forensically unique relative to the diatoms found in the collected samples. However, that assertion is simplistic and only valid within a spatial context (i.e., location). One must also consider temporal variations (i.e., time). Although the types of species may not dramatically vary at any given location, the population density will change as moisture and heat increase or decrease with time (e.g., greater in the peak of summer and lower during winter). Given warmth, moisture, sunlight, and time, more diatoms will grow. Samples must be taken at documented intervals (specified and marked locations) along nearby bodies of water immediately upon notification that a person is missing. Any test conducted later on after body recovery may not accurately reflect diatom populations as they existed at the time the victim went missing. That is why we have always advocated that water samples be taken as soon as possible when a victim is reported missing and an assumption can be made that he or she may be found in that body of water.

In the past, diatoms were considered a valuable means for determining whether a victim had died as a result of drowning or was simply recovered in a body of water. When a victim inhaled water into his or her lungs, the diatoms in that water would find their way into his or her bone marrow (DiMaio & DiMaio, 2001). An examination of the marrow could tell pathologists whether or not a victim perished as a result of drowning. An additional presumption was that if no diatoms were found, then the victim died in tap water. However, recent studies have discovered diatoms in the bone marrow of deceased persons who did not drown, and have also suggested that diatoms can be retained in the bone marrow indefinitely. Scientists, therefore, sought other indicators that might distinguish between saltwater, freshwater, and tap water drownings. They determined that the presence of diatoms along with fecal bacteria (pollutant markers) in a victim's blood were good indicators of drowning in treated water (Armstrong & Erskine, 2011; Lucci, Campobasso, Cirnelli, & Lorenzini, 2008). They have also learned to look in the pleural effusion fluid for differences in electrolyte concentration as well as the presence or absence of bacteria that are common to saltwater ecosystems (Armstrong & Erskine, 2011; Kakizaki, Takahama, Seo, Kozawa, & Yukawa, 2008; Usumoto, Sameshima, Hikiji, Tsuji, Kudo, Inoue, & Ikeda, 2009).

Budgetary constraints are the greatest hindrance to this area of forensic examination in our opinion. The amount of personnel labor time required to collect the initial samples and to microscopically examine each one is prohibitive. Although the diatoms in the bone marrow, blood specimen, pleural effusion fluid, or stomach contents should be relatively unique to the location of the drowning (if that was the cause of the victim's death), the amount of time that would be required to examine each sample and to identify the types and numbers of diatoms therein could be costly.

We have publicly advocated alternative testing and even suggested it directly to some medical examiners and coroners. We suggested that the fluid in the lungs, in the pleural cavity, and from the stomach contents be examined microscopically for diatoms and bacteria. A high concentration should suggest either saltwater or freshwater, and not tap water. Correspondingly, an absence might indicate tap water. If it is determined that the fluids do not reflect treated city tap water, then the medical examiners can return to a closer examination of the diatoms within the initial samples taken along the river of body of water. This would help them to identify a more precise location for the water entry location.

Medical examiners should also automatically use gas chromatographs or mass spectrophotometers to determine the chemical make-up of the fluids recovered from victims. They should examine the fluids recovered from a victim for the chemicals used in the treatment of local public waters, or for known environmental pollutants in the area that might identify the type of water, its possible source, and its possible location. For example, if a body is recovered downstream from a steel or paper mill, then the contaminants in the fluids drawn from the victim's lungs and stomach should be similar to those at the steel or paper mill. In farm country, pesticides and fertilizers should be found. Similarly, in rainwater run-offs and catch basins near roadways or in cities, chemicals associated with automobiles should be found (e.g., various fuels, oils, antifreeze, and so forth). Simply put, the chemical make-up of the fluids trapped in a victim's body should reflect the chemical make-up of the fluids in the environment from which that victim's body was recovered. Given the amount of industry in the area of Gary where Brian was recovered, as compared to the lack thereof where he was purported to have entered Lake Michigan in Chicago, the chemical composition of the water in Brian's lungs would have made it a relatively easy task to identify whether it came from Gary or Chicago.

Toxicology

Brian was recovered with a Blood Alcohol Concentration (BAC) of 0.084 grams per deciliter (gm/dL) or just over 3 drinks for a 145 pound male. Considering that he was in the water for approximately two and a half months or 77 days, then the alcohol in his system could have increased as a result of postmortem alcohol production by as much as 0.0375 to 0.0750. Erring on the side on caution, Gannon used the minimum amount to calculate Brian's actual BAC for the night he entered the water.

Estimated Postmortem Alcohol Production Values (gm/dL)

Period	Minimum	Maximum
1 month	0.0150	0.030
2 months	0.0300	0.060
3 months	0.0450	0.090
4 months	0.0600	0.120

Assessed BAC – Postmortem Alcohol Production Value
= Estimated Actual BAC
0.0840 – 0.0375 = 0.0465 gm/dL

Therefore, Brian's BAC was actually at about 0.0465 gm/dL or just under 2.5 drinks (since each drink equals about 0.02). Intoxication in most states is currently 0.08 (or 4 drinks). In one state (Michigan), the limit for legal intoxication is 0.10 (or 5 drinks). Technically, Brian was sober enough according to the law to operate a motor vehicle, yet he was too drunk according to authorities to make it back to his hotel. Brian was actually legally sober when he entered the water. Considering that Brian only had approximately 2.5 drinks in his system and was not even considered drunk by legal standards, it seems very unlikely for him to have wandered around aimlessly and then to have fallen into Lake Michigan.

Contrary to official press releases and other media reports, many of these young men were found to have some kind of debilitating drug (most often GHB) in their systems. What would have caused Brian to become so sick after drinking so little? Brian's behavior of staggering around and repeatedly throwing up after only having a small amount of alcohol in his system (0.0465 BAC) was reminiscent of someone who was on a type of debilitating drug (e.g., GHB, Rohypnol, or ketamine). Was he also drugged? Unfortunately, we will never know. No specific toxicology tests were done for these debilitating drugs as a part of the autopsy. There were three reasons that this did not happen.

First, these drugs are not included in the standard assays or drug screens requested for unattended deaths. These special drug tests will not be requested unless it is clear-cut and someone suspects that the death was not the result of natural causes. In addition to that, they cost extra money. We have assisted a couple families in their search for answers and coordinated and paid for these tests; they run about $600.

Second, unlike most autopsies, the pathologist (Dr. Young M. Kim) who conducted the autopsy for the Office of the Lake County Coroner did not collect multiple samples. Routinely, the persons responsible for an autopsy (i.e., the coroner, pathologist, or medical examiner) will collect blood from either the chest cavity, the thigh muscle, or an organ like the heart. In particularly suspicious cases, they may collect all of them for comparison studies. He or she will also collect tissue samples from major organs like the liver and brain, which can be quite valuable for forensic toxicology testing. Quite often, they will also collect vitreous humor from the eye. That did not happen in this case. No tissue or vitreous samples were collected. The Lake County Coroner, Dr. Thomas R. Philpot (Doctor of Podiatric Medicine), did not override the examining pathologist's decision and order extra blood samples, tissue samples, or vitreous humor to be taken. The importance of that investigative failure would become apparent.

Third, and we could not make up this kind of story, the first specimen container holding a blood sample broke during transit to the testing facility. Specimen Number 863315701 was sent to the Quest Diagnostics Regional Laboratory Facility in Wood Dale, Illinois. It was received on March 20, 2000 (3 days after Brian's recovery). A standard blood serum drug screen with confirmation and quantitation was to be performed. The toxicology report issued on March 21st showed that no test had been done since the specimen container had broken in transit. A second vial was then sent to the testing facility. Specimen Number 863430978 was received on March 21st. The official toxicology report was issued the next day (March 22, 2000) and reported the presence of ethyl alcohol in the blood at 84 milligrams per deciliter (a BAC of 0.084 gm/dL). None of the other drugs for which the standard drug screen tested were detected in Brian's blood.

Oddly, no acetone was detected either. A body produces various chemicals including alcohols as it decomposes. Acetone is one of the chemicals that is produced as the alcohols break down. We would have expected to see some measure of acetone in Brian's blood had he actually died on January 1st, which was 77.25 days before the blood sample was drawn at autopsy on March 18th. This suggested to us that Brian had not been deceased as long as everyone else had presumed.

Rigidity

Rigidity (*rigor mortis*) is the stiffening of the muscles after death that begins within 30 minutes after death and usually subsides within 24 to 36 hours on land depending upon the temperature of the medium within which the body is located and the body temperature itself (Shkrum & Ramsay, 2007). Environmental conditions may retard this process; the colder it is, then the longer it will take for rigor to relent. The autopsy report stated that rigor was no longer present in the body. This was consistent with both the period of time that Brian had been missing and presumed deceased, as well as the environmental conditions. Since the body was recovered in the water after missing for approximately 77 days, then there should not have been any rigor in the body regardless of the temperature. Therefore, rigor should have subsided long ago.

Body Position and Lividity

Lividity (*livor mortis*) is the pooling of the blood into the dependent capillaries and veins after death (Geberth, 2006). This process starts within 30 minutes after death and typically becomes "fixed" within a period of 10 to 12 hours. "Fixed" means the blood has settled in one position and cannot be significantly shifted or displaced by changing the position of the body. For example, if a body were left for 4 hours in a prone position (face-down) and then turned for another 4 hours to a supine position (on its back), then lividity would partially shift or displace from the front to the rear. At recovery, it would appear to have both anterior and posterior lividity. Generally, after 12 hours, lividity will not displace (Spitz & Spitz, 2006).

The position of lividity within Brian's body at recovery was inconsistent with the position in which he was recovered. The Pathologist described lividity in Brian's body as being fixed in his posterior side (on his back). Since most victims in a typical drowning scenario float on their anterior side (face-down), and since Brian was recovered lying face-down in the sand, then his lividity should have also reflected this position (Hendrick, Zaferes, & Nelson 2003). This information was a tell-tale sign that something was wrong. Brian's lividity did not reflect this and showed that he was on his back for a minimum period of no less than 10 to 12 hours postmortem (most likely longer than 12 hours) before being found face-down on the beach. Therefore, Dr. Young M. Kim (M.D., Pathologist) should have clearly noticed this and should have found this to be suspicious. This information clearly pointed to Brian being murdered and not accidentally falling into Lake Michigan on New Year's Eve.

We reviewed what we knew about deceased bodies and their floatation characteristics. First, bodies that are already deceased prior to entry into the water may often float for some time and may not sink immediately. Second, except for really obese people, most bodies sink and float face-down in the water after death. Next, human bodies are rarely flipped over except in exceptionally turbulent water (e.g., rapids, fast flowing rivers or streams, near the base of a dam, or waves crashing on an ocean beach). Fourth, the presence of fixed lividity requires stability of position and time during the period immediately following death. Therefore, Brian had to have been in one unchanging position on his back over a continuous period of time in order for lividity to fix there.

This told us that Brian had to have been lying on his back on the lake bottom, floating on his back on the surface, or lying on his back on the beach for more than 10 to 12 hours in order for lividity to fix posteriorly. Our analysis had to also consider whether he died in Chicago or in Gary. We also had to consider all the possible ways that he could have arrived at the beach: in a prone position (face-down) or in a supine position (face-up). We conceptualized several possible scenarios to account for Brian's posterior lividity.

Scenario 1: Brian was alive when he entered the water in Chicago. He then sank to the lake bottom and somehow ended up on his back for more than 10 hours and lividity became fixed. After about 72 hours, the decomposition process created gases that caused him to bloat. He resurfaced and then floated to Gary where he was recovered on the beach.

Scenario 2: Brian had just recently died before he entered the water in Chicago. He floated on his back for more than 10 hours and lividity became fixed. He floated in the waves across the surface of Lake Michigan for 30 miles to Gary where he was recovered on the beach.

Scenario 3: Brian died somewhere other than the Chicago beach and remained on his back for at least 10 hours while lividity fixed. He was then transported to the beach in Gary where he was recovered.

Scenario 4: Brian died at the beach in Gary and remained on his back for at least 10 hours while lividity fixed. He was later recovered at the same beach.

If the underwater wave action near the beach in Chicago was turbulent enough to flip Brian to his back while he was lying on the lake bottom, then they should have continued to flip him, over and over again. If the surface swells and troughs of Lake Michigan were turbulent enough to flip him to his back while he was floating, then they should have continued to flip him, over and over again, until he came to rest on the beach. If the waves of Lake Michigan were turbulent enough to flip him to his back while he was lying on the beach, then they should have continued to flip him, over and over again. In any case, Brian's lividity would not have been established on one side, rather it would have been mixed and indistinct throughout his body no matter the position in which he was recovered. Therefore, the likelihood of Brian having been flipped over only twice in Lake Michigan seemed even more than just a major stretch; it was almost an impossibility to say the least.

Larynx and Sand

The hyoid bone is a small (U-shaped) bone in the neck at the base of the tongue, just above the Adam's Apple. It usually breaks during strangulation. We read in the autopsy report that the laryngeal cartilages and hyoid bone were not fractured. Since they were intact, we reasonably concluded that Brian was not chocked to death.

Law enforcement officers with whom we spoke and media reports all suggested that Brian would have fallen about 15 feet into Lake Michigan. We found this assertion to be misleading and incongruent with the rest of the "accidental death" hypothesis. If Brian had walked straight down East Goethe Street across the obstacle course of traffic lanes, fences, and guardrails, then he would have come to a concrete apron that was about 10 feet above Lake Michigan. However, had he walked south along North Lake Shore Drive until he came to the pedestrian tunnel at Division Street, then he would have come out to an open beach that gradually went down to the lake shore. Brian's BAC was not high enough that it would have contributed to his death. At this location along the beach in Chicago even with the 0.084 BAC that the autopsy reported (or the actual 0.0465 gm/dL that he had) Brian could have crawled out of the water had he tripped and fallen down. In order for him to drown in this area, he would have had to intentionally walked out past the edge of the beach and laid down or then fallen and made no attempt to get back up. This was illogical and did not fit with his personality.

Although it does not occur in every drowning case, it is not unknown to find small amounts of mud, sand, leaves, or other debris from the water in a victim's nostrils or oral cavity (Armstrong & Erskine, 2011). These materials may be floating in the water and small amounts may get inside a victim when he takes a breath while on the surface or near the bottom. Drowning victims have been known to grab onto items around them (at the bottom) after sinking in a river or lake including mud, dirt or vegetation. It is thought that during the drowning process, from being disoriented in combination with the struggle to survive, drowning victims are reaching for anything to try and find a way out or to pull themselves to safety. They usually have these materials in their hands or under their fingernails upon recovery. Typically, they do not place these materials into their mouths (oral cavities).

It is less common to find these same kinds of material further back in a victim's airway by his larynx. In our opinion, there are only two ways for a victim to ingest sand into his larynx.

1. If there was a lot of sand present in the water as a result of something stirring up the bottom (e.g., the victim disturbing the river or lake bottom with his hands upon reaching the bottom), then he could have swallowed some sand when he inhaled water before drowning.
2. If the victim was drowned in a few inches of water in which sand was directly below his mouth and nose, then he could inhale it during the fight to save his life.

It is important to note that Brian was recovered face-down in the surf with a small amount of sand in his larynx on a remote beach over 30 miles away from where he supposedly went into Lake Michigan. There was no mention of any foreign material under Brian's fingernails. If he supposedly disturbed the soil enough for him to have swallowed the sand, then he could have had some of the sand from the bottom of Lake Michigan under his fingernails when recovered. Furthermore, there were no waves and no boat traffic in the area of the Chicago beach that could have stirred up the sand on the lake bottom since the lake was frozen over near shore at that time.

We found it more believable that Brian did not drown at the beach in Chicago. We asserted that he was either transported to Lake Street Beach in Gary and drowned at that location, or he was murdered at another unknown location and dumped at Lake Street Beach. Wherever it was, he was held down and ingested the sand before drowning, and was then left in the surf in Gary to make it look like a drowning. We opine that this same modus operandi was used again in 2010 to facilitate the death of another young man who was recovered in the Chicago River near the Wells Street Bridge with mud and leaves deep in the lumen of his trachea – which was basically impossible. The medical examiner also failed to test the material in that case. The parents discussed this with the Medical Examiner's Office and asked for reclassification of their son's case, and for an independent investigation into what happened to their son.

Unfortunately, the Coroner and the Pathologist never thought to examine the sand in Brian's larynx to see whether it matched the beach upon which he was found lying. Medical examiners are supposed to check for any signs of foreign material (plants, insects, dirt, sand, fibers, etc.) that would help an investigator to determine the initial crime scene or entry point in drowning cases. Foreign material should be checked when it is recovered anywhere on the person of a victim, specifically when it was ingested by the decedent. Representative fragments of the material in a victim's nostrils, sinuses, mouth, larynx, trachea, or stomach should be retained in cases of equivocal or suspicious circumstances. These samples can be compared to the sand and debris collected from the recovery site for the purpose of confirming or refuting the estimated point of water entry (Armstrong & Erskine, 2011). This would have also helped them to determine whether this case was truly an accident or a homicide. None of this was ever done in this case. If the Pathologist and Coroner truly believed that Brian drowned in Lake Michigan right off of North Lake Shore Drive in Chicago, then they should have obtained a sand sample from the beach there. They could have checked to see whether the sand in Brian's larynx matched the sand on the beach or lake bottom in Chicago. Since this was never done, we will never know if this scenario occurred.

Different Contexts

All of the aforementioned analyses were based on the 5 reports that we read, which stated that Brian had been found face-down on Lake Street Beach in Gary, Indiana. However, a different scenario all together may have existed since Sergeant Bill Fazekas (Gary Police Department) had told Gannon that he thought Brian was possibly recovered on his back. In considering this alternative scenario, we again looked at all possibilities and found only 3 contexts were possible.

Context 1: Brian arrived at the beach in Gary via Lake Michigan, and he was already deceased with lividity already fixed posteriorly (similar to Scenarios 1 & 2 above).

Context 2: Brian arrived at the beach in Gary having recently died elsewhere and lividity established while he lied on the beach on his back (similar to Scenario 3 above).

Context 3: Brian arrived at the beach in Gary alive and died there, whereon, lividity established while he lied on the beach on his back (similar to Scenario 4 above).

Prima facie, if Brian had been found lying on his back, then any one of these 3 contexts would solve the problem since lividity was fixed on his back. However, we now also had to consider and explain the sand in his larynx.

First, if Brian had drowned in Lake Michigan next to North Lake Shore Drive (Scenario 1), then he would have had to have sunk the 10 to 15 feet to the lake bottom and would have also had to have disturbed the bottom of Lake Michigan and then ingested sand into his larynx while drowning. Unfortunately, we will not know whether this occurred here since the sand was never collected and examined. Furthermore, when considering the first alternative context, we kept in mind that bodies tend to sink head first and remain in that position on the lake or river bottom until putrefactive gases form and cause the body to resurface. This decomposition process usually takes approximately 36 to 48 hours on land, or 72 to 96 hours in water. Since bodies tend to settle face-down on the bottom of a body of water, then an investigator would normally expect to see lividity fixed anteriorly in a typical drowning since the period of time for putrefaction to develop would have been days. Since Brian only had lividity on his back, then the likelihood of Scenario 1 within Context 1 happening was improbable.

Second, since bodies that are dead before entry into the water do not always sink right away, then Brian could have theoretically floated on his back all the way across Lake Michigan to the beach in Gary were he deceased prior to entering the water (Context 1). However, if Brian were deceased before going into the water as hypothesized in Scenario 2, then he would not have been physically capable of swallowing water admixed with sand from the Chicago beach or the bottom of Lake Michigan. We concluded that Brian could not have been dead before he ingested the sand. This meant that the likelihood of either Scenario 2 or Context 1 happening was improbable. We concluded that this had not occurred. Brian should not have arrived deceased at the beach in Gary with lividity already fixed posteriorly.

Of course, if Brian were dead before going into the water, then this would have proven that someone else was responsible for placing him in the water in Chicago. In the event that skeptics still did not want to believe that Brian was already deceased and placed in the water by another person (rather, that it was somehow a natural or accidental death), we considered two more possibilities. (A) Brian mysteriously died from unknown causes while walking the shore line of Lake Michigan in Chicago and fell in. (B) Brian slipped and hit his head on the concrete apron, died within seconds, and fell in. Since most bodies float face-down unless they are obese (which Brian was not) or are flipped over in turbulent water, then Brian should have been floating face-down for a period of time before being flipped over onto his back. Therefore, lividity should still have been present on both Brian's anterior and posterior when he was recovered. The Coroner should have witnessed some extent of shifted lividity. We opined that if one flip had occurred, then several could have and possibly should have occurred. Since no shifting of lividity was mentioned by the Coroner, we concluded that no flipping of Brian's body occurred in the water or on either beach. Fixed and consistent lividity suggested to us that his body had been predominantly in one stable position for an extended period of time, that was, on his back.

Even if one were to say that Brian floated the whole time on his back, and as such the lividity was fixed posteriorly as it should be, then there is no explanation for the sand in Brian's larynx. How did he ingest sand when he had not sunk and instead floated the whole time on his back from Chicago to Gary? Either Brian drowned, sank face-down and ingested sand (which would have fostered anterior lividity on his body before he resurfaced), or he never sank and floated the whole time on his back (which accounted for the posterior lividity, but did not account for the sand in his larynx). Neither scenario worked because Brian was probably murdered at this desolate location in only a few inches of water and gagged on the sand as he was being suffocated. We proposed then that he was placed on his back into Lake Michigan very close by, where he remained until recovery.

Decomposition and Maceration

According to the scenario that Brian's was an accidental death, he was presumed to have died in Lake Michigan from drowning shortly after he went missing at 03:45 hours on January 1, 2000. He was recovered at Lake Street Beach on March 17, 2000, and pronounced deceased at 18:08 hours. This meant that Brian was missing for a total of 76.6 days (76 days 14 hours 23 minutes, or 1,838 hours 23 minutes). He was autopsied 16 hours 22 minutes later at 10:30 hours on March 18, 2000. Altogether then, the period of time between when Brian went missing and when he was autopsied was 77.25 days (77 days 6 hours 45 minutes, or 1,854 hours 45 minutes).

The first clear signs of decomposition are color changes of the body and bloating from the gases forming in the abdomen (Geberth, 2006). In the first 12 hours on land (24 hours in water), the skin will change color (from blue to green) starting in the right lower quadrant (RLQ) of the abdomen and spreading to the entire body within 24 hours on land (48 hours in water). By approximately 36 to 48 hours on land (72 to 96 hours in water), bloating (within the eyelids, scrotum and penis) occurs along with marbling. Marbling is discoloration as a result of bacterial breakdown of red blood cells within the body. The face and body begin to swell giving the appearance of increased weight, obesity or bloating. The skin then becomes loose and markedly swollen. The rate and progression of decomposition will be retarded by cold water. However, a body recovered from water, even if it was refrigerated shortly thereafter, should be autopsied as soon as possible since decomposition will progress more quickly than a body that was recovered on land (Armstrong & Erskine, 2011).

In the autopsy report, the Pathologist stated that Brian's body was relatively well preserved and described the decomposition as slight to moderate. Decomposition should have been considerably more pronounced in light of the victim's time in the water. The fact that Brian's abdomen was not distended after presumably being dead and in the water for 77 days should have been an obvious sign that something was amiss. Considering the cooler water temperature, decomposition may have taken longer for Brian's body to decompose, but his abdomen should have definitely been distended even if it was in the water for only a few weeks much less 2.5 months. Brian was missing for 77 days and lying on a beach in shallow water. He should have been nearly unrecognizable as a result of putrefaction, maceration, and exposure to the sun and water. Considering his excellent postmortem condition, it certainly appeared that he had not been deceased and in the water for the whole 76.6 days. Although Brian's abdomen was not bloated with decomposition gases, his scrotum was. This extent of decomposition indicated that he had only been deceased for about a week.

Our assessment was confirmed by the Pathologist's description of the condition of Brian's skin. He stated that the skin on Brian's face showed signs of change and that the skin on his hands was wrinkled (Washerwoman's Hands or *Wauschaut*) and starting to separate from the fingers, which typically occurs between 48 to 96 hours after death. This meant that the skin on the hands had not yet degloved, which normally starts at around 72 to 96 hours postmortem and is completed by about the 168th hour postmortem (or 7 days after death). All of this showed that Brian could not have been in the water for an extended period of time since his abdomen would not only have been more distended, but his level of decomposition would have been more extensive the following day at autopsy after refrigeration. Either he had been held alive for a period of time, murdered, and then placed onto the beach, or he was murdered and preserved in a freezer for a period of time before his placement at the water's edge.

Documented Mistakes

Documents that possess inherent and significant legal importance must be proofread over and over to ensure that precise definitions, clear descriptions, and accurate empirical measurements are recorded. However, everyone makes a mistake once in a while, and a typographical error or transposition here and there can be excused on occasion. The care with which an autopsy report or coroner's inquest is prepared can speak volumes. It can indicate the level of attention to detail possessed by the person composing the document. It can also provide insight into the extent of professional knowledge and skill. And, it can offer a window into the amount of enthusiasm that a person has for his or her duties. Substandard work can betray underlying problems in the workplace such as an employee who perceives himself or herself to be underpaid, understaffed and overworked, underappreciated, or subjected to a hostile work environment. It may also indicate an employee's problems at home that are being brought to work such as depression or anger related to a divorce, a possible substance abuse issue, or a sleep-related matter (e.g., sleep apnea, working two jobs, or up all night with a sick child).

Numerous errors existed in the documents associated with Brian's forensic examination (i.e., the Coroner's Verdict, the Certificate of Death, and the Autopsy Report). It began on the Coroner's Verdict with a simple typo of the word "morning" and the date of death was listed as April 17th (in a fill-in-the-blank response) when it should have been March 17th. Further down on the same page, the Coroner narrative reported that Brian's death had been certified on March 17th and that the autopsy was performed on March 18th. Next Brian's date of birth on the Certificate of Death was listed as May 16, 1978, when it actually was March 16, 1978. Not a big deal to some, maybe. However, considering that he was recovered on March 17th, it puts the dates of birth and death into a new perspective. Like many of these young men, Brian disappeared just before his birthday.

Last, the body weight reported at autopsy was 257 pounds and had to be incorrect. We really do not believe that Brian's body weight was 257 pounds at the time of recovery. A body can absorb a lot of water depending on how much was ingested and the length of time that a victim was in the water. If Brian had accumulated this amount of water during drowning or through absorption, then his 145 pound body would have been very distended and bloated. In fact, the Coroner himself said that Brian's body was not distended. If Brian had gained 100 pounds, then we doubted that the Coroner would have said that his abdomen was not distended. At times, a medical examiner or coroner will weigh a drowning victim with the soaking wet cloths still on the body. Even this explanation could not account for a weight increase of over 100 pounds. The body should be weighed both ways before autopsy, but more importantly it should be weighed before autopsy with the cloths being completely off of the body. We believe this to be an error in reporting and an oversight. Brian's weight at autopsy was probably 157 pounds and not 257 pounds. When all of these reporting errors were added up, then we were left questioning the amount of diligence that went into this autopsy.

Ocular Changes

What was apparently missed by both the Coroner (Thomas R. Philpot, D.P.M.) and the Pathologist (Young M. Kim, M.D.) was the importance of the condition of Brian's eyes. In the autopsy report, Dr. Kim described the size of the pupils and the color of the irides in Brian's eyes. He stated that there were no signs of conjunctival petechiae and that the sclerae were cloudy. First, the period of time between when Brian went missing and the start of his autopsy was 1,854 hours 45 minutes. He was presumed to have been deceased and in Lake Michigan for a majority of that time. Therefore, the condition of his eyes should have been such that assessments like those made by Dr. Kim should have been nearly impossible due to decomposition. Second, ocular changes can be used to estimate time of death or Postmortem Interval (PMI). If the sclerae are cloudy, then this means that the victim was dead on land for a period of time, from within minutes to hours. Since Brian was recovered face-down in the surf on the beach, then the only way for his eyes to have been exposed to the air and to become cloudy was that he was dead on land lying on his back for a period of time before being entered into the water.

Internal Assessment

Once more, the condition of Brian's body was an indicator that events did not occur as they were presumed to have occurred. In addition to this, once again in this case, our assessment of Brian's body had to rely on the Pathologist's qualitative descriptions rather than quantitative measurements that are routinely made during autopsies. Traditionally, persons conducting autopsies will remove internal organs and weigh them. This is especially true for the lungs when the body is that of a presumed drowning victim. However, during Brian's autopsy, no organs were weighed. If they were weighed, then their weights did not make it into the official record known as "the autopsy report." This was another indicator of the quality of investigation associated with this case.

In a majority of drowning cases, the combined weight of adult lungs is over 1000 grams. The right lung usually weighs more than the left lung (Spitz & Spitz, 2006). Internal organ weights may increase during the first 6 hours postmortem as a result of ingested fluid or water seeping into the lungs. Prolonged submersion may actually decrease their weights as fluids dissipate out of the lungs (Shkrum & Ramsay, 2007). If the weight is less than 1000 grams, then there is usually some amount of pleural effusion, which is the passing of the ingested fluid into other parts of the body. The effusion is typically observed in the area surrounding the lungs, having accumulated within the right and left pleural cavities. Excess fluid may also be found in the area of the pericardial sac and peritoneal cavity.

According to the Pathologist's description of the internal condition of Brian's body, pleural effusion did not occur. The description in the autopsy report clearly stated that there was no evidence of abnormal levels of blood or fluids in and around the pericardial sac (the space containing the heart and about 25 to 50 cubic centiliters of fluid) and the peritoneal cavity (the space between the parietal and visceral peritoneum that contains about 50 milliliters of serous fluid). Specific mention was made that there was no ascitic fluid (an abnormal accumulation of fluid in the abdomen). Since we did not know the weight of the lungs at autopsy, then we could not estimate whether or not they contained excess fluid. However, in all likelihood, Brian's lungs had no water whatsoever in them because the Pathologist described them as well aerated and stated that they filled the pleural cavities. Had he inhaled lake water (i.e., a wet drowning), then his lungs would have shown an increase in weight. Given the period of time that Brian was presumed to be in the water, even if he had not inhaled water in to his lungs (i.e., a dry drowning), then some water would have seeped into his lungs and slightly increased their weight. However, in light of the Pathologist's qualitative description of the internal cavity and its organs, we interpreted it to mean that Brian was not a wet drowning and was not in the water for an extended period of time.

Gastrointestinal System

The big question was whether Brian had drank enough that night to become extremely intoxicated. His behavior indicated that he may have. We had heard that he had fallen asleep on the short ride back to the hotel and that he vomited repeatedly over the course of nearly two hours. However, the staff at the Irish Eyes pub recalled that he only had a couple drinks, and the autopsy report indicated that his BAC was 0.084 (or actually 0.0465). By these last two facts, Brian was relatively sober for a New Year's reveler. So, we turned to the odor of alcohol in the stomach and bowels, which is generally a good indicator of alcohol consumption, and in some cases, postmortem alcohol production (Armstrong & Erskine, 2011). Considering that Brian was reported to have vomited repeatedly, we took into account that his stomach would have been completely empty of any contents, food and alcohol. However, an odor of alcohol should have still been present in the body cavities were he drinking to a sufficient extent to explain his behavior.

The Pathologist confirmed that Brian had not had much to drink by performing the unpleasant task of determining the internal body odor. We learned that the autopsy report presented that the smell of alcohol was absent in the body cavities. The fact that there was no odor of alcohol in Brian's stomach showed that alcohol did not play a part in either his drowning or the seemingly intoxicated behavior that he exhibited outside the hotel.

During an autopsy, the smell of alcohol in a victim will alert the pathologist to the presence of alcohol and the possibility of it as a contributing factor relating to the death. This was not the condition with Brian's death.

Conclusion

Considering all the evidence in this investigation, we conclude that Brian Welzien was drugged, abducted, murdered, and dumped on a beach. Knowing how these debilitating drugs (especially GHB) work and their rapid absorption rate into the body (18 minutes to 1 hour) suggested that Brian was drugged within a relatively short span of time before he reached the hotel. Therefore, we assert that Brian was drugged sometime before he left the Irish Eyes pub. The level of ethyl alcohol in his system was insufficient to explain his behavior outside the Ambassador East Hotel. However, the physiological effects of a drug such as GHB can account for Brian's drowsiness and excessive vomiting. In all likelihood, it affected his cognition as well and he did not know where he was or to where he should return to sleep. This could also explain why he wandered off and the ease with which someone could abduct him.

We also considered the relationship between the sand in his larynx, the position in which he was recovered on the beach, the location of his fixed lividity, and the decomposition process. After looking at numerous drowning cases over the past decade, the fact remained that sand in the larynx was exceptionally rare and generally did not exist in accidental drownings. Logically, there were only two locations where Brian could have picked up the sand in his larynx: the edge of Lake Michigan in either Chicago or in Gary. However, were he murdered in some undisclosed location, then the sand could have come from another body of water like a retention pond or river, or even a puddle. The only theoretical way for him to have sand from the Gary beach in his larynx, was for it to have first somehow entered his closed mouth (recalling that he was deceased) and then to become trapped in the back of his oral cavity, and second to then manage to work its way back deeper into his larynx.

Since this was improbable, we had to look back to Chicago. Had he fallen into the water in Chicago, sank to the bottom in a normal fashion (face-down), come to rest on the bottom in a normal position (face-down), subsequently panicked and aspirated water and sand upon drowning, then that could have accounted for the sand in the larynx. However, since lividity was posteriorly fixed and it takes at least 10 hours to fix, then that would have meant that Brian would have somehow had to have been flipped while on the Chicago lake bottom. Given the fact that the decomposition process requires at least 36 hours on land (up to 72 in the water) to reach bloating from gases, then we could surmise that Brian was on the lake bottom for at least that period of time (which would have been more than sufficient to produce fixed lividity). It also meant that had he been flipped once already during that time, then there was sufficient time for him to be flipped again. Why had he not been flipped again? To complicate things, there was no water in Brian's lungs, which told us that he had not aspirated any water and therefore cast doubt on the assumption that he had simultaneously inhaled a small amount of sand.

We read 5 reports that stated Brian was recovered in a prone position (face-down) and 1 report that said he was found lying on his back. Therefore, the logical likelihood of Brian having been flipped over only a couple times in Lake Michigan (i.e., either while on the bottom in Chicago or while on the beach in Gary) seemed even more than just a major stretch of our imagination; it was almost an impossibility to say the least. We took into consideration that he would have either remained in a stable position over time and presented with identifiable fixed lividity, or he would have been repeatedly flipped (while on the lake bottom, while floating, or while lying on the beach) and presented with mixed or indiscernible lividity.

Brian's death seemed like a simple drowning case when one quickly read over the paperwork. However, close attention to detail told us that something was absolutely wrong. We conceptualized and discussed every possible scenario that we could think of in order to try and explain how someone could go missing in downtown Chicago and be found 30 miles away on an Indiana beach. That distance and the forensic evidence bothered us. Here are the scenarios that we constructed and examined at length.

Died at the Chicago beach of natural causes

1. Some natural physiological event overcame Brian (e.g., chronic fatigue, fainting or nacrolepsy). He lost his balance and fell into the water alive at the Chicago beach. Upon sinking to the bottom, he came to and struggled to survive, which stirred up the sandy bottom. Shortly thereafter, he ingested water and sand, and drowned. Lividity fixed while his body lie decomposing on the lake bottom. Eventually, his body bloated with putrefactive gases and resurfaced. It then floated across Lake Michigan to Gary.
2. Some natural physiological event overcame Brian (e.g., chronic fatigue, fainting or nacrolepsy). He lost his balance and fell into the water alive at the Chicago beach. Upon sinking to the bottom unconscious, he drowned but did not ingest sand. Lividity fixed while his body lie decomposing on the lake bottom. Eventually, his body bloated with putrefactive gases and resurfaced. It then floated across Lake Michigan to Gary.
3. Some natural cause of death immediately took Brian's life (e.g., cardiac arrest or a brain embolism). He lost his balance and fell into the water at the Chicago beach. He did not ingest any sand since he was already deceased. For some reason, he sank to the lake bottom anyway, where lividity fixed while his body lie decomposing. Eventually, his body bloated with putrefactive gases and resurfaced. It then floated across Lake Michigan to Gary.
4. Some natural cause immediately took his life. Brian fell into the water at the Chicago beach already deceased. Therefore, his body floated and did not sink to the bottom. As such, he did not ingest any sand. Lividity fixed and his body bloated with putrefactive gases while it floated across Lake Michigan, where it washed ashore in Gary.

Died at the Chicago beach of an accidental death

5. Some physiological event overcame Brian (e.g., sudden dizziness or nausea associated his intoxication). He lost his balance and fell into the water alive at the Chicago beach. Upon sinking to the bottom, he came to and struggled for his life; stirring up the sandy bottom, he ingested some sand. Shortly thereafter, he drowned. Lividity fixed while his body lie decomposing on the lake bottom. Eventually, his body bloated with putrefactive gases and resurfaced. It then floated across Lake Michigan to Gary.
6. Brian accidentally stumbled and fell, striking his head on the concrete apron at the Chicago beach and rendered him unconscious. He slipped into the water alive,

drowned and sank to the lake bottom. He did not ingest any sand. Lividity fixed while his body lie decomposing. Eventually, his body bloated with putrefactive gases and resurfaced. It then floated across Lake Michigan to Gary.

7. He accidentally slipped, struck his head on the concrete apron at the beach and immediately died. Brian's body then fell into the water. Even though he was already dead, he sank to the lake bottom. Lividity fixed while his body lie decomposing. Eventually, his body bloated with putrefactive gases and resurfaced. It then floated across Lake Michigan and washed ashore in Gary.
8. Brian accidentally slipped, struck his head on the concrete apron at the beach and immediately died. His body eventually fell into the water, but did not sink. While his body floated across Lake Michigan, lividity fixed and his body bloated with putrefactive gases. He washed ashore in Gary.

Died at the Chicago beach by suicide

9. Brian committed suicide by jumping into the water alive at the Chicago beach. He sank to the lake bottom, whereon, he struggled for his life and stirred up the sandy bottom. He ingested water and sand, and drowned. Lividity fixed while his body lied on the bottom in Chicago. Eventually, putrefactive gases bloated his body causing it to resurface. His body floated across Lake Michigan and washed ashore in Gary.

   Note: The following scenario (#10) demonstrated that any one of the natural death or accidental death scenarios (#1–8) could have occurred in the same manner, that is, that Brian could have first traveled to Gary and then died. We believed that variant to be ludicrous, and therefore did not construct additional and separate scenarios.

10. Brian somehow traveled to the Lake Street Beach in Gary (on foot, by city bus, cab, or hitchhiked). There, he committed suicide by wading out into the water alive at the Gary beach, sat down, and held his breath until he passed out. (He may have used some kind of narcotic or extreme alcohol intoxication to help him.) He fell over in the surf and sank to the lake bottom, whereon, he ingested water and drowned. Lividity fixed while his body lied on the bottom in Gary. Eventually, putrefactive gases bloated his body causing it to resurface and to wash ashore in Gary.

Murdered at the Chicago beach, dumped at the Chicago beach

11. Brian was walking along the concrete apron in Chicago that borders Lake Michigan. He was grabbed by a passerby and intentionally pushed into the freezing water alive and conscious. He struggled for his life until hypothermia and/or exhaustion overcame him. Whereon, he sank to the lake bottom, ingested water and sand, and drowned. Lividity fixed while his body lied on the bottom. It eventually bloated and resurfaced, and then floated across Lake Michigan to Gary.
12. Brian was walking along the concrete apron in Chicago that borders Lake Michigan. He was grabbed by a passerby and intentionally pushed into the freezing water alive and conscious. He struggled for his life until hypothermia and/or exhaustion overcame him. Whereon, he ingested water and drowned, but did not sink or ingest sand. Lividity fixed and bloating occurred while his body floated across Lake Michigan to Gary.

13. Brian was walking along the concrete apron in Chicago that borders Lake Michigan. He was jumped by a passerby, who clubbed him on the head and rendered him unconscious. The assailant then intentionally tossed Brian into the freezing water alive and unconscious. He sank to the lake bottom, ingested water but no sand, and drowned. Lividity fixed while his body lied on the bottom. It eventually bloated and resurfaced, and then floated across Lake Michigan to Gary.
14. Brian was walking along the concrete apron in Chicago that borders Lake Michigan. He was jumped by a passerby, who clubbed him on the head and rendered him unconscious. The assailant then intentionally tossed Brian into the freezing water alive and unconscious. He ingested water and drowned. In this case, he did not sink to the bottom or ingest sand, rather he floated out in Lake Michigan. Lividity fixed and bloating occurred while his body floated across the lake, where it washed ashore in Gary.
15. Brian was abducted from the street near the hotel. He was moved to the Chicago beach and thrown into the freezing water alive and conscious. He struggled for his life until hypothermia and/or exhaustion overcame him. Whereon, he sank to the lake bottom, ingested water and sand, and drowned. Lividity fixed while his body lied on the bottom. It eventually bloated and resurfaced, and then floated across Lake Michigan to Gary.
16. Brian was abducted from the street near the hotel. He was moved to the Chicago beach and thrown into the freezing water alive and conscious. He struggled for his life until hypothermia and/or exhaustion overcame him. He promptly ingested water (but no sand) and drowned. Rather than sinking like a body normally would, Brian's body floated to the beach in Gary. Lividity fixed and bloating occurred while his body floated across the lake, where it washed ashore in Gary.
17. He was abducted either near the hotel or the beach and then murdered by asphyxiation at the Chicago beach (i.e., held face-down in shallow water on the beach and ingested very little water and some sand). Brian was immediately placed into the water at the Chicago beach, where he sank to the bottom. Lividity fixed and putrefactive gases bloated his body while it lied on the lake bottom in Chicago. Eventually, it resurfaced and floated to Gary.
18. He was abducted either near the hotel or the beach and then murdered by asphyxiation at the Chicago beach (i.e., held face-down in shallow water on the beach and ingested little water and some sand). Brian was immediately placed into the water at the Chicago beach, where he sank to the bottom. Putrefactive gases bloated his body and caused it to resurface. Whereon, lividity fixed while it floated across Lake Michigan. He washed ashore in Gary.

Murdered elsewhere, dumped at the Chicago beach

19. Brian was abducted near the hotel or the beach. He was then transported elsewhere and murdered by asphyxiation (i.e., held face-down in shallow water and ingested sand). He was then immediately transported back to the Chicago beach and placed into the water. Whereon, even though he was already deceased, he sank to the bottom. Lividity fixed on his back while his body decomposed and bloated with putrefactive gases. His body eventually resurfaced and floated to Gary.
20. Brian was abducted near the hotel or the beach. He was then transported elsewhere and murdered by asphyxiation (i.e., held face-down in shallow water and ingested

sand). He was then immediately transported back to the Chicago beach and placed into the water. Since he was already deceased, he did not sink and floated out into Lake Michigan. Lividity fixed on his back and his body bloated with putrefactive gases while it floated to Gary. His body eventually washed ashore in Gary.

21. He was abducted and transported elsewhere, where he was murdered by asphyxiation (i.e., held face-down in shallow water and ingested sand). While he was still at that undisclosed location, lividity fixed on his back and his body decomposed. After a couple days, he was transported back to the Chicago beach and placed into the water. Since he was already deceased and bloated with putrefactive gases, he did not sink and floated out into Lake Michigan. The winds easily blew him across the lake, where he was recovered in Gary.

Murdered at the Chicago beach, dumped at the Gary beach

22. Brian was abducted and murdered by asphyxiation at the Chicago beach (i.e., held face-down in the beach and ingested sand). He was then immediately transported to the Gary beach and placed into the water there. While his body lied in the shallow surf, lividity fixed and his body decomposed filling it with putrefactive gases.

Murdered elsewhere, dumped at the Gary beach

23. He was abducted, transported elsewhere, and then murdered by asphyxiation elsewhere (i.e., held face-down in shallow water and ingested sand). He was then immediately transported to the Gary beach and placed into the water there. While his body lied in the shallow surf, lividity fixed on his back and his body decomposed filling it with putrefactive gases.
24. He was abducted, transported elsewhere, and then murdered by asphyxiation elsewhere (i.e., held face-down in shallow water and ingested sand). While his body lied at that undisclosed location, lividity fixed on his back and his body decomposed filling it with putrefactive gases. He was later transported to the beach in Gary and dumped in the surf.

Murdered at the Gary beach, dumped at the Gary beach

25. Brian was abducted, transported to the Gary beach, and murdered there by asphyxiation (i.e., held face-down in shallow water and ingested sand). He was then carried out into the freezing water a short distance. While his body lied in the shallow surf, lividity fixed and his body decomposed filling it with putrefactive gases.

We also conceptualized additional variations of the homicide scenarios that included a holding period after abduction. Those options were not displayed on the chart (Figure 6.8) for the sake of brevity and clarity. We calculated that 11 more scenarios were possible that may have involved a kidnap or hostage holding period. They included variants of scenarios 15 through 25. Including the additional 8 scenarios that would have repeated #1–8 with Brian being moved to Gary before dying, this meant that we analyzed a total of 44 scenarios (25 + 8 + 11).

Whether Brian was conscious or unconscious, he could have ingested water through his nose and drowned. However, there was no water in his lungs, which meant that he did not die as a result of a wet drowning. Additionally, we assert that in an unconscious state, Brian would not have been breathing through an open mouth and would not have swallowed

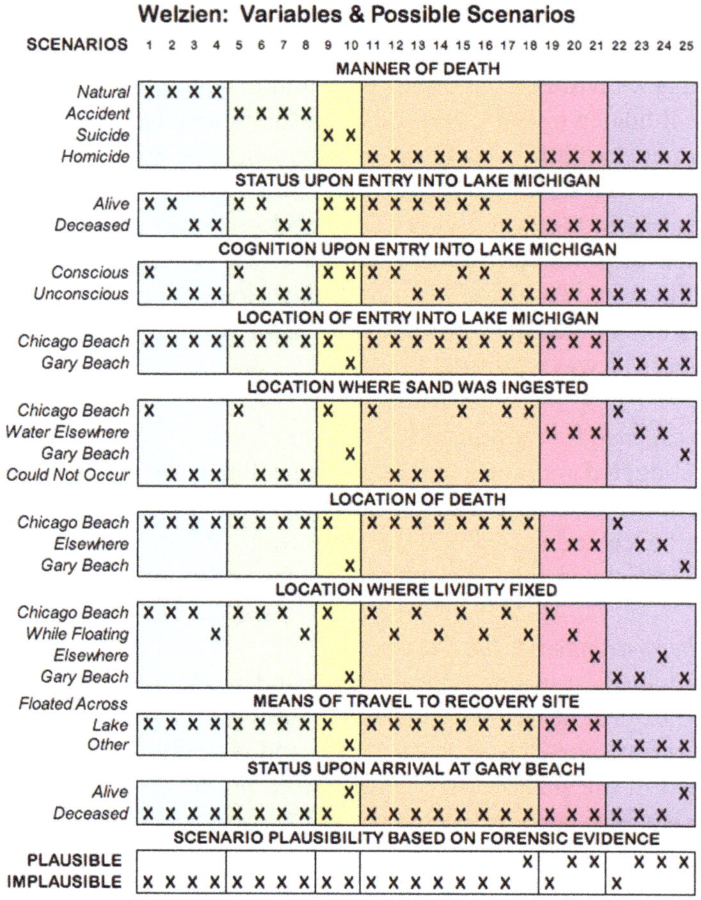

Figure 6.8 The 25 scenarios that were analyzed in order to explain Brian Welzien's death.

sand from the lake bottom. We also considered whether or not someone would attempt to murder another human being by suffocation (i.e., forcing his face into the moist sand) on the beach in Chicago. Given the volume of traffic on the 12 lanes of North Lake Shore Drive and U.S. Route 41 at any hour during the day, the proximity of high-rise housing and businesses, the extent of lighting, the expanse of open ground, we conclude that there would be entirely too great a possibility for someone to witness the homicide on the beach in Chicago. The beach in Gary was another matter. It afforded a location characterized by remoteness, one low-volume roadway, a small suburban housing area with low population, and poor to no lighting. In other words, the Gary beach was the perfect place to murder someone.

Furthermore, given the forensic evidence related to lividity and decomposition, it seemed to us that someone had pushed Brian's face into the sand in shallow water, which cut off his air supply and caused his death due to asphyxia. He probably did not put up a very effective fight since evidence pointed to him having been drugged. Given the face-down position of his body on the beach while lividity was fixed on his back, demonstrated to us that not only was this inconsistent with a normal drowning, but that Brian was dead for a period of time before he was entered into the water. He had obviously been deceased and lying on his back for no less than 10 hours before he was placed face-down in the surf on Lake Street Beach.

The hard forensic evidence related to putrefaction and maceration pointed us toward a conclusion of abduction and murder. The fact that Brian's eyes were cloudy suggested that he was dead on land for a period of time before being entered into the water. The presence of skin slippage and absence of skin degloving suggested that Brian had not been deceased more than a week. That finding was corroborated by the presence of a swollen scrotum and the absence of a bloated abdomen, which informed us that Brian had been dead about a week. And finally, the victims in all other drownings along the beaches and harbors of North Lake Shore Drive were recovered in the vicinity of where they were last seen and not 30 miles across Lake Michigan in another state. This told us that Brian had been transported to the beach in Indiana.

We could not discern whether Brian was murdered and preserved in a refrigerator or freezer and then dumped on the beach, or whether he was held and then murdered at a later date. However, we did conclude that Brian was most likely drugged, definitely abducted, and then entered into the water after he had been murdered. We posited that this drowning most likely occurred somewhere on that Indiana beach or very close by. Brian Welzien (in 2000), along with other unsolved cases in Chicago (e.g., Trevor Hoheisel in 1998, Albert Papandreou in 2002, Glen Leadley in 2003, Matthew Soumakis in 2005, Jesse Ross in 2006, Jay Pohill and James Burfisher in 2010, Philip Patnaude and Harsha Maddula in 2012) need and deserve an investigation. The commonalities among those cases should compel a coordinated multiagency investigation, not only by the Chicago Police Department, but by the Illinois Attorney General's Office, the United States Department of Justice and the FBI. Stephany Welzien, a mother who lost her only child, deserves a true investigation into her son's death.

7

Christopher Mark Jenkins*

February 17, 1981–February 27, 2003

Background

Like many of these young men, Chris Jenkins had a lot going for him in life and he was the kind of son any parent would be proud of. He had grabbed life by the reigns and taken control. Simply put, he was going places. He had been on several championship teams for high school football and was named an Academic All-American. At the time of his death, Chris was an undergraduate at the Carlson School of Management in Minnesota. He was an excellent student and was going to finish the program in less time than it takes most students (by a full year). Chris loved playing goalie and was a co-captain for the Lacrosse team at the University of Minnesota in Minneapolis. In 2002, the United States Lacrosse Intercollegiate Associates, Men's Division of Intercollegiate Associates (USLIA/MDIA), announced its All-Americans and listed Chris as an Honorable Mention in the position of Goalie.

Chris went to the Lone Tree Bar and Grill at 528 Hennepin Avenue in downtown Minneapolis with some friends on Halloween night in 2002; hereafter known by these aliases: Cassidy (the designated driver), Joslyn (who married Cassidy), Alvin, Cory, and Amber (Chris' girlfriend). He dressed in a faux buckskin "Indian" costume because of his deep admiration and respect for Native Americans (Figure 7.1). According to one witness (Jill, the bar manager), Chris was said to be very jovial, dancing by himself at times, milling around talking to a lot of people, and just having a good time. He mysteriously disappeared early on the morning of November 1, 2002. A passerby reported seeing a body in the water 4 months later near the Third Avenue Bridge on February 27, 2003. That body was recovered and identified as Chris.

* Photo courtesy of Steve and Jan Jenkins.

Figure 7.1 On Halloween night 2002, Christ Jenkins was last seen at the Lone Tree Bar and Grill wearing a faux buckskin Native American costume.

Gannon had become aware of the drowning cases across the country during early 2005 and they were reminiscent of cases he had in New York City. In April 2006, he and Duarte traveled to Minnesota and met with Steve and Jan Jenkins to discuss their son's case (Figure 7.2). What developed was the start of a relationship with the Jenkins and a tremendous amount of information sharing between Gannon, Duarte, Steve and Jan Jenkins. Thus began what would become the most organized investigation to date into the murders of young men by drowning across the United States and Canada. Gilbertson became aware of the cases at about that time while doing online research into the drowning death of Scot Radel in Saint Cloud (February 2, 2006). He used the information recovered from the Internet to formulate an assignment for two of his graduate students. Their final report was aired on Fox TV (May 19, 2006). Later that year (October 26, 2006), Gannon and Duarte surprised

Figure 7.2 The Jenkins family (from left to right): Chris, Jan, Sara, and Steve. (Photo courtesy of Steve and Jan Jenkins.)

Gilbertson by showing up at his office. Gannon had seen the work of Gilbertson and his graduate students on the Internet and wanted to talk to him. Not 4 days had passed when Steve Jenkins called Gilbertson (October 31, 2006) and they set up a meeting (November 5, 2006). As it were then, there was a convergence of independent events around Chris' case that brought everyone together. Steve and Jan Jenkins continued to challenge the label of "accidental" that had been put on Chris' case. On November 21, 2006, officials in the Minneapolis criminal justice system changed the manner of death to a "homicide."

Circumstances

Last Seen

Christopher Mark Jenkins ("Chris") was a White male, 21 years old at the time of his disappearance, 5 feet 8 inches, 185 pounds (Body Mass Index: 28.12), blonde hair and blue eyes. He was last seen in the Lone Tree Bar and Grill with numerous friends on Halloween night (October 31, 2002). He was removed from the bar by a bouncer for supposedly urinating on his costume. It was later confirmed that a drink had been accidentally spilled on him. Chris was escorted out of the bar at about 00:30 hours on November 1, 2002, and never seen alive again.

On October 31, 2002 (Halloween), Chris was up early that morning (09:00 hours). At 10:00 hours, he drove his girlfriend (Amber) to work as a waitress at the Lone Tree Bar & Grill. Between 10:00 hours and 15:00 hours, Chris did some shopping at Rosedale Shopping Mall; where he purchased an "Indian" costume. From 15:30 hours to 16:00 hours, a friend of Chris' (Marc) fell and injured his ankle while running. Chris got an ice pack for Marc to put around his injury and informed him that he was planning on going downtown that evening. Dressed in the costume that he had purchased earlier that day, he left at 16:00 hours to pick up Amber at the Lone Tree Bar and Grill. Chris had class to attend, so she dropped him off at school in his costume. At 17:00 hours, Chris returned home and picked up his friend Marc and brought him to his house. Sometime between 17:20 hours and 20:00 hours, a keg of beer showed up at Chris' house. At 20:00 hours, Chris drove to Amber's house, picked her up, and returned to his house. From 21:00 hours to 22:30 hours, Chris and Amber stayed at his house. At 21:40 hours, Chris called Marc's house and spoke with one of Marc's roommates and told him about the keg at his house.

At 23:00 hours, Chris and a group of friends (driven by Cassidy) headed for the popular warehouse/bar district of Minneapolis. They parked in the Block E parking ramp and then walked one block north to the Lone Tree Bar and Grill on the corner of 6th Street and Hennepin Avenue (Figure 7.3). Amber took possession of Chris' wallet and cell phone since his costume did not have any pockets. A second group of people also left Chris' house and met at the bar. At 23:15 hours, Marc made a call to Chris but got no answer. A female bartender, who was working close to her station inside the Lone Tree near the 6th Street exit door, reported seeing Chris seemingly happy and dancing by himself at approximately 00:00 hours (midnight). At 00:10 hours, the bar manager witnessed and overheard a conversation between Chris and a Minneapolis Police Department (MPD) officer who was working in the nearby Annex. She overheard the officer ask Chris whether he was okay since a spot on the front of his costume pants was wet. Chris replied that he was all right, and that he had accidentally spilled a drink on himself. Chris then walked

Figure 7.3 The last place that Chris Jenkins was seen alive was the Lone Tree Bar and Grill in the popular warehouse-bar district in downtown Minneapolis.

away. According to the manager, the police officer told a bar security supervisor to keep an eye on Chris.

Sometime between 00:15 and 00:40 hours, the bar manager, a server/bartender, a bouncer working the 6th Street exit door, and another bouncer who was working outside in front of the 6th Street exit door closest to Hennepin Avenue, all saw a white male in an American Indian costume being escorted out of the bar. It was approximately 20 °Fahrenheit outside, and Chris had no wallet, no money, no cell phone, no keys and most importantly no jacket or warm clothing. He was removed from the bar by the security supervisor to fend for himself. Chris was never seen alive again.

Recovery

Chris was recovered floating on his back in the Mississippi River on February 27, 2002, almost 4 months after he was last seen. He was recovered by Hennepin County Sheriff's Department Water Patrol officers at approximately 18:15 hours in the east side of the river just south of the Third Avenue Bridge in downtown Minneapolis (Figure 7.4). This part of the

Figure 7.4 Chris Jenkins' body was recovered on February 27, 2002, from a mass of frozen debris that had become hung-up on a sandbar just below the Third Avenue Bridge.

river is often referred to as the Horseshoe Dam area, which was made up of the Mississippi River cascading over the Upper Saint Anthony Falls, the Upper Saint Anthony Falls Lock and Dam, and the Saint Anthony Falls Laboratory at 30 Southeast 3rd Avenue. Although the river was clear of any ice in this area at the time of his recovery, Chris' body had come to rest amongst a clump of frozen branches and debris that was hung up on a sandbar just below the Third Avenue Bridge. He had a small amount of snow and ice on him.

Analysis of Evidence

Dog Searches

The police did very little initially when Chris went missing. Six days after Chris had gone missing, the Jenkins took action themselves and brought in (coordinated for, and personally paid for) dog handlers and their bloodhounds, and began conducting their own K-9 searches (Figures 7.5 and 7.6). Penny Bell and K-9 "Hoover" were the same handler-bloodhound team that conducted the 1999 search for Jeffrey Geesey in La Crosse, Wisconsin.

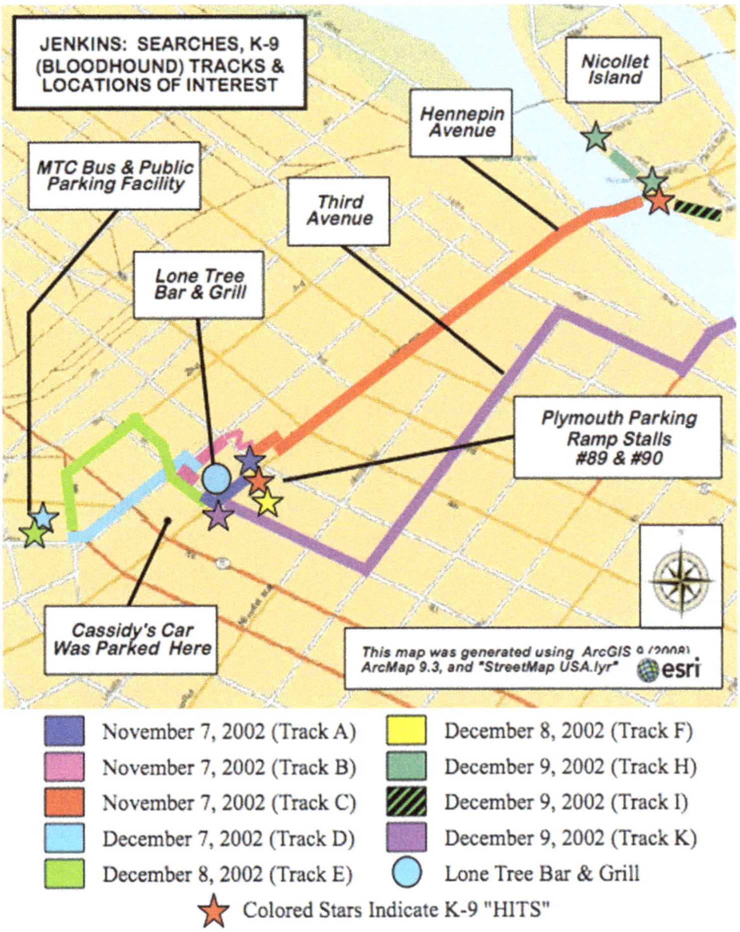

Figure 7.5 Two different teams of handlers and bloodhounds conducted several tracks in the downtown warehouse-bar district of Minneapolis in search of Chris Jenkins.

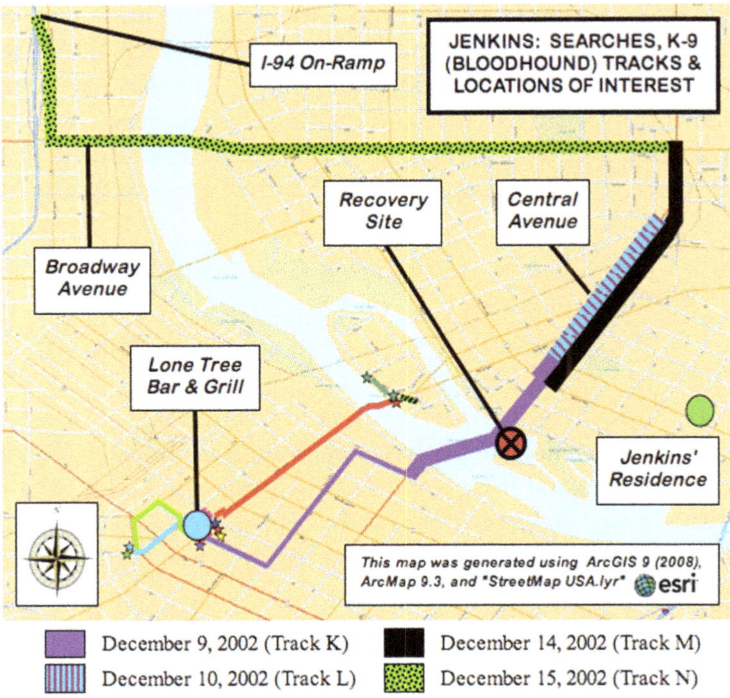

Figure 7.6 Twelve ground tracks and 4 premise searches were done as part of efforts to find Chris Jenkins. The tracks eventually led to northbound Interstate Highway 94.

During that search effort, a La Crosse Fire Department firefighter (Wallerich, now a Captain) commented to a local newspaper reporter regarding Hoover's uncanny tracking ability. He was quoted in the newspaper as having said that were he not present during the K-9 search, then he would not have believed the outcome. While tracking from a boat in the river, Hoover led them to the exact spot where Geesey's body was recovered. That same level of tracking skill was repeated in the search for Chris 3 years later.

In 2002 on November 7th, Annie Sherma and her bloodhound repeatedly led the search team from the Lone Tree Bar and Grill where Chris was last seen to an underground parking garage across the street and about a half block north on Hennepin Avenue (*Tracks A & C*). The bloodhound led them down to 2 particular parking stalls (#89 & #90) in the Plymouth Parking Ramp (517 Hennepin Avenue) and then indicated that something significant had happened to Chris at that location (Figure 7.7). The K-9 then led them out into the middle lane of traffic on Hennepin Avenue as though it was following a vehicle. This meant that Chris had most likely been transported in a vehicle and the dog was following his scent in the middle of a three-lane road.

A second round of K-9 searches with a bloodhound (Hoover) and handlers (Penny Bell & Terry Kaminski) started approximately 4 weeks later on December 7, 2002. Based on the documents that we read, it appeared that in all likelihood a total of 15 searches took place during the next week: 9 ground tracks, possibly as many as 5 premise searches, and 1 vehicle walk-by search. Two searches inside buildings, not presented on our maps (Figures 7.5 and 7.6), were conducted during the early morning hours of Saturday, December 7, 2002. The first search was conducted to test the accuracy and validity of the dog. It began between 00:00 and 00:45 hours in the morning and was initiated at Chris' apartment (611 4th Street

Figure 7.7 Both bloodhounds tracked Chris Jenkins' scent to stalls #89 and #90 in Plymouth Parking Ramp on Hennepin Avenue in downtown Minneapolis.

Southeast, Minneapolis). Hoover was introduced to Chris' scent outside his apartment building using articles of clothing and a Lacrosse helmet. The bloodhound proceeded into the apartment, through the first floor, up all steps to the back bedroom, bathroom, and the small front room. Chris' father, Steve, confirmed that these were in fact his rooms.

The second search was conducted to establish Chris' presence at the Lone Tree Bar and Grill (528 Hennepin Avenue). It began at 01:30 hours in order to avoid both pedestrian and automobile traffic. It started outside the bar, and the bloodhound was reintroduced to Chris' scent. The dog proceeded to all the places that a customer would be expected to be found: the front doors and inside the bar, all around the dance floor, to the bathroom, and then back to the bar. Next, Hoover tracked through the kitchen and directly to the office and scratched on door. The manager on duty opened the office door. The bloodhound went to a file cabinet, then back through the kitchen to the bar near Hennepin Avenue and back out the same glass doors. During the period of December 7th through December 14th, handler Penny Bell and her bloodhound Hoover completed 2 additional searches of residences, one of which belonged to Chris' girlfriend and the other belonged to an undisclosed third party (*Tracks G & J*).

A highlight of the K-9 searches were the locations of "hits" that were signaled by Hoover. Two hits occurred in the Metro Transit Commission Bus and Public Parking Facility at the intersection of 1st Avenue North and 8th Street North on December 7 and 8, 2002 (*Tracks D & E*; *Light Blue Star* & *Bright Green Star*). This was not where Cassidy had parked his vehicle on the night of October 31, 2002. He had parked it in the Block E ramp on 7th Street North at Hennepin Avenue; one block south of the Lone Tree Bar and Grill. These two hits were on the opposite corner of the block and at least another 2 blocks walking distance further from where the car had been parked.

Hoover also tracked Chris' scent from the Lone Tree Bar and Grill to an underground parking facility (the Plymouth Parking Ramp) just around the corner on Hennepin Avenue on December 8th. This track and hit (*Track F*; *Yellow Star*) confirmed earlier results of tracking and hits. It was the exact same spot (i.e., stalls #89 & #90) that Annie Sherma and her tracking dog had led them to and hit on back on November 7th (*Tracks A & C*; *Blue Star* & *Red Star*). Chris' scent was also in the vicinity of a small amount of blood residue, as well as a piece of red string and red feather fragments, which were similar to the components of Chris' Indian costume. The police dismissed the red string and feather, saying that it did not belong to Chris. As far as we could determine from official reports, the MPD investigators did nothing else with these potential pieces of evidence. However, one report indicated that someone from the Federal Bureau of Investigation contacted the store where Chris had purchased the costume, and then requested the same kind of feather from the company that manufactured it. No further reference to the string, feather, or blood was ever found in any other reports.

Several tracks led the search party outside the immediate downtown area (Figures 7.5 and 7.6). The first track by Annie Sherma and her bloodhound brought the searchers 0.7 miles down Hennepin Avenue and across the bridge over the Mississippi River on November 7th (*Track C*). Upon reaching the north end of the bridge, Annie and the K-9 tracked Chris' scent underneath the bridge, down to the water's edge, into the water, and indicated a hit (*Red Star*). Additional tracks and hits occurred in this area. On December 9th at 10:50 hours, when they first brought a different bloodhound (Hoover) to the north end of the Father Louis Hennepin Bridge, she began howling loudly and would not stop (Figure 7.8). The handler (Penny Bell) had to take the dog several blocks away in order to calm her. Upon returning to the north end of the bridge at 11:17 hours, the dog then led the search party northwest along the Mississippi River, hitting at the start of the trail and again a few hundred yards upstream at a small dock in the river (*Track H*; 2 *Dark Green Stars*). Later that same day, the bloodhound followed a scent to the southeast into an area of Nicollet Island with park benches that overlooked the Horseshoe Dam area (*Track I*).

Tracking efforts between December 9th and 15th proved to be quite interesting and exhausting for all involved (Figure 7.6). It began on December 9th when the bloodhound exited the underground parking garage on Hennepin Avenue, which was where the hits in stalls #89 & #90 had occurred (*Blue Star, Red Star,* & *Yellow Star*). At 20:50 hours, the searchers started a night track that lasted until almost midnight. The dog went out onto Hennepin Avenue into the middle lane of traffic as though it were following a vehicle (*Track K*). The bloodhound went eastbound on 6th Street and then northbound on Marquette Avenue to the U.S. Post Office, where it turned right onto 1st Street South and tracked eastbound until she reached 3rd Avenue South. The searchers continued northbound across the bridge, which started as 3rd Avenue South and became Central Avenue Southeast. There had been some speculation that Chris may have committed suicide by jumping from a local bridge. However, the handler and bloodhound tracked in the street past the location on the bridge that overlooked the body recovery site without incident or hit. Upon reaching

Figure 7.8 Both bloodhounds picked up Chris Jenkins' scent underneath the north end of the Father Louis Hennepin Bridge on Nicollet Island in downtown Minneapolis.

4th Street Southeast at nearly midnight, everyone showed signs of tiring (having tracked for 1.4 miles) and the search ceased for the day.

The search was resumed the next day at 09:30 hours (December 10, 2002). The bloodhound was brought back and restarted at the end-point (Central Avenue Southeast at 4th Street Southeast). Hoover continued northbound for 0.6 miles along Central Avenue Southeast until she reached Spring Street Northeast (*Track L*). The majority of the day was spent following up on hits along this route in parking lots and their associated businesses. Penny Bell and Hoover took a couple days off to recharge themselves after all the walking during the past few days. Then, on December 14th, Hoover was brought back to Central Avenue Southeast at 3rd Street Southeast. She started tracking northbound at 08:40 hours on Central Avenue Northeast and went 0.9 miles all the way up to Broadway Street Northeast (*Track M*). At that point, the search effort for the day was halted due to traffic and safety issues; Penny and Hoover had almost been struck by a passing motor vehicle.

The next day at 14:00 hours (December 15th), the bloodhound tracking was restarted at the intersection of Central Avenue Northeast and Broadway Street Northeast (*Track N*). Penny and Hoover tracked Chris' scent down the road as though they were following a vehicle westbound for 1.7 miles until they reached the intersection with Washington Avenue North. At that intersection, they turned northbound and tracked 0.4 miles up to the on-ramp to Interstate Highway 94 at North 22nd Avenue. This entire search track (the 4.4 miles from the Lone Tree Bar & Grill to the intersection of Central & Broadway, and then onto the I-94 on-ramp) went as though Chris had been in a vehicle and was being transported out of the area to somewhere else.

We found the similarities in the K-9 searches and the subsequent outcomes with law enforcement to be disturbing. Both searches were conducted with 2 different bloodhounds and 2 different handlers separated by a month. Both searches went from the Lone Tree Bar and Grill, where Chris was removed, to the same underground parking ramp and the exact same 2 stalls (#89 & #90) where a piece of red string, red feather fragments, and small amount of blood residue were recovered. Yet, report narratives seemed to indicate that the MPD investigators decided to ignore this information since they believed that the feather did not belong to Chris. They dismissed the red feather as potential evidence before Chris or the headband he was wearing were even recovered and a comparison could be made.

Common sense should have suggested to the MPD investigators that they needed to determine who rented those two parking stalls. It should have also directed them to determine whether the stalls were occupied by those persons on the evening that Chris disappeared. Were the stalls not occupied that night, then MPD investigatory protocol and/or Standard Operating Procedures (SOP) should have mandated that the investigators needed to discover where these individuals were during the evening that Chris went missing. If they, either person, had used those stalls that evening or were in the immediate area, would it not have been prudent for the MPD officers to question them regarding their whereabouts or to check their alibis for that evening? Information gleaned from an attendant at the Plymouth Parking Ramp showed that the individual who occupied one of the parking stalls not only lived within a few miles from the Father Louis Hennepin Bridge (2.9 miles), but he actually worked as a bouncer at the Lone Tree Bar and Grill. Furthermore, a walk-by on this person's vehicle with a bloodhound at about 11:43 hours on December 9th produced a mild hit for Chris' scent. As far as we know, no report stipulated the verification of the whereabouts and alibis of the individuals associated with the leasing and use of stalls #89 and #90. To what extent was this evidence followed up by investigators?

Ground Searches

In addition to the K-9 searches mentioned above, officers from the MPD conducted several ground searches on foot of premises and open areas. They searched Nicollet Island, specifically the park area and the restaurant (Nicollet Island Inn) on November 8, 2002. They also searched the shoreline around the Horseshoe Dam area down to the Stone Arch Bridge on foot that day. On November 11th, they continued their efforts on the east bank by the Stone Arch Bridge and searched the park area of Father Hennepin Bluffs. MPD officers also looked behind the main U.S. Post Office. They then searched underneath the Third Avenue Bridge, where Annie Sherma and her bloodhound had hit 4 days earlier on November 7th (Figure 7.5, *Track C*). No sign of Chris was found anywhere. Later, at about 14:30 hours on February 11, 2003, a Homicide Unit sergeant, along with other MPD police officers, searched the University of Minnesota dormitory room (Pioneer Hall) of an unidentified person of interest. According to reports, the whole thing turned out to be nothing and the individual was cleared as a potential suspect.

Video Recordings

Like most of the drowning cases of young college-age men in the United States that we have investigated, there was no recorded video evidence of them once they left the bar. Once again, it was as though a healthy young man simply vanished from the streets of a major city. Investigators from the MPD scoured the area for recorded video. As is also common with these cases, they encountered businesses with no CCTV (closed circuit television) security recording devices, broken equipment, recorders that were not turned on, tapes or digital memories that had already been recorded over, and erased video. Nothing useful was recovered in the way of video evidence. Here were some examples.

Sergeant Pete Jackson from the MPD Homicide Division received 2 CDs (compact discs) from Dave Gust at the University of Minnesota that presented video which covered the area around the university. One video was from the steam plant and the other from the coal plant. He viewed both CDs and stated that Chris was not on either of them. The CD from the steam plant had very good footage of the east end of the Stone Arch Bridge from 00:00 to 04:00 hours on November 1, 2002. No sign of Chris was found on any of the university's video CDs.

On November 8th, an MPD officer collected CCTV video-recordings from the Federal Reserve Bank on Hennepin Avenue next to the Mississippi River and the bridge where both bloodhounds had indicated hits for Chris' scent (Figure 7.9). The bank's outside security cameras captured the western approach to the bridge, the whole north side of the Father Louis Hennepin Bridge and the roadway, and part of the riverbank underneath the bridge on the east side of the river. In fact, the bank's CCTV cameras had a pretty clear view of the location where the bloodhound had done her persistent howling. This seemed to be a promising source of evidence. After close review, there was no evidence observed of Chris in his Native American ("Indian") costume. In the end, there was no evidence of anyone else who might be wearing such a costume, or even anyone who vaguely resembled his physical stature, walking on the roadway leading onto the Father Louis Hennepin Bridge, or on the bridge, or under it on the far side.

Another promising source of evidence was the Metro Transit Commission Bus and Public Parking Facility that was located at the intersection of 1st Avenue North and 8th

Figure 7.9 Security cameras on the Federal Reserve Bank were visible from this location under the Father Louis Hennepin Bridge where the bloodhounds had hit, in particular, where a K-9 had tracked Chris Jenkins' scent down into the river.

Street North. This was the spot where two bloodhound hits for Chris' scent had occurred on December 7 and 8, 2002 (Figure 7.5, *Tracks D & E*; *Light Blue Star* & *Bright Green Star*). Security video evidence was sought at the facility office, which was located at 33 9th Street North. Chris was not seen in any of the CCTV footage recorded on the night of October 31st and into the morning of November 1st.

Witness

The police informed Gannon and Duarte that they had one witness who, while riding his bicycle across the Father Louis Hennepin Bridge at approximately 02:00 hours on November 1st, said that he had seen an individual matching Chris' description walking across the bridge by himself (Figure 7.10). According to Detective Sergeant Pete Jackson of the MPD Detective Bureau, who was in charge of the investigation, the witness even stated that the person whom he had seen looked like he was looking for a fight. The witness' statement spoke to Chris' potential state of mind. Was he upset about being ejected from the bar? Or, was he angry after having observed his girlfriend flirting with another guy in the bar? This was the same male who had provided her with part of her sexualized Halloween

Figure 7.10 The view south down the Mississippi River in Minneapolis: the Father Louis Hennepin Bridge (*blue*), the Third Avenue Bridge (*white*), and the Stone Arch Bridge (*gray*).

costume. The witness' statement was supposed to foster a belief that Chris was distraught, and as such, lend credence to the law enforcement hypothesis that he took his own life by jumping from the Father Louis Hennepin Bridge, which is what Gannon and Duarte were told by investigators.

This hypothesis seemed to be strengthened by the tracking results from 2 different bloodhounds, which included 2 solid hits and 1 unrelenting howling. It is important to first note that bloodhounds follow scents, they do not follow people. Clearly, Chris' scent was there. That did not mean that he had been there. None of the hits were on the bridge. They were all near or under the north end of the bridge. The tracking behavior of both dogs suggested that Chris' scent was in or on a vehicle while it crossed the bridge. Thus, we concluded that the scent on the surface roadway of the bridge must have been either a transfer scent that was being carried by someone who had had contact with Chris that night, or he was inside a vehicle. The recorded video evidence from the Federal Reserve Bank cameras showed all activity near and on the bridge for the evening of October 31st into the morning hours of November 1st. Neither Chris nor anyone resembling him in any fashion (physical stature or costumed in the same manner) was ever observed in those videos. When we jointly examined the video information with the bloodhound searches, it proved that Chris never even made it to the roadway that crossed the Father Louis Hennepin Bridge that evening. In other words, Chris did not walk across the bridge that night. Since Chris was not there that night, he therefore could not have killed himself that night by jumping from the bridge. As such, the lone witness was mistaken and we assessed his testimony to be unreliable.

Recovery Location

Chris was discovered floating on his back in the Mississippi River just to the south of the Third Avenue Bridge and on the east side of the river during the afternoon of February 27, 2002. This part of the river was often referred to as the Horseshoe Dam area. It was formed by the natural geological feature of the Upper Saint Anthony Falls and the U.S. Army Corps of Engineers' Spillway, Lock and Dam, and associated Saint Anthony Falls Laboratory (Figure 7.11). Chris' body was recovered by officers from the Hennepin County Sheriff's Department Water Patrol at about 18:15 hours (approximately 118.7 days after he was last seen on November 1, 2002, at about 01:00 hours).

Some controversy existed as to when Chris arrived at that spot in the river and when he had first been seen there. Although Chris was recovered on February 27th, one witness stated that the first time he had seen the object in the water was about 15:00 hours on February 20th (seven days earlier). He did not report it because he thought it was just a prank and that someone had thrown a scarecrow or dummy into the river. He claimed that the next time he saw the object was around noon on February 27th. That was when he realized it was a body. The statements made by the witness suggested that Chris' body had potentially been at that spot in the river for some time; perhaps as long as seven days. However, another witness commented that the first time she had seen the body was at approximately 15:50 hours on February 27th. She professed that she had observed Chris' body floating down the river with the logs and then coming to rest against the debris where it was recovered. This statement clearly meant that his body was not there for seven days and had just arrived from somewhere upstream.

As we learned more about Chris' discovery and the recovery site, it became more clear to us that he must have entered the Mississippi River somewhere north of the Father Louis

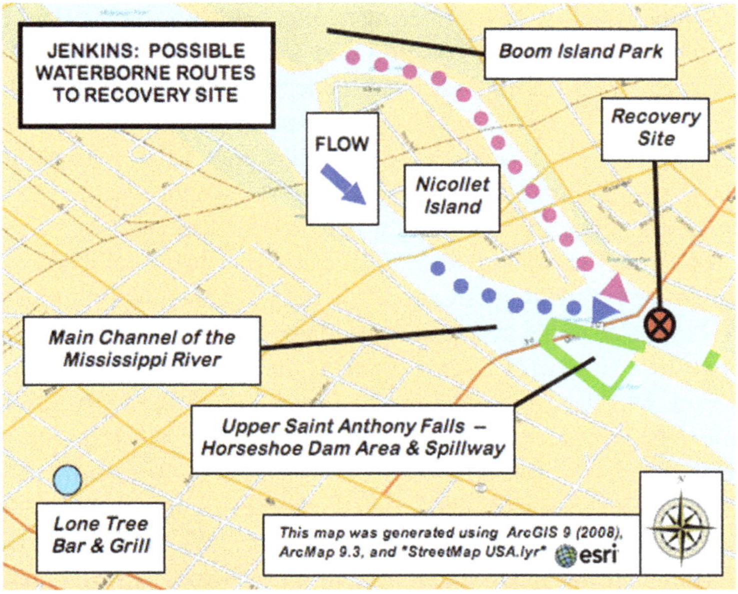

Figure 7.11 Chris Jenkins was recovered in the Horseshoe Dam area of the Mississippi River in downtown Minneapolis on February 27, 2002. Analysis proved that he had to have come to that location via the eastern most channel upstream (*Bright Purple Dotted Line*). He could not have arrived there via the larger west channel (*Blue Dotted Line*).

Hennepin Bridge. Investigatory reports stated that analysis of aerial photographs and reports from the Saint Anthony Falls Laboratory indicated that the body had most likely shown up in late February. According to those reports, the Horseshoe Dam area where the body had been recovered (specifically, the sandbar just south of the Third Avenue Bridge) was iced-over and photos presented only part of the debris frozen in the ice. It was not until later in the month, when melting opened up the waterway, that the logs and debris containing Chris' body dislodged from upstream and floated down to become entangled in the debris caught on the sandbar. Since there was no ice on the river at the time of his body recovery except at the shoreline in shaded spots, Chris had to have been close to shore in order for there to still be ice around the logs and debris containing his body.

An assessment of the river was conducted by the leading water experts in the country, Walter "Butch" Hendrick (President and dive expert) and Andrea Zaferes (Vice President, forensic specialist & trainer) of Lifeguard Systems, Inc. After numerous tests, Lifeguard Systems determined that there were 3 possible locations where the body could have been entered into the water to wind up where it did. One location according to the current was from Nicollet Island. However, considering the ice on the body and the lack of ice in the middle of the Mississippi River at this location (Upper Saint Anthony Falls), Hendrick and Zaferes concluded that the body most likely came from a mile or more upstream and north of the Father Louis Hennepin Bridge. They suggested that Chris should have come from an area further north of where he was recovered, possibly as far as 3.5 to 5 miles north. This information was reinforced during further conversations with Saint Anthony Falls Laboratory personnel.

Laboratory staff explained that surface currents and undercurrents in the main channel (the west channel) of the Mississippi River were governed by the pull of the water falling over the Horseshoe Dam at the Upper Saint Anthony Falls. It was unlikely that any object, no matter how closely it stayed floating to Nicollet Island, could drift past the island and end up along the east bank south of the Third Avenue Bridge (Figure 7.11, *Blue Dotted Line*). However, currents in the east channel tended to swirl just after passing under the Third Avenue Bridge and created an eddy, or dead spot, where logs and other debris would become trapped (Figure 7.11, *Bright Purple Dotted Line*). This phenomenon assisted in forming the sandbars in the area upon which objects would become marooned during low-water seasons like winter. Chris' body was recovered among debris that had snagged on one of the sandbars. Tests using a water dummy that had been thrown into the east channel back on June 9, 2003, suggested that Chris had come down the east channel.

Our analysis of the currents in that area reaffirmed the hypothesis that Chris had gone into the river north of the Third Avenue Bridge. Even though the bloodhounds had hit near and under the Nicollet Island end of the Father Louis Hennepin Bridge in the west channel, the information regarding river currents and flow characteristics during melt-off led to one conclusion only: Chris came down the east channel. We adamantly opposed any notion that Chris had jumped from either the Father Louis Hennepin Bridge in the west channel or the Third Avenue Bridge in the east channel. We ascertained that a fall from such a height would have inflicted serious antemortem (before death) injuries. Since there was no mention of antemortem injuries on Chris' body in the autopsy report, we posited that Chris did not jump from either bridge and commit suicide. In the end, our analysis also led us to propose that Chris may have gone into the Mississippi River at the bend in the east channel up by Boom Island Park on the north end of Nicollet Island.

Body Position and Posture

The position and posture that Chris' body was found in at recovery was extremely unusual. He was recovered floating in a supine (face-up) position in the Mississippi River. Typically, drowning victims float in a prone position (face-down). There is the occasional victim who is found floating on his back, but this is very rare and only occurs when a victim is either very obese or the body of water is very turbulent like that of a raging river (Hendrick, Zaferes, & Nelson, 2003). Chris was a muscular athlete and in great physical shape (5 feet 8 inches, 185 pounds, with a Body Mass Index of 28.12). In addition to the fact that he was not obese, it was winter in Minnesota and the Mississippi River was iced-up at the time. There were no surface currents or waves to flip his body. So, if this was a normal drowning, then Chris should have been found floating in a prone position (face-down).

We considered it preposterous that Chris was found in the macabre body posture that he was. His body posture was such that it resembled a mummy positioned in a sarcophagus with his hands clasped and his arms crossed over his chest. Drowning victims may occasionally present with cadaveric spasm, the instantaneous development of rigidity (*rigor mortis*) that results from intense muscular contraction at the moment of death (DiMaio & DiMaio, 2001). Rigor normally establishes and relents in 36 hours on dry land in a temperate environment (Spitz & Spitz, 2006). Cold weather may prolong this process, and water usually doubles its time. The amount of time from when Chris was last seen to when he was recovered was about 2,849 hours 15 minutes. Were he deceased and in the water that entire time as investigators wanted us to assume, then rigor should have relented a long time before he was recovered.

Winters in Minneapolis get cold enough to freeze the surface of a large moving body of water like the Mississippi River. Chris was missing for a 118-day period (November 1, 2002, to February 27, 2003). The average temperature for the entire period was 20.7 °Fahrenheit (University of Utah-Logan, 2011). Only 41 percent of the days reached a high temperature at or above freezing (32 °Fahrenheit). Taking into account overnight lows (as low as −14 °Fahrenheit on February 7th), only 11 percent of the days during that time averaged a daily temperature at or above freezing. From the day he went missing (November 1st) until January 9, 2003, most of the days reached highs above 32 °Fahrenheit that prevented the river from freezing solid. After that day, temperatures dipped and the surface of the river iced-over. However, there were 3 short periods of daytime thawing: 4 days (January 31st to February 3rd), 5 days (February 17th to 21st), and beginning the day Chris was recovered (February 27th). The temperature reached 37 °Fahrenheit on the day of Chris' recovery.

Given the daily temperatures, Chris could not have gone into the Mississippi River in November 2002 when he went missing. Had he gone into the water anytime during November or December, then he would have immediately floated downstream and been seen, reported to police, and recovered because the river was not yet frozen-over. Had he been placed into the river just before the first real freeze in January 2003, then he probably would have broken free and floated downstream during the first thaw (January 31st to February 3rd). Therefore, he had to have been placed into the river sometime during the first (January 31st to February 3rd) or second thaw (February 17th to 21st) in order to be recovered during the start of the third thaw (February 27th), which coincided with the day of Chris' recovery. Given the observed fact that he had a fair amount of snow and ice on him at recovery time and that very little precipitation occurred that winter, that meant that he was likely present in the river during the one major day of precipitation (i.e., 0.78 inches on February 3, 2003).

Chris' body was witnessed floating to the spot where it was recovered. It was recovered partially frozen, covered with some snow and ice, and frozen to a large tree branch. Our analysis suggested that there was only one way for those facts to have happened. We proposed that his body floated rather than sank since he was already deceased when his killers slid him into the water on his back. This was done at a spot along the river bank that presented an easy approach on foot while carrying a body. His body floated a short distance along the bank of the river before it became hung up on a tree branch just below the surface. Whereon, the river refroze, Chris was encased in the ice until the river thawed on February 27th. On that day, both he and the branch floated down to the eventual body recovery. The evidence suggested to us that Chris' arms were posed and that he was placed into the water on his back after death with the intent that he would be found in that ghoulish position and posture.

Head Position

After death occurs, the natural tension in the muscles relaxes and the head will normally fall to one side or the other before rigidity establishes. The literature on death investigations informed us that individuals who die on land will normally be found with their heads turned to one side, whereas drowning victims are found with their heads hanging forward due to the common position of floating face-down (Haupt, 2006). Nearly all drowning victims are found floating face-down with their arms extended forward and slightly down. Although victims who drown are usually found in a prone position (face-down), there is the occasional case where a victim is found in a supine position (on his back like Chris). As mentioned earlier, this generally only happens when a victim is either very obese and the water quite turbulent; neither of which were true in this case. In the event that a victim is floating on his back and given the relaxed state of the body and neck muscles and the buoyancy of water, the head generally sags straight back.

Gannon immediately noticed in the recovery photographs that Chris was discovered floating on his back with his head tilted to his right side. This suggested that Chris did not fall into the water, drown, and remain there to be recovered later. Since his head was tilted to his right side, it showed that when he died it was in a terrestrial environment (on land) and not an aquatic environment (in water). If Chris had accidentally fallen into the river, then his head should have been either straight forward with his chin tucked into his chest (as a result of his initial face-down position before somehow being flipped onto his back) or it should have been straight back with his chin pointed in the air. Since he was encased in ice, it made the evidence even more compelling. Even after rigor came and went, Chris would still have remained frozen in the position he was in when he entered the water. This directly contradicted the hypothesis that Chris died as a result of an accidental drowning. The titled position of his head told us that he was dead on land for a period of time before being entered into the water. Someone, therefore, was responsible for putting him into the water.

Rigidity and Lividity

Two external characteristics of a body that are routinely described by the official performing an autopsy (whether a coroner, medical examiner, or pathologist) are rigidity and lividity. Rigidity (*rigor mortis*) is the stiffening of the muscles that starts shortly after death (Geberth, 2006). Depending upon the temperature, rigidity is completely gone within approximately 36 hours on land to 72 hours in the water. Lividity (*livor mortis*) is the settling of the blood into the dependant capillaries after death (Armstrong & Erskine, 2011), which begins within 30 minutes and is fixed (resists being shifted or moved) within 10 to 12 hours.

Rigidity and lividity are extremely important for determining a postmortem interval (PMI) and identifying a time and manner of death. The examining official routinely provides an assessment of the extent of rigidity (going-in, established, relenting, not present) by describing whether rigor is in the jaw, arms, and legs. This is often determined by moving the joints and limbs carefully and slowly to feel resistance, if any, from rigor. Lividity is typically described relative to color (pink, red, purple, mixed, or unable to detect) and blanching, which is the reaction of capillary refill upon digital pressure (i.e., the speed at which the skin turns from white to its previous color after pressure was applied with a finger). It is also assessed for the extent to which it is "fixed" to one side of a body. Lividity is usually in the portion of a body closest to the earth relative to the position in which the body was discovered.

Since Chris was missing for 2,849 hours, then rigidity would have been unappreciable. It should have gone out weeks before his recovery and described by the Medical Examiner as not present or having already relented. Furthermore, because Chris was recovered floating on his back after a presumed extended period of time, then lividity should normally have been detected and described as being on his posterior side. Quiet surprisingly, there was no specific mention of rigidity or lividity in the 6-page autopsy report submitted by Dr. Raymond Rivera from the Hennepin County Medical Examiner's Office. He stated in the autopsy report that there was no unusual range of motion in the joints of the arms and legs. Perhaps, this was his reference to rigidity.

Beard Stubble

According to some witnesses, Chris was clean-shaven Halloween night. However, the Medical Examiner wrote in the autopsy report that there appeared to be early-growth facial hair on Chris' chin (the classic 5 o'clock shadow). If Chris had beard stubble when he was recovered, then that would show that he either had not shaved the night he went missing and drowned immediately after his removal from the bar, or he had shaved that day and was held alive for a period of time for the facial hair to grow before he was killed. On June 26, 2005, Andrea Zaferes (Lifeguard Systems) showed a professional in photography the picture of Chris that was taken in the Lone Tree Bar and Grill on the night that he went missing. He was asked to determine whether there was facial hair on Chris' face or whether he was clean-shaven. He said that after he used computer software to enlarge and enhance the photograph, that Chris was clean-shaven in the photo. He offered a possible explanation for the Medical Examiner's description in the autopsy report and said that human skin will shrink during the early stages of decomposition, which gives the facial hair the look of growth. We could not find anything in the research literature that verified the science of this assertion. Thus, it was left for debate.

Slip-On Shoes

The police stated that Chris had fallen or jumped from the Father Louis Hennepin Bridge. However, he was recovered still wearing his slip-on, clog-type shoes. We determined that the shoes would have definitely come off his feet had he fallen or jumped from any bridge. Even if he had accidentally fallen into the Mississippi River, then we asserted that the kicking of his legs while swimming would have removed the shoes during his struggle to survive. We felt that this was another example that proved that Chris was dead before entry into the water.

Mud and Chemistry

The Medical Examiner described Chris as being encrusted with black mud. It was on his clothing, in his hair, and on his shoes. It was described in a manner as to suggest that it was not just a film of dirt or slime, rather, there was a considerable coating of this black mud. We concluded that there were only four times when he could have acquired the mud: before he went into the river (Pre-Entry), as he was going into the river (At Entry), while he was in the river (While In), and as he was coming out of the river (During Exit). Since we know that the body recovery team performed professionally, then we surmised that the team members did not drag Chris' body through the mud along the river bank. So, the fourth option (During Exit) was precluded from further consideration. That meant that only 3 options remained and 5 scenarios were generated.

Pre-Entry: Chris was struggling for his life as his assailant(s) held his face down in water in a muddy area near the bank of the river. This would explain how the mud got into his hair and became such a matted, dense, tangled mass. Rolling around on his front and back during the struggle caused the mud to be worked into every part of his clothing and shoes. Having accomplished the task, the assailant(s) rested and left him to lie there in the mud.

At Entry A: Regardless of the reason, Chris decided to walk down by the banks of the Mississippi River in the middle of the night. He stumbled, rolled around in the mud, and ended up in the river, from which he could not retreat.

At Entry B: Since a person generally sinks head-first during the drowning process, Chris picked up the mud as he landed on the bottom of the river.

At Entry C: The person(s) responsible for his death posed Chris' hands across his chest while he laid on his back in the mud along the shoreline before slipping him into the Mississippi River.

While In: Chris' body was on the river bottom slowly decomposing in the cold water. Eventually, putrefaction began to generate gases that caused his body to slowly resurface. When a body begins to rise, there is the possibility that freshwater-postmortem wandering may occur. This is the case where a body may actually rub along the river bed for a period of time until enough gases are formed within the body to cause it to rise to the surface (Armstrong & Erskine, 2011). The river needs to be fast moving, which the Mississippi River can be at times and in certain spots.

Our analysis concluded that the 2nd scenario (*At Entry A*) would not have generated the extent of mud that covered Chris as seen in the body recovery photographs. One reason the 3rd scenario (*At Entry B*) did not happen was because Chris was dead before his entry into the water; as we will prove beyond a reasonable doubt in this chapter. This did not occur because victims who are dead before entry into the water do not always sink. They may likely float due to air trapped inside the lungs (Armstrong & Erskine, 2011). We found that the 5th scenario was unlikely (*While In*). If Chris had been dragged along the river floor by the current, then there should have been some sort of postmortem travel abrasions (usually to the facial area); but there were none. Also, if he had been dragged along the bottom in the fast-moving river, then he would have most definitely lost his slip-on, clog-type shoes that he was wearing that evening. When a person is killed in another location and allowed to begin the decomposition process, and is then dumped into a waterway, then the body usually does not sink. If it does sink, then the decomposition gases already forming will contribute to a sooner and quicker resurfacing. Even if the 2nd scenario (*At Entry A*) were combined with the 3rd scenario (*At Entry B*) and 5th scenario (*While In*), then Chris might have had mud on his feet and knees, maybe here and there, but not the pervasive coating and clumps of mud as were seen.

We concluded that the 1st scenario (*Pre-Entry*) and 4th scenario (*At Entry C*) were the only ones that could adequately explain the presence of so much mud. If Chris did not sink because he was already deceased before entry into the water (scenarios 2 & 3), and the mud affixed to his hair and clothing did not come from being dragged along the floor of the Mississippi River (scenario 5), that left only the 1st and 4th scenarios (*Pre-Entry* and *At Entry C*) – and both involved human intervention. Our assessment proposed that Chris' shoes would have come off in the water were he alive and trying to swim to safety, or simply from the force of the Mississippi River current. We also acknowledged that they would have likely come off during a struggle for his life on the bank of the river while someone was trying to suffocate him in the mud. However, Chris still had on his slip-on, clog-type shoes. Since the 4th scenario (*At Entry C*) involved human intervention and posing, we surmised that the shoes would have been put back on his feet as part of the body posing endeavor. Although Chris' murder may have occurred along the banks of the Mississippi River, we will never know for sure without a confession from the perpetrator(s).

Since the MPD changed the classification of Chris' case to a homicide, then it would have been imperative to want to know the specific location where Chris had acquired all that black mud. Given the fact that it was a potential crime scene, it would have been nice to have at least narrowed it down to even a general location along the river bank. However, the mud that had adhered to Chris' clothing was never tested. Had MPD investigators taken samples of the mud from the river and had them tested against the mud on Chris' clothing, then a determination as to where he had acquired the mud could have been made. This would have identified a water entry point for Chris and an actual crime scene for a case that police had initially labeled an accident and suggested was a possible suicide. The MPD investigators had this material (i.e., the black mud) and yet they did not perceive it as forensic material, much less test it. Much like our discussion of diatoms in the preceding chapter, no attempt was made to collect samples of river water, mud from the banks of the river, or mud from the bottom of the river.

This shortcoming in procedure is part of the overarching problem with present-day water-related investigations. We cannot emphasize this next point enough. The fact that water and mud samples were not collected was due to no fault of the MPD officers or investigators. It is a systemic problem that is associated with outdated policies and protocols that have not kept up with technology. Cops are not taught to look at evidence located in water with the same regard as evidence on dry land (Becker, 2000). They are not taught that it has any forensic value to an investigation or in court. Within the immediate area of recovery and at intervals around the scene, officers need to collect water samples and soil samples from along the water's edge and bottom. All samples can be chemically analyzed for related pH content, nutrients, animal and human wastes, industrial and agricultural pollutants. First, samples taken from the deceased can be compared to samples taken from the recovery site to determine possible "background contamination" (Becker, 2000). Comparisons can then be made with samples taken around the recovery site within the body of water. However, this whole effort is for naught when investigators lack the knowledge and foresight to collect samples at the time of recovery.

Injuries

The Medical Examiner described Chris' body as being free of any discernible internal or external hemorrhage (bleeding) or contusion (bruising). In light of the hypothesis that Chris may have committed suicide by jumping from a local bridge of that height, we found the absence of bruising to be unexpected. Bruising generally requires a beating heart that is pumping blood to injured capillaries. Had Chris leapt alive from a bridge the height of the Father Louis Hennepin Bridge or the Third Avenue Bridge, then he would have clearly sustained some bruising before expiring in the icy water. That is of course provided that he did not die instantaneously upon impact. Perhaps, the coolness of the water slowed or stopped the development of bruises. However, one would think that such an impact from that height would have at least dislodged his shirt from its tucked-in condition, caused his clog-type shoes to come off, and caused him to be found in any other disheveled position and posture other than neatly on his back with his arms crossed over his chest. Simply put then, Chris did not leap to his death.

The autopsy report presented that there were no injuries at all to Chris' body (anterior neck, hyoid bone, back, arms, legs, and so forth). We considered the absence of any bruising to be quite telling. Chris's mother (Jan) told us that she was surprised that there were no signs of bruising on Chris since he was the goalkeeper for the Lacrosse team. She said he was always getting pelted with balls, and that his thighs and arms were always black and blue for a few days after a practice or game. Chris had recently had Lacrosse practice only a day or two earlier. The fact that there were no injuries on Chris' body also led us to believe that he might have been held for a period of time before he died. Given the retarding affect of cold water on processes related to death and decomposition (i.e., rigor mortis, algor mortis, livor mortis, putrefaction, and maceration), we estimated that it would have taken anywhere from 4 days to a week to heal any bruises that Chris may have sustained from his position as a Lacrosse goalie. This meant that Chris did not die on the night of October 31st–November 1st.

We specifically noted that the Medical Examiner actually autopsied Chris' back looking for subcutaneous injuries (i.e., bruising below the surface of the skin). This is rarely done by medical examiners except in very suspicious cases. The fact that there were no soft tissue or subcutaneous injuries to Chris' body, specifically to the muscles in the front of his neck and on his back, revealed that Chris was not strangled and was not held face-down by someone kneeling or his back or pressing him to the ground. It also meant that he did not pull the hair from his own head in a spontaneous cadaveric spasm while he fought for his life and eventually drowned. This evidence spoke more to the possibility that Chris was murdered another way, that the hair in his hand was placed there as part of the act of posing the body, and that he was put into the river in the position in which he was eventually recovered. This occurred while the murderer(s) waited for rigor to stiffen the arm muscles, which took approximately 2 to 4 hours. The next question to be answered would be, how then was Chris murdered?

Empty Systems

Healthy human lungs are pinkish-red in color and present a somewhat sponge-like consistency. An average lung weighs between 325 and 570 grams. The right lung is normally slightly heavier than the left lung since it has 3 lobes instead of only 2 lobes. The heart takes up the remaining space. The combined lung weight in average adult males is typically greater than 1,000 grams in drowning scenarios due to inhaled water (Shkrum & Ramsay, 2007). However, if the combined lung weight is less than 1,000 grams, then one of two things probably happened: either a wet drowning and pleural effusion, or a dry drowning. Lung weights may drop in cases of wet drowning due to the passing of fluid from the lungs into the cavity surrounding the lungs (i.e., pleural effusion). In such cases, fluid may also be observed in the area of the pericardial sac and peritoneal cavity. A dry drowning is when no fluid is found in the lungs. This can occur in two ways. First, a victim may have a reflexive contraction, which prevents water from passing into the airway (i.e., laryngeal spasm). Or second, a victim may not have been breathing before entering the water due to unconsciousness or death. In either scenario, the person experiences hypoxia (i.e., oxygen depravation) and is considered to have "drowned" since he is underwater. The research literature suggests that dry drownings occur in about 10 to 15 percent of the cases (Lunetta, Modell, & Sajantila, 2004; Lunetta, Penttilla, & Sajantila, 2002). That statistic has been challenged by a more recent study, which found that as few as 2 percent of cases are actually dry drownings (Armstrong & Erskine, 2011, p. 248).

The condition and weight of Chris' lungs signified that his death was either a dry drowning or that he did not drown at all. They were also some of the smallest of lungs we have ever seen, especially for a young male athlete. As already presented, lungs typically weigh between 325 and 570 grams. We are used to seeing the water-filled lungs of drowning victims up around a combined weight of 1,000 to 1,200 grams at autopsy. Chris' combined lung weight was 695 grams. His right and left lungs weighed 355 and 340 grams, respectively. He did not have the pinkish froth in his trachea that is often found in drowning victims (i.e., an air bubble mixture of blood from ruptured small blood vessels and mucous). Also, his lungs did not have any water in them and there was no pleural effusion of any kind whatsoever. In simplest terms, his lungs and body cavities did not contain any foreign fluids from the environment that supposedly killed him.

Three other organs were reported to be empty by the Medical Examiner at autopsy: the bladder, the stomach, and the gallbladder. It is not uncommon for a body to empty or purge itself of urine and feces upon death. Since Chris was not exposed, then we precluded the idea that he had fallen into the river while attempting to relieve himself. It seemed that his empty bladder was most likely explained as part of the death process. However, Chris' stomach only contained 27 milliliters (0.913 fluid ounces – less than the volume of a shot glass) of a thickened, brownish-red liquid that contained a mixture of very finely chewed and unidentifiable food substance. According to the autopsy report, his gallbladder was empty.

Relative to the digestive system, very little emptying takes place during the first 20 to 30 minutes in the stomach, small intestine, and colon. Food usually leaves the stomach anywhere from 4 to 6 hours depending on the size of the meal, its density (e.g., steak or pizza, as compared to oatmeal or soup), and the extent of muscle action in the stomach and small intestine (Bowen, 2005; National Institute of Diabetes and Digestive and Kidney Diseases, 2008). The transit time of food through the digestive system may even be influenced by psychological stress, biological sex, and whether or not a person is pregnant (Bowen, 2006). Liquids leave more quickly than solid foods. About 50 percent of the stomach contents will be emptied in 2.5 to 3 hours post-ingestion, with total emptying in 4 to 5 hours (Bowen, 2006); some researchers suggest as long as 6 hours. This meant that Chris had to have been dead sometime within 6 hours after eating his last meal. No indication existed in any report that an attempt had been made to identify when and where Chris had eaten his last meal, and what he had eaten.

The finding that Chris' stomach was nearly empty of contents could be explained in a host of ways. But, that fact disturbed us when combined with the knowledge that his gallbladder was also empty. A digestive juice known as "bile" is produced by the liver and stored in the gallbladder between meals (National Institute of Diabetes and Digestive and Kidney Diseases, 2008). Before a meal, an average human gallbladder holds about 10.7 milliliters of bile. The first low (*early nadir*) or initial dump of bile occurs shortly after food intake begins. The gallbladder then refills (*early peak*) and begins to empty again very slowly to a second low (*late nadir*) at 146 minutes after ingestion, plus or minus 33 minutes (Howard, Murphy, & Dowling, 1991). It takes about 42 to 50 minutes for the gallbladder to refill (Mesgarzadeh, Krishnamurthy, Bobba, & Langrell, 1983).

This means that once a person starts to eat, then logically we should not see both an empty gallbladder and an empty stomach under normal conditions (see Figure 7.12). The empty stomach could have been explained away by vomiting or having eaten 6 or more hours earlier, but the empty gallbladder told another story. An empty gallbladder told us that Chris had to have eaten within the past 6 hours. His stomach had reached a point in time where it should have only emptied about 50 percent of its contents, and was also up to that point in time where his gallbladder had emptied (*late nadir*) but not yet started to refill. Having identified the presence of food remnants in Chris' stomach in conjunction

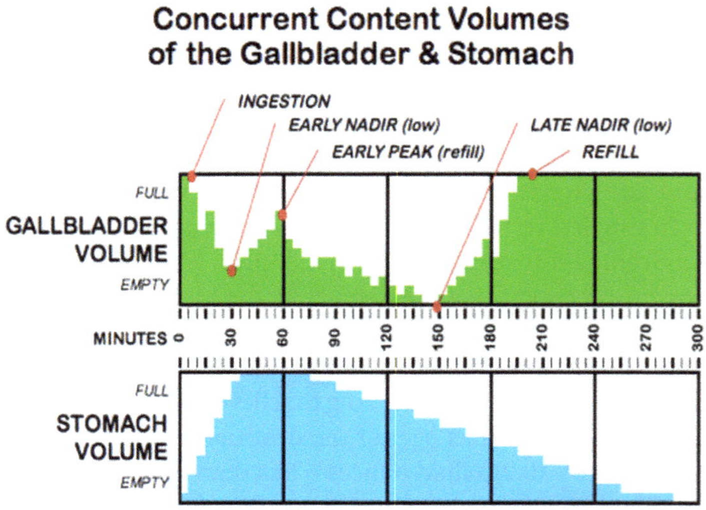

Figure 7.12 An empty stomach and an empty gallbladder should not occur naturally or simultaneously. The gallbladder provides bile to the stomach during the first 2.5 hours after ingestion. Once it is empty (*late nadir*), a short pause occurs and it then begins to refill. At that point in time, the stomach should have emptied about 50% of its contents.

with an empty gallbladder meant that he had to have eaten within about 3 hours of his time of death.

This was a shocking discovery in light of other forensic evidence. No report indicated anyone having witnessed Chris eating inside the bar after he arrived there around 23:00 hours. He could not have purchased a meal at a local fast food shop after leaving the Lone Tree Bar and Grill since he had no money on him; his girlfriend possessed his wallet and she was back in the bar. Unless someone fed him in the bar, then he had to have eaten after he left the bar. If he ate after he left the bar, then who fed him? Additionally, that delay in time would have lowered his blood alcohol concentration (BAC) and sobered him up somewhat. We knew from toxicology reports that Chris' BAC most likely did not cause nausea-induced vomiting. If he did throw-up, then it was most likely caused by the presence of some drug in his system (e.g., one of the side effects of GHB is nausea).

Toxicology

Blood alcohol concentration (BAC) can be a very important piece of evidence during the investigation of an unattended death, especially a drowning. It can be a difficult statistic to work with when one does not fully understand it from a biological, toxicological, or pharmacological perspective. Although there is some debate regarding whether or not alcohol increases after death as a result of decomposition, we found that sufficient research existed which supported an assertion of postmortem alcohol production (Athanaselis, Stefanidou, & Koutselinis, 2005; Canfield, Kupiec, & Huffine, 1993; Garriott, 1996; Gilliland & Bost, 1993; Heatley & Crane, 1990; Johnson, Lewis, Angier, & Vu, 2004; Kugelberg & Jones, 2007; Moriya & Hashimoto, 2004).

We also discovered that misinformation had been spread on certain web sites and blogspots about determining the level of alcohol in a victim at the time of death. That information probably led readers to believe that there was no way to accurately determine the intoxication level of victims with respect to these cases. Contrary to said Internet misinformation, we found more than an adequate volume of research literature which supported an assertion that alcohol levels can be determined. Again, there are of course many factors that affect the decomposition process (e.g., time, temperature, victim's musculature and weight, clothing, body and environmental temperatures, precipitation, direct sunlight or shade, buried in soil or exposed, or submerged in water).

There is a simple technique that many pathologists use to determine alcohol decomposition, that is, percentages. Some forensic pathologists have suggested at times that a victim's BAC had increased by a certain percentage (20% to 30%) due to putrefaction after death. Unfortunately, a percentage is not consistent enough in our opinion. When using a percentage, the amount of increase that can be attributed to postmortem alcohol production is based on the initial BAC level within a victim rather than the interaction of all the pertinent variables. For example, consider Victim A and Victim B who were identical in every possible demographic characteristic. Both were deceased and exposed in the open air, lying in the shade on land for 4 months. Their BACs were 0.100 and 0.040, respectively. Using percentages (20% to 30%), Victim A's BAC would have increased to a reading of 0.120 to 0.130. Victim B's BAC would have increased to a reading of 0.048 to 0.052. Logically and scientifically, the increase should have been the same, while mathematically they ended up different.

Gannon has examined hundreds of drowning cases over the past decade. He combined that experience with numbers he received from the medical community to develop a chart to determine postmortem alcohol production (Figure 7.13). We always error on the side of caution, and so, we use the numbers at the low end of the spectrum. Since alcohol increases after death during the decomposition process, we use the following chart to determine a victim's blood alcohol concentration (BAC) at the time of death.

These values were corroborated by Dr. Michael Baden, a world-renowned forensic pathologist, when he commented on two cases where both victims were missing for 4 months before their recovery from the water. One of those case was Chris Jenkins. In Chris' case (11/01/2002 to 02/28/2003) and another case in New York, the victims were

Estimated Postmortem Alcohol Production Values (gm/dL)

PERIOD	MINIMUM	MAXIMUM
1 month	*0.015*	*0.030*
2 months	*0.030*	*0.060*
3 months	*0.045*	*0.090*
4 months	*0.060*	*0.120*

(Assessed BAC) minus (Postmortem Alcohol Production Value) equals (Estimated Actual BAC)

0.120 – 0.060 minimum = 0.060 gm/dL
0.120 – 0.120 maximum = 0.000 gm/dL

Figure 7.13 Research shows that bodies produced alcohol after death as part of the decomposition process. An estimated actual BAC can be calculated using the values in the above table, which was compiled from Gannon's examination of hundreds of drowning cases combined with data from the medical community.

recovered with BAC levels of 0.120 (Chris) and 0.126 (the NY case). In both cases, Dr. Baden stated that the victim's alcohol level at the time of death was at 0.060 (Jenkins) and 0.066 (the NY case). This meant that in both cases the victims' BACs increased by about 0.060. Chris was recovered with a BAC of 0.12. Since alcohol increases during the decomposition process (which in this case was 4 months long), Chris' BAC could have increased by as little as 0.060 or as much as 0.120. This meant that he could have actually entered the river with a BAC at "Zero" (0.000).

Decomposition for 4 months was minimally 0.060 to 0.120 maximum, which meant that Chris entered the Mississippi River at no more than about 0 to 3 drinks since each drink equals 0.020 milliliters. In fact, since the legal limit to operate a motor vehicle in Minnesota is a 0.080 BAC as it is in most states, he was legally sober enough to drive a car when he died and entered the water with a 0.060 BAC. Chris was not some drunk kid who wandered into the freezing Mississippi River on the morning after Halloween. Considering that Chris had very little alcohol in his system when he entered the water, proves that alcohol was not the primary reason or contributing factor for his death. His death stemmed more from his intentional drugging and eventual abduction and murder then it did from his alcohol consumption. We posited that Chris was drugged, abducted, held for a period of time, murdered by induced hypoxia (drowned or suffocated), posed and placed into the Mississippi River on his back with his hands neatly placed across his chest.

Toxicology studies that are typically done at autopsy include alcohols (typically, ethanol and methanol), and a "drug screen" or "drug panel" that includes a laundry list of common classes of drugs of abuse (otherwise referred to as "recreational drugs"): amphetamines, barbiturates, benzodiazepines, cannabinoids, cocaine and metabolites, fentanyl, methadone and metabolite, opiates, oxycodone and metabolite, phencyclidine, propoxyphene and metabolite, analgesics, anesthetics, antibiotics, anticonvulsants, antidepressants, antihistamines, antipsychotics, cardiovascular agents, endocrine agents, gastroenterology agents, narcotics, neurology agents, sedatives and hypnotics, stimulants, and urology agents. Usually, a special request at additional expense must be submitted in order to test for date rape drugs like gamma-hydroxybutyric acid (GHB), flunitrazepam (Rohypnol or "roofies"), ketamine ("Special K"), and Clonazepam (a.k.a., Klonopin; another potential date rape drug used to treat seizures).

Unfortunately, most medical examiners do not test for date rape drugs because of budgetary constraints. They may order this additional testing, but only when specifically requested by the police or when a case is considered truly suspicious. However, most police and medical examiners classify drowning cases as accidents, suicides, or undetermined. That is why we have always recommended that any drowning death which is not physically or personally witnessed should be considered suspicious, and that medical examiners should be required to test for the presence of the more common date rape drugs (i.e., GHB, Rohypnol, and ketamine). In Chris' case, the Medical Examiner must have thought that the case was suspicious because he ordered liver tissue testing for GHB, Rohypnol, and Clonazepam.

We also discovered additional misinformation on the Internet about GHB. Some web sites presented that since these victims were not found for weeks or months, then drugs like GHB may not show up on a traditional toxicology screen and may be washed away with other evidence in the water. This is patently false. It is imperative to secure a body and any other physical evidence in a body bag or container on the bottom or floating where it is found since physical evidence can remain on the body (Armstrong & Erskine, 2011: Hendrick, Zaferes, & Nelson, 2003). As for GHB and other drugs, an investigator is presented with a problem much like that of alcohol. Some drugs may actually increase in measure as part of an endogenous production process associated with postmortem decomposition (NHTSA, 2012b; Nishimura, Moriya & Hashimoto, 2009). In fact, GHB and its analogs have shown up in numerous other drowning victims who were missing from as little as 5 days to as many as 118 days (and who were associated with the cases in this book).

Case in point, Chris was in the water longer than anyone else (4 months) and he still had GHB in his system. The liver tissue tests for Rohypnol and Clonazepam came back negative.

However, there were 57 micrograms per milliliter (mcg/mL) of GHB in his system at autopsy. Unlike some cases where this knowledge was buried in another report or even kept from the family and media, the Medical Examiner's autopsy report specified that the GHB was discovered by testing the liver tissue sample. This was important since liver tissue samples may generally provide more accurate test results than blood samples. GHB is an inhibitory neurotransmitter that causes memory loss and can render a victim debilitated and helpless. It can be used as a date rape drug and has a very short half-life of 18 to 60 minutes (0.3 to 1.0 hour). The specific amount of GHB in Chris (57 mcg/mL) would have rendered him in a light sleep (Figure 7.14; 52 to 156 mcg/mL = light sleep). In fact, considering that GHB has such a short half-life meant that 36 minutes to 2 hours earlier Chris could have had as much as 114 to 228 mcg/mL of GHB in his system, which would have made him considerably compliant and easy to abduct.

Given GHB's short half-life, the presence of GHB in Chris' system suggested that he died shortly after being drugged, perhaps within 1 to 2 hours. Events could have happened in one of two ways to foster a situation wherein Chris could appear at autopsy with

Gamma Hydroxybutyric Acid (GHB) Dosages & Half-Life

	DOSAGE IN MICROGRAMS	ELAPSED MINUTES	ELAPSED HOURS	
DEEP SLEEP / COMA	3,000,000	414	6.9	
	1,500,000	396	6.6	
	750,000	378	6.3	
	375,000	360	6.0	
MODERATE SLEEP	187,500	342	5.7	260 mcg/ml
LIGHT SLEEP	93,750	324 ☆	5.4	156 mcg/ml
WAKEFULNESS	46,875	306	5.1	52 mcg/ml
	23,438	288	4.8	
	11,719	270	4.5	
	5,859	252	4.2	
	2,930	234	3.9	
	1,465	216	3.6	
	732	198	3.3	
	366	180	3.0	
	183	162	2.7	
	92	144	2.4	
	46	126	2.1	
	23	108	1.8	
	11	90	1.5	
	6	72	1.2	
	3	54	0.9	
	1	36	0.6	
	1	18	0.3	
	0	0	0.0	

Typical GHB Dosage = 1 to 3 grams (1 gram = 1,000,000 micrograms)
GHB Half-Life = 18 minutes
☆ Christopher Jenkins had 57 mcg/ml of GHB at Autopsy

Figure 7.14 The level of GHB still in Chris Jenkins' system at autopsy (57 mcg/mL) would have caused him to be sleepy and very compliant with the demands of others. He would have also likely experienced some confusion and nausea.

GHB still in his system. First, presuming that he died during the early morning hours of November 1st, then he had to have been drugged, abducted and murdered within a couple hours, and then refrigerated until he was placed into the river. Or second, he could have been abducted and held, then drugged a second time in order to make his murder go more easily without a fight, and then placed into the river. Based on experience with other victims, the assailant(s) probably knew about the effects of GHB, its short half-life, and the likelihood that the medical examiner would not test for GHB. The assailant(s) may have misjudged the level of GHB in Chris' system and assessed it to be lower based on his behavior and cognitive state. At that point in time, he was suffocated without much of a fight, posed, and placed into the river.

Contrary to popular belief, GHB does not metabolize in the body during decomposition the same way alcohol does. The Medical Examiner told Chris' father (Steve Jenkins) that GHB is produced endogenously (by natural means within the body) and that it can increase a little during decomposition. However, it was at such a minute level that it could never have amounted to the 57 mcg/mL that was collected from Chris during autopsy. Some studies have shown GHB has increased by as much as 5 mcg/mL and in another study it increased by 10 mcg/mL. But in most cases, it was much less than 10 mcg/mL. Even if the GHB in Chris' system had increased by as much as 5 or 10 mcg/mL, he would still have had anywhere from 47 to 52 mcg/mL of GHB in his system when he entered the water, and double that amount (94 to 104 mcg/mL) 18 minutes to an hour earlier. The typical extent of postmortem GHB production that we have seen has been less than 5 mcg/mL.

In the Dan Zamlen case, his GHB level rose from 97 to 100 mcg/mL after a period of 1 year from the initial testing. This meant that Dan's sample of cavity blood, which was properly stored and refrigerated (40 to 44 °Fahrenheit), increased by about 1 mcg/mL for every 4 months as a result of natural postmortem GHB production. Even though Chris was assumed to have been in the river for 4 months, since he was pulled from the river covered in a piece of ice, then the extent of postmortem decomposition and endogenous GHB production would have been far less than the normal or expected amount, if any. The quantity that Chris had at autopsy was more likely the amount that he had in his system at the time of his entry into the water. Yet, if we accounted for the possible postmortem GHB production in accordance with results from Dan Zamlen's case (i.e., 1 mcg/mL for each 4 months that he was missing), then the amount that Chris may have actually had when he entered the river was likely about 56 mcg/mL.

If all of the GHB in Chris' system was caused by postmortem decomposition during his 4 months in the water, as the Medical Examiner would like to have us believe, then there should have also been other drugs present in his system. During the decomposition process, the body produces ethyl alcohol and GHB. It also produces additional amounts of n-propanol, n-butanol, isopropanol, methanol and acetone (Gilliland & Bost, 1993; Heatley & Crane, 1990; Johnson, Lewis, Angier, & Vu, 2004; Moriya & Hashimoto, 2004). There was no mention of these other drugs in Chris' body because there had been no postmortem production of them over the period of 4 months that he was in the water. This showed that the level of GHB collected from his body at autopsy was fixed at that level because it was the level at which it was when he entered the water. This meant that the measurement was a true and accurate quantification of the GHB that he had in his body when he entered the Mississippi River.

There was one other toxicological finding that told us that Chris had been abducted and held for a period of time. Actually, it was the absence of a finding that was important.

Without implicating any party, sources indicated that certain person(s) were in search of "grass" and went to Chris about 16:00 hours asking whether he had some. He did not, but stated that he would try to acquire some. We made no judgment about the morality of marijuana use. However, we surmised that Chris must have casually smoked marijuana often enough for others to assume he would be in possession of some amount. According to the literature, plasma concentrations of Delta9-tetrahydrocannabinol (THC) ranged from 7 to 18 nanograms per milliliter after even one puff or hit on a marijuana cigarette (NHTSA, 2012a). Peak plasma concentrations of THC measuring 100 to 200 nanograms per milliliter were found in habitual marijuana smokers. Although these plasma THC concentrations fell below 5 nanograms per milliliter in less than 3 hours, the elimination half-lives for plasma and urine were best estimated to be about 3 to 4 days. For infrequent or occasional users, plasma THC concentration levels fell below quantitation limits within 8 to 12 hours.

Since Chris had to go look for some marijuana at 16:00 hours, we did not know whether he found any or smoked any that night. No further mention of it was made in reports. We opined that he might have smoked some were it available at his house that evening during the keg party. Yet, we treated the matter as though he did not smoke any marijuana that night. Given the data presented in the research literature regarding THC plasma concentration levels in heavy and occasional users, we asserted that even an infrequent or casual user (which we estimated Chris to be) would produce a positive test result. The drug screens conducted on Chris' liver tissue sample and on his aortic blood sample came back negative for Cannabinoids. We concluded, therefore, that Chris either did not smoke during the 4 days prior to his abduction, or he was held alive for a period of at least 4 days, in order for the THC to clear his body.

Ocular Changes

Physical changes to the human eye following death (i.e., postmortem ocular changes) can be difficult to interpret. They can be used to some extent to determine the length of time since death (i.e., Postmortem Interval or PMI), and should always be considered as approximations. There are six anatomical features of an eye's anatomy that an investigator must know in order to correctly interpret autopsy findings (Figure 7.15). The pupil is the black center diaphragm that regulates the amount of light entering the eye. The iris (or iride) is the part that gives color to an eye. The cornea (corneas – plural) is the clear dome-shaped covering over the eye. The sclera (sclerae – plural) is the white portion of the eye. The conjunctiva (conjunctivae – plural) is the thin coating that lubricates and protects the eye. This is the component that is associated with "pink eye." It also covers the inside of the eyelids. Lastly, vitreous fluid is the liquid contained within the eye that can be used for toxicological testing.

There were four common ocular postmortem artifacts of interest in Chris' case: corneal film, corneal cloudiness, corneal opacity, and *taches noires sclérotiques* (Shkrum & Ramsay, 2007). When the eyes remain open at room temperature (68 °Fahrenheit), a thin film will appear over the cornea within 1 hour. This is followed by corneal cloudiness, which can be visible to investigators as a milky white fog over the cornea within 2 hours or less after death. Next, a dense white coating over the cornea called corneal opacity can be seen as early as 2 hours and is generally established by at least 6 hours postmortem. Because this process is affected by environmental temperature and humidity, it is typically slowed considerably when the eyes remain closed. If the eyes remain closed after death, then a film may not appear until about 6 to 12 hours. Cloudiness will take

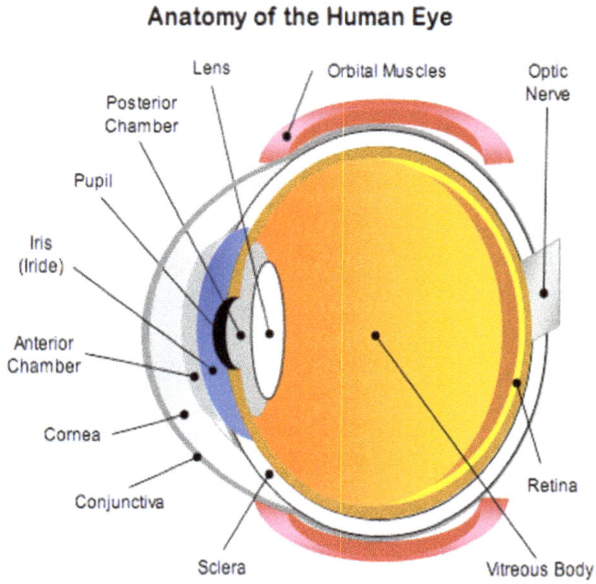

Figure 7.15 The cornea will begin to dry out after death on land. The process of corneal opacification with the eyes closed involves establishment of a film by 6 to 12 hours, cloudiness by 12 to 24 hours, and then complete opacity by the 60th hour postmortem.

approximately 12 to 24 hours to appear, followed by opacity being established by 24 to 60 hours.

Another postmortem artifact is *taches noires sclérotiques*, which is the drying of the sclera. It appears as increasing shades of tan to brown across the portion of the sclera that was exposed to air due to an open eyelid. It begins immediately and is usually quite detectable by 6 hours postmortem. It is important to note that it does not affect the cornea. If a deceased person's eyes were open, then it is possible to have corneal opacity and *tache noir*. If a deceased person's eyes were closed, then there should only be corneal opacity. If a deceased person was found with his eyes closed and both corneal opacity and *tache noir* were present, then his eyes were initially open and someone or something closed the eyelids several hours after his death. *Tache noir* on a drowning victim is a red flag for investigators since it means that the deceased person died on dry land, remained there long enough for *tache noir* to develop, and was then dumped in the water.

Forensic pathology textbooks and reference manuals typically present only the four postmortem artifacts concerning eyes that we have just discussed: corneal film, corneal cloudiness, corneal opacity, and *taches noires sclérotiques*. They are associated with whether the eyelids were open or closed, the temperature and humidity of the environment, exposure to air, and time. There is one more phenomenon that occurs which is more closely associated with decomposition. A body will produce putrefactive gases as it decomposes. Warm environments with moderate to high humidity will speed decomposition and cause gases to be produced more quickly, which causes a body to bloat (i.e., the abdomen, scrotum, face, and eyes). Very warm or cold environments (e.g., a dessert or polar region), which tend to also be very dry or arid, will slow decomposition and encourage mummification of a corpse. A final postmortem artifact that is often overlooked by investigators is that the decomposing eye may bloat or swell with fluid in a drowning scenario or damp environment. Whereas, an eye in a dry or arid environment may shrivel and wrinkle as moisture escapes it. This is a condition that affects the whole eye and should not be confused with *tache noir.*

When we looked at the Medical Examiner's description of the colors related to postmortem decomposition of Chris' eyes, we read that there was a greenish-black discoloration of the irises and a green discoloration of the sclerae. In an autopsy photograph of one of Chris' eyes, we noticed that the sclera appeared to be dark pinkish-tan, the cornea was clouded and dark, and the conjunctiva was dark pink. Both the autopsy description and our observation supported an assertion that Chris was not in the water for the whole time he was missing. Even as cold as the air and water temperatures were during the period he was missing, the level of decomposition of Chris' eyes was not representative of someone who had been in the water for 4 months. Had he been deceased for any extended period of time, then his eyes would have exhibited corneal opacity instead of just corneal cloudiness. This demonstrated that Chris was recovered within a very short time after death.

Furthermore, even though he was lying in water, Chris' cornea had begun to wrinkle as though it had been exposed to dry air and losing moisture. Given this last artifact and knowing that he was found lying in water, we could only conclude that he had been exposed to a warmer and dryer environment for a period of time after death and prior to being found in the river. Additionally, Chris' eyes were free of injury and petechiae, which meant that he was not strangled. Petechiae are the small red to reddish-purple spots that form as a result of the rupture of blood vessels within the eyes. They will typically develop when a victim was strangled.

Decomposition and Maceration

One of the first signs of decomposition is a green (blue-green) discoloration of the skin (DiMaio & DiMaio, 2001), which usually starts in the right lower quadrant (RLQ) of the abdomen within the first 12 hours on land (24 in water). It spreads to the entire body within 24 hours (48 in water) of death; and presents as dark green, dark red, and dark purple within 24 to 36 hours on land (48 to 72 in water). The next stage is called "marbling," which usually appears postmortem around 36 to 48 hours on land (72 to 96 in water) and ranges in color from dark yellow, to orange, to dark red. A common characteristic of marbling is the dark purple appearance of the veins below the skin surface. About this same time, the body will begin to bloat from decomposition gases. The first indications will present in the scrotum, then abdomen, face and eyes. By 72 hours after death, decomposition on land will have consumed the entire body and the purging of fluids from the body may be evident around orifices (Spitz & Spitz, 2006).

Maceration of a corpse also occurs in stages and can indicate time of death. As a body decays, it starts to fall apart. It may start by loosing skin and hair, then mass, and then bones. On land, skin will start to come loose from a body ("skin slippage") after about 48 to 96 hours postmortem and should be apparent over major portions of a body by 96 to 168 hours postmortem (Armstrong & Erskine, 2011). It is usually most visible on the chest and abdomen, back, front and back of legs, and the face. The scalp will typically lose hair during this time too. Much like a glove, the skin on the palms of the hands and soles of the feet will eventually shed; this is referred to as "degloving" (Geberth, 2006). The onset of degloving of exposed skin on land typically occurs at about 72 to 96 hours (3 to 4 days), with completion around 144 to 168 hours (6 to 7 days) after death.

Although water may retard the decomposition process and cause it to take twice as long when compared to a body on land, it may actually have no affect on the timetable associated with maceration or may even accelerate certain aspects of it. In many cases, water may hasten skin slippage. Since water softens skin tissue, it shortens the amount of time required to advance toward complete degloving. The degloving process often occurs more quickly in water and begins when the hands show signs of mild maceration known as *Wauschaut* ("Washerwoman's Hands") within an hour after immersion. It may be possible to have signs of skin slippage on exposed skin sooner than one would expect. On land, the early signs of skin slippage usually appear anywhere between 48 to 96 hours. In the water, this would probably be closer to the 48-hour mark.

For example, if a person died outdoors on dry land during early November in a northern Midwest state, then 48 hours after death, an investigator would expect to see indications of bloating with extensive marbling combined with greens and reds across the whole abdomen and body, as well as early signs of skin slippage. However, if this body had fallen into the water, then the low temperature of the water coupled with the cooling properties of the water will have slowed decomposition, while the softening affects of the water will have maintained a steady rate of maceration (or may have even accelerated it). Therefore, an investigator may likely encounter only signs of early decomposition in the RLQ (some blues and greens typically seen at 24 hours on land) along with early signs of skin slippage (typically seen at 48 hours on land). This is why confusion can often set in. It is imperative for investigators to keep in mind that there are two timetables running concurrently here, one for decomposition (i.e., bacterial putrefaction & enzymatic autolysis) and another for maceration. This becomes even more complex when incorporating the timetables for tepidity, lividity, rigidity, ocular changes, and anthropophagy (Appendix D).

Chris was last seen at about 00:40 hours on November 1, 2002. According to the accidental drowning hypothesis offered by authorities in Minneapolis, a person could propose that Chris died shortly thereafter and no later than about 01:00 hours on November 1, 2002. He was recovered at about 18:15 hours on February 27, 2003. He was autopsied at 09:00 hours on February 28, 2003. Therefore, Chris was missing and presumed to be in the water the bulk of 118 days 17 hours 15 minutes (2,849 hours 15 minutes). It was an additional 14 hours 45 minutes between recovery and autopsy. So, Chris may be presumed deceased for a total of 119 days 8 hours (2,864 hours). As we have noted in other chapters, a body decomposes at half the rate (a delay ratio of 2:1) in water when compared to on land (Armstrong & Erskine, 2011). We have also noted that bodies which have been in water or frozen tend to decompose more quickly after recovery (Shkrum & Ramsay, 2007). Given all things equal, then the extent of decomposition presented in Chris' body at autopsy should have been about the same as a body on land after 59 days 16 hours (1,432 hours). In other words, decomposition and maceration should have been relatively advanced in either time span (i.e., 2,864 hours or 1,432 hours).

The Medical Examiner estimated the extent of decomposition to have reached a moderate state. He qualified this assessment in his description of Chris at autopsy. Relative to the color of decomposition, Chris presented with a generalized green skin color across his entire body. Although no mention of marbling was made in the autopsy report, we could see that his forearms presented with what appeared to be early marbling. The areas of skin that were unprotected by clothing or were not submerged in the water were documented as having appeared green-black-brown (left side of his face) and as black-brown (dorsum or back of the hands). The description of the palms of his hands reflected the characteristic wrinkled, white skin of "Washerwoman's Hands" with only partial degloving. Extensive skin slippage was recorded to have occurred. The Medical Examiner noted hair loss on the back of the head in two areas: the occipital scalp, which is near the base of the skull, and just above it in the parietal scalp. Putrefactive gases had started to bloat Chris' face, genitals, and abdomen.

The extent of decomposition with which Chris' body presented at the time of autopsy was inconsistent with the 119.3 days (2,864 hours) that he had been presumed deceased. Even after taking into consideration that this case involved both water and a Minnesota winter (two factors that could definitely delay timetables), the condition of Chris' body was a lot better than we would have expected to see. Decomposition should have been more extensive after 4 months in the water compared to what it was. It should have progressed a lot further than to the extent to which it had. Decomposition of Chris' body reflected about 2 to 2.5 days (48 to 60 hours) postmortem on land. Using a delay ratio of 2:1 for decomposition in water as compared to land, this would have extended time estimates out to about 4 to 5 days (96 to 120 hours) in the water. Even if we gave the greatest benefit of a doubt and multiplied the delaying affect of water and cold weather by an unreasonable factor of 10 (i.e., a delay ratio of 10:1 for water compared to land), then Chris' decomposition would have still only resembled that of someone who had been deceased and in cold river water for 20 to 25 days (480 to 600 hours). That meant that 94.3 to 99.3 days (2,264 to 2,384 hours) were still unaccounted for by the accident hypothesis.

Also, the amount of maceration (especially, skin slippage and degloving) recorded by the Medical Examiner suggested that Chris was not in the water for the whole period of time that he was missing, much less deceased for that whole timeframe. The autopsy stated that Chris' hands and feet only showed skin wrinkling and that there was only partial degloving. This clearly reflected approximately a period of 72 to 120 hours after death. The skin on the hands and feet of a body that had been, presumably, in water for about 2,849 hours should have been completely degloved. In fact, so much time would have elapsed that the skin from the hands would have even likely washed away downstream. As with decomposition, the state of Chris' maceration could not account for the entire period of time that he was missing. However, the extent of decomposition after adjusting for water and cold temperatures (i.e., 96 to 120 hours) coincided with the extent of maceration (i.e., 72 to 120 hours), and corroborated our analysis of timetables. We concluded that this evidence confirmed that Chris truly was murdered and that this was what police call a "staged scene."

Anthropophagy

The Medical Examiner described Chris as presenting with small lesions and burrows, some that exposed the subcutaneous fat. The larger lesion on his left temple was oval in shape and measured 0.9 centimeters by 0.8 centimeters (about 1/3 inch by 1/3 inch). There were numerous smaller lesions that measured 0.2 centimeters by 0.4 centimeters (just slightly larger than 1/16 inch by 2/16 inch) on his upper arms, back, and the backside of his legs. The Medical Examiner stated that these wounds were consistent in appearance with postmortem anthropophagy (i.e., insect or animal predation or eating of the corpse).

This evidence should have been an overhead flare in the night sky for investigators. Fish and crayfish do not create lesions and wounds that appear as small oval burrows when they feed on human corpses submerged in their watery habitat. There were only a few insects that could have caused that kind of wound, and neither insect would have been active outdoors at that time of the year in Minnesota and in those wintery temperatures. Furthermore, we opined that it was an impossibility for insects to have made the lesions on Chris' body after he entered the water. If Chris had fallen into the Mississippi River and then died as proposed by adherents to the accidental death hypothesis, then that meant that the insects had to have been active underwater in order to cause the burrowed lesions on the posterior of Chris' legs and back since he was found floating on his back. However, the two species of insects that we were aware of that make that kind of burrowing lesion were not aquatic. That demonstrated that the insects had to have found his corpse and began their work on land in a warm place (likely an enclosed building) before being placed into the water with him. That was the only logical way for them to find his body, crawl under his clothing, burrow under his skin to create the lesions, before he was thrown into the river.

The Medical Examiner collected and vouchered (i.e., labeled and placed in plastic evidence envelopes) samples of the mud, fingernail clippings, hair extracted from the scalp, as well as various specimens from internal organs. No description of the insects was offered by the attending pathologist, Dr. Rivera. Even though he succinctly identified the lesions as anthropophagy and described their size, no specimens of the insects were collected so they could be taken to a forensic entomologist in order to identify the species and to determine their stage in life. That analysis could have contributed to a better understanding of the postmortem interval (PMI) and how long Chris was deceased on land before being placed into the Mississippi River.

Foreign Matter

In April 2006, Gannon and Duarte met with Steve and Jan Jenkins in Minnesota to discuss their son's case. On June 29, 2006, Gannon received and e-mail from Jan asking him to take a look at one of Chris' autopsy photographs that a family friend (Gary Huber) had enlarged. To that date, Gannon and Duarte had only been shown the body recovery pictures. Gary, who was a neighbor, had asked Steve Jenkins one day how the investigation was going. Steve replied by telling him how difficult things were with the police, and that the family felt that nothing seemed to fit correctly with Chris' case. The Jenkins informed Gannon that Gary was a professor of mortuary science and had been involved in thousands of autopsies and was willing to look at the autopsy photographs for them. No one was prepared for what Gary had uncovered. He had enlarged one of the autopsy photographs to focus on Chris' slightly open left hand. Jan Jenkins e-mailed that picture to Gannon on June 29, 2006. Gannon was stunned. There, in plain sight, was what appeared to be strands of wet, matted, dirty blonde or light brown human hair in Chris' hand.

Keep in mind that this event (the discovery of the hair in Chris' hand) took place in June 2006, about 40 months after his body had been recovered and autopsied. Had it been tested? Where was it now? Had MPD investigators and the Medical Examiner truly missed this important evidence during the autopsy? Even though the autopsy report contained precise descriptions of all other vouchered evidence, there was no mention of finding hair in Chris' hand. The Medical Examiner, Dr. Rivera, wrote in the autopsy report that he had vouchered foreign matter that was found clinging to Chris' body. Since he never provided a description of the foreign matter, and never used a different term to refer to it somewhere else in a report, and never mentioned what part of the body it had been recovered from, we could not assess whether or not this was an attempt to document the hair.

Obviously, any foreign matter found on a corpse should be vouchered due to its potential value as investigatory evidence. This should have been a major red flag to everyone in the autopsy room, especially when the foreign matter was hair that came from inside the closed fist of the decedent who was found floating on his back in a posed position. Chris was postured much like one would expect to see a body in a casket. His clutched left hand containing the hair rested on the center of his chest, while the right hand was placed such that it clasped the left wrist and held the left arm firmly against the chest. Of course, there was no further mention of this material or any reference to test results in either the police, autopsy or toxicology reports.

Gannon then asked Jan, "Is this material (hair) even still available to be tested?" The report suggested that it had been put into a sealed envelope. But, we did not know whether it was still available since so much time had passed. Had it been destroyed in accordance with department guidelines for the preservation and maintenance of evidence? This was important and something we needed to find out quickly. Gannon then e-mailed the picture to the rest of the team and got the same response from everyone. Duarte, Gilbertson, and Carlson could not believe what they saw, and the first question out of their mouths was always, "Has it been tested?"

Jan then asked Gannon how something like this could have happened, and how and from where did Chris get the hair in his hand? Gannon shared his professional assessment with her. In his opinion, there were only three ways that this could have possibly happened. Either way, it provided further evidence that Chris had been murdered and also showed the possibility that he may have been fighting for his life before he drowned.

1. The simplest explanation was that it was intentionally placed there. The person(s) responsible for Chris' abduction and murder could have placed some hair in his left hand, closed his hand tightly, posed his arms across his chest, waited for rigor mortis to set in, and then slid him into the river.
2. Another explanation for the hair in the hands was that while the assailant(s) attempted to drown Chris, he fought vehemently for his life. While the attacker(s) forcibly held him face-down in the water to drown him, Chris reached back in an attempt to remove the hands of his murderer(s) from his head and neck. He inadvertently pulled some hair from his own head during the struggle. He may have had a cadaveric spasm upon the moment of death, which would instantaneously locked the hair into his own hand.
3. The last explanation for the hair in the hands was that Chris fought ferociously to ward off the assailant(s). Chris reached out and inadvertently pulled some hair from the head of the assailant(s) during the struggle. A cadaveric spasm subsequently locked the hair in the grasp of his own hand.

A cadaveric spasm is the stiffening and rigidity of a single group of muscles occurring immediately after death; instantaneous rigor mortis as it were (Geberth, 2006). This is the incident portrayed in movies where a victim's hand is locked around a gun or knife, and has to be pried open, or at times the fingers broken, in order to release the muscles and to obtain the weapon from the victim. It is often referred to as a "death grip." It was illogical that Chris could have pulled some of his own hair while accidentally drowning and then had a cadaveric spasm. First, this would have required instantaneous death and would not have explained how his arms ended up back across his chest. Second, if his thrashing about in the river was so violent that he pulled some of his own hair, then his costume would have become untucked and his shoes would have come off his feet. This meant that the hair in Chris' left hand and the posturing of his arms had to have been the result of a controlled event involving human interaction.

The Medical Examiner had collected and vouchered hair samples from the top of Chris' head and reported their length in the autopsy report as 4 centimeters (about 1.57 inches). Chris kept his hair short. This was evidenced by testimony from his family and pictures of him, including the photograph taken that night at the Lone Tree Bar and Grill (Figure 7.1). Using the forensic scale in the autopsy picture, we estimated that the hair in Chris' left hand appeared to be a lot longer than the hair on his head; perhaps as long a 3 inches or more. If this were the case, then the hair in his left hand may have been purposely placed there by the murderer(s) as taunting of the police and the forensics community. Perhaps, the mindset of the killer(s) was such that evidence was left for the police to find:

a. knowing that they would never discover it right in plain sight, or
b. knowing that they would never find it because they would not look for it, or
c. knowing that they would find it and then do nothing with it.

Another question needed to be answered: Whose hair was it anyway? Was it Chris' hair or was it from someone else? Had investigators tested it and discovered that it was from yet another victim, then that would have definitely been a way to taunt the authorities.

Now, the hair had been collected and vouchered on February 28, 2003. It was discovered and reported to the family for the first time 40 months later in June 2006. We continued to support the Jenkins in their quest and to pressure local authorities to test the hair from Chris' left hand in an attempt to identify its owner. It took another 16 months (until December 2007) to get the authorities to test the hair. We finally received the test results nearly 2.5 years later during an exchange of e-mails between Gannon and Jan Jenkins during the period of July 12 to July 24, 2010. Jan informed us that she had been told that Mitochondrial DNA (mtDNA) had been used to identify the hair as belonging to Chris. They tested the hair from Chris' left hand and compared it with the hair specimen collected from the top of his head at autopsy.

All humans have coded hereditary material called deoxyribonucleic acid (DNA) (National Library of Medicine, 2011b). The classic DNA double helix looks like a twisting ladder. It is built from two spiraling strands of nucleotides, which are made up of a base, a sugar molecule, and a phosphate molecule. DNA has 4 chemical bases: Adenine (A), Guanine (G), Cytosine (C), and Thymine (T). There are about 3 billion bases in human DNA (National Human Genome Research Institute, 2012a). The chemical bases form up in pairs ("base pairs"). More than 99 percent of those bases are the same in all people. Even though it is only about 1 percent that makes each human unique, that small percent can be used to identify us (Biological and Environmental Research Information System, 2009).

There are several forms of genetic material. The genetic material that is traditionally used in court as evidence comes from one's father, and is often called Y-DNA. There is also mitochondrial DNA (mtDNA) which comes from one's mother (National Human Genome Research Institute, 2012b; National Library of Medicine, 2011a). When the DNA material that was collected as evidence is insufficient for testing or has been damaged, then mtDNA can be used. In fact, over a dozen states have accepted mtDNA into evidence in court cases (Kreeger & Weiss, 2003; National Commission on the Future of DNA Evidence, 2002).

However, the mtDNA of two sisters will be identical (FBI DNA Analysis Unit II, 2012; Isenberg, 2002). The mtDNA of a son and his father will be the same. Only Y-DNA is unique to an individual. Mitochondrial DNA traces the genetic lineage through mothers back in time. These are organized into haplogroups. A test for mtDNA will tell a medical examiner from which haplogroup a person's genetic material descended. Within a region of a continent, thousands of individuals will have the same mtDNA, but each will have an unique Y-DNA. As such, mtDNA cannot be used to specifically identify a piece of genetic material as coming from a specific individual (Fourney, 1998; Linch, Whiting, & Holland, 2001). Only Y-DNA can do that. It was for that reason, that we expressed our opinion to the Jenkins family that this was not a definitive DNA test. Anyone of similar ancestry could potentially be from the same haplogroup as Chris and possess the same mtDNA. We encouraged them to have the hair retested for Y-DNA. To the best of our knowledge, the hair was never tested again.

Conclusion

We believe from the evidence that we have uncovered, that Chris Jenkins was definitely murdered. Specifically, he was drugged with GHB, abducted near the Lone Tree Bar and Grill, held for a period of time, suffocated, posed on his back with his hands placed across his chest, and then slid into the Mississippi River on his back north of the Father Louis Hennepin Bridge.

Chris was drugged. The police investigation into Chris' death centered on activity at the Lone Tree Bar and Grill. However, some documents that we reviewed suggested that at some point during the evening he had gone over to Brothers Bar and Grill (which was 1 block north through a parking lot) and then returned to the Lone Tree Bar and Grill where he continued to drink. Photographs of Chris that were taken that night right before he was escorted out of the Lone Tree (e.g., Figure 7.1), as well as statements made by those in contact with him that night, clearly indicated that he was extremely intoxicated. He was staggering and slurring his speech. Yet, the toxicology report revealed that Chris incredibly ended up with only an estimated actual 0.060 BAC (about 3 drinks) at the time of his death after accounting for postmortem alcohol production. It also showed that there was no THC in his system, but he did have 57 mcg/mL of GHB in him. Where he received a dose of the date rape drug is a question for law enforcement to figure out. The fact remained that Chris had a nonrecreational drug in him, which is typically used to facilitate the involuntary date rape of females.

Chris was not deceased the entire time he was missing. The condition of Chris' body at autopsy indicated that he had been deceased on land for a period of time before entering the water. Although he had been missing and presumed deceased for 119 days 8 hours (2,864 hours), his eyes evidenced clouding and drying, and had not swollen to the extent that they should have due to decomposition and exposure to the water. The color and condition of his body due to decomposition was not as advanced as one would expect to see. At autopsy, the extent of decomposition presented in Chris' body should have been about the same as a body on land after 59 days 16 hours (1,432 hours). However, it only showed signs of early marbling, which was equivalent to about 36 to 48 hours on land. Additional evidence also pointed to a short timetable. None of the evidence indicated that Chris had been deceased for the entire time that he had been missing. The bruises that he always had from playing lacrosse were healed, which suggested that he had been held for at least 3 to 4 days before being killed. The stomach was empty and the gallbladder was also empty, which meant that he probably died within 3–5 hours after his last meal.

Chris died indoors and on land. The head position, body position, and body posture at recovery, were consistent with a death on land. When a person dies lying face-up on land, his head will often tilt to one side. Whereas, a drowning victim will usually float face-down and the head will remain pointed straight ahead. Chris' head was tilted to his right. Recorded evidence of rigidity and lividity did not provide any additional clues to position or posture. Insects burrowed their way into his body. This could not have happened in the water. It could not have happened outdoors in those temperatures at that time of the year in Minnesota. That proved that Chris had to have been deceased on land and indoors for a sufficient period of time for the insects to find his body. This also meant that his death and presence in the river was no accident.

Chris did not drown – he was suffocated. The light weight of his lungs, the absence of a pinkish froth in his trachea, and no pleural effusion of any kind whatsoever, indicated that neither a wet or dry drowning had taken place. When we considered the lack of injuries, specifically subcutaneous injuries, then we came to a realization that a struggle had not transpired. This told us that Chris was murdered using a form of suffocation that did not involve a fight for his life and the horrific gasping for air like in a manual strangulation. He could have been murdered using a less combative form of suffocation that involves placing a bag over a sedated victim's head. The oxygen contained within the bag is gradually replaced with carbon dioxide and leads to respiration failure and death. Chris had 57 mcg/mL of GHB in his system at autopsy, which meant that just 36 minutes to 2 hours earlier the level of GHB could have been as much as 228 mcg/mL. Since this procedure probably took longer than 36 minutes, Chris would have been in a definite state of relaxation and confusion. He would have quietly laid there, consuming all the oxygen in the bag until his body shut down. There would have been no struggle, or signs associated with such, which would suit the murderers' purpose (i.e., an intoxicated male with no signs of foul play).

The hair in his hand did not resemble the hair on his head. To begin with, it was too long to be Chris'. Furthermore, investigators did not prove beyond any margin of doubt that it was Chris' hair, since they did not use the correct kind of DNA in their comparative analysis. They used the mitochondrial DNA from the mother (which identifies the continental region of origin for a groups of people) rather the DNA from the father (which identifies individuals). The evidence told us that only a scenario which involved human intervention could have led to his death. The hair was placed in his hand and his arms crossed over his body shortly after he was deceased.

Chris did not fall into the river from a bridge. His slip-on, clog-type shoes would have come off his feet during the fall or upon impact with the water's surface. Had he fallen into the river from a bridge and then acquired the mud from the river bottom, then he certainly would not have been recovered in the unnatural posture that he was (i.e., floating on his back with his legs straight and arms crossed). Drowning victims are normally found floating face-down with their arms out in front of them. On the rare occasion that a victim is recovered floating on his back, then the arms are generally extended out to the side – not crossed over the chest. In fresh water, the body typically floats just below the surface. It will float higher in salt water. Whether floating face-up or face-down, the posture of the body while floating would place both hands underwater and protect them from the air.

Chris' right hand was desiccated. Butch Hendrick and Andrea Zafares (Lifeguard Systems, Inc.) shared photographs of Chris' hands with some forensic pathologists. They all agreed that in order for his right hand to be dried out while his left hand was not, then his right hand had to have been exposed to air while his left hand was protected by something. Since deceased bodies do not float on their sides, this told us that Chris was most likely very close to shore, lying on his back with only half of his body exposed to the air. He had to have entered the water at the river bank. We conclude that he picked up the mud from the river bank during the process of being placed into the Mississippi River. Chris was slid into the river on his back, which accounts for his body posture in the river as well as the mud on his person and in his hair. As could be seen in the recovery photos, the left side of his body was encrusted with ice and snow. Since the river had thawed and was open at the time of recovery while snow and ice remained along the river banks, this told us that Chris' deceased body had dislodged from the edge of the river where his killer(s) had left it. There were other clues that supported this finding.

Chris was most likely entered into the water north of the Father Louis Hennepin Bridge. The K-9 searches clearly demonstrated that Chris' scent went from the Lone Tree Bar and Grill to the vicinity of stalls #89 and #90 in the Plymouth Parking Ramp, then by vehicle to I-94 northbound. His scent was also picked up under the north end of the Father Louis Hennepin Bridge where the bloodhound essentially did a "trauma roll" hit and continuously howled. However, there was no feasible way for a body to enter the water there and to float to the location where Chris' body was recovered. This suggested to us that he had probably been temporarily taken to that spot and tormented or tortured there. The currents and eddy formed by Nicollet Island and the Horseshoe Dam told us that in order for Chris' body to reach its final resting spot, it could not have floated down the west side of Nicollet Island in the main channel of the Mississippi River. Rather, it had to have floated down the eastern channel along Nicollet Island. This suggested that Chris was placed into the water along the eastern channel at a location that offered easy on-foot access to the river bank. We found such a site at the south end of the Boom Island Park.

Even though Chris was dead before entry into the river and as such did not sink, he was not spotted immediately by passersby. His murderer(s) probably presumed that his death would be judged an accidental drowning no matter where his body was recovered in or along the river. Therefore, they were not concerned with hiding him. While attempting to slide him into the river, the mud most likely prevented the assailant(s) from getting him far enough out into the water. Not wanting to end up in the icy waters too, the killer(s) left Chris' body in the mud next to a pile of fallen tree branches at a relatively secluded location along the Boom Island Park. He was most likely placed into the river during the thaw between January 31st and February 2nd, and then became fixed to the debris when the river refroze. As spring thaw opened up the river and the water level rose, his body and the debris thawed out and dislodged from their position along the river bank. Chris' body and the debris then floated down the eastern channel along Nicollet Island to the recovery site below the Third Avenue Bridge. His body was recovered on February 27, 2002. Therefore, although Chris was in the water for 24 to 27 days, his body presented with decomposition and maceration that was consistent with 4 to 5 days due to the ice in which he had become trapped and the coldness of the water. His death was originally labeled an accidental drowning. As far as anyone in the Jenkins family or the public knows, no further investigation has taken place regarding Chris' death even though the status of his case was changed to "homicide" on November 21, 2006.

Jelani Dante Brinson*

8

Background

Jelani Brinson was a wonderful young man who was not ashamed to tell others about his love for Jesus Christ and his family. He had great hope for humanity and openly advocated diversity issues. Although he was raised Catholic, he was very active in a nondenominational church and had graduated from Fourth Baptist Christian School in north Minneapolis in 2003. He was very athletic. Not only did he enjoy playing soccer, he was good at it. In 2004, during the 1/2 year that he was at Faith Baptist Bible College (Ankeny, Iowa), he was listed as an Honorable Mention All-American in the National Christian College Athletic Association (NCCAA) Men's Division II (Figure 8.1). Jelani had also attended emergency medical technician training at Hennepin Technical College, and was most recently attending Crown College in Saint Bonifacius, Minnesota, where he was a solid B student.

He greatly respected his parents Donnie Brinson and Alyce Hamilton, who were divorced at the time. His mother is an emergency room doctor at a major hospital in the Twin Cities. He and his girlfriend had already had a daughter whom they named from the Old Testament. Jelani loved them both deeply and often spoke about marriage. Although they lived apart, he routinely took care of his daughter 2 to 3 days during the week. The day before his body was recovered in April 2009, his girlfriend learned that she was expecting. A son was born in December 2009 and named in honor of his ancestry. Jelani had worked for the Sprint Corporation for 5 years and had recently been promoted and received a raise in pay. He was working as a sales consultant on the floor at the stores on Jolly Lane and Colorado Lane in Brooklyn Park. His promotion moved him to the Edina store. One day

* Photo courtesy of his parents, Alyce Hamilton & Donnie Brinson.

Figure 8.1 Soccer was one of Jelani Brinson's passions. (Photo courtesy of his parents, Alyce Hamilton and Donnie Brinson.)

while he was at work in Edina and his car sat in the parking lot, the tires on Jelani's car had been slashed.

The family contacted us in late September 2009. On October 9th, Gilbertson met at the Anoka County Sheriff's Office with Alyce Hamilton and Mamie Singleton (Jelani's godmother and a retired police detective). They spoke with Detective Dan Douglas, who was very open during the meeting, sharing his knowledge of the case material and his concerns about the evidence. We were not allowed to retain copies of any reports at that time since this was still an open investigation. Gilbertson continued to meet with the family and assisted them with obtaining a copy of the autopsy report and photographs. We strongly advocate that victims or surviving family members should receive one free copy of autopsy materials upon request due to their cost. When Gilbertson contacted the Anoka County Medical Examiner's Officer, he discovered that there were 227 photos, which would have cost the family $544.39 including all fees and taxes. He arranged to preview all of the photos on November 18th and to pay for only those that were selected (n = 46). Prior to leaving that day, he had an opportunity to go through the photos with the Medical Examiner who performed the autopsy (Dr. Janis Amatuzio) and learned that they shared many of the same interpretations of the forensic evidence. Between January and March 2010, Gannon and Gilbertson helped the family to contact producers from America's Most Wanted, as well as technicians from viaForensics to have Jelani's cellular telephone examined.

Circumstances

Last Seen

Jelani Dante Brinson was an African-American male, 24 years old at the time of his disappearance, 5 feet 10 inches, 167 pounds (Body Mass Index 23.96), black hair and brown eyes. Jelani was seen in five different locations on the night he disappeared. His evening (April

17, 2009) started at his father's home in north Minneapolis, where the two of them were taking care of Jelani's daughter. Around 19:30 hours, Jelani arrived at Mad Jack's Sports Café in Brooklyn Park, where he was seen by a group of girls that he went to meet. He then met a colleague from the Sprint store on Jolly Lane at about 20:00 hours and the two of them went over to another Sprint store on Colorado Lane, where he talked to two other coworkers. Next, at about 20:30 hours, Jelani briefly interacted with his younger brother at his home in Brooklyn Park. He then returned home to his father's place and played with his daughter for a while. At approximately 21:00 hours, he left there to go visit with the girls some more (Figure 8.2, *Blue Dotted Line*). They had moved to Victory Grill on Colorado Lane, which was near the Sprint store. According to witnesses, he never made it there. Instead, Jelani ended up at a house party in Anoka (Figure 8.2, *Green Arrowed Line*; Figure 8.3). Present at the party were 2 coworkers and a brother of one of them. According to them, Jelani arrived at the party around 22:00 hours. Shortly thereafter, he received a phone call and abruptly left the house. They went outside about 5 minutes later to look for him when he did not return. So, by their estimates, Jelani was last seen about 22:05 hours on Friday, April 17, 2009.

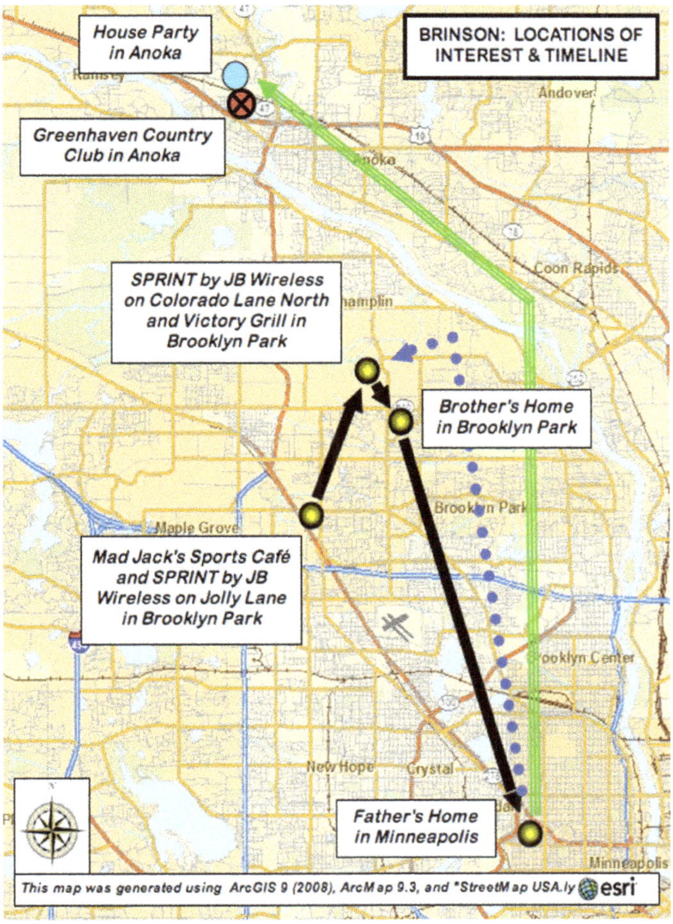

Figure 8.2 On the evening of April 17, 2009, Jelani Brinson was constantly moving and seen in numerous locations by multiple people, then he suddenly dropped off the radar.

Figure 8.3 Jelani Brinson was last seen at this home in Anoka at about 22:05 hours, Friday, April 17, 2009.

Figure 8.4 Jelani Brinson was recovered from this pond at Green Haven Golf Course in Anoka at about 13:30 hours, Saturday, April 25, 2009.

Recovery

On Saturday, April 25, 2009, "Bob" was playing golf at Green Haven Golf Course in Anoka. He was an employee there and it was his day off. At about 13:04 hours, he noticed something floating in the middle of the large pond on the west side of the clubhouse between holes 10, 11, and 18 (Figure 8.4). He went to take a closer look and discovered that it was a body. Bob immediately called 911. Law enforcement arrived and found Jelani floating supine (on his back) in approximately 2 to 3 feet of water. He was found with his face exposed above the water and his right hand sticking up out of the water. The back nine holes were temporarily closed for about an hour while officials recovered Jelani's body. They marked the spot where he was found with a metal rod.

Analysis of Evidence

Timeline

Spatio-temporal analysis of events for April 17, 2009, disclosed conflicts in witnesses' statements and engendered additional questions. In other words, a quick review of events and locations seemed to fall into order quite well: Event A, then B and C, and so forth. However, the order of events, the timing of events, and the location of events and actors on that Friday evening, as well as Jelani's reported behavior, just did not make any sense to us. Once we analyzed the proposed timeline and kept track of who was supposed to be where and when with whom, then things started to unravel (Figure 8.2).

19:00 hours: The evening started out in north Minneapolis at Donnie Brinson's home where Jelani lived. His daughter was over for the night. Jelani was supposed to meet some girls he knew at Mad Jack's Sports Café (8070 Brooklyn Boulevard, Brooklyn Park) at 19:00 hours. He arrived there at about 19:30 hours and stayed for 1/2 hour. While he was there, he called his mother (Alyce), who coincidentally was also there. Yet, she did not hear her phone ring due to the noise level and the two did not see each other.

20:00 hours: An ATM transaction in Brooklyn Park was recorded on Jelani's debit card. He went over to the Sprint store that was nearby (7639 Jolly Lane, Brooklyn Park). He picked up a colleague from work ("Edgar") who punched out at 20:10 hours. The two of them then drove over to the other JB Wireless Sprint store (9634 Colorado Lane, Brooklyn Park) to meet a third colleague ("Mark"). Another co-worker ("Lorraine") stated that they came into the store around closing time. Jelani stayed there briefly and then left. He stopped by his brother's residence in Brooklyn Park around 20:30 hours. Jelani asked him whether he wanted to go with him to a party at Edgar's house. He told him that they would be smoking marijuana there. His brother declined and tried to convince him not to go. Next, Jelani went back at his dad's house and played with his daughter.

21:00 hours: Jelani asked his father to watch his daughter for a bit because he wanted to go back and visit with the girls some more. Donnie really liked a particular dish that the restaurant prepared, so he asked Jelani to bring an order "to-go" back for him. Jelani agreed to do that for his dad. Jelani called his mom at 21:18 hours, but made no contact. At 21:21 hours, Jelani sent the last text message recorded on his phone. Around 21:30 hours, Donnie looked out the window and saw Jelani sitting in his car along the curb holding his cellular phone. During this same time period, the girls had left Mad Jack's Sports Café and driven over to Victory Grill (9690 Colorado Lane, Brooklyn Park), which was near the Sprint store on Colorado Lane. The girls stayed there from 21:00 to 23:00 hours. While the girls were there, Jelani's brother and a friend of his stopped by Victory Grill. They asked where Jelani was and no one had seen him there. At 21:48 hours, Jelani made his last *facebook* entry on his account. He wrote, "expect the unexpected."

22:00 hours: According to those individuals who were present at the house party in Anoka, Jelani arrived around 22:00 hours. The house was rented by a coworker at the Sprint stores in Brooklyn Park (Mark). Mark's half-brother ("Dick") lived with him. Statements to investigators indicated that one of the activities was to be smoking marijuana. The story was that Jelani received a cell phone call at about 22:05 hours that seemed to upset him. He left the house through the front door. He supposedly went outside to smoke a cigarette. At 22:10 hours, when Jelani did not come back into the house, the three of them went to look for him on foot throughout the nearby yards. Dick told investigators that he was in the basement at the time of Jelani's arrival. But, he did see Jelani leave out the front door and run southbound.

That is why they went off on foot in that direction to look for Jelani. Alyce returned her son's earlier phone call at 22:20 hours, but made no contact. At that time, the three guys from the house party claimed that they were still walking around the neighborhood looking for Jelani. They even told investigators that they went out driving around looking for Jelani that night. He was never seen alive again.

23:00 hours: The last call made from Jelani's cell phone was at about 23:00 hours on the night he disappeared (April 17, 2009, Friday) to another cell phone whose signal was transmitted via the tower located near geodecimal coordinates 44.7713 (west), –93.8121 (north), which was about 30 miles southwest from the house in Anoka. The tower (federal antenna structure registration number 1212287) was owned by STC Five LLC (Sprint) and had a height of 250 feet above the ground. It was located next to the Carver County Soil and Water building at 11360 Highway 212 in Cologne. Given the tower's location and height, and the surrounding terrain, a signal could have easily reached out about 10 miles. Sprint pinged Jelani's cell phone at 00:57 hours on April 19, 2009 (Sunday), and it was not returned.

To begin with, Jelani's behavior was erratic that evening. If everyone's accounting of time and Jelani's whereabouts was correct, then he was flitting around like a bee in a clover field. He could not have spent any appreciable amount of time at any one location. If one considers that he arrived at Mad Jack's around 19:30 hours and then arrived at the house party at about 22:00 hours, then that amounted to 2.5 hours or 150 minutes of time within which to go to all the places he was reported to have been. As can be seen (Figure 8.5), there just was not much time for any one person or activity in his life that evening.

Assuming knowledge of the area and the location of road construction, and using the shortest distances possible on surface roads, and accounting for speed limits, vehicle traffic and traffic lights, Jelani would have driven about 35.2 miles. We have personally driven these routes and verified the data. If only 150 minutes were available that night within which to drive and 95 minutes were spent driving, then Jelani would have had only 55 minutes to be physically present at all of those locations. This estimate did not include time to get in and out of his vehicle, to park it, or to walk up to each location from his

Brinson: Estimated Driving Distances and Times Based on Information from Interviews

LOCATION	MILES	MINS.
Mad Jack's - Sprint on Jolly	*0.3*	3
Sprint on Jolly - Sprint on Colorado	*4.1*	12
Sprint on Colorado - Jelani's Brother	*1.3*	5
Jelani's Brother - Donnie's	*10.0*	25
Donnie's - Victory Grill	*11.7*	30
Victory Grill - House Party	*7.8*	20
Estimated Miles Driven	*35.2*	
Estimated Minutes Spent Driving		95

Figure 8.5 Jelani Brinson would have driven 35.2 miles and spent 95 minutes of a possible 150 minutes driving back-and-forth on the evening of April 17, 2009.

parked car. This may sound like a trivial analysis, but each second added up to numerous minutes. Jelani would have literally been in-and-out of each location. His demeanor should have been somewhat agitated or extremely focused. He was a man on a mission so to speak. Was something going on that evening that no one else knew about, or were some witnesses lying?

Statements made by his family were corroborated by his cell phone record. The calls his mother said she had made were there. His father said that he saw Jelani sitting in his vehicle texting at about 21:30 hours. A time estimate that was off by about plus or minus 10 minutes was pretty good. Perhaps, Donnie saw Jelani while he made the phone call to his mother at 21:18 hours and sent the final text message at 21:21 hours. However, the location referenced by Jelani in that message concerning his whereabouts did not match. In that text message (Figure 8.6), Jelani stated that he was "Over around my moms place at my old co workers crib." The person on the other end replied, "Cool. When we watching splinter, tonight or tomorrow night?" There was no reply. Why did Jelani misrepresent his location? Was it a white lie that already committed him to another activity and excused him from watching a movie that night? Even so, then why did the texting conversation abruptly cease on Jelani's end?

For some reason, when Jelani left Donnie's home at about 21:21 to 21:30 hours, he must have driven straight to the house party in Anoka. The most direct routes were 17 to 22 miles and about 35 minutes either way. This would have placed him there at about 22:00 hours as reported by persons at the house party. Had Jelani suddenly realized what time it was, stopped texting at 21:21 hours and set the phone down, and then driven to the house party, then he would have arrived around 21:56 hours. Yet, it begs the question, why was he in such a rush to get to the house party that evening?

This was another part of the timeline that was puzzling. Jelani had told his dad that he was going to go spend more time with the girls at the bar (Figure 8.2, *Blue Dotted Line*), which was about halfway to the house party. Perhaps, this was yet another white lie to politely conceal his real activity. According to the girls and his brother, Jelani never made it to Victory Grill. The timeline did not allow any time for him to stop at the bar to visit with the girls. So, he must have driven straight from his father's residence in Minneapolis to the

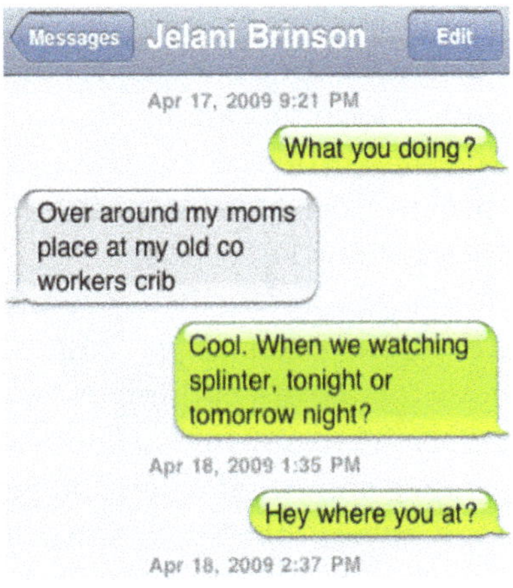

Figure 8.6 The last text message conversation via Jelani Brinson's cell phone ended abruptly on his end at 21:21 hours, April 17, 2009. (Screen capture courtesy of his mother, Alyce Hamilton.)

house party in Anoka (Figure 8.2, *Green Arrowed Line*). But, we were supposed to believe that he did go back to the parking lot near the Sprint store and Victory Grill in order to leave his vehicle and to get a ride to the party. He had left one coworker (Edgar) with another coworker (Mark, who was hosting the house party) at the Sprint store on Colorado Lane North near the bar where the girls were. Edgar told investigators that he gave Jelani a ride to the party. That meant that Edgar had to have been waiting inside the Sprint store after closing, or in his own vehicle in the parking lot, for Jelani to return. Was the fact that Edgar was waiting for him the reason why Jelani was in such a rush?

There was a logistics problem here. If one or both of the coworkers had waited at the Sprint store for Jelani to stop and pick them up in order to take them to the house party, then Jelani's car would have been at the house in Anoka. If the coworkers had gone home earlier on their own and Jelani drove straight to the house party from his dad's home, then his car would have been at the house in Anoka. However, Jelani's vehicle was recovered on April 18th in the parking lot near Victory Grill and the Sprint store on Colorado Lane North. Since he reportedly left the party on foot, then how did his car get to the parking lot?

One possible answer was that the he drove there, parked it, and then got a ride to the party from someone. Who gave him the ride? We were told that Edgar had stated to investigators that he gave Jelani a ride to the house party. This option was completely contrary to Jelani's nature. He did not like being stuck somewhere and dependent upon others to take him home. He always drove himself so he could leave when he wanted to leave. Had he left his car in the parking lot and accepted the ride from Edgar to the house party, then Jelani would have eventually needed a ride back to his car. To us, that did not sound like a move that was well though out, and did not sound like a decision that Jelani would have made. It placed him completely dependent on people at the house party for transportation. Furthermore, if the phone call informed him of some emergency the required his immediate action, then only three behaviors were logical responses. Jelani should have either (1) asked for a ride back to his car, (2) asked to borrow a car to get to wherever it was that he need to be, or (3) called a taxi cab.

In our opinion, the whole story about him leaving abruptly without an explanation never made any sense. Statements offered to police are never 100 percent accurate regardless of whether they are given by witnesses or suspects. Years of experience conducting interviews and interrogations taught Gannon and Duarte that each statement will contain both fact and fiction. The amount of each that an officer records is correlated to the extent of an individual's innocence or guilt. Portions of the truth will be woven into the fabric of a story along with memories that are incomplete or inaccurate, false or fantasy, or outright attempts at deception. The only way to make sense of all this was to accept as fact that the statements given to police had to be grossly less than accurate.

This meant that Jelani had to have driven straight to the house party. His vehicle had to have been brought back to the Victory Grill's parking lot by someone else after his disappearance. We came to this conclusion because investigators were told that Jelani had given Edgar a ride from one Sprint store to another at about 20:10 hours. They were later told by Edgar that he had given Jelani a ride from the Sprint store to the house party. Had Edgar left his vehicle at the second Sprint store earlier in the day? Furthermore, no reason was offered for why Jelani would opt to get a ride to the house party rather than driving himself there. This was exactly what Gannon and Duarte were talking about regarding the creation of various shades of truth in statements to police.

We could only identify three reasons for why Jelani would leave the party in such a hurry. First, as already discussed, the phone call could have informed him of some emergency that required his immediate attention (e.g., something was wrong at home with his child). Second, the phone call could have been to tell him that someone (i.e., who posed a threat to his health and life) was headed to the house party to take action against him. We surmised that this scenario would have caused him to secure a ride away from the party as quickly as possible. Leaving on foot would have exposed him to being spotted by the inbound aggressor(s). We acknowledged the fact that the path south through the backyards and golf course would have partially concealed his escape, but there would have been no reason to take a path over numerous obstacles and to abandon clothing (i.e., his hat and shoes). Perhaps, the aggressor(s) was already waiting outside for Jelani and a foot-chase ensued. The subsequent struggle would have been loud and violent, and would have subjected the aggressor(s) and Jelani to observation by neighbors.

Only one reason made sense to us for why Jelani would leave the party so abruptly. That third reason was that he wanted to escape something that was going on at the party which presented a danger to his life. Had he succeeded in leaving the house, then a pursuit on foot may have occurred, wherein Jelani lost clothing along the way. As already pointed out, the violent commotion would have attracted the attention of neighbors. Therefore, we opined that Jelani never actually left the house at all. He had to have been assaulted in the house and bound. His car was driven back to the Victory Grill parking lot with the intent to add to the confusion of events for investigators.

Search Efforts

This was sort of an unique case when it came to searches. Usually, a lot more searches using K-9s are conducted and areas are repeatedly searched on foot. Part of that might be explained by the fact that not much time existed within which to carry out multiple searches since Jelani was found in about a week. The search efforts in this case reflected Gerald Smith's case in some respects. In both cases, investigators presumed that the victim had intended to go to his residence and then continued on toward the river. As a result, search efforts were directed in those areas and in accordance with that line of thinking.

The first search occurred the very night that Jelani went missing (at about 22:30 hours on Friday, April 17, 2009). The guys at the house party (Edgar, Mark, and Dick) reported to investigators that they went out on foot looking for him in the neighborhood (Figure 8.7, *Blue Line*). They did not find him. So, they drove around and ended up back where his car was parked in the parking lot next to Victory Grill in Brooklyn Park. Again, they did not find him and returned to the house in Anoka. Saturday came (April 18th) and Jelani did not show up for work at the Sprint store in Edina. At 14:00 hours, his mother (Alyce) reported him missing to the Anoka Police Department. Family and friends went door to door asking about Jelani. They drove all through the neighborhood and scoured backyards (*Yellow Box*). No one had seen him. The guys also looked for him again later in the day around 19:00 hours. At that time, they retraced their path in the neighborhood looking for clues. They also explored further out and ended up behind the neighbors' homes to the south. There, behind a tall wooden fence, they found Jelani's winter hat and a shoe (*Bright Purple Dot*).

The greatest search effort took place on Sunday, April 19th. Early in the day, about 50 to 60 volunteers got together and began searching roughly a 3,000 feet by 3,000 feet box (Figure 8.7, *Bright Green Box*) that extended from the home where Jelani was last seen

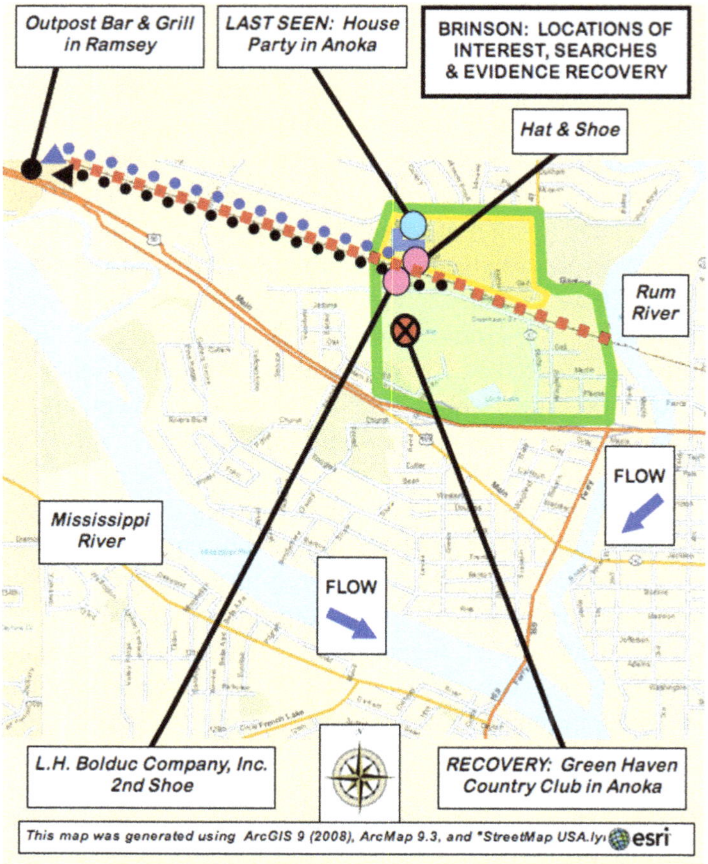

Figure 8.7 Search efforts on foot (*Blue Line*) for Jelani Brinson began immediately the night he disappeared (April 17, 2009). Within the first 4 days after he went missing, family and friends had covered a 9,000,000 square-feet search area on foot (*Bright Green Box*), plus K-9 tracks (*Blue, Black*, and *Red Dotted Lines*) and several searches by vehicle. Law enforcement had explored along the Mississippi and Rum Rivers.

(*Light Blue Dot*) south to the local Perkin's, and then eastward to Highway 47 (a.k.a., Ferry Street). Jelani's girlfriend took part in this search effort and wore one of Jelani's hooded parkas (i.e., "hoodie"). She walked from a spot on the train tracks near where his hat and shoe had been found to the river on the east, and then west down to the Outpost Bar and Grill in the nearby town of Ramsey, and finally back to the starting point (*Red Dotted Line*).

Three police K-9s began searching that Sunday morning. A handler and her K-9 from Minnesota Search and Rescue Dog Association ran 2 tracks. The first started at about the 400-block of West Garfield Street and proceeded west to the entrance of the L. H. Bolduc Company, Inc. (649 West Garfield Street). The dog then went through the property and onto the train tracks that ran along the north side of the property (just to the south of where Jelani was last seen). The K-9 headed west along the tracks for approximately 1 mile until it came to about 100 yards from the Outpost Bar and Grill in Ramsey (6141 Highway 10). The handler returned to the house where Jelani was last seen and restarted her dog. The K-9 tracked Jelani's scent south to the tracks near the L. H. Bolduc Company and then went west along the tracks to the Outpost Bar and Grill again. We did not hear of any other bloodhound that tracked Jelani's scent from the house on Kennedy Street into the golf course or anywhere south of the Bolduc Company and West Garfield Street. Therefore, we assessed that K-9 handler and her dog had hit on a scent dropped by Jelani's girlfriend when she walked that route earlier that day while wearing one of his hoodies. This was significant since Jelani's other shoe was recovered that day on the property of the Bolduc Company amongst a pile of steel tubing (Figure 8.7, *Bright Purple Dot*).

Anoka Police Department and Anoka Fire Rescue crews began searching in and around the Rum River on Monday, April 20th. Law enforcement also began preliminary searches along the Mississippi River. Anoka police officers executed a search warrant that day at the residence where Jelani was last known to be, but did not find any clues. The next day, Tuesday, April 21st, the Anoka County Sheriff's Office officially joined the search effort. At 15:00 hours, the family, friends, and a group of volunteers met in the parking lot of the Champlin Super Target (11990 Business Park Boulevard next to U.S. Highway 169) in order to organize search parties. They spread out from there in their vehicles, covering all of the locations where he had been reported as well as the routes in between. They found no clues. We discovered no other formal search efforts.

Bearing in mind that hindsight is 20/20, it still struck us as somewhat odd that no K-9s were ever taken to any of the bridges leading out of the city of Anoka area. Given that investigators were operating under a premise that Jelani may have attempted to walk home or to his girlfriend's residence, then the bridges would have served as choke-points and restricted his route. He would have had to have walked across 1 of 3 vehicle bridges or a train trestle (Figure 8.7). In many of these cases, the victims do not walk toward home, rather, they walk about 150 to 210 degrees in the opposite direction. So, we also found it unusual that no dogs or foot searches were conducted to the north of the Kennedy address. It also seemed anomalous to us that no K-9s were used during the warrant search of the house on Kennedy Street where Jelani was last seen. We expected both a bloodhound and a cadaver dog to have been run through the house. Lastly, we especially found it peculiar that a bloodhound and a cadaver dog were not immediately brought to Jelani's recovery site in order to back-track to wherever he had previously been. Had he walked to Green Haven Golf Course under his own power, then a bloodhound hit on his scent would have told us that. Had someone else carried Jelani to the pond because he had already died, then a cadaver dog hit would have disclosed that information as well.

We also kept in mind that Green Haven Golf Course was open the entire time that Jelani was missing. It was not the peak part of the golfing season, but there were golfers out on the course everyday since the weather was especially nice. Daytime high temperatures during the period of April 17th to April 25th were as low as 50 and as high as 85, with an average of about 62 °Fahrenheit. There were only 4 days of measurable precipitation that totaled a mere 0.085 inches of rain. For Minnesota after winter, it was beautiful early golfing weather. Although it was not "searched" as such, the pond where Jelani's body was recovered was definitely "under observation" during the daylight hours. We firmly believed that someone would have seen his body floating in the pond were it there prior to the day it was discovered.

Recovered Property

To the best of our knowledge, all of the property that Jelani had with him on the night he went missing was recovered at some point. It was either found on the ground or on his person. The first items to be recovered were personal clothing. During the evening of April 18th, the day after Jelani disappeared, the guys from the house party assisted in the search efforts. They were walking behind the houses that were across the street. Next to a tall wooden fence at about 19:00 hours, Edgar spotted and recovered Jelani's winter hat (Figure 8.8) and one of his athletic shoes. As previously discussed, rather than selecting a route with no fences, we were supposed to believe that he chose to take on this obstacle course. We were also required to accept that, shortly after successfully scaling the wooden fence, this hat fell off Jelani's head and one shoe slipped from his foot, and he did not recover either. When discussing this, Alyce stated that the knit Andian hat with ear flaps was not the type that would easily slip off her son's head; it routinely stuck to his head and had to be pulled off (Figure 8.8). For that matter, Alyce asserted that the hat could not easily slip off the head of anyone with cornrowed hair. Instead of leaving the hat and shoe where they were in the grass and calling police, Edgar picked both of them up with his bare hands and then turned them over to investigators.

The next item of Jelani's personal property that was recovered was his other athletic shoe during the ground search effort on Sunday, April 19, 2009. His girlfriend's brother-in-law found the second shoe amongst a stack of steel tubing in the materials yard at the L. H. Bolduc Company. Instead of leaving the shoe where it was and calling police, he recovered it, placed it in a paper bag, and then turned it over to police. According to Detective Douglas, the athletic shoes were not analyzed for fingerprint evidence because they had been handled so many times by different people. We found this chain of events to be an absolutely preposterous farce. What television-watching American over the age of 6 does not know well-enough to leave evidence alone when it is found? Common sense alone should have told all involved parties not to touch any of Jelani's recovered personal property since it may be potential evidence. Even if the person who picked up the evidence was oblivious to the proper treatment of potential evidence, then someone else in the search party should have known and should have prevented contamination of the evidence. Were

Figure 8.8 Jelani Brinson's winter cap was of an Andian style. It was a tight-fitting, knit cap with ear flaps and draw strings. It was not the kind of hat that would easily fall off his head. (Photo courtesy of his parents, Alyce Hamilton and Donnie Brinson.)

the shoes and the hat intentionally touched knowing it would make them unusable as evidence, and explain the presence of their fingerprints?

The remainder of Jelani's personal property was recovered with his body from the golf course pond. His wallet was found on his person with no cash in it. However, it contained his Minnesota Driver's License, all of his known debit and credit cards and an unidentified paper receipt (the ink had become illegible, but the paper had not yet begun to deteriorate). Also enclosed in his wallet were a picture of his daughter and two medical insurance policy cards under his policy number (one for him and one for his daughter), which demonstrated his commitment to her as a part of his life. His pockets also contained a small package of dental floss, all of his keys on two small carabiners, and his cell phone (BlackBerry Model 8330). His iPod with ear-buds was found in the left side pocket of his cargo shorts.

Jelani was dressed in two T-shirts and briefs, cargo shorts with a leather belt, a sock on each foot, and an unzipped hooded jacket. The Medical Examiner, Dr. Janis Amatuzio, demonstrated great attention to detail in her reports. She described every item of clothing by color and whether or not it was found in a normal position as when worn. Specifically, she noted that the zipper on the shorts was zipped and that the belt was through all of the belt loops. She also provided her observations regarding debris and foreign matter on the body. In short, it appeared that Jelani was recovered with everything that he should have had on his person.

Body Position and Lividity

Lividity (*livor mortis*) is the settling and pooling of blood in a body to the lowest points after death (DiMaio & DiMaio, 2001). It creates an appearance of paleness in elevated portions of a body and red to dark purple in the lowest portions. Areas where a body is in contact with the surface or is lying across on object will leave a white shape resembling the object. The rate at which lividity establishes is related to movement of the body and gravity, body and environment temperatures, and the speed of decomposition. As time passes, the ability to displace or blanch lividity decreases.

Generally speaking, lividity starts within 30 minutes postmortem and is detectable within 2 hours on land. It can be displaced from one side to another by moving or rolling a body. This will shift the blood and may cause confusion due to mixed lividity (i.e., the presence of both anterior and posterior lividity). Lividity is said to be "fixed" when it can no longer be displaced. The exact time for lividity to fix varies among the forensic authors (Figure 8.9). However, all sources agree that lividity is fixed by the 12th hour postmortem for bodies on dry land in a temperate environment (68 to 75 °Fahrenheit). Blanching occurs when someone (e.g., a medical examiner or investigator) applies digital pressure to an area of lividity on a decedent. The color of the skin will blanch (turn white) under the forceful pressure of a finger. When the pressure is released, the color may return to the body. In living persons, this is a test for capillary refill. Eventually, as the blood becomes clotted, there will be no blanching regardless of the amount of pressure exerted on a body.

The fixing and blanching of lividity are inter-related artifacts. Fixing can tell an investigator relatively how long a deceased person has been lying in a given position, and whether or not the body has been moved. Blanching can tell an investigator relatively how long the person has been deceased. Although there is disagreement among forensic authors about the precise timing of blanching, a consensus exists that the extent to which a deceased body will resist blanching will become greater with the passage of time. A body will not blanch after the 12th hour postmortem.

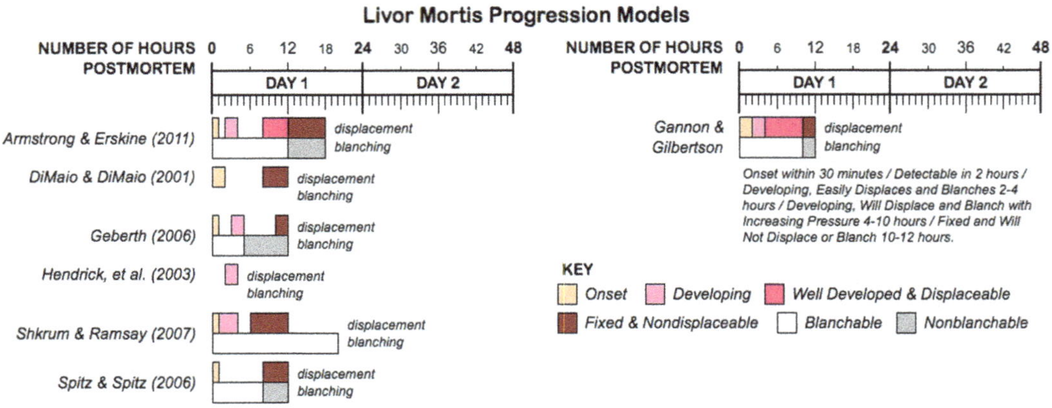

Figure 8.9 Although forensic authors may not agree on precise times for lividity to displace, blanch, and fix, there is a general consensus that all movement of the blood within a body ceases 12 hours after death in temperate conditions.

The Medical Examiner clearly recognized the importance of lividity. Jelani was discovered in the pond lying in a supine position (on his back) in 2 to 3 feet of water. She specifically pointed out that the body was transported and stored in a supine position (an observation that we have not seen in any other autopsy report). Then, at the time of the autopsy, Dr. Amatuzio described anterior lividity (on his front) on the trunk of his body, all extremities and face, and stipulated that lividity would not blanch. During his discussion with Dr. Amatuzio, Gilbertson learned that she knew immediately that the position of Jelani's body at recovery was incongruent with his lividity. She stated that, in order for lividity to fix anteriorly on Jelani's body, he had to have been deceased and lying on his chest somewhere for a period of about 12 to 18 hours. Since he was found lying on his back in the pond, then that meant that someone had to have moved his deceased body to the pond. Furthermore, the fact that lividity did not displace while he was transported and stored in a supine position for a period of about 47 hours (recovery to autopsy) indicated that lividity was fixed before Jelani went into the pond at the golf course.

Rigidity

Rigidity (*rigor mortis*) is the postmortem stiffening of a body. It takes 6 to 12 hours on land for rigor to completely establish in a body (Armstrong & Erskine, 2011). Rigor persists between 12 to 24 hours. It starts to relent at about the 24th hour postmortem and is it typically gone by the 36th hour in a temperate environment on dry land. As such, rigor progresses at a constant rate of about 12 hours to establish, 12 hours to persist, and 12 hours to relent. Water carries heat away from a body more quickly than does air. So, the timeline for rigor is typically extended to twice the normal values when a body is in water – like during a drowning scenario. This is routinely called a 2:1 time delay ratio for water. Therefore, the rigor timeline can be extended to about 72 hours when a body is recovered from the water (Figure 8.10). A cold environment – like that in a morgue cooler – can also retard the progression of rigor, as does obesity. Warm weather or a slim build (lack of body fat) can accelerate the rigor process. It is all related to heat as it contributes to the rate of decomposition, and subsequently to the rigor process. Rigor starts in the whole body at the

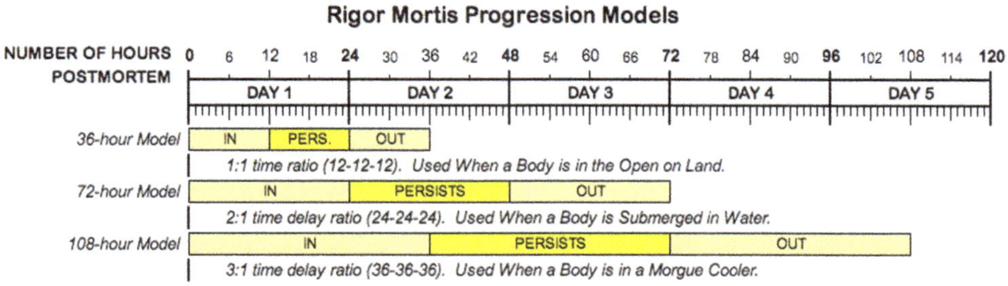

Figure 8.10 Rigidity typically develops in a body within 12 hours, persists for 12 hours, and then takes another 12 hours to relent. Water and cool air temperatures prolong this process.

same time. It takes hold in the smaller muscles first (e.g., the jaw) and then the larger ones (e.g., arms then legs). It relents in the same order, smaller to larger muscles.

The Medical Examiner assessed rigidity in Jelani's body at both recovery and autopsy. This afforded us the opportunity to make a reasonably accurate estimation of the progression of rigor relative to time. She stated that rigor was just starting to relent at recovery and described the position of his right arm. Jelani was found floating high in the water supine (on his back) with his arms down at his sides. His right arm, part of his chest, and the front of his face were out of the water. His right arm was flexed 90 degrees at the elbow and pointed skyward. At autopsy, Dr. Amatuzio wrote that rigor had subsided from the jaw, the arms, and the legs, which meant that rigor was completely gone.

The extent of rigor in Jelani's body established a time bracket for us. Jelani was of average height and weight (5 feet 10 inches, 167 pounds). The weather was fairly mild during the period that he was missing; daytime temperatures ranged between 50 to 85 °Fahrenheit. Therefore, given an average body and a temperate environment, had Jelani died on land, then he would have gone into and out of rigor in about 36 hours. If this was truly a drowning scenario and Jelani had died in the water, and since he was recovered from water, then it was logical to use a 2:1 time delay ratio for water when calculating time estimates. This would have resulted in a 72-hour model (Figure 8.10).

Since Jelani was out of rigor at autopsy, that told us that he probably died about 72 hours prior to autopsy in order to go through the whole rigor cycle before autopsy. That meant that the latest possible time of death for Jelani could have been around 12:00 hours on April 24, 2009 (Figure 8.11, *Turquoise Dot*). Since rigor was in Jelani's body when he was recovered from the pond, that meant that rigor had most likely not started any more than 72 hours prior to his recovery. That also meant that Jelani could not have died more than 72 hours prior to recovery. However, the Medical Examiner had described rigor as just starting to relent. So, an adjustment was made to the chart in order to position the rigor bar where it would reflect rigor just going out at the time of recovery (Figure 8.11, *Adjustment 1*). Furthermore, Dr. Amatuzio had suggested that, in order for lividity to fix prior to him being placed in the water, Jelani had to have been deceased on land for a period of 12 to 18 hours. A second adjustment was made to the chart to reflect Jelani being on land for the first 12 hours while rigor developed in his body (Figure 8.11, *Adjustment 2*). That meant that the earliest possible time of death for Jelani could have been around 01:00 hours on April 24, 2009 (Figure 8.11, *Red Star*). Using these estimates of time, Jelani could have passed away sometime between April 24th at 01:00 hours and April 24th at 12:00 hours.

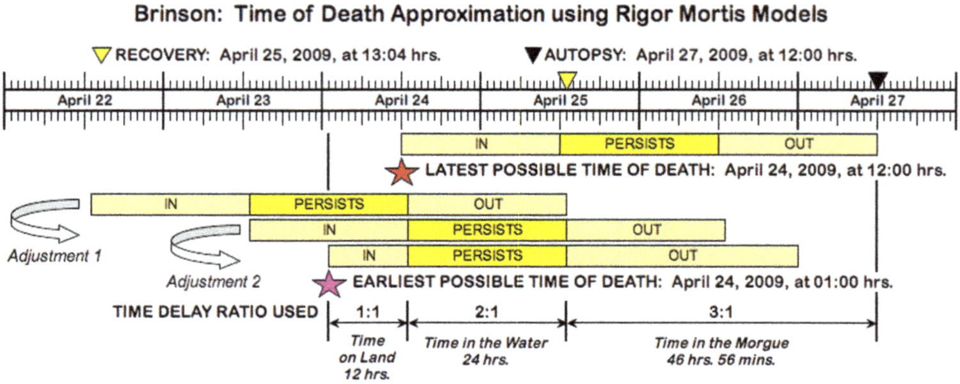

Figure 8.11 Rigor was described at recovery as just starting to relent. It was completely absent at the time of his autopsy. Charting maximum time periods and then adjusting for the Medical Examiner's descriptions created a potential time window for Jelani Brinson's death.

A closer examination of the parameters of the case suggested a narrower window of time for Jelani's death. We noted that lividity indicated Jelani had been deceased on land for 12 to 18 hours prior to being placed in the water. Therefore, a 2:1 time delay could not be used for the first 12 to 18 hours. The typical 1:1 time ratio had to be used for the period of time during which lividity fixed and rigor set in, and while Jelani was still on land. Furthermore, Jelani was found floating high in the water and the air temperatures were fairly warm during the day, especially the days just prior to his recovery. He was not completely submersed in the water and was exposed to the warming rays of the sun. That caused us to consider discarding the use of a 2:1 time delay for calculations related to the period of time that he was in the water. But, since Jelani was recovered from water, we used the longer periods of time in order to better account for unknown variables.

We also had to consider the period of time that Jelani was out of the water and held in cold storage. A total of 47 hours elapsed between recovery and autopsy. The research literature does not suggest a numeric value or time delay ratio for morgue coolers like it does for water (i.e., a 2:1 time delay). There are two kinds of cold storage, above freezing (positive temperature about 2 to 4 °Celsius, or 35.6 to 39.2 °Fahrenheit) and below freezing (negative temperature about −15 to −25 °Celsius, or 5 to −13 °Fahrenheit). The Anoka County Medical Examiner's cooler was positive temperature and would have delayed decomposition and slowed the progression of rigor. Research suggests that the extent of time delay varies greatly depending on the condition of the body when it is brought into the facility (Huntington, Higley, & Baxendale, 2007). We deduced that a time delay ratio of 3:1 for the affect of the Medical Examiner's cooler on retarding decomposition may have been appropriate in Jelani's case.

Our analysis up to this point included only lividity and rigidity. Our findings were that Jelani would have been facedown on land for at least 12 hours, but no greater than 18 hours, in order for lividity to fix and rigor to fully set (death to fix/set). This was followed by a short period of time to move him to the pond (fix/set to water entry). Next was an unknown period of time in the water (water entry to recovery), and then 47 hours on land again in refrigeration (recovery to autopsy). All of these calculations may seem excessive or unnecessary, but they did prove two points beyond a reasonable doubt: (1) Jelani could not have been deceased any longer than 2 days before his body was recovered on April 25th, and (2) Jelani did not die on April 17th.

Ocular Changes

There are five parts of the human eye that are of interest during forensic analysis; the pupil, the iride (iris), the cornea, the sclera, and the conjunctiva. We were interested in the Medical Examiner's description of the cornea in this case. After a person dies on land and the tear ducts cease rehydration of the eyeballs, the corneas will begin to dry out and cloud over (Geberth, 2006). This process begins immediately when the eyelids are open and changes can be detected within 1 hour. It begins as a thin film over the corneas, and becomes opaque by about 2 hours after death. By the 6th hour postmortem, the corneas may appear completely covered over (similar to the appearance of cataracts). This is referred to as corneal opacity or corneal opacification. A concurrent change to the sclerae (i.e., the white parts) will occur when the eyelids are open (Shkrum & Ramsay, 2007). As the eyes dry out, the sclerae will turn progressively browner and darker in the areas that were exposed to the open air. This will be established within 2 hours and is called *Tache Noire* (a.k.a., "the line in the eye"). Although this particular phenomenon will not occur when the eyelids are closed, the eyes can still experience corneal opacification. Even when the eyelids are closed, a film can form over the corneas by 6 to 12 hours. Cloudiness will establish in 12 to 24 hours, followed by complete corneal opacity by the 60th hour after death.

The Medical Examiner described Jelani as presenting with brown irides at autopsy. There were no items of interest concerning the sclerae or conjunctivae, such as petechiae or other small hemorrhages. She stated that she could not discern the size of his pupils due to early corneal opacity. Since his eyelids were closed, this suggested to us that Jelani had been deceased less than the equivalent of 60 hours. In fact, since her description was that of "early" corneal opacity and not complete opacity, that meant that Jelani had likely been deceased slightly longer than 24 hours (Figure 8.12). Jelani's face and part of his chest were floating high out of the water. Yet, sufficient moisture in the pond produced a mildew over his exposed body. This covered and moistened his closed eyelids. Therefore, we assessed that the time in the pond could be considered a holding period concerning further opacification of Jelani's corneas. The time between recovery and autopsy, when Jelani was back

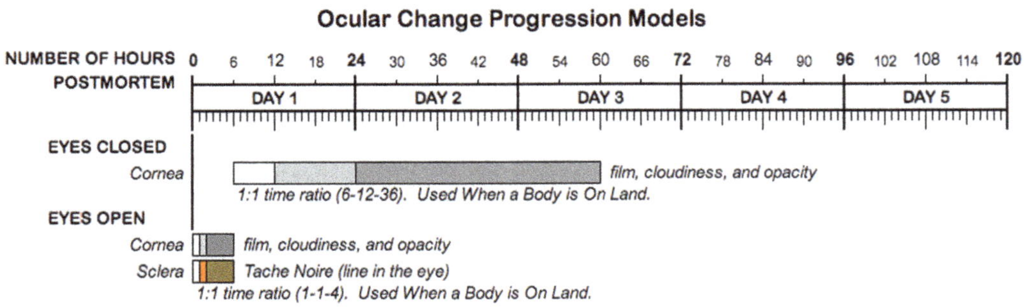

Figure 8.12 Changes to the corneas and sclerae are governed by whether or not the eyelids were open after death, and by time of exposure to air or moisture. Whereas warm dry air will accelerate these processes, cool moist air will retard them.

on land and exposed to air, was 47 hours. That left about 13 hours to account for, which fit well with the Medical Examiner's assertion that Jelani had been deceased for 12 to 18 hours on land prior to being placed in the pond. Since Jelani's body was moist when brought in and remained so at autopsy (as evidenced by the mildew and fungi on his body), we opined that the Medical Examiner's cooler retarded ocular changes during the clouding phase. This further helped to explain Dr. Amatuzio's description of Jelani's corneas as presenting with early corneal opacity.

Decomposition and Maceration

Decomposition begins moments after a person passes away (DiMaio & DiMaio, 2001). There are two aspects of decomposition: bacterial putrefaction and enzymatic autolysis. This is eventually followed by maceration, which is basically the coming-apart of a body. The first signs of putrefaction, which usually start within 12 hours, are a blue-green discoloration of the abdomen in the Right Lower Quadrant (RLQ) followed by the Left Lower Quadrant (LLQ). It typically takes 12 hours for the entire abdomen to become this color. The body will then transition over the next 12 hours to blue-green and darker green, with blotches of red to dark red-orange, and occasionally purplish areas. At about 36 hours after death, decomposition gases built up in the veins will appear as dark red to purplish lines under the skin. This phenomenon is called marbling. The next step is advanced discoloration, which signals the onset of maceration. At this point (approximately 48 hours after death), a body's color will begin to turn black as skin, fingernails, and hair begin to fall off.

Each of these stages of decomposition discoloration takes about 12 hours to progress on dry land and forms a simple taxonomy: early discoloration 12 to 24 hours postmortem, intermediate discoloration 24 to 36 hours, marbling 36 to 48 hours, and advanced discoloration 48 to 72 hours. Maceration starts in the form of Washerwoman's Hands (*Wauschaut*), which is the whitening and wrinkling of the skin on the finger tips and palms, as well as the toes and soles. It can be detected within minutes after immersion in water. Skin slippage may be detected as early as 48 to 96 hours, and is clearly evident by 96 to 168 hours. The hands may begin to shed their skin as early as 72 to 96 hours, and will have completely degloved by 144 to 168 hours. Feet in socks or shoes are not protected from this process and may actually deglove more quickly. Exposure to a damp or moist environment (e.g., a basement, a forest during the rainy season, a bog or swamp) or submersion in water may accelerate this process.

The Medical Examiner depicted Jelani's body with green discoloration in both the RLQ and LLQ, as well as marbling across the whole of his body. She stated that the skin on his abdomen was taught. Our examination of autopsy photos confirmed her description and also recorded that no bloating was present in the abdomen or scrotum. There was some initial and minor skin slippage on his torso. Jelani's hands and feet appeared to be in quite good shape. They presented with minor Washerwoman's Hands (*Wauschaut*) and no indication of degloving. His body and head hair were intact. We also noted that a slime of mildew had begun to form on Jelani while he was in the pond; this predominantly covered exposed flesh on his face and neck. At the time of his autopsy, Dr. Amatuzio commented on a white fungus (yeast form) that had grown on exposed skin. This too was observable in autopsy photos. A full-body radiologic scan indicated that there were no cracked or broken bones, and that there were no foreign objects in his body (e.g., a bullet, a broken-off knife blade, or a surgical pin or screw).

Brinson: Known Postmortem Artifacts and Assessed Conditions

EVENT & ARTIFACT	ASSESSMENT
AT WATER ENTRY	
Livor Mortis - Completely Fixed, Anterior	*Deceased > 12 hrs*
Rigor Mortis - Completely Set In	*Deceased > 12 hrs*
AT BODY RECOVERY	
Rigor Mortis - Beginning to Relent	*Deceased > 24 hrs*
AT AUTOPSY	
Livor Mortis - Fixed, Anterior	*Deceased > 12 hrs*
Rigor Mortis - Relented	*Deceased > 36 hrs*
Ocular Change - Early Corneal Opacity	*Deceased 24 - 36 hrs*
Putrefaction - Marbling, No Bloating	*Deceased about 36 hrs*
Maceration - Minor Skin Slippage, No Degloving	*Deceased < 48 hrs*

Figure 8.13 Summary of the known postmortem artifacts related to Jelani Brinson's death and assessments of their condition if he had been deceased on land for the entire time.

The condition of Jelani's body at the time of autopsy, and the rate at which it was decomposing, confirmed for us that he had not been deceased any longer than the equivalent of about 36 to 48 hours (Figure 8.13). Fixed anterior lividity told us that he had been dead at least 12 hours prior to entry into the water. Rigor had completely fixed and locked his right arm in a bent position, which meant that Jelani had been dead at least 12 hours prior to entry into the water. Rigor that was just starting to relent when Jelani was recovered informed us that the time between his death and recovery was the equivalent of at least 24 hours. However, rigor had relented by the time of his autopsy, which placed Jelani on a timeline somewhere just after his 36th hour postmortem. His eyes were described as presenting early corneal opacity, which would have been consistent with the 24th to 36th hour postmortem (which may have been interrupted and retarded since he was lying in water for part of that time). The presence of marbling and absence of bloating, suggested that he was at about the equivalent of his 36th hour after death. This was reinforced by the near nonexistent signs of maceration. Jelani only presented with early skin slippage across his body, mild *Wauschaut*, and an absolute absence of any degloving. This told us that maceration had just begun and that placed Jelani at sometime less than his 48th hour postmortem.

The problem was that Jelani had been missing for 8 days, but the postmortem artifacts showed that he could have only been dead for a period of approximately 36 to 48 hours. Analysis was complicated by the fact that he was deceased on land, then in the water, and then back on land in the Medical Examiner's cooler. Each of those environments would have affected the development and progression of postmortem artifacts differently: land with no time delay, water with a 2:1 time delay, and the cooler with a 3:1 time delay. The presence of moisture would have specifically had an impact on ocular changes and maceration.

A heuristic device was conceptualized to help in mathematically analyzing each location and time period. Four models were constructed around the Medical Examiner's assertion that Jelani had been deceased on land for at least 12 hours, and possibly as long as 18 hours, prior to being placed into the water. The models were operationalized by sites and their corresponding time delay ratios as punctuated by specific events. Since our assessment of the postmortem artifacts had suggested that Jelani had been deceased for the

Brinson: Estimation of Unknown Time Durations for Events

SITE	TIME DELAY RATIO	EVENT	MODELS 12 / 36		12 / 48		18 / 36		18 / 48	
LAND	1:1	*Death*	*0.0*	*0.0*	*0.0*	*0.0*	*0.0*	*0.0*	*0.0*	*0.0*
		Lividity Fixed & Rigidity Set In	*11.0*	*11.0*	*11.0*	*11.0*	*17.0*	*17.0*	*17.0*	*17.0*
		Transport & Water Entry	*1.0*	*1.0*	*1.0*	*1.0*	*1.0*	*1.0*	*1.0*	*1.0*
WATER	2:1	*Supine in Pond*	*15.4*	*7.7*	*39.4*	*19.7*	*3.4*	*1.7*	*27.4*	*13.7*
LAND	1:1	*Recovery & Transport*	*1.0*	*1.0*	*1.0*	*1.0*	*1.0*	*1.0*	*1.0*	*1.0*
COOLER	3:1	*Storage Until Autopsy*	*46.0*	*15.3*	*46.0*	*15.3*	*46.0*	*15.3*	*46.0*	*15.3*
		Actual Elapsed Time (hrs)	*74.4*		*98.4*		*68.4*		*92.4*	
		Equivalent On-Land Time (hrs)		*36.0*		*48.0*		*36.0*		*48.0*

MODELS: *Death* to *Water Entry* = 12 or 18 hours; *Equivalent On-Land Time* = 36 or 48 hours.

NOTE: *Transport & Water Entry* and *Recovery & Transport* were approximated at 1 hour, then *Supine in the Pond* was calculated to bring the *Equivalent On-Land Time* to either 36 or 48 hours.

Figure 8.14 Four models were set up to test the relationship between the Medical Examiner's assertion (that Jelani Brinson had been deceased between 12 and 18 hours before being placed into the pond) and the postmortem artifacts (which depicted a body that had been deceased between 36 and 48 hours).

"Equivalent On-Land Time" of at least 36 hours, but no more than 48 hours, then each model had to total either 36 or 48 hours. This resulted in 4 models: 12/36, 12/48, 18/36, and 18/48 (Figure 8.14).

Internally, certain times were static and governed by either the modeling or known events. Since we had deduced 12-hour and 18-hour postmortem periods prior to entry into the water, then "Lividity Fixed & Rigidity Set In" plus "Transport & Water Entry" had to equal either 12 or 18 hours. We also knew that Jelani had been recovered at 13:04 hours on April 25th and not autopsied until 12:00 hours on April 27th. This meant that "Recovery & Transport" plus "Storage Until Autopsy" had to be entered as 47 hours. We then adjusted the entry for "Supine in Pond" until the total under "Equivalent On-Land Time" reached 36 or 48 hours. Internally, the table then used the "Time Delay Ratio" that corresponded to each site and event to auto-estimate the amount of time that Jelani might have spent at each site. Totaling the column provided an overall approximation of the "Actual Elapsed Time" for all events to occur.

Using the estimates from the table, the following dates and times for a possible *Time of Death* and a *Time of Water Entry* were identified.

Model	*Time of Death*	*Time of Water Entry*
Model 12/48	09:40 hours on April 23rd	21:40 hours on April 23rd
Model 18/48	15:40 hours on April 23rd	09:40 hours on April 24th
Model 12/36	09:40 hours on April 24th	21:40 hours on April 24th
Model 18/36	15:40 hours on April 24th	09:40 hours on April 25th

An analysis of Models 18/36 and 18/48 was in order. If Jelani had been murdered at about 15:40 hours, then he would have been placed into the water around 09:40 hours. There were some trees and ground cover nearby, but we believed that the golf course grounds personnel and golfers would have seen the assailant(s) placing Jelani's body in the pond at this time of the morning. Additionally, if he was placed there at 09:40 hours on April 25th, then he would have only been in the water for a period of approximately 3 hours 24 minutes (Model 18/36). He would have been found in full rigor at the time of his body recovery. Had he been placed in the pond at 09:40 hours on April 24th, then he would have only been in the water for a period of about 27 hours 24 minutes (Model 18/48). This meant that Jelani would have been out of rigor and decomposition would have been more progressed. Furthermore, he would have been visible to golf course staff and patrons for 11 hours of daylight on April 24th as well as 7 hours on the morning of April 25th. These two models were discounted.

The most difficult times of the day to see are the half-hour before sunrise and after sunset. These periods are referred to in the military as Begin Morning Nautical Twilight (BMNT) and End Evening Nautical Twilight (EENT). Shadows are at their worst and the eyes experience difficulty adjusting to the vast variations in available light within the field of view. During this part of the year and month, the sun was rising shortly after 06:00 hours and setting just after 20:00 hours. So, by 21:40 hours, it would have been reasonably dark and outdoor activities in backyards and on the golf course would have pretty much been wrapped up.

Thus, we turned to an analysis of Models 12/36 and 12/48. If Jelani had been murdered at about 09:40 hours, then he would have been placed into the water around 21:40 hours. Had he actually been placed into the pond at 21:40 hours on April 23rd, then Jelani would have been exposed to the sun and to human observation for the full 14 hours of daylight on April 24th as well as 7 hours on the morning of April 25th. However, had Jelani been slipped into the pond at 21:40 hours on the night of April 24th, then several key factors fell into place. First, his abductor(s) would have worked under the cover of darkness, and right at the time of day when people would have been turning their attention and activities to inside their homes and wrapping up their daily affairs. Second, Jelani's body would have only been visible for 7 hours of daylight on the morning of April 25th. The question remained as to how well the observed postmortem artifacts could be explained.

We surmised that the assailant(s) had to put Jelani into the pond during a period of time that was both dark and absent of any potential witness. We started this portion of the analysis with a stereotypical assumption. We posited that Jelani had to be placed in the pond during the quietest time of night, which would have been shortly after midnight but before morning activity started to pick back up (00:00 to 05:00 hours). By 03:00 hours in the morning, things are pretty quiet in the backyards and on the streets around the Green Haven Golf Course. Thus, we concluded that a 03:00 hours time for entry into the water was the most logical. A post-midnight model was adjusted to set the time for entry into the water at 03:00 hours on April 25, 2009. That action increased the time that Jelani was deceased on land to 16 hours. He was then in the pond for about 10 hours, followed by 47 hours in the morgue cooler before autopsy.

Of the 15 models that were constructed and tested, this model accounted for all postmortem artifacts pretty well (Figure 8.15). Lividity was fixed and rigor had set in prior to entry into the pond. Rigor had relented by the time of autopsy. Greens and dark reds were present on the body with early signs of marbling. Bloating was just beginning and may not have been detectable. Ocular change had been interrupted and retard by exposure to the

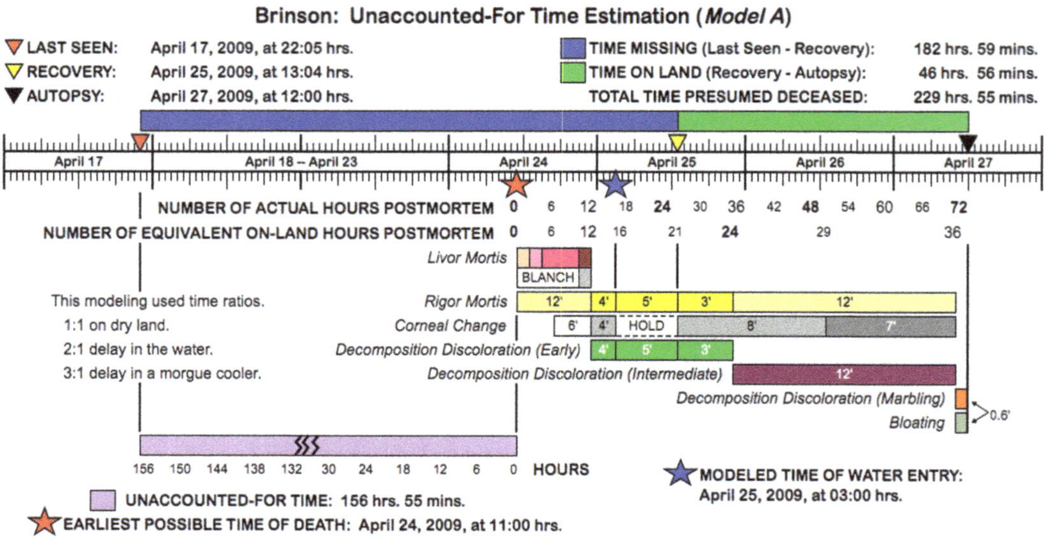

Figure 8.15 The 03:00 hours model for estimating a time of death and water entry for Jelani Brinson was close, but it did not have rigor relenting at the time of body recovery.

water. The cool dry air in the morgue cooler restarted the opacification process. The only postmortem artifact that was off a bit was rigor. The Medical Examiner described rigidity as starting to relent at Jelani's recovery. In this model, it did not relent until after 9 hours in the morgue cooler (i.e., the equivalent of 3 hours on land). However, the daytime high temperatures for Anoka were 85 and 72 °Fahrenheit on April 24th and 25th, respectively. The sky was mostly clear with only a trace (0.005 inches) of precipitation on April 25th. This would have warmed the water in the pond considerably. The warm water and the sunshine would have heated Jelani's body and accelerated the progression of rigor during the 10 hours that he was in the pond. This would have moved all colored bars in the graphic to the left, which would not have caused any major conflict with the Medical Examiner's description or our observations of postmortem artifacts.

Rather than adjusting the bars based on a presumption that the sun would warm the water and Jelani's body, we decide to move the graphic based on a shift in time. However, was it logical to move the *Time of Water Entry* event to a pre-midnight time slot? According to the United States Naval Observatory (USNO, 2011), the Sun set at 20:11 hours on April 24th. The half-hour period leading up to End Evening Nautical Twilight (EENT) was from 20:43 to 21:13 hours. So, the time proposed by Model 12/36 (21:40 hours, April 24th) would have come just after darkness had set in. The Sun did not rise until 06:11 hours on April 25th. It was at its highest point overhead at 13:11 hours; Jelani was recovered at 13:04 hours. No illumination was available from the Moon, which had set at 20:13 hours that night. In fact, a New Moon occurred at 22:23 hours on the night of April 24th. We decided to run a model with the *Time of Water Entry* set to 23:00 hours on April 24th.

In this new model (Figure 8.16), Jelani would have been deceased for an *Actual Elapsed Time* of about 18 hours before entry into the water. He would have been dead for a total of approximately 32 hours at the time of his body recovery. Adding in the time that it took to recover him and to transport him to the Anoka County Medical Examiner's morgue, as well as the time in the cooler (47 hours), then Jelani would have been deceased for a total *Actual Elapsed Time* of around 79 hours, and a total *Equivalent On-Land Time* of roughly 40.5 hours.

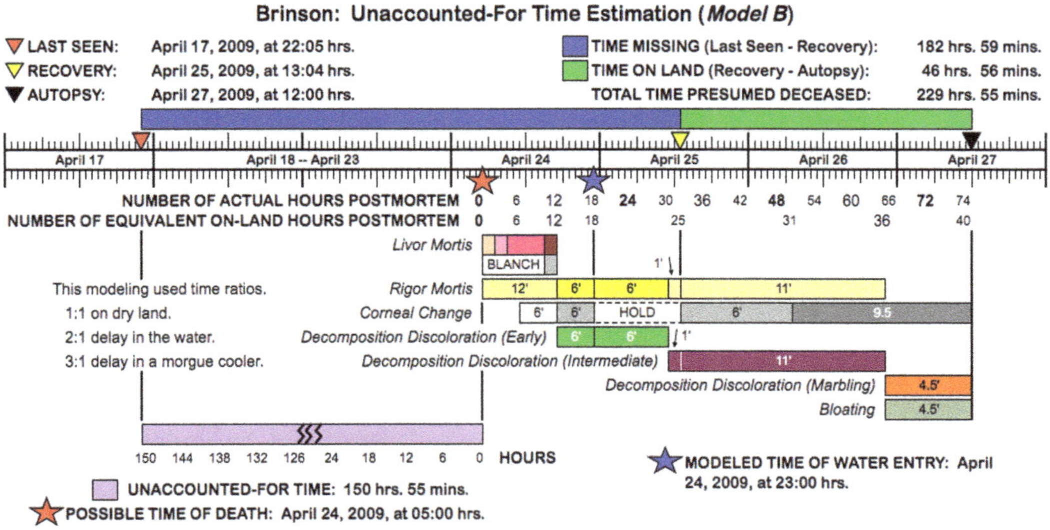

Figure 8.16 The 23:00 hours model accounted for both rigor relenting at the time of body recovery and having relented by the time of autopsy.

This new model also accounted for the differential time delay affects of the environments in which he had been. He had been deceased on land (1:1), in water (2:1), and then back on land in the morgue cooler (3:1). At autopsy, Jelani's body would have been out of rigor. Being in water would have retarded the ocular change process; then being back on land in a dry air environment would have continued it. This would have placed Jelani's ocular change at about 33.5 hours into a 60 hour process and ocular opacity would have appeared to be in its early stages. Jelani's level of decomposition would have included dark greens and reds across his entire upper body and likely early indications of marbling. Since he was 4.5 hours into a 12 hour phase of decomposition, there would have been some bloating in his face that was exposed to the air and Sun while in the pond, but no sign of bloating of his abdomen and scrotum that were covered with clothing and underwater. For maceration, Jelani would have presented with Washerwoman's Hands and some skin slippage would have started on his chest, arms, and legs. No degloving of the hands or feet would have been detectable. This extent of postmortem putrefaction and maceration was a precise description of the autopsy photos that we witnessed and that Gilbertson discussed with Dr. Amatuzio.

Internal Assessment

Since Jelani's body was recovered from water, we naturally started by looking at the condition of his respiratory system. A pinkish foam or froth will quite often appear in the airway as a result of small blood vessels breaking under the pressure exerted by the body during the drowning process (Spitz & Spitz, 2006). It is typically found exuding from a victim's mouth. If drowning contributed to a victim's cause of death by means of asphyxia or hypoxia, then the alveoli (i.e., the tiny air sacks) should be congested with water or at least with this pink foam. There may often be debris from the river or lake in the trachea, left and right main stem bronchial tubes, and bronchioles. The human body is an amazing design of packaging to maintain integrity and to control cross contamination. Component parts are contained in sacks (e.g., the lungs in the pleural cavity, and the heart in the pericardial sac). Then, all of the organs are packaged in a larger double-layered sack (i.e., peritoneal cavity). Fluid in the lungs may seep out into the pleural cavity. The heart may engorge with water and eventually some effusion will be evident in the pericardial sac. The longer a body is in the water, then the greater the likelihood that there will also be some effusion into the peritoneal cavity.

We also looked at the esophagus and stomach contents while examining the airway. Many times, debris or vomitus can also be found in the esophagus. Undigested food, beverage, or pill fragments in the stomach are also of interest. One reason we look at this is because when a victim fights the urge to inhale water, he or she will instead swallow the first few gulps of water during a drowning. Therefore, the stomach may contain some liquid. The liquid in the stomach should be analyzed to ensure that it contains the same chemicals and pollutants as the water in which the body was found. It should also contain the same species and count of diatoms. Jelani's stomach contained 60 cubic centimeters (or 60 milliliters) of a white-flecked, brown liquid, which equated to only 2.03 fluid ounces (about 2 shot glasses). There was no indication in the autopsy report as to whether or not this was ever tested. The description sounded like it could have been anything from chewed up pills to partially digested and curdled dairy creamer from the coffee that Jelani liked so much.

The Medical Examiner's detailed description of Jelani continued throughout the autopsy. She illustrated a young man in excellent physical health. He was a classic human specimen, with all internal organs at or about their expected size and condition for his age. In fact, Jelani's body demonstrated near perfect symmetry. The left and right kidneys are usually about the same weight. Typically, their combined weight is about that of the heart. In Jelani's case, the kidneys weighed 180 gram each and his heart weighed 380 grams. Jelani's esophagus was intact and presented nothing out of the ordinary. Jelani's left and right lungs weighed 380 and 420 grams, respectively. There was no foam or froth in his nasal passages or airway, but it did have the expected amount of mucus. There was no pulmonary edema and the pulmonary arteries were in perfect condition (i.e., smooth, glistening, free of thrombi and plaques). There was no effusion in the pleural cavity, pericardial sac, or peritoneal cavity.

An absence of foam or froth in the airway does not completely rule out drowning as a cause of death, but it should alert investigators that something else might have been a cause of death with a victim. Such was the case with Jelani. During his discussion with Dr. Amatuzio, Gilbertson discerned that she was troubled and puzzled by this case. He could tell that she was truly upset that this perfectly healthy young man had been cut-down in the prime of his life and she could not find any explanation for his cause of death. The Medical Examiner was glad to know that the case was still being investigated by law enforcement. She knew that lividity and rigidity pointed to any of manner of death other than suicide or accident at the pond. At the very least, Jelani had died elsewhere and someone had brought him to the pond at Green Haven Golf Course. But, what had killed him? There was no physical, medical, or forensic shred of evidence to tell us why he had died or how he had perished. Although she had no proof, Dr. Amatuzio opined that Jelani's brain may have been slightly swollen. This might have suggested some sort of trauma to the head, but there was no evidence of external or internal injury to the scalp, skull, or brain. She was confident that Jelani did not drown and that human intervention played a role in his death. But, the Medical Examiner could not identify a cause of death.

Injuries

The media has unwaiveringly released that Jelani had no injuries. This was consistent with all of these cases. There was always "no sign of foul play" in all of these cases. There were no physical injuries to the bodies of these young male victims. This forensic "fact" reinforced the belief that the cases were accidental deaths. Hypothetically speaking, why might law enforcement investigators not tell the public when there really were injuries on a victim? False confessions are not uncommon in homicide cases, but only the true assailant would have specific knowledge of the injuries. By withholding information pertinent to wounds, then that information can be used by investigators to verify the real attacker. Only the true aggressor (or anyone present who observed the assault) will have knowledge of how the wounds were generated, where they were, and how bad they were. Another reason to withhold information about a victim's injuries might be that detail of the injuries could be unnecessarily graphic or they could be embarrassing to a victim (i.e., a case that involved rape or sexual dismembering of a body). A final explanation may be that investigators wanted to dump the case and close it as an accident - which was not the situation in Jelani's case.

Microscopic Examination

The Medical Examiner described Jelani's liver and kidneys as presenting mild sinusoidal congestion. A sinusoid is a tiny blood vessel within the structure of an internal organ such as the liver or heart. While researching this condition, Gilbertson discovered that sinusoidal congestion in biopsies of liver tissue can be attributed to venous outflow impairment. Furthermore, sinusoidal congestion can be caused by physiological disorders with sinusoidal infiltration and destruction of the reticulin framework. One of those disorders is sickle cell anemia (Bauer, Moore, & Hutchins, 1980; Kakar, Kamath, & Burgart, 2004; Mills, Mwakyusa, & Milner, 1988).

Upon this discovery, Gilbertson examined the measurements recorded for Jelani's heart. His left ventricle had a diameter of 2.0 × 3.0 centimeters and his aortic valve circumference was 8.0 centimeters. These measurements were relatively the size that a person would expect (Sim, Muskawad, Lim, Yeo, Lim, Grignani, Durrani, Lau, & Duran, 2003). However, the thickness of the left ventricle was 2.0 centimeters, and the thickness of his right ventricle was 0.5 centimeters. These seemed rather thick. Having the same diameter with thicker walls would decrease the interior space, and as such, decrease the volume of blood that could pass through the ventricle.

Sickle cell trait may also contribute to death during times of extreme physical exertion. In one Florida case (Stephany, 2008), a 19-year-old African-American male with sickle cell trait died as a result of dysrhythmia. Perhaps, Jelani had symptoms associated with an undetected sickle cell trait, which were compounded by a rapid heart rate that he experienced due to the psychological stress of life-threatening danger and physical stress from the attempt to flee the house. All of this was magnified by the reduced blood flow through his left ventricle. We must emphasize that this hypothesis has not been discussed with Dr. Amatuzio and we have sought her feedback.

Recovery Location

The fact that Jelani was recovered in the middle of the golf course pond and not along its perimeter was a major clue for us. There were no water currents in the pond. It was not on flat ground and unprotected. It was in a low-lying area and protected by trees. So, the wind had not blown Jelani from the edge to the near-exact center of the pond. There were four possible explanations for why Jelani was found in the middle of a pond at the Green Haven Golf Course. He could have ended up there as a result of a pure accident, a suicide, an accidental death and cover up, or a homicide. We have discussed all of these scenarios with Detective Douglas and the family. The possibility existed that this was a purely accidental death. Jelani could have stumbled into the pond while trying to walk back to his car in the parking lot at Victory Grill. Although it did not make sense relative to a rational and sober person, it could have been explained by substance intoxication. The house party was supposed to be about booze and pot, but the toxicology report showed that Jelani had not been drinking alcohol or smoking marijuana. Many of the victims we have investigated were discovered with gamma-hydroxybutyrate (GHB) in their systems. GHB causes short-term memory loss and great confusion. A person may make a decision to walk in a given direction, and then two steps later, forget why the action was initiated.

Even if Jelani's death was a drug-induced accident, then a lot of poor decision making had to happen. He had to have decided for some unknown reason to leave the house party only minutes after arriving. The route along which his personal property was recovered was not the most direct path "as the crow flies" back to Victory Grill where his car was parked (a walk of 7.5 miles). It zigzagged its way through properties, presenting the greatest possible number of obstacles and requiring the most physical effort. Had Jelani gone directly across the street, he could have walked through a yard with no fences. Instead, he seemed to have chosen a route that required going between the houses to his left, which caused him to climb over the neighbor's 3.5 feet high chain-link fence at the front of the yard and a 6 feet high wooden fence at the back of the yard without being seen or heard by residents. This was where he lost his hat and a shoe. He then had to walk down a slight embankment and cross two sets of railroad tracks.

At that point, Jelani would have faced another decision. The property of L. H. Bolduc Company, Inc., was in front of him (649 West Garfield Street, Anoka). This business specialized in driven piles and earthen retention systems. The property contained stacks of pipe, timber, H-beams, and steel sheeting. The business was fenced on only three sides (i.e., east, south, and west). As he faced south, just to his right was the west edge of the business. Jelani could have walked around the end of the fence and past the obstacles that the property posed to him. Rather than going to one side or the other as he had done before, he again had to have chosen the more difficult path and gone straight ahead into the yard full of pile driving material. While crossing this property, he lost the other shoe near a stack of tubing, which left him in his stocking feet. Jelani would have then encountered yet another fence that was well over his head in order to get out of the business' yard on the south side. He would have then wandered through the golf course and entered the pond. Logic would suggest that entering the nearly waist-deep water should have told him that this was the wrong way to go. But, if we were to believe this accidental death scenario, then we were to also believe that he continued on into the middle of the pond before falling over backwards and drowning. Somehow, he supposedly accomplished all this without his shoes and without getting the bottoms of his socks impregnated with mud from the pond. We did not accept this scenario.

Suicide was another scenario that we did not accept. Based on what we had heard from family members and others about Jelani's character and spiritual beliefs, we could not even imagine that this was an option for him. He was absolutely happy in life. He loved Jesus, he loved his family, especially his new baby girl, and he had just been promoted at work. Life was going really well for Jelani. Some might suggest that stranger things have happened and that no one can claim to know all that was going on in his life. That may be true; but, neither us, Detective Douglas, nor the family could accept this scenario. One piece of forensic evidence that clearly led us to this conclusion was the lack of mud on the bottom of his socks. Furthermore, how could he walk all the way from the house party to the middle of the pond without wearing down the fabric of his socks or without getting any soil, mud, or even a single blade of grass worked into the fabric? He could not. So, he could not have killed himself.

There was also the probable scenario that Jelani could have accidentally died in the presence of others, either at the house party or on his way home. The person(s) who discovered him could have panicked for any number of reasons (e.g., did not want to have contact with law enforcement), and would have had to have chosen to dispose of his body by leaving it in the pond at the golf course. Perhaps, they wanted people to believe it was an accidental death. The person(s) who put Jelani in the pond had to have carried him to the middle of the pond. We knew that he did not float around after being placed in the pond. We concluded that where he was recovered was where he had been placed since his feet were resting on the bottom of the pond, anchoring him to that spot. This scenario remained a probability until we saw the autopsy report and photographs.

That meant that only a homicide and body dump scenario remained reasonable enough to be believed or accepted. Two factors related to the body recovery location contributed to that conclusion: physical evidence and body condition. No matter what scenario we considered, we kept coming back to the socks. The only way for Jelani to get to the middle of the pond without soiling the bottoms of his socks was for him to be carried there. It made no sense that he could have arrived at the middle of the pond alive given that lividity had already fixed and rigor had set. So, the pure accident and suicide scenarios were not options. It made no sense that he accidentally died at the house party or anywhere else on the night he went missing due to the condition of his body. He was in too good of condition; that is, the extent of his putrefaction and maceration did not correlate with the period of time that he was missing and presumed dead. So, the accidental death and body disposal scenario was also not an option. Jelani had to have died several days after he went missing, laid in a prone position for at least 12 to 18 hours, and then been carried to the middle of the pond.

Toxicology

Americans like to alter their cognitive state through the instrumental use of substances (i.e., sugar, caffeine, nicotine, and alcohol). Some are legal, while others are illegal. Coffee-based and energy drinks help us to wake up in the morning and reinvigorate us during the day. Cigarettes and smokeless tobacco calm our nerves and suppress our appetites. Some beverages are associated with emotional events and help us to outwardly display our inner feelings, like champagne that is used to help us celebrate, or we may "cry in our beer." The use of some substances is considered "recreational" (i.e., alcohol, marijuana, and other illicit drugs). Many of these same substances are specifically used to relax us and to counter the day's stressors and the chemicals we had put into our bodies throughout the day.

We did not judge the reason(s) why Jelani used certain substances. What was important is that we knew what substances Jelani used on a regular basis. He drank a beer now and then, but it was not high on his list of things to do. Rather, Jelani thoroughly enjoyed his coffee. In fact, he drank so much coffee from a particular national brand name that it was uncommon to see him without their paper cup in his hand. He also occasionally smoked cigarettes. He had tried marijuana in the past and liked it, and had been asking to smoke pot during the last 2 weeks he was alive. Jelani had never used, and never expressed any desire to use harder drugs and narcotics that are commonly abused among today's youth to intensify their "buzz" experience, to enhance their sexual prowess, or to facilitate date rape: cocaine, crack, heroin, codeine, hydrocodone, oxycodone, and psilocybin mushrooms ("magic mushrooms"), methamphetamine, 3,4-methylenedioxy-*N*-methylamphetamine (MDMA, "ecstasy"), flunitrazepam (Rohypnol, "roofies"), ketamine, gamma-hydroxybutyrate (GHB), and gamma-butyrolactone (GBL).

The toxicology screens found cotinine in Jelani's system. Cotinine is an alkaloid and metabolite of nicotine (Wall, Johnson, Jacob, & Benowitz, 1988). It typically shows up during toxicology tests of smokers and has even be used in research studies to demonstrate exposure to second-hand tobacco smoke among nonsmokers. For more detailed information, a thorough discussion of cotinine was presented in Chapter 5 (Smith). The toxicology test for cotinine was not quantitated, and therefore could not be used for any definitive analysis.

As anticipated, caffeine was also present in Jelani's body at autopsy. The toxicology report from National Medical Services (NMS) included information about average dose-dependent peak plasma concentrations that could be detected after 30 minutes; that is, a 120 milligram (mg) dose averaged 3.0 micrograms/milliliter (mcg/mL), a 300 mg dose averaged 7.9 mcg/mL, and a 500 mg dose averaged 14 mcg/mL. The average half-life of caffeine in the blood of a healthy individual is about 5.7 hours (Statland & Demas, 1980). Some sources suggest caffeine half-lives between 5 to 7 hours, with 75 percent being eliminated from the blood by 8 to 10 hours. The NMS report showed that a *Caffeine, Blood* (test code 0930B) had been performed. It indicated that 0.55 micrograms per milliliter of caffeine were present in Jelani's blood. This small amount in Jelani's blood suggested to us that considerable time had elapsed between his last coffee drink and his death. Clearly, more time had passed than would have been required to run out of the house party and into the pond on Green Haven Golf Course.

No form of alcohol was reported in postmortem toxicology tests. So, Jelani's death could not be written-off as another "accidental drowning associated with acute alcohol intoxication" as many of the other cases had been that we have examined. The absence of alcohol told us that alcohol intoxication had not contributed to his strange behavior and purported abrupt departure from the house party that night. Some postmortem alcohol production would have begun even though Jelani had been missing for a period of only 8 days (April 17th to April 25th). The complete absence of any form of alcohol (specifically, isopropanol, n-propanol, and n-butanol) told us that no statistically significant postmortem alcohol production had occurred as of yet. That fact confirmed our proposal that Jelani had only been deceased no more than 2 days before his body was recovered.

Since Jelani had been asking to smoke marijuana and it was supposed to be present at the house party that night, we expected to see some level of tetrahydrocannabinol (THC) in his toxicology test results. The drug screen of Jelani's urine sample from autopsy indicated no finding of cannabinoids. This did not mean that there as no THC in his body. It simply meant that the amount in his body, if any, did not meet or exceed the reporting cutoff level of less than or equal to 50 nanograms/mL. So, if Jelani's bizarre behavior that night could not be explained by alcohol or marijuana, then what may have contributed to it? Was any other substance or drug found in his system that may have contributed to his death?

Urine is generally considered to be the most reliable specimen for accurate gamma-hydroxybutyrate (GHB) measurements because it does not produce GHB after death like blood does. GHB occurs endogenously in the human body at very low levels as a metabolite of the inhibitory neurotransmitter named gamma aminobutyric acid (GABA). Numerous studies have been conducted to determine a cut-off value for distinguishing between endogenous and exogenous GHB in the urine and blood. In one study (Moriya, Nishimura, Furumiya, & Hashimoto, 2006), the urinary level of GHB in male smokers was 0.52 mcg/mL (plus or minus 0.37 mcg/mL). Another source (National Highway Traffic Safety Administration, 2012) suggested that 10 mcg/mL be used as a cut-off for urinary GHB since postmortem urine specimens from non-GHB using subjects were typically below that mark.

Like many of these cases, GHB was found in the victim during the autopsy. GHB causes memory loss and can render a victim debilitated and helpless. It can be used as a date rape drug and has a very short half-life of 18 to 60 minutes (0.3 to 1.0 hour). The NMS quantitated toxicology test of Jelani's urine (*Gamma-Hydroxybutyric Acid Screen, Urine (Forensic)*, test code 9326U) revealed a level of 22 mcg/mL. MEDTOX laboratories (Saint Paul, Minnesota) reported a slightly higher serum level of 35.1 mcg/mL of GHB in Jelani as the result of blood test *Gamma-Hydroxybutyric Acid, Serum*. In their toxicology report, the amount of GHB in Jelani would have equated to a wakeful state.

Wakefulness	<52 mcg/mL
Light Sleep	52 to 156 mcg/mL
Moderate Sleep	156 to 260 mcg/mL
Deep Sleep	>260 mcg/mL

However, even at that level (22 to 35 mcg/mL), Jelani would not have had complete control of his faculties. He would have been euphoric, confused, sleepy, demonstrating poor judgment, and compliant to the wishes of others. He would have been slightly clumsy, but could have moved under his own power and easily directed to where others wanted him to go. Considering that GHB has such a short half-life (18 to 60 minutes), Jelani could have had as much as 140 mcg/mL of GHB in his system 36 minutes to 2 hours earlier, which would have rendered him extremely easy to control and abduct. The Medical Examiner recognized this and made special comment about the level of GHB in Jelani's system in her final autopsy report.

Conclusion

The entire analysis of postmortem artifacts that we presented herein may have seemed well beyond what was necessary. However, the findings that it generated were extremely important to Jelani's case. We pointed out that the anterior lividity did not correspond with the supine position in which Jelani's body had been recovered. The recorded observations of rigidity at recovery and again at autopsy afforded a unique opportunity to develop a timeline for rigor. That postmortem artifact coupled with ocular changes and the progression of putrefaction and maceration clearly portrayed a person who had not been deceased for the whole 8 days that he had been missing. The presence of GHB in Jelani's system suggested human involvement in Jelani's death.

Our analysis proved beyond a reasonable doubt that Jelani did not die on the night of April 17, 2009, when he went missing. So, he could not have died in the house in Anoka that night. It also meant that Jelani did not die elsewhere that night. Our analysis demonstrated that he had to have died much later than proposed by any accidental death scenario. Furthermore, it confirmed that Jelani did not walk around in his stocking feet for 7 days before finding his way into the golf course pond. This brief study clearly found that Jelani had to have been abducted on April 17th, held somewhere for 7 days, murdered on April 24th and dumped into the pond within about 18 hours, and then recovered shortly after lunchtime on April 25th.

Our forensic findings also brought into question the discovery and recovery of Jelani's two shoes and hat. They were either lost during Jelani's flight from his abductor(s) on the night of April 17th, or they were taken to those locations and planted as evidence. We have seen victims' personal property returned to the scene in several other cases. The fact that the shoes and hat were discovered strung out along a path between the house party and the golf course pond without any scent of Jelani demonstrated criminal intent. The person(s) who placed the shoes and hat where they were discovered knew that the property had to be found in key locations that supported a hypothesis that Jelani had walked to the golf course pond, fallen in, and drown. The person(s) who placed the shoes and hat in the search area knew on April 17th that Jelani would ultimately be found deceased in the golf course pond sometime later. This is also why there was no scenting of Jelani anywhere near where the items were discovered.

The Medical Examiner may not have known the exact cause of death, and so, classified Jelani's case as "Undetermined." Yet, Dr. Amatuzio and Detective Dan Douglas both knew that this case was clearly a homicide. Jelani's case remains open and is being investigated by the Anoka County Sheriff's Department. Jelani was a strong and fit individual. He was, however, somewhat sedated by the GHB that was given to him – probably to take some of the fight out of him. Jelani Brinson was definitely murdered and his family definitely deserves those responsible for this heinous act to be brought to justice. Hopefully, the Anoka County Sheriff's Office will be able to accomplish this task.

Should you have any information about Jelani Brinson's death, then please contact the Anoka County Sheriff's Office: call (763) 323-5000, or e-mail sheriff text "TIP674" and your tip to 274637 (*CRIMES*), or call (800) 222-8477 (222-*TIPS*). You may also submit a tip using a fill-in-the-blank form that is available online at https://www.tipsubmit.com/webtips.aspx?AgencyID=674&DSID=674).

Todd Douglas Geib*

9

Background

Todd Geib lived with his cousin next to Half Moon Lake in Casnovia, Michigan. His sister described him as a good guy who was fun to be around and who was very athletic. Todd was a natural athlete and enjoyed playing baseball, football, and basketball. He was also an avid outdoorsman and could handle the trail, the woods, or the lake. He spent many hours bonding with his dad while deer hunting. He loved to fishing; his trophy fish is proudly displayed in his parents' home to this day. He would also go dirt biking at a track by Lansing with his friends. Todd commuted about 30 miles one-way to work at Hager Distribution, Incorporated, a wholesale lumber company in Wyoming southwest of Grand Rapids.

He often went home to nearby Ravenna on weekends to visit his parents, sisters, nieces and nephews. According to his mother (Kathy Geib), Todd had a dry sense of humor and often teased her, especially when she bummed a cigarette. He liked to listen to country music and the oldies. Todd's parents described their religious background to us as consisting of Protestant and Catholic upbringings, but considered themselves to be more or less nondenominational Pentecostal. Like many of these young men, Todd believed in an afterlife, a final judgment, and salvation through Christ.

Circumstances

Last Seen

Todd Douglas Geib was a White male, 22 years old at the time of his disappearance, 5 feet 11 inches, 180 pounds (Body Mass Index 25.10), black hair and brown eyes. His ancestral heritage

* Photo courtesy of his parents, Doug and Kathy Geib.

Figure 9.1 Todd Geib (right) with his parents Doug and Kathy. (Photo courtesy of his parents, Doug and Kathy Geib.)

was drawn from a mix of German and Polish. Saturday evening (June 11, 2005) started out for Todd Geib at home with his parents (Figure 9.1). Between 16:00 and 17:00 hours, he ate pepperoni and sausage Hobo Pies with them at their home in Ravenna. Todd was back at his residence on Moon Court between 18:00 and 18:30 hours talking with his cousin. By about 19:30 hours, he had arrived at the Half Moon Bar and Grill along Newaygo Road (a.k.a., M-37) (Figure 9.2). Todd's best friend (hereafter, Dave) and 2 other associates (hereafter, Chuck and Theodore) were also there drinking with him. Todd left the bar with the 3 guys and 2 gals (one known and a Jane Doe) at about 21:30 hours and headed to an outdoor keg party in an abandoned orchard just under 2 miles away and just to the north of White Road.

The party had become an annual event with over 50 people attending according to his family. One report stated that Todd told his friends (i.e., the ones who had come to the party with him) that he was going home at about midnight and started to walk towards his

Figure 9.2 Before going to the outdoor keg party in the orchard, Todd Geib was drinking and enjoying the company of friends at the Half Moon Bar and Grill on June 11, 2005.

residence that was just over 1 mile away. However, a rumor existed which suggested that Todd was involved in a fight at about 00:45 hours (Sunday, June 12th) while at the orchard party. It was unclear whether the fight was with one individual or a group of people. Some witnesses reported seeing a small group of unidentified young men from Kent City at the party who were strutting around like they were looking for a fight. Todd left the orchard and was never seen alive again. He vanished after a brief and mysterious phone call to Theodore's sister (hereafter, Patricia). Todd was then recovered 21 days later in Ovidhall Lake in the opposite direction from where he was last seen walking.

Recovery

A married couple, who were out to enjoy an afternoon of fishing, discovered Todd's body 3 weeks later at about 17:00 hours on Saturday, July 2, 2005, in the approximately 20-acre Ovidhall Lake. At its deepest point, the lake was about 20 to 25 feet deep. Todd's body was recovered by members of the Muskegon County Sheriff's Department and the Muskegon County Marine Department with assistance from the Michigan State Police. Matthew Kempf from the Muskegon County Medical Examiner's Office was present in his investigative role. The body was taken to the morgue at Sparrow Hospital by the Muskegon County Body Removal Team. Todd was discovered floating in a rather odd posture. Although he was in the expected prone position for a drowning (face-down), his head and shoulders were out of the water. This baffled members of the recovery team and investigators so much that they looked for an explanation of this phenomenon. Having found none, the investigator (Matthew Kempf) wrote in his Death Scene Investigation Report that nothing was found tied to the body or anchored the body in such a manner as to contribute to Todd's unusual upright floating posture.

Analysis of Evidence

Search Efforts

Todd Geib went missing during the early morning hours of Sunday, June 12, 2005. That same day, his mother (Kathy Geib) filed a missing person complaint at about 20:00 hours. Unlike many of the cases we have examined, the officer who took the complaint in Michigan listened to the information that family members and friends brought forward and agreed that something was not right. Rather than waiting a couple days to see whether Todd would show up somewhere, Trooper Casey Trucks with the Michigan State Police (MSP) exercised the kind of urgency needed in these cases and immediately sprung into action. We commend him for his swift actions. Having received the missing person complaint in less than 19 hours of when Todd was last seen, Trooper Trucks had the Muskegon Central Dispatch Supervisor (Becky) call the West Michigan Search and Rescue (WMSAR) in Muskegon right away on Sunday evening. She coordinated with Chuck Stark, who arrived at the search area later that same night. Upon his arrival, he informed them that more search assets could be brought to bear on the following morning (Monday, June 13th), such as bloodhound teams and, weather permitting, a helicopter.

On Sunday, June 12th at 23:00 hours, Trooper Trucks, Deputy Rideout (Muskegon County Sheriff's Department K-9 Unit), Chuck Stark and members of the WMSAR, representatives from the Casnovia Fire Department, as well as members of the Michigan-based

Missing You Foundation, and about 20 other volunteers (mostly family and friends) met at the scene of the orchard party. They broke up into 4 search groups of about 6 to 8 persons each and went into the woods. That night, they covered an area leading in the direction of Todd's residence that was bounded by White Road on the north, North Newaygo Road (M-37) on the east, Moon Road on the south, and Peters Road on the west (Figure 9.3, *Purple Area*). Nothing was found. There was no sign of Todd, no sign of any of his property, and no sign of someone having walked through the area.

The Michigan State Police continued search efforts on Monday morning, June 13, 2005. At the direction of Detective Sergeant Harris, Sergeant Waterway contacted all area hospitals to see whether Todd had been admitted: Gerber Hospital in Fremont; Holland Hospital in Holland; North Ottawa Community Hospital in Grand Haven; Mercy General Hospital, Hackley Hospital, and Hackley Behavioral Health in Muskegon. He also called to see whether Todd had been picked up and brought into one of the surrounding county jails: Muskegon County Sheriff's Office in Muskegon, Newaygo County Sheriff's Office in White Cloud, and Ottawa County Sheriff's Office in West Olive.

Suzanne's Law (42 U.S.C. § 5779(a)) was enacted in April 2003 and changed the reporting age of missing persons from 18 to 21 years old. The law affected reporting policies in Michigan and required all missing persons under the age of 21 to be entered into the Law Enforcement Information Network (LEIN) within 2 hours of taking a report. They were to be entered as either Endangered, Catastrophe, Involuntary, or Disabled. As of the day he was reported missing (June 12, 2005), Todd was 22 years 9 months and 23 days old.

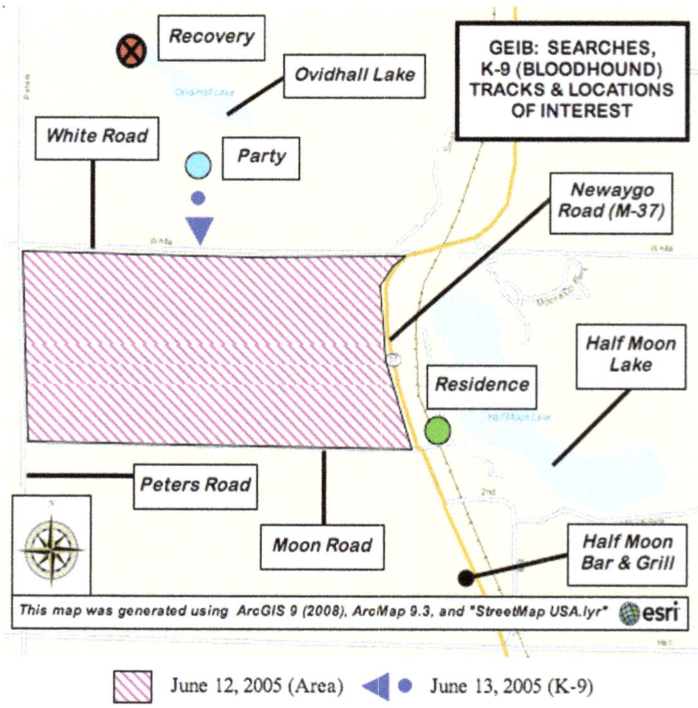

Figure 9.3 On June 12, 2005, less than 24 hours after Todd Geib was last seen, the area between the orchard party and his residence (*Purple Area*) was being searched on-foot by about 20 to 25 people, which included law enforcement officers, qualified search and rescue personnel, family and friends, and other volunteers. Bloodhounds tracked Todd's scent to the edge of White Road, where it vanished (*Blue Dotted Arrow*).

Despite Todd's age being greater than 21, Sergeant Waterway entered him into LEIN as an "endangered missing person." Another common characteristics of these cases is that many of these young men disappeared a week or two before their birthdays.

On Monday, June 13th, assets from the WMSAR arrived and were deployed into the field to search for Todd. An airboat (to navigate the swampy areas) and a helicopter were used and joined by just under 100 people on the ground. Bloodhounds from the WMSAR tracked Todd's scent from the area of the bonfire party down an unimproved dirt road that lead through the orchard to the edge of White Road (Figure 9.4). At that site, the tracking dogs lost his scent. It was as though he had been picked up and transported by vehicle away from that location. This was important because it, coupled with rumors, contributed to investigators' premise that Todd may have been struck by a car and then taken away by its occupants. They believed so strongly that he might have been struck by a car that they checked local body shops for vehicles coming in with damage that could be attributed to a collision with a human body.

Search efforts continued all day on Tuesday, June 14th. Every possible kind of asset was used on that day to search for Todd: helicopters, boats and airboats, search dog teams, horse-mounted searchers, and 4-wheel ATV search teams. About 50 people were involved in the ground search efforts. Officials were there in force to search and to help coordinate family members, friends and volunteers as they scoured the woods, marshy areas, and waist-high grass. Areas were searched and re-searched. Yet, no sign of Todd or any trace of him. Law enforcement pulled out its resources on Wednesday and left the Geib family and friends to search on their own.

On June 19th shortly after 20:00 hours, MSP Troopers Trucks and Green met at the site of the orchard party bonfire with a small contingent of the Geib family and a self-proclaimed psychic ("Spicer"). Spicer claimed that Todd was already deceased. She suggested that he was near a lone tree and partially underwater in an open area that was located in the southwest corner of a small marsh or swamp, which was situated about 300 yards (900 feet) to the north of the bonfire. Trooper Trucks recorded that he, Trooper Green, Spicer, and those Geib family members who were present, searched that night until darkness hindered their efforts. We found no further record of whether or not the northwest corner of the lake was searched on any subsequent date as a result of Spicer's statement. No mention

Figure 9.4 Bloodhounds tracked Todd Geib's scent from the site of the orchard party down a dirt path, and then lost it at this location next to White Road. Todd was headed in the right direction to get back to his home.

of a psychic's input was ever made to us by the Geibs, so we do not know whether or not they even searched the northwest corner.

If the psychic was correct and Todd was there deceased and partially submerged, then he probably would have been spotted had someone gone there. Investigators would later discover that Spicer's description was pretty much spot-on with a few exceptions. The recovery location was marshy and Todd was recovered partially submerged. The lake was the only lake within a short distance to the north of the orchard. However, the site was actually about 1,500 feet to the north of the party and Todd was recovered in the northwest corner of Ovidhall Lake.

Possible Altercation

Multiple sources had told MSP investigators that Todd may have had an altercation with an individual prior to leaving the party. Further probing discerned that the involved person was from Grant, Michigan (hereafter, Randy). On Tuesday morning, June 14th, Detective Sergeant Harris went to Randy's home to conduct an interview. Randy was not home, so he left a business card in the door requesting that he be contacted by telephone as soon as possible. Randy called the MSP office at 20:30 hours saying that he was available for an interview that evening. Troopers Trucks and Dunlap went to Randy's home at 21:30 hours and interviewed him in his kitchen.

Randy provided details of his evening starting with dinner at the Half Moon Bar and Grill around 22:30 hours. He stated the names of persons with whom he had been in contact during the night in question. His timeline of events was punctuated by "last call" at the Kazz Bar in Casnovia, which occurred at about 01:30 hours on Sunday. Randy stated that he then returned to the orchard party and accidentally bumped into a dark-complexioned white male about 20 minutes later around 02:05 hours. He was not sure who had bumped into whom, but the other guy was very intoxicated and wanted to fight. Randy talked him down and walked away. He then offered additional times, locations, activities, events, and witnesses to his whereabouts through 04:00 hours when he left the party on into the remainder of Sunday. The MSP Troopers requested and were granted permission to search Randy's home, and found nothing that could link him to Todd. They were also allowed to examine the clothing that Randy wore to the party and found no tears, stains or indications of a physical fight. They were even allowed to examine the palms and backs of Randy's hands, his chest, and the inside of his mouth and lips for injuries that might be associated with a fist fight. They found no injuries.

Since Todd had supposedly left the party (00:50 hours) before the time of the altercation as reported by Randy (02:05 hours), and the description of the bellicose and drunken man did not match Todd very well, we determined that the verbal confrontation had not involved Todd. Troopers Trucks and Dunlap had been quite thorough, and Randy had been exceedingly cooperative. Everything suggested that Randy had not been in contact with Todd that night and that he most likely had nothing to do with Todd's disappearance. On the other hand, Randy's responses to the Troopers' questioning were highly detailed, perhaps too detailed and rehearsed. This could be cause for concern. Since Randy had been forewarned of the interview and its purpose, he had all day to reflect on events and to verify facts with others. From another perspective, one might also say that he had time to get his story together and his alibi firmed-up. We found no record of whether or not MSP investigators followed up and interviewed those who could confirm Randy's story.

Cell Phone Records

Todd's body was recovered with all his property except his baseball cap, his cell phone, and one shoe. The hat and phone are two items of personal property that have repeatedly played an important role in establishing physical evidence that was supposed to convince investigators and onlookers that the case was an accidental drowning. These items have typically shown up within areas that had already been searched. A prime example of this was Adam Falcon's case. Even though Todd's hat and cell phone were never found, this case was no different. Cell phone records indicated that the final 4 calls were made between 00:45 and 01:00 hours on the morning of June 12, 2005. We believed that these last cell phone calls were merely a ruse to convince investigators that Todd was engaged in conversation with someone until he supposedly lost his way and fell into the lake or his phone's battery went dead. Furthermore, we surmised that Todd had probably already been abducted by the time these calls to and from his phone were made.

The 4th to last call (#4) was made to one of Todd's female friends. She told investigators that she answered her phone and heard someone say twice, "I'm in a field." She thought the person was Todd and commented that he sounded winded or out of breath. The call lasted only 3 seconds before it dropped out. So, she returned the call (#3). Someone answered Todd's phone but did not speak. She reported hearing either heavy breathing or wind. Internet research for historical weather data in the area of Casnovia disclosed that the maximum recorded wind speed between 23:00 hours on June 11th and 01:00 hours on June 12th was 17 miles per hour with gust to 24 miles per hour. So, given that Todd had pretty good physical conditioning (i.e., heart rate and breathing) and that it was reasonably windy that night, it may have been possible that it was just wind that she heard. After 39 seconds, that call also dropped out.

The last two calls (# 2 and #1) were made to Todd's long-time friend (Dave). Both calls lasted for 0 seconds, which meant that they accounted for a "ping" from Todd's phone.

Call	Time	Duration	Call From	Call To
4	00:47:24 hrs.	3 sec.	Todd	Patricia
3	00:51:06 hrs.	39 sec.	Patricia	Todd
2	00:56:12 hrs.	0 sec.	Todd	Dave
1	00:59:41 hrs.	0 sec.	Todd	Dave

Generally speaking, people associate cell phone activity from a specific phone number with a specific living human. The two are not necessarily correlated. If a phone has been stolen, then it is no longer under the control of its owner and all activity coming from it should not be automatically associated with its owner. Therefore, we asserted that these last two calls were only made from Todd's cell phone in order to register a ping on a cellular tower and to create the electronic appearance that they had been generated by Todd himself. There was never a message left on Dave's phone or even any amount of time that was recorded except for the momentary contact (ping). This was intended to reaffirm the illusion that Todd was still in control of his phone, and that it was losing power and could not maintain a signal.

Recovery Location

Not only was the recovery location (Figure 9.5, *Red-X Dot*) in the opposite direction of where Todd was last seen walking to (*Black Arrow*), it was also at the opposite end of

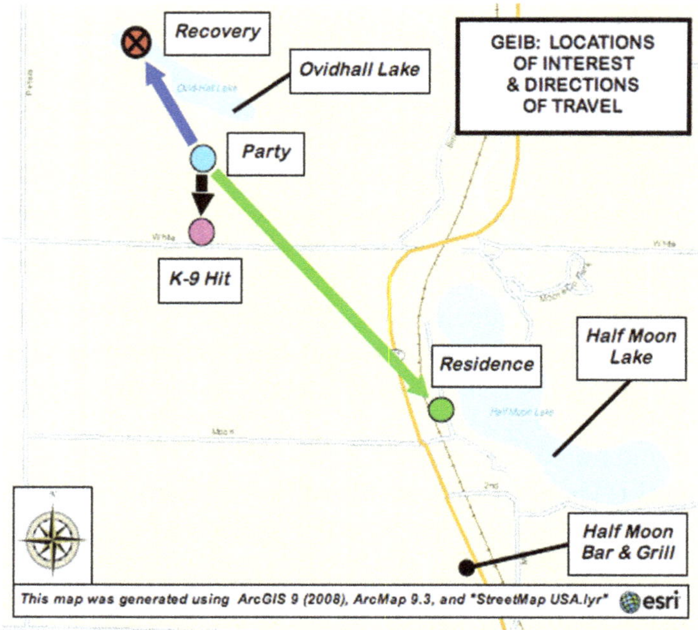

Figure 9.5 Like so many of these cases, the evidence trail in Todd Geib's case (*Black Arrow*) led in a direction that was inconsistent with either the way home (*Green Arrow*) or the path to the body recovery site (*Blue Arrow*). The pattern of opposing directions to recovery and home was also reinforced.

Ovidhall Lake relative to the orchard party. The pattern of opposing directions that has been so well established among these cases was also reified. The straight-line direction to the site where Todd's body was recovered (*Blue Arrow*) was nearly 180 degrees as the crow flies from the straight-line direction of travel he would have taken to get back to his home (*Green Arrow*). The area where Todd's body was recovered would have been very difficult to reach. A person would have to cross swampy terrain along the south side of the lake near the party. The spot where he was found could not be observed from the roads or nearby residences since the lake was completely surrounded by woods. There were no homes or cabins directly on the lake from which a person could have witnessed or heard anything.

There was only one way to access the lake by road. That route would have taken Todd further away from his residence. He would have walked 0.3 miles west along White Road to the intersection with Peters Road; both of these roads are improved and graded gravel surfaces. This intersection was referred to by locals as "Witches' Corner" due to the number of ritualistic animal sacrifices and Satanic graffiti found there over the years by law enforcement. This fact may have been picked up by other individuals on the Internet and media personalities, and then spun as part of the urban legend of the smiley face drownings. We did not find any dominant Satanic theme as part of the motive for the linked homicides that we have investigated. From that infamous intersection, Todd would have walked an additional 0.7 miles north on Peters Road until he arrived at a gated, unimproved dirt road on the northwest side of Ovidhall Lake (Figure 9.6). After climbing over the gate or the adjoining wooden fence, he would have walked another 0.3 miles to the edge of the lake. There was absolutely no logical reason for Todd to walk 1.3 miles in the opposite direction of his home to a lake in the middle of the woods. It made no sense.

Figure 9.6 On June 12, 2005, Todd had to have gone through this gate in order to get to the lake where he was recovered.

Recovered Property

Todd was recovered with all of his property except his baseball hat, his cell phone, and one black shoe. These were all items that a person could lose while trying to negotiate the rough terrain in the dark while intoxicated. The waxing crescent moon was at 20 percent illumination on the night of June 11, 2005. However, it set at 01:11 hours on June 12th. This meant that very little ambient light was available to Todd as he walked on-foot down the dirt path back to White Road. Had he stumbled and dropped his hat or phone, or somehow lost a shoe, it would have been very difficult to see it in the darkness and deep grass. We opined that this was the story the assailant(s) wanted people to believe. They reinforced that lie by leaving money, credit cards, identity cards (i.e., driver's license and social security card), and car keys in Todd's wallet; thus, ruling out robbery, identity theft, and car jacking (motor vehicle theft) as a motive.

Body Position and Lividity

Lividity (*livor mortis*) appears as a discoloration of the body after death. It is caused by gravitation of the blood to the lower parts of a body. Simply put, it is the pooling and settling of the blood that starts within 30 minutes after death (Spitz & Spitz, 2006). It takes about 12 hours (usually 10 to 12 hours) for lividity to "fix," which means that the blood has settled in one position and can no longer be significantly "displaced" or "shifted" by changing the position of the body. If a body is moved during the time that lividity is fixing, then its color can appear diffused (i.e., in two locations). As time passes, lividity will become increasingly resistant to displacement. It is normally completely fixed and will not displace after 24 hours in the water. Body and environmental temperatures may have some marginal affect on this process.

The Death Scene Investigation Report was prepared by Field Investigator Matthew Kempf from the Medical Examiner's Office. It was based on his observations at the scene beginning at about 17:40 hours on July 2, 2005. In the section for "Livor," he checked the box indicating that lividity was as expected. This indicated that he had made an empirical assessment of the position of lividity. It also made perfect sense. There should have been recognizable lividity on his body considering the amount of time that Todd was presumed to be in the water (i.e., about 497 hours or 20.7 days). This initial assessment was contradicted by the autopsy report written by Dr. Brian Hunter, who was a trained forensic pathologist. He wrote in the autopsy report that the position of lividity could not be determined. Less than 20 hours passed between the body recovery and autopsy. As such, discoloration of the body due to decomposition should not have been a factor in masking the position of lividity. Only one of the reports could have been correct.

This whole matter came down to an analysis of the position of the body relative to time. It was, however, confounded by the reported position of the body at the time of recovery and that had to be sorted out first. Field Investigator Kempf had checked the box on the Death Scene Investigation Report indicating that lividity was as expected. He wrote in the report that the body was discovered floating face-down on one page, and floating in a prone position with his head and shoulders out of the water on another page. Initially, one might interpret this to mean that Todd was floating high in the water much like Jelani Brinson. In other words, could this have meant that Todd was not completely submerged in the water? Instead, was he sticking partially out of the water – like a body in a life jacket floating in salt water?

Although the report used the words "prone" and "face-down" to describe the posture of Todd's body at recovery, Gannon had discovered another description. From conversations Gannon had with Detective Sergeant Gary Miles (Michigan State Police) over an 8-month period (September 2008 to April 2009), he learned that Todd was actually found floating standing straight-up. This "bobber in the water" or buoy posture was inconsistent with a normal drowning and was something which was very suspicious to Detective Sergeant Miles and the other investigators at the recovery scene. This also explained why comments had been included in the Death Scene Investigation Report concerning the absence of any anchors or lines tied to Todd to hold him in that bizarre posture. Oddly, this was the same posture that Michael Noll was found in when he was recovered in 2002 from Half Moon Lake in Eau Claire, Wisconsin. In Noll's case, the standing position of his body (with his head and shoulders out of the water) was attributed to the ice which had surrounded his body. But, there was no ice on the lake in Todd's case.

This begged further questions. If lividity was observed at the time of the body recovery to be in the position it was expected to be, then did this mean that lividity was anterior (i.e., on the face and chest as it should be since most drowning victims float face-down)? Or, was lividity assessed to be from the waist down considering the actual recovery position of the body (which was with the head and shoulders out of the water)? If lividity was anterior at the time of recovery, then that meant that Todd had to have been deceased and lying someplace face-down (most likely on land) for a period of time before being entered into the water. It takes 10 to 12 hours on dry land for lividity to completely fix and to cease displacement. However, he had apparently not been deceased and face-down long enough for lividity to completely fix. This told us that the timing in Todd's case involved three time periods and not two. The two periods that are typically associated with a drowning are (a) in the water, and (b) in the morgue. The postmortem artifact of lividity in Todd's case suggested three periods: (a) on land, (b) in the water, and then (c) in the morgue.

Rigidity

Rigidity (*rigor mortis*) is the stiffening of the muscles after death which usually subsides anywhere from 24 to 36 hours on dry land in a temperate environment, to no later than 48 to 72 hours in water (DiMaio & DiMaio, 2001). The autopsy report stated that no rigor was present in Todd's body at the time of the autopsy. This was consistent with the time of year (mid-June into early July), the outdoor air temperatures (73 to 91 °Fahrenheit), and the period of time that he was presumed deceased (21.5 days). We have established the scientific use of time delay ratios of 3:1 for morgue coolers and 2:1 for water in this book. Since Todd's body was in Sparrow Hospital's morgue for 20 hours, this would have been an on-land time equivalent of about 6.7 hours and in the water equivalent of about 10 hours. That meant that he had to have been deceased the equivalent of about 29 hours on land or 62 hours in the water, or some mathematical combination thereof.

Ocular Changes

In some respects, the human eye can act like a stopwatch for estimating a postmortem interval (Figure 9.7). The corneas will begin to dry out and cloud over shortly after death (Geberth, 2006). Changes can be detected within 1 hour when the eyelids are open. The process of corneal opacification starts as a thin film over the corneas, and start to appear cloudy by about 2 hours after death. By the 6th hour postmortem, the corneas may appear completely clouded-over. At the same time when the eyelids are open, the sclerae (i.e., the white parts) will start to change (Shkrum & Ramsay, 2007). Even when the eyelids are closed, a film can form over the corneas by 6 to 12 hours. Cloudiness will establish in 12 to 24 hours, followed by complete corneal opacity by the 60th hour after death.

The Forensic Medical Examiner who performed the autopsy described Todd's eyes in greater detail than we have seen in most of the other cases. Doctor Hunter wrote that he could not determine the color of the irides because of decomposition swelling of the eyelids and the extent of corneal opacification. He stated that the corneas appeared slightly

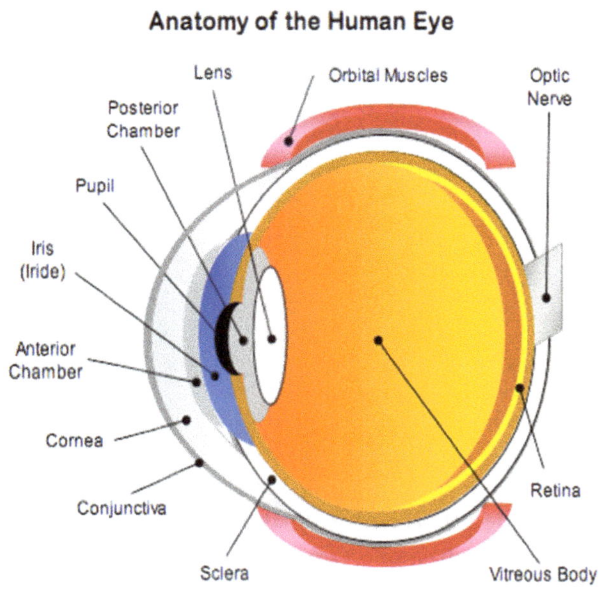

Figure 9.7 The cornea will begin to dry out after death on land. The process of corneal opacification with the eyes closed involves establishment of a film by 6 to 12 hours, cloudiness by 12 to 24 hours, and then complete opacity by the 60th hour postmortem.

opaque and the sclerae were green. In his opinion, the color of the sclerae was due to decomposition and not liver disease. The Medical Examiner commented on the condition of the conjunctivae, which was something we rarely read in autopsies. The conjunctiva is a highly vascular (blood vessels) and clear membrane that covers and protects the inside of the eyelid and the sclera of the eye (white part). He portrayed the conjunctival vasculature as congested, which meant that the small blood vessels covering the front of the eyeball had excess blood or fluid.

Doctor Hunter added that identification of petechial hemorrhages (a.k.a., petechiae, tiny spots that result from ruptures of minute blood vessels) could not be made due to the condition of the overall eye. This was unfortunate because it meant that he could not infer as to whether or not Todd had been strangled. Had Todd been strangled, then petechiae would have typically been present. It is important to note that the phenomenon of petechial hemorrhaging does not always occur in cases of suffocation.

The Medical Examiner's empirical observations and descriptions of Todd's eyes were extremely important and useful in estimating a time of death. Since water would have hydrated Todd's eyes and considerably slowed opacification, the simple fact that his eyes were any extent of opacity meant that he had most likely been deceased on land for a period of time. That also meant that he had to have been placed into Ovidhall Lake. However, Todd's head and shoulders were out of the water. So, one could argue that this exposed his eyes to air and contributed to corneal opacification; this is a strong and logical argument. But, as we have seen (e.g., Brinson), the proximity of the face and eyes to water and moist air when a body is floating in water will either arrest or retard ocular opacification in most incidences.

It is imperative to note that postmortem artifacts do not always progress at the same rate. In other words, they do not always change at a 1-for-1 progression. This case was a classic example of that principle. When a body is in water, decomposition will continue at a slower rate (2:1 time delay) and maceration (skin slippage and Washerwoman's Hands) may actually hasten, while ocular changes will most likely be suspended. The number of hours that eyes were exposed to air should not be confused with the number of hours a person was dead. Since closed eyes are generally cloudy by the 24th hour postmortem and are completely opaque by the 60th hour, this meant that the condition of Todd's eyes suggested that his eyes had been exposed to the air for at least 24 hours after his death, but not greater than 60 hours. The next step was to examine the extent of putrefaction and maceration of Todd's entire body and compare that with the condition of his eyes. A timeline was starting to develop.

Decomposition and Maceration

Decomposition and maceration are good indicators for estimating time since death (Armstrong & Erskine, 2011). This is especially true when an investigator knows the environmental conditions within which the body has been resting. There were 5 postmortem artifacts that needed to be identified with regard to Todd's body.

Decomposition (bacterial putrefaction and enzymatic autolysis)

- Color: What color was the body?
- Bloating: Was there any bloating and to what extent had it developed?
- Purging: Was there any purging of bodily fluids?

Maceration (softening and breakdown of tissue)

- Skin Slippage: Was there any skin slippage, and to what extent had it progressed?
- Degloving: At what stage was degloving of the hands and feet?

If an investigator only knows the environment from which a body was recovered, then these postmortem artifacts can be used to estimate any other unidentified environment(s) that the body may have been in before discovery.

Putrefaction is the decomposition of soft tissues. After death, bacterial flora from the gastrointestinal tract spread throughout the body producing putrefaction (Shkrum & Ramsay, 2007). The extent of decomposition relative to time varies depending on the environmental temperature, amount of clothing worn by the deceased, the proportion of fatty tissue relative to the size of the body, and so forth (Geberth, 2006). Generally speaking, the first colors to appear are blues and greens (Shkrum & Ramsay, 2007). They start in the Right Lower Quadrant (RLQ) and then the Left Lower Quadrant (LLQ), and take about 12 hours to appear. Green discoloration of the entire body should be clearly evident by approximately 24 hours. The body will then gradually change during the next 12 hours after death to darker hues of bluish or grayish-greens, then darker reds and purples (i.e., 24 to 36 hours postmortem). This is followed by shades of dark orange and yellow with highlighted dark purple veins. This affect is called "marbling" and occurs during the period of 36 to 48 hours postmortem. At the same time, the decomposition process progresses and the micro-organisms continue to grow, the body begins to swell from the gases that they produce (Spitz & Spitz, 2006). The purging of bodily fluids usually begins around the 48th hour after death, and can be seen seeping predominantly from the nose and mouth.

The color of the body will now shift to browns and blacks as the skin begins to come apart. Skin slippage should now be identifiable across the body, especially in exposed areas. It will appear spotty between 48 and 96 hours postmortem, and be clearly evident between 96 and 168 hours. If the body was in water, then Washerwoman's Hands (*Wauschaut*) should be well developed. The start of degloving may be seen on the palms near the wrists and fingertips as early as 72 to 96 hours. Degloving is when the top layer of skin (epidermis) separates from the second layer of skin (dermis). It presents like a loose glove lifting and pulling away from the hands. On the feet, it begins to deglove at the heel. Typically, exposed hands will have completely degloved sometime between 144 and 168 hours after death on land. The timing of decomposition and maceration events is typically doubled when a body is found in the water (i.e., the 2:1 time delay ratio for the affect of water).

However, our observation of empirical facts has informed us that times related to skin slippage and degloving may actually either remain constant or shorten. Therefore, erring on the side of a conservative estimate and doubling the time for degloving to occur in Todd's case (which would be 336 hours), then we still could not account for the entire time that Todd was missing. That meant that Todd could not have been deceased the entire time that he was missing, and therefore his death did not occur that night and was not accidental.

The Medical Examiner continued his thorough description of Todd's body as it appeared to him at the time of the autopsy. As had become routine in these cases, no injury was reported to the body (i.e., atraumatic). Most of them were recorded as "no sign of foul play" even though some clearly did have indicators of human-generated injury (e.g., McNeil). When it came to colors, Dr. Hunter described the face, neck, and torso as green.

He assigned no colors to the lower extremities. This sounded like the forensic characteristics of about 24 hours postmortem.

However, even though he did not use colors like dark or purple, the adjectives that he used to described the abdomen suggested to us that decomposition had actually advanced. Doctor Hunter wrote that decomposition was intermediate to moderate. We also discovered that he discussed bloating of the head and face, neck, and scrotum. This typically occurs about the same time that marbling becomes detectable. Yet, he presented no reference to marbling anywhere. These combined postmortem artifacts of decomposition told us that Todd had not been deceased any longer than about the equivalent of 36 hours on land (or 72 in the water taking into account the 2:1 time delay ratio).

The autopsy report also discussed skin slippage over much of the body in the expected areas, particularly on the torso, upper and lower extremities. Todd's palms and feet were described as presenting with an affect of Washerwoman's Hands, but no degloving had started. In addition to this, the body still retained head hair and eyebrows. These postmortem artifacts of maceration placed the body at less than the 72-hour mark.

Gastrointestinal System

There is general consensus among experts concerning the timing of emptying for the stomach and gastrointestinal tract (DiMaio & DiMaio, 2001; Shkrum & Ramsay, 2007). Small or light meals, like a sandwich, will digest and leave the stomach in about 2 hours. A medium meal will clear it in approximately 3 to 4 hours, while a heavy meal will pass in about 4 to 6 hours. Fluids will pass through the stomach more quickly than solids. The partially digested food will complete its journey through the small intestine by about the 12th hour (Geberth, 2006). It can take some foods, like a large portion of beef steak, up to 24 hours or more to pass completely through a human depending on that person's metabolism and the type of liquid that was drank with the meal. Also recall that it takes about 3 to 3.5 hours from the start of taking in food for the gallbladder to completely refill (as discussed in Chapter 2, McNeil & Chapter 7, Jenkins).

The autopsy report stated that Todd's stomach was empty and the gallbladder contained bile (a precise measurement was not recorded). We knew that Todd started out Saturday evening (June 11, 2005) at his parents' home eating pepperoni and sausage Hobo Pies. That meal took place between 16:00 and 17:00 hours. Although the volume of that food may have been large considering Todd's appetite, the pies were not an especially dense food and could be considered a medium meal. Since we could not claim to know his metabolism, we had to consider the broader window for digestion and passing. That meal could have cleared Todd's stomach as early as 20:00 hours and as late as 23:00 hours. Considering what he was drinking that night, his gallbladder could have easily refilled by midnight.

Our analysis of the stomach and gallbladder in this case did not disclose any information that contradicted a hypothesis that Todd had drowned during the early morning hours of June 12, 2005. The time between his last known meal and when he was last seen at the orchard party were sufficiently far enough apart that no stomach contents remained. In fact, Dr. Hunter even commented that there were no pill fragments in Todd's stomach. Even Todd's bladder was empty (part of the genitourinary system). Had the stomach contained some partially digested food particulates, then their stage of digestion could have aided in determining a postmortem interval. Furthermore, had the stomach contained anything other than the remnants of pepperoni and sausage Hobo Pies, then investigators would have had to find an explanation for the source of this new food and a time for when it had been consumed.

Unfortunately, we have yet to read an autopsy wherein the attending medical examiner opened and examined the small intestine and the large intestine (a.k.a., colon). If the Medical Examiner had checked the small intestine and found food was present there, then we would have known that Todd had died sometime after 6 hours, but less than 12 hours, after eating his last meal. If the small intestine was empty, then we would have known that Todd had died at least 12 hours after eating his last meal. This expanded examination of the gastrointestinal system would have told us whether or not Todd had been held for more than 24 hours without being fed.

Respiratory System

The medicolegal literature and our experience reading autopsies informed us that when the lungs of a person who was recovered from water weigh more than 1,000 grams (gm), and pleural effusion is present, then that individual probably experienced some extent of drowning and ingested water into his lungs (Zhu, Quan, Li, Taniguchi, Kamikodai, Tsuda, Fujita, Nishi, Tsuji, & Maeda, 2003). The autopsy report presented the weight of the right lung as 560 gm and the left lung as 450 gm, for a combined weight of 1,010 gm. This indicated that Todd most likely inhaled a small amount of water shortly before he died.

In addition to that, the Medical Examiner wrote that both lungs presented with moderate congestion due to pulmonary edema. He described the pleural cavities as containing 25 to 50 milliliters (mL) of decomposition fluid with no visible sign of blood. Pleural effusion is the collection of fluid in the space between the two linings of the lungs (i.e. the pleura). Studies suggest that statistically significant findings exist for the assertion that the duration of time that a body spends in water is correlated to the amount of pleural fluid produced (Morild, 1995; Yorulmaz, Arican, Afacan, Dokgoz, & Asirdizer, 2003). Therefore, the small amount of pleural effusion in Todd's body suggested that he had only been in the water a short period of time. Another possible medical explanation for the congestion and pulmonary edema was a drug overdose (Armstrong & Erskine, 2011).

A final item related to Todd's lungs was Dr. Hunter's observation that the subpleural spaces contained mild to moderate amounts of anthracotic pigment. Simply stated, anthracosis (i.e., the presence of anthracotic pigment) is an accumulation of carbon pigment from breathing dirty air. The most pronounced anthracosis can be found in smokers. There are several reasons for finding carbon-laden macrophages in pleural fluid cytologic samples. One of those explanations is smoking crack or freebase cocaine (Pantanowitz, Warren, & Goulart, 2009). Thus, we were left asking whether Todd was a smoker, had he recently breathed smoke-filled air somewhere, or had he smoked some form of cocaine in his past?

Toxicology

Toxicology results in this case were very important in understanding what had happened to Todd and how he died. Tests were performed by the Toxicology Testing Center (St. Lawrence Campus) at Sparrow Hospital in Lansing, Michigan. Iliac artery blood was used to conduct the initial drug screen, and then femoral blood was used to perform quantitation testing for specific drugs.

The general drug screen showed that cotinine was present in Todd's bloodstream at the time of his death. Cotinine is an alkaloid and metabolite of nicotine and it routinely shows up in the blood work of smokers during toxicology tests (Wall, Johnson, Jacob, & Benowitz, 1988). Cotinine is completely eliminated from the bloodstream by day 5 after smoking cessation (Feyerabend, Bryant, Jarvis, & Russell, 1986; Jarvis, Russell, Benowitz, & Feyerabend, 1988; Sepkovic, Haley, & Hoffman, 1986). We knew that Todd smoked because his mother (Kathy) had mentioned how he teased her when she bummed cigarettes from him. How much he smoked was irrelevant for two reasons. First, had he died during the early morning hours of June 12th, then cotinine should have been in his blood. Second, had Todd been abducted and murdered a couple days later, then cotinine would have still been in his blood. And lastly, the presence of cotinine in this case told us nothing because his captor(s) could have given him a cigarette at any time before his death and caused the positive test result.

The toxicology tests also disclosed a blood alcohol concentration (BAC) of 0.12 for ethanol. This was the equivalent of about 6 drinks. Todd was an experienced drinker. He started drinking beer that evening at about 19:30 hours at the Half Moon Bar and Grill with his friends, and was not drinking heavily. Considering he was physically last seen by some of those same friends at about midnight heading back home on foot, that meant that he had only been drinking for about 4.5 hours. Given what we knew of Todd's physical build (5 feet 11 inches, 180 pounds, at a Body Mass Index of 25.10), personality, and drinking prowess, we did not believe that a 0.12 BAC was sufficiently intoxicated to contribute to Todd ending up deceased and floating in a lake nearly 180 degrees from his home.

Furthermore, utilizing the table that Gannon developed to estimate the affect of the postmortem production of alcohol on BAC test results, Todd's BAC would have increased by about 0.0150 during the first month that he was in the water. Knowing that Todd was supposed to be in the water for approximately 3 weeks (20.7 days), his BAC from decomposition would have risen by only 0.011. This meant that Todd's actual BAC at the time of his death would have been 0.109 or just under 5-1/2 drinks. Basically, Todd was recovered with such a low BAC that he was almost sober enough to drive.

Another important point we learned from the toxicology tests for alcohol was the negative finding for all other volatiles of alcohol. The absence of n-butanol and n-propanol was of particular importance (Armstrong & Erskine, 2011). Their absence strongly suggested that no postmortem alcohol production had occurred. This meant that Todd had apparently not been deceased for nearly 3 weeks or some amount of these chemicals should have come up positive in the tests.

On page 1 of the Death Scene Investigation Report, the first decision required of Field Investigator Kempf was under the section entitled "Primary Rationale for Medical Examiner Activity." He was offered 8 options plus "other." He could have checked "Cause of Death Not Determinable by Attending Physician" or "Accidental Death." He did not. Rather, he checked the box for "Suspicious Circumstances." The Medical Examiner was equally as cautious and had examined Todd's stomach for pill fragments. This level of suspicion was even held by the lead investigator, Detective Sergeant Gary Miles. During the course of numerous conversations with Detective Sergeant Miles from September 2008 to May 2009, Gannon learned that every inch of Todd's body was painstakingly examined to see whether there were any needle marks. When Gannon asked him why that was done, Detective Sergeant Miles stated that they were looking for anything that might help to explain what had happened to Todd. Given that the relatively pristine appearance of Todd's body was inconsistent with the outdoor temperatures and weather conditions, especially considering the extended period of time that he was missing, Todd should have been very badly decomposed. Since he was not, Detective Sergeant Miles told Gannon that he had taken every step to look for clues into Todd's death. Obviously, Miles knew that something suspicious had occurred with regard to Todd's case.

On the morning of June 14th, Trooper Jay Sweetland (Michigan State Police) was approached by a man in the staging area for the day's search efforts. The man said that his son had shared information with him that may shed light on what happened to Todd. Trooper Sweetland then interviewed the young man in the presence of his father. The young man said that he had used drugs himself. So, it was logical that someone might come to him asking about a possible source to make a purchase. He claimed that Todd had approached him on Friday, June 10th, requesting whether he knew where he could buy some cocaine. He informed Todd that he had quit some time ago and that all of his connections had dried up. He further stated that he believed Todd had made a purchase from "Mr. X" (he provided a name), who also happened to be at the orchard party that night. The young man described "Mr. X" as a student at Michigan State University (MSU) in East Lansing who comes to the Muskegon-Casnovia area on occasion.

In a study to identify patterns of cocaine and metabolite elimination after cessation (Moolchan, Cone, Wstadik, Huestis, & Preston, 2000), all of the volunteer human research subjects self-reported having smoked cocaine and their last use ranged from 2.5 to 63 hours. Testing during the initial processing phase (with a detection limit of 1 nanogram/mL) found cocaine in only 60 percent of the subjects. However, two metabolites were detected at higher proportions: ecgonine methyl ester (EME) in 80 percent, and benzoylecgonine (BE) in 100 percent. That same study also reported findings for plasma half-lives and Mean Residence Time (MRT, the average time for all drugs to reside in the body) for cocaine, EME, and BE. They found that the plasma half-lives were 3.8, 5.5, and 6.6 hours, respectively. The MRT values were 5.7, 7.7, and 9.6 hours, respectively.

As previously discussed, the Medical Examiner noted that Todd's lungs presented with mild to moderate amounts of anthracotic pigment, which could be attributed to smoking cigarettes and crack or freebase cocaine (Pantanowitz, Warren, & Goulart, 2009). The toxicology report showed negative findings for cocaine and its metabolites. We did not know what the reporting cut-off or limit of detection was for that test. However, had Todd purchased cocaine on June 10th as the young man professed to Trooper Sweetland, and used or smoked it that evening or at any time prior to his presumed death during the early morning hours of June 12th (a timeframe of less than 48 hours), then the metabolites of cocaine should have still been at high enough levels to be detected and to trigger a positive hit on the drug screen conducted at autopsy. Either Todd did not purchase or use cocaine as asserted, or he was held long enough for the cocaine and its metabolites to achieve terminal elimination from his blood before he was murdered.

The most important finding in the toxicology report was the detection of desipramine (495 ng/mL) and amitriptline (51 ng/mL). Desipramine (desmethylimipramine) is a tricyclic antidepressant drug and has been around since 1965. It is a metabolite of imipramine and has many side effects. Intoxication, especially overdose, can be fatal (Dahlin, Låstbom, Blomgren & Ryrfeldt, 1997; Hughes & Rome, 1984). In one case (Bickel, Brochon, Friolet, Herrmann & Stofer, 1967), the authors narrated a story of a 2-year-old girl who had accidentally swallowed 100 tablets of desipramine. The child presented with mild convulsions of the arms and legs about 1 hour from ingestion. Within 1/2 hour, the parents rushed her to the local pediatric clinic. By the time they got her there, she presented with unconsciousness, cold skin with bluish discoloration, an abnormal dilation of the pupils with absence of light reflex, an absence of other reflexes, an absence of muscle tone and jerking of the extremities, and a pulse that was almost undetectable (Bickle, et al., 1967). The child died due to progressive bradycardia about 6.5 hours after ingesting the drug (i.e., a heart that kept beating more and more slowly until it could no longer sustain life).

The important part of their study's findings centered on an increased fluid volume and whether or not they could find physical evidence of the pills in the child's stomach. The researchers reported that several steps were taken to counter the slowing heart rate and other symptoms. Part of the life-saving measures involved trying to clear her airway and stomach. They stated that bronchial intubation removed a large volume of gastric juice (Bickel, et al, 1967). This may be explained by the fact that, prior to being taken to the clinic, the child was sitting at the dinner table. Even though she showed very poor appetite and felt tired, perhaps the routine act of sitting at the dinner table triggered the gallbladder to start releasing bile into the stomach; kind of like Pavlov's dog and the bell (Pavlov, 1927). However, this explanation could not account for the presence of so much fluid. The child was also administered an anesthesia and "gastric lavage yielded copious gastric contents without recognizable remnants of the tablets" (Bickel, et al, 1967, p. 431). In layperson terms, they flushed her stomach with water and could not find physical evidence of the 100 tablets that she had swallowed.

In another study (Zuckerman & Conway, 1993), a 14-year-old girl had ingested 54 tablets of 50 mg desipramine. She had a history of suicide attempts. As a result of the doctor's treatment, she survived this one as well. They treated her using fluid restriction, tracheal intubation, application of positive end-expiratory pressure, and vasopressors. She presented with several symptoms. Initially, she had cardiac dysrhythmia and hypotension, and eventually developed pulmonary edema with clinical symptoms reflecting acute respiratory distress syndrome (ARDS). Of particular interest in this article was the researchers' discussion of the development of pulmonary edema and ARDS, and a potential relationship with the sequelae associated with swallowing the tablets (e.g., cardiac disturbances, hypotension, acidosis, gastric aspiration, pneumonia). They suggested that her lung injury may have been related to any number of these symptoms as well as a direct affect of the desipramine on her lung parenchyma. According to Armstrong and Erskine (2011), individuals who have survived a drowning event and received therapeutic intervention may present similar symptoms (e.g., encephalopathy, pulmonary edema, pneumonia, or ARDS). Aspirated gastric contents or inhaled fluids may cause direct lung injury that evolves into ARDS and which may result in the development of aspiration pneumonia (Armstrong & Erskine, 2011).

There are certain overdose symptoms of tricyclic antidepressants – like the desipramine and amitriptyline that were discovered in Todd's system – that could complicate an autopsy related to drowning. The fact that the Medical Examiner could not find any evidence of pill fragments in Todd's stomach was entirely possible. Todd's system may have been at an extremely high level of the drug (495 ng/mL), but the few desipramine tablets or capsules that he may have been given to raise his system to that level was minimal when compared to the 100 tablets taken by the child. If those were not found in the child's stomach, then the pills in Todd's stomach were long gone as well. Another example was cyanosis brought on by ARDS; that is when a person does not have enough oxygen in his or her blood and the skin and mucous membranes present a waxy-bluish color. To what extent might this mask or contribute to an inability to determine the location of lividity? To what extent might this be confused with the gray, blue, and green colors during early stages of decomposition? If it did, then this might explain why Dr. Hunter, the Medical Examiner who performed the autopsy, stated that he could not determine lividity.

The Geib family sought a second opinion to review the original autopsy report and photographs that were produced by Dr. Hunter. They brought in a board-certified medical examiner, Dr. Michael Sikirica, the same medical examiner who performed Adam Falcon's autopsy. Doctor Hunter expressed that he thought Todd had been deceased the entire time that he was missing. Once he publicly released his professional assessment of Dr. Hunter's autopsy report (February 2010), Dr. Sikirica agreed with and reiterated a statement that Gannon had made 10 months earlier during a *Garage Logic* radio program broadcast on 1500 ESPN (April 2009). During that radio interview, Gannon declared that Todd had only been deceased a few days at the most. To the best of our knowledge based on reading various websites, no one (i.e., no medical examiner, law enforcement or media investigator) has ever offered an alternative or definitive explanation to Doug and Kathy Geib for Todd's death. Doctor Sikirica never explained the drugs in Todd's system in any public statement, or in any private discussion with the Geibs. If he had, then the Geibs would have known about the lethal amount of drugs that Todd had in his system (which we explained to them during our visit at their home on November 14, 2012). Also, it may have been possible that Dr. Hunter's finding of drowning as a cause of death was influenced by the presence of the symptoms associated with desipramine overdose. To what extent might the symptoms of a tricyclic antidepressant overdose contribute to an increased lung weight? Specifically, what role was played by pulmonary edema, pneumonia, and a general production of excessive fluids? To what extent might the presence of fluid in the lungs be confused with a wet drowning?

The Medical Examiner (Dr. Hunter) reported that the pleural cavities contained fluid (50 mL on the left side and 25 mL on the right side). Todd's lungs weighed slightly more than we would have been expected for someone of his size. His left lung was 450 gm and his right lung was 560 gm. Although the desipramine overdose symptoms of pulmonary edema and acute respiratory distress syndrome were of interest to us, pneumonia was the key symptom of focus here in our analysis. Pneumonia can trigger pleural effusion and fluid in the lungs. Both of these symptoms would easily account for the small amount of fluid in the pleural cavities and the lung weight gains. Neither Dr. Hunter nor Dr. Sikirica mentioned any of the symptoms of desipramine or amitriptyline overdose. Therefore, we surmised that neither of the two doctors considered examining Todd's body in light of desipramine or amitriptyline overdose symptoms.

It was unusual that someone would take this particular prescribed medication to get high; although, it could not be ruled out entirely. Desipramine is a neurotransmitter that helps to balance certain brain chemicals. This medication is given to help relieve the symptoms of major depression (of which Todd had none) after other types of antidepressants have not been effective. This is not the type of drug one takes recreationally to get high. The amount of this drug in Todd's system was double the highest recommended dosage. The typical dose for a person with a chemical imbalance or psychosis ranges from 5 ng/mL up to 125 ng/mL, with 250 ng/mL being the maximum amount recommended for depression. This maximum amount is to be administered over the course of an extended period of time and under the care of a physician. The second drug, amitriptyline, is also a neurotransmitter for the brain and does relatively the same things. It is given to help regulated the chemicals in the brain to ease major depression. Again, Todd was not suffering from any form of depression.

Considering the inherent danger associated with these type of drugs and the excessive quantitations of them in Todd's system, we believed that he was at least unconscious if not dead before his entry into the water. Gannon and Duarte drove to Pennsylvania to meet world renowned forensic pathologist and medical examiner Dr. Cyril Wecht. They showed Todd's autopsy and toxicology reports to him. He read them, paused, confirmed the lethal dosages of the drugs by reviewing a large reference book, and then stated his assessment. Doctor Wecht stated, "Considering the amount of drugs in his system, there was enough evidence to substantiate that this individual [Todd Geib] was at least unconscious if not dead before entry into the water." He had confirmed our earlier assessment and statements. When you consider the unusual type of drugs in his system, it would lead one (including Prosecutor Tony Tague) to believe that all indications were pointing to this case being a homicide and not an accident.

Suspicious Material

During Todd's autopsy, a small piece of white plastic was found on his buttocks. The precise location was not recorded. This evidence was not mentioned at all in the Medical Examiner's autopsy report. Neither the discovery of it nor the securing of it in a manila envelope as evidence (labeled "Prop 0015") was mentioned anywhere in the autopsy. The only reason we knew about it was because of the fact that it had been vouchered as evidence was mentioned in a Supplemental Incident Report that was filed by Trooper Michele Dunlap.

Although this small and seemingly insignificant piece of plastic was secured like evidence, it was treated like a piece of litter. No attempt to identify its chemical makeup or its origin was ever made. Was it packing material or was it some form of a raw material used to construct another product? Was it stiff or flexible? What were its dimensions? No other report even speculated as to how it got there. Unfortunately, we have never seen the recovery or autopsy photographs. So, we have never seen this piece of white plastic and do not know whether or not a picture of it was even taken. Gannon had filed a Freedom of Information Act request for the pictures and permission had been granted by the Geib family. However, in the 11th hour, someone convinced the Geibs that they could do a better job of bringing Todd's story forward and we were denied copies of the photos.

We found this plastic to be significant in light of the massive rip in the backside of Todd's blue jeans (Figure 9.8). The rip was not running along a seam, as such, it was not a "blow out" one might get from sitting down or bending over in tight pants. It was clear to us that the rip had been created by something that snagged his jeans and then tore them in two. Having grown up working on farms and hunting in rural farmlands, the rip reminded Gilbertson of one that a person might get from barbed wire. The only difference being, that when a person gets snagged by barbed wire, he typically stops his forward motion. This rip looked like Todd had been snagged and then continued his forward movement with great speed and/or force. Much like one would do when being chased and fearing for his life.

The picture of the pants was taken by Gilbertson and Carlson during their visit to Casnovia on August 31, 2008. The family had contacted Gannon about a week earlier. Gilbertson and Carlson drove the 13-hour trip straight through to Casnovia and met with the family at the Half Moon Bar and Grill. Doug and Kathy Geib took them to all the important sites, and encountered a local property owner at "Witches' Corner." Prior to their departure, the Geib's shared all of their documents and allowed them to photograph the pants. To the best of our knowledge, Todd's boxers were not also torn. So, this begged a

Figure 9.8 Todd Geib's blue jeans had a snag near the top of the left back pocket and a massive tear running down the middle along the right back pocket.

couple questions. How did the piece of plastic get inside Todd's boxers and on his buttocks? From where did the plastic originate?

Suspicious Events

When something like the unexplained death of a child happens to a family, it becomes pretty easy to start seeing conspiracy under every rock. It is a natural human tendency that investigators must self-monitor and be alert for when listening to the stories passed along by traumatized family members and curious members of the public. Todd's case was not without its fair share. In fact, it exceeded what one would have expected for an "accidental drowning."

Like most parents, the Geibs were quite vocal in the surrounding communities trying to get the word out about their son. Then one night, after the Geib family had gone on television to report that they believed their son's death was suspicious, the weekly telephone contact with Gannon suddenly became nightly contact with 2 to 3 calls. Gannon received a call from Kathy. Her voice sounded urgent and frantic. A strange vehicle had followed her daughter home from work late at night. He tried to calm her down and to gather facts in order to determine whether this was intentional or just circumstantial. This behavior continued for several nights. The stalking behavior was even reported to a police officer who was sitting in his car in the parking lot of a convenience store, and he did nothing. One evening, the same vehicle was seen from a window in their house by the son-in-law. The car sped off as he ran outside, so he chased in its direction with his car for a short distance down the road. Realizing he had lost sight of it, he returned home. The driver of the unidentified vehicle tried to run the daughter off the road one evening and 911 was called. That call finally generated a police response and the stalking abruptly stopped.

Another suspicious event involved the Geibs' nephew. He too was quite vocal about his cousin's death. He publicly declared that Todd's death was no accident; it was murder. While he was on vacation in Florida, his home burned down. Fire and police investigators ruled it arson, but no one was ever prosecuted for the crime. Thankfully, no one was at home at the time and the only loss was to property.

On the night that Todd went missing, he was out drinking with Theodore and Chuck. Both of them were employed. Chuck owned his own landscaping business. It just seemed

Figure 9.9 Someone placed a 4 inch smiley face disc on Todd Geib's headstone at the time of the third anniversary of this death (June 12, 2008). (Photo courtesy of Doug and Kathy Geib.)

odd to us and others that Theodore and Chuck left together for Pensacola (Florida) shortly after Todd disappeared and before he was recovered. This was never followed up.

The most suspicious event happened shortly after the third anniversary of Todd's disappearance and death. [Important Note: Although Todd's headstone shows his date of disappearance (June 12, 2005), the death certificate shows Todd's body recovery date as the official date of death (July 2, 2005).] Whether the person who did this was involved in his death or not remained to be seen. Either way, whomever it was that did it had some serious issues with what is considered appropriate or humorous. As they did on every previous anniversary of Todd's death (2006 and 2007), the Geib family went to the gravesite to pray and reflect on Todd's life. In fact, they sometimes went there during the week and often on weekends. So, it was no secret that they would be at the cemetery about every 4 to 5 days. Upon arrival on July 18, 2008, the Geibs discovered a 4 inch smiley face disc on Todd's headstone (Figure 9.9). No one ever came forward to claim responsibility for placing it there. Was this the act of a sick-minded sense of humor, or a taunt of the police? Was it a coincidence or intentional that this occurred about 81 days after Gannon and Duarte's April 28th appearance on *Good Morning America* and the team's first national press release?

Graffito and Spray Paint Can

In early July 2008, the Geib family had just come from the cemetery where they found the smiley face disc lying on top of Todd's headstone. At that time, they did not know what it meant. Was it a sick joke or was someone trying to say that Todd was in a happier place now? All they knew is that it was kind of strange to find it there. They shared the finding with a friend, who in turn told them about some additional drownings that had been associated with a smiley face being left at the scene. It was at this point that Kathy first called Gannon (July 20, 2008).

Gannon told Kathy about some of the other cases with which he had been involved. He shared with her how our team had been able to provide families with some hard-sought answers once we had been provided all of the case-related documents and photographs. He discussed how in a majority of the cases the team had proven homicide (as in the Jenkins case). Kathy asked him about the smiley face graffiti. After Gannon answered her question, she then informed him of what had transpired at Todd's gravesite just a couple days earlier. Gannon told her that the disc was very different from any of the other cases; this was the first case to involve an object and not a graffito. He suggested that the disc was a taunting of everyone involved in Todd's case, from the police, to the family, and possibly even to his team for having recently presented the smiley face theory on national television.

Gannon then asked Kathy whether there was a smiley face painted anywhere near where Todd had gone missing. She informed him that there was an eerie smiley face with horns spray-painted on a tree near where the orchard party had been held. She said that it was in such a location that it could be seen from the road by anyone passing by. Gannon was keenly aware of the timing and significance of this and other events.

The smiley face that we had shared in confidence with KSTP was presented during the local broadcast of an interview that had been conducted with the whole team (March 21, 2008). It was shown again on *Good Morning America* (April 28, 2008). That smiley face was reflective orange, but did not have horns. Gilbertson photo-shopped the original digital photo after discussing it with the whole team. Initially, we had all agreed to specifically withhold information that only the offender(s) would know. The original photograph of that smiley face was taken in Ames (Iowa) by Carlson on May 29, 2007, during our cross-country field research. It was associated with Abel Bolanos' disappearance (March 31, 2007) and body recovery (April 3, 2007). Since this smiley face had been publicly released, we decided to present the unaltered, original photo of the reflective orange, horned smiley face during our national press conference on April 28, 2008 (Figure 9.10). Although every member of the team knew the ideological meaning of the smiley face icon at the time of the press conference, Gannon only explained the cultural meaning of the words next to the graffito. We knew then that the smiley face was an important symbol and would come to learn that it was the most important symbol to this group of murderers.

The timing of events told us that the smiley face graffito in Casnovia was not the result of a copy cat offender. The reflective orange, horned smiley face that we presented was spray-painted in April 2007 and shown on television in April 2008. However, the reflective orange, horned smiley face in Casnovia had been spray-painted on the tree prior to Todd's body recovery in July 2005, and prior to the release of our photo in April 2008. Thus, the orange smiley face disc that had been left on Todd's headstone on July 18, 2008, had to be the act of a sick mind who saw it on television, or a direct taunt of police and connected to the other cases, or from those individuals involved with the painting of the horned smiley face on the tree 3 years earlier (who were most likely responsible for Todd's abduction and murder). In either case, the person who left the smiley face disc at the gravesite knew that

Figure 9.10 The photograph of the smiley face graffito that we presented during our national press conference in a New York City (April 28, 2008).

it, as an icon, was important to the group, to the cases, and should have been equally as important to law enforcement investigators.

In the beginning (2007), Gilbertson's analysis of the graffiti left in towns (and not just near the body recovery site) disclosed that the smiley face graffito came in many styles. Each group had a style that it used, and some groups used similar styles. The smiley face icon comprised 1 set of graffiti out of a total of 13 identified sets. Others (i.e., law enforcement investigators, media reporters and subject-matter experts, and Internet bloggers) have either never grasped the significance of this icon, or have backed away from it claiming that it was no longer important. Some have even asserted that it should have never been a part of the analysis of these cases. On the other hand, at the time of our press conference in April 2008, we knew its deeper meaning and had discovered that it was the most important symbol used by the group.

That is why Gannon asked Kathy Geib whether the horned smiley face graffito was still on the tree near Casnovia when she called him on July 20, 2008. Kathy volunteered to check and said she would go back to the scene and photograph it for us. He asked her to also take photographs of any additional graffiti and to see whether anything may have been left behind by those responsible for the graffiti. Kathy and some family members went back to the location and called Gannon. They found the tree where the smiley face had been spray-painted. Only a faint smudge of it remained. Someone had painstakingly scrubbed it and most of the bark from the tree (most likely the owner of the property). They took several pictures of it anyway with a cell phone camera; the file size and resolution of the photos made them difficult to see and to include here. At Gannon's direction, they also took a sample of the painted wood from the tree and put it into a paper bag for him (just in case law enforcement ever became interested in determining what kind of paint it was and if it was anything that might be of an exotic or specific nature and easily identifiable). We still retain that sample today.

In the meantime, Gilbertson and Carlson cleared their schedules at the university and planned a trip out to Casnovia. On August 30, 2008, they drove the 13-hour trip to Grand Rapids, Michigan. The next morning (August 31st), having slept well and refreshed, they drove up to Casnovia and met Doug and Kathy Geib at the Half Moon Bar and Grill. They spent about 2 hours at the bar getting familiar with Todd's life and his family's story. They then drove over to Todd's cousin's home where Todd was living and interviewed him. From there, they inspected the entire route to the entry to the orchard. Along the way, they found graffiti that was representative of the type of organizations that were responsible for these murders – but, they kept that information to themselves.

The Geibs then took them to Witches' Corner where the horned smiley face graffito had been found spray-painted on a tree. Upon arrival, the Geibs surprised them by presenting a paper sack. Gilbertson and Carlson were told that the contents of the sack had been found about 15 feet from the tree. Doug walked over and showed them the exact spot on the ground where it had been found. It had been found between the time Kathy had last spoken with Gannon and the team's arrival. The bag contained another, smaller paper sack (Figure 9.11). Inside that sack, was a can of reflective orange "marking" spray paint. It was the same color paint as the horned smiley face on the tree (as well as the ones in several other locations). Kathy told them that they had recovered it very carefully using the paper sacks and making sure not to touch it as Gannon had requested. Gilbertson still maintains custody of that spray can in a secure area at his place of work.

The spray can was brought back to Saint Cloud State University in Minnesota. Gilbertson took it to Dr. Lakshmaiah Sreerama, Chair of the Chemistry Department and Director of

Figure 9.11 A reflective orange, horned smiley face graffito was visible on a tree near Witches' Corner. Nearby, a matching spray paint can was discovered. The Geibs secured the spray can inside 2 paper sacks without touching it. It was later fingerprinted and then secured by Gilbertson in a locked storage area in order to maintain the chain-of-custody.

the Forensic Science Minor, who previously worked for Minnesota's Bureau of Criminal Apprehension (MnBCA). Gilbertson explained the background of the spray can and asked that it be fingerprinted. The can was handled and dusted for prints with the same level of care that Dr. Sreerama would have given to evidence at the MnBCA. What made this really suspicious was that there was not one single fingerprint on the spray can or its cap.

Logically, this was impossible under normal conditions. The can would have been packaged in a factory by a machine – no prints. It would have then reached a store, where the box was cut open and the can handled to be placed on the shelf by a Stocker – 1st Set of Prints, Person 1. A customer would have picked up the can and placed it in a basket or cart – 2nd Set of Prints, Person 2. That same person would have picked it back up and placed it on the counter – 3rd Set of Prints, Person 2. The cashier would have picked up the can, scanned its barcode, and placed it in a plastic bag – 4th Set of Prints, Person 3. The customer would have gone home. At some point in time, the can would have been taken to the woods, retrieved from the plastic bag, the cap removed, used to spray-paint the horned smiley face, recapped, and then tossed into the woods – 5th Set of Prints, Person 2. In all then, a total of 5 sets of fingerprints should have overlapped on the spray can from a total of at least 3 different individuals. Yet, the spray can was as clean as it was the day it went into the box at the factory.

Gannon called Bode Laboratories to see whether they could do "Touch DNA" testing on the spray can; they confirmed that they could. Gannon informed them of the fingerprinting and asked whether that could, in anyway, affect the DNA testing. The laboratory technician stated that it would not affect anything. Furthermore, the fingerprint powder would in fact protect the DNA sample on the can if one existed. Gannon asked whether they would do a test pro bono. He was informed that, unfortunately in this case, they would not be able to assist him. Without the assistance of law enforcement or someone who could run the findings through the Combined DNA Index System (CODIS), then the DNA evidence would be useless. However, if an individual becomes a person of interest in the future, then the DNA results could at least add some evidentiary weight to the fact that a specific person was present in the woods at that location and was in all likelihood connected to a potential "smiley face homicide." We still have that spray paint can available for testing.

Linked Events and Information

In early April 2009, the executive producer of the 1500 ESPN radio program *Garage Logic* invited Gannon and Duarte to be on a show about the smiley face murders. The team was in Saint Paul assisting with the search for Dan Zamlen at the request of the parents. Gannon and Duarte headed over to the KSTP building where the program was broadcasted. They announced who they were upon arrival and were quickly ushered into the sound booth. On that day, Todd's case was discussed. When asked a direct question by the show's host Joe Soucheray, Gannon replied, "We can prove that Todd Geib was at least unconscious if not dead before he went into the water." Kathy Geib called Gannon within a few days after the radio broadcast and said that she had never heard that information before from anyone. Gannon said, "Kathy, I told you we could prove Todd was either dead or was unconscious when he entered the water." She asked Gannon how he knew this and whether it was from the photos or something else. Gannon then told her that it was from a combination of things.

Shortly after Gannon and Duarte's radio interview on 1500 ESPN, Kathy requested the autopsy photographs from the Michigan State Police; she had never looked at them before. During the summer of 2009, those photos made their way into the hands of Walt "Butch" Hendrick and Andrea Zaferes of Lifeguard Systems out of Shokan (New York). Butch and Andrea took Todd's story to an annual conference for medical examiners and pathologists. The case photographs were shown to the participants during one of the sessions. They unanimously agreed that Todd had not been in the water for more than 2 to 5 days at the most according to his level of decomposition. Since Todd was missing for 20-plus days, that meant that he was held anywhere from about 15 to 18 days before being placed into the water. Whether he was alive or dead during this period was not mentioned.

The Medical Examiner was incorrect in stating that there was very little known information about why the decedent was in the water or how he got into the water. How Todd got into the water was easy – Todd was in the water because someone put him into the water. The reasoning as to why he was in the water is also easy – Todd was murdered. Normally, the Medical Examiner could say that he did not know specifically how a victim died (i.e., "cause of death"). But in this situation, someone definitely put him into the water at a much later time. This was technically at least the improper disposal of a human body or tampering with a deceased body. Of course, Todd could have died from natural causes and then his friends panicked and put him into the water to make it appear to be an accident. Although extremely unlikely because of the amount of time involved, most medical examiners still would not classify the case a homicide without more evidence.

Given that the group of forensic experts had concluded that Todd was not placed into the water until approximately 15 to 18 days after he went missing, was this not enough reason to classify Todd's case as a homicide? Most people (friends or enemies) do not hold a dead body for an extended period of time before deciding what to do with it. This was not a situation of someone accidentally dying of a drug overdose (e.g., Len Bias where the friends panicked and did not call 911 immediately while they cleaned up the area). This was not even a fistfight where one of the fighters died and the body was placed into the water to make it appear as though an accident had occurred. This was the intentional holding of a body for an extended period of time before disposing of it.

If the forensic experts were correct in their observation and the decomposition of Todd's body was inconsistent with the length of time that he was missing, then that meant only one of two things could have occurred.

1. Todd did not die on the morning he went missing and was held alive somewhere during the 15 to 18 days prior to his death and entry into the water.
2. Todd died on the morning he went missing was held somewhere for 15 to 18 days at or near Zero (0) °Fahrenheit in order for his body not to decay.

Both scenarios pointed to someone being involved with the abduction and holding of Todd (alive or deceased) until his placement into the water at a later date. All of the facts in this case pointed more towards homicide than any other plausible explanation. We opined that any medical examiner or police detective should have known this.

Cascading events occurred in 2009 and 2010. First, Gannon made statements regarding Todd's death during a radio interview on 1500 ESPN and then discussed those statements with Kathy Geib over the phone (April 2009). Next, the Geibs made contact with New York attorney Trish DeAngelis with whom we had previously conferred during another case in Albany. DeAngelis drafted a letter for the Geib family that was addressed to Prosecutor Tague and requested that he consider reopening Todd's case and classify it as a homicide (dated October 7, 2009). In order to strengthen Todd's case, Ms. DeAngelis had contacted Dr. Michael Sikirica to see whether he would concur with the assessment offered by the group of medical examiners (i.e., that Todd had only been dead for a period of 2 to 5 days). Doctor Sikirica agreed with their findings.

About 4 months later (February 12, 2010), we put out forensic information about Todd's death that included references to the toxicology test results. That information was picked up by a popular Internet blogspot (February 13, 2010). The next day (February 14, 2010), Dr. Sikirica did an interview on a national radio program and reaffirmed the information that we had previously put out. Kathy Geib also told us that Todd had gone to East Lansing the previous week. East Lansing is important because there have been numerous other suspicious drownings and disappearances in and around East Lansing since 1990 that reflect similar victimological parameters.

Year	Name	Disappeared	Last Seen Location	Recovered	Recovery Location
1990	Dale Shields	November 1990	Near Owen Graduate Hall	November 18, 1990	Red Cedar River[a]
1994	Morgan White	March 12, 1994	Just north of MSU campus	March 16, 1994	Red Cedar River[a]
1997–98	Ryan Getz	December 31, 1997	Cedar Village Apartments	April 18, 1998	Red Cedar River[a]
2001	Eric Blair	October 20, 2001	Cedar Village Apartments	October 23, 2001	Red Cedar River[a]

[a] All of these young men were recovered in the Red Cedar River between the Bogue Street bridge and the Farm Lane bridge (flow direction). The Bogue Street bridge is about 500 feet north of Owen Graduate Hall and 100 feet south of the Cedar Village Apartments.

In addition to the aforementioned cases, there were a couple other cases associated with the Lansing-East Lansing area and Michigan State University (MSU). Franklin Gottschalk, an English major at MSU, was last seen at his residence in Mason (February 2, 1997). Frank drove off in his brother's car without permission. The vehicle was later found in a parking lot near the intersection of East Grand River Avenue and North Cedar Street in Lansing. Frank is still missing. Glen Leadley was a graduate of MSU in supply chain management. He was last seen at a party in Chicago (February 8, 2003) and was recovered from Lake Michigan (February 23, 2003). Was he followed to Chicago or was he murdered by the organization (group) there? Corey Williams from Lansing went missing (January 2008) and was recovered from the Grand River near Frances Park in Lansing (March 18, 2008). Stephen Mbidzo was last seen the day after his birthday at a party north of East Lansing on Hunsaker Street (March 13, 2009). He was originally from Zimbabwe, and was a member of the MSU African Students Association. His body was recovered from an isolated section of the Grand River in Eagle Township wearing only socks (April 9, 2009). Law enforcement is still investigating this as a suspicious case.

There were two suspicious cases in the Muskegon area. Jeffrey Stratton, originally from Virginia, was working in Michigan on the Palisades Nuclear Plant in Covert. He was last seen about 00:45 hours at Jake's Beach House restaurant in downtown South Haven where he refused a cab ride (November 6, 2010). His cell phone was found in the parking lot of the Curve Inn bar. His body was found about 2 miles north of the bar between 102nd and 107th Avenues on the shore of Lake Michigan (November 7, 2010). There was no wallet or keys recovered on him, and investigators were trying to figure out how he made it to that location since his car was at the bar. The body was so badly bruised around the face and neck area that a family member identified him by his clothes while waiting for dental records. Yet, the police say there was nothing conclusive that pointed to foul play. Lastly, there was the recent case of Travis Trowbridge in Ravenna, which was only 17 miles west of Todd's residence on Half Moon Lake near Casnovia. Travis was last seen at an outdoor party (October 1, 2011). His body was recovered from water about a half-mile west of the party (October 2, 2011).

These deaths were within about a 60-mile radius of where Todd resided, and they occurred immediately after the Geib family became vocal about Todd's death being a homicide rather than an accident. In early February 2010 after information was released about Todd's death, there was a lot of local media coverage. An online letter writing campaign was also initiated to call for the reopening of Todd's case. Jeffrey Stratton disappeared on November 6, 2010, followed a year later by Travis Trowbridge on October 1, 2011. Both of those dates were significant. Several young men have gone missing during the two 5-day periods of September 29th through October 2nd, and November 5th through 9th. November seemed to be especially important.

Name	Location	Date Disappeared
Ryan Katcher	Oakwood, IL	November 5, 2000
Christopher Nordby	Minneapolis, MN	November 7, 2001
Michael Noll	Eau Claire, WI	November 6, 2002
Joshua Guimond	Collegeville, MN	November 9, 2002
Kyle Fleischmann	Charlotte, NC	November 9, 2007
Matthew LaCrosse	Bangor, ME	November 9, 2007
Trevor Boehm	Evanston, IL	November 5, 2008

Both deaths occurred in cold weather when there was no reason for either of the victims to be near water, especially in the freezing cold of west-central Michigan. We believe these deaths were a taunt of the community, police, and especially the Geib's for their continued pursuit for an investigation into their son's death. By that point in time, we surmise that the group/organization of murderers knew that no one would ever be brought to trial and justice. They did not need to continue "drowning" young men around the state. Rather, the group decided to commit a murder in the vicinity of the Geib family, which was getting nowhere with its challenging of authorities, and to throw another "drowned" body in the face of those same authorities.

When Gannon spoke with him (September 2008 to April 2009), Detective Sergeant Gary Miles of the Michigan State Police had no idea of these additional drowning cases. Gannon described the suspicious nature of the drownings, as well as the similarities of the victims and the extraordinary coincidences among the cases. Gannon asserted that an active killer resided in the area of Lansing-East Lansing and he was using the MSU campus as a hunting ground to identify and stalk his prey. We found it more than coincidental that Todd just happened to be taken to East Lansing the week before he drowned. We also found it suspicious that "Mr. X" from MSU in East Lansing (who was the person that Todd had supposedly attempted to score cocaine from) was in Casnovia the weekend of the orchard party. Considering the number of drowning deaths specifically attributed to East Lansing, we believed that Todd was introduced to the organization there for approval before his murder (drowning) or sacrifice.

New Information

After his initial reading of the autopsy report, Gannon said that if he were to give an estimate based on the postmortem artifacts, then he would say that Todd was deceased for a combined equivalent period of time of about 2-1/2 days (60 hours); some of that was on land and some was in the water. Our analysis of the postmortem artifacts confirmed that initial assessment. Our model employed three time ratios: a direct 1:1 for on land, a 2:1 time delay for in water, and a 3:1 time delay for in the morgue. For example (Figure 9.12), rigor takes 12 hours to establish, 12 hours to persist, and 12 hours to relent. The period of time related to rigor relenting occurred in the water and in the morgue. Although the portion of that time that was spent in the water actually lasted 16 hours, it was the equivalent of 8 hours on land (2:1 time delay ratio; *Light Yellow Bar*). Likewise, the portion of time in the morgue related to rigor relenting actually lasted 4 hours, but it was equivalent to 1.3 hours on land (3:1 time delay ratio).

Once again, the postmortem artifacts clearly defined a postmortem interval (Figure 9.12). Lividity was fixed, unchanging and nonblanching, which meant that Todd had been deceased at least 12 hours on land. Rigor had completely relented, which meant that the body had reached the 36-hour mark on land (72 hours in the water). The confusing postmortem artifact was early corneal opacity. The process of opacification takes between 24 and 60 hours. The fact that Todd's corneas were starting to appear opaque meant that his eyes had been exposed to air. Decomposition characteristics due to putrefaction and autolysis (i.e., greens, slight distension of the abdomen, bloating of the scrotum, and an absence of marbling) suggested that Todd's body was somewhere between the 36th and 40th hour postmortem on land (72nd and 80th hour in water). These findings were confirmed by the

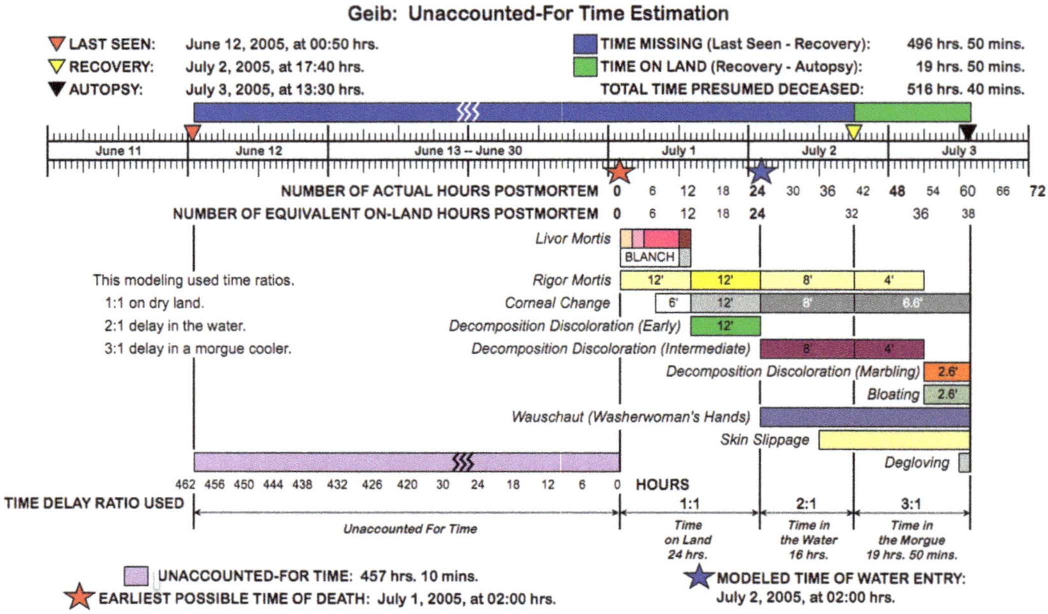

Figure 9.12 The modeled timeline for Todd Geib's case was an approximation. The colored bars could be adjusted up to 2 hours to the right and still maintain the characteristics of the postmortem artifacts as descried in the autopsy report. This would suggest a water entry time between July 2nd at 02:00 and 03:00 hours.

postmortem maceration artifacts of skin slippage and degloving, which pointed to a body that had not been deceased any longer than 72 hours.

Given the facts of the case, we asserted early on that Todd was abducted during the morning hours of June 12th. Our analysis of the postmortem artifacts led us to conclude that he was held for approximately 18 to 19 days, depending upon the amount of time that he was deceased on land. A conversation we had with the Geibs at their residence confirmed our original assessment (19:00 to 23:00 hrs. on November 14, 2012). Gannon summarized the findings from our analysis of the postmortem artifacts and explained our estimate for the postmortem interval (i.e., a PMI of 2-1/2 days). That meant that Todd had been held alive for several days before being murdered. He explained that since deceased bodies do not usually sink, and since Todd was found floating with little decomposition, then he was probably only placed into the lake the night before he was recovered. Furthermore, this meant that Todd was actually only in the lake for approximately 14-plus hours. This placed his possible time of entry into the water sometime between 02:00 to 03:00 hours on July 2nd.

On November 14, 2012, Gannon and Gilbertson went to Ovidhall Lake and spoke with the two witnesses who had discovered Todd's body (Jim and Brenda Wilde). Gannon spoke with them again by phone to confirm their information (May 7 & 8, 2013). Their son (Chad) said that he and his friend were fishing on the lake Friday morning July 1, 2005. They searched for fish using a depth finder and an underwater ice fishing camera, which gave them clear images of the lake and the lake bottom. They explained that they had been on all areas of the lake while fishing and that there was definitely no image of a body in the water anywhere in the lake. That same evening (July 1, 2005), Al Wilde (Jim's brother), along with his son (Jace), were on the lake fishing until 21:00 hours that night. They went back and forth

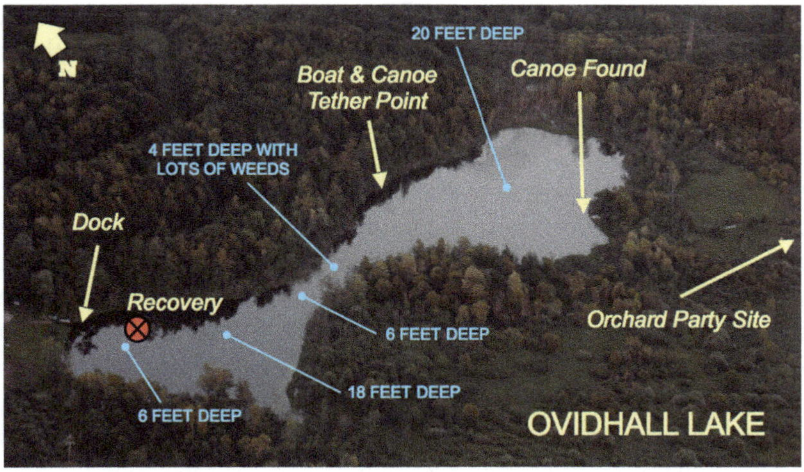

Figure 9.13 Photograph of Ovidhall Lake taken by Jim Wilde from a small airplane after Todd Geib's body was recovered on July 2, 2005. Since he had been fishing on the lake during the week before Todd's recovery, Jim knew the condition and depth of the lake at specific locations. (Photo courtesy of Jim Wilde (2005). Figures added by Gilbertson.)

through the narrows twice and never saw any sign of Todd's body. At 21:00 hours, Al tied his boat off at the dock near where Todd was found the next day. Then on Saturday morning July 2nd at approximately 07:00 hours, Jim and his son Chad went to Ovidhall Lake to fish before the day got too hot and the fish quit biting. The weather had been extremely warm during the past few days and it was having an adverse affect on their fishing.

They arrived at the northeast end of the lake where their boat and canoe were usually tethered (Figure 9.13). Upon arrival, they noticed that their canoe was across the lake on the southeast side in the direction of the orchard party. They took the boat and rowed across to the other side to retrieve their canoe. When they got to the other side, they noticed that there were beer cans in the canoe. Apparently, someone had taken the canoe the previous evening, floated around in it while drinking, and then abandoned it. After returning their canoe to it is normal mooring point, Jim and Chad continued to fish in the east end of the lake until around 10:30 hours and then called it quits for the day. They never ventured anywhere near "the narrows" or the west end of the lake, so it would have been impossible for them to see Todd's body if it was there.

However, that same evening around 17:00 hours (Saturday, July 2, 2005), Jim and Brenda Wilde went to the lake to fish. This time, they entered the lake from the northwest side where Al Wilde kept his boat. While walking down the hill to the lake, Brenda asked Jim what that was in the lake. At first, Jim said that it was probably a beaver. Brenda was not so sure and said, "I hope it isn't what I think it is!" (referring to a body). When they got closer, Jim could see that it was a body and assumed that it might be Todd. Jim is an avid photographer. So, he took his brother's boat out to the location where Todd's body was and took pictures of the scene for the police. He was cautious not the disturb anything. He told Gannon that Todd was "floating like a bobber in the water, almost straight up and down, and his feet were stuck in the weeds." He then came back to shore and phoned the police. The police secured the lake and asked Jim and his wife to leave. He informed them that he had taken photos and eventually forwarded them to the police. We have since learned that most of those pictures were somehow misplaced.

Jim also told the police that his canoe had been taken and abandoned the previous evening and that thieves had been drinking in his canoe. He informed them that he dumped the beer cans on the shore next to the path that led to the orchard party where Todd was last seen. Jim was astounded that the police seemed to disregard this crucial and critical piece of information, especially since his brother and son were both at this exact location at different times during the previous day. The presence of the beer cans in the canoe and its displacement to the south side of the lake could not be attributed to a loose knot and strong winds. Those facts meant that the canoe had been stolen, moved, and abandoned sometime during the early morning hours of July 2nd. The location of Todd's body in the northwest end of the lake coupled with its time of discovery told us, and the Wildes, that Todd was most likely placed into the water earlier that morning using their canoe. He was taken out and dumped into the water that was only 6 feet deep. Whereon, he shot to the bottom, his feet became stuck in the weeds, and he floated in an unusual position. From an evidentiary standpoint, the police never thought about examining the beer cans or the canoe for fingerprints or DNA. They never even considered bringing out a cadaver dog to confirm or disprove the fact that Todd's deceased body might have been in the canoe, or possibly in the boat.

Todd's body was discovered by Jim and Brenda Wilde at approximately 17:00 hours on the evening of July 2, 2005. The Wildes told us that Todd could not have come from the south side of the lake since the weeds in the narrows were 4 feet tall and he would have never floated through them without becoming entangled. Chad Wilde told us that the lake narrows into a bottle neck with lilly pads and weeds; it is extremely difficult to even paddle through that area much less to float through it. In his opinion, if Todd was already dead, then he would never had floated through the narrows and would have more likely been caught up in the vegetation. Todd had to have gone into the water near the location where he was found. According to Chad, Todd was recovered in an area that was approximately 6 to 10 feet deep, although the lake is as deep as 20 feet in certain spots in the northeast end of the lake (where their boat and canoe were normally secured, and the path to the orchard party was located).

Todd's body was in pretty good condition considering that he had been presumed deceased for 21-1/2 days, and that it had been quite warm. Gannon mentioned to Jim Wilde that he had learned about a cold spring that fed into the lake. He commented on how this could preserve Todd's body. Jim quickly dispelled that remark and stated that the water was extremely warm that summer, which accounted for the fact that fishing was pretty poor. Jim said that was the reason why he and his wife were only looking for Bluegills and why his son was unable to find any decent fish the day before. Jim also stated that turtles were feeding in the lake during that time. Thus, had Todd been in Lake Ovidhall for an extended period of time (21 days), then there would have been extensive anthropophagy (animal feeding) on his body. We now know exactly what had transpired with regard to how long Todd had been in the lake.

Conclusion

In summary then, on or about July 1st, Todd was given a couple of cigarettes to smoke and a few alcohol-based drinks to calm him down and to entice him into compliance. The drinks probably contained the desipramine (495 ng/mL) and amitriptline (51 ng/mL). After Todd had slipped into unconsciousness, his killers placed him face-down where he suffocated as a result of either the pulmonary edema induced by the massive drug overdose, or he was placed in shallow water and succumbed to hypoxia. Having killed him, they left him lying face-down for about 24 hours. Lividity began to fix and rigor established. Rigor had not only established, but had already started to relent. They then transported him to Ovidhall Lake under the cover of darkness and placed him in the water sometime during the early morning hours of July 2nd. His body remained in the water for about 15 hours until it was recovered on July 2nd. Todd was preserved in the morgue for almost 20 hours before autopsy. During this time, rigor relented while marbling, bloating and ocular changes progressed, and the hands began to deglove.

Although knowing the timeline for Todd's case may have been an important part of understanding what happened to him, it was not ultimately important to the matter of justice for Todd and his surviving family. Within the scope of final justice, it did not matter whether Todd was held for 3, 11, or 19 days before being placed into the water, because any number of days proved that someone was responsible for abducting and holding him (alive or dead) for an extended period of time before disposing of his body. Our finding that Todd was abducted and held automatically erased all notions of an accidental death on the night of June 12, 2005. The next logical step was to apply practical knowledge of victimization, which resulted in the inference that Todd was murdered. Considering all of the physical and forensic evidence in this case, we concluded that Todd was drugged, abducted, held for a period of time, murdered, and then placed into the water. The fact that the spot in the lake where Todd was recovered was rather remote and that there was restricted access to the lake should not go unnoticed. Todd did not just leave the party, get lost in the dark, fall and hit his head, roll into the water and drown. This was a cleaver, well thought out, and premeditated murder.

We assert that the type of drugs in Todd's system pointed to murder. Normally, an investigator could say that the type of drugs that were in Todd (i.e., prescribed for a chemical imbalance or psychosis) were not the usual type of drugs that someone might take to get high. However, most people know that individuals in today's society who are looking to get high will take almost any kind of drug(s) without regard for any potentially adverse pharmacological affects, from drinking cough syrup to sniffing hazardous cleaning solutions to injecting untested designer drugs. In light of this fact and considering that Todd may have wanted to get high, we cannot rule out the possibility of him taking this type of medication in order to alter his cognitive state.

We conclude that the amount of drugs in Todd's system pointed to murder. When presented with a drug that is new or unfamiliar, a rational person would not take large amounts at first since he does not know its toxic or lethal dose. He would experiment over time with larger and larger doses, or ask someone who has experience with the drug how much is safe to take. However, rationality does not always carry the day when it comes to substance abuse and overuse. With or without knowledge of the drugs, for Todd to have taken that much of these drugs the first time out would have equated to attempting suicide. Furthermore, we know that he was put into the water almost 19 days after his abduction. Therefore, the high dosage in his system was nothing more than an intentional act. The goal was to debilitate and incapacitate Todd. His abductor(s) needed to reduce his physical strength to a point that he could be easily placed into the water without a fight. We also believe that the assailant(s) wanted to either debilitate him to the point of unconsciousness so he would not struggle to survive the drowning, or kill him from the medication alone.

The fact that he was held for such a long period of time before entry into the water showed real psychopathology that could only come from individuals who are involved in some sort of orchestrated or ritual killing. What makes us say this was not that Todd was held for an extended period of time before he was put into the water, rather, because of how pristine his body was at autopsy. We would expect some signs of torture or binding on a victim after nearly 20 days of abduction. The fact that he had no burns, no ligature marks, and no cuts or bruises, demonstrated real planning and precaution on the part of the abductor(s).

This was the kidnappers' way of taunting the authorities. Through the condition of Todd's body, these individuals were sending a message to law enforcement and medical examiners right up front. Yes, he was murdered. Yes, he was held for an extended period of time (alive or dead) before putting him into the water. Yes, we are putting it right in your face. So, what are you going to do about it? Unfortunately, those involved are not too worried about being caught since after all these years the medical community and law enforcement have not recognized what is happening or responded. The offender(s) know that local authorities will write off each death as a tragic accident fueled by alcohol. Therefore, they are not worried that a different type of conclusion may be reached.

The organization's members are getting more and more blatant in what they are doing. They are daring the authorities to take another look at or to reclassify these cases as homicides. They are above reproach. They cannot be touched. They cannot be caught. They are superior. This is the collective mentality of an organization of killers. The victims represent cases that can be linked, not by association to the same killers, rather by association to the same ideology and purpose for their murders. The extent of this organization is not restricted to only the United States, but includes Canada and some European countries.

Unfortunately, these cases were all considered to be "accidental drownings" in the beginning. Except for a handful of families, friends and concerned others, few people get all worked-up about accidental deaths. If these were hate crimes, then a lot of people would be rallying to the cause. In a crowd of tens-of-thousands, a mixture of complacency and anonymity foster inaction and silence. Everyone assumes that someone else will be moved to act. This phenomenon is known as the diffusion of responsibility (a.k.a., the bystander effect or the Genovese Syndrome). Thus, no one acts because he or she does not want to stand out and be "the odd one" (Darley & Latané, 1968; Levine & Thompson, 2004; Manning, Levine, & Collins, 2007).

On the other hand, individual members of small groups (minority populations) realize that their actions are required for the whole group to survive and that they can make a difference. The Buddhist concept of dependent origination (a.k.a., causal interdependence) proposes that every event is somehow interconnected to other events (Payutto, 1994). Using old adages and clichés to explain this, a sense of "we are all in this together" should prevail since "what goes around, comes around," and when no one speaks up "we'll all go down together" with the ship. If no one speaks up and starts the conversation, then there is no discussion for anyone else to join. Some minority populations are well organized and do a good job of starting important conversations and of making themselves to be heard when it comes to hate crimes.

This group of mostly college-aged, Euro-American male victims, who were drinking and then found drowned, represents a very small demographic population. More importantly, these victims have a very small lobbying group to represent their wrongs before lawmakers and to tell their stories through the media. Therefore, their deaths go largely unnoticed. If this were a bunch of college-aged females being drowned, then there would already have been an investigation. In fact, the FBI has already formed a task force to combat the murder of women along America's highways. The "Highway Serial Killer Initiative" was formally established in 2007 to track the 500-plus suspicious slayings of prostitutes by suspected long-haul truck drivers.

Part of the problem of not being able to successfully gather a lobbying force is a general lack of understanding of precisely who these victims were and who they have become. In the beginning, most of the victims were White males of European ancestry. An occasional minority victim occurred, but they were not cognitively clustered with the others simply because of their racial differences. Newspaper and television reporters, authors of periodicals and books, and Internet bloggers all discussed the "White male victims" associated with the urban legend of a serial killer. Over time, the minority victims have been brought into the conversations about the drownings, but the authors' and readers' understanding of the victims has not changed. People just do not realize that members of minority communities have been the victims of this murderous organization all along, and probably from the very first case. The victims have been from every color of skin, religion, and sexual preference describable. It is time for action! Perhaps, political action will come from the members of those minority lobbying groups who are already organized and do so well at speaking for themselves and others. Perhaps, they will cry loudly enough that an official investigation by federal law enforcement will finally happen.

There are many misnomers and misconceptions being spread by those who know nothing about this investigation, who never looked at a single autopsy report, or have never been to a single scene. Some "experts" (i.e., law enforcement investigators, criminal profilers, university professors, researchers, and investigative reporters) even say these cases are not homicides, or if they are, then they are not connected. Those statements are being made by people who have not personally uncovered one single shred of forensic evidence to substantiate their own claims. Simply claiming that another person's argument is unfounded does not make it so. Patterns can only be seen once several dozen cases in multiple locations have been examined. How many of the experts have truly looked at more than a couple or a handful of cases in one town? Some experts now suggest to forget graffiti (specifically, the smiley face), claiming that it has nothing at all to do with these killings or who is responsible for them. We are here to state categorically that graffiti was and is the key to this investigation, and the smiley face is the most important graffito. Not only did it help us to identify those who were committing these murders, it also told us about their ideological basis for it occurring in the first place. It was clearly the reason for the words, "Evil Happy Smiley Face Man."

This group is intent on violence and they are at war with anyone who does not subscribe to their ideology. They are a group of equal opportunity killers whose belief system fuels behaviors that are becoming more and more violent with each passing day. They continue to work in small semiautonomous cells (that are not affiliated with any publicly known organization) while encouraging independent operatives for more dramatic effects. We believe that they will play a major role in our next domestic terror threat. We only hope that it does not take the blowing up of another federal building like in Oklahoma City for this country, and specifically the FBI, to get involved. In that incident, 168 people tragically lost their lives. So far to date, there are well over 200 plus young men who were probably victims of this organization. How utterly brilliant it was for them to do this one person at a time while still fulfilling their mission without drawing attention to themselves and by staying below the radar.

Hopefully, someday soon, someone with the power to act will hear the cries of the parents who demand an investigation into their sons' deaths. The parents may have to join forces with an established lobbying group from one of the minority populations (e.g., African-American, Latino, Asian, Jewish, or Gay, Lesbian, Bisexual and Transgender communities). Their greatest challenge will be to develop empathy or sympathy among the masses and to then motivate them to orchestrated and goal-oriented action. Until that day comes, the mass of anonymous and unorganized Americans who know about these drownings will continue to go about the routine of daily life while asking questions driven only by emotionless curiosity. WHO, WHAT, WHEN, WHERE, HOW and WHY?

Who died? What was his name? When and where did it happen? What were the circumstances? How did it happen and why?

Thomas James Booth, III* 10

August 18, 1983–February 3, 2008

Background

Tommy Booth was last seen on the night of January 19–20, 2008, and was recovered 14.5 days later in Ridley Creek on February 3, 2008. After our team's appearance on the ABC program *Good Morning America* (April 28, 2008, at approximately 07:30 hours), the supervising Detective Sergeant in Ridley Township, Scott Willoughby, called and asked us to confer with him regarding the suspicious circumstances of the disappearance, death, and recovery of Tommy. The team arrived in Woodlyn (Ridley Township, Pennsylvania) on May 2, 2008, and met with Willoughby to go over case materials and to examine associated sites. Before leaving, the team provided an initial assessment of its findings and conclusions. That analysis was based on recovery and autopsy photographs, an examination of the sites where Tommy was last seen and where he was recovered, as well as information shared with us by the Ridley Township Detective. Our initial conclusion was that Tommy had been in the water for no more than 36 hours. The medical examiner's autopsy report was finally released on August 2, 2008, and verified our findings of three months earlier.

The team has remained in contact with the Detective and Medical Examiner. We returned to Woodlyn on May 21, 2008, and reexamined the sites and discussed our new evidentiary findings. We met first with Dr. Frederic Hellman, Delaware County Chief Medical Examiner, in Lima, Pennsylvania. After that meeting, the team drove to Woodlyn and met again with Detective Sergeant (now Lieutenant) Scott Willoughby. We discussed our additional forensic findings related to Tommy's abduction and death, and proposed persons of interest for investigation. We went back to Woodlyn a third time on March 21, 2009.

* Photo courtesy of Barbara MacKay-Bush.

Figure 10.1 Tommy Booth (right) with his mother Barbara MacKay-Bush. (Photo courtesy of Barbara MacKay-Bush.)

Ridley Township Police have been very open and cooperative every time we contact them. The agency's representative wrote that he had no issues with our use of investigative documents and related pictures, in part or as a whole, as needed to accomplish this work provided that Tommy's mother was okay with it (Figure 10.1). Gannon has maintained communication with Tommy's mother (Barbara) over the years. After showing her which photos we wanted to use, she gave us clear permission to use them and any documents that we needed. We compiled this chapter about Tommy's death from law enforcement reports, our notes taken during meetings with the Detective and Medical Examiner, on-site observations, examination of body recovery photographs, and our analysis of the autopsy and toxicology reports.

Circumstances

Last Seen

Thomas James Booth, III ("Tommy"), was a White male, 24 years old, 5 feet 11 inches, 185 pounds (Body Mass Index: 25.80), with brown hair and hazel eyes. He resided in Wilmington, Delaware. Tommy was last seen about 01:00 hours (1:00 a.m.) on Sunday, January 20, 2008. The following timeline and facts were established using police reports (RTPD, 2008) and notes developed by a private investigator who was hired by the family. Tommy's family members stated that he did not drive because he had a medical condition (Epilepsy) and was taking prescribed medications (Xanax and others). Additionally, he was not familiar with the Woodlyn area. Members of the group with whom he traveled that night stated that they had discovered the bar "Bootleggers" online and wanted to check it out (Figure 10.2). The group traveled in 3 separate vehicles from Delaware to Pennsylvania that night. The 1st vehicle contained a 22-year-old White Male (DRIV-1.1), a 24-year-old White Male (PASS-1.2), another 24-year-old White Male (PASS-1.3) and his girlfriend, a 21-year-old White Female (PASS-1.4). In the 2nd vehicle, were a 23-year-old White Male (DRIV-2.1), a 21-year-old White Female (PASS-2.2), and a 24-year-old White Male (PASS-2.3). Riding in 3rd vehicle were a 25-year-old White Male (DRIV-3.1), and Tommy Booth (PASS-3.2).

Figure 10.2 The front entrance to Bootleggers.

Tommy entered Bootleggers (in Woodlyn, Ridley Township, Delaware County, Pennsylvania) with these 6 male associates and 2 female associates at 22:55 hours on January 19, 2008 (identified on videotape by his mother). PASS-1.3 and PASS-2.2 stated that they had been smoking marijuana in the bar and were kicked out at about 00:45 hours. PASS-1.3 then called his brother (DRIV-1.1, who was inside the bar) and told him that he wanted to leave. At about 00:52 hours, PASS-1.2 left the bar and met up with DRIV-1.1, PASS-1.3, PASS-1.4, DRIV-2.1, PASS-2.2, and PASS-2.3 in the parking lot of the bar. The group stated that they told DRIV-3.1 that they were leaving, and that he should make sure he drove Tommy back to PASS-1.3's home back in Delaware when the bar closed. This meant that all 7 people from the 1st and 2nd vehicles were supposed to have left the bar at about 01:00 hours, an hour before bar closing (Figure 10.3).

However, DRIV-3.1 (whose responsibility it had become to give Tommy a ride back home) seemed to be somewhat confused about the timing of events that night. We acknowledge that this is a common occurrence when asking people to perform retrospective recall

Figure 10.3 At the back entrance to Bootleggers, the team (left to right, Carlson, Gannon, and Duarte) stopped to discuss its findings and to check with Detective Sergeant Willoughby for any updates on Tommy Booth's case.

of events. Truthful people will try to get the time elements correct – sometimes trying to be too precise – but generally miss it by 10 to 20 minutes. One element they do not normally get wrong is the ordering of events; and rarely do truthful people incorrectly state the location of events. In one report, DRIV-3.1 told police that the last time he recalled seeing Tommy was at about 01:00 hours, and Tommy was in the Hip Hop section of Bootleggers. He contradicted himself during another interview, wherein he told the interviewing police officer that he thought Tommy had left with the group at about 01:00 hours. In yet another police interview, DRIV-3.1 told police that the last time he saw Tommy was around 01:30 hours heading to the bathroom in Bootleggers. However, during an interview with the Private Investigator, DRIV-3.1 contradicted the statement he had given to police and stated that he was outside the bar between 01:25 and 01:40 hours where he had observed an altercation while speaking with other friends he knew from Bootleggers. DRIV-3.1 stated that he walked back into the bar at about 01:45 hours and at about 02:00 hours, when the bar was closing, he walked around inside the bar and was unable to physically locate Tommy. Searching for Tommy at 02:00 hours would have occurred only if DRIV-3.1 thought that Tommy was still there, which contradicted his other statement that he thought Tommy had left at 01:00 hours. Lastly, DRIV-3.1 said during yet another interview that he thought Tommy may have hooked up with a girl and left the bar.

Personally leaving the bar that night was not so confusing for him. According to DRIV-3.1, he then left the bar and drove himself back to PASS-1.3's home in Wilmington without calling Tommy's cell phone to ascertain his location. Tommy was never viewed on a security camera leaving the bar. This meant that he had to have exited the bar through the front emergency doors that were not monitored by video cameras. All of Tommy's associates stated that they did not realize that he was really missing until about noon on Sunday, January 20, 2008. It was then determined that Tommy never made it back home to Delaware County and a subsequent missing persons report was prepared and a search ensued for him.

Recovery

The spot where Tommy had been found, as well as the area surrounding where he had been found, had been thoroughly searched by humans and dogs repeatedly during the time he was missing without any positive results (RTPD, 2008; SARD-PA, 2008; Figure 10.4). The first search occurred on Tuesday, January 22, 2008, and was conducted by his mother (Barbara MacKay-Bush), his stepfather (Timothy Bush) and an aunt. They searched along Ridley Creek and the wooded area behind Bootleggers. The first K-9 search was not conducted until 6 days after Tommy went missing; it was done at 09:00 hours, on Saturday, January 26, 2008, by Search & Rescue Dogs of Pennsylvania, and concluded at 12:30 hours with negative results (SARD-PA, 2008). The team deployed 4 cadaver search dogs and no evidence, trace, or scent of Tommy, alive or deceased, was located during the search.

Fourteen (14) days after his disappearance at approximately 13:45 hours on February 03, 2008, Tommy was found deceased, prone (face-down) in Ridley Creek directly behind Bootleggers by the Greater Philadelphia Search and Rescue Service in an area that had been previously search by 2 K-9 teams; he was due south of center field at the Widener softball field with dense brush between the field's fence and the creek. Detective Sergeant Willoughby and Detective Philip Turner were notified, and they contacted Lieutenant Greg Seltzer with the Criminal Investigation Division (CID) to request its assistance. Delaware County CID

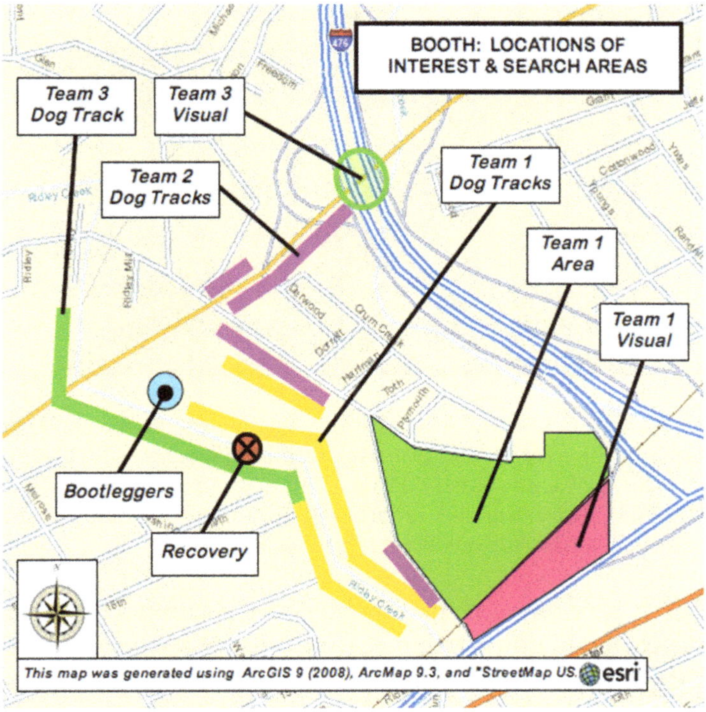

Figure 10.4 Three teams searched for Tommy Booth using area searches on foot, visual searches, and K-9 teams (SARD-PA, 2008).

personnel responded at approximately 14:30 hours, and Investigators Ferguson and Lafore from the Delaware County Medical Examiner's Office arrived about 14:45 hours. His body was removed from the area about 15:50 hours.

Analysis of Evidence

Recovery Location

The body recovery location, when assessed in light of information related to the extent of decomposition of Tommy's body (a deeper analysis of this will follow later in this chapter), was our first clue that he had not accidentally fallen into the creek 14.5 days earlier. On land in a temperate environment, bloating from decomposition gases can be detected between 36 to 48 hours (1.5 to 2 days). In water, especially cool water, this process may take twice as long (3 to 4 days). Cold air (e.g., refrigeration) can even retard decomposition. No matter what estimator of time one uses, Tommy was presumed to have accidentally fallen into the creek 14.5 days earlier and should have presented with considerable bloating due to decomposition. In a warm environment, Tommy's body would have risen to the surface full of decomposition gases (i.e., refloated). Furthermore, Ridley Creek was known to overflow its banks (approximately 5 feet high) after a rainfall, and was believed to had done so during the week prior to Tommy's recovery. Thus, the creek would have flowed at a greater speed and depth than was visible in the police department's recovery photographs (Figure 10.5). In all likelihood, the depth of the creek during flood stage

Figure 10.5 Although quite shallow when Tommy Booth was recovered, Ridley Creek reportedly overflowed it banks on a regular basis during rainfall. (*Special note:* Use of this photograph was approved by Barbara MacKay-Bush.) (From Ridley Township Police Department (RTPD). 2008. *SUPPLEMENTAL* [Investigation reports dated January 23, 2008 through February 6, 2008]. Woodlyn, Pennsylvania: Various Police Officers.)

could have been 5 feet or more. Hypothetically, this would have easily swept Tommy's bloated and refloated body downstream. Given this knowledge of bloating and Ridley Creek's history of flooding, our analysis concluded that Tommy's body should have never been recovered where it had been.

We knew right away that only 3 hypothetical scenario options were possible in Tommy's case. Had he actually left Bootleggers by going out the back door and then fallen into Ridley Creek that night as presumed, Tommy's body should have bloated from decomposition in no more than 3 to 4 days given the environmental conditions during the time that he was missing (relatively cool February temperatures). But, his body would not have refloated during that time since it was resting in the shallow waters of Ridley Creek. During the second week, the flood waters in the creek would have taken his bloated body quite a ways downstream as it refloated (Figure 10.6, *Hypothetical Scenario Option A*). However, Tommy was not found some great distance downstream from Bootleggers as expected; he was found near it. Since the flooded creek would have been deeper and the current running more swiftly during the week prior to Tommy's recovery, that meant that he would have had to have gone in further upstream in order for his bloated body to be recovered anywhere near Bootleggers (Figure 10.6, *Hypothetical Scenario Option B*). Even if one were to believe that Tommy went into the water further upstream (although no scent of him was ever recovered by K-9 teams in that vicinity), then it would be preposterous to accept the possibility that his body coincidently stopped near Bootleggers and would not have traveled even further downstream during flood stage.

That left only one remaining possible option (Figure 10.6, *Hypothetical Scenario Option C*): Tommy's body was recovered in the exact spot where it had entered Ridley Creek. We believe this to be what really happened. As previously discussed, persons who are deceased before being entered into a body of water will generally float. But, persons who fall into a body of water alive and then drown will sink to the bottom and stay there despite any extent of water current or turbulence until they decompose and refloat (Hendrick, Zaferes, & Nelson, 2003). The creek overflowed its banks before the first search on January 26th. That meant that if Tommy had actually entered the water during the early morning hours of January 20th, then his body would have decomposed, washed away in flood

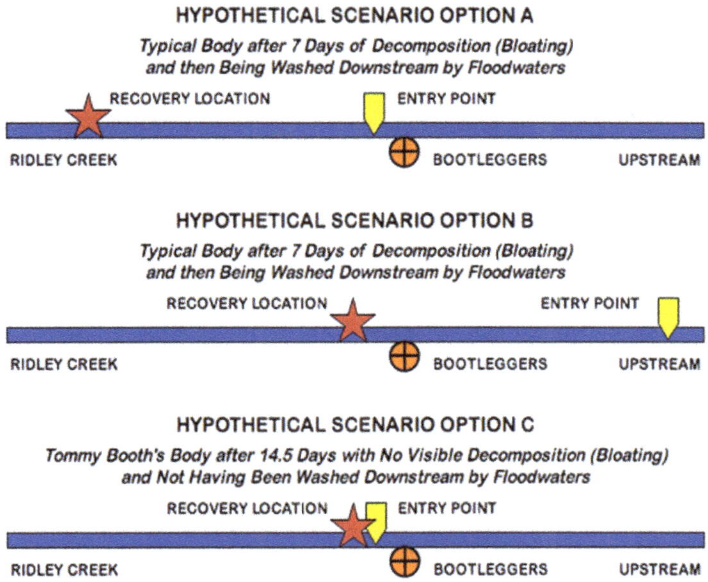

Figure 10.6 Only 3 scenarios were possible for Tommy Booth's recovery location.

waters, and floated for approximately a few days until either he became lodged against something (e.g., logs, tree branches, or a strainer in the creek) or came to rest on the sandy bottom when eventually the creek subsided. Assuming this was an accidental drowning, had Tommy fallen into the creek behind Bootleggers 14.5 days earlier, then he would have surely decomposed during the first week, refloated during the early part of the second week, then traveled downstream during the creek's flood stage, where he would have continued to decompose even more. Since none of the expected decomposition was evident, that meant that Tommy had to have gone into the creek after the flood stage in order to avoid being swept downstream. Considering the location of Tommy's recovery and the absence of bloating, as well as the fact that he was not stuck on any obstruction, this meant that his body was recovered very near where it had entered the creek.

Furthermore, a mathematical equation can be used to approximate how far a sinking body may travel in water before it comes to rest on the bottom (i.e., *Distance Traveled*). First, the estimated *Drop Time* must be calculated. *Drop Time* equals the *Depth* divided by the *Body Drop Rate*. Next, *Distanced Traveled* equals the *Drop Time* multiplied by the *Current Speed* (Figure 10.7). In fresh water, a body drops at 2 to 2.5 feet per second; and it drops at 1.5 to 2.0 feet per second in salt water (Hendrick, Zafares, & Nelson, 2003, p. 83).

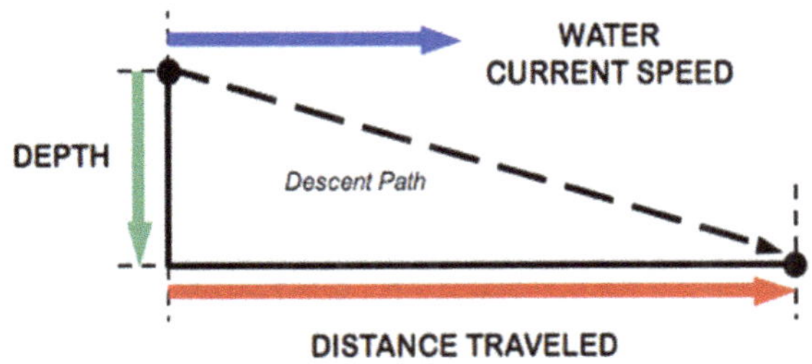

Figure 10.7 The location of a body underwater can be calculated by knowing where the body was last known to be on the surface, the depth of the water, and the speed of the current.

A *Body Drop Rate* of 2 feet per second is generally used as a standard for all calculations regardless of water type. Water current speed is measured in knots: 1 knot = 100 feet per 60 seconds, or 1.7 feet per second. For example, since Tommy was in fresh water, a *Body Drop Rate* of 2 feet per second can be used. If Ridley Creek had a water depth of 5 feet at flood stage with a 2-knot current (200 feet per 60 seconds, or 3.3 feet per second), then Tommy would have been located about 8.3 feet from where he entered the water. For example:

Depth ÷ Body Drop Rate = Drop Time
5 feet divided by 2 feet per second = 2.5 seconds

Drop Time × Current Speed = Distance Traveled
2.5 second multiplied by 3.3 feet per second = 8.3 feet

Even if the creek was raging at 10 knots (1,000 feet per 60 seconds, or 16.7 feet per second), then Tommy would have traveled only 41.3 feet before coming to rest on the creek bed behind Bootleggers. In other words:

(Depth ÷ Body Drop Rate) × Current Speed = Distance Traveled
(5 feet divided by 2 feet per second) × 16.7 feet per second = 41.3 feet

It is inconceivable that the 4 cadaver dogs and both search and police personnel, who canvassed the area looking for Tommy on January 26th, would have missed not only his scent but also his body directly behind Bootleggers.

Added to all this was the fact that he was not found on the bottom submerged in water, rather laying along the shoreline with only a portion of his body in about 6 inches of water. That meant that the standard adjustments to calculating decomposition in water versus on land no longer applied. It meant that Tommy had been in open air – and not under water – for several days, which would have contributed greatly to the decomposition process. His abdomen should have been observably bloated at recovery. Furthermore, Tommy's body showed very little decomposition at all and no indication that it had even started to bloat with gases. Taking all of these empirical observations into consideration (i.e., a general absence of appropriate decomposition, an absence of bloating and refloating, and also an insufficient water volume to carry him away), we asserted that Tommy's body remained in one general spot in Ridley Creek because it had only recently been placed there. This told us that he had likely died sometime during the past 2 days or less and had been placed into the creek at that location.

Body Staging

Our team concluded that Tommy's body had been staged. He was found in the prone position (face-down) on the east side of Ridley Creek with the creek running along the west side of Bootleggers. The right side of Tommy's body was in approximately 6 inches of water and the left side of his body was resting on a sandy area. Tommy's arms were flexed at the elbow and tucked underneath his body. Three sticks (small, broken-off tree branches) were discovered stuck into the soil of the creek bed and lodged against Tommy's body (Figure 10.8). The 1st stick was standing in between his legs and up against his groin. The 2nd stick was standing straight up between his body and his right arm. The 3rd stick was

Figure 10.8 Tommy Booth was found facing downstream with three sticks firmly stuck into the creek bed: one at his crotch, one at his armpit, and one a few feet downstream. (*Special note:* Use of this photograph was approved by Barbara MacKay-Bush. All yellow graphics were added by Gilbertson.) (From Ridley Township Police Department (RTPD). 2008. *SUPPLEMENTAL* [Investigation reports dated January 23, 2008 through February 6, 2008]. Woodlyn, Pennsylvania: Various Police Officers.)

also upright a few feet away from his head to the front and left. Tommy was facing downstream. Therefore, he could not have floated up against the sticks, and they could not have floated up against him and lodged themselves so securely in the creek bed soil. Clearly, the sticks had been placed there by human intervention, which supported our assertion that Tommy's body had been staged.

Drag Mark and Shoe Tracks

The Medical Examiner knew from the beginning that something was not right with this case. In his postmortem report, Dr. Hellman wrote that there was no sign of injury to the body to indicate foul play. But, the circumstances surrounding his disappearance and recovery were cause for suspicion. He described a depression in the creek bed that led up to Tommy's head as a "drag mark" (Figure 10.9). He also suggested that there were shoe tracks in the soil of the creek bed running upstream along both sides of said drag mark. Furthermore, Dr. Hellman concluded that they had probably been made no more than 1 to 2 days before Tommy's recovery. Examination of the photograph suggested that faint shoe tracks may have also been visible near the shoreline at the beginning of the drag mark (lower left-hand corner of photo).

We posited from the recovery photo that the mark in question was indeed a drag mark created by Tommy's head and not a natural phenomenon caused by the water current carrying sand particles downstream around Tommy's head. As can be seen, the drag mark curved toward the east bank of Ridley Creek, and not directly downstream as would have appeared due to water current and displaced sand. During conversations with the Medical Examiner, we learned that Dr. Hellman had a local university physicist (name undisclosed) examine the creek's soil for its erosion properties. The physicist determined that any shoe tracks in the creek bed would have been erased by the flowing water within 48 hours. This analysis of the shoe tracks combined with the drag mark suggested that 2 individuals had dragged Tommy upstream by his ankles to the spot where his body had been staged and recovered. We propose that some effort should be taken in future investigations to create

Figure 10.9 A drag mark led upstream from the creek bank to Tommy Booth's head. (*Special note:* Use of this photograph was approved by Barbara MacKay-Bush. All yellow graphics were added by Gilbertson.) (From Ridley Township Police Department (RTPD). 2008. *SUPPLEMENTAL* [Investigation reports dated January 23, 2008 through February 6, 2008]. Woodlyn, Pennsylvania: Various Police Officers.)

a record of the presence of the shoe tracks found in shallow water. At a minimum, an attempt should be made to photographically record their existence. Perhaps, a dam could be fashioned using plywood that is placed around the body and the shoe tracks, and then the water could be hand-pumped out. Forensic photographs and/or plaster casts could then be made.

Mud, Detritus, and Insects

While reading the reports, we found additional information that confirmed our assessment of the drag mark. The reports stated the Tommy had a lot of mud on his head, face, and under the jaw as well as on his neck. Additionally, Tommy had some mud stuck to the lower front of his body and in the area between the groin and navel. However, there was very little mud on both legs down to the socks and shoes; it was especially light on the buttocks and front of his thighs. The Medical Examiner reported that mud, wet leaves, and other detritus (organic debris formed by the decomposition of fauna and flora) was found on Tommy's anterior side in between his shirt and long-sleeved pullover jersey. The Medical Examiner also commented on the presence of a few insects.

This information clearly demonstrated to us that Tommy had been dragged face-down by his ankles into the creek, which caused the mud and other materials to become lodged under his chin. His chin acted like a plow, thus leaving a furrow in the soil of the creek bed (i.e., the distinctive drag mark; Figure 10.9). The mud was sparse on his legs since they only came in contact with the creek bed once he was dropped by the two people dragging him. What was not mentioned was whether an entomologist was ever called to determine what kind of insects they were and at what point they were in their life cycle. This would have assisted in making an even more accurate estimate of the time that Tommy was placed into Ridley Creek. This is a standard procedure, which should be done in every case when a deceased body is recovered with insects regardless of whether it is found indoors or outdoors, but is especially important in a case that is considered suspicious or when it is clear that the victim was readmitted to the scene.

Most insects are attracted to the orifices or cavities of the body (i.e., eyes, ears, nose, mouth and open wounds) of the victim. Since Tommy was face-down in the water, then the insects should not have been able to be attracted to any area other than possibly his exposed ear canal if the temperature was warmer. While Tommy was missing, the average daily high temperature was 40.3 °Fahrenheit and the average daily low was 25.6 °Fahrenheit. Considering the outdoor temperatures, it seems more likely that Tommy was dead indoors for a period of time as it was too cold outdoors (under 50 °Fahrenheit) for the insects to be attracted to any part of his body.

Rigidity

The presence of rigidity (*rigor mortis*) in Tommy contradicted an accidental drowning hypothesis. Rigor sets first in the small muscles and then the larger; it relents in the same order (i.e., smaller muscles then larger) (Geberth, 2006). Dr. Hellman described Tommy's jaw, arms and legs as still presenting full rigor. Since the small muscles of Tommy's jaw were still in rigor, this meant that the rigor process had not started to relent. Clearly, Tommy had not been dead very long since he was in full rigor at both recovery and autopsy. Had he actually died during the early morning hours of January 20th (about 369 hours 40 minutes before his autopsy), then Tommy should have been in and out of rigor before his body was autopsied.

Rigor usually dissipates within 24 to 36 hours in temperate climes. Environmental conditions can retard this process by several days. The cooler or colder it is, then the longer it may take for rigor to relent (Shkrum & Ramsay, 2007). On the day of recovery, it was generally sunny and the air temperature was about 50 °Fahrenheit. At 13:45 hours on February 3rd, Detective Sergeant Willoughby was notified that Tommy's body had been discovered. According to a report filed by Investigator Lafore (Delaware County Medical Examiner's Office), Tommy's body appeared to be in full rigor (350 hours 50 minutes after he went missing). His body was not removed from the scene until 15:50 hours. Since Ridley Creek was not at flood levels during the previous 3 to 4 days, then Tommy was not submerged in water. Thus, the affect of immersion in cold water on retarding the relenting of rigor would have been marginal at best. No logical explanation based on environmental conditions could be used to fully explain why Tommy was still in full rigor 14.5 days after having gone missing.

We performed a simple analysis of the available data (Figure 10.10). Tommy went missing on January 20th at 01:00 hours (*Red Triangle*). He was recovered on February 3rd at

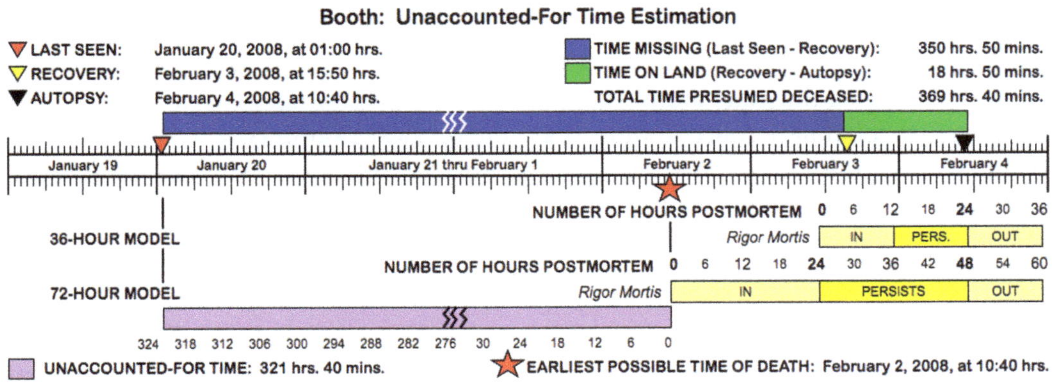

Figure 10.10 The presence of full rigor in Tommy Booth's body at autopsy meant that he did not drown 14.5 days earlier. In order for Tommy to still be in rigor at autopsy, he had to have died sometime after 10:40 hours on February 2nd.

15:50 hours (*Yellow Triangle*). And, he was autopsied at 10:40 hours on February 4th (*Black Triangle*). Tommy was missing for 350 hours 50 minutes (*Blue Bar*) and was autopsied 18 hours 50 minutes later (*Green Bar*). A total of 369 hours 40 minutes had elapsed between the time that Tommy went missing to when he was autopsied. Tommy was in full rigor at recovery and at autopsy. To begin the analysis, we aligned the autopsy (*Black Triangle*) at a point along the normal 36-hour rigor process (*Yellow Bar*) that would equate to full rigor just about to begin relenting. This showed that Tommy would have been going into rigor at recovery (i.e., the *Yellow Triangle* aligned with the *IN* segment of the *Yellow Bar*). Since we knew that this was not the case (he was in full rigor), then we also knew that the environmental conditions had retarded the rigor process. Therefore, we concluded that the rigor process would probably take no more than 72 hours: 24 hours going in, 24 hours persisting, and 24 hours going out. Giving everything the benefit of a doubt, we aligned the autopsy (*Black Triangle*) at a point along the 72-hour rigor process (*Yellow Bar*) that would equate to full rigor just about to begin relenting (i.e., the 48th hour mark). We could then clearly see, going backwards in time, that Tommy could not have died any later than February 2nd at about 10:40 hours (*Red Star*) in order to still be in rigor at autopsy on February 4th. This meant that 321 hours 40 minutes of unaccounted-for time existed (*Purple Bar*). Where was Tommy?

Body Position and Lividity

Lividity (*livor mortis*) also contradicted any notion of an accidental drowning. The Medical Examiner described lividity within Tommy's body as being fixed and as being on both sides of Tommy's body. He reported that it was present but spotty on Tommy's anterior (face, arms and legs) and posterior (only on his back, and not on the back of his legs). How does one explain a presence of both anterior and posterior lividity? Generally, the pooling and settling of the blood starts within 30 minutes after death, and fixed lividity occurs after 10 to 12 hours. Prior to lividity being completely fixed, some extent of shifting or displacement can occur when a body is repositioned. Information from the autopsy report and photographs suggested that Tommy was deceased and on his back for over 8 hours in order for lividity to have become partially fixed posteriorly. The presence of some anterior lividity was accounted for by his having been found face-down in the creek. Arguably, one could posit that Tommy was rolled in the water from his back to his stomach by the force of the current. In light of the previous discussion concerning bloating and refloating, and the conclusion that Tommy had been placed in the creek after the flood stage had subsided, as well as the depth of the water at the time of his recovery, then Ridley Creek was not a raging river that could have rolled Tommy over. The Medical Examiner reported observable lividity on both the anterior and posterior portions of Tommy's body. We concluded that this was the result of Tommy having been dead on his back for a period of time somewhere on land before being placed face-down in Ridley Creek. This flipping of the body would engender repeated shifting of lividity, thus obfuscating the original lividity and body position at the time of death.

Ocular Changes

The autopsy report stated that Tommy presented with corneal clouding that had obscured the color of his irides to some degree. Corneal film and cloudiness are two postmortem changes that can be used to estimate a time of death; this is done relative to eyes open or eyes closed. If the eyes are open and cloudy, then death usually occurred within 2 hours or less. When a body is discovered with the eyes closed and a film is present, then death occurred in 6 to 12 hours. If the eyes are cloudy, then death occurred within 12 to 24 hours. Since Tommy's eyes are found closed at recovery and cloudy, then these characteristics stipulated that he was dead for a period of 24 hours or less at the time of recovery. Since it was most likely that he was entered into the water at night, then Tommy was placed into the water the night before his recovery (i.e., the night of February 2–3, 2008). This evidence corroborated our opinions concerning rigor (Figure 10.10).

Decomposition and Maceration

The extent of decomposition of Tommy's body was inconsistent with 14.5 days postmortem given the weather and water conditions, and the fact that he was not completely submerged (Figure 10.11). Observable forensic facts supported our assessment (Armstrong & Erskine, 2011). On land in a temperate environment (i.e., 68 to 72 °Fahrenheit), a decomposing body will start to change skin color from blue to green in the Right Lower Quadrant (RLQ) of the abdomen within 12 hours, and then spread over the entire body within 24 hours after death. A dark green, red, or sometimes dark purple color will even appear within 24 to 36 hours. Next, marbling of the larger muscle areas and bloating from decomposition gases can be detected between 36 to 48 hours. Skin slippage (usually 2 to 3 days) and eventual degloving of the hands may appear as early as the 3rd day, but no later than the 7th day after death.

Tommy was found in a prone position with only a portion of the anterior side of his body immersed in water. An examination of the recovery and autopsy photographs disclosed that Tommy's arms, hands and face were just starting to present changes associated with immersion in water. He did not present with any sign of putrefaction, maceration, marbling, bloating, or skin slippage that would be consistent with 14.5 day postmortem on land or in the water. Along with his clothing, Tommy's body was almost pristine.

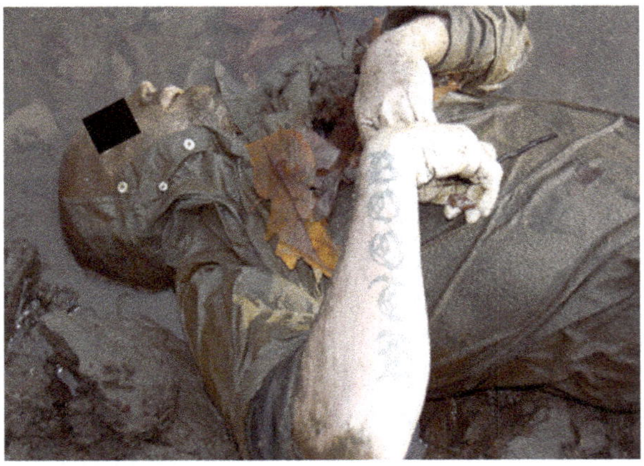

Figure 10.11 Tommy Booth's condition was inconsistent with 14.5 days postmortem. (*Special Note:* Use of this photograph was approved by Barbara Mackay-Bush.) (From Ridley Township Police Department (RTPD). 2008. *SUPPLEMENTAL* [Investigation reports dated January 23, 2008 through February 6, 2008]. Woodlyn, Pennsylvania: Various Police Officers.)

The Medical Examiner described him as having an early grey discoloration in the RLQ. Considering the condition of the body, he could not have been at this location for more than 12 to 24 hours, which was the assessment that our team had given the Ridley Detective Bureau on May 2, 2008, three months before the Medical Examiner's postmortem report was finalized and released on August 2, 2008.

Fluids, Weights, and Time

Unlike most autopsies that we have read, this medical examiner was really on the ball when it came to describing fluids within the body. All of these were very important empirical observations. In the autopsy report, Dr. Hellman noted normal amounts of blood-tinged fluid in the pleural cavities, pericardial sac and peritoneal cavity. He commented on finding a moderate amount of blood-tinged fluid in the lungs and distal airways that was associated with swelling. Pleural effusion can result from disease, multiple organ failure, postmortem liquefaction, or inhaled water seeping from the lungs into the surrounding cavity (Armstrong & Erskine, 2011; DiMaio & DiMaio, 2001). The longer a body is immersed in water or deceased, then the greater the likelihood of pleural effusion occurring. A blood-tinged foam or froth present in the larynx, trachea, or bronchial tree is indicative of an antemortem reaction. A pink foam in the airway usually begins to disappear after a body has been in the water for more than 1 week (Shkrum & Ramsay, 2007).

The autopsy report also presented that the Medical Examiner aspirated several milliliters of a blood-tinged fluid from the sphenoid sinus. The research literature suggests that this may be up to 5 milliliters (Armstrong & Erskine, 2011, p. 251). Although this can occur in nondrowning cases, it is often indicative of a wet drowning and aspirated volumes are greater in wet drowning cases. The fluid in the sphenoid sinus can be examined for and compared with the debris, chemicals (such as man-made pollutants), and diatoms that were present in the body of water from which the deceased was recovered. Diatoms are microscopic, single-celled organisms that are primarily made up of silicon-based exoskeleton unique to each species. Thousands of species exist and they can be found alive or as fossils (Spitz & Spitz, 2006). Unfortunately, to our knowledge, this fluid was never examined.

According to the Medical Examiner, Tommy had a mixture of a brown fluid (100 milliliters or 3.4 ounces) and softened food particles (tan-yellow) in his stomach at autopsy, which he kept for toxicological testing. He reported that the gallbladder contained 20-plus milliliters of bile (about 0.7 ounces). We could find no record of whether or not the fluid from the stomach had ever been examined for chemicals or diatoms that were consistent with Ridley Creek. We could find no record of whether or not law enforcement ever sought out any information about what Tommy had to eat in the past 24 hours, when, where, and with whom. Please recall the discussion in Chapter 2 (Figure 2.6) concerning gastrointestinal contents, the gallbladder, and the digestive process. The Medical Examiner's description told us that Tommy's gallbladder had passed *Late Nadir* and was refilling because he was nearing the end of the digestive process that involved the stomach, and that he had most likely eaten within 4 to 6 hours prior to death.

The weights were presented for most organs in the autopsy report (heart, right lung, left lung, liver, spleen, right kidney, and left kidney). However, Dr. Hellman only commented on the size of the heart, right and left lungs, liver, right and left kidneys. He noted that Tommy's lungs had expanded in size, but presented with normal weights (Left 390 grams and Right 490 grams). In all likelihood, they did not contain any water from Ridley

Creek. For the heart, liver, right and left kidneys, he recorded the same assessment: that the organs were the correct size but slightly heavier in weight relative to the size of Tommy's body. This observation was extremely important. Relative to asphyxiation and drowning cases as compared to other types of trauma, if the time between submersion and recovery is short (within 6 hours of death), then the weights of certain organs (i.e., lungs, kidneys, liver, and spleen) may be increased (Shkrum & Ramsay, 2007).

All of these empirical facts suggested that only a short period of time had elapsed between Tommy's death and his recovery. He had been missing for 14.5 days and presumed deceased for most of that time. That presumption could not be correct. The biological evidence was: (a) the absence of pleural effusion, (b) the presence of a blood-tinged fluid in the lungs and airways, (c) the existence of food particles in the stomach, (d) the refilling gallbladder, and (e) the increased internal organ weight. Clearly, Tommy had not been in Ridley Creek for more than 1 week. Since cooler temperatures can delay and prolong processes associated with the Postmortem Interval (PMI), then these fluids and weights may have actually indicated that Tommy was only in the creek somewhere between 12 and 24 hours prior to his recovery on February 3rd at 15:50 hours.

Injuries

Tommy sustained several small injuries that normally might have been overlooked. The autopsy report indicated that the injuries were located in 4 areas on his body: the face, knees, back of the right hand, and neck strap muscles (Figure 10.12). The Medical Examiner described two areas of abrasion near the bridge of the nose. These were not descriptions of the same injury since Dr. Hellman had specifically referred to the second abrasion as an additional one. The first injury was on the bridge of the nose (about 3/8

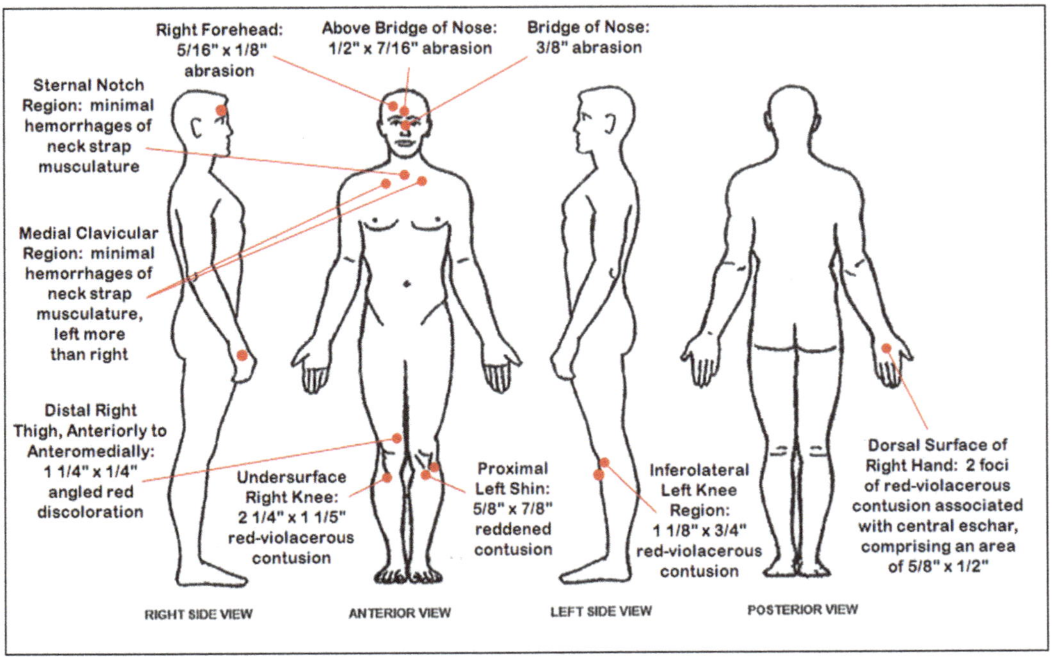

Figure 10.12 Injuries on Tommy Booth's body at autopsy; artist rendition is from observations of autopsy photographs and reports.

inch in diameter) and the second injury was just over the bridge of the nose (1/2 inch by 7/16 inch). The third injury on Tommy's face consisted of an abrasion on his right forehead (5/16 inch by 1/8 inch).

A second area of injury was Tommy's knees. Both knees had been injured and presented with violaceous-red (purplish) marks. The Medical Examiner labeled these discolored areas as contusions (i.e., bruises). The first bruise (1-1/8 inch by 3/4 inch) was located in the inferolateral region of Tommy's left knee, which is the area immediately below his knee cap and to the outside. A second bruise (5/8 inch by 7/8 inch) was just below this in the proximal left shin region, which is the part of the shin nearest the knee cap. The right leg presented with a significant bruise (2-1/4 inch by 1-1/2 inch) in the area below the knee cap, as well as another bruise (1-1/4 inch by 1/4 inch) above the knee cap that ran diagonally from the front (anteriorly) to the inside of the thigh (anteromedially).

The third area of injury was the dorsal surface (back side) of Tommy's right hand, which had two small areas of purplish bruising. The largest of these two bruises (5/8 inch by 1/2 inch) was nearly circular in shape and presented with a central eschar, which is a dry scab formed on skin that has been burned or cauterized.

Lastly, the fourth area of injury centered on Tommy's neck strap muscles. The Medical Examiner described these injuries as minimal hemorrhages that involved the muscle tissue connecting the head to the trunk of the body. Hemorrhages are similar to contusions, in that, they involve a loss of blood from ruptured blood vessels and produce a similar "bruised" appearance. Tommy's neck strap musculature was injured in the area of his sternal notch and medial clavicular region, which is the soft spot at the base on one's neck where the collarbones meet the breastbone. Hellman stated that the musculature on the left side had been damaged more than the right side.

All of these injuries could be easily explained were this an accidental drowning. The bruising on Tommy's knees could have been caused when he fell down the embankment into Ridley Creek. The torn neck strap muscles could occur during a regular drowning. And, the abrasions on his face were merely travel abrasions from scrapping along the bottom of the creek. Sounds reasonable until one stops and really thinks about how bruises and abrasions develop, and considers alternative explanations for the torn muscles. Simply put, bruises require a beating heart to develop. Had Tommy stumbled and fallen into the Creek and then drowned shortly thereafter, then he would not have had bruises. Had Tommy sustained the abrasions while being swept downstream by the creek at flood stage, then he should have had more abrasions that just a few on his nose and forehead. And, how does one explain the injury on the back of his hand? The size and shape of the eschar described by Dr. Hellman sounded to us like a cigarette burn. Had Tommy inflicted this upon himself in a show of macho tolerance to pain before his peers or to impress women? According to family members, Tommy had no previous history of such behavior or burn marks on his arms or hands.

We posited that these injuries were the result of the abduction process, torture, and being dragged into the creek. First, the torn neck strap muscles indicated to Gannon that a right-handed person had ambushed Tommy from behind by grabbing him about the neck with a choke hold. That is why the musculature was hemorrhaged more on the left side. An assault from behind that forced him to the ground would have accounted for the multiple injuries to Tommy's thigh, knees and shins. Second, the small burn marks on the back of Tommy's right hand were the result of a cigarette that was used during his torture. His abductors sought to determine what Tommy knew, or whom he told, about their gang by subjecting him to the pain of burning the soft flesh on the back of his hand. Lastly,

Gilbertson posited that the abrasions on his face (the bridge of his nose and forehead) were the result of being dragged along the sandy bottom of Ridley Creek. It was Tommy's face that had carved out the drag mark in the creek bed (see above, Figure 10.9). Tommy had to have been assaulted and held alive for a period of time in order for the bruising to develop before being murdered and placed into Ridley Creek.

Video Recordings

On the night in question, the girlfriend of one of Tommy's associates was celebrating her birthday. According to statements made by the young men in this group, they had discovered Bootleggers online and went to check it out that night. Tommy was observed at 22:55 hours on Saturday, January 19, 2008, entering Bootleggers through the front door, which was covered by a CCTV security camera and a bouncer.

Statements made by members of this group indicated that everyone except DRIV-3.1 and Tommy left the bar at approximately 00:50 hours because a couple of them were caught smoking marijuana in the bar. DRIV-3.1 provided conflicting statements to police concerning when and where he last saw Tommy. They ranged from seeing Tommy at about 01:00 hours in the Hip Hop section of Bootleggers, to around 01:30 hours when Tommy was heading to the bathroom in Bootleggers. DRIV-3.1 stated that at about 02:00 hours, when the bar was closing, he walked around inside the bar and was unable to physically locate Tommy.

Statements

The Ridley Detective Bureau did not thoroughly interview or follow-up with any of the people who were with Tommy that night. They only conducted an initial cursory investigation when Tommy first went missing. They never reinterviewed either PASS-1.3 or DRIV-3.1. They never interviewed the birthday girl (PASS-1.4) or her friend (PASS-2.2) at all regarding anything that happened the night of Tommy's disappearance. They did, however, track down and interview the Hispanic girls with whom Tommy had been seen talking to that night in the bar. This information was given to the police by PASS-1.3 who went back to Bootleggers the following Saturday (January 26th) and spoke with the 3 females who remembered very little about anything pertaining to Tommy.

Statements concerning chronological events generally do not include precise recall of time to the minute. This is particularly true when such statements are given under stressful conditions or the events occurred during periods of intoxication. Recall of events that are precise relative to time are either indicative of a person with a great attention to detail (and a history of such should be demonstrated) or are a sign of deception.

DRIV-3.1 statements disclosed his intent to cover up the truth. The private investigator hired by the family recorded in his notes that DRIV-3.1 said he was out front between 01:25 to 01:40 hours with other friends whom he knew from Bootleggers. This statement brought to light three issues. First, DRIV-3.1's recall of events that night to 5-minute intervals is suspect. Second, if it were correct, then DRIV-3.1 could not have seen Tommy headed to the bathroom at 01:30 hours, as he stated earlier, since he was outside. Third, DRIV-3.1 had let it slip that he knew people from Bootleggers, which meant that his statement about discovering the bar online and wanting to check it out with this group of friends must have been false.

The bouncer's statement was most likely correct and conflicted with those provided by the group that was with Tommy that night. Members of the group adamantly stated that Tommy did not leave the bar with them that night and that he stayed behind with DRIV-3.1. Tommy was never seen on CCTV security camera exiting the bar. The bouncer working one of the exit doors, which was not covered by a CCTV security camera, stated that someone resembling Tommy may have exited the bar with the birthday girl (PASS-1.4) and the others at 00:50 hours. This was supported by analysis of Tommy's cell phone records for that night.

Cell Phone Records

Two (2) brief calls were made at 00:54:32 hours on January 20, 2008. Unfortunately, Tommy's cell phone record did not indicate the GPS coordinates for these two calls. The first call was from Tommy's phone to (302) 4XX-XXXX, which was identified during our first analysis (2010) as a cell phone with a Southwestern Bell Mobile Systems service provider in Dover, Delaware. Current analysis (2011) identified this number as an Cingular/AT&T "back door" voice mail number. Some of these backdoor numbers were recently reassigned, changed, or disconnected. Their original purpose was to give users access to their local wireless carrier's voice mail system, and could allow users to leave a voice mail message for one of the carrier's subscribers without ringing his or her phone.

The second call at 00:54:32 hours on January 20th was from (302) 9XX-XXXX. This number came back during both analyses (2010 & 2011) to a Verizon Delaware landline (i.e., home phone) associated with the residence of DRIV-2.1 in Wilmington, Delaware. This last call confirmed that someone was at DRIV-2.1's home and made a call to Tommy's cell phone at 00:54:32 hours. This call should not have been made by DRIV-2.1 or any other member of the group, because a statement given by PASS-1.2 declared that he, DRIV-2.1 and 5 others (i.e., DRIV-1.1, PASS-1.3, PASS-1.4, PASS-2.2, & PASS-2.3) had departed the bar at about 00:52 hours and met in the parking lot to return to Wilmington. According to the bouncer, he had seen members of the group leave the bar at about 00:50 hours. Thus, the bouncer's recall confirmed the timeline of events, but he could not accurately recall who in the group left the bar. This also demonstrated that the bouncer's relative memory of events with regard to time indicates that he probably told the truth. Since it is about a 20 to 25 minute drive south down Interstate Highway 95 from Bootleggers back to Wilmington, had someone from the group left the bar about 00:15 hours, returned to Wilmington, and lied about it? What would an analysis of the cellular records for everyone on the group reveal?

Spatial analysis of the last call made from Tommy's cell phone did not confirm anything, especially his presence in Bootleggers. All it confirmed was that Tommy's cell phone (and not necessarily Tommy) was in closer proximity to one cell tower than it was to another tower at that time. The last call was made at 00:59:07 hours on January 20, 2008. It was presumed to have been made from Bootleggers. The wireless carrier (Cingular/AT&T) had 3 cellular towers within range of Bootleggers. The final call was transmitted via *Tower #1* (Figure 10.13). The concentric circles are 250 feet apart. Bootleggers was actually closer to *Tower #2* than it was to *Tower #1*. Establishing concentric circles determines the line at which you are closer to *Tower #1* than to other cellular towers. In order to hit off *Tower #1*, Tommy's cell phone would have likely been anywhere to the south of the bold *Green Line*.

This analysis demonstrated that Tommy's phone should have used *Tower #2* that was to the north of Bootleggers. There were two possible reasons for his cell phone to use *Tower #1*:

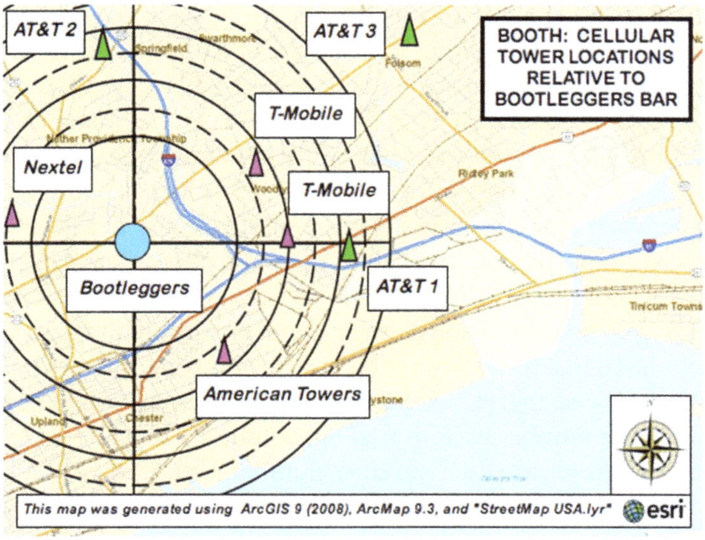

Figure 10.13 In 2008, there were 7 cellular towers in the vicinity of Bootleggers. Tommy Booth's last cellular call (at 00:59:07 hours on January 20, 2008) was presumed to have been made from Bootleggers, and was transmitted via *Tower #1*.

(1) his phone was at Bootleggers and something blocked its signal to the north; and (2) his phone was not at Bootleggers and was actually somewhere south of the bold *Green Line*. His phone (and by inference, Tommy himself) did not have to be at Bootleggers (Figure 10.14). In fact, both could have been on the Interstate Highway system on their way out of the area.

The police analysis of Tommy's cell phone records was inaccurate and raised even more questions. A supplemental report was logged by a detective at 17:22 hours on February 6, 2008. First, Tommy's cell phone number was (302) 559-XXXX and serviced out of Wilmington,

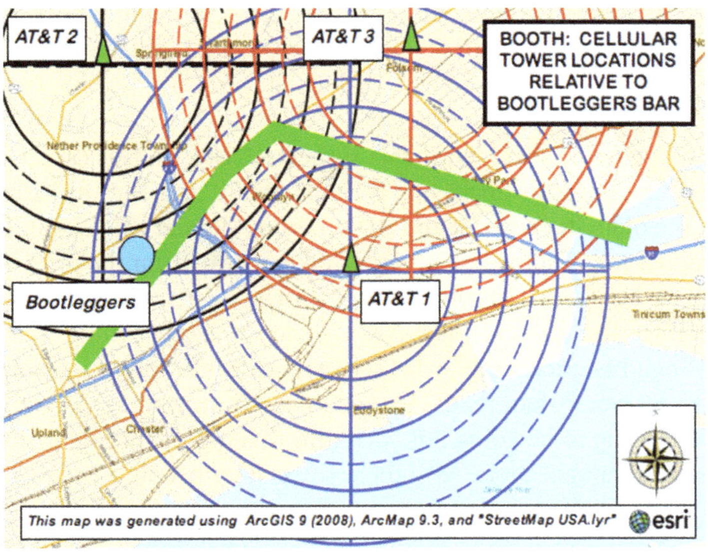

Figure 10.14 The concentric circles are 250 feet apart. Bootleggers was closer to *Tower #2* than it was to *Tower #1*. In order to transmit a cellular call via *Tower #1*, Tommy Booth's phone would have had to have been in an area that favored a signal to that tower; that is represented here by the area south of the *Green Line*.

Delaware (his place of residence). However, this police report listed his cell phone number as (610) 529-XXXX, which is a cell phone serviced out of Ardmore, Pennsylvania (northwest of Philadelphia). Second, the report suggested that both calls at 00:54:32 hours were made by friends to Tommy's cell phone. When in fact, one was an out-going call from Tommy's cell phone to (302) 4XX-XXXX, and the other call was an in-coming call to Tommy's phone from (302) 9XX-XXXX. Third, the police said that Tommy was checking his voicemail and deleting them. But, when a person wishes to hear voicemails and to delete them, that action will show up on cell phone records as a call to the same phone. The call at 00:59:07 hours was made to (777) 1XX-XXXX, and not to Tommy's own phone. Thus, Tommy or someone else was not listening to voicemails and deleting them. Further analysis of this 777 area code phone number disclosed that it was not a valid private number anywhere in North America. An online search indicated that it had been used on occasion for commercial purposes. When people called the number back to find out whom it was who had called them, they would hear "dead air" (as reported at "nuisance number" websites).

Toxicology

A relative of Tommy's told Sergeant Palo that he (Tommy) used cocaine on a regular basis and drank alcohol in excess. However, the toxicology report stated that no toxicologically significant types or measurements of cocaine were detected. Tommy was recovered with a 0.220 percent Blood Alcohol Concentration and a 0.101 percent Vitreous Fluid Concentration. Also, the level of Tommy's medication (Alprazolam) within his system was measured at 0.01 micrograms per milliliter of blood, which is at the low end of a peak dose plasma range (0.01 to 0.02) for a 1 milligram oral dose. In fact, no report indicated whether or not the police or the Medical Examiner ever determined what the dose level of Tommy's medication was supposed to be, or how it compared with his blood level. The toxicological report did not support his relative's assertion about cocaine and alcohol, or that of others who claimed that excessive alcohol and drugs may have contributed to Tommy's death.

Potential Suspects

Evidence strongly suggested that identifiable suspects existed in this case. On July 12, 2009, Major General Booth (Tommy's uncle) told Gannon that he and Tommy had a phone conversation earlier on the night he went out and went missing (January 19, 2008). Tommy had told him, "that he wanted to get some new friends and get away from the ones he was currently with. He stated that they were into some strange things." When his uncle asked what kind of things were they into, Tommy said, "like AK-47s and some other things that he didn't want to be around." When his uncle asked whether they were into robberies, Tommy responded with, "No, it was a lot worse than that." His uncle asked him whether any of the guys he had spoken about were going to be going out with him this night. Tommy confirmed that they were, but that he would not be alone with them since other people would also be around.

Conclusion

Our team believes that the facts in this case lead to a conclusion that Thomas James Booth, III, was abducted, murdered, and then disposed of by placing his body in Ridley Creek to create the appearance of an accidental death. During our March 2009 visit, the Medical Examiner stated to us that he was 99 percent sure that this was a homicide, but that he could not state with 100 percent surety how the victim died. All evidence in the Medical Examiner's autopsy report and photographs clearly pointed to this case being a homicide regardless of whether he could state categorically how the victim died. The condition and position of the body along with the lividity, rigidity, the head drag mark, and the shoe imprints in the creek bed soil, demonstrated to us and the Medical Examiner that Tommy's death involved human intervention. We believe that Tommy's death may actually be one of the few cases of dry drowning. The evidence (i.e., blood-tinged fluid in the airway and the absence of fluid in the lungs) suggested that he likely struggled to not inhale water while being held face down. When all of that was coupled with the condition of his eyes and abdomen with respect to decomposition, then we concluded that Tommy was in Ridley Creek for less than 24 hours.

We believe the cell phone activity that night was intended to misdirect investigative efforts. The calls at 00:54:32 hours were made to create the appearance that Tommy was still at the bar while others (who may become logical suspects and needed an alibi) were 20 miles away. The last call at 00:59:07 hours was intentional and designed to send a taunting message to police – if they caught it. The police never questioned DRIV-3.1 as to why he did not call Tommy's cell phone an hour later when he was leaving the bar at 02:00 hours; first, to see where Tommy was, and second, to leave him a voice message stating that he was getting ready to leave and return back to Wilmington. "Tommy, where are you? Hey man, Let's go! I'm getting ready to leave. Tommy, if you made other plans, give me a call. Let me know where you're at." Nada! Nothing! None of this ever occurred. There was no message about leaving or any concern for Tommy whatsoever.

One possible reason that there was no call or concern for Tommy could have been because DRIV-3.1 already knew where Tommy was and with whom he was – he was already abducted and in the company of those who would ultimately be responsible for his death. So, why would DRIV-3.1 need to make a call to Tommy's phone, unless of course he needed to make some kind of alibi for himself or the group. This information also confirmed to us that Tommy was not at Bootleggers or anywhere in the area near Bootleggers as the previous cell phone records (00:59:07) had shown. If he was still there, then DRIV-3.1 could have made a call to Tommy's phone and shown that he was in the vicinity of Bootleggers if not exactly inside. This would have also accounted for Tommy's body being found later behind Bootleggers and would also have provided a possible alibi. The only problem with this scenario was that Tommy was nowhere near Bootleggers.

A second possible scenario existed for why there was no call to Tommy that night. Perhaps, DRIV-3.1 knew that Tommy was nowhere near Bootleggers, and he also knew that he could not make a call to Tommy's phone because it would leave a digital finger-track. The authorities could have then requested Tommy's cell phone records, which would have come with incoming and outgoing phone numbers, times, duration of calls, types of call, and either the GPS coordinates for the phone or the antenna data (i.e., the Federal Communications Commission Antenna Structure Registration Number, directional indicator code, and GPS coordinates). If the authorities could get their hands on Tommy's actual cell phone, then they would have had access to all of the metadata on the internal memory chip/card. This would have included times and GPS coordinates for each phone call, as well as each time Tommy's phone checked-in with the cellular system and "pinged" a tower. Authorities could have literally "connected the dots" as the phone traveled past cellular towers giving them a road map of exactly where Tommy's cell phone was at that moment, if not Tommy himself. This was something the killers could not allow to happen.

In our collective professional opinion, this was the reason why there was never a call made to Tommy's phone at 02:00 hours, and also why there was never a recovery of the phone in the Tommy Booth case. In many of the cases that we have looked at, the cell phones were found in a location that was inconsistent with where it should have been. Interestingly, they were found in areas that had been previous searched numerous times. To not have the phone at all for someone who was recovered right behind the bar speaks volumes as to what the killers' intentions were. We believe that an attempt was made to recruit Tommy for membership in this organization. When he declined the offer, those responsible for his death knew they had to specifically find out whom Tommy may have told about their organization and activities. Examining his cell phone's call history and phonebook would have been a good place to start. They had to make sure that they got rid of Tommy and left no digital trace as to who was responsible for this heinous act.

We believe that his cell phone had been taken from him by his abductors and left with someone at the bar to create the digital appearance that he was still there at closing time. Information gleaned from police reports and our own work not only supported a conclusion that a homicide had been committed, it also suggested that potential suspects were among those individuals who were with Tommy on the night he disappeared. Barbara MacKay-Bush (Tommy's mother) stated that on the day before the search and rescue dogs found Tommy, her husband's coworker had searched the area and the creek and did not find Tommy's body. Yet, Tommy was recovered the following day behind Bootleggers. This confirms that Tommy was placed at this location within the previous 24 hours. The case needs to be changed to an active homicide investigation.

Cullen Fortney* 11

Background

Cullen Fortney is at least one case that we know of where someone actually survived an attempted drowning by the Smiley Face Killers. Scoffers and skeptics have all declared that even serial killers make mistakes and someone survives. They have asked, "Where, then, is your survivor if this is a serial killer?" First off, these cases are not the work of one killer, and they are not serial. They are not the work of a serial killer, and therefore, do not fit neatly into the profile of a serial killer that these professionals are trying to force them into for their media sound bites and commentaries. Second, the evidence that we present in this chapter clearly demonstrates that this was no accident, rather, that an attempt was made to extinguish Cullen's life that night.

It was appropriate that this case happened in La Crosse, Wisconsin, where nearly a dozen other young men have perished since 1997. Although this was not the first case of interest to occur in La Crosse and it is out of chronological sequence, it serves as the perfect case to introduce 4 other La Crosse cases and is significantly important for three reasons. Cullen's case gave us greater insight into how and when the abductions were taking place, and whether or not our assumptions about what was taking place were actually correct or not. It was also important in that it clearly showed how the local police made honest-to-goodness errors in investigating Cullen's attempted drowning.

There are skeptics who do not believe that any of the La Crosse drowning cases were homicides. Some folks absolutely refuse to acknowledge any evidence presented to them, while others in authority refuse to present all of the existing evidence for others to scrutinize. Rather, these naysayers cling to blood alcohol concentration (BAC) levels, especially the high ones, and declare that these were nothing more than tragic accidents wherein intoxicated college males unconsciously wandered down to Riverside Park and fell into the Mississippi River. There are even some whose attempts to be sagacious writers came across as crass humorists. One example of this was found on the official website for the La Crosse County Medical Examiner (LCCME). He produced and posted a PowerPoint presentation at his website (River Drowning.ppt) in order to counter the "urban legend" of a La Crosse serial killer (LCCME, November 11, 2005). On the last slide, he responded to the question of whether or not there was a serial killer. He stated that the evidence had led him to the conclusion that there was a killer in La Crosse. Furthermore, not only was the killer responsible for the deaths of these young men in La Crosse, he was also

* Attempted Drowning, January 8, 2006. [Even though Fortney's name appeared in the media, we have chosen to not present his photograph in order to preserve his public anonymity.]

responsible for the deaths of thousands more annually. He even provided the name of this killer: *Al Cohol.*

The La Crosse County Medical Examiner, administrators and investigators of the police department, and others in La Crosse adhere to the argument that the presence of so many bars so close to the river is a primary contributor to these deaths. There are 30 drinking establishments in the downtown bar district within about an 8 square block area (see Figure 11.1, the *Blue Dots*). There used to be more, but some have been consolidated into larger bars. For example, Ringside and Legends were sold and are now one bar called Whiskey River Saloon. There are approximately 23 bars in the immediate vicinity of the primary drinking corridor (the heavy *Green Line*), which is about 1050 feet long. That means that there is another bar roughly every 50 feet along the corridor. That is a lot of drinks when you are a college student out doing a pub crawl. These figures do not include those businesses where a college student could get a mixed drink, wine, or beer; that is, places like restaurants, pizza joints, and hotel lounges. One can see why the argument of a critical mass of bars does have its appeal as a partial explanation for these deaths. That is until one stops and thinks about all the universities and colleges in the United States – particularly the upper Midwest – that are not only closer to a body of water, but right next to it with larger student populations. Yet, they do not have the same "drinking and drowning problem" that La Crosse has.

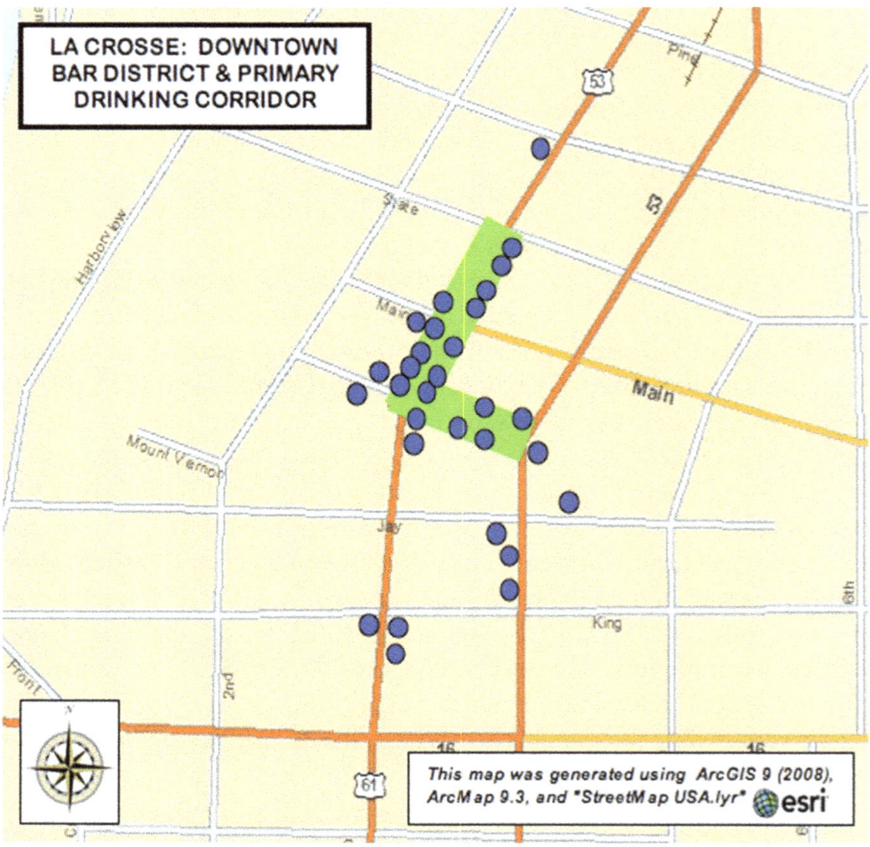

Figure 11.1 The La Crosse downtown bar district and its primary drinking corridor (*Green Shaded Area*) included about 30 drinking establishments (*Blue Dots*) in 2006.

Circumstances

Last Seen

It was Saturday, January 7, 2006, and Cullen was back home in Viroqua from the University of Wisconsin – Madison for the holiday break. Cullen drove that night and picked up a friend (hereafter, Randy). The pair then went to La Crosse to meet up with another guy (hereafter, Jason). The plan was to go downtown for some drinks and to stay overnight at Jason's afterwards. Cullen was last seen on the dance floor of John's Bar at approximately 01:45 hours on early Sunday morning, January 8, 2006. Cullen did not remember anything after dancing except that he woke up swimming for his life in the freezing January waters of the Mississippi River.

Finding Cullen

Gannon needed a survivor. At that point in time, our team did not exist. The path of Gannon and Duarte had not yet crossed with the path of Gilbertson and Carlson; yet, their trajectories were now drawing them closer each day. Although Gannon was convinced in late 2004 that something sinister was going on and wanted to investigate these deaths, he had mentioned to Duarte that he needed to speak with someone who had survived one of these attacks. Then in January 2006, Gannon called Duarte and told him that they had a survivor, in La Crosse of all places. They were on their way to Wisconsin.

Finding Cullen was not difficult. Gannon and Duarte had a phone number and address for Cullen's home of record in Wisconsin. The pair went to Viroqua and attempted to reach Cullen there first. They discovered that this address was for a nice old, two-story colonial style home in a quiet neighborhood. When they knocked on the door, there was no answer. So, Duarte called the phone number they had while Gannon listened at the door for the phone to ring; which it subsequently did. They left a hard-copy message at the door identifying themselves and their desire to speak with Cullen. When they received no answer, Gannon called back later that evening. Cullen's parents informed him that they did not want to speak with anyone, and that they wanted to put this incident behind them.

As part of their search for any local information concerning Cullen, they went to the University of Wisconsin – La Crosse, 1 of 3 area academic institutions (the others are Viterbo University and Western Technical College). They gleaned no information on Cullen. Duarte, who can find anyone, searched the Internet for a possible address for Cullen in Madison since he was attending the University of Wisconsin – Madison. He found Cullen. So, off they went to Madison to interview the young man whom the La Crosse Tribune appropriately labeled "the one that got away."

Cullen's Interview

They found Cullen at his residence in Madison. As the interview began, Cullen related the following story. Cullen remembered being at John's Bar dancing around closing time and then waking up in the freezing Mississippi River swimming for his life. Everything in between those events was a mystery. He told them how he was fortunate enough to swim with the current and toward shore where he saw something that he believed to be a concrete slab near the Isle La Plume. He grabbed onto it and was lucky enough to pull himself out of the water onto shore, where he collapsed from exhaustion.

Gannon could see right away how nervous Cullen was when they were speaking to him. So, he asked him whether he was nervous and Cullen responded, "Some people and the police thought I was making this story up." Both Gannon and Duarte assured him that they did not believe he was making this story up and that they just wanted to hear his recollection of the events of that evening as best as he could remember them. Gannon explained that from his recollections it might aid them in figuring out what was happening to these young men in La Crosse.

Cullen was acting like a victim and Gannon did not want to revictimize him. So, he initiated a tension-relieving discussion about golf based on items he saw around Cullen's apartment. Gannon asked him what clothing he had on and he said that he had lost his shoes, $20.00 cash and his favorite hat. Gannon asked him whether it was a golf hat and Cullen said it was. He said, "It was a Titleist hat." Gannon then asked whether he was a golfer and Cullen said he was. They exchanged a few comments about golf, and then Gannon informed him about how far Duarte could drive a ball (over 300 yards). Cullen appeared to be a pretty good golfer himself from the conversation that ensued.

Cullen then told them how he laid on the shore for a while and then awoke quickly, like in a bad dream, from the cold and fright of knowing something terrible and traumatic had happened to him and knowing that he needed to get help. He heard the early morning traffic (Sunday morning) and within minutes got up and ran toward it. He then spotted the Gundersen Lutheran Medical Center and ran to it for help (Figure 11.2). He ran inside without his jacket, shoes, or cell phone and told the hospital personnel that he almost died and that someone had almost killed him. This happened around 07:00 hours on January 8, 2006. The police were notified and responded to the hospital to conduct an investigation.

The importance of the facts in Cullen's next statement proved to Gannon and Duarte that not only were they right about these cases not being accidents, but also that in the majority of them, the victims had to have been drugged before being thrown into the water in order for this to have happened without them being able to remember it. It also proved to them that their original assumption was correct, that is, that some of the victims were being held for a period of time before being deposited into the water. Gannon asked Cullen how long he was in the water before he was fortunate enough to get out. He said he was in

Figure 11.2 Once Cullen Fortney reached the main road, he could see Gundersen Lutheran Medical Center. He ran directly to the Emergency Room.

the water for approximately 5 to 10 minutes maximum and then collapsed "on the rocks" next to shore. Gannon then asked Cullen how long he was on shore before he woke up and heard the traffic and ran toward it. At that point, Cullen related the most important piece to this whole case. He said, "I was on shore for what seemed like it was only for 10 to 15 minutes, but it must have been hours since I walked into the hospital at around 7 o'clock."

Analysis of Evidence

Entry and Exit Locations

Cullen was able to get out of the water close enough to Gundersen Lutheran Medical Center that he could see it once he reached the main road (see Figure 11.3). The police went to the location that Cullen identified as the spot where he pulled himself from the water and located some of his personal property near the river's edge. That location is in the general vicinity of where several of other victims (i.e., Kapfer, Geesey, and Dion) were recovered. The police purport that all of those victims entered the water at Riverside Park. If the victims had entered the water at Riverside Park, then they would have continued floating south past Isle de la Plume in the current of the main channel of the Mississippi River. The only way for the victims to have been recovered in the side channels and sloughs was for them to have been put into the water near the Niedbalski Bridge at Hood Street, at the 7th

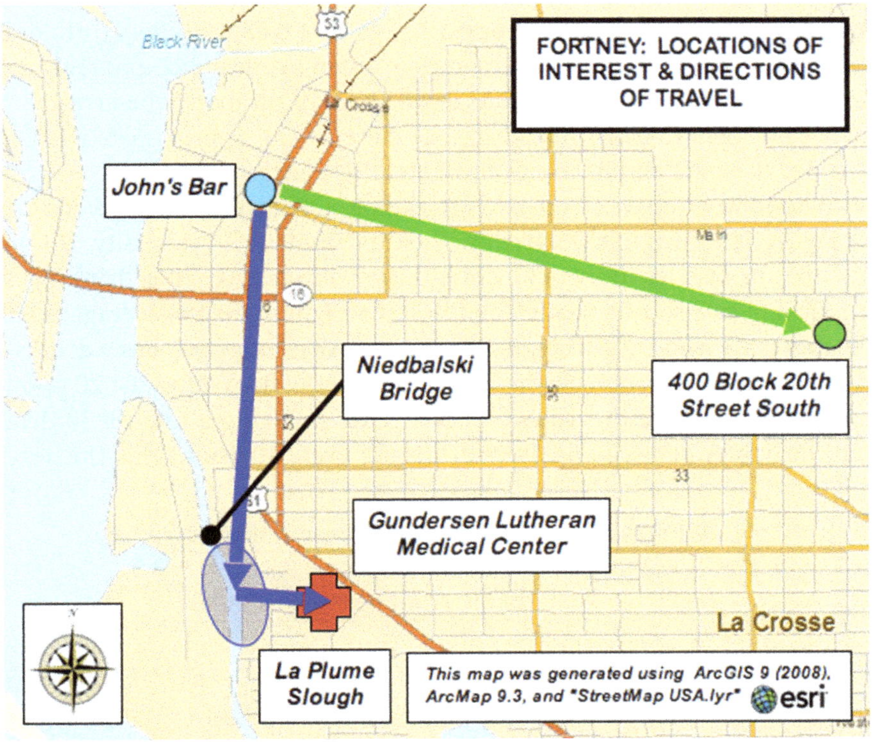

Figure 11.3 January 7–8, 2006: Cullen Fortney was last seen at John's Bar (*Blue Dot*) and should have returned to the 400 block of 20th Street South (*Green Dot*); instead, he ended up in La Plume Slough (*Blue Shaded Ellipse*) where he rescued himself from the river and ran to Gundersen Lutheran Medical Center (*Red Cross*).

Street boat landing further to the south, or in close proximity to the locations where they were recovered. Given their extremely high level of alcohol intoxication, they should have been in severe stupor and near unconsciousness. It is, therefore, also unlikely that they walked the 1.5 plus miles south to these locations (Figure 11.3). They had to have been driven there, which means human intervention. This dilemma for the La Crosse police was compounded by Cullen's survival.

Cullen stated that he swam with the river current toward shore. Thus, it was unlikely that he stumbled and fell into the water close to the east bank of the main channel of water that runs through La Plume Slough. Somehow, he ended up far enough out in the water that the current was carrying him along and sweeping him away. This suggested to us that he most probably entered the water from the middle of Niedbalski Bridge on Hood Street, or from a boat. This would explain his having to swim with the current and coming to shore further south in La Plume Slough. Additionally, he could not have fallen in by Riverside Park as the police proposed; since he would have succumbed to hypothermia and died as a result of the time required to travel that distance and the freezing temperature of the water.

Toxicology

The police were called and responded to the Gundersen Lutheran Medical Center and conducted an interview with Cullen around 08:00 hours. The police requested a blood sample and a blood alcohol concentration (BAC) test. Cullen's BAC was 0.043 at that time or approximately two drinks (0.02 milliliters = 1 drink). Alcohol intoxication in most states throughout the United States is based on a BAC level of 0.08 milliliters (mL) or approximately 4 drinks (see Figure 11.4). If a person were tested by the police and registered a 0.08 BAC, then he is considered too drunk to drive and will ultimately be arrested. A drink of alcohol is equivalent to 0.02 mL and stays in the body for approximately 1 hour before being dispersed (Centers for Disease Control and Prevention, 2011).

Physical build would have an affect on the amount of alcohol that a person could consume (see Figure 11.5; Virginia Polytechnic Institute and State University, 2011). A taller, more muscular, or heavier individual would have a lower BAC after drinking the same amount of alcohol as a shorter, leaner, and lighter weight man. The average is based on a 5 feet 10 inches male who weighs about 180 pounds. An average guy has 9 drinks and is at a 0.19 BAC. A male of the same height (5 feet 10 inches) who weighs just 20 pounds more at 200 pounds, would have the same 0.19 BAC after drinking a total of 10 drinks. This means that the lighter male could have 9 drinks for every 10 drinks that the heavier male

What is a Standard Drink in the United States?

A standard drink is equal to 13.7 g (0.6 oz) of pure alcohol. Generally, this amount of pure alcohol is found in:

- 12 oz beer
- 8 oz of malt liquor
- 5 oz of wine
- 1.5 oz or a "shot" of 80-proof distilled spirits or liquor (e.g., gin, rum, vodka, or whiskey)

Figure 11.4 The relative equivalent volumes of alcohol in different types of drinks. (From Centers for Disease Control and Prevention. 2011. *Alcohol and Public Health.* Frequently Asked Questions. [Online.] Available: www.cdc.gov/alcohol/faqs.htm#howAlcoholAffect.)

BAC Table for Men

DRINKS	BODY WEIGHT IN POUNDS 100	120	140	160	180	200	220	240	CONDITION
0	.00	.00	.00	.00	.00	.00	.00	.00	Only Safe Driving Limit
1	.04	.03	.03	.02	.02	.02	.02	.02	Driving Skills Significantly Affected -- Possible Criminal Penalties
2	.08	.06	.05	.05	.04	.04	.03	.03	
3	.11	.09	.08	.07	.06	.06	.05	.05	
4	.15	.12	.11	.09	.08	.08	.07	.06	
5	.19	.16	.13	.12	.11	.09	.09	.08	
6	.23	.19	.16	.14	.13	.11	.10	.09	Legally Intoxicated -- Criminal Penalties
7	.26	.22	.19	.16	.15	.13	.12	.11	
8	.30	.25	.21	.19	.17	.15	.14	.13	
9	.34	.28	.24	.21	.19	.17	.15	.14	
10	.38	.31	.27	.23	.21	.19	.17	.16	Death Possible

Figure 11.5 A table for approximating the blood alcohol impairment of men. (From Virginia Polytechnic Institute and State University. 2011. *Blood Alcohol Impairment Table for Men.* [Online.] Available: www.alcohol.vt.edu/Students/alcoholEffects/estimatingBAC/index.htm.)

could consume in order for them both to have the same 0.19 BAC. In fact, every male who is heavier than the average 180-pound male could consume one extra drink for every 20 pounds heavier (e.g., 200, 220, and 240 pounds) to reach a 0.19 BAC. Similarly, every male who is lighter than the average 180 pound male could consume one less drink for every 20 pounds lighter (e.g., 160, 140, and 120 pounds) to reach a 0.19 BAC.

BAC Mathematics

Since the drowning cases of college-age males in La Crosse were reported by the police and medical examiner to be accidents fueled by alcohol intoxication, this meant that Cullen must have been really drunk. The police proved this presumption by performing some simple mathematics to estimate Cullen's level of intoxication earlier in the evening. Alcohol disperses in the human body at approximately 1 drink per hour for the average male or about the equivalent of 0.02 mL of alcohol. The La Crosse Police Department started with Cullen's 0.043 BAC at 08:00 hours. He was last seen about 6 hours earlier at around 02:00 hours in John's Bar. Since Cullen was missing for 6 hours, his body would have dispersed approximately 6 drinks or 0.12 mL. Thus, the police added the 0.12 mL to Cullen's 0.043 mL and concluded that he must have had about a 0.163 BAC (see Figure 11.6). The police concluded that Cullen had consumed 8 drinks by the time he went missing (01:45 hours) and that his BAC showed him to be at twice the legal intoxication level of 0.08 mL. Therefore, he was just another drunken kid who fell into the water and fortunately just happened to survive. Or, was he?

Hypothermia

The water temperature for the Mississippi River that evening was 32 °Fahrenheit – literally, ice water. Hypothermia is the lowering of the body core temperature, which results in the slowing of brain, organ, and muscle functioning. Ultimately, it can lead to death.

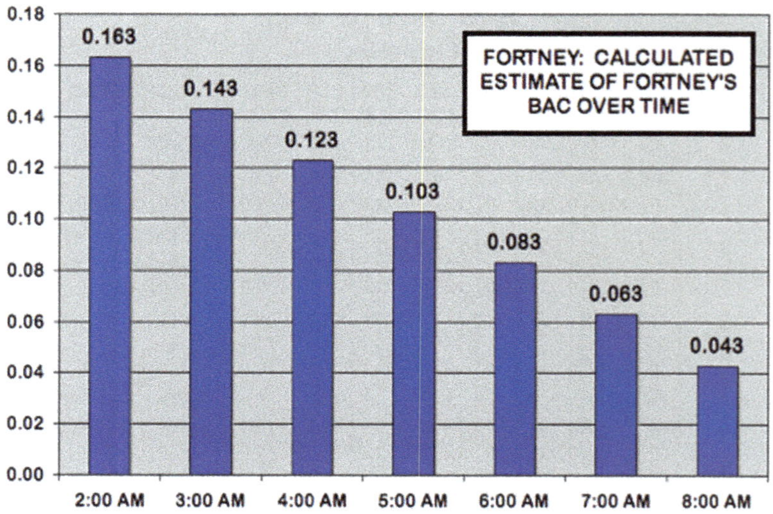

Figure 11.6 Knowing that Cullen had a 0.043 BAC at 8:00 a.m., the police calculated that he must have been at about an estimated 0.163 BAC at 2:00 a.m. when he left John's Bar.

When it comes to estimating time, the police were wrong and Cullen was correct. Cullen stated that he was in the water for approximately 5 to 10 minutes. He was absolutely correct and could not have been in the water any longer and survived. If the water temperature is 32.5 °Fahrenheit (see Figure 11.7; Ohio Department of Natural Resources), then a person in the water would be unconscious in under 15 minutes. Cullen stated that the length of time that he laid on the rocks was 10 to 15 minutes. In actuality, it may have been shorter – this whole scenario may have only lasted 5 minutes. Cullen may have experienced peritraumatic temporal distortion; in other words, 30 seconds may have seemed like 3 minutes because his brain and nervous system were racing with adrenaline trying to assess the situation and to keep him alive (Hancock & Weaver, 2005; Ursano, Fullerton, Epstein, Crowley, Vance, Kao, & Baum, 1999).

The police led him to believe that he was on the rocks for hours rather than minutes considering the time that he was last seen and the time that he entered the hospital. This, of course, is absurd. Hypothermia can occur in air as well as water. Had he actually fallen into the water shortly after bar closing and then climbed out to lay on the rocks in his

Survival Times for Immersion in Water

TEMPERATURE °F	EXHAUSTION	DEATH
32.5	*under 15 minutes*	*15 minutes or less*
32.5 - 40	*15 - 30 minutes*	*30 - 90 minutes*
40 - 50	*30 - 60 minutes*	*1 - 3 hours*
50 - 60	*1 - 2 hours*	*1 - 6 hours*
60 - 70	*2 - 7 hours*	*2 - 40 hours*
70 - 80	*2 - 12 hours*	*3 hours - indefinite*

Figure 11.7 The Mississippi River was 32 °Fahrenheit on the night that Cullen found himself struggling to survive. (From Ohio Department of Natural Resources. 2011. *Surviving a Cold-Water Accident.* [Online.] Available: www.dnr.state.oh.us/watercraft/safetytips/accident/tabid/2876/Default.aspx.)

wet clothing, then he would have succumbed to hypothermia there and died well before 07:00 hours came around. A person who falls into a body of water at 32.5 °Fahrenheit has 15 minutes or less before death may occur (Ohio Department of Natural Resources, 2011). If Cullen had entered the water sometime after bar closing like the police had presumed, then he would have most likely been dead within 15 minutes (no later than 03:00 hours) had he not been immediately rescued and received medical attention. These facts about water temperature and hypothermia clearly demonstrate that there was no way possible for Cullen to have been in the water sometime after bar closing (02:00 hours) and to have walked into the hospital at 07:00 hours since he would have been dead for over 4 hours.

The police had to have known this since they were smart enough to calculate his BAC from the time he was in the hospital back to when he was last seen at the bar. Of course, the police could always say that Cullen was walking it off or sleeping somewhere for 4-1/2 hours until 06:30 hours when he awoke and entered the Mississippi River without remembering the whole event. The problem with this scenario, however, is that Cullen's BAC would have been 0.073 or 3-1/2 drinks at 06:30 hours. At 07:00 hours, his BAC would have been 0.063 or 3 drinks. Cullen would not have been intoxicated at 06:30 hours, so there would have been no reason for him to fall into the Mississippi River; much less not remember how it occurred. Cullen would have been legally sober at that time and according to the letter of the law would have been physically capable of driving a motor vehicle.

Gannon's own BAC and hypothermia calculations relative to time concurred with Cullen's version of events rather than the police's. Gannon's analysis revealed that Cullen had to have entered the Mississippi River sometime after 06:30 hours in order for him to have been able to survive both the time in the water and the period of time on the shore, and still have been able to walk into the hospital at approximately 07:00 hours. The only explanation for Cullen to have entered the Mississippi River at 06:30 hours and to have no recollection of how it occurred, was to have been drugged in the bar sometime around 01:00 hours and escorted out of the bar, whereon he was held for a period of at least 4-1/2 hours while the pedestrian traffic subsided. Cullen had to have been given a debilitating date rape-type drug like GHB, Rohypnol, or ketamine, which has a very short half-life and can be completely out of the system in a period of 3 to 6 hours. He was then thrown into the freezing Mississippi River between 06:30 to 07:00 hours (Sunday morning) just as the drug was wearing off. He was shocked back to reality by his body hitting the freezing water of the Mississippi River and was just fortunate enough to survive. This is also why he had no memory of what happened to him until he hit the freezing water and awoke (i.e., GHB eliminates short term memory).

Suspicious Incident

John's Bar was the last seen location for another individual and his suspicious incident that evening. A friend of Cullen's from Viroqua (hereafter, Nate), was out on the town that night and was last seen drinking at John's Bar. The next day, Nate had trouble piecing together his activities during the previous evening. He had parked his pickup truck in Wettstein's lot, ended up drinking in John's Bar, and then wound up at the Gundersen Lutheran Medical Center passed out in the lobby. Nate had no idea how he got there. Additionally, his pickup truck was missing. The vehicle was located 4 days later on Thursday, January 12th, in the 900 block of King Street (see Figure 11.8). According to La Crosse Police Captain Robert

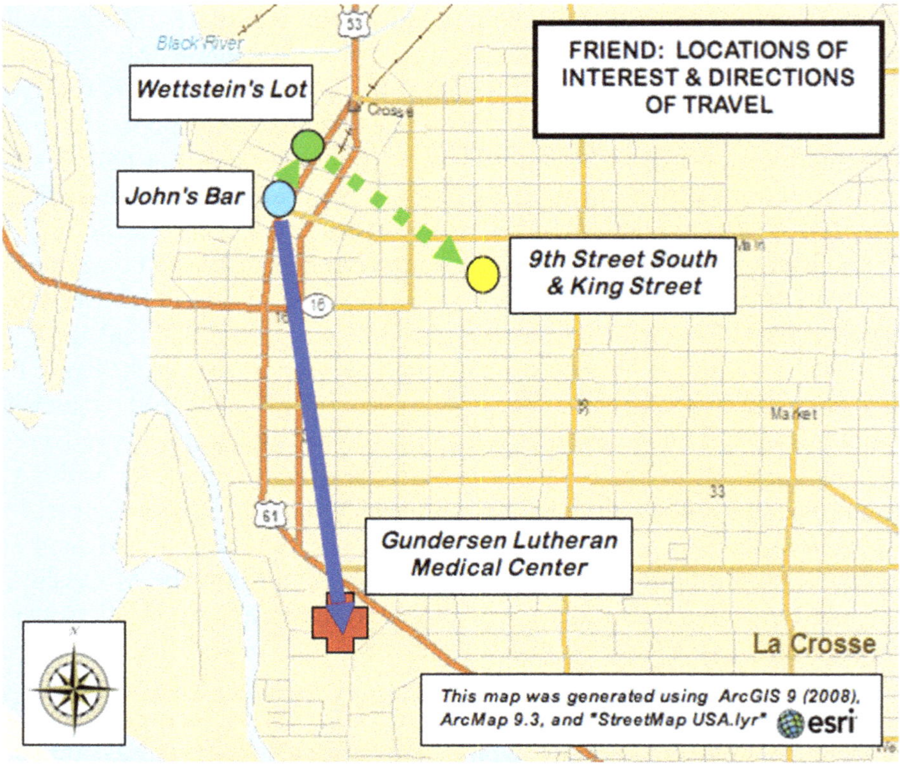

Figure 11.8 January 7–8, 2006: Cullen Fortney's friend Nate was last seen at John's Bar (*Blue Dot*) and should have returned to Wettstein's lot (*Green Dot*) to get his pickup; instead, he ended up at Gundersen Lutheran Medical Center (*Red Cross*); they finally found his pickup 4 days later by 9th Street South and King Street (*Yellow Dot*).

Abraham, the video footage from the parking lot showed a man entering the vehicle with keys around 03:00 hours on Sunday, January 8th, and driving away. Unfortunately, the footage was not sharp enough to make out a face. But, police surmised that the man who entered the pickup and the man who wound up at the hospital were the same man (Nate) – even though his vehicle was nowhere near the hospital when it was found. Obviously, Nate did not drive himself to the hospital. So, how did he get there?

Conclusion

Cullen Fortney's case was clearly an attempted murder and the police had to know this since they were smart enough to figure out the alcohol dispersal chart. If they could figure out the alcohol chart, then they should have been able to figure out the hypothermia chart. The La Crosse police investigator's timeline of events can only suggest that Cullen should have died from hypothermia and not survived the freezing waters of La Plume Slough that night. If the police say that Cullen entered the water sometime after bar closing at 02:00 hours, then he would have been dead by 03:00 hours as a result of 32 °Fahrenheit water and hypothermia. He would not have been alive to walk into the hospital some 4 hours later. However, according to the timeline offered by Cullen, he did not enter the water until much later.

Although the La Crosse police investigator's BAC mathematics and timeline demonstrated that Cullen was really drunk and over twice the legal limit (0.163 BAC) when he left John's Bar, it also ignored Cullen's level of sobriety when he walked into the hospital. Cullen's BAC at Gundersen Lutheran Medical Center at 08:00 hours was 0.043 (legal to drive). Even though a BAC of 0.163 is drunk, it is not so severely inebriated that it would wipe out all memory in most drinkers of any age. Thus, we can understand how a person may not recall all events between 02:00 and 04:00 hours due to intoxication, but a complete blank needs to be explained. Keep in mind that Cullen was at a BAC of 0.043 by 08:00 hours. He was not the 0.163 BAC "Drunk" upon which the police wanted people to focus. How does an individual who is not legally drunk have no recollection of how he got into the water at about 06:30 hours? Also, how could he not recall at least one piece of information from the time period between 01:45 and 07:00 hours when he climbed out of the water? The only possible and reasonable explanation for this to have occurred is that he was drugged. Although the testing may have been done, unfortunately, there is no information about any drug test having been administered.

We assert that Nate was also drugged that evening. We believe he was drugged either to separate him from Cullen or to help the police explain the circumstances of Cullen's disappearance and intended drowning. Two separate incidents happened on the same evening; one individual wound up in the water (which should have resulted in death), and the other one fortunately survived and did not wind up in the water. The pattern that evening for both Cullen and Nate included drinking at John's Bar, along with missing time and no memory of events after being at John's Bar, followed by an unscheduled walk-in visit to the Gundersen Lutheran Medical Center.

We conclude this to be true due to the comparative facts of the Lucas (Luke) Homan investigation later that year (September 30, 2006). In that case, Luke's friend ("Allen") also wound up at the hospital on the same evening that Luke was reported missing and later found drowned. Allen had no recollection of events after leaving the bar. (Luke's case is covered in greater detail later in this book.) We opine that this scenario was used in both cases as a way to physically separate these young men at the time of their abductions. The scenario also logically connects their investigations. By showing that the same scenario played out earlier in Cullen's case as later in Luke Homan's, the police were supplied with an example, or excuse, about how one man drowned while the other man was fortunate to survive.

Either way, in the Cullen Fortney case, he was clearly abducted, held for a period of time and then deposited into La Plume Slough to drown. This case is clearly an attempted murder and the police cannot have it both ways. The FBI Supervisory Special Agent (BAU-2) who signed off on the La Crosse Police Department's investigation into the drowning deaths of young men needs to take another look at their investigation. When the FBI reviewed the drowning cases in La Crosse at the request of the police department, he did not review material related to or associated with Cullen – probably since he was found alive. To law enforcement, this appeared to be just another tragic accident fueled by alcohol, and not an abduction and attempted murder – which it clearly was. In closing, this was one case wherein we did not have photographs to examine. We did not have autopsy photographs because Cullen survived. We also did not have evidentiary photographs. Not because he survived, rather because he was not considered to be a victim. La Crosse investigators declared from the start that Cullen had experienced an accidental fall into the water as a result of his alcohol intoxication. When no crime is suspected to have been

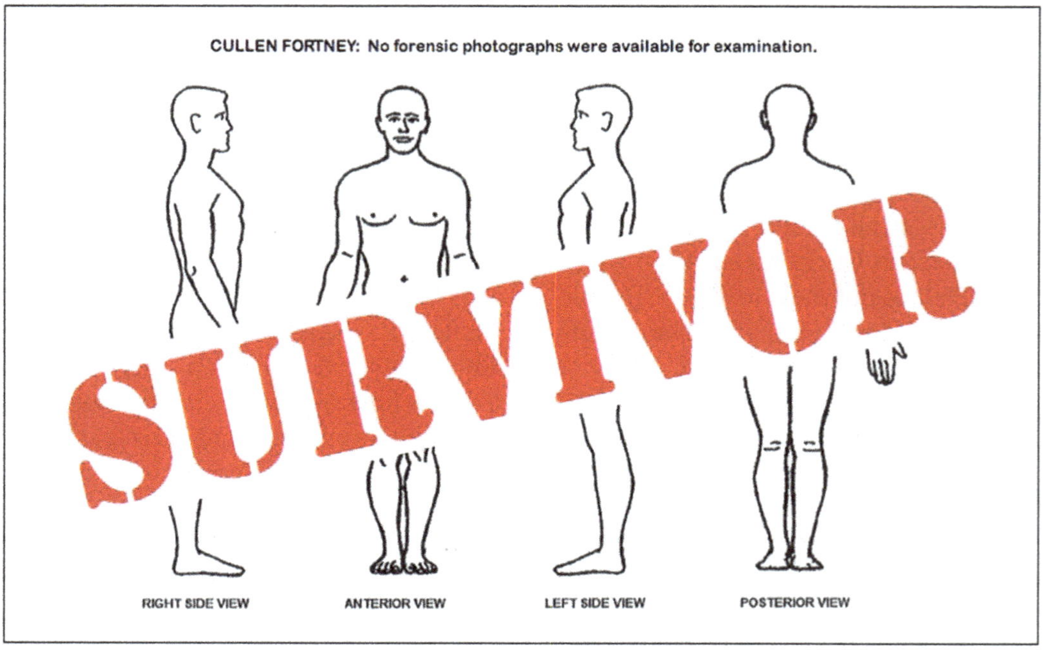

Figure 11.9 No artist rendition was possible. The police did not believe Fortney's earlier statements about someone trying to kill him. They presumed he was the survivor of a potential accidental drowning and not the victim of an attempted homicide.

committed or civil liability or tort matter exists, then no film is expended in documenting injuries related to an accident. Thus, rather than taking Cullen at his word when he said earlier that someone had tried to kill him that night, the police investigator's presumption of an accident determined the procedural course that was taken gathering potential evidence – or should we say, in not gathering potential forensic evidence (e.g., drug screen and photographs of physical injuries; Figure 11.9).

12

Nathan Allen Kapfer*

Background

Skeptics always spin the numbers. They point to the fact that the disappearances and "drowning" deaths of a handful of college-age men in the city of La Crosse have occurred over a 15 year period (1997 to 2011). The truth of the matter is that they are wrong. Nate Kapfer was 3rd in a series of suspicious disappearances and deaths to occur in La Crosse over a 5 month period (148 days).

1. Charles Blatz disappeared on September 28, 1997, then 12 days later,
2. Anthony Skifton disappeared on October 10, 1997, then 135 days later,
3. Nate Kapfer disappeared on February 22, 1998.

Nate was recovered on April 4th, but Dr. Lindsey Thomas did not conduct the autopsy until 3 days later on April 7th. Just like most of the other cases, Nate's case was closed with the cause of death listed as drowning; supporting documentation associated the death with alcohol intoxication.

The initial investigation was directed by Lieutenant Brohmer of the La Crosse Police Department. In fact, based on the records that we reviewed, he personally conducted 34 interviews and filed associated case reports. As a Detective Sergeant, Gannon found this great extent of involvement by a lieutenant in an investigation of a missing person to be somewhat irregular. Typically, this routine police work would be done by patrol officers during the conduct of their daily tours or by more junior detectives.

* Photo courtesy of his parents, Mark and Doris Kapfer.

Circumstances

Last Seen

Nathan Allen Kapfer ("Nate") was a White male, 19 years old, 5 feet 10 inches, 160 pounds (Body Mass Index: 22.95), brown hair and blue eyes (Figure 12.1). He grew up in Montana with his parents, Mark and Doris, and brother Brian. He was a member of Our Savior Lutheran Church. Nate was an excellent student who graduated 3rd in his high school class. He was a member of the National Honor Society and a scholarship recipient. He enjoyed spending time with family and friends, as well as hunting, fishing, and participating in sports. Nate was an accomplished free safety and wide receiver for Dawson County High School, which finished 2nd in state his senior year. He was an assistant coach for the Glendive American Legion baseball team (the Blue Devils) for two seasons. He was a pitcher at Viterbo College in La Crosse. His nickname was "Coch" (short for Cochise). One thing that stands out in people's memories of Nate was his genuine and infectious smile. The epitaph on his headstone reads, "Another Smile in Heaven."

He had baseball practice during the afternoon (Noon to 16:00 hours) of February 21, 1998. He had spoken to numerous friends about attending a party at a friend's house (hereafter, Keith Morris) later that evening (207 South 9th Street). Nate was one of the first people to arrive at the party; he showed up around 18:00 hours. He was reported by many witnesses to be running the music at the party, which was attended by approximately 40 to 50 people. He was said to have had a few beers.

According to Lieutenant Mitch Brohmer's report on his interview with Keith Morris and several others, Nate stayed at the party until around 23:00 to 23:30 hours, at which time he then walked downtown to The Library bar (where most of his friends said they usually hung out). By midnight, Nate was at the bar drinking with friends, some of whom were from the basketball team. He was drinking "Long Island Iced Teas" according to police reports and witness statements. The police reports include information that these mixed drinks are made with 4 shots of alcohol in each drink. Nate was said to have had 3 Long Islands with one friend (hereafter, Malcom) and 2 shots with another friend (hereafter, Rich). Everyone described him as pretty intoxicated. He stayed at The Library bar until around 01:30 hours (February 22, 1998) and then went with others to Brothers Bar and Grill (Figure 12.2).

Figure 12.1 Nate Kapfer had natural athletic ability and loved to play baseball. (Photo courtesy of his parents, Mark and Doris Kapfer.)

Figure 12.2 Nate Kapfer was drinking at The Library in downtown La Crosse on the night he disappeared (February 21–22, 1998). He then went over to Brothers Bar and Grill where he was denied further alcohol and was escorted out of the business.

Brothers was out the front door of The Library and to the left, around the corner, and just across the street. Video surveillance shows a young male (identified as Nate) staggering while entering Brothers just before last call at about 01:30 hours, and then exiting the establishment shortly thereafter. Nate's short time at Brothers was explained in statements given to police by bar employees. A Brothers bouncer said that Nate had a difficult time keeping his balance and that he could not tell the difference between his university identification card and his Wisconsin Driver's License. A Brothers bartender gave Nate a drink of water. According to the bouncer's statement, Nate became very belligerent and was dry heaving. He was then escorted out of the bar, whereon, he started shouting obscenities at multiple bouncers, opened his jeans, and grabbed his crotch. At that point, the police were called to assist.

At 01:42 hours, Police Officer Secord and Officer Flatten were dispatched to respond to a call for service regarding trouble with a patron at Brothers. The officers recovered multiple identification cards from Nate. They determined that he had used a friend's ID card to gain entry into the bar (since he was underage at 19 years old), and that he was denied a drink from the Brothers bartender for being overintoxicated. He was given a Portable Breathalyzer Test (PBT) in which he registered a 0.077 BAC. Nate was found to be sober enough to legally drive. He was issued four citations (Incident #98-0008731, Dated 02/22/98).

1. Underage Drinking Summons #M749526
2. Disorderly Conduct Summons #M749527
3. False ID Summons #M749528
4. Being in a bar Summons #M749529

After issuing the citations, the two police officers released Nate at the intersection of 2nd Street South and Pearl Street, and observed him while he walked east on Pearl Street. The police later learned that Nate spoke briefly with a few friends at the corner of 3rd Street South and Pearl Streets next to Coconut Joe's (Figure 12.3). According to statements provided by those friends, Nate never mentioned that he had just received the four summons from the police. He was last seen walking north on 3rd Street South from Pearl Street at approximately 02:30 hours. Nate was never seen alive again by his friends.

Figure 12.3 Nate Kapfer was last seen walking north (to the right) from the corner of 3rd Street South and Pearl Streets next to Coconut Joe's, where he had stopped to talk to a few friends after receiving 4 citations from La Crosse police officers.

Recovery

Nate's body was discovered about 41.5 days after he went missing. Official reports stated that he was discovered at about 15:00 hours on April 4, 1998. One report stated that his body was found just out of the main channel of the Mississippi River in Running Slough south of the Bayside Court Condominiums. Running Slough is approximately 3.5 miles south of Riverside Park. Another report described the recovery location as being near a gravel pit in Running Slough – the exact spot where Jeffrey Geesey was recovered a year later on May 24, 1999. John Steers, the La Crosse County Medical Examiner, referred to the spot where Nate's body was discovered as being near the 3200 block of East Avenue South in the town of Shelby. This would have placed it behind the Dairyland Power Cooperative and in the south end of Bluff Slough.

Nate's body was up against a large mass of debris that had collected within the slough. It is important to note that he was not snagged in the debris, rather he had floated up against it and was held there by the current. His head and upper torso were out of the water and the rest of his body was underwater. The Minnesota Regional Coroner's Office representative, Investigator Schatzley, took photographs of the body before it was removed from the river. Nate's body was removed from the water at 17:36 hours and an initial examination occurred. It was placed into a body bag at 18:47 hours. Nate's body was taken to the 7th Street Boat Landing (a public waterway access point), where it was removed from the water for transport.

Analysis of Evidence

Recovered Property

Nate's property (i.e., wallet, baseball cap, keys, and 4 municipal ordinance citations) was recovered early Monday morning, February 23, 1998. It was discovered by a young man who was searching with other Viterbo baseball teammates for Nate since he did not return home on Saturday night (February 21–22). The personal property items were found on the north end of Riverside Park near the iconic statue of Chief Hiawatha. More

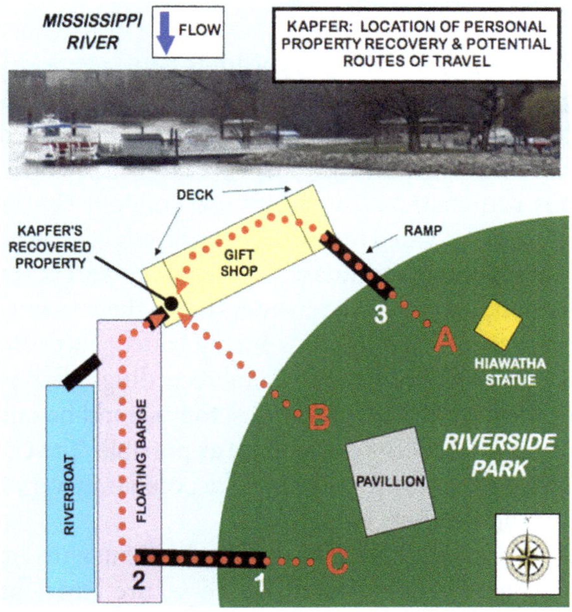

Figure 12.4 Nate Kapfer's personal property was recovered on the west deck of the floating Gift Shop during the morning the day after he went missing. Three possible routes (A-C) could have been taken to place it there.

specifically, Nate's property was found neatly placed on the west deck of the La Crosse Queen Gift Shop.

In his reports, Lieutenant Brohmer described three possible routes that Nate could have taken in order to place his property at that location (Figure 12.4). Route A was possible but extremely arduous since it required Nate to overcome a gated fence (#3) climb onto the roof of the Gift Shop, traverse it, and then to climb back down to the west deck – all without falling into the water or becoming scratched up. Route B was the least likely since it would have required Nate to swim the short distance to the Gift Shop and then climb out of the water. Since Nate's belongings showed no sign of having gotten wet (specifically the citations), then this route was not used. Route C was the most likely path even though it would have required Nate to climb over 2 gated fences at opposite ends of the ramp (#1 & #2). Once on the floating barge, it would have been relatively easy for him to reach the deck of the Gift Shop.

Investigators' thinking about the case was shaped by the fact that Nate's personal property had been found in this location, neatly folded and stacked, as though it was displayed and waiting for others to find. As demonstrated by their behavior, investigators could not, or would not, shake the presumption that Nate had walked to this location and committed suicide that night. At 09:02 hours on February 23rd, Sergeant Kloss and Officer Coady responded to the report that items had been found in Riverside Park. After determining that the items belonged to Nate, the La Crosse Fire Department (LCFD) arrived at the scene and dragged the immediate area for Nate's body. They found nothing. According to an FBI report, the water around the Gift Shop where Nate's personal property was found was not covered by ice at the time of the incident. The LCFD dragged the surrounding water again on February 24th for 2.5 hours and LCFD divers searched the area on February 25th. Nothing was found.

Video Recordings

Closed Circuit Television (CCTV) video recordings can have a dramatic affect on any investigation. Their presence on a street corner or building can reduce crime by creating a general deterrent influence for potential offenders before the fact, and they can provide an evidentiary influence in court by showing a suspect's face and behavior after the fact. Their use and effectiveness is demonstrated in the city of London, United Kingdom. When it comes to missing persons cases, video recordings can be vital for determining and tracking a person's route and direction of travel, last seen location, and corresponding behaviors. A lot of businesses, like bars, install video recorders to aid them in pursuing charges against wrongdoers or to protect them from liability during court proceedings. Many businesses record over older tapes (i.e., VCRs) or erase digital recordings after a period of time. Since these timeframes vary from a few days to months, they should be one piece of intelligence information that an investigator seeks out as early as possible. The CCTV recordings from 2 locations for the night of February 21st–22nd were potentially very important, especially those from The Library and Brothers bars.

On February 25th (3 days after Nate disappeared), Lieutenant Brohmer met with one of the co-owners of Brothers bar (hereafter, Ed) to secure any possible video recording that the bar might have. This was the last bar that Nate was known to have been in that night. Ed was able to provide a video recording, which was taken as evidence. The recording showed Nate on the night of February 21st–22nd. One could clearly see him coming in and being escorted out. A Brothers bartender refused to serve Nate because he felt that he was too intoxicated. The bartender gave him a glass of water, which apparently made Nate angry. According to a police report, the bartender said that Nate was asked to leave the bar after the episode with the water because he began to "dry heave."

On March 3rd (which was 9 days after Nate disappeared), Lieutenant Brohmer finally contacted a co-owner (hereafter, Matt) of The Library 6 days after he had spoken with Ed. This was the bar that Nate was at prior to going around the corner to Brothers. Ed and Matt are brothers and co-own both The Library and Brothers bars. Matt told Lieutenant Brohmer that they only had a few tapes at The Library and that the staff had already recorded over the tape from the night of February 21st–22nd. The police officer took the tape as evidence at that time with hopes that the former recording could be recovered. No prior images were ever recovered from the videotape.

It took the police 10 days to retrieve the tape from the bar where Nate was drinking most of the evening (The Library) when they already had the tape from the last bar that he was removed from because of his supposed intoxication (Brothers). Since Nate was not served anything other than a glass of water at Brothers and he blew a 0.077 on the PBT, were investigators not interested in ascertaining whether something else had contributed to Nate's demise and whether that "something" was given to him in another bar? Also, this was now the 3rd case in a period of 5 months, which should have alerted the authorities to the possibilities that something else – possibly sinister – might be taking place in La Crosse. This whole scenario engenders several questions. Since both parties (the police and the bar owners) knew that Nate was missing from those bars, then why were all tapes not recovered or voluntarily turned in immediately? Did Ed not tell his brother Matt, a co-owner of both bars, that police were interested in securing their CCTV tapes? Was this simply the result of a general lack of concern and a sense of urgency, or just a terrible lack of attention to detail?

Reported Sightings

Two people called into the police department to report that they had possibly seen Nate on the night in question. On February 25, 1998, Sergeant Joholski interviewed the first caller regarding his sighting. The caller stated that he had seen a young White male in his 20s wearing a green shirt while he was driving home on February 22nd. At about 01:00 hours as he crossed the bridge over the La Crosse River near the 700 block of North 3rd Street, he observed the young man standing on the east side of the bridge staring at the water and seemingly oblivious to his surroundings.

According to one of Nate's friends who was drinking with him at The Library, Nate said he was going to the bathroom at about 0:45 to 01:00 hours and never returned. The distance from the bar to the bridge was about 1.2 miles round-trip and would have taken about 20 minutes to walk. Since Nate was known to have gone from The Library to Brothers just before 01:30 hours, then there was just barely enough time for him to have walked directly to and return from the bridge. Everyone's estimates of time had to have been exact and Nate would have practically had to run the entire distance. This sighting could not have been Nate.

Another possible sighting was reported by a second caller (hereafter, Tim). Officer Nedland met with him on February 24th and took his statement. Tim said that he had encountered a young White male near the Kwik Trip at 1333 Rose Street during the early morning hours of February 22nd at about 06:00 hours. Tim said that the young was very intoxicated and had spoken his name, which sounded something like "Jason." The two chatted as they walked south along the road to Hardee's at 1311 Rose Street. He paused briefly and watched as the young man struggled to enter Hardee's. Lieutenant Brohmer followed up by interviewing 3 Hardee's employees on February 24th. The distance from Coconut Joe's (where Nate was last seen walking north) to the Kwik Trip was 2.2 miles one-way. Since it occurred at 06:00 hours, there was plenty of time for Nate to walk from one location to the other. Could "Nathan" when uttered by someone who was intoxicated be mistaken for "Jason?" Possible, perhaps. However, the bars closed shortly after Nate walked off to the north, alone, and away from his group of friends. This "Jason" was highly intoxicated according to Tim. That would mean that the individual in question, were he Nate, would have had to acquire a lot more alcohol after 02:00 hours. Where would he get it without valid IDs? It was unlikely that this sighting involved Nate.

Clothing

One point of confusion was the clothing that Nate was wearing that night. Several witnesses commented on Nate's green T-shirt that he wore to the house party. It resembled a popular sports drink logo and displayed the words, "Get Lade Lust Quencher." He was also reported to be wearing that same green T-shirt and a white undershirt when his body was recovered and at the time of his autopsy. However, at the time he received the citations that night, Nate was described as wearing a brown long-sleeved shirt and a white T-shirt with an unidentified design or image on the front of it. This description was also entered into the National Crime Information Center's (NCIC) system for Nate as a missing person.

Since Nate's car was several blocks away, there was not enough time for him to leave The Library, walk to his car to retrieve the brown shirt, then enter into Brothers. He would have then had to walk back to his vehicle to get the green t-shirt after interacting with the police and before entering the water. He was last seen walking north and his car was east of the downtown bar district. There was no report that he was carrying or wearing both the green t-shirt and the brown shirt during the evening. This cannot simply be a lack of attention to detail by the officers who encountered Nate at Brothers. They most likely recorded exactly what they saw him wearing.

Although this might have seemed to be trivial, it was a strange and unexplained part of the events that night. The temperature that night dipped to 33 °Fahrenheit and did not get above 35 °Fahrenheit until 08:00 hours on February 22nd. The wind was about 5 miles per hour out of the south-southeast with gusts to 12 miles per hour. So, with the wind chill factor, it was a brisk night. It was unlikely that he took off the long-sleeved shirt, unless of course he was overheating due to some drug in his system like GHB which could cause that symptom (i.e., hyperthermia). Since everyone was supposed to believe that Nate had neatly folded and placed his personal property at the riverboat Gift Shop, then he would have also left his folded brown long-sleeved shirt there rather than discarding it. The long-sleeved shirt was never recovered, and the differing descriptions of his clothing that night remained a mystery.

Vehicles

Nate had driven to Keith Morris' house and intended on driving home. His vehicle was recovered a few days later right where he had parked it on the east side of the 200 block of South 9th Street. Nate was a very mature and responsible young man. He would never operate a motor vehicle under the influence of alcohol. This was why he walked to the bar from Keith's house and why his BAC was so low at bar closing time (as evidenced by the police officer's PBT results of 0.077). This also leads to the theory that Nate was abducted. By all accounts offered by those who knew Nate, he would not become so drunk that he would have had to leave his vehicle at someone else's house. Furthermore, he would not have gone off drinking someplace else to the point of almost 3 times (0.22) the legal intoxication level.

A police report (#98-8847) also mentioned an incident regarding another of Nate's friends (hereafter, Mark). Mark stated that he observed Nate walk into the bar (The Library) around midnight with a few friends just after he had arrived there himself. Shortly after Nate and some others left The Library and walked over to Brothers, Mark left the bar (The Library) around 01:40 to 01:45 hours and began walking home. He said that at the intersection of 5th and King Streets, he became aware of a vehicle behind him going real slowly. He could see only one person in the vehicle (Figure 12.5).

As he was walking east along King Street and just before reaching 6th Street, the vehicle pulled across his path in front of him into the parking lot of Wells Fargo Bank. Instead of using the ATM machine, the driver pulled straight through and back out to King Street, where he stopped at the stop sign and just sat there like he was waiting for Mark. When Mark reached 7th and King Streets, he looked at the truck and the party inside. Because he believed that the driver in the truck was stalking him, he turned and ran south down 7th Street South and did not see the vehicle again. Mark had been walking in the direction of the party at Keith Morris' house and Nate's parked car.

Mark described the truck as a dark-colored (navy blue or black), smaller pickup like a Chevrolet S-10 with a topper. He said there was a little light on the dashboard that may have been a Citizens' Band (CB) radio or a radar detector. Could the item on the dashboard

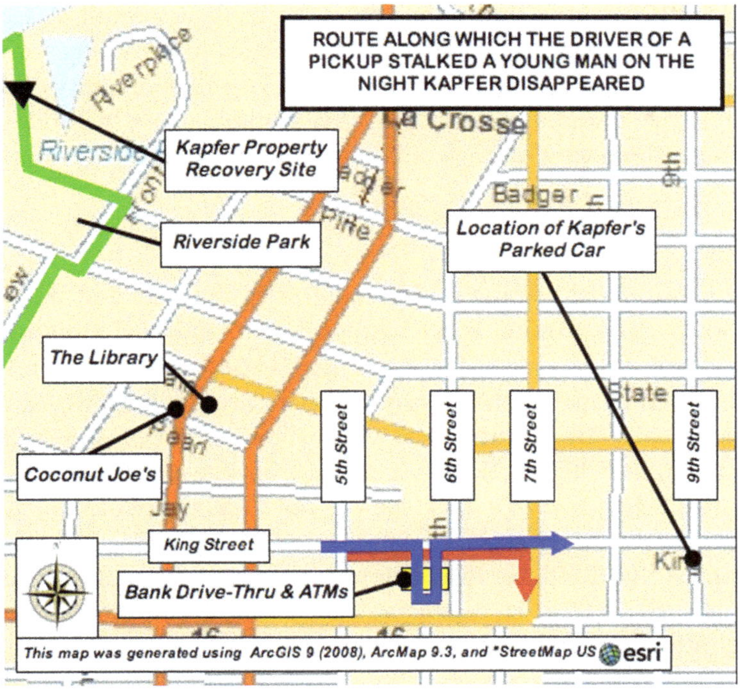

Figure 12.5 On the night that Nate Kapfer disappeared, his friend Mark was stalked by a dark-colored pickup with a topper (*Blue Arrow*). Mark was walking (*Red Arrow*) in the direction of the house party and Nate's parked car.

have been a police scanner to monitor activity in the area? Mark said that the truck was in very poor shape, and he was not able to get a license plate number. This description matched the vehicle that bloodhounds hit on during the subsequent investigation into the disappearance and death of Jeffrey Geesey the following year in April 11, 1999. Could this vehicle have been attempting to abduct Mark and failed, and then came across Nate later? Or, was Nate the primary target and the incident with Mark had nothing to do with Nate's abduction? Could this vehicle have been attempting to abduct two young men? Wherein, one is drowned and the other is found alive or in the hospital; as in the previous Fortney case and the subsequent Homan case. Considering that Nate was probably drugged in the bar, which was evidenced by his uncharacteristic behavior that night at the bar, we believe that both Nate and Mark were intentionally targeted.

Any way one looks at this, La Crosse Police Department investigators never followed up on this information as something of a matter of importance. They never considered this as a possible lead and something that required further investigation. This pattern played out again in 2006 with the cases of Cullen Fortney (January 8, 2006) who fortunately survived, and Lucas Homan (September 30, 2006) who drowned. In both of those cases on the same night in La Crosse, a second person also went missing and ended up at a local hospital without any memory or clue of how he had gotten there.

We believe that this modus operandi had two underlying goals. The first goal reaffirmed the belief that these were just drunk college males who met with an unfortunate accidental drowning death. This was done to show how easy it would be for someone to drown. Their criminal modus operandi provided police and the media with the stories of two young men who became extremely intoxicated on the same night, one who ended up dead and the other in a detoxification center or emergency room. A second goal was to increase the likelihood of producing a suitable victim that evening. By drugging two individuals on the same night, they could be assured of an opportunity of separating one of them from his friends and drowning him. This would increase their odds of securing a victim in case something went wrong with one of the abductions.

Body Position

Nate's body was discovered floating in the slough with the head and shoulders protruding from the water. This position is uncommon for drowning victims who are usually recovered face-down in the water. One may argue that this phenomenon was caused by the current pressing him against the mass of debris in the slough. However, in many of the other cases that we have investigated, the river current did not cause a similar effect. For example, Gerald Smith (Chapter 5) was recovered from the storm-swollen Wabash River floating up against debris next to a dock. He was not sticking out of the water. Todd Geib (Chapter 9), on the other hand, was found in this same posture (i.e., floating like a fishing bobber). We proved that Todd was dead before entering the water. The research literature has clearly established the fact that persons who are deceased prior to water entry will most likely not sink, rather they will float (Armstrong & Erskine, 2011).

Dog Searches

Four searches for Nate's scent were conducted using a bloodhound on the water from a boat and on land during the end of July 1999. Officers Kirby and Thompson brought scent articles related to Nate. Mark and Doris Kapfer, as well as Barry Blatz (the brother of Charles Blatz who had mysteriously disappeared in La Crosse less than 5 months earlier in 1997 and drowned) were present, as was Fire Fighter Smith and the driver of the boat, Dohlby. The dog handler was Penny Bell and her assistant was Terry Kaminski. The bloodhound, Hoover, was also used in the Christopher Jenkins and Joshua Guimond cases in Minnesota in 2002.

Although some controversy existed concerning the use of K-9s so long after an event in question and the longevity of a scent's viability, the results produced by Hoover were exceptional and confirmed known locations. They launched the boat from the public access next to the bridge where 3rd Street North becomes Copeland Avenue (a.k.a., Highway 53), and traveled west down the tributary passing underneath an old railroad trestle to the area of the riverboat dock and Gift Shop. Hoover hit on the dock near the back of Gift Shop, the side railing deck of Gift Shop, and the ramp to the boat. The bloodhound repeatedly cried and demonstrated excited behavior when near the river bank, ramp, and back deck of the Gift Shop. This was an indicator that something traumatic, like a physical struggle, had happened in that location. A fight will cause more dead skin cells from the combatants to drop to the ground and to spread in the air. This in turn fosters a stronger scent that can be picked up by the bloodhound and which will last longer.

Once out in the open channel of the Mississippi River, Hoover demonstrated great interest in the sandy beach at Pettibone Park. Had Nate accidentally fallen into the river at the dock, then his scent should not have been 1,000 feet away on the opposite side of the river and 2,250 feet downstream. They drove the boat south in the Mississippi River to Houska Park, where the K-9 showed no interest in the walkway bridge at Market Street,

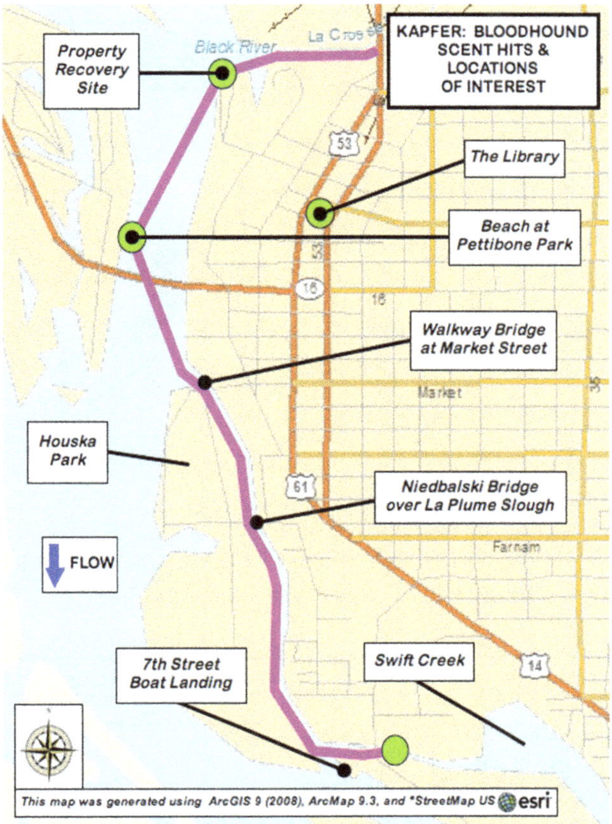

Figure 12.6 A bloodhound picked up Nate Kapfer's scent in four general locations (*Bright Green Dots*): in the bar district (at The Library, Brothers, and Shooters); near the La Crosse Queen riverboat dock and Gift Shop; near the beach at Pettibone Park; and near the 7th Street boat landing.

or the Niedbalski Bridge at Hood Street (Figure 12.6). However, upon reaching the area on Swift Creek behind the 7th Street boat landing, Hoover looked up at Mark Kapfer, sniffed him, cried and cuddled with him. This was the same area mentioned in the Fortney case from 2006 (Chapter 11). Fire Fighter Smith said that Hoover had hit at the same place that a K-9 had hit earlier, but he would not say exactly where that was.

A bloodhound search for Nate was conducted on land by Penny Bell, Hoover, and Terry Kaminski, which tracked his scent coming from The Library to Brothers (Figure 12.7, *Blue Line*), and then to Shooter's bar (*Black Line*). No video or eyewitness evidence of Nate ever having entered Shooter's was uncovered. However, K-9 search indicated that his scent had entered Shooter's bar through the front door and then went out the back door, through the alley, across the parking lot, (Figure 12.7, *Bright Purple Line*) and then north to Riverside Park by the iconic 12-foot statue of Chief Hiawatha (Figure 12.8, *Bright Purple Line*). This end-point in the track was the same location where the bloodhound had earlier indicated a traumatic event had happened to Nate. Perhaps, this track was not left by Nate, rather by someone who had been in direct physical contact with him earlier that night.

Nate had left Brothers bar that night in the back of a police vehicle. The officer then dropped him off a block west at the intersection of 2nd Street South and Pearl Street (Figure 12.7, *Red Star*). There was no record of an attempt to use the bloodhound to track

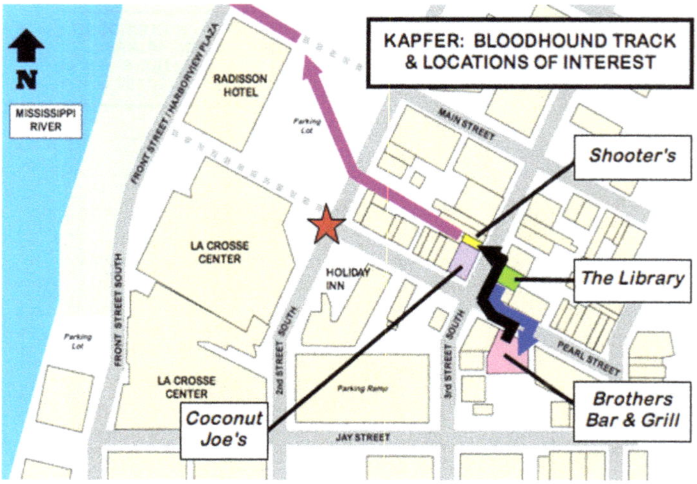

Figure 12.7 Nate Kapfer's scent was tracked on land by a bloodhound from The Library bar to Brothers (*Blue Line*), then to and through Shooter's (*Black Line*), and then to the north end of Riverside Park near the statue of Chief Hiawatha (*Bright Purple Line*).

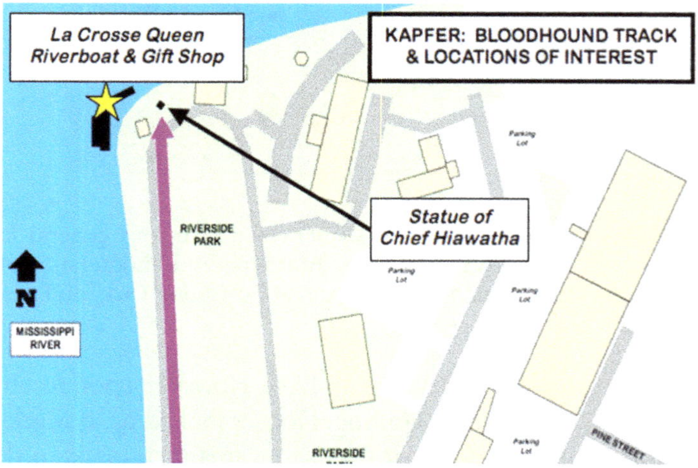

Figure 12.8 A bloodhound tracked Nate Kapfer's scent into Riverside Park and then to the north end near the statue of Chief Hiawatha (*Bright Purple Line*). His personal property was recovered at the La Crosse Queen Gift Shop (*Yellow Star*).

Nate from this intersection to the corner near Coconut Joe's (where he spoke to a group of friends), and then north along 3rd Street South where he was last seen walking.

Recovery Location

Running Slough is approximately 1.5 miles south of Riverside Park (Figure 12.9). One official law enforcement report stated that Nate was discovered just out of the main channel of the Mississippi River in Running Slough near a gravel pit, which would have placed his body at about the 4400 block. Another law enforcement report placed the recovery site a short distance south of the Bayside Court Condominiums between the 3300 and 3400 blocks. The La Crosse County Medical Examiner, John Steers, referred to the recovery site

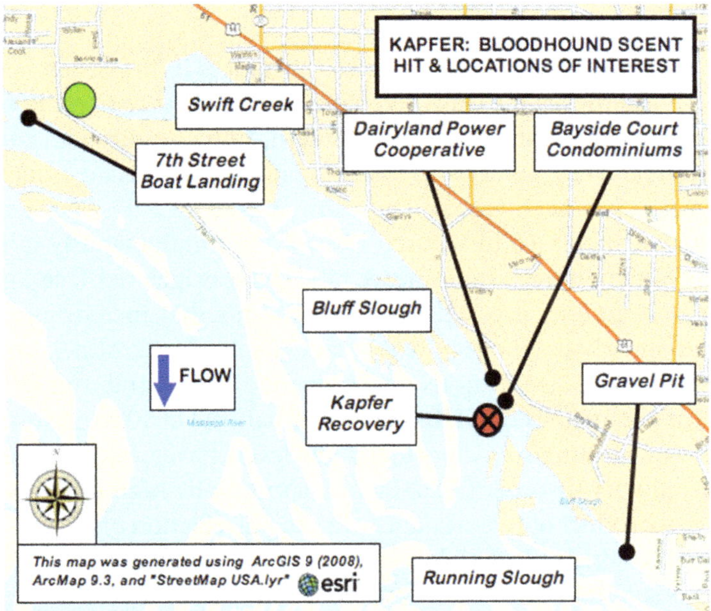

Figure 12.9 Nate Kapfer's body was recovered in the southern part of Bluff Slough, which meant that he was likely entered into the water in Swift Creek somewhere near where the bloodhound hit on his scent (*Bright Green Dot*).

as being near the 3200 block of East Avenue South in the town of Shelby, which would have placed it behind the Dairyland Power Cooperative in the southern part of Bluff Slough north of Running Slough. This location matched the site that Mark Kapfer had indicated for his son's body recovery.

Water current tests concluded that objects which entered the Mississippi River near Riverside Park usually remain in the main channel. However, objects may occasionally enter Running Slough from the main channel and then float south. Objects may also enter Running Slough when they are placed into the water at the 7th Street boat landing, which ramps into the main channel. Objects in the water do not float against the current of the Mississippi River and north into Bluff Slough. Objects will also occasionally leave the main channel of the Mississippi River and drift into Swift Creek when they entered the water near the walkway bridge at Market Street over the north end of La Plume Slough next to Houska Park. However, since the bloodhound did not hit on Nate's scent in La Plume Slough, it was reasonable to conclude that his body had not been in that stretch of water.

The only way to ensure that an object would end up in Bluff Slough was to enter it into Swift Creek anywhere to the east side of the 7th Street bridge. The only way for an object to leave the main channel and come to rest in Bluff Slough at the precise spot where Nate's body was recovered, would be for it to pass through Running Slough and then to float against the current several hundred yards. In other words, Nate may have been drowned elsewhere, but he did not enter the water near the La Crosse Queen riverboat dock and Gift Shop, or anywhere along Riverside Park or Houska Park for that matter. He had to have been brought to the 7th Street bridge and entered into Swift Creek there. This would account for the fact that the bloodhound was unable to pick up his scent anywhere along La Plume Slough.

Toxicology

The toxicology report states that Nate had two substances in his system: phenethylamine and n-propanol. Phenethylamine (PEA) is a colorless liquid at room temperature and soluble in water, ethanol, and ether (Shulgin & Shulgin, 1991). Studies indicate that PEA acts on the human brain and central nervous system in many ways. It can induce self-perceived clarity or sharpness of mind, euphoria and calm at moderate dosages. Extracellular levels of dopamine were increased by infused PEA, while simultaneously inhibiting neuron firings. High doses may induce rapid heart rate and a bright red face and upper chest. Substituted phenethylamines are a class of compounds that include neurotransmitters, hormones, stimulants, hallucinogens (e.g., plant alkaloid mescaline), entactogens (e.g., MDMA or Ecstasy and MDA), anorectics, bronchodilators, and antidepressants. PEAs include drugs that are analogs of GHB and have a half-life of 10 to 15 minutes. It may be found endogenously in humans. Abnormally low levels have been associated with attention deficit hyperactivity disorder (ADHD) and abnormally high levels with schizophrenia. PEA is the end product of phenylalanine in the putrefaction of tissue.

N-propanol is a colorless alcohol. It is a flammable liquid and toxic when inhaled. It is a moderate skin irritant and causes severe eye irritation. However, it is not harmful in small amounts and is endogenous to the human body. N-propanol is sometimes used as a solvent in pharmaceuticals. It is also used to dissolve predatory drugs like PEA, Rohypnol, or GHB for use in eyedroppers, which can then easily facilitate the administration of the drug into any beverage in a bar (Porrata, 2013). The human body produces small amounts of n-propanol during the decomposition process. There is usually the simultaneous production of other chemicals in the body such as, acetone, ethanol, methanol, isopropanol, and n-butanol.

Of all the substances, acetone was the most important to this analysis. A body produces ethanol and n-propanol as it decays. The ethanol subsequently breaks down into acetone. Rather than testing the blood (which was done in this circumstance), a test can be conducted to measure the amount of ethanol in the tissues of the body in order to determine the extent of postmortem production of n-propanol caused by decomposition. An indicator that the presence of tissue ethanol is the result of postmortem production by micro-organisms is the detection of low-molecular-weight alcohols such as n-propanol, n-butanol, and isobutyric acid (Armstrong & Erskine, 2011). Furthermore, research suggests that the presence of n-butanol is a good indicator of postmortem ethanol production. This is especially true for deceased bodies that have been in the water for extended periods of time.

Since Nate was assumed to be deceased the entire time between when he went missing and when he was autopsied (44 days 7 hours 45 minutes), then the levels of methanol and isopropanol should have also increased due to postmortem production and reached the reporting limit. Likewise, the breaking down of alcohols would have likely produced measurable levels of acetone. None of this occurred; the toxicology results for methanol, isopropanol, and acetone were all negative. Therefore, the n-propanol and PEA in Nate's system could not be the result of postmortem production. Rather, they had to be present as a result of an external source.

Lieutenant Brohmer initially reported that a full toxicology screen had been completed and no drugs were found to be present in Nate's system. He later provided a caveat and stated that there were no drugs in Nate's system that contributed to his death. In her final pathology report and diagnoses submitted in April 1998, Dr. Lindsey Thomas described this case as a drowning. She did not present the BAC results and did not even list alcohol intoxication as a contributing factor. Two months later in June 1998, John Steers (the La Crosse County Medical Examiner) listed the cause of death as drowning and the manner of death was undetermined. Although he mentioned the 0.077 alcohol level obtained by the police officer during a PBT field test, the final 0.220 BAC was not mentioned. In every other case that we have examined, the investigating officials and medical examiners have always commented on the amount of alcohol in the victims. In fact, they have always reported the highest levels found. Why was the matter of alcohol and BAC not mentioned in the final reports for Nate's death?

If the n-propanol and PEA in Nate's system were to be attributed to postmortem production during decomposition and putrefaction, then corresponding increases in all alcohols should have been noted. The 0.220 BAC reported for Nate at autopsy would have been lower at the time of death after subtracting the amount due to postmortem production. Did investigators fail to consider this aspect of the toxicology results and BAC analysis, or did they choose not to acknowledge it? A person cannot ascribe the presence of n-propanol and PEA as a result of postmortem production while simultaneously trying to explain the absence of methanol, isopropanol, and acetone. The only way to explain the levels of all substances is to recognize that Nate had a drug in him, either voluntarily or surreptitiously against his wishes. Was this an attempt to disguise the fact that there were not only drugs in his system, but debilitating drugs that are not recreational in nature (e.g., GHB dissolved using n-propanol).

All of Nate's friends and acquaintances who were interviewed by Lieutenant Brohmer and who had seen Nate that night thought he was intoxicated. The bartender and bouncer at Brothers bar thought Nate was overly intoxicated. The video tape recovered as evidence from the Brothers bar clearly showed a young man who was out of control and not acting like his normal self. Everyone said that Nate was generally a calm person, and that his demeanor did not dramatically change when he was drinking. The one exception was that night at Brothers. He was dry heaving, hanging on the bar and using it for support, loud, vulgar, and aggressive right before police took him away in their vehicle.

Nate was recovered with a 0.220 BAC; almost 3 times the legal limit. Since the bars were closed when Nate was given and passed the field breath test by the La Crosse police officers, where did he get the alcohol to drink to bring his BAC from 0.077 up to 0.220? There was no mention of Nate drinking with anyone or even being in the company of anyone after he was seen walking north on Pearl Street. No one mentioned another house party that they went to, or even going back to Keith Morris'. Nate's behavior indicated that he had most likely been drugged.

Nate arrived at The Library around 23:30 hours and left 2 hours later at about 01:30 hours. The information about him having drank 3 Long Island Iced Teas with 5 measures of alcohol each (Figure 12.10), plus 2 shots of hard liquor, was inconsistent with the 0.077 result from the Portable Breathalyzer Test (PBT). The 3 mixed drinks and 2 shots would equate to 9.5 shots of alcohol at 0.020 per shot, which would account for a total reading of 0.190 BAC for a 180-pound male. Since Nate weighed approximately 160 pounds, then he would have had about a 0.210 BAC. Most of that would have been in his bloodstream by the time he reached Brothers bar. In order for Nate's BAC to be at 0.077 or just under 4 shots of alcohol (0.080), he would have needed enough time for 0.133 of alcohol (or 6.65 additional shots) to have been dispersed from his body. Since it takes about 1 hour for a shot (0.020) to disperse from the average male body, it would have taken Nate about 6 hours 39 minutes for him to be at 0.077 BAC. Nate registered a 0.077 on the PBT that was given to him at approximately 02:00 hours. That meant that he had to have stopped drinking about

Long Island Iced Tea

INGREDIENT	MEASURE	ABV	VOLUME
Vodka	*1.5*	*≥ 40*	*0.5*
Tequila	*1.5*	*35-55*	*0.5*
White Rum	*1.5*	*40*	*0.5*
Gin	*1.5*	*> 40*	*0.5*
Triple Sec	*1.5*	*15-40*	*0.5*
Lemon Juice	*2.5*	*0*	*0.8*
Gomme Syrup	*3.0*	*0*	*1.0*
Dash of Coke	*1.5*	*0*	*0.5*
Totals	*14.5 cL*		*4.8 fl.oz.*

MEASURE is in centiliters / VOLUME is in fluid ounces.
ABV = Percent of Alcohol By Volume, 40% = 80 Proof.

Figure 12.10 People who saw Nate Kapfer in The Library said he drank 2 shots of hard liquor and 3 Long Island Iced Teas; the equivalent of 9.5 shots of alcohol in under 2 hours.

13 hours earlier at around 13:00 hours the afternoon before. Since he was drinking at the house party at 18:30 hours, that did not occur.

The sequence of events regarding Nate's BAC involved 3 variables and formed 8 cause-and-effect models (IV 1 + IV 2 = DV, Figure 12.11). Independent Variable 1 (DRINKS) centered on the accuracy of eyewitness reporting regarding the number and type of drinks that Nate had consumed that night. Did he really have that many of those particular mixed drinks and shots? Independent Variable 2 (ALCOHOL) focused on whether or not those drinks actually contained the amount of alcohol that should normally be in them. In other words, did the amount of alcohol in Nate's system accurately reflect the amount of alcohol associated with the beverages that he was presumed to have drank? An example of this was the statistical probability that the bartenders' pours could have been long or short, which would vary the amount of alcohol in a mixed drink. Another theoretical probability could have been that the drinks were watered-down, which would have reduced the amount of

Kapfer: Possible Sequence of Events Models

	IV 1 +	IV 2 =	DV	
NUMBER	DRINKS	ALCOHOL	PBT	POSSIBLE
1	*True*	*True*	*True*	*No*
2	*True*	*True*	*False*	**Yes**
3	*True*	*False*	*False*	**Yes**
4	*True*	*False*	*True*	**Yes**
5	*False*	*True*	*False*	**Yes**
6	*False*	*True*	*True*	**Yes**
7	*False*	*False*	*True*	**Yes**
8	*False*	*False*	*False*	**Yes**

DRINKS: The number and type of of drinks reported by witnesseses was accurate.
ALCOHOL: The actual amount of alcohol in those drinks was accurate.
PBT: The Portable Breathalyzer Test resutls were accurate.
POSSIBLE: Logical or physical possibility that the model could exist.

Figure 12.11 Eight theoretical cause-and-effect models were examined in order to determine which possible sequence of events could explain Nate Kapfer's BACs (0.077 and 0.22).

alcohol. The Dependent Variable (PBT) in the models was always whether or not the PBT produced accurate results.

Model 1: No – logically and physically impossible. The number and type of drinks was accurate, and the amount of alcohol in those drinks was accurate. Subsequently, the PBT device worked properly and provided accurate results.
Model 2: Yes – logically and physically possible. The number and type of drinks was accurate. The amount of alcohol in those drinks was accurate, but the PBT device malfunctioned and provided inaccurate results.
Model 3: Yes – logically and physically possible. The number and type of drinks was accurate, but the amount of alcohol in those drinks was inaccurate (less than presumed). Additionally, the PBT device malfunctioned and provided inaccurate results.
Model 4: Yes – logically and physically possible. The number and type of drinks was accurate, but the amount of alcohol in those drinks was inaccurate (less than presumed). The PBT device worked properly and provided accurate results, reflecting the reduced alcohol content.
Model 5: Yes – logically unlikely, but physically possible. The number and type of drinks was inaccurate, but the amount of alcohol in those drinks was accurate. The PBT device somehow malfunctioned and provided inaccurate results.
Model 6: Yes – logically and physically possible. The number and type of drinks was inaccurate, but the amount of alcohol in those drinks was accurate. The PBT device worked properly and provided accurate results, reflecting the reduced alcohol content of the drinks actually consumed.
Model 7: Yes – logically and physically possible. The number and type of drinks was inaccurate, and the amount of alcohol in those drinks was inaccurate (less than presumed). The PBT device worked properly and provided accurate results, reflecting the reduced alcohol content.
Model 8: Yes – logically and physically unlikely, but possible. The number and type of drinks was inaccurate, and the amount of alcohol in those drinks was also inaccurate (less than presumed). Additionally, the PBT device malfunctioned and provided inaccurate results.

This whole issue could easily become a big critical thinking exercise. Proponents and their supporting arguments could probably be found for each model. However, it all came down to one simple observation: the PBT device registered a 0.077 BAC despite Nate's reported obnoxious behavior and impaired physical coordination. Either the PBT device was working properly or it was not. This meant that only 3 possible scenarios could have happened that night.

Scenario 1: It did not matter whether or not the PBT device was working properly or provided accurate results. Given the behavior that Nate was presenting at the time, due diligence on the part of the police officers compelled them to conduct a field sobriety test in order to confirm or refute the PBT results. Having confirmed the PBT results (0.077), the officers cited and released Nate.
Scenario 2: It did not matter whether or not the PBT device was working properly or provided accurate results. The police officers ignored Nate's behavior and accepted the PBT results (0.077), gave 4 citations to Nate, and released him.

Scenario 3: The PBT device was working properly and provided accurate results (> 0.080), reflecting the amount of alcohol that Nate was reported to have consumed according to witnesses. However, police officers falsified the PBT results, cited and released Nate in an intoxicated state.

Clearly, no police officer would allow Scenarios 2 or 3 to happen because that would expose him or her to extensive liability issues. That meant that Scenario 1 had to be the correct set of circumstances if the police officers were doing their diligent duty that night while processing the complaint concerning Nate and his disorderly conduct in public. This also meant that the only way to explain Nate's surly and cantankerous behavior was drugs.

External Assessment

Bodies recovered from water are usually assessed twice, once at recovery and a second time at autopsy. The initial assessment is normally done by a representative or investigator from a medical examiner's office. In some jurisdictions, the actual coroner or medical examiner may even show up to perform the initial assessment. The assessment always includes an attempt to identify the race and biological sex of the body, and an estimation of the age. It typically involves a simple description of any clothing worn, how it is worn, whether or not it is torn, and whether or not it has any blood, mud or other debris on it. A comment is usually made about the clothing on the body at recovery relative to a comparison with the clothing that was known to be worn at the time the person was last seen. Any personal possessions on the body are described (e.g., jewelry, cell phones, watches, money, wallet and contents). In most cases that we have investigated, the person writing the assessment will state where on the body the property was found (e.g., left front pants pocket).

The external assessment will also include a description of the condition of the body concerning physical damage (e.g., missing limbs, and lacerations), anthropophagy (i.e., land and aquatic animal feeding), insects, skin color, decomposition and bloating, hair and skin loss (i.e., maceration). The report will also state the tepidity (*algor mortis*) or cooling of the body's temperature relative to touch or feel. The assessor will also attempt to determine the extent of rigidity (*rigor mortis*) by looking at the body and lightly manipulating the limbs. The report generally presents a *prima facie* assessment of whether lividity (*livor mortis*) is on the front (anterior), on the back (posterior), or to one side. This may include a statement about whether or not the lividity corresponded with the position in which the body was recovered.

The initial assessment was done during recovery on April 4, 1998. Nate's body was assessed by Investigator Schatzley (La Crosse Police Department) and Mike Poellinger (Houston County Medical Examiner), but not at the recovery site. Nate's body was not assessed until it arrived at the Franciscan Skemp Medical Center in La Crosse. The body was described as that of a white male. The weight was estimated at about 197 pounds in soaking wet clothing and inside two bags. It was wearing a green "Get Lade Lust Quencher" T-shirt similar to that which Nate was seen wearing at the house party. The 2 rings and braided necklace that Nate was wearing were thoroughly described. Poellinger wrote that the body was covered in mud. Schatzley stated that Nate's body was covered with mud and sand, and small insects. The body was bloating and presented with a purple-green discoloration, as well as signs of marbling (all of which typically occur at 72 to 96 hours in water). Skin slippage was observed on the hands and torso, but no mention of degloving was made (which typically occurs at 72 to 96 hours in water).

The second assessment was done by Dr. Lindsey Thomas and began at 09:00 hours on April 6, 1998. She wrote that this was the first time that she had seen Nate's body. The body was presented to her in a body bag that had been sealed with evidence tape. Although the body had been kept in a standard morgue cooler, she opened the bag and discovered that Nate's body was frozen solid. Therefore, she left Nate's body out so it could thaw in room temperature. His body remained there thawing overnight (for 25 hours).

At 10:00 hours on April 7th, the Medical Examiner concluded that Nate's body had sufficiently thawed in order for her to continue with the autopsy procedure. She reported the body to be that of a 19-year old white male, 160 pounds, at 5 feet 10 inches, and that Nate was initially identified using jewelry and clothing. Doctor Thomas thoroughly described the rings, necklace, and clothing. She specifically addressed the green "Get Lade" t-shirt. She also recorded that no contradictions were found when comparing dental records with dental x-rays of the body.

Rigidity (*rigor mortis*) is the stiffening of the muscles that occurs after death. On land, it usually takes between 24 to 36 hours to set in and to completely go out depending on the environmental conditions (DiMaio & DiMaio, 2001). In the water, this process can take twice as long (i.e., a 2:1 time delay ratio) and is normally complete by 72 hours (Figure 12.12). By the time the autopsy was performed, rigidity had completely relented in Nate's body. That was appropriate since he had been missing and presumed deceased in the water the whole time (i.e., 41-plus days).

Lividity (*livor mortis*) is the settling and pooling of the blood into the dependent capillaries after death (Geberth, 2006). It starts within 30 minutes and becomes completely fixed within 10 to 12 hours for bodies on land. Fixed means the blood cannot be significantly shifted if the body is moved. The Medical Examiner stated that lividity was not readably identifiable in Nate's body. This could not have been attributed to the upright position in which he was found floating in the water. If it were, then all of the blood would have settled into his legs and feet and she would have reported it. Instead, she could not tell whether it had pooled on Nate's anterior, posterior, or to his left or right sides. This

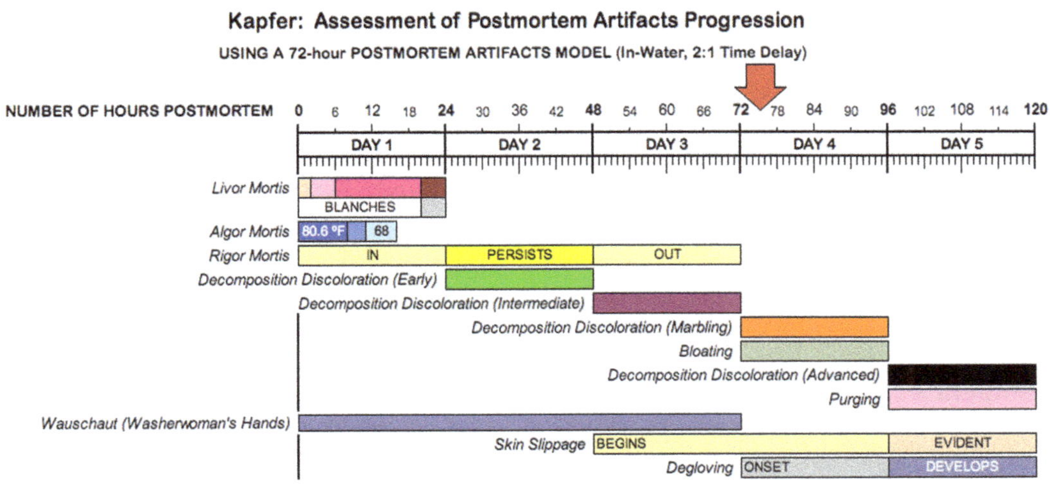

Figure 12.12 The postmortem artifacts for Nate Kapfer's body at autopsy suggested that decomposition had progressed to the equivalent of or slightly beyond the 72nd hour in water after death (*Red Arrow*).

indicated that someone or something had rotated or rolled him periodically after death in order to prevent lividity from becoming detectable.

In the early stage of decomposition on land, a body will turn green within the first 12 hours, starting in the Right Lower Quadrant (RLQ) and spreading to the entire body within 24 hours (Shkrum & Ramsay, 2007). In the intermediate or mid-stage of decomposition, a body will appear dark green, then red, and gradually become a dark purple discoloration within 24 to 36 hours. Marbling and signs of bloating usually occur within 36 to 48 hours on land. All of these times are doubled when a deceased is in water (Figure 12.10). Degradation of the skin begins within minutes of death and is accelerated when a corpse is in the water. Skin slippage will normally start to occur 48 hours after death, with degloving of exposed hands and feet beginning at about 72 hours postmortem.

Decomposition changes on the body were portrayed as green discoloration with marbling, bloating of the abdomen, Washerwoman affect on the hands and feet (*Wauschaut*), and extensive skin slippage with no mention of degloving. She thoroughly described the color and length of the hair on the head and face, but made no mention of it sloughing off. That meant that maceration had not progressed very much at all. Logically, a 2 to 1 time delay could be used to calculate his rate of decomposition since he was found in water. Collectively, the postmortem artifacts demonstrated that Nate had been deceased and decomposing in the water for the equivalent of about 72 hours (Figure 12.12). This did not correspond with the total amount of time (about 1,063 hours 45 minutes) between when he went missing (approximately 02:30 hours on February 22, 1998) and when the Medical Examiner described him at autopsy (10:00 hours on April 7, 1998). However, when estimating a Postmortem Interval (PMI) for Nate, we also had to keep in mind the empirical fact that he was found frozen, which meant that he did not decay at all while in the water. Therefore, instead of being deceased for as long as 72 hours, he was actually only deceased for about 36 hours on land before being frozen.

Perhaps the strangest part of her external description was the small (up to 1 millimeter) bright pink marks that she noticed on the tips of Nate's left thumb, 2nd and 3rd fingers, and on his right thumb, 2nd, 3rd, and 4th fingers. Nate also had two injuries on his left leg that were described much like relatively new bruises (i.e., purple discolorations). One was on the front of his left knee measuring 20 millimeters (mm) by 15 mm (approximately 0.8 inches × 0.6 inches). The second was on his left shin about 150 mm (about 5.9 inches) below his knee and measured 10 mm (0.4 inches) in diameter. They were mentioned as superficial injuries by the Medical Examiner who performed the autopsy, Dr. Lindsey Thomas. Although they were only small contusions, their locations suggested that Nate may have fallen onto his left knee during a struggle with an abductor. It was also possible that they could have been received during baseball practice. In any case, they did not occur at the moment of falling into the water. Elapsed time and a beating heart are required for bruised tissue to appear purple. The injuries were clearly sustained before death.

Temperatures

Tepidity (*algor mortis*) is the temperature of a body as it cools down after death. This progresses at a generally predictable rate. People with less body fat cool more quickly than people who carry extra weight, as do persons with little clothing compared with those individuals who are heavily clothed. The general rate at which a body cools (known as the Glaister Equation) is 1.5 °Fahrenheit during the first 12 hours and then cools at

1.0 °Fahrenheit until it is the same temperature as the environment in which it rests. However, none of that mattered in this case since Nate's body was found to be frozen solid at the time of autopsy (09:00 hours on April 4, 1998). This empirical fact was recorded in the autopsy report by Dr. Thomas. Nate's body was so frozen through-and-through that she left it sitting out in the morgue at room temperature for 25 hours before she conducted the autopsy at 10:00 hours on April 7, 1998. *Prima facie*, it seemed like this may confound the interpretation of forensic evidence relative to the postmortem interval. However, in reality, it actually helped to clarify the timeline and to firmly establish that Nate was murdered.

A total of 41 days 16 hours 32 minutes (41.7 Days) had passed between when Nate was last seen (about 02:15 hours on February 22, 1998) and when his body was resealed in the bags at Franciscan Skemp Hospital (at 18:47 hours on March 4, 1998). During the last 10 days that Nate's body was supposedly in the water, the coldest air temperature was 30 °Fahrenheit and the warmest was 75 °Fahrenheit. In fact, 6 days reached highs of at least 60 °Fahrenheit and only 1 night dropped below 37 °Fahrenheit. The last 10 days were relatively mild and warm, and it even rained. March 29th received 0.24 inches of rain, followed by 0.51, 0.52, and 0.11 inches over the next 3 days. So, between March 29th and April 1st, 1.38 inches of rain fell in the La Crosse area. In fact, during the entire period that Nate was missing, the coldest recorded temperature was 6 °Fahrenheit with all overnight lows averaging out at 30 °Fahrenheit. Certainly, these were not the kind of temperatures that would have been required to turn a human body into a block of ice that took 3 days to thaw out (from recovery on April 4th at 15:00 hours to autopsy on April 7th at 10:00 hours).

When Nate was recovered, rigor had already fully relented. Had he actually fallen into the river on February 22nd and then drowned, then it could have taken as long as 72 to 96 hours for rigor to relent due to the delaying affect of water (i.e., a 2:1 delay ratio). Had the river been cold enough to thoroughly freeze Nate's body after he fell into the water, then rigor should have been suspended at some stage in the process rather than relented. Since he was not in rigor after thawing out for 3 days, this meant that rigor had completely gone out of Nate's body prior to becoming frozen solid. Furthermore, if the water temperature was sufficiently cold enough to completely freeze a human body, then this also meant that Nate had to have been dead on land for at least 36 hours prior to being entered into the river.

However, as can be seen by the previously reviewed temperatures, the river was not frozen over and was not cold enough to freeze a body solid. A cold storage facility like a typical morgue or walk-in cooler used in a butcher shop would have been cold enough to preserve his body, but not cold enough to freeze it (i.e., with temperatures typically at or about 36 to 39 °Fahrenheit). A cold storage facility like that used to store frozen foods may have been cold enough to eventually freeze Nate's body (i.e., with temperatures above 0 °Fahrenheit but below 20 °Fahrenheit), but not to the extent that it would have taken 3 days to thaw. We believe that the kind of cold storage facility required to freeze his body through-and-through would have been one like those at a frozen foods processing plant where temperatures are at about −45 °Fahrenheit and are capable of flash-freezing products. Another possibility was a cold storage facility with dry ice (−109.3 °Fahrenheit).

Had Nate been placed into the river at any interval of time greater than 24 hours prior to the discovery and recovery of his body, then he would have thawed out in the river and not in the autopsy room. This meant that he had to have been deceased on land for a period of 24 to 36 hours in order for rigor to set in and to relent prior to being placed into a deep freezer. He was then removed from the freezer and placed into the river about 24 hours prior to recovery. The fact that he had to have been in a deep freezer at some point in time between when he went missing and when his body was recovered indicated human involvement in Nate's death. His tissues could have been examined under a microscope to identify damage to cell walls as a result of ice crystals and the freezing process. This might have aided in determining how cold the freezer was, since extremely cold temperatures freeze more quickly (i.e., flash-freeze) and produces smaller ice crystals with less cellular destruction (a technique improved upon by Clarence Birdseye for frozen foods).

Taking into account that we concluded that Nate was dead on land before being frozen, then his decomposition would have progressed in a typical manner. It would have started with a blue-green discoloration in the right lower quadrant (RLQ) within 12 hours that spread to the entire body within 24 hours (Spitz & Spitz, 2006). Rigor would have started to relent by the 24th hour after death and completely relented by the 36th hour. By that time, dark red and dark purple discoloration would have also been visible on the body. Bloating of the scrotum and abdomen, as well as marbling, would have begun to appear in approximately 36 to 48 hours after death. However, these discolorations and bloating did not occur because he was frozen about that time. Decomposition discoloration and bloating therefore resumed during the 3 days that he was thawing out in the morgue cooler and in the autopsy room. Skin slippage would have also resumed and become detectable while he was thawing.

The aforementioned (i.e., our model of postmortem processes) was a perfect match for the description recorded by Dr. Thomas at the time of the autopsy. The Medical Examiner portrayed Nate's body as presenting with bloating and a purple-green discoloration, as well as signs of marbling. Skin slippage was observed on the hands and torso, but no mention of degloving was made. Decomposition precluded assessment of the irides and cornea. In light of the known weather variables, the condition of Nate's body relative to decomposition and maceration told us that he had to have been frozen in an environment external to the Mississippi River. Had his body become frozen in the river, then the decomposition and maceration processes would have been retarded or suspended, and would have explained the condition of his body at autopsy. However, since Nate was missing and presumed dead for 41-plus days and the weather conditions (i.e., specifically, air temperature and radiant sunshine) were not conducive to becoming frozen in the river, then the extent of decomposition and maceration should have been more advanced. This fact was not supported by the recovery photos or the Medical Examiner's description at autopsy. Hair on the head of a corpse in water is typically falling off or gone by the end of the second week. Nate's hair was still intact which suggested that he had not been deceased and in the water for more than 2 weeks. At the very least, his body should have been purging fluids, degloving, and should have appeared black, especially in the head and shoulders that were floating out of the water.

Insects

Another key piece of evidence that centered on temperature was insects. Officials who were present at the body recovery were Investigator Schatzley and Sergeant Kabat (La Crosse Police Department), Chief Stinson and other La Crosse Fire Department personnel, John Steers and Ken Kolbe (respectively, Medical Examiner and Deputy Medical Examiner, La Crosse County), and Mike Poellinger. Poellinger was the medical examiner from Houston County, which is the Minnesota county across the river from the City of La Crosse and La Crosse County, Wisconsin. In his investigative report (dated April 6, 1998), Poellinger recorded his initial April 4th assessment of Nate's body as he witnessed it at recovery. He described it as being covered with small insects, as well as mud and sand. Oddly, Dr. Lindsey

Thomas, the medical examiner who performed Nate's autopsy on April 7th, made no mention of any insects in any report.

Insects on any deceased body recovered from water should be a warning flag for medical examiners and investigators. The insects may suggest that the victim was killed on land, remained there long enough for the insects to find the corpse, and the body was then dumped in the water to mask the crime (Armstrong & Erskine, 2011). If there were small insects on Nate's body, then why was there no record of an examination of the insects or even any attempt to identify what kinds of insects they were or what stage of development they had reached. An entomologist could have told the authorities whether or not the insects could survive outdoors at that time of winter in Wisconsin. An entomologist could have also described for them the general habitat for such insects during that time of the year. No record existed that indicated that any samples of the insects had been kept for later study.

Insects are generally drawn to a decomposing corpse when environmental temperatures are at or above 50 °Fahrenheit. Since insects usually are not active in temperatures under 50 °Fahrenheit, and the high and low temperatures were respectively 46.9 and 32.0 °Fahrenheit the night Nate went missing and supposedly drowned, then it would have been extremely unlikely that any insects would have been attracted to his body outdoors. If our assertion that Nate did not go into the water until the day before he was recovered when the temperature was warmer (50 °Fahrenheit) and there was a possibility for insects to be active, then the insects still would not have been attracted to Nate's body since it was frozen solid. Therefore, the insects must have been attracted to his body during the period that it was on land and began to decompose, went in and out of rigor, and before it was frozen. Mike Poellinger (Houston County Medical Examiner) is a trained professional. It was unlikely that he added fictitious evidence to his report, especially evidence as important as insects on a corpse. If there were insects on Nate's body as reported, then there were only 4 scenarios to explain how this may have occurred.

Scenario 1: Nate was dead and left outdoors for a period of time in order for the insects to appear on his body before entry into the water.

Scenario 2: Nate was dead and kept indoors for a period of time in order for the insects to appear on his body before entry into the water.

Scenario 3: Nate was dead before entry into the water, and then floated on top of the water whereon insects were attracted to his decaying body.

Scenario 4: Nate fell into the river and drowned, and then floated on top of the water whereon insects were attracted to his decaying body.

Since Nate's body was so completely frozen, it was exceptionally unlikely for either of the last two scenarios to occur since insects typically seek a damp and warm place to lay their eggs. We believe that Nate was dead somewhere on land for a period of time first (before he was frozen) and before his entry into the water. There was no mention of the insects in the police reports. Also, there was no report of the insects by the Medical Examiner who performed the autopsy. There was only a one line statement from Mike Poellinger (Houston County Medical Examiner in Minnesota), who was the only person to have written a report and was not employed by or associated with agencies whose jurisdiction and interest rested in the City of La Crosse or La Crosse County. Furthermore, we do not know whether the insects were alive or dead at the time that Poellinger wrote his report, or whether their stage of development was suspended due to the freezing. Any evidence of this nature should have been collected for examination by an entomologist in order to provide additional information regarding the postmortem interval and to assist in determining a time of death. Obviously, the bugs should have still been on Nate when he was brought in for the autopsy. Was this just another accidental oversight? It certainly reflected on the quality of the initial investigation into Nate's death.

Mud and Sand

Investigator Schatzley wrote in his supplementary report that he saw mud on Nate's face and stomach at recovery. Mike Poellinger (Houston County Medical Examiner) confirmed that observation in his report and added that there were also insects and sand. None of these artifacts were discussed in any other law enforcement or autopsy report. No samples were taken and kept in secured storage for later analysis. Why not? Was the presence of sand really that significant to this investigation? Mud on the face and stomach of a victim who drowned in a body of water such as the Mississippi River with a muddy bottom would make sense. Under normal circumstances, a victim could possibly pick up some mud while laying on the river bottom and decomposing.

However, two variables made Nate's case anything but normal. First, we determined that he was decomposing and then frozen solid before entry into the water. He would not have sank to the river bottom and would floated the entire time until recovery. He would not have picked any mud from the river bottom. Second, Nate was found floating with his head and shoulders protruding out of the water. As previously presented, the La Crosse area received 1.38 inches of rain between March 29th and April 1st. Nate was not discovered until April 4th. It is likely that most of the mud would have washed from his face during that time. This meant that he had to have been entered into the water after April 1st, which confirmed our premise that he had been entered into the water within 24 hours of discovery and recovery.

Perhaps most important, was the presence of sand on Nate's body. The river bottom of the Mississippi River in the region is composed primarily of various forms of soil and pollutants. It is muddy, not sandy. There are locations of sand along the river bank. During one of our visits to La Crosse, we found one such site along the north shoreline of Swift Creek, which was back upstream from the body recovery site. Another sandy site that we found was at an approach into the river (perhaps an unimproved boat ramp) on the west end of Division Street. The most distinct location of sand that we could find was on the beach at Pettibone Park, which was where the bloodhound had detected Nate's scent. Had the sand on Nate's body been collected, analyzed, and compared with any of these locations (particularly, Pettibone Park beach), then the police might have identified a possible water entry point and potential crime scene.

Internal Assessment

At the time of his autopsy, the weight of Nate's lungs indicated that he had probably inhaled some sort of fluid. A combined weight of the lungs that exceeds 1,000 grams is a good indicator that a "wet" drowning may have occurred. Nate's combined lung weight was 1,070 grams. His right and left lungs weighed 510 and 560 grams, respectively. The left lung typically weighs less (i.e., about 50 to 100 grams less) since the heart takes up some of the cavity space on that side. The fact that Nate's left lung weighed more than it should have in comparison to his right lung should be viewed as an anatomical pathology. The additional and unnatural weight of the left lung can be attributed to the presence of a non-biological substance. In this particular case, that substance was presumed to be water from the Mississippi River. However, we will never know whether or not it was river water or tap water since no sample was ever taken and preserved for testing. A test for the typical chemicals used at a public water treatment plant would have resolved that question.

Pleural effusion is also a good indicator of drowning. If an excessive amount of fluid has entered the lungs and heart, then that fluid will eventually seep out into the protective sacs that contain the lungs, heart, and internal organs. Over time, some fluid will be produced in these cavities as a result of decomposition. The Medical Examiner described an accumulation of fluid in each pleural cavity around the lungs, in the pericardial sac around the heart, and in the peritoneal cavity containing the organs. This can be interpreted as clear evidence of pleural effusion related to drowning.

Nate's stomach contained 120 cubic centiliters of red fluid, which was about 40.6 fluid ounces (fl.oz.), 5.1 cups, or 1/3rd gallon. Witnesses had claimed that Nate drank 3 Long Island Iced Teas (about 4.9 fl.oz. each) and 2 shots (1 fl.oz. each) of hard liquor while at The Library bar. That would account for approximately 16.7 fl.oz. of liquid in his stomach. The color of the liquid in his stomach was correct considering what he had been drinking. The remaining 23.9 fl.oz. might have been river water that he had swallowed. The fluid could have been tested for public water treatment chemicals and river water pollutants. If the fluid came from the river, then it would have most likely contained diatoms as well, which would have been visible under a microscope. However, here again, this simple and inexpensive procedure was not performed. This is a systemic problem that centers on the fact that most medical examiners and investigators automatically presume that victims drowned in the water from which they were recovered. Thus, no testing to verify or refute that presumption occurs.

FBI Report

The La Crosse Police Department requested the involvement of the Federal Bureau of Investigation (FBI) as a result of renewed media coverage and public discussion about a possible serial killer in the city during the Summer and Fall of 2006. Several cases were reviewed by FBI Supervisory Special Agent (SSA) Hilts from the Behavioral Analysis Unit 2 (BAU-2) at the National Center for the Analysis of Violent Crime (NCAVC). He was assisted by other members of the NCAVC. The final report was released in June 2007 and discussed in the local newspaper.

Nate's case was number 4 in that report. Important times, locations, and events for Nate's case were summarized by SSA Hilts. He then presented Nate's BAC at the time he received the citations (0.077) and at the time of his autopsy (0.220). Hilts commented that he did not know how to interpret the BACs. It appeared that even this FBI agent could not explain the increased BAC considering that the bars were closed and there was no report of anyone drinking with Nate after bar closing. In the report, SSA Hilts made special note that obstacles had to be overcome in order to place Nate's personal belongings (i.e., wallet, baseball cap, keys, and 4 municipal ordinance citations) on the rear deck of the Gift Shop. It appeared that even this FBI agent had a problem with the location of the recovery of Nate's property, especially considering that Nate was almost three times the 0.08 legal level for intoxication.

The BAU-2 specializes in the study of the psychology associated with behavior. Given that, we found it odd that no comment was made by SSA Hilts about the fact that Nate did not mention the citations to his friends on the street corner minutes after receiving them. One would expect that sharing the outcome of this recent event with friends would have been a normal part of conversation amongst friends, especially when one of them was drinking and upset, perhaps depressed, or hypothetically considering suicide – which seemed to be the premise under which the police were working.

It must be inferred that the FBI did not see all the paperwork pertaining to this case. The Medical Examiner's autopsy report did not present certain information that is normally contained within such documents. No manner of death was presented in Dr. Thomas' autopsy report. Additionally, the autopsy report did not present any discussion of toxicology test results. There was not even one mention of the BACs in the autopsy report. However, 4 separate documents (2 from the Regina Medical Center Laboratory, and 2 from the Clinical Laboratories at the Hennepin County Medical Center) clearly presented the presence of n-propanol and phenethylamine). Yet, the FBI report stated that no drugs were found in Nate's body.

We believe that had SSA Hilts seen the toxicology documents for Nate's case, then he would have referenced the drugs in his report and commented on them as he had in case number 7 of his report (i.e., Jared Dion). The La Crosse County Medical Examiner (John Steers) stated on camera and in print that there were no drugs in Jared Dion's system. However, during a subsequent conversation some 5 years later, Mr. Steers informed Bryan Dion (Jared's father) that there was in fact GHB in Jared's body; which he now attributed to postmortem decomposition. Even though there was no medical report of GHB anywhere in the publicly available Dion file, SSA Hilts mentioned the presence of GHB in Jared's system in his report on La Crosse. Obviously, he had seen a toxicology report that had been held earlier as "confidential" from public eyes and included the information in his report as he should have.

The fact that n-propanol and phenethylamine were not mentioned at all in the FBI report suggested to us that the SSA Hilts had not seen all the pertinent material related to this investigation. Considering what the FBI apparently did not see with respect to the investigation of Nate's death, we assert that the FBI should revisit the drowning deaths of the young men in La Crosse again. It should make every effort to conduct an unobstructed, full accounting of all the facts pertaining to these cases.

Conclusion

In our opinion, Nate Kapfer's death was written off by authorities as just another one of the accidental drowning deaths in the City of La Crosse that was associated with the irresponsible drinking habits of a young male student full of macho athleticism. Given what we know about the forensic and circumstantial evidence of the case, we could not disagree more with the conclusion of an accidental drowning.

The bloodhound searches did not confirm a linear route of travel for Nate from the bars to the recovery site. The K-9 hits did not create a scent trail. Rather, they portrayed a spotty pattern that jumped from location to location (i.e., a connect-the-dots path as it were). This suggested that he was transported from site to site and did not walk or float there leaving a scent trail in between locations. Downtown, however, Nate's scent was tracked from The Library through Shooter's bar. Regardless of whether the scent was personally left by Nate or by someone who had contact with him that night was irrelevant. The fact remained that the scent went through Shooter's and ended near the statue of Chief Hiawatha. The police did not follow up by investigating why the scent went through Shooter's. Furthermore, the K-9 scent hit at Pettibone Park coincided with the finding of sand on Nate's body at recovery. How did Nate's scent get across the river to the park? Did the sand at the beach match the sand on his body? These pieces of evidence should have been followed up by police.

Like in many of these cases, the police told the families and the media that the young man was so drunk that he did not know any better, wandered too close to the river, fell in and drowned. However, in this case, the FBI even considered it suspicious that a drunk individual had to circumvent numerous locked security gates in order to gain access to the location where his property was recovered. The same guy who could not stand on his own two feet in the presence of police officers somehow managed to climb over gates and fences. All the while, Nate supposedly climbed over all these obstacles in his intoxicated state in order to voluntarily jump into or to accidentally fall into the Mississippi River without incurring any type of physical injury to his body or damage to his clothing.

Also, considering that bodies normally sink when they drown and remain there until putrefaction occurs (i.e., decomposition gases in the abdomen form and the body rises to the surface), Nate's body should have been recovered by divers who searched the area around the Gift Shop – but, it was not. A floating object could not possibly get into Running Slough from the north end of Riverside Park. However, it cannot get, via Running Slough, from the north end of Riverside Park to the spot in Bluff Slough where it was actually described to be without floating against the current several hundred yards. It would need to be somewhere further south in order for it to come to rest near Bayside Court Condominiums.

The PBT administered earlier by police after the bars closed indicated a 0.077 BAC. The postmortem toxicology test quantitated his BAC at 0.220. No one could account for Nate's whereabouts or the different levels of alcohol in his system, which made the second BAC level very suspicious. Where was Nate drinking for this to occur? With whom was Nate drinking in order to achieve such an extremely high BAC after the bars were already closed? Since no one ever came forward to say that he or she was drinking with Nate, and since none of his friends ever said that he went to another party or that they even saw him again, where was he for this to occur?

We opined that this pointed to someone else being involved with the elevation of the level of alcohol in Nate. Yet, the police did not feel this was suspicious enough or that it warranted further investigation. The police officers who responded to Brothers bar learned from interviews with the complainants that Nate's behavior included staggering, using the railing to stabilize himself, uncharacteristic vulgarity, and dry heaving. After giving him a field sobriety test and then finding that his BAC was only 0.077, Nate's behavior did not match his level of intoxication. How was it that the responding police officers at the scene did not find the facts to be suspiciously inconsistent and sufficient to take Nate to a hospital for further assessment? The outcome of events that night would have been dramatically different.

The presence of n-propanol and phenethylamine (an analog of GHB) in Nate's system did not raise enough suspicion for the law enforcement authorities or medical examiners to cause them to pursue further investigation. The empirical facts were that a student athlete, who only had a 0.077 BAC after drinking all night (over 8 hours) with his friends, decided to drink by himself after bar-close to the point of almost three times the legal limit of intoxication for operating a motor vehicle, and then ingested n-propanol and a GHB analog. We were astounded that not one agency or its representative found this information and scenario to be worthy of further investigation.

Considering that we did not know the exact amount of n-propanol, we normally would not be able to say whether this came from the decomposition process or not. But, considering the fact that Nate was frozen to the point that it took 3 days for his body to thaw out, and that the production of n-propanol does not occur in frozen bodies, we did not believe that this was a normal decomposition scenario. We assessed that the n-propanol was present in Nate's system because it was used as a medium to transport a GHB analog (i.e., phenethylamine) from a portable dispenser into one of his drinks that night.

Nate had driven to a house party that evening and had intended on driving home. His vehicle was recovered on the east side of South 9th Street a few days after he went missing. He never operated a motor vehicle under the influence of alcohol. Since Nate was a very mature and responsible young man, this is why he had walked to the bar from the house party and why his BAC was within the legal limit to drive at the time of bar closing. This also lends credence to the theory that Nate was abducted. It was illogical and would have been out of character for him to have remained legally sober enough to drive home after bar closing only to then go and drink himself until he was nearly 3 times the legal limit.

The physical postmortem condition of Nate's body suggested that he had only been deceased on land for no more than about 36 hours before being frozen. The fact that he was frozen solid would have suspended all postmortem processes. Nate was so frozen that it took 3 days to thaw out. Unfortunately for advocates of the hypothesis that he was frozen after falling into the river, the outdoor weather conditions did not support this possibility. Air temperatures and sunny skies during the 3 weeks prior to Nate's recovery would have caused his body to thaw in the water. This empirical fact indicated that Nate's frozen body had to have been placed into the water no more than 24 hours prior to recovery, otherwise he would have thawed out in the water and have been very badly decomposed. This meant that human intervention was required in the disposal of Nate's body after death. In addition, our examination of recovery photos indicated that very little if any decomposition had taken place during the 6 weeks that he had been missing. A comparison of the recovery and autopsy photos demonstrated that most of Nate's decay occurred during the 25 hours that he was left out to thaw at room temperature in the morgue. This made sense, since bodies retrieved from water decompose more quickly than bodies on land, and frozen bodies decay even more rapidly as they thaw.

Furthermore, the presence of insects on Nate's body suggested that he had been dead on land prior to becoming frozen. Since we knew that he had to have already been a frozen mass during the 24 hours prior to recovery, then outdoor insects would not have been attracted to his corpse. This logically required that the insects were drawn to his body prior to freezing. Since outdoor air temperatures were not significantly above 50 °Fahrenheit during the first weeks that Nate was missing, then outdoor insects may not have been active. We therefore concluded that the insects (which were not collected for forensic analysis) had to have been indoor insects.

Thus, prior to being place into the Mississippi River, Nate was either (a) held for weeks, murdered, frozen, or he was (b) murdered, frozen, and then held for weeks. No matter how one specifies the order of events, the scenarios always involve human intervention in order for things to fall into place. In light of all the evidence and investigative information, we concluded that Nate's death involved involuntary drugging, abduction, being held for a period of time without consent, murder by some form of asphyxia that induced hypoxia, being frozen at temperatures below −30 °Fahrenheit, and then being placed into the Mississippi River at a later time.

Jeffrey Forest Geesey*

13

March 9, 1979–May 24, 1999

Background

Jeffrey Forest Geesey was the fourth in a series of suspicious disappearances and deaths to occur between 1997 and 1999 in the City of La Crosse, Wisconsin. The first three disappearances occurred within a 5 month period beginning with Charles Blatz (September 1997), then Anthony Skifton (October 1997), and then Nathan Kapfer (February 1998). Jeff was last seen on the night of April 10–11, 1999. He was recovered some 43 days later from the Mississippi River during the morning hours of May 24, 1999.

By the time Jeff disappeared, rumors had spread throughout the La Crosse area that a serial killer was on the loose, stalking college-aged men, and drowning them in the nearby Mississippi River. This was reinforced by the 14-month period between the Kapfer and Geesey disappearances that could be interpreted as a serial killer's "cooling off period" (i.e., as criminal profilers refer to such breaks in time between events). Over the next 8 years, local fears and the belief that a serial killer was afoot grew as a result of 13 more mysterious deaths in Wisconsin.

- 2001 – Patrick Runingen in La Crosse
- 2002 – Craig Burrows in Eau Claire
- 2003 – Michael Noll in Eau Claire; Nathan Herr in Sheboygan
- 2004 – Jared Dion in La Crosse
- 2005 – Joshua Snell in Eau Claire; Joseph Koebach in Oconto Falls
- 2006 – Kenji Ohmi in Madison; Max Walker in Milwaukee; Lucas Homan in La Crosse
- 2007 – Christopher Melancon in La Crosse

* Photo courtesy of his father, Richard Geesey.

- 2010 – Craig Meyers in La Crosse
- 2013 – Neala Frye in Onalaska

During that timeframe, many more cases occurred in Minnesota, Iowa, Illinois, Indiana, and Michigan. Various conspiracy theories and Internet web sites developed that centered on the mysterious disappearances of more than 40 other college-aged men under similar circumstances and their subsequent body recoveries from rivers and lakes.

Jeff's body was autopsied by Dr. Lindsey Thomas from the Minnesota Regional Medical Examiner's Office in Hastings at 10:45 hours on Monday, May 24, 1999. She indicated that the cause of death was probably drowning, but offered no assessment for a manner of death in this case. The final determination and official explanation of Jeff's death was issued by John Steers, the La Crosse County Medical Examiner, on Tuesday, July 20, 1999. He stipulated the cause of death to be cold water drowning with acute alcohol intoxication, and the manner of death as undetermined. The date and time of death was recorded as 08:15 hours on May 24, 1999. It is about 115 to 140 miles from La Crosse to Hastings, and takes about 2.5 hours to drive the distance at the posted speed limits. It was interesting to note that Jeff was recovered from the water at 08:15 hours and autopsied precisely 2.5 hours later at 10:45 hours on the same day.

Gannon and Duarte met with Dr. Richard Geesey (Jeff's father) in La Crosse in October 2006. At that time, Professor Geesey taught forestry science at the College of Natural Resources, University of Wisconsin-Stevens Point. He had assembled a wealth of intelligence concerning his son's case. He had obtained documents from the United States Army Corps of Engineers for Mississippi River Lock and Dam 7. The documents that he shared with us presented data on the local air temperatures in degrees Fahrenheit, the river water temperatures in degrees Fahrenheit, the amount of local precipitation in inches, water depth fluctuations in feet, and the water flow rate in cubic feet per second. He also provided Gannon and Duarte with copies of the La Crosse County Medical Examiner's report, the Minnesota Regional Medical Examiner's Office autopsy report, as well as several body recovery and autopsy photographs. Having seen and studied related case materials, this chapter was based on our hand-written notes and collective recall, as well as additional investigation and analysis that our team has done.

Circumstances

Last Seen

Jeffrey Geesey ("Jeff") was a White male, 20 years old, 6 feet 1/2 inch, 200 pounds (Body Mass Index: 26.75), brown hair, and brown eyes. He started out the evening of Saturday, April 10, 1999, at Hanson Hall. At approximately 17:30 hours, Jeff walked to Taco Bell (315 West Avenue North) and spoke with the manager, whom he informed that he was going to a girl's apartment on Pine Street for a house party. He then left the restaurant and walked to the house party. Upon leaving the house party, Jeff walked down State Street to Third Street with the girl and her father, and two young men (hereafter, Scott and Bill) to Big Al's pizzaria (115 3rd Street South) where the father bought the group something to eat and drink. Jeff had never met the two young men before that evening.

Around 22:30 hours, the girl and her father left to go home, while Jeff and the other two young men walked over to the Bodega Brew Pub (122 4th Street South). Jeff was introduced

Figure 13.1 Interviews with employees of the "Bodega Brew Pub" confirmed that Jeffrey Geesey had been drinking there on the night of April 10–11, 1999.

to a third young man (hereafter, Steve) for the first time at approximately 23:30 hours while at the Bodega Brew Pub. A brunette female bartender gave Jeff some free drinks since he did not have any money left. Not only did she remember Jeff when questioned by the police, she also recalled the names of the others he was with along with the fact that they were rugby players. This served to confirm that they were in fact in the Bodega Brew Pub (Figure 13.1). They stayed there until around midnight (00:00 hours).

According to Steve, he and the others (Scott, Bill, and Jeff) left the Bodega Brew Pub around midnight and walked over to the Club Millennium (121 3rd Street South - just across the alley from Big Al's) where they shared a pitcher of beer (Figure 13.2). After the pitcher of beer at about 01:00 hours, Bill and Scott started walking home. Meanwhile, Steve went to The Library and Jeff supposedly stayed at Club Millennium speaking to a brunette female there until closing.

Conflicting stories regarding Jeff's whereabouts that night placed him at the Bodega Brew Pub, the Club Millennium, and The Library bar. Bill and Scott had no recollection of what bar they were in and stated only that it started raining on their way back toward

Figure 13.2 Across the alley from Big Al's pizzaria (on the extreme left in this photo) to the south (going to the right), was The Club Millennium (now the location of the Cognac Club), which was located next to The Library bar.

campus. They said because of their degree of intoxication and the heavy rains that evening that they got disoriented and had a difficult time finding their way back to campus. Scott said that the last time he saw Jeff, he was talking to a brunette female in a bar. Bill said the brunette was petite in size.

An online check for available National Weather Service data located a digital copy of the original "Record of River and Climatological Observation" (WS Form B-91) for weather station 4N-NW (USC00474366) for the month of April 1999. It indicated that 0.80 millimeters (0.32 inches) of rain fell between 22:00 and 23:59 hours on April 10th, and an additional 13.00 millimeters (0.51 inches) between 00:00 (midnight) and 09:00 hours on April 11th. This was corroborated by the data discovered by Dr. Geesey for Lock and Dam 7. Although this was not a monsoon rain, there were periods of heavy rain from 01:00 until 02:30 hours with lighting starting at approximately 02:00 hours. Wind speeds averaged about 10 knots with gusts to 15 knots, and the outside air temperature was about 45 °Fahrenheit. In other words, it was not a pleasant night outside relative to weather conditions. It was not the kind of night that one would expect to find anyone out wandering around for no apparent reason.

The owner of Club Millennium stated that the young people who live in the apartments above his bar have a practice of throwing their keys down to people on the street. That way, they can unlock the outside entrance door that leads to the upstairs apartments and come upstairs to continue partying after bar closing time. In fact, the occupant of the front apartment (119 3rd Street South) frequents The Library bar and parks his vehicle in front of the building. While in La Crosse from May 14–15, 1999, Richard Geesey (father) and a friend observed the occurrence of this actual procedure (i.e., tossing the keys to young people on the street to come up and party after bar closings). Also, there were two, young, brunette women hanging out of the window of the front apartment; who, according to the owner of the Club Millennium, also frequented The Library bar.

We also learned that at the time of Jeff's disappearance and death the Club Millennium was frequented mostly by Black males in their 30s and 40s. Furthermore, no one remembered Jeff (a young, White male) being in the bar that night. As discussed below, bloodhound tracking indicated that Jeff was in The Library bar and that Steve may have been mistaken about who was where that night. Considering all this information and what we personally observed about both bars during numerous visits to La Crosse, we believe that Jeff was not in the Club Millennium that night and was in The Library bar until closing, whereon he then made contact with someone from the apartments above the Club Millennium.

Recovery

Jeff's body was discovered about 43 days after he went missing. According to official reports, Jeff was recovered at 08:15 hours on May 24, 1999. His body was found in Running Slough, an inlet of the Mississippi River near the Town of Shelby. He was snagged amongst some river debris that had collected near a gravel pit roughly 3.8 miles south of Riverside Park as the crow flies. This location was only about 3,400 feet (0.64 miles) south of where Nathan Kapfer had been recovered on April 4, 1998. The La Crosse County Medical Examiner wrote that Jeff's blood alcohol concentration was 0.420 and that he had 130 micrograms (mcg) of gamma-hydroxybutyrate (GHB) in his system. As typically reported, no signs of trauma were discovered on the body.

Analysis of Evidence

Dog Searches

The first K-9 search was conducted on May 27, 1999, which was 3 days after Jeff's recovery. Upon their arrival in La Crosse, the bloodhound (Hoover) and her handlers (Penny Bell and Terry Kaminski) were initially taken to the campus of the University of Wisconsin-La Crosse where Jeff was enrolled in classes. There, the dog scented Jeff's baseball cap that had been provided by the campus security. The search party then went to Sanford Hall. Hoover proceeded to the 2nd floor and alerted on a window sill. She then proceeded to the 3rd floor and checked Room #312. She backed out and continued down the hall to Room #329. Having checked that room, the bloodhound backed out and continued down the hall, whereon, she alerted on the baseboard area of the closed door to Room #330 – Jeff Geesey's room. Hoover entered the room, alerted on a backpack on the left side of the room (Jeff's side) and alerted on the top bunk (Jeff's bunk).

Later that same day (May 27, 1999), a bloodhound search indicated the presence of Jeff's scent in The Library bar and not in the Club Millennium. Jeff's scent was all over the inside of The Library bar and in its restroom. The bloodhound indicated that Jeff had walked around inside The Library and that he had used the men's room. From the location of the scent on the wall of the toilet stall, it was surmised that Jeff may have been throwing up at this time right before bar closing.

Next, Jeff was scented outside The Library. There, the bloodhound designated that Jeff's scent was associated with a truck and a van that were both parked near The Library (i.e., one in front of the bar and one in the alley). The truck parked in front of The Library bar was a blue Ford Ranger pickup with a Wisconsin vehicle plate, which was owned by a male individual (hereafter, Karl) who frequented The Library. Karl and his roommate lived in the front apartments above the Club Millennium. During the evening, he parked his Ford Ranger in the parking ramp located diagonally across from The Library bar. According to numerous witnesses, after bar close, he often moved his truck from the parking structure to the street in front of The Library. Jeff was scented by the bloodhound as being inside Karl's pickup.

A similar vehicle was described by "Mark" as having followed him from The Library bar just moments before Nathan Kapfer disappeared. Mark had identified the suspect vehicle as a dark-colored, navy blue or black, smaller pickup like a Chevrolet S-10 with a topper. At night and to a person who had been drinking, A Ford Ranger and a Chevrolet S-10 could be mistaken for each other. A comparison of some basic "Specs" (specifications) shows how easily the two vehicles could be confused by someone who was not a "car guy" (Figure 13.3). The K-9 also signified that Jeff's scent was present inside a Plymouth minivan that was parked in the alley between Big Al's and the Club Millennium. The van was owned by a female individual (hereafter, Karen) who also frequented The Library. Additionally, Karen happened to be a brunette and was in the process of divorcing her husband at that time.

The bloodhound also indicated that Jeff's scent was in a parking structure adjacent to the Holiday Inn (Figure 13.4, *Red Star*), which was about 1 block southwest of The Library and Club Millennium (near the intersection of Jay Street and 3rd Street South). There, Jeff's scent was associated with a vehicle on the 2nd floor of the parking structure. Since a description or license plate number was not recorded for that vehicle, we could not discern

Pickup Size Comparison

SPECIFICATION	FORD RANGER	CHEVROLET S-10
Width	*69.4 inches*	*67.9 inches*
Height	*64.9 inches*	*62.0 inches*
Length	*187.5 inches*	*190.0 inches*
Wheelbase	*112.0 inches*	*108.0 inches*
Wheels	*15 inches*	*15 inches*
Curb Weight	*3,030 pounds*	*3,016 pounds*

NOTE: Specs are for the 2-door, 2002 Model of both vehicles.

Figure 13.3 The bloodhound hit on a Ford Ranger pickup while tracking Jeffrey Geesey's scent. The vehicle that stalked "Mark" (Chapter 12) was described as being small like a Chevrolet S-10 pickup. A side-by-side comparison of the "Specs" shows how similar the two vehicles are.

whether or not it was the same vehicle parked in front of The Library bar in which Jeff's scent had been detected (Figure 13.4, *Red Dot*). Investigators should always record this kind of information as it becomes available, because one never knows when it may become an important part of a case analysis.

The K-9 also hit in the northwest corner near an entrance leading from the parking ramp into the hotel. While searching for Jeff's scent, the bloodhound also designated that

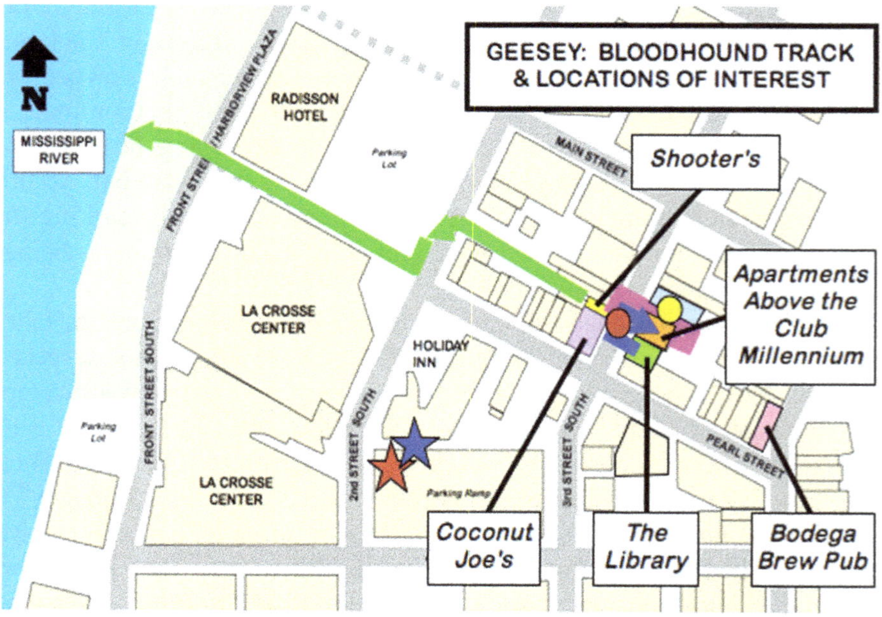

Figure 13.4 A bloodhound tracked Jeff Geesey's scent from The Library to the apartments above the Club Millennium (*Blue Arrow*), then out the back door and through the alley (*Bright Purple Line*). It went across the street to Shooter's, through the bar and out the back door (*Bright Green Arrow*). After negotiating the interior of the block, the K-9 crossed 2nd Street South and tracked past the Radisson Hotel to Riverside Park and the bank of the Mississippi River. The bloodhound also demonstrated positive hits on a Ford Ranger pickup (*Red Dot*) and a Plymouth minivan (*Yellow Dot*), as well as an unidentified vehicle in a parking ramp (*Red Star*) and vomitus in a shrub bed (*Blue Star*).

a heavy scent was located in the shrub bed directly below the area where it had hit on the northwest corner of the 2nd floor of the parking ramp. At ground level (Figure 13.4, *Blue Star*), the dog hit on some vomitus in the shrub bed (which was recovered, but never tested). It appeared that Jeff had vomited over the wall while standing on the second floor of the parking structure directly above.

When the bloodhound tracked Jeff's scent inside the apartments above Club Millennium, she did not go into Karl's apartment because the door was locked. However, Jeff's scent was located on material inside a collection bag of a custodian's sweeper that was stored in a locker closet. Jeff's scent trail was found in the front entrance to the apartments and on the front stairway leading up to the 2nd floor where the apartments were located. The K-9 also followed his scent along the 2nd floor hallway. It indicated that Jeff's scent was present on the front window sill in the hallway that overlooked the street and the bars, as well as in the communal bathroom on the 2nd floor. The bloodhound then tracked Jeff's scent through the rear entrance door on the 2nd floor and then down the back stairs.

Once outside, the tracking dog traveled west through the alley between Big Al's and Club Millennium and crossed 3rd Street South (Figure 13.4, *Bright Purple Line*). There, it went through the front door of Shooter's Bar and out the back door (Figure 13.4, *Bright Green Arrow*). The search party then followed the K-9 west down a short alley and across a parking lot to 2nd Street South. Upon crossing the street, they reached a chain link fence along the east side of a parking lot. The bloodhound then continued west to the Radisson Hotel (200 Front Street; also listed as 200 Harborview Plaza). After going around the hotel, it tracked through Riverside Park toward the river and stopped at a spot along the Mississippi River.

It was interesting to note that the track followed by the bloodhound while tracking Jeff's scent led it west down a short alley and through a parking lot to 2nd Street South, where it walked past the Radisson Hotel to Riverside Park. This route was very similar to the one taken by the tracking dog while following Nathan Kapfer's scent (Chapter 12, Figure 12.7). However, when tracking Nate, the search party went north through Riverside Park to the statue of Chief Hiawatha. Another curious fact was that the point along the Mississippi River where the bloodhound had tracked Jeff's scent was the exact location where Lucas Homan would be recovered 7 years later in 2006 (Chapter 15, Figure 15.5).

The bloodhound then returned to the fence at the east side of the Radisson Hotel parking lot along 2nd Street South. There, it indicated that Jeff had entered a vehicle and was transported south down 2nd Street to where it ends and becomes Front Street South. The K-9 continued along Front Street South to where it became Norplex Drive at Jackson Street. The search party followed the tracking dog south down Norplex Drive until it stopped at the Niedbalski Bridge at Hood Street (Figure 13.5, *Bright Purple Arrow*). The bloodhound did a trauma roll at that location, which indicated that some type of physical incident or traumatic event involving Jeff had occurred there. Niedbalski Bridge was also the body recovery site for Anthony Skifton (October 10, 1997), and was just north of the spot where Cullen Fortney pulled himself from the water (Chapter 11, Figure 11.3).

Hoover (the bloodhound) was considered to be one of the best tracking dogs ever seen by all those who had observed her performance in numerous cases. There are K-9s that search with their noses to the ground, and air-scent dogs who track with their noses in the air. There are also cadaver dogs that are specifically trained to track and indicate the scent of deceased humans (from a drop of blood to decomposing bodies). According to the next scenario, Hoover was apparently an air scent dog.

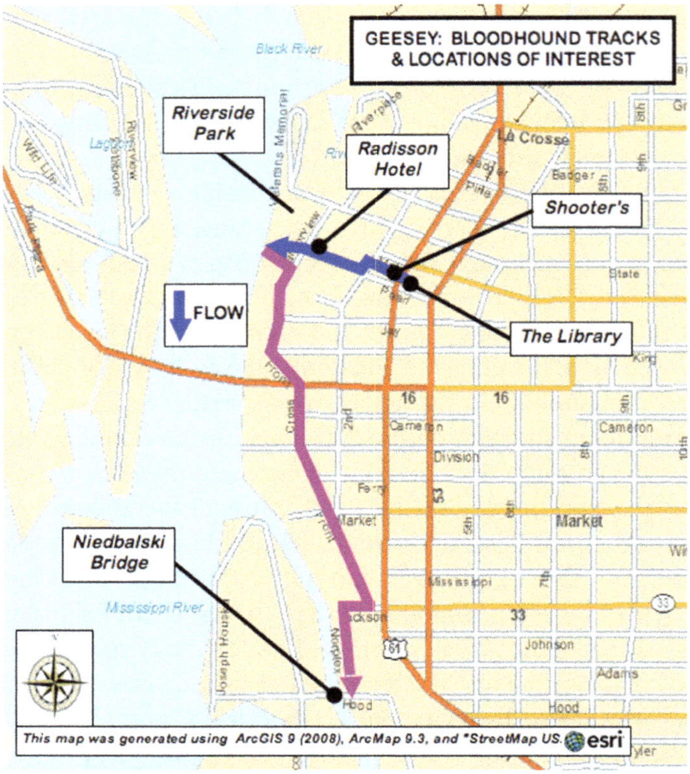

Figure 13.5 After tracking Jeff Geesey's scent to the edge of the Mississippi River (*Blue Arrow*), the bloodhound followed his scent south to the Niedbalski Bridge (*Bright Purple Arrow*). The K-9 did a trauma roll at that location, indicating that some type of physical incident or traumatic event involving Jeff had occurred there.

The second search was conducted almost two months after Jeff's recovery. The La Crosse Fire Department provided a boat which was launched from Pettibone Island in order to conduct a waterborne K-9 search. Prior to the start of the search, Richard Geesey wanted to confirm the dog's tracking ability considering its previous findings during the first search. In particular, he wanted to determine the extent of validity of the K-9's tracking that suggested the possibility of Jeff having been transported by vehicle to his eventual body recovery location. While Hoover was still in the holding truck, Dr. Geesey asked the two firemen whether one of them would hide Jeff's hair brush inside his fire department raincoat. Professor Geesey then put Jeff's hair brush inside two plastic freezer-type bags and gave it to one firemen, who opened his coat and placed the double-bagged hair brush under his sweatshirt, closed his rubber raincoat, and buttoned it up. When Hoover was released from the truck, she immediately started to air-scent and went directly over to Dr. Geesey and sniffed him. Hoover then went directly to the fireman who had hidden the hair brush and jumped up on him. She scratched on the chest of his raincoat where he had hidden the hair brush. This pretty much confirmed the dog's proficiency to all those present.

The waterborne search was then started with Hoover going to the front of the boat. After everyone was onboard, the dog looked back at the driver of the boat as if to say, "Let's go!" The boat departed the shoreline and they went south on the Mississippi River. When the boat got to the Niedbalski Bridge, Hoover attempted to reach the low-hanging bridge by jumping up and indicated a positive scent hit by barking. As the boat continued south down the Mississippi River, the dog looked back at the driver, went to the left side of the boat, and barked. This meant that he should steer the boat to the left, which would take them into Running Slough. The boat driver made the left into Running Slough and continued until they reached the gravel pit near the town of Shelby. The K-9 jumped out of the boat at that point and sat on the gravel pit. Richard Geesey asked a fireman whether this was the location where his son had been recovered. According to Dr. Geesey, the fireman responded that it was with a tone in his voice of amazement at the dog's ability.

Hoover then followed Jeff's scent out of the gravel pit over land as though someone who had contact with him had left that location. Jeff was recovered with only one sneaker on (as is the case in a few of the other "drownings" we have investigated). He was missing his left sneaker. Did he accidently loose this sneaker while floating in the river or was it taken by those responsible for his murder as a trophy, which is often common among serial killers? Could this have been the reason that Hoover tracked Jeff's scent leaving the location of his body recovery?

At that point in time, all occupants were back in the boat and were leaving when the bloodhound started to bark again from the front of the boat. She gave an indication to continue in the direction that she was barking. The boat driver continued over to a small island near the gravel pit. At that location, Hoover got out of the boat and sat on the island. Richard Geesey asked a fireman what had occurred there. The fireman – again in amazement – replied that they could not get his son into the boat since he was lodged in between some debris which had collected near the gravel pit. So, they had to pull Jeff by hook over to the island. They placed him into a body bag at that spot and then hauled the body into the boat.

Gannon personally spoke with that fireman by phone on August 6, 2007. He confirmed his statement to the local newspaper that he would have never imagined that kind of skill possible had he not seen it with his own eyes. However, he would not speak with Gannon about other information regarding what he had seen or believed with respect to Jeff's case. The fireman stated that he was told by the police Supervisor in Charge of Jeff's investigation to not speak with anyone regarding this case and to refer all inquires to law enforcement.

The third search for Jeff was conducted on November 17, 1999 (Figure 13.6, *Bright Green Line*). The bloodhound started to track from the Niedbalski Bridge, where it had previously alerted on some sort of traumatic event having transpired. It went east on Hood Street back out to the T-intersection with Norplex Drive, turned left, and tracked back north up Norplex Drive (about 975 feet). At that location, the road formed a T-intersection with Jackson Street. The bloodhound turned right and tracked east a short distance (about 275 feet) until it arrived at a major 4-way intersection that was regulated by a semaphore light (i.e., where 3rd Street South becomes South Avenue, and overlaps with both U.S. Highway 14 and U.S. Highway 61). From there on, the search party walked south towards the Gunderson Lutheran Hospital (Figure 13.6, *Red Cross*) following the dog that was hot on a scent. The manner of tracking suggested that the K-9 was following Jeff's scent in a vehicle. The dog continued tracking in the direction of the gravel pit, but the search was broken off due to heavy traffic and a lack of a police escort. This was in the same general area where Cullen Fortney (Chapter 11) had walked after pulling himself from the water and running to the hospital.

The entire route that Jeff would have walked was about 4.9 miles long using the bloodhound's scent track and then the most direct path on foot to get to the body recovery site. It was approximately 0.2 miles from the downtown bars to the spot in Riverside Park (Figure 13.5, *Blue Arrow*), 1.1 miles to the Niedbalski Bridge (*Bright Purple Arrow*), and then another 0.8 miles to Gunderson Lutheran Hospital (*Bright Green Line*). Had Jeff walked

Figure 13.6 The bloodhound left the area of the Niedbalski Bridge and continued to track Jeff Geesey's scent back out onto the main road (*Bright Green Line*). The search party followed the dog south toward Gunderson Lutheran Hospital (*Red Cross*), but had to stop due to heavy traffic. The most likely and direct path to the body recovery site would have been an additional 2.8 mile walk (*Red-X Dot*).

all the way, then he would have walked another 2.8 miles from Gunderson Lutheran to the vicinity of the gravel pit in Shelby (Figure 13.6, *Blue Dotted Line*). That meant that he would have walked about 25,872 feet (4.9 miles). A completely sober person of his age could have walked the route in roughly 90 minutes, which equated to 3.27 miles per hour. That was not a blistering pace, rather, a steady pace at about 287.5 feet per minute (e.g., the length of a football field). This would have been an impossible task for Jeff keeping in mind that the La Crosse County Medical Examiner reported that Jeff's blood alcohol concentration was 0.420 and that he had 130 micrograms of GHB in his system.

Obviously, these 3 separate search incidents showed the dog to be more than proficient at following a scent. They also showed a consistency of location with respect to the other victims. Gannon and Duarte spoke face-to-face with local law enforcement officials in April 2007 regarding the proficiency of the tracking dog. They were told that, unfortunately, the dog was a bust. Investigators had heard good things about her (i.e. Hoover the bloodhound). But, when she was brought there, she did not do anything for them.

Recovery Location

Jeff's body was recovered at approximately 08:15 hours on Monday, May 24, 1999. It was found near a gravel pit in Running Slough, which came off the main channel of the

Mississippi River. The body recovery site was only about 3,400 feet (0.64 miles) south of where Nathan Kapfer had been recovered on April 4, 1998. That spot was within the jurisdiction of the City of La Crosse. The location of Jeff's recovery was often described in the official documents as being near the small town of Shelby. The main part of Shelby was at about the same geographic latitude as the body recovery site (i.e., horizontal to it), but it was about 3 miles east of the recovery site. However, the geopolitical boundaries of the area claimed by the Town of Shelby wrapped around and included the area of land with the gravel pit, which was surrounded (on the north, east, and south) by the boundaries of the City of La Crosse. This meant that the body recovery location actually rested within the jurisdictional area of the Town of Shelby and La Crosse County.

Jeff's body recovery was difficult since he was found in an area where debris had collected in the river. The firemen were unable to properly bag his body at the spot where he was floating. So, they pulled his body over to an adjacent island where it was placed into a body bag (a fact that was reaffirmed by the bloodhound). It was then transported back north to the 7th Street boat landing, where it was removed from the river. Jeff's body was then taken directly to the Regina Medical Center in Hastings, Minnesota, where it would be autopsied.

The big question right up front that had to be answered was how did Jeff's body get to that location. As a result of research related to Nathan Kapfer's death, we had learned about local river currents and patterns related to floating objects. Jeff, much like Nate, could not have walked to Riverside Park, fallen into the river, and floated to this general area of the Mississippi River. Both had to have been taken there or very close by. We also knew from the La Crosse County Medical Examiner's report that Jeff was extremely intoxicated that night with a 0.420 BAC and 130 mcg of GHB in his system. We concluded that this magnitude of substance abuse would have made it nearly impossible for anyone to stand or much less walk to the Town of Shelby. We induced four possible scenarios based on the toxicology information and the bloodhound searches, which repeatedly suggested that a vehicle had been involved.

1. Jeff was driven by his abductor(s) to the Niedbalski Bridge and put into the river alive, most likely unconscious. He subsequently drowned and then floated into Running Slough and to his eventual body recovery location near the gravel pit.
2. Jeff was driven by his abductor(s) to the Niedbalski Bridge where he was murdered. He was then placed into the river at that location and floated into Running Slough and to his eventual body recovery location near the gravel pit.
3. Jeff was driven by his abductor(s) to the Niedbalski Bridge where he was murdered. His body was then taken by boat into Running Slough and dumped near the gravel pit, where one or more of the boat's occupants went ashore and left the location on foot.
4. Jeff was driven by his abductor(s) to the Niedbalski Bridge where he was murdered. His body was then taken by vehicle to the gravel pit site, carried to the river bank, and dumped into Running Slough.

The next item to explain at the recovery site was Jeff's scent leaving the area of the gravel pit. Since Jeff was deceased at that location and obviously not moving, one possible reason for a scent trail to lead away from the gravel pit was that someone who had contact with his body must have been there and then left the area. Therefore, as a transfer scent on the other person, Jeff's scent was tracked by the K-9 as leaving this location. Two possible scenarios were envisioned regarding the transfer scent.

1. Someone had spotted Jeff's body at the gravel pit before he was recovery and then walked away without notifying the authorities. The individual who had discovered Jeff may have been afraid or apprehensive to come forward and so walked away – which was unlikely.
2. The scent leaving the gravel pit area was left there by those who were responsible for Jeff's death and the placement of his body into the river as they departed on foot – which was more likely.

Lividity and Rigidity

Lividity (*livor mortis*) and rigidity (*rigor mortis*) are extremely important characteristics for estimating the postmortem interval (PMI; how long it has been since death occurred). Lividity and rigidity are typically one of the first things recorded by medical examiners under "External Examination" while describing the appearance of a body at the beginning of an autopsy. Lividity is commonly described by its color and location. Rigidity is often assessed in terms of whether or not it is present. When present, a written discussion of the extent to which certain muscles may still present rigor helps the medical examiner to define the victim's state of rigidity as establishing, as set, or as relenting.

Lividity is the settling of the blood to the lowest portion of the deceased after death (Geberth, 2006). Normally, the body of drowning victim floats face-down and lividity is therefore anterior. A body may occasionally flip in the water due to wave actions from passing boats or strong winds. In those cases, the body ends up floating face-up and lividity is posterior. Since Jeff was supposed to have been dead and in the water for a period of 43 days, then there should have been clear signs of lividity on his body that were consistent with the position in which he was recovered. In fact, blood becomes fully settled to a specific position in a body after a period of 10 to 12 hours and cannot be significantly shifted. Therefore, there should have been some mention of lividity in the autopsy report.

Unfortunately, there was no mention of lividity in any report written by the Medical Examiner who performed the autopsy in Hastings or the La Crosse County Medical Examiner. The autopsy photographs showed no typical sign of lividity. It could not be determined as anterior or posterior. Observation of the pictures disclosed that the very top of Jeff's shoulders into his neck displayed early marbling and dark red discoloration. Rather blotchy dark green and dark red discoloration could be identified across the back. If this was the lividity, then that would mean that Jeff would have been in a head-down and feet-up position (*Trendelenburg Position*) for a period of at least 10 hours while the blood settled towards his head. This would not have resembled any standard position for a drowning victim, who should have lividity in both the head and feet.

Rigidity is the stiffening of the muscles after death. It relents (i.e., leaves a body) within 24 to 36 hours on land in temperate weather, and in 48 to 72 hours in the water (DiMaio & DiMaio, 2001). During the period that Jeff was missing and presumed to be in the river (April 11th through May 24th), the average outdoor air temperature was 56 °Fahrenheit with the lowest temperature at 36 °Fahrenheit and the highest at 81 °Fahrenheit. In fact, during the 5-day timeframe of April 30th to May 4th, the temperature ranged from 77 to

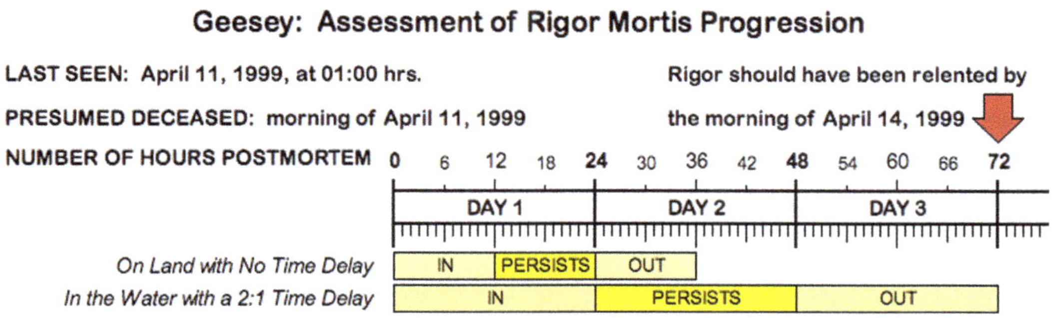

Figure 13.7 When a body is immersed in water, rigidity typically relents in about 72 hours. That meant that rigidity should have completely relented by the morning of April 14th since Jeff Geesey was presumed to have drowned during the early morning hours of April 11, 1999.

82 °Fahrenheit with no precipitation. In other words, it was quite warm outside and Jeff was supposedly laying in the sun while floating in the river for 43 days.

At the known temperatures, Jeff should have been coming out of rigor in approximately 52 to 56 hours after death. We knew this to be a scientific fact given the environmental conditions and time in another La Crosse case; that of Luke Homan who went missing and was recovered from the Mississippi River approximately 56 hours later with rigidity relenting in his body. Since there should have been no sign of rigor in Jeff's body after 43 days, then any record of rigidity in official reports should have indicated that it had completely relented before he was recovered and autopsied (Figure 13.7). Unfortunately, rigidity was not mention at all in any report.

Quite shocking was the discovery that Jeff was found with his arms still in rigor. This fact was suggested by the photographs taken during the body recovery. Furthermore, it was verified by statements made to Gannon by individuals who were present at the body recovery. Jeff's right arm was raised above his shoulder. It was so stiff that they could not get it into the black body bag with the rest of his body. They had to place another bag over it. Rigidity starts in the smaller muscles and progresses to the larger muscles, and then relents in the same order (Spitz & Spitz, 2006). The empirical observation that Jeff's arms were in rigor indicated that he was still coming out of rigor. Given the 2:1 time delay ratio fostered by immersion in water, this meant that Jeff had likely not been deceased longer than 72 hours by the time of his recovery (Figure 13.7).

Had he actually fallen into the river and drowned during the early morning hours of April 11th as presumed, then rigidity should have completely relented sometime during the morning of April 14th. The autopsy photographs suggested that rigidity had not relented by the time of his autopsy on May 24th, which indicated that Jeff had not been deceased any longer than about 72 hours. Our analysis of the progression of rigor relative to Jeff suggested that he died sometime on or about May 21st (Figure 13.8). This foreboding finding revealed that he had to have been abducted on April 11th, held for 39 to 40 days, murdered and placed into the river on or about May 21st, and recovered on May 24th.

Internal Assessment

With the exception of signs of decomposition, the internal cavities and a majority of the internal organs appeared normal in size, weight and shape. No signs of internal injury or trauma were identified during the autopsy.

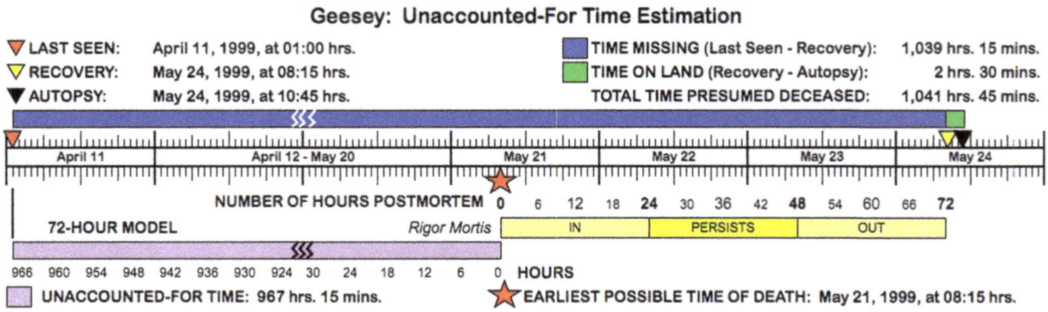

Figure 13.8 Jeff Geesey's body was still in rigor at the time of recovery, which meant that he could not have been dead for any longer than about 72 hours.

At autopsy, Jeff had 10 cubic centimeters (cc) or about 0.338 fluid ounces (fl.oz.) of a sludgy, brown substance in his stomach. This could have been a combination of the pizza he had eaten at Big Al's just prior to 22:30 hours and the beer he had drank later on at the bar. Food leaves the stomach within 4 to 6 hours depending on the meal. This near empty state of Jeff's stomach suggested that he probably died sometime within 4 to 6 hours after his last meal. However, his gallbladder contained 1 cc or about 0.034 fl.oz. of bile, which meant that it had not refilled after eating. Since his gallbladder had not refilled and his stomach was nearly empty, that meant that Jeff had to have thrown up. It also suggested that he did not swallow any significant amount of water after going into the river. Therefore, it was anyone's guess whether his last meal was pizza at Big Al's and he was then murdered, or whether he was abducted and held alive for a period of time, fed, and then murdered.

Jeff's lungs were exceptionally light in weight for a drowning. The right lung weighed 400 grams (gm) and the left lung was 340 gm. Typically, lungs in a drowning collectively weigh over 1,000 gm. Some decomposition fluid was present in the pleural cavities, the pericardial sac, and the peritoneal cavity. The lung tissue (parenchyma) showed some signs of congestion when sectioned and a small amount of bloody fluid could be squeezed out when pressure was applied to it. Congestion was definitely a sign that some sort of trauma had been experienced by the lungs and strongly suggested that a drowning had occurred. Furthermore, the low lung weight and the minimal presence of pleural effusion and fluid in the lungs demonstrated that only a small amount of water had entered the lungs during the drowning process, which suggested that Jeff was likely unconscious upon submersion in the water.

Decomposition and Maceration

In the water, early decomposition causes discoloration (blue-green) that starts in the Right Lower Quadrant of the abdomen within 24 hours and spreads to the entire body within 48 hours. Intermediate decomposition changes the color to dark green, dark red, and sometimes dark purple, within 48 to 72 hours. Marbling of a body (i.e., the development of red, purple or green-black discoloration along the blood vessels) becomes detectable within 72 to 96 hours after death. Bloating (gaseous swelling) of the abdomen occurs within 72 to 96 hours when a body is in water (Shkrum & Ramsay, 2007). It is especially visible in areas of loose skin like the scrotum, penis, and eyelids. The "Washerwoman's" affect (*Wauschaut*) to the hands and feet usually begins within 20 minutes of immersion into water, and continues to develop until approximately 72 hours (3 days) (Armstrong & Erskine, 2011). Skin slippage is noticeable within 48 to 96 hours (2 to 4 days), and is clearly evident by 96 to 168 hours (4 to 7 days) after death. After 72 to 96 hours (3 to 4 days), Jeff's hands and feet should have started to deglove. His hands should have completely degloved by about 144 to 168 hours (6 to 7 days) postmortem.

Jeff's postmortem condition at recovery was described as presenting with moderate decomposition, "washerwoman's" hands and feet, skin slippage and considerable hair missing from the scalp, abdominal bloating, and discoloration. No antemortem injuries were noted to the body except four scars on the inside of his lower left arm (0.6 to 1.8 inches), which law enforcement interpreted as associated with an earlier suicide attempt. An area of about 2.4 by 2.8 inches in the Lower Left Quadrant of the abdomen was identified as possible postmortem aquatic anthropophagy (i.e., marine life feeding on the body of the deceased).

Since no definitive description of the color of decomposition was offered in the autopsy report, and no mention of marbling was recorded, we had to rely on our observation and interpretation of available photographs and postmortem indicators. Jeff's color had advanced to dark green in some spots, which meant about 48 to 72 hours postmortem. Bloating was detectable in the eyes, mouth, and abdomen, but no marbling was visible in the Right or Left Lower Quadrants was noted. That suggested that he had reached a point in time at about 66 to 78 hours after death.

Hair had fallen off the top of his head, but remained on the sides. Skin slippage was mentioned in the autopsy report, but degloving was not. The skin on the right foot, which was protected by a sock and shoe, was starting to come off. Although it was difficult to discern due to the camera angles, the hands appeared as though the skin may have actually completely degloved. This was logical since exposure to moisture can accelerate skin slippage, particularly degloving of the skin on exposed hands and feet. Since Jeff was already losing hair and the exposed hands may have already sloughed their skin, then these characteristics indicated that decomposition had likely reached the 96 hours (4 days) postmortem, but had not exceeded 144 hours (6 days). This explained the mixed interpretation of the appearances of decomposition indicators. It also suggested that Jeff's actual postmortem interval may have been about the average of the interpretations, that is, at about 120 hours (5 days) (Figure 13.9).

Jeff disappeared during the early morning hours of April 11th and was recovered on the morning of May 24th. He was missing for 43 days. All government officials associated with this case (i.e., law enforcement investigators and medical examiners) designated Jeff's death as a drowning and considered it to have happened on April 11th. Therefore, Jeff was presumed to have been deceased for 43 days and in the Mississippi River for 43 days. The

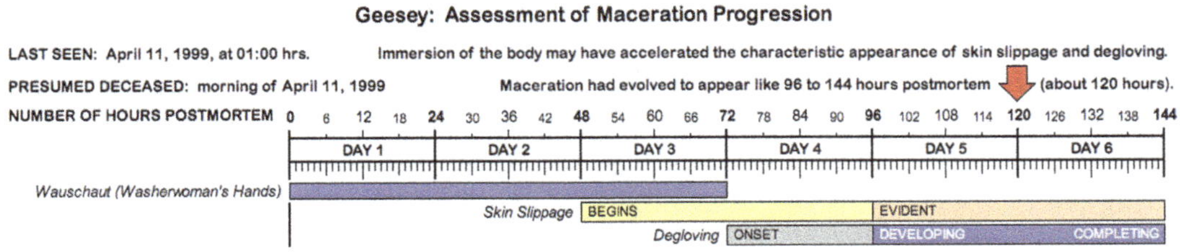

Figure 13.9 Immersion in water likely accelerated the maceration process for Jeff Geesey, and may have contributed to mixed interpretations of decomposition characteristics. The appearance of those indicators suggested that he had been deceased no less than 96 hours and no more than 144 hours; we averaged it out at 120 hours (5 days).

postmortem condition of Jeff's body at recovery suggested that he had been deceased no less than 72 hours (3 days), but no more than 96 hours (4 days).

Since we always error on the side of caution, we took into account the environmental conditions. The average outdoor air temperature during the time that Jeff was missing and presumed to be in the river (April 11th through May 24th) was 56 °Fahrenheit. The coldest it got was 36 °Fahrenheit and the warmest was 81 °Fahrenheit. In fact, there was a 5-day period (April 30th to May 4th) when the temperature reached daily highs of 77 to 82 °Fahrenheit. Thus, it was quite warm outside and Jeff should have been in a much more advanced state of decomposition than he was. Regarding the water temperature, we analyzed the data gathered by Dr. Geesey from the United States Army Corps of Engineers for Mississippi River Lock and Dam 7. The water temperature ranged from approximately 48 °Fahrenheit on April 11th to about 64 °Fahrenheit on May 24th.

All of the calculations already mentioned above were based on the 2:1 time delay ratio for the retarding affect of water on decomposition. Therefore, the estimate that Jeff had been deceased no less than 72 hours (3 days) and no more than 96 hours (4 days) was already twice the estimate needed for an on-land time since death (i.e., postmortem interval). That meant that if Jeff had only been deceased for 4 days, then he had to have been alive for 39 of the 43 days that he was missing. When we doubled the time for the possible retarding affect of the cooler water on decomposition (i.e., from 96 hours to 192 hours or 8 days), then that meant that Jeff was still held alive for 35 days. To demonstrate how preposterous this was, even if we quadrupled the postmortem interval to 384 hours or 16 days, it still meant that Jeff had been held alive for 27 days before he was killed.

Gilbertson demonstrated this mathematics to a forensics expert during a visit to the National Center for Missing and Exploited Children on October 21, 2009. Gannon and Gilbertson have since shown the recovery and autopsy photographs, and specified the dates for disappearance and body recovery, to several other forensic pathologists. When asked for their professional opinions of how long the young man had been deceased, the experts always concurred with a finding of 4 days, but no more than 7 days. When asked whether they would need 14 or 21 days, their response was always in the negative and they asked us what our point was. When we informed them that he was missing for 43 days they were all astounded and emphatically insisted that he may have been missing, but not deceased. Regardless of whether Jeff was held for a period of 1 or 39 days did not really matter. What did matter was that Jeff was held for a period of time before being entered into the Mississippi River.

Toxicology

When Jeff was recovered, his Blood Alcohol Concentration (BAC) was reported to be 0.420 grams per deciliter (gm/dL). Each alcoholic drink equates to about 0.02 milliliters of BAC in a 180 pound man. Since Jeff weighed 200 pounds, then it would have required an extra drink in order for him to reach the same level. Therefore, he would have had to have drank about 22 drinks in order to reach a 0.420 BAC that night. However, Jeff's body would have been metabolizing some alcohol during that same time. The body of a 180 pound male disperses about 1 alcoholic drink per hour (Centers for Disease Control and Prevention, 2011). If Jeff started drinking alcohol around 18:00 hours at Big Al's and continued until the bars closed at 02:00 hours, then he would have been drinking for 8 hours and metabolized about 0.16 of BAC or 8 drinks. This would have to be added back into the equation in order to figure out how much he hypothetically drank that night. He would have drank 22 drinks over the 8-hour period in order to reach 0.420 plus the 8 drinks that he dispersed for a total consumption of 30 drinks, which equaled about 3.75 (3 to 4) alcoholic beverages per hour over the 8 hours that elapsed. That would have been 1 drink every 15 minutes for 8 hours without stopping.

The La Crosse County Medical Examiner told the La Crosse Tribune that a person who typically does not drink alcohol would probably be dead at a 0.42 BAC. He suggested that a person who drinks a lot and often would certainly have trouble walking and standing on his own two legs. That information was consistent with what we knew about that affects of alcohol poisoning. This level of inebriation is considered to be coma-inducing by some medical professionals and researchers. Thus, we believed that Jeff was either very close to being unconscious – if not fully unconscious – at the time he was supposedly walking toward the river. In light of the amount of alcohol in Jeff's system and the tracking paths of the bloodhound following his scent, we assessed that Jeff never could have walked to the Niedbalski Bridge. We concluded that he was abducted and driven to that location. We asserted, given his alcohol intoxicated state, that it was highly unlikely that he could have been able to walk the distance from downtown to the bridge.

Jeff's BAC was determined by testing his spleen – technically, it was not a BAC. This was done because there were no available specimens for blood, urine, or vitreous fluids according to the autopsy report. Apparently, there was not even enough blood in Jeff to retrieve a sample from an artery or vein, an internal organ, or muscle tissue. It was very possibly for there to be no urine in his body at death. He could have urinated before death or may have released his bowels during the death process. There was no reason for Jeff's body to not contain any blood, especially since he was not mummified due to a dry environment. The autopsy photographs displayed clearly showed how dry and bloodless everything was. It appeared as though his body had been exsanguinated (drained of its blood) by someone who was proficient enough to not only remove the blood, but to also remove the vitreous fluid from within both eyeballs.

Gilbertson spoke with two morticians and asked them how to remove the blood from a body. They stated that small incisions (about 2 inches) is made along the side of the neck next to the Right Common Carotid Artery and left Internal Jugular Vein. In Jeff's case, no such incision or other wound was described by the Medical Examiner who performed the autopsy. The removal of all fluids from Jeff had to have been done without making any noticeable marks that a forensic pathologist would have clearly observed and noted as suspicious in an autopsy report. Since no such remarks were entered into the autopsy report, we could not reach a conclusion as to how the fluids had been removed.

Perhaps, the absence of blood in Jeff's body can be better understood by recalling that lividity seemed to be in his shoulders and neck as the possible result of being placed in a head-down position (*Trendelenburg Position*). This position would have also facilitated drainage of the blood via his Right Common Carotid Artery and left Internal Jugular Vein. Furthermore, we wondered whether the bruising under Jeff's armpits and around his waist could explain his exsanguination. These bruises could not have come from his clothing. They appeared to be more like the result of grabbing, holding, or restraining. Were these the points at which the blood left his body? Exsanguination would also account for why Jeff did not have any recognizable lividity on his body.

There are typically three specimens that are used when calculating how much ethanol is in a body: Blood (BAC), which is the best way to test and returns 100%; Vitreous (VAC), which usually returns 90% of the blood level; and Urine (UAC), which is substantially higher and returns 130% of the blood level. In fact, we have argued that in order to get the

Comparative Relative Concentrations of Alcohol

SPECIMEN	CONCENTRATION
Urine	*1.30*
Whole Blood	*1.00*
Vitreous	*0.90*
Liver	*0.85*

Figure 13.10 The amount or level of ethanol naturally varies within a body. (From Spitz, W., & Spitz, D. (Eds.) (2006). *Spitz and Fisher's Medicolegal Investigation of Death* (4th ed.), Table XXIII, p. 1222. Springfield, IL: Charles C. Thomas.)

most accurate BAC level, the blood should be tested from 3 parts of the body and compared (i.e., the heart, the torso cavity, and a thigh muscle).

When taking into account that Jeff's ethanol level was calculated by using the spleen instead of his blood, one must recognize the Jeff's actual BAC would have been substantially higher (Figure 13.10; Spitz & Spitz, 2006). The spleen is the backup system for the liver, which usually returns 85% of the blood level. Everything filtered through the liver would be left in the spleen. If the liver had been used for calculating the amount of ethanol rather than the spleen, then the level would have been slightly higher than it was reported. Therefore, Jeff's actual "Blood" Alcohol Concentration (BAC) before being filtered through the liver and into the spleen would have been substantially higher than the 0.420 that he registered. Could it have been as high as 0.50 BAC? This fact further convinced us that Jeff did not, and could not have, walked anywhere in that state much less to the Niedbalski Bridge.

The standard drug tests requested by medical examiners during an autopsy include general "screens" that report a positive or negative hit when a substance is found to be present above a cutoff value. The screens search for the presence of broad classes of drugs: amphetamines, barbiturates, benzodiazepines, cannabinoids, cocaine and metabolites, methadone, opiates, phencyclidine (PCP), propoxyphene (e.g., Darvon), and salicylates (e.g., aspirin). The medical examiners often also ask for tests to determine volatiles: acetone, ethanol, methanol, isopropanol, n-propanol, and n-butanol on occasion. At the time of an autopsy, a medical examiner does not typically request toxicological tests that measure and report the precise amount of a specified substance in a sample (referred to as "quantitation"). Those extra tests can be expensive and impact an agencies budget if requested too often.

Four toxicology tests were performed in association with Jeff's autopsy (Figure 13.11). The first test was a standard drug screen and was performed using a liver specimen. It

Geesey: Toxicology Tests & Reports

TEST	SPECIMEN	REQUESTED	1st REPORT
1) Drug Screen	*Liver*	*May 25, 1999*	*July 7, 1999*
2) Volatile Screen	*Spleen*	*May 25, 1999*	*July 7, 1999*
3) Flunitrazepam - Quantitated	*Liver*	*May 26, 1999*	*June 16, 1999*
4) Gamma Hydroxybutyric Acid - Quantitated	*Liver*	*May 26, 1999*	*June 16, 1999*

NOTE: The Final Toxicology Report was issued on July 14, 1999.

Figure 13.11 Four separate toxicology tests were performed for Jeff Gessey's autopsy.

tested for the common drugs of abuse, except marijuana. The drug screen returned negative results, indicating that no drugs were present in Jeff's body. A second test was done using a spleen specimen to identify the volatiles (i.e., acetone, methanol, isopropanol, ethanol, and n-propanol). Only ethanol (drinking alcohol) came back with a reading (0.420 gm/dL). Some debate exists as to whether or not alcohol increases after death due to decomposition. There is plenty of support for the assertion of postmortem alcohol production (Athanaselis, Stefanidou, & Koutselinis, 2005; Canfield, Kupiec, & Huffine, 1993; Garriott, 1996; Gilliland & Bost, 1993; Heatley & Crane, 1990; Johnson, Lewis, Angier, & Vu, 2004; Kugelberg & Jones, 2007; Moriya & Hashimoto, 2004).

N-propanol is a colorless alcohol. It is a flammable liquid, toxic when inhaled, is a moderate skin irritant, and causes severe eye irritation. It is sometimes used as a solvent in pharmaceuticals. It is also an industrial solvent used in many consumer products. The research literature suggests that the neo-formation of ethanol after death may be indicated in blood by the presence of n-propanol at a proportion of 20:1 to 25:1 (Wigmore & Chow, 2000). As a body decomposes, it breaks down, ferments, and produces alcohols. These (specifically, ethanol and isopropanol) eventually break down as well and convert to acetone. After 43 days of decomposition at these temperatures, Jeff's body should have produced all of these substances.

Decomposition peaks and n-propanol were noted in the toxicology report for volatiles (dated July 7, 1999). However, acetone, methanol, and isopropanol returned negative findings. Since Jeff had an extraordinary amount of alcohol 0.420 gm/dL in his system, then he definitely had enough alcohol in his system to produce some amount of acetone, methanol, and isopropanol during the decomposition period. Since none of these chemicals were in his system, it more than confirmed the fact that Jeff was not deceased or in the water for the whole period of time that he was missing. It also suggested that the n-propanol in his system had to come from an external source.

Jeff's body was recovered on May 24th and autopsied right away. Samples of his liver and spleen were taken since no blood or vitreous was available. The standard screens were ordered the next day, May 25th (Figure 13.11, Tests 1 & 2). Typically, additional testing for specific substances is only ordered for two scenarios: (1) when medical examiners or law enforcement investigators have a reasonable suspicion that a crime occurred, or (2) the first set of screens indicated the presence of a class of drugs and they seek specific identification and quantitation of the substance. In this case, such suspicion must have existed since quantitation tests (Figure 13.11, Tests 3 & 4) were ordered for flunitrazepam and its metabolites (the date rape drug named Rohypnol – "roofies"), as well as for γ-hydroxybutyric acid or gamma-hydroxybutyrate (GHB). To request them so soon was an anomaly and most likely not an accident. Something at the autopsy must have convinced the Medical Examiner (Dr. Lindsey Thomas) to ask for those extra tests.

GHB is a naturally occurring substance in the human body that resembles the inhibitory neurotransmitter gamma-aminobutyric acid (GABA) that is found in the brain. Some evidence exists that it functions as a neuromodulator in the central nervous system of mammals. On the street, it is used as a debilitating drug to render victims helpless (Figure 13.12). It is also produced postmortem during decomposition. Research suggests that GHB at higher doses may slow the rate at which the human body eliminates ethanol (Vree, Damsma, van den Bogert, & van der Kleijn, 1978). Heavy drinking in conjunction with taking GHB has been associated with respiratory arrest (Einspruch & Clark, 1992).

The presence of GHB in a body is generally very minimal if at all. In Chapter 8 (Brinson), we established that postmortem urinary concentrations of GHB are typically

General Effects Associated with Gamma-Hydroxybutyrate (GHB)

CONCENTRATION	EFFECT
< 52 mcg/ml	*Wakefulness*
52 - 156 mcg/ml	*Light Sleep*
156 - 260 mcg/ml	*Moderate Sleep*
> 260 mcg/ml	*Deep Sleep/Coma*

NOTE: Terminal Half-Life of 18 to 60 minutes.

Figure 13.12 The toxicology report from the National Medical Services laboratory (dated June 16, 1999) included this information on how to interpret the GHB finding for Jeff Geesey.

less than 10 mcg with the majority of values less than 5 mcg. When the toxicology report for those two tests was released (June 16, 1999), it indicated that no flunitrazepam was present in Jeff's system. However, it also showed that he had been recovered with 130 mcg of GHB in his system.

Therefore, if acetone, ethanol, isopropanol, methanol, n-propanol, and GHB are all produced postmortem during decomposition, then all of them should have been found during toxicological testing. Only ethanol, n-propanol and GHB were found, which suggested that the larger portion of all three substances must have come from an exogenous (external) source rather than an endogenous (internal) source like decomposition. N-propanol is not harmful in small amounts. It is sometimes used to pre-dissolve the predatory drug GHB for use in an eye-dropper, which facilitates easy administration into a drink at a bar. The amount of GHB determines the level of incapacitation. Since Jeff had 130 mcg of GHB in his system and 156 mcg normally causes moderate sleep, then he was very close to being in a moderate sleep.

Combining Jeff's alcohol concentration level (0.420 gm/dL) with the amount of GHB in his system (130 mcg) makes it very unlikely that he walked any distance, much less the 3.8 miles south along the bloodhound track to the gravel pit where his body was recovered. The extremely high levels of both alcohol and GHB in Jeff's system at the time suggested that he was driven to those locations by his abductor(s). At the time of his transport, he was most likely unconscious, close to death, or already deceased due to respiratory and/or cardiac cessation. Furthermore, recalling that he had little to no blood in his system (as evidenced by the fact that the Medical Examiner could not collect a blood sample), he was most likely dead when he was entered into the Mississippi River.

Assuming that it would have taken at least 1/2 hour in Jeff's intoxicated condition to walk the distance to the gravel pit, and considering the very short half-life of GHB (18 minutes to 1 hour), it meant that Jeff's level of GHB could have easily been as high as 260 mcg 18 minutes earlier. This level would have bordered on a deep sleep or coma. And, this does not take into account the amount of alcohol in his system, which was also at a coma-inducing level. In fact, the level of GHB in Jeff's body could have been 520 mcg approximately 36 minutes earlier. This more than proves that Jeff did not walk anywhere in this inebriated state, rather, he was clearly abducted and transported.

Ocular Changes

Physical changes to the human eye following death can be used to some extent to determine the postmortem interval (i.e., the length of time since death). Textbooks and reference manuals generally present only the four postmortem artifacts concerning eyes (i.e., corneal film, corneal cloudiness, corneal opacity, and *taches noires sclérotiques*). These artifacts are associated with whether the eyelids were open or closed, the temperature and humidity of the environment, exposure to air, and time. A fifth artifact will be discussed herein (i.e., eyeball bloating due to decomposition gases).

There are three sequential, postmortem ocular artifacts: corneal film, corneal cloudiness, and corneal opacity (Shkrum & Ramsay, 2007). A thin film will appear over the cornea almost immediately when the eyes remain open at room temperature (68 °Fahrenheit). This is followed by corneal cloudiness, which can be visible to investigators as a milky white fog over the cornea within 2 hours or less after death. Next, a dense white coating over the cornea called corneal opacity can be seen as early as 2 hours and is generally established by at least 6 hours postmortem. If the eyes remain closed after death, then a film may not appear until about 6 to 12 hours. Cloudiness will take approximately 12 to 24 hours to appear, followed by opacity being completely established by 60 hours on land.

Taches noires sclérotiques is another possible postmortem ocular artifact. It appears as increasing shades of tan to brown across the portion of the sclera that was exposed to air due to an open eyelid. It begins immediately and is usually quite detectable by 6 hours postmortem. It is important to note that it does not affect the cornea. It is possible to have both corneal opacity and *tache noir.* If the deceased was found with his eyes closed and both corneal opacity and *tache noir* were present, then his eyes were initially open and someone or something closed the eyelids several hours after his death. *Tache noir* on a drowning victim is a red flag for investigators since it means that the deceased person died on dry land, remained there long enough for *tache noir* to develop, and was then dumped in the water.

There is one more postmortem phenomenon associated with the eyes that is often overlooked by investigators. A body will produce putrefactive gases as it decomposes. Very warm or cold environments (e.g., a dessert or polar region) tend to also be very dry or arid, which will slow decomposition and encourage mummification of a corpse. Warm environments with moderate to high humidity will speed decomposition and cause gases to be produced more quickly, which causes a body to bloat (i.e., the abdomen, scrotum, face, and eyes). Whereas, a decomposing eye in a dry or arid environment may shrivel and wrinkle as moisture evaporates, the eye may bloat or swell with fluid in a drowning scenario or damp environment. This is a condition of the whole eye and not a result of *tache noir.*

The Medical Examiner described Jeff's irides as dull brown and wrote that the pupils were indiscernible. There were no distinctive injuries to the conjunctiva. The body recovery and autopsy photographs showed that his eyelids were closed. Dullness of the irides with the eyelids closed denoted corneal opacity, which meant that Jeff had been deceased for a period of about 60 hours before entry into the water. Bloating of Jeff's eyes from decomposition gases was visible in the photographs, which suggested that he had been deceased between 72 and 96 hours.

FBI Report

A report was prepared for the La Crosse Police Department by an FBI Supervisory Special Agent from the Behavioral Analysis Unit 2 (BAU-2) at the National Center for the Analysis of Violent Crime (NCAVC). He was assisted by other members of the NCAVC. The final report was released in June 2007 and discussed in the local newspaper. Jeff's case was number 5 in that report. In his summary of the important times, locations, and events for this case, the Agent pointed out that Jeff's associates had left him at the bar because he would not leave with them. He also noted the fact that Jeff had been missing for 4 days (from April 11th to April 15th) before he was reported missing.

The agent reviewed the discoveries from an interview with Jeff's parents. Nothing was ever recorded in any document to explain the scars on Jeff's left forearm that had occurred less than 4 months earlier in January 1999. Law enforcement labeled these scars as the result of a suicide attempt. However, our conversation with Dr. Geesey disclosed that Jeff had not attempted suicide. Rather, he had turned to cutting himself as a way of dealing with certain issues. It was also learned that Jeff talked more about suicide when he drank. His parents also told authorities that Jeff had been drinking since he was 15 years old, and that he had been depressed because he had tried but could not stop. In addition, Jeff had been arrested for drinking and driving on two occasions, and once for public intoxication.

The report presented the 0.420 gm/dL alcohol concentration level in Jeff, but only mentioned the presence of GHB in his system. The report pointed out that the Medical Examiner who had performed the autopsy (Dr. Lindsey Thomas) had attributed the amount of GHB in Jeff to postmortem decomposition. The report presented that fact that the La Crosse County Medical Examiner (John Steers) had concluded that the cause of death was cold water drowning with acute alcohol intoxication. Yet, the report's author made no comment about the amount of GHB or the extent to which it may have contributed to Jeff's demise.

Although the case review had clearly illustrated a life tormented by alcohol abuse and an earlier suicide attempt, the report's author did not challenge the La Crosse County Medical Examiner's (John Steers) conclusion of an undetermined manner of death. Given the facts (i.e., that police had wrongly believed that Jeff had recently attempted suicide, that he had an on-going substance abuse problem, and that he was presumed to be exceptionally intoxicated on the night of April 10th–11th), the agent made no comment on, nor provided any opinion regarding, the apparent lack of concern for Jeff's well-being on the part of his associates. The review of Jeff's case concluded with the suggestion that, absent new leads, there was no reason to proceed with further investigation into his death.

Graffiti

The specific location and the types of graffiti found in Riverside Park by Professor Richard Geesey (Jeff's dad) were significant. It was found inside the pavilion at the north end of the park near the statue of Chief Hiawatha. The location was significant because other victims' personal possessions were recovered there and their scents had been tracked to the site or nearby (i.e., Nathan Kapfer & Jared Dion). The empirical fact that victims' property was repeatedly found in the same area of the park demonstrated a definite connection among the La Crosse victims that was more than just circumstantial or spurious. The specific nature of the graffiti demonstrated its relationship to those who were responsible for these deaths. These graffiti were also recovered at numerous other locations where victims had gone missing and drowned. A photo of one graffito was actually on a victim's cell phone with a phrase that signified the meaning of the graffito (i.e., Gerald Smith).

The relevance and value of these graffiti to the investigation and their meaning to those responsible for Jeff's abduction should not be overlooked. Jeff went missing in April 1999. Gannon and Duarte met Dr. Geesey in La Crosse on October 26, 2006 (Figure 13.13). He took them to the pavilion at that time and showed them the graffiti that he had found years

Figure 13.13 Gannon and Duarte met Dr. Geesey in La Crosse on October 26, 2006. He took them to the pavilion at that time and showed them the graffiti that he had found 7.5 years earlier (April 1999).

before (April 1999). It was still there 7.5 years later (October 2006). During the end of May 2007, just after the 8th anniversary of his son's death, Richard Geesey notified a local law enforcement agency that there were graffiti painted on a wall inside the pavilion that he believed were possibly connected to the murder of his son. He informed them that it was still there in the pavilion after 8 years.

A little over a week later (specifically, June 8, 2007), our team was back in La Crosse doing a follow-up. We stopped at the pavilion to find that not only had the graffiti been painted-over, but that the paint was still damp and we could smell it in the air. This suggested to us that the repainting of the pavilion had only recently occurred, perhaps within the previous few days. We photographed the spot on the wall where the original drawings had been in order to document that the area was now completely clear of any graffiti (Figure 13.14). Upon seeing that the graffiti had been painted over, Gannon remarked that he had always heard of detectives attempting to rejuvenate a case that was languishing in obscurity by putting a "fresh coat of paint" on it.

Figure 13.14 On June 8, 2007, after comparing the wall with photos taken in October 2006, Gannon indicated the precise spot on the wall where the significant graffiti had been just days before. The smell of fresh paint was in the air.

Figure 13.15 The team noted a new graffito during a trip to La Crosse on April 18, 2009. A pair of eyes now filled the blank space on the wall as if to say, "We're watching you!"

We are in no way or by no means suggesting that the law enforcement agency had anything to do with repainting of the pavilion and the destruction of what we considered to be important evidence. It may have finally come to the attention of the parks department after nearly 8 years without fresh paint. A similar circumstance occurred in a case near Chicago. A smiley face graffito had been painted on the cut-off stub of a large tree branch. After it was pointed out to law enforcement by a news reporter, the graffito disappeared along with about 2 inches of the remaining cut-off stub.

Subsequently, a new graffito was painted where the old graffiti had been. During our visit to La Crosse to meet with the Homan family (April 18, 2009), we photographed the new graffito as well (Figure 13.15). The graffito told us that the group was letting us know that they were not only aware of what was going on at this location and were watching it, but that they were probably watching the authorities and us as well. This same graffito was still there 4 years later when we were there again on June 18, 2013.

Conclusion

We believe that the forensic evidence and investigative information concerning the disappearance of Jeffrey Geesey clearly proved that he was drugged, abducted, held for a period of time, murdered, and then placed into the Mississippi River.

The coma-inducing level of alcohol in Jeff's body (0.420 gm/dL) proved that he could not have walked anywhere. To be at that level of alcohol intoxication and found in the river meant that he would have been chugging down alcoholic beverages while either standing in the river or right next to it. In light of the fact that the level of ethanol alcohol in his body was calculated using a sample from his spleen, his true "BAC" would have been much higher. This confirmed that Jeff did not walk anywhere, not to Riverside Park, not to Niedbalski Bridge, and not to the gravel pit in Shelby.

If the GHB and n-propanol in Jeff's system had been caused by endogenous means or through decomposition as stated by the La Crosse County Medical Examiner, then some of the alcohol (i.e., ethanol) in his body must have been caused by decomposition as well. If some of the ethanol was produced during the 43 days that Jeff was presumed to be in the water, then the other volatiles (i.e., isopropanol, methanol, & acetone) should have been produced and present too. Since there was no postmortem production of the other volatiles in Jeff's body, then there was no postmortem production of either GHB or n-propanol. Therefore, the presence of both GHB and n-propanol in Jeff's body lent credence to the hypothesis that he was drugged. In all likelihood, the n-propanol was used to dissolve the predatory GHB in order for it to be more easily administered into a bar drink by means of an eye-dropper.

Once a victim is under the influence of GHB, he is basically a walking zombie who will do almost anything he is directed to do, including walking across an icy body of water like the Mississippi River. Since GHB robs a mind of its short term memory, a person can be at one place one minute, and then suddenly realize that he is someplace else with no recollection of how he got there. He may then black out again and wake up in the Mississippi River swimming for his life (i.e., like Cullen Fortney) or walking across the icy river (i.e., like Craig Meyers). At that point in time and space, he blacks out again and continues walking until the ice breaks. Whereon, he is unable to escape the freezing river and drowns. The case becomes a tragic accident and is quickly closed by the medical examiner and local police. This also seems to have been the case in a few other deaths that we have researched in the USA and in Canada.

Having succumbed to the affects of GHB, why then would a person not continue to drink when someone hands him a bottle of liquor? Could this have happened to Nathan Kapfer a year earlier who was completely sober at bar closing time, or to Jeffrey Gessey whose actual alcohol level was above comatose? Since Jeff was drugged and held for over 30 days before being entered into the Mississippi River, was it not possible that he was given alcohol while under the influence of GHB? Was he forced to drink excessive amounts of alcohol in order to increase his BAC, such that it made his death appear to be an accident and therefore easier for the authorities to write off as such?

Since we knew that Jeff could not have walked anywhere at that level of intoxication, then the expertise of the bloodhound was crucial. The tracking K-9's discoveries showed that Jeff was not only driven to the location where he was eventually recovered, but that he was placed into the water by someone who probably left the area with Jeff's scent on him. The bloodhound's abilities and the extent of its proficiency at tracking were not only confirmed by those in attendance (i.e., family members and friends), but specifically by La Crosse Fire Department personnel who were present and their subsequent statements made to the La Crosse Tribune.

Contradictions were plenty in this case. The tracking ability of the K-9 was firmly established. However, the dog tracked Jeff's scent to locations that did not coincide with witness statements. The 3 young men (whom Jeff met for the first time that night) were assertive that he was in the Club Millennium. Yet, the dog did not confirm those statements and indicated that he had been all over the inside of The Library bar. Furthermore, his scent was followed into a building and to apartments that he had no reason to be in, as well as inside 2 vehicles within which he had no reason to be. Were these scent hits indicative of his presence or a transfer scent? Jeff's scent was also detected a block away in a parking ramp. Since the dog hit on vomitus there, that was not a transfer scent. What was Jeff doing that night in the parking ramp by the Holiday Inn? Relative to the downtown area, how did his scent get into and through Shooter's bar? This was reminiscent of the bloodhound track in Nathan Kapfer's case.

Regarding the bloodhound tracking, if the tracks were accurate, then Jeff did not remain next to the river. The dog tracked him to Niedbalski Bridge and then back inland to the main road south near Gunderson Lutheran Hospital. That meant that he did not fall into the Mississippi River at Niedbalski Bridge. Since we knew that he could not have physically walked from Niedbalski Bridge to the gravel pit in his intoxicated state, then that meant that he had to have been transported by someone else. Either that, or he did not go into the river that night. Simply put, then, he did not die of an accidental fall into the river on the night of April 10–11, 1999.

The condition of Jeff's body cannot be overlooked. Clearly, it was not in the Mississippi River for the period of time that he was missing. Lividity was indiscernible, perhaps, partially due to the fact that his body had been exsanguinated. It was unusual that the Medical Examiner did not describe rigidity in the autopsy report. However, the recovery and autopsy photos, as well as witness statements, indicated that Jeff was still in rigor at recovery and most likely at autopsy. Discoloration due to decomposition, skin slippage and degloving of the hands and feet, minimal bloating (i.e., present in the abdomen, but marginal in the scrotum), along with a general absence of marbling, all suggested that Jeff had been deceased and in the water for no more than about 5 days. That meant that approximately 38 days were unaccounted for when he was missing.

The obvious answer was that he had been abducted and held before being murdered. If Jeff was not in the water for 30+ days, then obviously he was abducted and held somewhere either alive or dead before his entry into the water (i.e., frozen & preserved like Nathan Kapfer). We believe that Jeff's death was painless and that he went without a fight. He was probably not even aware of what was happening to him. The light weight of his lungs, the minimal build-up of fluid in his cavities and sacs (pleural, pericardial, & peritoneal), in combination with his extreme level of intoxication, as well as the absence of blood and vitreous fluid from his body, all suggested that he was unconscious – if not already deceased – when he was entered into the river. The Geesey family deserves a more thorough investigation into his murder. The FBI needs to take another look at this case.

Jared Phillip Dion*

14

March 7, 1983–April 15, 2004

Background

Jared Dion was the fifth young man to die in a series of suspicious drownings that occurred over a 7 year period (1997 to 2004) in the City of La Crosse, Wisconsin. He was a sophomore at the University of Wisconsin-La Crosse and majored in marketing. He was also a star wrestler and in excellent physical shape. Although his hometown was Pewaukee (Wisconsin), Jared attended Arrowhead Union High School in nearby Hartland. Jared was the captain of the high school wrestling team and was a State Runner-Up in the 135 pound weight class in 2000. Matthew Kruziki was from Hartland and on the same varsity wrestling team with Jared. Matthew was recovered deceased in March 2006 from the Mississippi River in East Dubuque, Illinois. Lucas Homan (the next chapter) lived just 15 miles down the road from Hartland in the town of Brookfield. He was recovered from the Mississippi River in La Crosse during October 2006. Mark Wegener, a 2009 Arrowhead Union alumnus, mysteriously died in May 2011 in Whitewater. Benjamin Fuder, a 2009 Edgerton High School graduate attending the University of Wisconsin-Whitewater, was found deceased in July 2012 at the same location as Wegener. Possible linkages or spurious relationships?

Jared's body was autopsied by Dr. Lindsey Thomas from the Minnesota Regional Medical Examiner's Office (MRMEO) in Hastings at 13:00 hours on Thursday, April 15, 2004. She indicated that the cause of death was freshwater drowning and noted acute alcohol intoxication. She provided no diagnosis for a manner of death. An official finding of "undetermined" was recorded by John Steers, the La Crosse County Medical Examiner (LCCME), as the manner of death for Jared. The LCCME stipulated the cause of death to be freshwater drowning with alcohol intoxication. The date and time of death was recorded as 07:30 hours on April 15, 2004. It is about 115 to 140 miles from La Crosse to Hastings, and

* Photo courtesy of his mother, Kim Dion.

takes about 2.5 hours to drive the distance at the posted speed limits. Jared was recovered from the water at about 07:50 hours on April 15th and autopsied approximately 5 hours later at 13:00 hours on the same day.

After Jared's death, the police orchestrated and held a special meeting for local students (April 22, 2004) to discuss the river drownings with a panel of university officials, La Crosse police officers, Wisconsin Division of Criminal Investigation (DCI) officers, and other local stakeholders who were addressing the issue. This meeting also included the area media corps, as well as family and friends of the victims. During that meeting, officials stressed the importance of personal responsibility with regard to drinking and safety. They assured the community that a serial killer was not on the loose, rather youthful male bravado and irresponsible binge drinking were the cause of area drownings.

This message was repeated two more times. One attempt to assuage public fears was in an open letter to the "Campus Connection" that was jointly written by two University of Wisconsin-La Crosse professors. In that letter, the professors stated that they were 99.9 percent sure that the cause of the drowning deaths was not a serial killer (Morgan & Vogt, 2004). Rather, they sought to convince readers that these deaths were unfortunate accidents fueled by alcohol binge drinking. Another effort to reassure the local community that the deaths were not the work of a serial killer was posted at the LCCME's department website in November 2005. John Steers started work on the 20-slide PowerPoint presentation on April 25, 2004, shortly after Jared's body was recovered. On the closing slide, the author attributed the drowning deaths of the young men in La Crosse to a killer named "Al Cohol" (Steers, 2004).

Circumstances

Last Seen

Jared Phillip Dion was a White male, 21 years old at the time of his disappearance, 5 feet 9 inches, 172 pounds (Body Mass Index: 29.40), reddish-brown hair and hazel eyes. Jared started wrestling in the 1st Grade. He placed second at State during his junior year at Arrowhead High School in Hartland. A terrible case of Mononucleosis adversely impacted his promising senior year. Jared weighed in at 164 pounds as a freshmen at the University of Wisconsin-La Crosse. He got a chance to wrestle the 1st and 2nd place State High School Champs and beat them both; proving to himself that he was a champ (Figure 14.1). His mom (Kim) said they never doubted him. Jared never missed a day of running in the morning, followed by wrestling practice and weights after class. With all that, he maintained a 3.5 GPA with hopes of going into law.

He was last seen near John's bar (Figure 14.2). The day (April 9, 2004) started out at 08:30 hours with Jared speaking to his mother (Kim Dion) by phone about coming to the university the next day (Saturday, April 10th) and about making plans for the upcoming Easter weekend. At 21:00 hours, he spoke with his girlfriend about going out with some friends. Around 23:30 hours, Jared and a group of friends went to the downtown bar district around 3rd Street North. At bar closing time, he and a male friend (hereafter, Mitch) were standing outside of John's bar (109 3rd Street North) waiting to catch a free ride back to campus on the Safe Ride bus. Mitch verbally objected to Jared's suggestion that they try to get one more drink. Mitch stayed on the bus, and he thought that Jared was there with him. As the bus pulled away from the curb, he looked back and Jared was not there. So, the last time that Mitch saw Jared alive was around 02:20 hours on Saturday, April 10, 2004.

Figure 14.1 Jared Dion was a champion in life, both athletically and academically. He weighed in at 164 pounds at the University of Wisconsin-La Crosse and maintained a 3.5 GPA. (Photo courtesy of his mother, Kim Dion.)

Figure 14.2 Jared Dion was last seen alive on April 10, 2004, at John's bar in La Crosse.

The Safe Ride bus was provided by the University of Wisconsin-La Crosse to make sure that those students who went downtown to the bar district got back to campus safely. That night, Jared skipped the bus and went back inside John's bar right at closing time. A member of the band that was playing there that night observed him speaking to a person with blonde hair. The band member could not distinguish whether the individual was a male or a female. Jared had mentioned to a band member that he was going to an after-hours party, but did not specify where that party was being held.

Recovery

Jared's body was recovered from the Mississippi River on Thursday, April 15, 2004. It had been located by tracking the global positioning system (GPS) data from his cell phone. The police had used thermal imaging to search the parks and surrounding areas, but found no trace of Jared. His body was found by the La Crosse Dive and Rescue Team and the La Crosse Fire Department about 07:50 hours. Reports at the time stated that Jared was

Figure 14.3 Jared Dion's body was recovered on April 15, 2004 (*Red Arrow*), near the Courtyard by Marriott Hotel in La Crosse. His Boston Red Sox baseball cap was found near the statue of Chief Hiawatha (*Yellow Arrow*) in Riverside Park (*Green Arrow*).

recovered by Riverside Park. The LCCME report offered an address of 99 State Street, which was probably a generic address for Riverside Park and was actually the nearest road intersection about 300 yards from the river's edge (State Street & Front Street at Harborview Plaza). Onsite interviews that were conducted by Gannon and Gilbertson separately on different occasions suggested that Jared had been recovered near 322 Front Street South (Figure 14.3, *Red Arrow*; geodecimal coordinates 43.81030, –91.25805).

Jared's body recovery site was within a stone's throw of where Craig Meyers' body was recovered in February 2010. Meyers' recovery location was listed as near the Courtyard by Marriott Hotel (500 Front Street South), but it was actually right next to the pier (i.e., at the top of the *Red Arrow* in Figure 14.3). This was reminiscent of McNeil and Andrews in New York City (Chapters 2 and 3), wherein, two young men were found a year apart and within yards of each other.

Analysis of Evidence

Recovery Location

There are 6 principles when it comes to bodies in water (Armstrong & Erskine, 2011; Hendrick, Zaferes, & Nelson, 2003).

1. When a living human enters the water and then perishes, the body may float a short distance on the surface before it sinks to the bottom as a result of a current or surface winds. As the body sinks vertically, it will travel some horizontal distance relative to the speed of the current (a.k.a., *Body Drop Rate*). A human body sinks in fresh water at about 2 to 2.5 feet per second, and at approximately 1.5 to 2 feet per second in salt water.
2. Once a body is on the bottom, it will not move unless it is in a turbulent location like next to a dam, in river rapids, or in a pounding surf.
3. As a body begins to decompose and bloat with gases, it will rise slightly off the bottom and may be carried along by underwater currents. This may cause "travel

abrasions" on the anterior portion of the body (i.e., nose, forehead, eyebrows, knees, elbows, and back of hands and feet) before it resurfaces.

4. The greatest distance that a body may travel will occur after it has bloated from decomposition gases and resurfaced. Like an unsecured buoy, a body will float freely at the speed of the current or surface winds until it becomes snagged on a tree, dock, or other obstruction in the water.
5. If a body bursts after resurfacing or the gases escape by some other means, then it may sink again to the bottom never to return.
6. When a deceased human enters the water, the body will typically not sink and remain afloat. If it does sink, then it will usually refloat more quickly. This phenomenon is related to the length of time that the person was deceased on-land and the extent to which decomposition has occurred and gases produced in the body. The longer the dead body was on land, the greater the decomposition and the greater the likelihood that it will not sink. The shorter the time between death and entry into the water, then the greater the likelihood that the body will sink (like Luke Homan in Chapter 15).

Jared's body was found in the Mississippi River about 30 feet from shore. Officials commented that it was likely that he had not drifted very far from where he fell into the river. In fact, the La Crosse County Medical Examiner (LCCME) proposed that the body only drifted 75 yards from the point where it entered the water. Officials also suggested that even a seasoned and physically conditioned swimmer would experience difficulty making it to shore since the river was about 18 feet deep in that spot and the current was rather swift. Jared was a decent swimmer, but he was intoxicated and the water was cold. The environment and circumstances worked against him.

We could not agree more with the LCCME regarding the estimated location of water entry. Either Jared sank right where he went into the river or he swam a short distance before succumbing to the cold water and treacherous current. As will be thoroughly discussed, he was not missing long enough and the environment was not warm enough to sufficiently decompose his body and cause it to bloat, resurface, and float. The LCCME was correct in his assessment, Jared went into the river near where he was recovered. We assert that Jared did not enter the river up near the statue of Chief Hiawatha where his baseball cap was discovered. His body did not sink, bloat, and resurface at the north end of Riverside Park, and then float south down the Mississippi River.

This is why it is so important to collect samples of the material found on the bottom of a body of water at various locations. One reason centers on using the bottom samples as laboratory controls in identifying the possible source of evidence found on a body. By comparing the bottom samples with material found on a body, an investigator may determine whether or not an item of interest (e.g., a white fiber) came from the bottom of a body of water or from an external source like a carpet or pet (Becker, 2000).

Relative to the investigation of drownings, we recommend that samples should initially be taken at any suspected or potential water entry points, and specifically near all locations where evidence was discovered on land. For example, in this case, since Jared's property was found near the statue of Chief Hiawatha, then bottom samples should be collected from both the Black River and the Mississippi River near the statue. Absent these types of sites, samples should be taken at regular intervals along the bottom of the body of water to the left and right of the point along the body of water that is nearest to the last seen or known location of the missing person. Samples from the body of water and the material on a victim's clothing should be analyzed to see whether and to what extent they match. This process will aid in identifying a possible water entry point, as well as points of contact with the bottom of the body of water.

Recovered Property

Jared was last seen on Saturday, April 10, 2004. On Wednesday, April 14th (4 days later), an individual jogging in Riverside Park discovered Jared's Boston Red Sox baseball cap hanging neatly on a pole near the statue of Chief Hiawatha (Figure 14.4). Local law enforcement told Gannon and Duarte that a jogger had found the cap and placed it on the pole. However, the runner stated that he had heard local television news report descriptions of the baseball cap owned by the missing young man. While he was out jogging in Riverside Park, he came across such a cap that had been left hanging on a pole as though someone wanted it to be found. The man declared that he ran by this location everyday, but only noticed the hat hanging there on the fourth day after Jared went missing. A subsequent search of the whole park was conducted with specially trained dogs and no additional evidence was found.

This was a part of the overall pattern in the cases that we have examined. The police would conduct a thorough search of the area using dogs, human searchers, and sometimes infrared. They would find nothing. Then quite often, items of property belonging to the victim would be discovered the next day in those areas that had been previously searched. Items of personal property were routinely recovered near the statue of Chief Hiawatha in the La Crosse cases. Another quality was that the property was usually found as though displayed, that is, neatly folded or arranged and placed in plain sight. This characteristic is typically associated with a sober person, and not someone who is intoxicated beyond a 0.08 BAC. It is also a trait that indicates an organized offender taunting authorities.

Figure 14.4 Jared Dion's Boston Red Sox baseball cap was found by a jogger 4 days after he went missing (April 14, 2004) near the statue of Chief Hiawatha in Riverside Park.

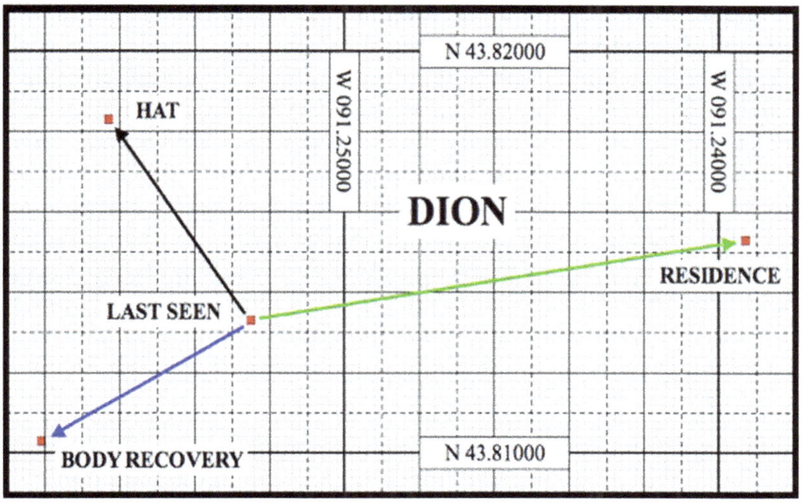

Figure 14.5 Three directions of interest for Jared Dion: his route to return to his apartment (*Green Arrow*), an evidence trail along which personal property was recovered (*Black Arrow*), and the direction in which his body was recovered (*Blue Arrow*).

Evidence Trails

The three directions of interest were inconsistent with each other (Figure 14.5): the direction to return to his apartment (*Green Arrow*), the direction of recovered personal property as an evidence trail (*Black Arrow*), and the direction of Jared's final body recovery (*Blue Arrow*). One would expect the evidence trail for personal property to lead in either the direction of home or the direction of the body recovery. Taking into account that the young man was intoxicated and may have been confused (even though he had walked home in the right direction hundreds of times before), one would at least expect the personal property trail to lead toward where the body was recovered. However, we were not surprised to learn that the three directions of interest were pointing in different directions just like many of the cases that we have investigated (e.g., Chapter 4). in fact, this is one of the patterns in the cases.

Witnesses

A witness statement made by a band member stated that he had last seen Jared speaking or leaving with a person with blonde hair. He did not know whether it was a male or female. It was not unlike Jared to be talking to someone, even a stranger. A friend of his stated that Jared was very social and was never alone. However, it was also very uncharacteristic for him to go off alone and not let someone know where he was going. Furthermore, the Dion family received an unsolicited letter on February 23, 2008. This was two months before Gannon and Duarte appeared on *Good Morning America* (GMA) and presented the idea of linked homicides, which the media labeled the "smiley face" cases. The letter to the Dions stated:

> *Dear Bryan and Kim Dion,*
>
> *This has taken me a lot of guts to write this letter. What has happened to your son has haunted me for years. I even told some of the La Crosse police officers on the street, but because I was a*

collage [sic] student at the time, my word meant nothing. I said something to my friends, and they told me I did all I could and that is all I can do.

The night that your son disappeared, I was walking home from work going home. By the Dell's Bar on third [sic] and Vine Street walking east home. By the courthouse on the bench was your son all passed out from drinking. There were a few people 7 or ten people that looked in there [sic] young 20's. They picked your son up and I watched them for a block as they carried him towards Riverside Park. I did not think about it at the time that this was going to happen. I thought they all knew one another and for the fact that there was one of me and more of them. I also did not say one word to them. After the one block, I turned around and continued walking home in the opposite direction they were heading. It did not dawn in my head until I heard the news and has haunted me quite bad since. I now there is nothing I can do. This is the only way I think I can get this off my conscious and bring peace that the truth be told.

Sincerely,
Someone who cares and hope the world one day has peace.

A short time after appearing on GMA (April 28, 2008), Gannon was asked to call Bryan Dion regarding Jared's case. He spoke with Bryan who told him about the letter that he received from someone who claimed to have seen a group of individuals carrying his son away. It sounded like a great break in the case, and Gannon reminded him that we might get all kinds of tips like this since we just went on national television and referred to these cases as murders rather than as accidents. Gannon remarked that had Bryan received the letter before we went on television, then that would give it more credence or validity. Bryan then informed Gannon that he did get the letter before we went on television. In fact, Bryan received it over two months earlier on February 23, 2008.

Rigidity

Rigidity (*rigor mortis*) is the stiffening of the body after death due to the disappearance of adenosine triphosphate (ATP) from the muscle tissues. It becomes detectable within 2 to 4 hours after death. In the water, rigidity normally begins to disappear after about 48 hours after death and is completely gone in the average individual within 72 hours. Rigidity progresses from the head to the feet and is first noticed in the neck and jaw (Geberth, 2006). Naturally, larger muscles present with rigidity last and are also the last from which rigor relents.

Jared was last seen by his friend at around 02:20 hours on April 10, 2004. His body was recovered at about 07:54 hours on April 15, 2004. He was supposedly in the river the whole time. Thus, Jared was presumed to be deceased and immersed in water for approximately 5 days 5 hours 30 minutes (125.5 hours). His body was autopsied by Dr. Lindsey Thomas about 5 hours 10 minutes (5.2 hours) after being recovered from the Mississippi River near La Crosse and transported to Hastings, Minnesota. This meant that he had been missing and presumed dead for a total of 5 days 10 hours 40 minutes (130.7 hours).

At the start of Jared's autopsy, Dr. Thomas assessed the quality of rigidity as developed. She did not offer any discussion of which muscle(s) presented with rigor and which did not. Having read this kind of description in other autopsy reports and clearly knowing the extent of rigor, we surmised in this case that her narrative meant rigidity was still present in Jared's legs and arms, and probably still in his neck and jaw. Since rigidity subsides within the average male individual by about 72 hours postmortem in water, and Jared was

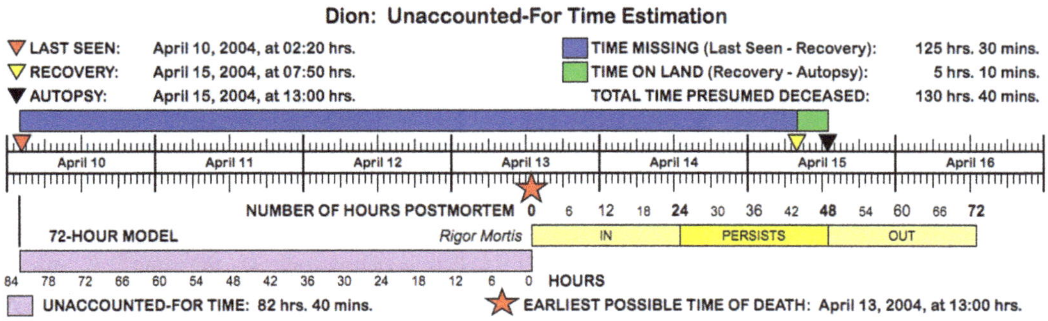

Figure 14.6 Jared Dion's body was still in rigor at the time of autopsy and no mention was made that it was relenting. That meant that he could not have been dead for any longer than about 72 hours, and most likely not much more than 48 hours.

missing and presumed deceased for nearly 130.7 hours, then why was his body still in rigor some 50 plus hours after it should have relented (Figure 14.6)?

The only reasonable explanation for this anomaly was that Jared could not have entered the water on the night of April 10, 2004. In fact, it meant that he could not have entered the water until sometime after 13:00 hours on April 13th. Even if the timeline for rigidity was pushed back a full 72 hours so that rigor was just about to completely relent at autopsy, then Jared still would not have died any earlier than about 13:00 hours on April 12th. This left approximately 58 to 83 hours (58 hours 40 minutes to 82 hours 40 minutes) of unaccounted-for time between when Jared was last seen and when he died.

Body Position and Lividity

Lividity (*livor mortis*) is the postmortem discoloration of a body due to gravitation of the blood into the dependent capillaries and veins at the lowest point in a body (Spitz & Spitz, 2006). Lividity begins within about 30 minutes after death and becomes "fixed" within 10 to 12 hours. Fixed means that the blood has settled in one position and can no longer be significantly shifted by changing the position of the body. In drownings, lividity is usually fixed and anterior since bodies almost always float in a prone position (face-down).

When lividity is described as "diffusely present," it means that there is detectable lividity in more than one part of the deceased's body. The only way for there to be lividity in multiple parts of a body is for it to be moved or rolled on a regular basis after death during the first 12 hours. When this happens, the blood does not completely settle to any one side of the body. We have seen some cases where victims were recovered on their backs and diffuse lividity could be explained. That was usually when the bodies were recovered from the torrent of flood waters, rivers with swift currents, oceans with breaking surfs or waves, or the body was trapped near the strainer or base of a dam. It is generally a phenomenon that is more often associated with obese persons, which was obviously not the case with Jared.

We have also repeatedly seen diffuse lividity, and inconsistent lividity, while examining these drowning cases. It is clearly a characteristic of the "smiley face" homicides. Jared was described as presenting with mostly fixed anterior lividity, but it was also partially detectable in other parts of his body. That meant that he had to have been moved from a prone position sometime around the 10th hour after death in order for the blood to shift to other positions. In this situation, in order for lividity to be fixed and anterior meant that

Jared was either floating face down or laying face down on land for about 10 hours. Since lividity was diffusely present (on other parts of his body), that meant that Jared had to have been flipped over to his back for a period of time.

Ocular Changes

Changes to the eye after death can be used to determine the length of time since death and should always be considered as approximations. Postmortem ocular changes can tell an investigator whether or not the deceased person's eyes were open or closed and exposed to air (Shkrum & Ramsay, 2007). There are three ocular changes worthy of noting: corneal film, corneal cloudiness, and corneal opacity. Obviously, these are important postmortem artifacts when it comes to a drowning case. An additional artifact of the eye is petechial hemorrhages (i.e., ruptures of the small blood vessels) in the sclera or conjunctivae, which usually mean that death was caused by strangulation.

Unfortunately, there was no mention as to whether Jared's eyes were open or closed, whether there was a film or cloudiness on the cornea or sclera, or whether there was any indication of ocular opacity. The Medical Examiner did, however, described the color of the irides as hazel and assess both pupils at 6 millimeters (mm) or about 1/4 inch. She also reported that blue-tinted soft contact lenses were on each eye. This told us that the pupils were dilated and that the eyes were closed. It also told us that a film, cloudiness, or opacity probably did not impair her ability to assess the condition of Jared's eyes.

The size of the pupils is regulated by the iris as it reacts to the amount of incoming light. It behaves like an electronic light meter that regulates the aperture on a camera (i.e., adjusting the f-stop). Since the stiffening of the muscles during rigor contributes to the dilation of the pupils, this postmortem artifact corroborates our assessment that rigor had not yet started to relent. Also, the fact that the contact lenses had not washed out of Jared's eyes only suggested that his eyelids had remained shut after entering the water.

Injuries

Injuries to Jared's hands and body were minimal. On his hands, only his right hand showed signs of damage (Figure 14.7). He presented with two small areas where the epidermis had

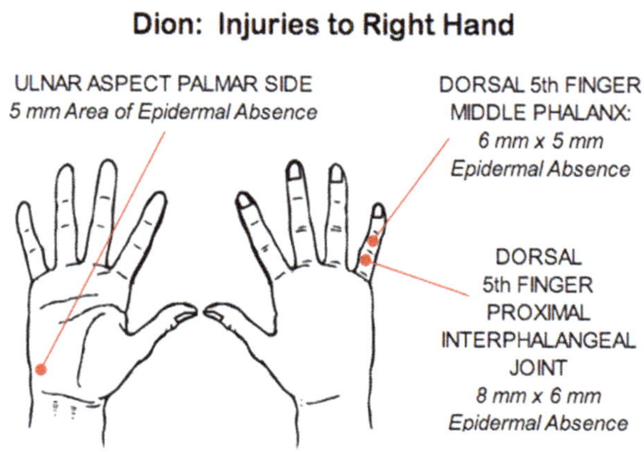

Figure 14.7 Although the injuries to Jared Dion's hands were minimal, they may not have been the result of an accidental fall.

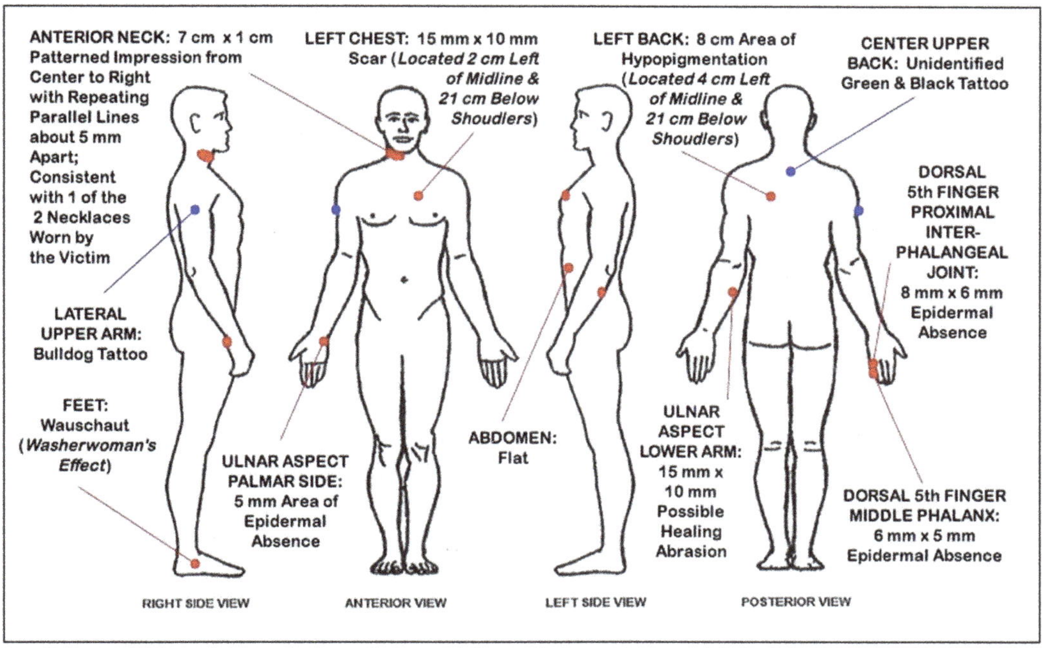

Figure 14.8 Jared Dion's body at autopsy; the artist rendition is from observations of autopsy photographs and reports.

recently been removed from the 5th finger (little finger). One was 8 mm by 6 mm (5/16 inch × 4/16 inch) on the proximal interphalangeal joint, which is the second knuckle next to the hand. The other was 6 mm by 5 mm (4/16 inch × 3/16 inch) over the middle phalanx (the area between the second and third knuckles). On the palmar side of the right hand at the ulnar aspect (the side opposite the thumb), Jared had a 5 mm area of missing epidermis. On the opposite side of his body, there were no wounds on his left hand. However, he had sustained an injury to the ulnar aspect of his left forearm that was about 80 mm (3-1/8 inches) below his elbow (Figure 14.8). The Medical Examiner identified it as possibly being an abrasion that was healing and measured it at 15 mm by 10 mm (9/16 × 6/16 inch).

There were also several blemishes that could not be identified by the Medical Examiner as old scars or as new postmortem artifacts. One of those marks was described as a linear area of hypopigmentation that was 80 mm in length (3-1/8 inches). It was located in the left mid-back about 40 mm (1-1/2 inches) from the midline and 210 mm (8-1/4 inches) below the shoulder line. Hypopigmentation is the change in a person's skin color that is usually caused by a genetic condition or increased exposure to sunlight. It may also be caused by various drugs, including some antibiotics, antiarrhythmics (used for defibulation), and anti-malaria. This mark was quite suspicious since the Medical Examiner could not determine whether it was a pre-existing condition (antemortem), sustained during the death process, or developed after death (postmortem). Could this subcutaneous lack of color in the skin of the mid back have been caused by a person kneeling on Jared in order to hold him down while attempting to drown him?

Oddly, there was another mark almost perfectly opposite the hypopigmentation. On Jared's chest, about 20 mm (3/4 inch) from the midline and 210 mm (8-1/4 inches) below the shoulder line, was a 15 mm by 10 mm scar (9/16 × 6/16 inch). The Medical Examiner also examined Jared's wrists and elbow regions. She reported that no marks were present on the antecubital fossae (inside bend at the elbows) or on either wrist, which suggested there was no indication that any type of binding of the arms had occurred.

Arguably, the wounds to Jared's right hand and left forearm could have come from stumbling and falling to the ground or upon rocks. We assert that they could have been acquired during a fist fight. In particular, the injury to the right palm and to the ulnar aspect of the left forearm resembled possible defensive wounds. Furthermore, the injury on the left forearm was the same size as the mark on Jared's left chest (i.e., 15 mm × 10 mm). When the left arm is raised to block and protect the face, then the placement of the wound on the left forearm aligned with the mark on the chest.

One final mark on Jared's body that was suspicious was on his neck. It was described as an impression being on the front of the neck, beginning in the center and running to the right. The mark was measured at 10 mm in height by 70 mm in length (approximately 6/16 × 2-3/4 inches) with repeating parallel lines about 5 mm apart (3/16 inch). The Medical Examiner suggested that the mark's pattern matched 1 of the 2 necklaces that Jared was wearing. Having not seen the necklaces that he was wearing when he was recovered from the river, we could not confirm or deny her assessment. However, based on our analysis of other postmortem artifacts, we did not believe that the mark was evidence of a ligature.

Decomposition and Maceration

Decomposition is a process of dissolution of the body as a result of bacterial putrefaction and enzymatic autolysis. After death, the bacteria in the gastrointestinal tract invade the vascular system and spread throughout the body causing decay (Shkrum & Ramsay, 2007). As the putrefaction process advances and the micro-organisms continue to grow in number, the body will begin to swell from the gases that are produced and the body will become discolored (Spitz & Spitz, 2006). Hemolysis and hydrogen sulfide gas production cause the bluish-green to dark green discoloration that shows up as part of decomposition (Shkrum & Ramsay, 2007). It starts in the Right Lower Quadrant (RLQ) and then the Left Lower Quadrant (LLQ), and takes about 24 hours to appear in water. Green discoloration of the entire body takes approximately 48 hours in water.

"Marbling" is the next stage and typically appears around 72 to 96 hours postmortem in water with colors ranging from dark yellow to orange to dark red. A classic appearance of marbling is the dark purple veins below the skin surface. Coinciding in time with marbling is bloating. When a body begins to bloat, it can be seen first in the scrotum, then the abdomen, face and eyes. By 96 hours after death in water, a body will show signs of fluid purging around orifices (Spitz & Spitz, 2006).

Maceration is the coming apart of a corpse and occurs in stages. As a body decays, it will lose skin and hair, then mass, and then bones. In water, skin will start to come loose from a body ("skin slippage") after about 48 to 96 hours postmortem and should be apparent over major portions of a body by 96 to 168 hours postmortem (Armstrong & Erskine, 2011). The scalp will typically lose hair during this time too. The skin on the palms of the hands and soles of the feet will shed as well ("degloving"). The onset of degloving of exposed skin typically occurs at about 72 to 96 hours, with completion around 144 to 168 hours after death. The extent of decomposition relative to time varies depending on the environmental temperature, amount of clothing worn by the deceased, the proportion of fatty tissue relative to the size of the body, and so forth (Geberth, 2006).

Although Dr. Thomas examined and described portions of Jared's body at the beginning of the autopsy, she made little mention of putrefaction or maceration characteristics normally associated with 130 hours after death. She described the overall appearance as free of distinctive color changes. She reported the absence of the bluish color of the skin (i.e., cyanosis), as well as the yellowing of the whites of the eyes, skin, and mucous membranes (i.e., jaundice). The Medical Examiner reported the color of the irides and the size of the pupils, but made no mention of ocular changes. She illustrated the genitalia, particularly the testes, without mention of bloating of the scrotum. The abdomen was described succinctly as flat. She stated that the feet presented with Wauschaut Effect (*Washerwoman's Hands*), but did not comment on whether the hands showed a similar condition.

We assert that she made no mention of certain decomposition artifacts because they were not present. A total of 5 days 10 hours 40 minutes (130.7 hours) elapsed between the time when Jared was last seen by his friend in front of John's bar and the moment he reached autopsy. The weather in La Crosse during the time that he was missing was mild. There was only a trace of precipitation on April 15th. Temperatures ranged from an overnight low of 24 °Fahrenheit to a daily high of 77 °Fahrenheit. Jared should have displayed advanced discoloration, bloating, fluid purging, skin slippage and degloving (Figure 14.9, *Red Arrow*). He did not. Instead, he was not bloating, he had not discolored, he was still in rigor, and skin slippage had not started. Jared's condition at autopsy resembled that of a body that had been in the water less than 48 hours (*Green Arrow*). Therefore, he could not have accidentally died on April 10th when he went missing.

Gastrointestinal System

The stomach contained approximately 200 cubic centimeters (6.76 fluid ounces) of watery, partially digested food. This showed that not only did Jared ingest a large volume of water, but that he had likely eaten sometime within the previous 4 to 6 hours. Under ordinary circumstances, the stomach empties its contents within 4 to 6 hours after a meal (Geberth, 2006). Our assessment that he had eaten within 4 to 6 hours was confirmed by the 5

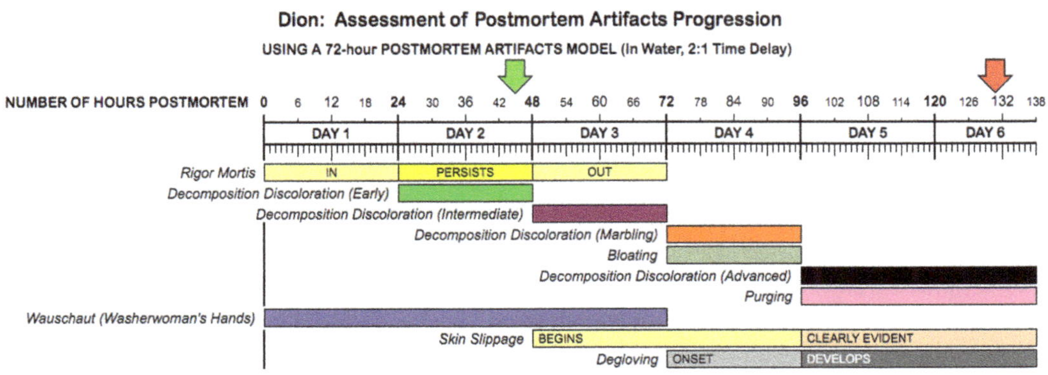

Figure 14.9 Given that Jared Dion had been presumed deceased and in the water for 130 hours (*Red Arrow*), as well as the mild environmental conditions, the postmortem condition of his body should have reflected advanced discoloration, bloating, purging, skin slippage and degloving. It did not. Rather, postmortem artifacts indicated that decomposition had not even reached the conditions typically seen on Day 2 (*Green Arrow*).

cubic centimeters (0.17 fluid ounces) of green bile that remained in his gallbladder, which indicated that he had not completed the digestion process and that his gallbladder had not yet refilled.

All of this meant that Jared had drowned within 6 hours after eating his last meal. The two questions that needed to be answered were, "What was Jared's last meal?" and "When was Jared's last meal?" As in all cases that we have examined (even those where stomach contents have been preserved as evidence), no attempt was made to test the stomach contents in order to determine whether they matched with the victim's last known meal. In fact, in most cases, no record existed of any attempt to identify the ingredients of the last meal. Since we knew that Jared was not in the water for the first 3 days after he went missing, only two scenarios were available.

Scenario 1: Jared was abducted and murdered by drowning shortly after he ate his last meal and held for a period of time in a sub-zero freezer in order to preserve his body.

Scenario 2: Jared was abducted and held for a period of 3 days, given food and lots of alcohol to drink, then murdered by drowning and placed into the Mississippi River.

Respiratory System

Jared clearly drowned. The combined weight of human lungs is typically less than 1,000 grams. However, in a wet drowning where a victim inhales water, the lungs will usually exceed 1,000 grams. Jared's left lung weighed 660 grams and his right lung 760 grams, a collective weight of 1,420 grams. The Medical Examiner recorded that the parenchyma was congested an wet, and that plentiful bloody fluid exuded from the lungs when manual pressure was applied to them. She further wrote that there was no obstruction in the tracheobronchial tree and made no reference to pink froth in the airway. This all pointed to a wet drowning, wherein, the victim inhaled water without fighting the process. This caused the water-logged lungs and the absence of pink forth (which is created by the admixture of water with blood from ruptured vessels in the lungs and bronchial tube).

Since most medical examiners never check to see whether the water in a victim was consistent with the body of water from which he was retrieved, or whether it came from local tap water, then we had to assume that the water in Jared's lungs was from the Mississippi River. However, he may have been drowned somewhere else (outdoors or indoors) before being entered into the water.

Toxicology

La Crosse authorities originally released a 0.40 BAC to the local press for Jared. Later, they reported that his BAC was 0.27. Actually, neither one was Jared's true Blood Alcohol Concentration (BAC). Alcohol concentrations differ based on the source or sample used during testing. If the results for blood (BAC) are considered a 100 percent value, then urine (UAC) typically returns a reading of 130 percent of the BAC. Vitreous fluid from the eyeball returns results that are 90 percent of the BAC, while liver tissue returns results that are 85 percent. The 0.40 reading reported for Jared was the result of a test of his Urine Alcohol Concentration (UAC), and the 0.27 was from his Vitreous Alcohol Concentration (VAC). Therefore, his true BAC was lower.

Formulas for Alcohol Concentration Equivalencies

SPECIMEN	%	CALCULATION #1	CALCULATION #2
Urine (UAC)	1.30	UAC x 0.769 = BAC	UAC x 0.692 = VAC
Blood (BAC)	1.00	NA	NA
Vitreous (VAC)	0.90	VAC x 1.111 = BAC	VAC x 1.444 = UAC

Dion: Calculations for Alcohol Concentration Equivalencies

SPECIMEN	TEST	CALCULATION #1	CALCULATION #2
Urine (UAC)	0.40	0.40 UAC X 0.769 = 0.31 BAC	0.40 UAC X 0.692 = 0.27 VAC
Vitreous (VAC)	0.27	0.27 VAC X 1.111 = 0.30 BAC	0.27 VAC X 1.444 = 0.39 UAC

Figure 14.10 Given a known value, mathematical estimates can be calculated for the other types of alcohol concentration. In Jared Dion's case, the known values ("TEST") for UAC (0.40) and VAC (0.27) demonstrated that sufficiently accurate estimates can be calculated for each other ("CALCULATION #2"). Thus, the arithmetic estimates for BAC should also be correct at 0.30 to 0.31 ("CALCULATION #1").

A note on the toxicology report from the laboratory at the Regina Medical Center (where Jared's autopsy was performed) suggested that a BAC value could be mathematically calculated by multiplying the VAC value by 0.90. This was incorrect; the reverse is the correct arithmetic equation. Since a VAC is 90 percent of a BAC, then a VAC may be calculated by multiplying a BAC by 0.90. In order to calculate a BAC from a known VAC, then the VAC must be multiplied by about 1.111 (Figure 14.10). In order to calculate an estimated UAC from a VAC, the VAC must be multiplied by 1.444. As a check of these mathematical equations, a calculated UAC of 0.39 can be obtained using the known 0.27 VAC. Likewise, a calculated VAC of 0.27 can be obtained using the known 0.40 UAC. Both estimations are acceptable findings.

In one official document, Jared's BAC was reported as 0.289. We did not use this BAC value since we were uncertain of its origin. Had officials used the arithmetic on the Regina Medical Center toxicology report to calculate the BAC, then they would have used a 0.270 VAC and multiplied it by 0.90 which would have equaled a 0.243 BAC. The accurately calculated mathematical estimate was about 0.30 to 0.31 BAC (Figure 14.10). The purpose of all this math was to demonstrate that Jared was not as drunk as officials first reported (0.40). Yet, he was in fact more drunk than their latter reports had suggested (0.27).

Not only was Jared highly intoxicated with alcohol at the time of his death, he also had gamma-hydroxybutyrate (GHB) in his body. There was just enough GHB in his system to make him manageable and compliant. He was recovered with 11 micrograms per milliliter (mcg/mL) of GHB. Given the half-life of GHB (18 to 60 minutes), then the level in Jared's system could have been as high as 252 mcg/mL just 90 minutes earlier. That level would have rendered him exceptionally compliant with the demands of an abductor(s), since he would have been in a deep sleep or possible coma-like state. These were the same substances recovered in both Nathan Kapfer's and Jeffrey Geesey's systems (i.e., ethanol and GHB).

GHB occurs naturally in the human body. Research suggests that it functions as a neuromodulator in the central nervous system. It is also commonly used on the street as a "date rape drug" to render victims helpless. The postmortem decomposition process produces small amounts of GHB. Postmortem urinary concentrations are typically less than 10 mcg/mL with the majority of values less than 5 mcg/mL. A Regina Medical Center report stated that 11 mcg/mL of GHB was consistent with endogenous production, which meant that it was naturally occurring in Jared's body at that level.

We have investigated numerous cases of victims with GHB. We have found that when GHB was detected in a victim it had hardly increased due to decomposition. In one case, GHB-specific tests quantitated the original amount at 97 mcg/mL at autopsy and at 100 mcg/mL when tested a second time a year later. That showed that the level of GHB produced postmortem had increased by only 3 mcg/mL over a whole year's time, or 1 mcg/mL every 4 months. Considering these facts, we found it extraordinarily difficult to believe that Jared's body produced 11 mcg/mL of GHB when he was presumed to be deceased and in the water for only 5 days (i.e., the equivalent of 2.5 days on land).

The literature suggests that the postmortem production of ethanol may be identified in blood by the presence of n-propanol (Wigmore & Chow, 2000). As a body decomposes, it breaks down and produces alcohols. Ethanol and isopropanol eventually break down and convert to acetone. Therefore, all of them (i.e., acetone, ethanol, isopropanol, methanol, n-propanol, n-butanol, and GHB) should be found during an autopsy's toxicological testing of bodies that have definitive decomposition. Only ethanol and GHB were reported to have been found in Jared. No other forms of alcohol were reported. Therefore, this suggested that the alcohol and GHB must have come from an exogenous (external) source rather than an endogenous (internal) source like decomposition.

The Medical Examiner even supported this finding and stated that she believed Jared's BAC did not change throughout the entire time that he was deceased. She told a reporter, "'With decomposition, bodies can produce small amounts of alcohol . . . and tends to be only with really marked decomposition,' Thomas said. 'I don't think that is a factor at all in this case.'" (Springer, 2004). It was unlikely that Kapfer, Geesey, and Dion took the GHB freely. The ingestion of GHB probably occurred at the hands of someone else who administered it into their drinks. The fact that the same substance (GHB) was present suggested the possibility of the same offender(s) being involved in these murders. Clearly, these were not accidents.

The toxicology finding that Jared had GHB in his system was not initially made public. During a town hall meeting in 2004, the LCCME stated that no drugs were found in Jared. He reiterated this point to a local newspaper reporter stating that Jared "had not consumed any drugs" (Springer, 2004). Specifically, he told the reporter, "Tests came back negative for any abuse drugs. Tests also found Dion did not have any chloroform in his system and had not ingested common 'date rape' drugs like GHB and Rohypnol" (Springer, 2004). It is not uncommon for law enforcement agencies to withhold information from the media and the local community in order to preserve special or inside knowledge of the commission or nature of a crime under investigation. That way, only the person who actually perpetrated the crime, or someone who was present at the time the crime was committed, will have that specific knowledge about the crime. This helps to identify individuals who may falsely confess to the crime. It also aids in distinguishing between offenders and their MOs (methods of operation or *modus operandi*), as well as copycats.

Withholding the fact that there was GHB in Jared's system suggested to us that the local authorities may have believed that there was something suspicious about his death. Otherwise, someone would have probably announced the presence of GHB at the town meeting and press conference held on April 22, 2004. Law enforcement agencies also often withhold specific information from families because some family members may begin investigating the crime themselves and may compromise or contaminate evidence or witnesses. Thus, we were not surprised to learn that the father (Bryan Dion) first heard about the presence of GHB in his son's system some 5-1/2 years later on May 8, 2009 – when Gannon informed him. After repeated phone calls to various officials, Bryan finally received a copy of the toxicology report from the LCCME's office 5 months later on October 7, 2009.

FBI Report

The La Crosse drowning cases are numbered 1 through 8 in the report written by an FBI Supervisory Special Agent (SSA) from the Behavioral Analysis Unit 2 (BAU-2) at the National Center for the Analysis of Violent Crime (NCAVC). He compiled the report in conjunction with other members of the NCAVC. Jared Dion was case number 7.

Most of the information that we had learned from official reports was reiterated in that report. Specifically, that a member of the band playing at John's bar that night had been told by Jared that he was going to a party after bar closing. That same witness also reported seeing Jared at about 02:30 hours talking to a blonde, whom the witness could not identify as male or female. The report also presented the discovery of Jared's hat in Riverside Park and that his clothing and personal items were found intact during recovery on April 15, 2004.

The report reviewed the Medical Examiner's ruling on cause of death (freshwater drowning with alcohol intoxication as a contributing factor) and manner of death (undetermined). The SSA did not present Jared's 0.40 UAC, rather he commented on his 0.27 VAC. He acknowledged the GHB in Jared's system, but he did not provide any specific quantitation (i.e., 11 mcg/mL) or assessment of the amount (e.g., minimal, marginal, or insignificant). He remarked that the Medical Examiner had attributed the presence of GHB to postmortem production as a result of decomposition.

The report was thorough, in that, the author reflected on past interactions that Jared had had with La Crosse police officers regarding alcohol related issues. One such incident centered on officer's finding Jared passed out in a stranger's yard. On that occasion, Jared did not know how he got there or where he was. The SSA closed with recommendations should further investigation become warranted. He proposed that the information provided by the band member be followed up since no official record existed which indicated that it had been pursued (specifically, the identity of the blonde individual with whom Jared was seen speaking and the location of the after-hours party).

Conclusion

We find that the evidence in the Jared Dion case indicated that he was not deceased any longer than 3 days (72 hours) prior to autopsy, and was most likely deceased no more than 2 days (48 hours). This meant that Jared's case was clearly suspicious since he was missing for a total of 130 hours 40 minutes. We assert that sufficient forensic evidence exists to support a deeper investigation into his death. Furthermore, we conclude that his death was most likely a homicide by drowning that resulted after being drugged and abducted. We believe that Jared was held alive for a period of time, at least 2-1/2 days, before being murdered and placed into the Mississippi River.

The forensic artifacts told us that this was a homicide. We assert that the Medical Examiner's description of the body was not in error and was not lacking. It was an accurate illustration of Jared's body. No mention of discoloration due to decomposition or bloating due to putrefactive gases was made because those postmortem characteristics were not present. The condition of Jared's body meant that it did not sink upon entering the water. It floated a short distance to a spot where it became hung up on debris in the river. His body did not sink because he was already deceased before being placed into the Mississippi River. The inconsistent directions of interest were suspicious and told us that someone had tried to throw off the search efforts. Jared should have attempted to go home that night. Instead, his body was recovered almost 180 degrees in the opposite direction. His property (a baseball cap) was found at about 90 degrees to that line of travel.

The condition of Jared's body at autopsy was a clear indicator that he had not been deceased since April 10th (approximately 5.4 days). If this truly was an accidental death, then he would have died on April 10th and been deceased a total of approximately 130 hours by the time he reached the autopsy table. Four artifacts pointed to a short postmortem interval: (1) bloating, (2) decomposition discoloration, (3) ocular changes, and (4) rigor. Jared's abdomen was described as flat and no significant bloating was noted in his eyelids, scrotum, or elsewhere. The absence of marbling meant that he was deceased less than 72 hours. The general lack of discoloration of Jared's body as a result of the decomposition process (specifically in the Right Lower Quadrant) told us that he had not even reached the intermediate stage (about 48 hours postmortem in water or 24 hours on land).

Ocular changes did not provide significant information relative to the postmortem interval, but they told us 3 things. First, given Dr. Thomas' description of Jared's eyes, neither cloudiness nor opacity had formed. That meant that he had not been deceased on land for more than about 24 hours. Second, it told us that his eyelids were closed after he passed. Third, the dilation of his pupils suggested that he was still in rigor. This was confirmed by the Medical Examiner's assessment that rigor was present and developed. She did not describe it as relenting or going out. Collectively, then, these artifacts pointed to a postmortem interval of 24 to 48 hours in water.

An earlier model that estimated a possible time of death as April 13th around 13:00 hours considered only the progression of rigidity in water as part of the analysis (Figure 14.6). In order for that model to be valid, Jared's abductor(s) would have had to murder him and then immediately place him into the river in broad daylight. That did not seem feasible. Therefore, a new model was needed.

In order to estimate a time of death, we started with 2 variables. The first was a forensic fact: Jared had not been deceased any longer than 48 hours in the water or the equivalent of 24 hours on land. The second was a criminological axiom: his abductor(s) would have placed him into the Mississippi River under the cover of darkness. That time would most likely be after bar closing and should allow enough time for the streets to clear; 03:00 hours was used (Figure 14.11, *Bright Green Star* and *Blue Star*). Two periods of darkness (*Black Bars*) existed within the 48 hours prior to Jared's autopsy. The first was between 20:17 hours (End Evening Civil Twilight – EECT) on April 13th and 05:53 hours (Before Morning Civil Twilight – BNCT) on April 14th. The second period of darkness was between 20:18 hours (EECT) on April 14th and 05:51 hours (BMCT) on April 15th.

Had Jared been entered into the water on April 15th at 03:00 hours (Figure 14.12, *Model A*, *Blue Star*), then he would have been in the water for about 5 hours before being recovered. Since water retards the decomposition process, we applied a 2:1 time delay ratio

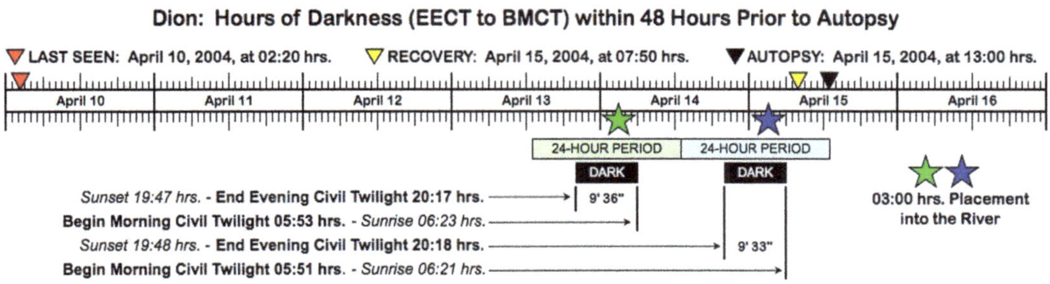

Figure 14.11 Jared Dion's abductor(s) would have entered him into the river under the cover of darkness (*Bright Green Star* & *Blue Star*). The forensic assessment of his postmortem condition suggested a time of death that was less than 48 hours prior to autopsy. Therefore, only two periods of darkness (*Black Bars*) were available to the assailant(s).

to obtain a 2.5 hour on-land equivalent time. He was on land in transit to the morgue, and then in the morgue awaiting autopsy for total of approximately 5 hours. So far, this would account for 7.5 hours. Since Jared was still in rigor at autopsy, then this 7.5 hours was subtracted from 24 hours (i.e., 12 hours for rigidity to develop, and 12 hours for it to persist before beginning to relent). Working backwards then, rigidity would have persisted for an additional 4.5 hours and would have taken another 12 to develop.

According to Model A, Jared's time of death would have been at about 10:00 hours on April 14, 2004 (Figure 14.12, *Red Star*). He would have been deceased and on land for 16.5 hours before being placed into the river (*Blue Star*). He would have been in the water for 5 hours before being recovered (*Yellow Triangle*) and on land for another 5 hours until autopsied (*Black Triangle*). This would account for the 12 hours required for rigidity to develop (*Tan Bar*) as well as the 12 hours for it to persist (*Yellow Bars*), and keep him in rigor until he reached autopsy.

Had Jared's abductor(s) put him into the river on April 14th at 03:00 hours (Figure 14.12, *Model B*, *Bright Green Star*), then he would have been in the water for about 29 hours (*Tan Bar* & *Yellow Bar*) before his body was recovered (*Yellow Triangle*). Applying a 2:1

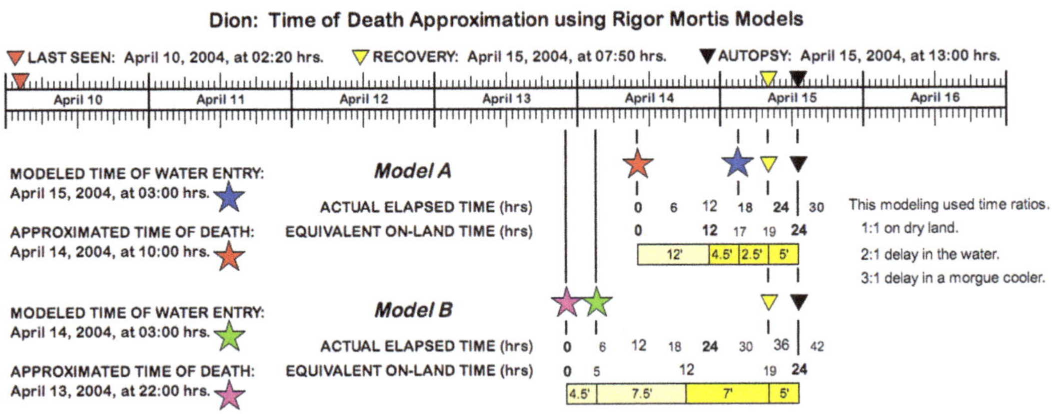

Figure 14.12 Jared Dion's kidnapper(s) likely entered him into the river under the cover of darkness (*Blue Star* & *Bright Green Star*). Since the Medical Examiner described rigidity at autopsy as developed and not as relenting, the time of death must have been less than 48 hours prior to autopsy. Two estimates can be calculated for the postmortem interval and the time of death (*Red Star* & *Bright Purple Star*).

time delay ratio for the retarding affect of water on decomposition, this equated to 14.5 hours on land. His transport and morgue time was a total of 5 hours. The total time in the water and morgue would then be 19.5 hours (i.e., 14.5 hours. + 5 hours.). Keeping in mind that Jared was in rigor at autopsy, then the 19.5 hours was subtracted from 24 hours (i.e., the time for rigor to develop and persist).

According to Model B, Jared's time of death would have been at about 22:00 hours on April 13, 2004 (Figure 14.12, *Bright Purple Star*). He would have been deceased and on land for only 4.5 hours before being dumped in the river (*Bright Green Star*). He would have been in the water for a period of 29 hours until his body was recovered (*Yellow Triangle*), which would have accounted for the equivalent of 7.5 hours of rigidity development on land (*Tan Bar*) and 7 hours of persisting rigor on land (*Yellow Bar*). And lastly, he would have been on land for another 5 hours until autopsied (*Black Triangle*).

Jared did not die on the night of April 10, 2004. The postmortem artifacts clearly demonstrated that Jared had not been deceased the entire 125 hours 30 minutes that his whereabouts were unknown. However, the analysis at this junction did not indicate a manner of death. His death could have still been an accident that happened sometime after April 10th. Only by examining the cause of death could we conclude a manner of death.

The extreme weight of Jared's lungs told us that he had inhaled some sort of fluid. Typically, a set of human lungs weighs less than 1,000 grams. Jared's lungs weighed 1,420 grams (about 42% greater than expected). They were described as being full of fluid. Pleural effusion was also present with 650 cubic centimeters (21.97 fluid ounces) of fluid in the pleural cavities. The human heart normally weighs about the sum of the two kidneys. Jared's kidneys weighed 370 grams and his heart weighed 440 grams (19% more than anticipated), which suggests that a small amount of fluid may have also reached his heart. The absence of any obstruction in his airway, specifically a pink froth, indicated that Jared had likely inhaled the fluid without a struggle. Strangulation had probably not occurred since the hyoid bone and laryngeal cartilage were intact.

The cause of death was hypoxia and cardiac cessation induced by suffocation that was facilitated using a fluid. We use the term "fluid" rather than "water" because the substance filling his lungs was never tested. We assert that when a victim is recovered from a body of water, then the fluid in his or her lungs and stomach should always be chemically evaluated in a laboratory in order to determine whether or not it truly was from that body of water. This investigative step should be a part of every agency's protocols. Since the fluid in Jared's lungs (21.97 fluid ounces) and stomach (6.76 fluid ounces) was not tested, we referred to it as a fluid and not water. In our opinion, if the gastric contents that were preserved at autopsy still exist, then they should be tested. If that specimen has been destroyed according to standard operating procedures, then Jared should be exhumed and his remains tested for chemicals. Specifically, he should be assessed for those chemicals used at the La Crosse water treatment plant. His body should also be examined for chemicals associated with pollutants in the Mississippi River. The remains of his lungs, pleural cavity, and stomach should be microscopically observed for diatoms.

In order to specify a manner of death, 3 questions needed to be answered. Why was Jared in the intoxicated state that he was? From where did he get the alcohol and GHB? How did he come to be near the river 3 to 4 days after he was last seen? We assert that the answer to these queries proved homicide as the manner of death.

We calculated that Jared had a 0.30 to 0.31 Blood Alcohol Concentration (BAC). Alcohol (ethanol) increases in the blood due to decomposition at a minimal rate of 0.0150 to 0.030 percent every month that a body is in the water. Obviously, cold water can retard this process and warm weather can accelerate it. An investigator should always error on the side of caution and use the minimum values.

Estimated Postmortem Alcohol (Ethanol) Production Values (gm/dL)

Period	*Minimum*	*Maximum*
1 month	0.0150	0.030
2 months	0.0300	0.060
3 months	0.0450	0.090
4 months	0.0600	0.120

We agree with the local officials who expressed that the BAC had remained steady and had not risen as a result of postmortem production during decomposition. The relatively pristine condition of Jared's body informed us that little decomposition had taken place and that no alcohols could have been produced during the 1 to 2 days that he was deceased. Thus, he died after having consumed a lot of alcohol.

It was possible that he had purchased the alcohol somewhere before April 10th. Since he was not seen back at his local residence, that indicated that he had to have hidden it. That did not seem too plausible. Perhaps, he purchased it somewhere after he was last seen on April 10th and the merchant never came forward to identify Jared as a customer out of fear over potential legal liability issues it might cause for the business. Recalling the band member's statement about Jared's plans to attend an after-hours party, maybe he stayed for 3 to 4 days at the house where it was held before he wandered off and accidentally fell into the river. Again, perhaps, no one from the house came forward to police out of fear of possible criminal charges or civil law suit stemming from Jared's death. All of these scenarios were theoretically possible, but logically and psychodynamically improbable given what we learned about Jared's personality, level of responsibility and interconnectedness with others, and demonstrated past behavior.

Jared also had 11 mcg/mL of GHB in his system. This was definitively contrary to his character and prior behavior. He would not have taken GHB voluntarily. There was some controversy regarding the source of the GHB. Some local officials attributed it to postmortem production as part of decomposition. However, Dr. Thomas (the Medical Examiner who performed Dion's autopsy) stated that the alcohol in Jared's system was not a result of postmortem production (Springer, 2004). It is a simple fact that if no alcohols were produced postmortem, then no GHB was produced as a result of decomposition. Furthermore, the absence of measurable amounts of n-propanol, isopropanol, n-butanol, and acetone, combined with the presence of GHB, was suspicious. This meant that the GHB had to be from an external source. This increased our skepticism that Jared had voluntarily drunk any of the alcohol which engendered his high BAC.

Although only a small amount, the 11 mcg/mL of GHB would have been enough to sedate Jared a little and at least take the fight out of him during the abduction process. Furthermore, considering the 18 minute half-life of GHB, Jared would have been extremely sedated and compliant just 36 or 54 minutes earlier. Any abduction process would have appeared like a buddy escorting his intoxicated friend. The abductor(s) would not have had to fight or struggle with Jared. Rather, he could have been led by the arm in any direction the abductor(s) wanted him to go. The injuries to Jared's hand, forearm and chest may have been defensive wounds and incurred during the 3 to 4 days that he was held captive. Given his high level of alcohol intoxication and the presence of the GHB, it was unlikely that he got them from a fight during the actual act of his murder.

We firmly believe that the forensic evidence in this case told a story. Jared Dion was abducted shortly after he was last seen by his friend (Mitch) in front of John's bar at about 02:20 hours on the morning of April 10, 2004. Where and how his kidnapping occurred is a matter for further investigation; perhaps, it was at the after-hours party, or on the street. He was held alive somewhere until April 13th. Probably around 18:00 hours, he was administered a dose of GHB. Once he was complaint due to the drug, he was handed a 500 mL bottle of alcohol to consume (16.9 fluid ounces of whiskey or flavored vodka). After a couple hours had elapsed, most of the liquid had passed from his stomach and the alcohol had made it into his blood stream (which would account for the 6.76 fluid ounces in his stomach and the 0.30 BAC that would have required about 15 shots of alcohol). At about 22:00 hours on April 13th, drugged and intoxicated on alcohol, Jared's life was taken from him by means of drowning. His murderer(s) transported his body to the dock near the Courtyard by Marriott hotel (500 Front Street South) at about 03:00 hours on April 14th. Jared's body was spotted the next morning (April 15, 2004) and recovered (Figure 14.12).

The forensic evidence in this case, specifically the condition of his body at autopsy combined with the fact that he was still in rigor after 130.7 hours (last seen on April 10th and autopsied on April 15th), clearly indicates that Jared had not died on April 10th, 11th, or 12th. That means that something is suspicious about Jared's death and that it demands further investigation. The band member who spoke with Jared at John's bar needs to be re-interviewed. The identity of the blonde with whom Jared was seen speaking as well as the location of the rumored after-hours party needs to be determined. Since all of his autopsy specimens have probably been destroyed, his body should be exhumed and examined for water treatment chemicals and diatoms. Jared's memory and his murder await justice.

Lucas Gerard Homan*

15

Background

Luke Homan was last seen on the night of September 29–30, 2006, and was recovered 2 days later in the Mississippi River on October 2, 2006. Any story about the untimely death of an upstanding young man cut down in the prime of his life is a sad one. However, this story may be the saddest one among a string of nine mysterious drowning deaths in La Crosse, Wisconsin, dating back to 1997. It is one thing to not find any evidence because it is not there. It is another to not find it because one does not know how to look for it. It is yet another to know how to look for it, find it, and then walk away from it.

The autopsy was performed by Dr. Lindsey Thomas at the Minnesota Regional Medical Examiner's Office (MRMEO) in Hastings for the City of La Crosse. In the October 24, 2006, letter accompanying her autopsy report, Dr. Thomas concluded that the cause of death was acute alcohol intoxication and drowning, and did not state a manner of death. Then, on October 30th, the La Crosse County Medical Examiner (LCCME; John Steers) repeated this cause of death (cold water drowning with acute alcohol intoxication) and ruled the manner of death as an "accident." Autopsy reports and photos were generated by the MRMEO. When we contacted the MRMEO who was the author of the materials, Dr. Thomas passed responsibility for granting permission to cite those materials to the LCCME's office. Although that office (John Steers) gave us permission to cite a PowerPoint presentation that he had posted online, he never responded to our letters requesting permission to cite the autopsy reports and photos.

* Photo courtesy of Jerry and Patti Homan (2012).

Figure 15.1 The Homan family: Jerry, Luke, and Patti (left to right). (Photo courtesy of Jerry and Patti Homan, 2012.)

Members of our team were first in La Crosse in March and December 2006, again in January 2007, and several times since then. We were in contact with the Homan family (from eastern Wisconsin) for over a year by telephone and by email prior to a meeting on April 18 and 19, 2009, in La Crosse. At that meeting, the team disclosed its findings to Jerry and Patti Homan (Luke's parents; Figure 15.1), other family members, and family friends, and conducted interviews with Luke's friend who was with him the night he disappeared (hereafter, Allen). Patti Homan provided our team with all official documents used to construct this case summary. The Homan family gave us permission to use and to show discreetly excerpted photos and the reports associated with Luke's autopsy. Thus, this analysis of Luke's case was based on our notes taken during personal observation of case photos and while reading official law enforcement and autopsy documents. All on-site photographs in this report were taken by members of our team.

Circumstances

Last Seen

Lucas Gerard Homan ("Luke") was a White male, 21 years old, 6 feet 2-1/2 inches, 205 pounds (Body Mass Index: 25.97), brown hair, and green eyes. It was September 29th and the City of La Crosse was celebrating its German heritage with its regionally famous Oktoberfest. Luke and a couple associates had a few drinks and then departed for the fest grounds around 10:30 hours to attend the tapping of the Golden Keg. He returned home about 13:00 to 13:30 hours with a barrel of beer for a house party, and laid down for a nap around 16:00 hours. At about 18:00 hours, Luke and a couple friends went to the Blimpie Sub Shop on campus and returned home around 19:00 hours. Shortly thereafter, Luke and two others (hereafter, the aliases Allen and Scotty) left in Scotty's car for the downtown bar district. According to witnesses, Luke was going to The Vibe bar for its $5 all-you-can-drink special from 19:00 to 22:00 hours.

Figure 15.2 On the night that he went missing, the last place that Luke Homan was reported to have been seen was in The Library bar in downtown La Crosse, Wisconsin.

Luke was seen going from The Vibe to The Library bar at approximately 01:30 hours on Saturday, September 30, 2006, by two of his friends (hereafter, Jack and Jim) (Figure 15.2). At approximately 01:30 hours when Jack was leaving The Vibe, he saw Luke talking to two unknown white males. Jim stated that he saw Luke enter The Library bar around 01:30 hours. Luke was seen talking with a taller white male whom Jim believed had previously worked as a bartender at the Rhino Bar, which is now called the Animal House. The subject had an injured knee and Jim felt this may be a way for police to identify him. There is no mention of the police ever attempting to contact or question this individual at all with regard to Luke's disappearance and whether he was with him or saw him that evening. There is also no mention of the police ever contacting the owners or personnel of either establishment to see whether this person had ever worked there.

Recovery

Luke was recovered from the Mississippi River at approximately 10:00 hours on October 2, 2006. Divers discovered him at 09:45 hours on the bottom in approximately 10 feet of water, about 37 feet north of the south end of the levee, and about 20 feet out from the levee. A temporary memorial was quickly set up nearby on shore (Figure 15.3).

Figure 15.3 A memorial was established along the Mississippi River at the spot where Luke Homan was recovered in Riverside Park.

Analysis of Evidence

Vehicle Search

On October 1st, the La Crosse Police Department (LCPD) received the name of the band that played at The Vibe bar on the evening Luke went missing (September 29th–30th). Additionally, police learned about an altercation between band members and an unknown male who was urinating next to their amplifier in the alley after bar closing. At the suggestion of agents from the Wisconsin Division of Criminal Investigation (DCI) who were assisting in the investigation, the police contacted members of the band who had already left the area and asked them to return to La Crosse. A member of the band returned to the main La Crosse Police Department parking lot at approximately 18:30 hours with his silver 4-door Sport Utility Vehicle with Wisconsin plates (Figure 15.4). It was parked in the lot east of the police department and municipal building. The vehicle contained three occupants (two females and a male) who consented to a search of the vehicle.

The vehicle search began with dog handler Fred Carsky along with K-9 Samo (a cadaver dog from People and Paws) who presented positive alerts on the right rear passenger compartment of the vehicle. This information suggested that a dead human body had been in that seat. Next, at 18:40 hours, dog handler Lynn Gardiner scented K-9 Tasha (a tracking Bloodhound) with an innersole from one of Luke's running shoes. The dog showed mild interest in the left rear passenger seat and moderate interest in the right rear passenger seat where the cadaver dog had hit. This information was consistent with a person having entered the back bench seat (rear passenger) of the vehicle from the driver side (left rear) and moving over to the passenger side (right rear). Since the bloodhound showed more interest (moderate) on the right rear passenger side and the cadaver dog had also hit on the right rear passenger side, this information was consistent with what appeared to be a victim (i.e., Luke) being slid across the back passenger seat from the left side to the right side.

The on-scene investigators (which included members of the LCPD and the DCI) then decided to black light the area of the vehicle to see whether there was any confirming forensic evidence in the vehicle to substantiate the dogs' hits in the vehicle. Black light is typically used to detect blood, urine, semen and saliva. The police report stipulated that the

Figure 15.4 During the La Crosse Police Department's search of an SUV similar to the one pictured here, both tracking and cadaver dogs had positive "hits" for Luke Homan inside the vehicle. They then examined it with an alternate light source and found human DNA material.

black light illuminated multiple white stains on the back of the right front seat and on the right rear passenger seat. At this point, there had been both tracking and cadaver dog hits for Luke as well as alternative light source evidence of the presence of human DNA material. At this juncture in an investigation, most law enforcement protocols would require the vehicle to be seized and searched for further forensic evidence of a possible crime. Depending on the circumstances of the case and the flight risk, the occupants of said vehicle would likely be detained for further questioning. The DCI investigators were only there as consultants. In this particular case, the LCPD investigators who were on-scene and in charge of the investigation released the three occupants and their vehicle, allowing them to leave and to drive back to Green Bay.

A "closed case" report prepared by a Special Agent with the Eau Claire Special Assignments, Wisconsin DCI, has only recently come to light in 2011. During the vehicle search on the night of October 1, 2006, the DCI Special Agent, along with an Investigator from the La Crosse Police Department, conducted an interview with the owner and driver of the vehicle concerning the bloodhound and cadaver dog positive hits for Luke's presence. Unfortunately, the precise line of questioning (i.e., a transcript of the exact questions and answers) was not presented in the report and only a summary existed. It did, however, show the suspicious nature of the evidence and the amount of diligence that was afforded the Homan family during this investigation.

Based on the summary report, the driver was asked whether anyone had ever been injured or suffered any loss of blood in the vehicle. The driver replied in the negative. The driver was then informed that a search dog (cadaver) had provided some type of alert, which meant that there may have been either blood or bodily fluids on, or in, the vehicle. Initially, the driver said there was no reason for blood to be in his vehicle. The driver then added that both female occupants (his girlfriend and her friend) were approaching the point of beginning their menstrual cycles.

Even if one were to believe this to be true and that he knew not only his girlfriend's cycle but the cycle of the other young woman, it still does not explain the presence of blood in his vehicle since he had said that they were only approaching their cycles and not having them. Furthermore, even if the driver of the vehicle wanted to say that one or both of the two young women had "spotted" while in the vehicle, it should have only helped to understand the presence of blood on the area of the right rear seat upon which one would sit. It would not have explained the presence of blood on the backside of the right front seat unless one of the young women had pressed herself against that area. This seemed very unlikely to us. Either way, the driver's response to the questioning clearly showed that the he was attempting to formulate a reason, hypothesis, or excuse for the presence of blood in his vehicle.

Lastly, unlike tracking dogs that scent only blood or skin cells related to a missing victim, cadaver dogs specifically scent the cells of human remains. They can smell decomposing flesh as well as an item as small as a single drop of blood. The cadaver dog would not have hit on the girls' blood or skin cells. The material scented by the cadaver dog in the vehicle was not related the living girlfriend or her living friend, rather it was related to a deceased body that had previously been in the vehicle.

The investigators should have asked the driver (and owner of the vehicle) whether he could explain why any human bodily fluids might be in his vehicle without any reference to the search dog results or the type of material. According to the interview summary, the investigator never pursued or probed with questions about other forms of human DNA material except blood. In fact, that is why the driver never provided any statement about any other human DNA material other than blood. The investigators should have also asked about urine, semen and saliva, and not focused solely on blood. A generic question concerning DNA material should have been asked. They led the interviewee to respond regarding only one type of material and conducted an incomplete interview. Had the driver of the vehicle been asked to explain why semen may have been found using a black light, then he might have suggested that he or others used to have sex in the back seat of the vehicle. This would have been a believable answer. Instead, knowing that there probably was blood in the vehicle, the driver came up with an alibi for the presence of blood in the vehicle that he believed would satisfy the police.

Tracking Luke

The first water search by boat was conducted on October 1st by the La Crosse Fire Department, which was sent out at 20:50 hours. Dragging occurred from about 21:15 to 22:15 hours without success. However, in a Jon Boat out on the river, K-9 Samo (a cadaver dog) indicated a hit (see Figure 15.5, *Hit #1*) for Luke in an area just south of the eroded

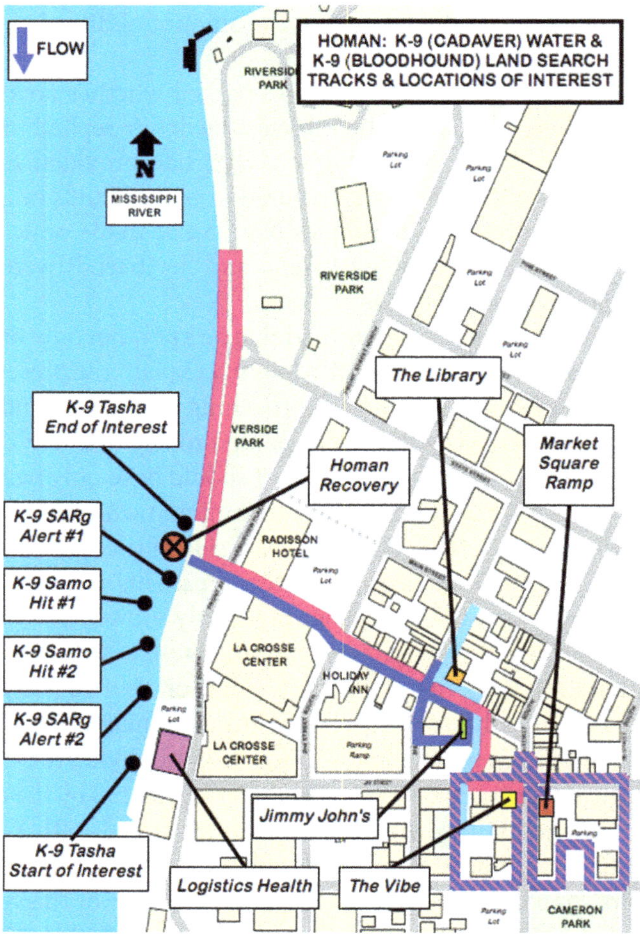

Figure 15.5 Bloodhound tracking dogs and cadaver dogs were used to locate Luke Homan's body in the Mississippi River (*Red-X Dot*): 3 water searches by K-9s and 4 land searches by K-9s (*Blue & Light Blue Lines*, and *Pink & Striped Lines*).

brick walkway in the south end of Riverside Park. This spot had been the end-point for K-9 Tasha (a tracking dog) during a land search for Luke that night. The next morning, October 2nd, three search teams with bloodhounds launched in boats to search for Luke. At about 07:45 hours, handler Fred Carsky and K-9 Samo (a cadaver dog) launched their boat. Later that morning at about 09:00 hours, K-9 Samo indicated another hit (*Hit #2*) for Luke in approximately the same location as the previous evening. Between 08:15 and 09:00 hours, Wisconsin K-9 SOS dog handler L. David Griffin along with K-9 SARg (a cadaver dog) searched the area along the riverbank near Riverside Park. K-9 SARg demonstrated interest in an area stretching from the south end of the levee to behind Logistics Health and gave two formal indications (see Figure 15.5, *Alert #1* and *Alert #2*). This same area was designated at approximately 09:15 hours by dog handler Lynn Gardiner when K-9 Tasha (a tracking Bloodhound) showed two areas of interest from their boat along the Mississippi River's east shoreline going south to north beginning near the grassy area behind Logistics Heath. This is the same general location where both Jared Dion (April 15, 2004) and Craig Meyers (February 16, 2010) had been found drowned and their bodies recovered.

All dogs had hit on a specific spot in the Mississippi River, so SCUBA diver Bill Powell was deployed. Luke's body was recovered shortly thereafter, brought to the surface, and then bagged in the water to prevent the loss of possible forensic material. Diver Powell also recovered 2 lengths of steel re-bar just off the levee wall in Riverside Park near the location where Luke was discovered. The items were stuck in the bottom standing straight up towards the surface. There had recently been some construction on Front Street according to police; although, their position in the water was unusual according to the diver.

Tracking Allen

On October 4th, People and Paws dog handler Lynn Gardiner along with K-9 Tasha (a tracking dog) returned to the scene at the request of a La Crosse Police Department (LCPD) Captain. The dog was scented using running shoes from Allen. While traveling east, the K-9 demonstrated a distinct interest in the entrance to the Market Square Ramp (a city-operated parking garage) at about the middle of the 400-block of Jay Street, and across the street from The Vibe bar (Figure 15.6, *Blue Line*). Dog handler Jody Disher and K-9 Pollie also showed interest in this parking garage when searching for Luke (see Figure 15.5, *Striped Line*). People and Paws did track Allen's scent from The Vibe bar to the front of Jimmy John's restaurant and followed the same path that Luke took and ended up at the same spot where Luke was found. The La Crosse Police Department utilized two other bloodhounds from Wisconsin K9 SOS to verify what People and Paws had indicated. These two bloodhounds also tracked Allen's scent from Jimmy John's directly to the point where Luke was recovered. For some reason, the police seemed blinded by this information (and never considered that this could have been Allen's transfer scent on Luke) and focused all their attention on Allen as a possible suspect and failing to see and follow up on the important leads that were right before their eyes (e.g., the vehicle search).

Wrong Suspect

Conflicting information existed relative to the nature and extent of Allen's intoxication, his whereabouts, his actions that night, and the degree to which the La Crosse Police

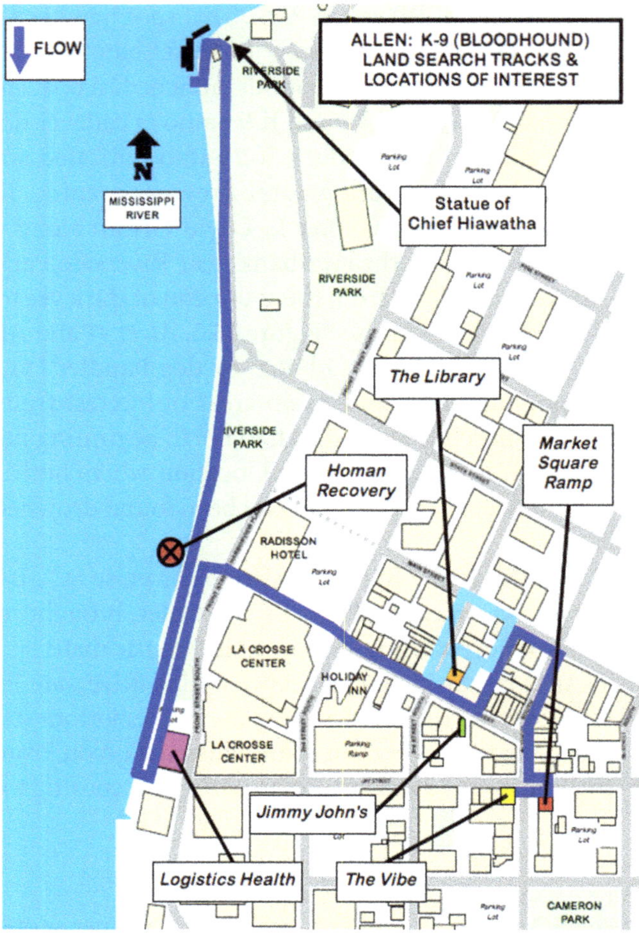

Figure 15.6 Using a tracking dog (K-9 Tasha), La Crosse police attempted to determine where Allen had been relative to Luke Homan's recovery location (*Red-X Dot*).

Department focused on him as a potential suspect. Since Allen's time was accounted for during the evening, he was not involved with Luke's disappearance and death. Confusion was generated by information provided in the department's own reports.

A La Crosse police sergeant filed a report dated October 5, 2006, that commented on findings from an interview that an Investigator conducted with the Radisson La Crosse Hotel night manager. In that report, the night manager was said to have observed Allen in the alcove near the hotel after walking eastbound from Riverside Park across Front Street to the Pearl Street walkway on the evening of September 29, 2006. A police patrolman filed a report dated 21:58 hours on September 29, 2006, wherein Allen was discovered stumbling through the south end of Riverside Park. The officer recorded that Allen had a bump on his head and some blood. Since Luke had been seen without injuries later that evening in several bars downtown, this earlier injury to Allen could not be attributed to some fight that occurred later in the evening that may have been related to Luke's death.

Allen registered a 0.266 Blood Alcohol Concentration (BAC) on a portable breathalizer and was transported to St. Francis Hospital (a.k.a., St. Francis Medical Center, or Franciscan Skemp Healthcare) where he was placed on detox hold by the police officer. Another sergeant filed a report dated October 4, 2006, wherein Franciscan Skemp administrative records indicated that Allen was released from the hospital at 02:40 hours on Saturday, September 30, 2006. A taxi voucher confirms this and indicates that, at 02:45 hours on September 30th, an individual was taken from the hospital to Sanford Hall (Allen's dormitory) at 1815 Farwell Street on the University of Wisconsin–La Crosse campus. The A-1 Taxi voucher and a photocopy of the handwritten log from the cab driver were placed into an evidence envelope, sealed, and placed into Evidence Locker 9C.

The time of Allen's release from the hospital was further confirmed by a police interview with the Sanford Hall Resident Advisor, wherein she stated that she heard a commotion in the hallway between 02:30 and 02:45 hours and that Allen spoke about the cut he had sustained above his eyebrow. She gave him an ice pack for it. At 03:00 hours, the front door to Sanford Hall was not physically staffed by a security guard, but was operated by a key card lock. Anyone could exit the building. However, unless they piggy-backed in with someone else, residents needed key cards to re-enter. There was no key card data record or human witness of Allen ever leaving and then re-entering the building that evening after returning home.

Gilbertson called Franciscan Skemp (608-785-0940) on August 7, 2010, and spoke with an employee at 17:17 hours regarding the detoxification center's present-day release criteria (it may have been different in the past). She told him that all admissions are held until they drop to at least 0.05 BAC. Also, there is no time limit on voluntary admissions, and those individuals who were brought in by police or ambulance may be held for up to 72 hours. The BAC in an average adult male is reduced at a rate of about 0.02 per hour. At this rate, Allen would have needed just over 10 hours of detoxification to reach the necessary level for hospital release. Something out of the ordinary occurred that night relative to how the police and the hospital handled Allen. Only 1 of the following 5 possibilities could have happened.

a. **Allen was admitted to the hospital earlier than reported.**
   If Allen had been admitted with a 0.266 BAC and released at 02:40 hours, then he would have had to have been admitted at about 16:40 hours the previous afternoon in order to allow sufficient time to reduce his BAC to the acceptable 0.05 level per hospital policy. This did not happen.
b. **Allen was released from the hospital later than reported.**
   If Allen had been admitted with a 0.266 BAC at about 22:00 hours and placed on detox hold, then he would have had to have been released at about 08:00 hours the next day in order to allow sufficient time to reduce his BAC to the acceptable 0.05 level per hospital policy. This too did not happen.
c. **Allen was released from the hospital in a drunken state.**
   If Allen had been admitted with a 0.266 BAC at about 22:00 hours and released at 02:40 hours as reported, then he would have experienced a BAC reduction of only about 0.092 and was released with a BAC of about 0.174 (twice the legal limit to drive). This should not be what happened due to legal liability issues and hospital policy.
d. **Allen was not as intoxicated with alcohol as had been reported.**
   The only way for Allen to be released at 02:40 hours with a 0.05 BAC was for him to arrive at 22:00 hours with about a 0.125 BAC. This would mean that the police PBT device was not functioning properly. Since the devices are routinely calibrated for accuracy, this should not have happened.

e. **Alcohol was not the source of Allen's intoxication.**
The behavior that Allen demonstrated must have been attributable to some other intoxicating substance in his system other than alcohol. Is this what happened?

Per the patrolman's field sobriety assessment, Allen was sufficiently intoxicated to require transportation to the hospital. However, his intoxication could not have been attributable to alcohol or the hospital would not have released him so soon. Something else was in his system that presented similar symptoms and dissipated more quickly than alcohol (e.g., GHB, which dissipates in 3 to 5 hours), and the portable breathalizer test (PBT) provided a higher than true BAC as they often do. As pointed out in Chapter 2 (Figure 2.5), alveolar air often presents an alcohol concentration level that may be twice that of urine or whole blood. Allen repeatedly stated during later interviews (with La Crosse police officers and our team members) that he had an area of uncertainty that revolved around whether or not he was with Luke at the river's edge as the police had attempted to convince him. Per the police department's own reports, Allen could not have been with Luke from 22:00 to 03:00 hours since he had been under continuous observation by two law enforcement officers, a taxi driver, numerous hospital detox staff, and a dormitory resident advisor. Allen was most likely not with Luke during the time that he entered the water (i.e., sometime after 01:30 hours). Allen has no recollection of what happened that evening to Luke or himself, and requested to take a lie detector test, which was administered by the police. Considering the time line, it appeared as though Allen was telling the truth and may have actually been drugged as had been the scenario in another abduction 9 months earlier that same year (i.e., January 8, 2006, when the victim was held for a period of 4.5 hours and the friend was admitted to the hospital and did not remember a thing).

It may have been reasonable under normal circumstances for the police to focus some of their attention on Luke's friend, Allen, because of the bloodhounds' responses. However, this case did not demonstrate many of the typical investigative characteristics that one would expect. It appeared that the lead law enforcement investigators from the La Crosse Police Department and the Wisconsin Division of Criminal Investigation practiced a double standard when it came to interpreting investigative results and establishing probable cause. They ignored the findings in the vehicle (i.e., the tracking dog's and cadaver dog's "hit" responses that were confirmed by an examination using an alternative light source) and released both the occupants and the vehicle. Subsequently and conversely, they clung to the findings of a tracking dog's "hit" response and focused undue attention on Allen because of it. The finishing touch to this whole sad irony is that the handler and tracking dog used to search the vehicle for Luke was the same handler and tracking dog used to track Allen (i.e., People and Paws dog handler Lynn Gardiner and K-9 Tasha). Search dogs are either a viable investigative tool or they are not; law enforcement officers cannot pick and choose.

Not only was Allen with Luke during the early evening hours on the night that he went missing, he was also involved in subsequent searches for him the following days. Thus, his scent could reasonably have been at some of these locations. Since Allen was with Luke during the early part of the evening, his scent in the vehicle could have been a transfer scent from Luke being placed into the vehicle later by his abductors. If the La Crosse police believed in the validity of the dogs to the extent that they felt that Allen may have played a role in Luke's demise (i.e., been in the vehicle or at the river's edge with Luke), then why did they not also feel that the owners of the vehicle may have been suspects?

Instead, the La Crosse police pursued Allen as a potential suspect and eventually arrested and charged him on May 7, 2007, with "Obstructing" (Wisconsin Statutes §946.41) for providing false information to an Investigator and other officers. Allen consistently insisted that he could not accurately recall all of the events that transpired that fateful night. In the face of police pressure and their evidence against him, Allen pled "No Contest" to the charges against him. During our interview with Allen, we asked him whether he had ever heard of an "Alford Plea." Not surprisingly, he had no knowledge of it; probably because he had never been told about it. Both are types of a guilty plea, but neither is an admission of guilt. Both expose a defendant to the imposed punishment. However, there is a distinct difference in the two types of pleading. A guilty plea of "No Contest" (*Nolo Contendere*) is not an admission of guilt, rather, it is an agreement to not challenge the prosecution's assertion that the act was committed by the defendant and allows for denial of alleged facts of the case in subsequent proceedings. An Alford guilty plea is not an admission of guilt, rather, it is recognition that the prosecution will likely convince the jury to find the defendant guilty even though the defendant does not admit committing the act and asserts innocence. Should Allen have pled Not Guilty or used the Alford Plea? He was sentenced and served 1 weekend in county jail plus 1 year of probation according to a Federal Bureau of Investigation report.

Recovery Location

Divers discovered Luke's body at 09:45 hours submerged in about 10 feet of water and resting on the river bottom, about 37 feet north of the south end of the levee, and about 20 feet out from the levee. The location where Luke's body was recovered was consistent with the location where several K-9s had tracked his scent to the water's edge. When a body enters the water (freshwater) it sinks after death and remains at the bottom and will not move until decomposition occurs, the body fills with gases, and the body resurfaces (i.e., refloat). It will then travel on the water's surface according to which way the wind pushes it (usually in a lake) or the direction and speed of the current of the body of water (usually in a river) (Hendrick, Zafares & Nelson, 2003). A human body may stay on the surface of a body of water for long periods of time without sinking when a deceased person is kept on land until the decomposition process is established (Armstrong & Erskine, 2011). Although Luke was deceased before he was entered into the river, he would have floated for a period of time and then sunk to the bottom. We discerned this because the period of time between when he went missing and when he was recovered was too short for decomposition gases to form, which was confirmed by the recovery and autopsy photographs. This was where the consistency ended.

The local police ardently pushed a storyline that suggested that Luke had staggered down to the waterfront to the area near the south end of the levee, where several cobblestones had been undermined by erosion in the corner and along the edge of the levee. Whether or not he had an altercation with Allen at that location was another question. What was important, though, was the assertion that Luke had lost his footing in the uneven and loose cobblestones, and accidentally fallen into the Mississippi River at that point in space and time. The police supported their premise with 13 on-site evidentiary photographs dated October 3, 2006. They presented 2 photos of the eroded corner with its loose and missing cobblestones at the extreme south end of the levee's walkway. This was followed by 3 photos that showed the loose and eroded cobblestones at a spot about 9 feet further north along the levee walkway, which was the exact location of Luke's impromptu memorial (Figure 15.3). This was set into context by 3 photos up and down the levee walkway, which demonstrated that there were no railings or fences to prevent someone from falling into the water. There were also 5 photos that showed the purported straight-line and ever-important downhill path from the bar area through the park to the southern end of the levee at the waterfront. More than a handful of times during television interviews, people associated with La Crosse have commented on this route in connection with the drownings as though they were anticipatory events that resulted from the combination of drunken students succumbing to the downhill pull of gravity toward the water (e.g., like a helpless marble rolling downhill).

Here was the inconsistency between the facts and the proposed storyline. Luke was recovered in about 10 feet of water and resting on the river bottom, about 37 feet north of the south end of the levee, and about 20 feet out from the levee. The location where the cobblestones were missing, loose, and undermined by erosion was in fact along the levee and was the same location where the dogs had tracked Luke's scent. Police would like us to believe that the dogs tracked Luke to that spot because he had walked to that exact spot and had fallen into the river there. However, the dogs did not track him to that spot because he had walked there. Rather, they tracked Luke to that spot because he was on the bottom of the river just upstream of that location. His scent was being carried downstream. Furthermore, it is physically impossible for a body to fall into a river and float upstream against the current. Instead, a body enters the water and travels downstream with the current as it sinks. It takes time for a body to descend from the water surface to the river bottom (Armstrong & Erskine, 2011). The *Body Drop Rate* of a human sinking in fresh water is about 2 to 2.5 feet per second. In salt water, a human body descends a bit more slowly at about 1.5 to 2 feet per second (Hendrick, Zaferes, & Nelson, 2003, p. 83). This becomes a basic physics vector problem that involves identifying the approximate location of a descended body based on the water entry location, the water flow direction, the water current's speed, and the water depth (Figure 15.7).

A body recovery team must first identify the *Depth* of the body of water through either estimation based on local knowledge, geological survey maps, or direct measurement (i.e., dropping a weighted rope to the bottom). Next, the *Current Speed* of the water in that location must be empirically identified. *Current Speed* is reported in "Knots" and equates to 100 feet per minute or 100 feet per 60 seconds (Hendrick, Zaferes, & Nelson, 2003, p. 83). This can be determined by tossing a tennis ball or other floating object into the water and timing it as it travels along the shoreline for 50 or 100 feet. An algebraic equation can then be used to calculate the approximate distance that a body may have traveled during its descent to the bottom: *Distance Traveled* equals *Depth* divided by *Body Drop Rate*, which is

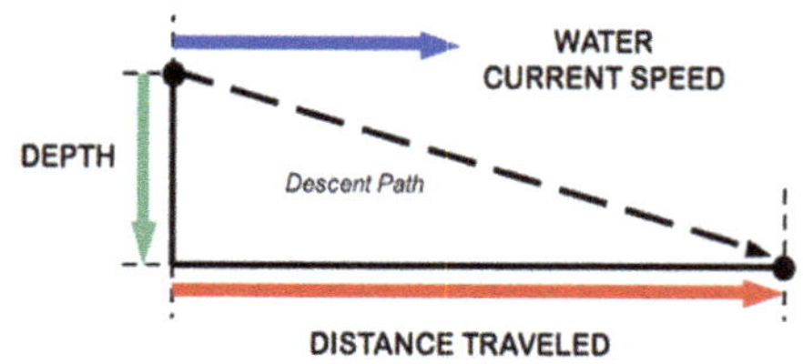

Figure 15.7 A physics vector problem: the location of a body underwater can be estimated by knowing the water depth and the speed of the current.

Approximate Distance Traveled Downstream in Feet using a 2 ft/sec Body Drop Rate

		CURRENT SPEED (Knots)									
		1	2	3	4	5	6	7	8	9	10
DEPTH (Feet)	10	5	10	15	20	25	30	35	40	45	50
	20	10	20	30	40	50	60	70	80	90	100
	30	15	30	45	60	75	90	105	120	135	150
	40	20	40	60	80	100	120	140	160	180	200
	50	25	50	75	100	125	150	175	200	225	250
	60	30	60	90	120	150	180	210	240	270	300
	70	35	70	105	140	175	210	245	280	315	350
	80	40	80	120	160	200	240	280	320	360	400
	90	45	90	135	180	225	270	315	360	405	450
	100	50	100	150	200	250	300	350	400	450	500

Distance Traveled = [(Depth) / (Body Drop Rate)] x (Current Speed)

Figure 15.8 The distance that a body may travel from its point of entry while descending to the bottom of a body of water can be estimated by knowing the water depth and current speed.

then multiplied by the *Current Speed* (Figure 15.8). When applying this approximated distance traveled near an ocean, a body recovery team must keep in mind potential changes caused by the affect of tides upon the water flow direction and depth.

In order for Luke to have been recovered on the river bottom at that location, he would have had to have fallen into the river further upstream. In fact, since he had been recovered on the bottom about 37 feet north along the levee from the site where the cobblestones were loose, then that meant that he had to have gone into the river further upstream. Additionally, Luke was recovered about 20 feet out from the levee. Since the levee presented an abrupt drop off of 6 feet into the river (Figure 15.9), then that meant that Luke had to have gone into the river even further upstream. This would have allowed for sufficient time for him to drift further out into the current – unless he fell off a boat. Lastly, had Luke fallen into the river in a conscious state at either of the locations along the south end of the levee's walkway where the cobblestones had been disturbed, then he could have climbed out of the water and onto the exposed rocks along the base of the levee that were less than

Figure 15.9 The levee in La Crosse presented an abrupt drop off of 6 feet. Luke Homan was recovered near where this photo was taken and about 20 feet out from the levee.

15 yards downstream from his recovery location. Our analysis concluded that this meant Luke had to have gone into the Mississippi River a reasonable distance upstream from the south end of the levee.

If nothing else, then the 13 evidentiary photographs of the levee walkway clearly demonstrated potential neglect and liability on the part of some government administrators or employees. One could clearly see and determine from the photos that the erosion and displacement of the cobblestones was not something that had occurred overnight. It took a while. Why had the department responsible for maintaining the levee's walkway not done so prior to Luke's death? The 13 photos were taken by the local police on October 3, 2006. Our team's photo of that same location along the levee (Figure 15.3) clearly showed that the cobblestone problem had still not been addressed when that picture was taken nearly 3 months later on January 10, 2007. In fact, when we met with the Homan family on April 18, 2009, we took photographs of the cobblestones which still had not been repaired (2 years and 6.5 months after Luke's death). Assuming that the police storyline was correct and Luke stumbled on missing, loose, or undermined cobblestones, then to what extent is someone partially liable for negligent maintenance of the levee's walkway and for allowing environmental conditions to exist that may have contributed to Luke's death? (Note: On June 13, 2012, Gannon and Gilbertson visited the site and confirmed that the cobblestones had finally been repaired.)

Decomposition and Maceration

The decay processes (putrefaction) generally take longer underwater when compared to on land. It may be further retarded by the refrigerating affect of cold water (Armstrong & Erskine, 2011). Generally, decomposition first becomes visible in the right lower quadrant (RLQ) by the 12th hour after death. It then typically spreads to the entire body within the first 12 to 24 hours after death. The visible signs of decomposition will usually change in color within 24 to 36 hours from hues of green to dark red and purple (Geberth, 2006). Slippage of the skin from the hands and feet (maceration) normally occurs within 4 to 7 days after death. The standard rule for the decomposition of human bodies in water (depending on the temperature) is that 2 days in water equal one day on land (Dix & Graham, 1999).

According to the U.S. Army Corps of Engineers (2011) searchable database for the Mississippi River Lock and Dam 7, the air and water temperatures were well above freezing during the period of time that Luke was missing (Figure 15.10). Thus, these temperatures would have had some, although minimal affect, on the rate at which Luke decomposed.

Homan: Daily Temperatures at Mississippi River Lock & Dam 7 near La Crosse, WI

DATE	AIR MAX	AIR MIN	WATER MEAN
September 29, 2006	*61*	*44*	*58*
September 30, 2006	*64*	*48*	*57*
October 1, 2006	*75*	*45*	*57*
October 2, 2006	*80*	*66*	*58*

Figure 15.10 Air and water temperatures were above freezing during the period that Luke Homan was missing. (From U.S. Army Corps of Engineers. 2011. Mississippi River Lock and Dam 7. [Online.] Available: http://www.mvp-wc.usace.army.mil/projects/Lock7.shtml.)

The water itself would have had a greater affect. Thus, the decomposition processes may have taken twice as long for Luke.

We examined the recovery and autopsy photographs repeatedly. No determination of changes to the cornea or sclera (i.e., ocular changes) could be made by us. We saw no color change in the RLQ or LLQ. There was a tennis ball-sized discoloration on the right side of Luke's abdomen, which appeared to be an older bruise from perhaps a week or more. Other than that, the only discoloration that could be seen was attributable to lividity. Washerwoman's Hands (*Wauschaut*) was consistent with having been immersed in the Mississippi River for less than 2 days. In fact, it appeared to have barely begun. As expected, skin slippage had not begun.

The Medical Examiner's (Dr. Thomas) autopsy comments concerning ocular changes, decomposition, and maceration on Luke's body were out of the norm. Typically, medical examiners will compose a short description of these postmortem artifacts. Relative to Luke, the only comments made by Dr. Lindsey Thomas were about the color of his eyes (i.e., green irides) and that Washerwoman's Hands was present on the hands and feet. There was absolutely no comment anywhere about a film, cloudiness, or opacity of Luke's eyes. We do not understand how the color of Luke's eyes could be described and then no comment made on the condition of the cornea or sclera. No description could be found anywhere in the autopsy report concerning discoloration of Luke's abdomen. This was reasonable since we concurred that there was no change to be observed and then described. Applying the principle of a 2:1 ratio for water to land, if decomposition color changes normally become visible in the RLQ within 12 hours postmortem on land, then they should have become visible on Luke in about 24 hours coming out of the water. From the time Luke went missing to the time of autopsy was 61.5 hours. Certainly, some extent of ocular change and decomposition color change should have been detectable at autopsy – it was not.

Rigidity

Rigidity (*rigor mortis*) is the result of the stiffening or contraction of the body muscles related to chemical changes occurring within the muscles after death (DiMaio & DiMaio, 2001). On land, the process of going into rigor usually starts within 30 minutes after death. Rigor takes about 6 to 12 hours to become completely fixed and it is normally out by 24 to 36 hours after death in a temperate environment (i.e., 68 to 72 °Fahrenheit). Although rigor starts at the same time throughout a body, it is first observed in the jaw and neck muscles. It progresses in a head-to-foot direction. Rigor also leaves a body in the same order and manner. Therefore, if rigor is in the jaw and arms but not the legs, then it is just starting. If rigor is not in the jaw but is still in the arms and legs, then it is starting to relent. Also, if there is no rigor in the jaw, arms and upper torso area but it is still in the legs, then rigor is almost completely relented. The rigor process is associated with the extent of decomposition and time (Shkrum & Ramsay, 2007). Other factors, such as body temperature and blood pH levels, will affect the speed at which rigor goes into and out of a body. As discussed earlier, submersion in water may slow the rigor process by a ratio of 2:1 (2 days in the water equals 1 day on land).

According to the MRMEO Medical Examiner, rigor was beginning to relent in Luke at autopsy. This observed fact may not have been entirely consistent with someone who had purportedly been deceased for approximately 61.5 hours. Further examination of the

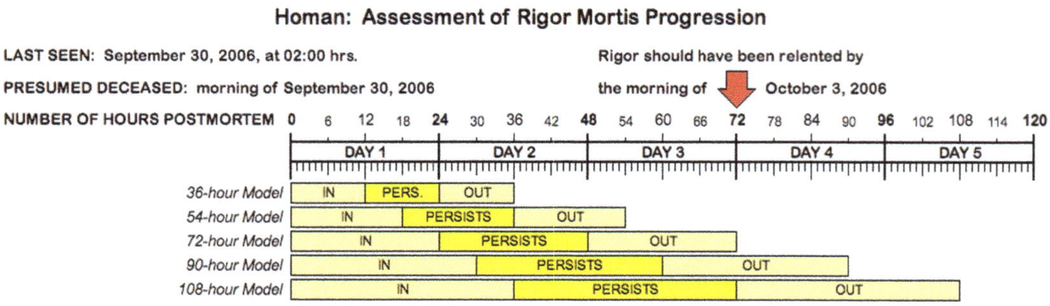

Figure 15.11 According to the MRMEO Medical Examiner, Luke Homan was just starting to come out of rigor at autopsy. The only model that fit that description was a 90-hour Model.

recovery and autopsy photographs suggested that there was some rigor in Luke's arms, but this did not confirm that rigor was only beginning to relent as stated by the MRMEO Medical Examiner. The water temperature was 58 °Fahrenheit when Luke was recovered on October 2nd, and the weather that day was sunny with a high of 80 °Fahrenheit. Given the air and water temperatures, and the 2:1 rigor dispersal ratio for days in the water compared to days on land, then the process of going into and coming out of rigor could have taken slightly longer with Luke. On land in a temperate environment, the stage of rigor that was described by the MRMEO Medical Examiner (i.e., beginning to relent) could be reached in about 24 hours (2/3rds of a 36-hour Model). Since Luke was in cool water, this may have taken up to 48 hours (2/3rds of a 72-hour Model). However, starting with an assumption that Luke died shortly after he was last seen at 02:00 hours on September 30th (Figure 15.11, *Red Triangle*), one would have to use no less than a 90-hour Model (*Yellow Bar*) in order to get Luke's body to a point where it would be just starting to relent by the time he reached autopsy (*Black Triangle*).

The progression of rigor is associated with other postmortem artifacts. Thus far, this analysis suggested that only a 90-hour Model could be used to account for the stage of rigor that the MRMEO Medical Examiner had described. Had Luke actually died during the early morning hours of September 30th (Figure 15.12, *Red Triangle*) and then presented with rigor beginning to relent at autopsy on the afternoon of October 2nd (*Black Triangle*), then Luke should have also presented at autopsy with considerable *Early* (*Green Bar*) and *Intermediate* (*Maroon Bar*) decomposition discoloration. Typically, a medical examiner will describe whether rigor is in the jaw and arms, as well as the extent

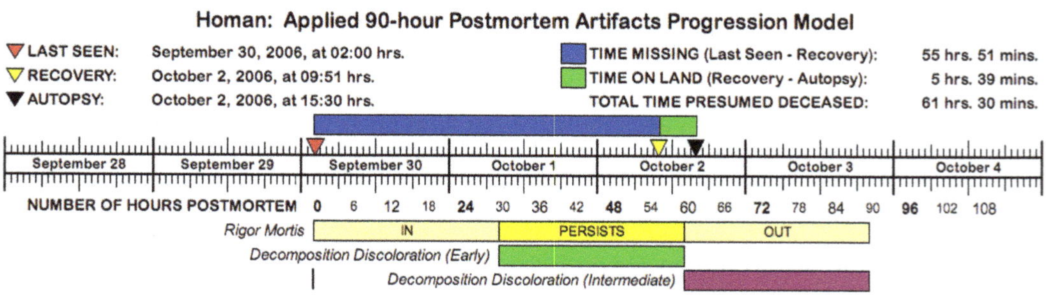

Figure 15.12 The MRMEO Medical Examiner's description of Luke Homan at autopsy was incongruent among simultaneously occurring postmortem processes. Luke could not be coming out of rigor at autopsy as described while not presenting decomposition discoloration.

of decomposition discoloration and corneal change. In this case, none of these items were described.

Body Position and Lividity

Lividity (*livor mortis*) is a postmortem discoloration due to the gravitation of blood into the dependent capillaries and veins; basically, it is the pooling and settling of the blood that starts within 30 minutes after death (Spitz & Spitz, 2006). It takes about 12 hours (usually 10 to 12 hours) for lividity to "fix," which means that the blood has settled in one position and can no longer be significantly "displaced" by changing the position of the body. Movement of a body during this period can cause lividity to appear diffused (i.e., in two locations). Another characteristic of lividity during this time is its resistance to "blanching." Blanching is the term used when an investigator presses his or her hand firmly against the discolored skin and it produces a change in the skin color, from a dark color to a pale color, and then back to the darker color. While lividity is establishing, it blanches under minimal pressure and displaces easily and rather quickly. Once lividity is fixed, it requires greater amounts of pressure as time passes in order to create blanching and will be increasingly more resistant to displacement. Body and environmental temperatures may have some marginal affect on these processes.

The MRMEO Medical Examiner described lividity in Luke as being anterior (on his front) and blanching when pressure was applied. This was consistent with someone who had been face-down in the water as are the majority of drowning victims. Gilbertson noticed that lividity was clearly evident on the front of Luke's face in the pictures taken at recovery on October 2nd. However, in the first pictures taken in the autopsy room some 3 to 4 hours later, lividity had partially displaced to the back of Luke's neck and away from his face. Furthermore, it was indistinguishable anteriorly on his abdomen; some discoloration associated with lividity could be seen posteriorly on his abdomen. Thus, some 61.5 hours postmortem, lividity was still blanching according to the MRMEO Medical Examiner's own description and it was still capable of displacement within a 4-hour period according to our observation of evidentiary photographs. This was improbable as blanching and displacement of lividity should have ceased some 30 hours prior to autopsy had Luke died during the early morning hours of September 30th (Figure 15.12). Any investigator knows that you cannot have rigor relenting with lividity still blanching (Geberth, 2006). You cannot have rigor relenting with no decomposition discoloration.

The only way to account for a majority of these postmortem characteristics as empirically observed in the recovery and autopsy photographs, and from what could be drawn from the MRMEO Medical Examiner's description at autopsy, was to phase-adjust a 90-hour Model (Figure 15.13). Shifting the start times for postmortem artifacts to line-up with the time of autopsy (*Black Triangle*) created a congruent scenario: blanching and displacing lividity, no corneal cloudiness or opacity, no decomposition discoloration. This meant that the MRMEO Medical Examiner's description of the stage of rigor mortis in Luke at autopsy had to have been wrong – it was just setting in rather than just relenting. Had she provided a typical autopsy description of rigor in the muscles of the jaw, arms and legs, then we might have agreed with her assessment. But, she did not provide such a description and departed from standard practices we have seen in hundreds of other autopsy reports. Why was this autopsy done differently? Did a trained professional misinterpret the signs of rigor?

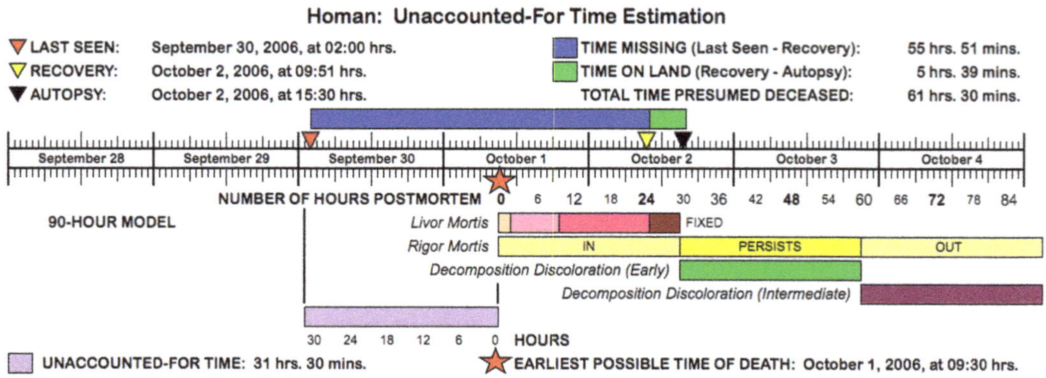

Figure 15.13 The only way to get all of the postmortem artifacts to line-up in the Luke Homan case was to adjust a 90-hour Model to coincide with the time of autopsy (*Black Triangle*) and to ignore the MRMEO Medical Examiner's description of rigor.

Tepidity

Tepidity (*algor mortis*) is the cooling of the body after death. Slender persons cool more quickly than obese persons, as would persons with little clothing compared with those individuals who are heavily clothed. Known as the Glaister Equation, the general rate at which a body cools is 1.5 °Fahrenheit during the first 12 hours and then cools at 1.0 °Fahrenheit until it is the same temperature as the environment in which it rests. Since the water that Luke was recovered in was 58 °Fahrenheit, then this process would have occurred over a total period of 34.5 hours. Starting at 98.6 °Fahrenheit, he would have cooled to 80.6 °Fahrenheit during the first 12 hours, and then cooled another 22.6 °Fahrenheit during the next 22.5 hours to match the 58 °Fahrenheit water temperature. Obviously, since Luke was missing for 56 hours, the police and medical examiner assumed that there was no need to check Luke's body temperature after being removed from the water. This simple procedure – which should be done with all deceased bodies, especially ones in water – was never done in La Crosse for any of the drowning cases of interest.

Measuring Luke's body temperature upon recovery and at autopsy would have confirmed or refuted forensic evidence related to decomposition that suggested that he was only in the water for a period of approximately 24 hours. In a 24 hour period, Luke's temperature would have only gone down by 30 °Fahrenheit (18 degrees during the first 12 hours + 12 degrees during the second 12 hours). This meant that Luke's body temperature would have been at 68 °Fahrenheit. If the water temperature was 58 °Fahrenheit and his body temperature was still at 68 °Fahrenheit after missing for a period of 56 hours, then the MRMEO Medical Examiner and the police would have known immediately that something was terribly wrong. Unfortunately, this simple procedure of determining a decedent's body temperature was never done.

Gastrointestinal System

Luke's stomach contained partially digested food (150 milliliters, or 5.07 fluid ounces), which was identified as ground meat by the MRMEO Medical Examiner who performed the autopsy. The stomach usually empties its contents within 4 to 6 hours after a meal. If the small intestine is empty, then death probably occurred at least 12 hours or more after the meal. Luke supposedly ate at the Blimpie Sub Shop on campus between 18:00 and 19:00 hours on Friday, September 29th. Gilbertson checked with the restaurant and the only item on its menu that contained ground meat was the Meatball Parmigiana sub sandwich. Since several search dogs had demonstrated an interest in Jimmy John's restaurant, Gilbertson also checked with the restaurant's manager and found that the menu did not contain any ground meat recipes. We concluded from the known timeline and available evidence that the meal that Luke had eaten at the Blimpie restaurant between 18:00 and 19:00 hours had probably passed from his stomach by 01:00 hours, which would have been a half-hour before he was seen entering The Library bar and a full hour before bar closing. No comment was made by the MRMEO Medical Examiner regarding the contents of Luke's small intestine or large intestine (colon), which would have helped to better establish the stage of digestion relative to Luke's time of death.

All this engendered potential issues with the investigation and the handling of evidence, and even more questions. First, local investigators did not verify that Luke did in fact eat a Meatball Parmigiana sub sandwich at the Blimpie restaurant. If he did eat a meatball sub, then how much did he eat since a large food volume would have prolonged the digestive timeline? Did he consume a 6 or 12 inch sandwich? Did he ask for double meat? The volume of material that remained in Luke's stomach amounted to 5.07 fluid ounces (just slightly more than 1/2 cup). This meant that, in all likelihood, less than 6 hours had passed since his last meal of ground meat since it was found partially digested in his stomach. Thus, the following conclusion was logically constructed: beginning with (a) the axiom that Luke had not eaten ground meat at either the Blimpie Sub Shop or Jimmy John's, and (b) given an understanding of the digestion process and the fact that partially digested ground meat was reported by the MRMEO Medical Examiner to be in Luke's stomach, then (c) this meant that Luke did not die until at least 4 hours had passed after he had eaten ground meat at some other location after bar close at 02:00 hours, which also meant (d) that Luke was alive until at least 06:00 hours, and (e) did not go into the water and die that night as presumed by police.

A second issue was the factual presence of the ground meat in Luke's stomach. He could not have consumed ground meat at Jimmy John's since it was not on the restaurant's menu or even in its refrigerated storeroom. If he did not eat a Meatball Parmigiana sub at Blimpie, then when and where did he eat the ground meat that was found in his stomach? This was never pursued by any investigating law enforcement agency; not local, not state, and not federal. This second issue raised a third issue for us. The third issue: if the material in Luke's stomach was ground meat and Jimmy John's did not have ground meat on its menu, then Luke did not eat there that night. So, why did the search dogs show an interest in Luke's scent in Jimmy John's restaurant? Four possible answers to this question existed.

a. Luke was in Jimmy John's with his friends, but did not eat there.
b. Luke was in Jimmy John's after his abduction, and was walked through Jimmy John's by his abductors.
c. Luke was not in Jimmy John's, but a person who had contact with him that night, and who had picked up a transfer scent, had eaten there or had walked through Jimmy John's.
d. Luke was not in Jimmy John's, but a person involved in his abduction, who had picked up a transfer scent during the abduction process, had eaten there or had walked through Jimmy John's.

Respiratory System

Whether a wet or a dry drowning, there is almost always some extent of hemorrhaging of the small blood vessels in the alveolar lining cells and capillary lining cells (endothelium). This causes red blood cells and proteins to leak into the alveoli, which is referred to as pulmonary edema (Armstrong & Erskine, 2011). This mixture of bodily fluids in a struggling individual usually turns into a pink froth or foam in the airway.

Evidence suggested that this was not a wet drowning, but it did not clarify whether or not it was a dry drowning. In our experience reading the autopsies of young men, normal lungs weigh about 325 to 570 grams (lack of symmetry is common and biologically explainable). They can sometimes weigh more than 1,000 grams when filled with water. According to Dr. Thomas' autopsy report, Luke's left lung weighed 450 grams and his right lung weighed 500 grams. She described his lungs as hyperinflated and made no mention of any foreign fluids. In other words, Luke's lungs may not have contained any water from the Mississippi River. Although she stated that the tracheobronchial tree and upper airway were unobstructed, she wrote in her autopsy report that there was foam in the airway. Her description was unclear as to a location in the "airway" for the foam; no foam was visible in Luke's nostrils or mouth in the autopsy photographs. Additionally, the Medical Examiner did not provide any description of the foam as to its color, nor any indication of the amount of blood present in it. She made no attempt to identify a source or cause for the foam. Most likely, she presumed its presence was due to drowning and left it at that.

Toxicology

Luke was a 6 feet 2 inch male who weighed 205 pounds. His blood alcohol concentration (BAC) was listed at 0.32 grams per deciliter (gm/dL). Further investigation revealed that this value was actually obtained from vitreous fluid, which technically made it a Vitreous Alcohol Concentration (VAC). As we have repeatedly pointed out in this book, vitreous levels are substantially higher than a true BAC (referring to blood), which would have been approximately 0.28 for Luke. The level of alcohol in Luke's urine was 0.39 gm/dL, which is referred to as a Urine Alcohol Concentration (UAC). Although 0.28 BAC is still quite drunk, it is still less than the 0.32 that was reported to the family and the public.

In La Crosse, an ongoing debate concerning the responsibility for these deaths has always centered on two possibilities: (1) an uncontrollable human killer, and (2) a controllable social problem of excessive drinking among college students. Attempts have been made to quell the public's anxiety and fear with statements made by officials, experts, and academics. The problem has been redefined as less threatening by labeling any idea of a human killer or killers as a ridiculous "urban legend." The public generally believes anything an "expert" has to say on television or in the newspapers, regardless of whether or not the problem is within their areas of expertise. These deaths have been labeled as "accidents" and blame placed on nothing more than really drunk young men who foolishly wandered into the Mississippi River. In any other crime or situation, if an expert suggested that a victim had caused, or even contributed to, the act of his own victimization, then people would be in an uproar – especially, if the victims were females. However, these victims were males. So, the public kept quiet and did not challenge the experts. Stories and statistics have been used to support assertions in the media. This included a consistent practice of announcing a drowning victim's highest level of alcohol concentration, whether that be from the urine (UAC) or vitreous (VAC), instead of his true blood alcohol concentration (BAC).

Naturally, we were interested in whether or not drugs were present in Luke's system when he died. A standard toxicological screen was performed that tested for classes of common substances of abuse: amphetamine, methamphetamine, barbiturates, benzodiazepines, cannabinoids (THC), tricyclic antidepressant, cocaine, opiates, and phencyclidine (PCP). This type of test only detects the presence (*positive*) or absence (*negative*) of the drugs, and does not report approximate or precise amounts (quantitation). In Luke's case, the drug screen came back with all negative results, which meant that none of those types of drugs were in him.

Strangely, the MRMEO Medical Examiner also ordered a test for chloroform. This test was not requested in any other case that we investigated. Chloroform enjoyed a brief period of recreational use in the early 1800s after its discovery. However, chloroform is rarely used today by anyone "to get high" because overdose or misuse is almost always immediately lethal. Simply put, it is not commonly used as a recreational drug by present-day youth. On the other hand, chloroform can be used to sedate someone in order to facilitate an abduction. Was this why Dr. Thomas ordered the test? Did she suspect foul play? What influenced her thinking to cause her to order the test for chloroform? The laboratory results came back "negative."

Typically, medical examiners do not order special tests for gamma-hydroxybutyric acid (GHB) during an autopsy. This was generally true in all of the cases. However, Dr. Thomas specifically requested a GHB screen right away. GHB causes memory loss and can render a victim debilitated and helpless. It can be used as a date rape drug and has a very short half-life of 18 to 60 minutes (0.3 to 1.0 hour). It usually becomes undetectable in plasma or blood after 6 to 8 hours. The forensic research literature confirms the postmortem production of GHB (Nishimura, Moriya, & Hashimoto, 2009). In addition, GHB is an endogenous compound (i.e., naturally occurring) in the human body at very low levels as a metabolite of the inhibitory neurotransmitter named gamma-aminobutyric acid (GABA). It can be found in the brain, cerebrospinal fluid, vitreous humor, liver, and kidneys. Urine is generally considered to be the most reliable specimen for accurate measurements because it does not produce GHB after death like blood does.

A GHB screen using a urine specimen was performed by the National Medical Services Laboratories (NMS Labs) and had a reporting limit of 2.0 mcg/mL. The test result indicated the additional testing was required in order to verify an amount. Thus, the screen was followed up with a "confirmation" test that provided a precise measurement as long as the findings met the reporting limit of 5.0 mcg/mL. The GHB value reported by the NMS Labs quantitation test actually included both GHB and gamma-butyrolactone (GBL). The research literature informed us that GBL breaks down into GHB in the body (NHTSA, 2012). It is an industrial solvent that is used in making cleaners, paint removers, and engine degreasers. It is also sold in some health stores, gyms, and on the Internet as a supplement. Some body builders use GHB as a substitute for anabolic steroids to stimulate muscle growth (Porrata, 2011). Like many of these cases, GHB was discovered in the victim when it was sought through toxicological testing. The NMS Labs GHB quantitation test of Luke's urine revealed a level that did not reach the reporting limit of 5.0 mcg/mL.

Numerous studies have been conducted to determine a cut-off value for distinguishing between endogenous and exogenous GHB in the urine and blood. We found no agreement on GHB when it came to cut-off values for postmortem production levels in blood. In one study (Moriya, Nishimura, Furumiya, & Hashimoto, 2006), the urinary level of GHB in males was 0.52 mcg/mL (plus or minus 0.37 mcg/mL, which is a range of 0.15 to 0.89 mcg/mL). As a general rule, the level of GHB concentration that can be found naturally occurring in living humans was typically below 1.0 mcg/mL (NHTSA, 2012), and ranged from 0.9 to 3.5 mcg/mL (Wang, Giang, Lu, & Kuo, 2006). Since the amount of GHB in Luke was greater than 2.0 mcg/mL, but less than 5.0 mcg/mL, one could argue that its presence may have been nothing more than endogenous or the result of postmortem production. However, postmortem production could be ruled out since no acetone, isopropanol, methanol, or n-propanol, were reported. If the GHB had been produced postmortem during decomposition, then all of them should have been found during toxicological testing. Therefore, we could not rule out an exogenous (external) source for the GHB discovered in Luke's urine.

Injuries

Luke's injuries were minimal and unremarkable when taken separately. But, when consider as a whole, they helped to paint a picture of what had transpired. Luke primarily sustained damage to his hands, arms, and head (Figure 15.14). There was also a yellowish-green bruise on his anterior, lower right side, which was about the size of an orange or fist. This was clearly an older injury that Luke had probably received while playing basketball. He was recovered with areas of blistered epidermis on both his right and left wrists. He had several lesions of the epidermis on the dorsum of his right hand: metacarpal proximal phalangeal joint of the 2nd finger (the large knuckle) and the proximal phalanx (the bone below it), and proximal interphalangeal joint (the middle knuckle) of the 3rd finger. There

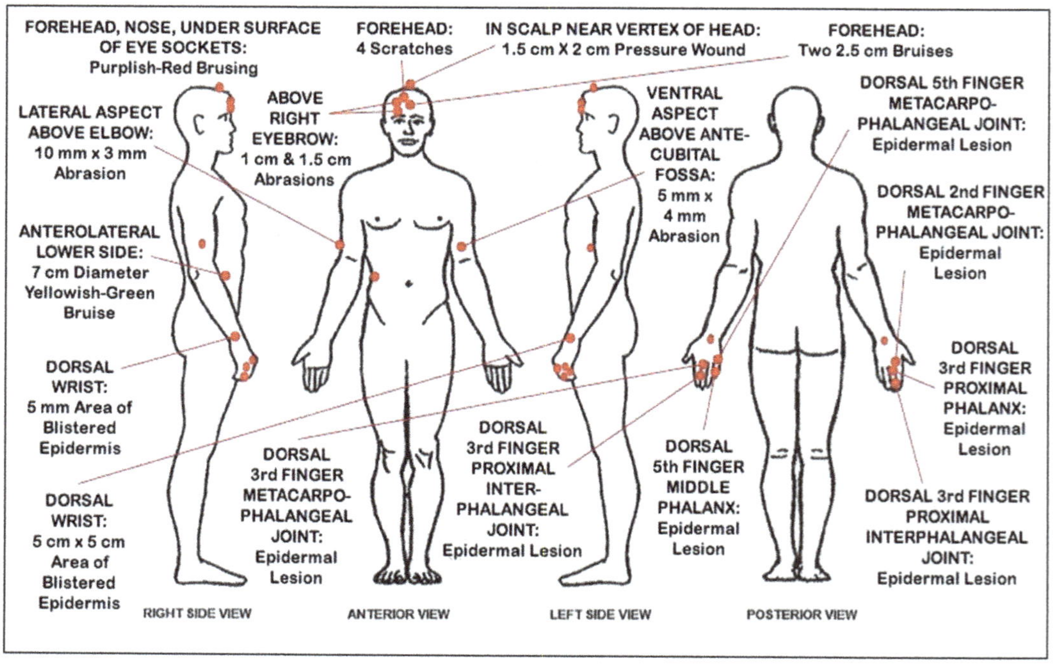

Figure 15.14 Luke Homan's body at autopsy; artist rendition is from observations of autopsy photographs and reports.

were similar lesions on the dorsal aspect of his left hand: metacarpal proximal phalangeal joint (the large knuckle) and the proximal interphalangeal joint (the middle knuckle) of the 3rd finger, the metacarpal proximal phalangeal joint (the large knuckle) and middle phalanx (middle bone) of the 5th finger. Luke had a minor 10 millimeter (mm) by 3 mm abrasion just above his elbow on the lateral aspect (outside) of the upper right arm. On the ventral aspect (under surface or inside) of his left arm, he had a 5 mm by 4 mm abrasion just above the antecubital fossa (anterior elbow).

Most distinctive was the blotchy purple-red discoloration that spread across his entire forehead (about a 120 square centimeter area), across the under surface of his eye sockets, and over his entire nose. Although some discoloration of Luke's face may have been attributable to lividity, the purple-red discoloration was not observed in his chin or around his mouth. In fact, lividity was not all that discernible on his abdomen. Sometimes, bruising can be mistaken for lividity. The blood in lividity will displace or shift to another location, but the blood in bruises will not (Shkrum & Ramsay, 2007). Therefore, if an investigator can get the lividity to displace away from suspected bruising, then it will become more visible. The blotchy purple-red discoloration that spread across Luke's entire forehead was barely detectable in the photographs taken upon his body recovery. However, it was clearly visible in the photographs taken at the autopsy some 4 hours later. Why? Luke was recovered facedown. He was on his back for 3 to 4 hours during transportation from La Crosse to Hastings. The lividity displaced from anterior to posterior during that time (as previously discussed under "Lividity" in this chapter), thereby, exposing the bruising.

There was a 1.5 centimeter (cm) area of abrasion and discoloration 2.5 cm above the right eyebrow. About 6 cm up on the right side above the eyebrow was a small abrasion of 1 centimeter in diameter. Just above this and slightly toward the center of the forehead (extending from 7 to 10 cm above the eyebrow), was an area of 1 shallow and 3 deep scratches that extended outwardly 3 cm to his left side. The most obvious injuries that could not go unnoticed on first viewing the autopsy photographs were the 2 bruises near the upper-center of Luke's forehead. Each injury measured about 2.5 cm and did not appear to be abrasions. We assessed the injuries to be pressure wounds since the epidermis did not look disturbed. There was also an injury well inside Luke's hairline near the vertex of his head that measured about 1.5 cm to 2 cm in diameter. It was described by the Medical Examiner as an abrasion (i.e., it was presumed to be a postmortem travel abrasion from the river bottom). However, we observed that the epidermis was not damaged in a pattern that was consistent with what one would expect from an abrasion. The hair follicles in the area had not been dislodged by an abrasive action, and the skin in the wound area did not appear to be damaged except where the blood vessels had been ruptured. Taking into account the surrounding bruising, we concluded that it too was an antemortem pressure wound (Figure 15.15).

During the course of our research into this case, we heard three possible explanations from law enforcement for the damage done to Luke's forehead, the crown of his head, and his hands. One proposed explanation was that the injuries were incurred during the fall into the river. The next theoretical suggestion was that the injuries were the result of travel abrasion. The last hypothesis was that he had been in a fight with his friend Allen that night (September 29–30, 2006).

We adamantly disagreed with any finding that Luke's wounds were the result of falling into the river or from travel abrasions. It is a simple scientific fact that bruises require elapsed time and a pumping heart in order to form. Some blood may be present in either

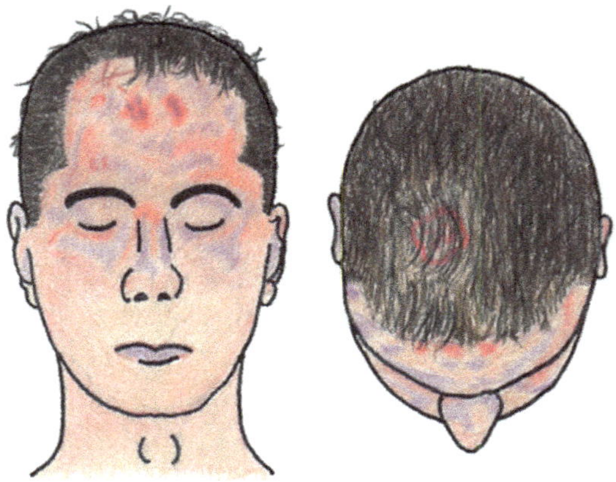

Figure 15.15 Injuries on Luke Homan's forehead and head; artist rendition from observations of autopsy photographs and reports. Bruising and damage characteristics indicated that they were antemortem pressure injuries and not postmortem travel abrasions.

antemortem (before death) or postmortem (after death) wounds due to the release of blood that was within surface tissue and vessels. This blood is generally released by the tissue and then washed away on victims who have entered a flowing body of water such as the Mississippi River. Postmortem injuries can be found on the exposed skin surfaces of recovered victims who skipped along the bottom of the river as they started to refloat (a.k.a., travel abrasions). These postmortem wounds present as damaged tissue without bruising.

On the other hand, wounds acquired antemortem generally present as damaged tissue with bruising. Had Luke sustained the injuries during a fall into the water or from scrapping along the river bottom, then the wounds would not have also bruised. Also, recall that Luke was recovered firmly on the river bottom and had not even begun to refloat. As stated earlier in the book, a body that has sunk to the bottom of a river will not move until decomposition gases cause it to become positively buoyant and to refloat (Armstrong & Erskine, 2011). Travel abrasions can only occur during the refloating process. In the autopsy photographs, the injuries and bruising on Luke's face and hands were consistent with someone who had been in a fistfight and not someone who had accidentally fallen less than 10 feet into the water at Riverside Park. Although the police made every effort to emphasize the diver's finding of 2 lengths of steel re-bar just off the levee wall in Riverside Park near the location where Luke was discovered, those objects could not have caused these kinds of injury. Rather, they would have impaled Luke.

Furthermore, had Luke received the injuries during a fight with Allen, then that fight would have had to have taken place prior to 22:00 hours and Allen's transport to the detoxification center by the La Crosse police officer. Luke's associates who reported having seen him in The Vibe and The Library bars around 01:30 hours would also likely have commented on the serious bruising that would have been clearly visible by that time. Additionally, we found that the damage to the knuckles and fingers on Luke's hands more closely reflected injuries acquired during a fist fight with defensive wounds to his arms and body. Due to the presence of bruising, the wounds on Luke's forehead were clearly inflicted antemortem. The position of the injury on the top of Luke's head could only have come from either someone striking him or something falling and striking him directly on the top of his head and not from any type of fall (Figure 15.15). The type (circular) and size of the injury appeared to be consistent with being struck with what NYPD detectives call a

"Slapper" or "Black Jack," which is a leather sleeve or pouch with a weighted metal insert. Thus, all 3 of these explanations from law enforcement were improbable.

Blood

Blood stains were found on the Cameron Avenue Bridge. Upon investigation, police found a trail of blood (various spots of it) along the walkway on the south side of the bridge. The police report suggested that it was similar to a trail that would be left by someone who was walking with a cut hand or nose. A patrolman from the La Crosse Police Department used swabs to collect samples of the blood, vouchered them, and placed them in Evidence Locker 9C. Even though the samples were placed in the same locker where the taxi voucher and log relating to Allen were stored (i.e., Evidence Locker 9C), Captain Brohmer told the Homan's that this blood referred to another case. There was neither a report that related the blood to another case, nor any report that stipulated whose blood it was. Further research by the team disclosed that a Special Agent (who worked for the Wisconsin DCI out of an Eau Claire office) assisted in the Homan investigation and had stated that the blood on the Cameron Avenue Bridge was never tested.

At the very least, the La Crosse Police Department should have typed the blood found on the bridge to see whether it could have possibly been Luke's, and then proceeded to DNA testing if necessary. They did not. As stated already, the blood was never examined. It was apparent from Luke's multiple injuries to his head that he would have had some sort of bleeding. Head wounds bleed profusely. If the blood on the bridge was Luke's, then the injuries he sustained had to have occurred prior to him supposedly falling into the river at Riverside Park. If he was bleeding from his head wounds, then why was there no blood whatsoever near his point-of-entry into the water at Riverside Park? Could the reason that there was no blood at that location be due to the fact that Luke had already stopped bleeding because he was deceased by the time his body reached Riverside Park. We asserted this since Luke's blood was in the vehicle where both the bloodhound and cadaver dog had hit, and because Luke was already dead in the vehicle. Furthermore, Luke could not have entered the water near the spot in Riverside Park where he had been recovered. He had to have gone in further upriver in order to sink to that location on the river bottom based on the mathematics of water current, depth and distanced traveled.

Flecks and Fibers

The Medical Examiner demonstrated her ability to notice details. She employed an ultraviolet light source to locate and retrieve tiny flecks of orange florescent material from the left side of Luke's face and hooded sweatshirt during the postmortem examination. According to reports, these orange flecks were inventoried and preserved, but we could not identify where they were stored (perhaps, in Evidence Locker 9C). Also, our research could not find any record or even indication that these orange flecks had ever been tested or identified. We did discover, on the other hand, that an orange florescent smiley face had been spray-painted on Front Street underneath the Cass Street Bridge (Figure 15.16), which was the first structure over the Mississippi River just to the south of where Luke was recovered. No sample of that paint was ever tested and compared with the material on Luke's body.

Upon examination of the autopsy photos, Gannon and Gilbertson noticed a minimum of 4 white fibers or hairs on the right sleeve of Luke's hooded sweatshirt and 1 on his chin.

Figure 15.16 At autopsy, Dr. Lindsey Thomas discovered and secured samples of orange fluorescent flecks on Luke Homan's jacket; but, she never tested or identified them. Interestingly, a smiley face graffito was found spray-painted in hunter orange fluorescent paint on the road nearby.

Based on their length and coloring, these samples appeared to be possible dog hairs, like those found on an Alaskan Husky (Figure 15.17). No record existed that would indicate whether the Medical Examiner or anyone present at the autopsy also noticed them, or whether they were collected, vouchered, tested, or identified by anyone. Since Luke's body was bagged in the water (which is the proper procedure for a body recovered in water), we may assume that the body as an item of evidence was not contaminated during transport or prior to examination. Thus, these white fibers were either present before Luke's body was placed into the body bag, which would mean that potential evidence was missed, or the white fibers became attached to the body after it was removed from the body bag, which

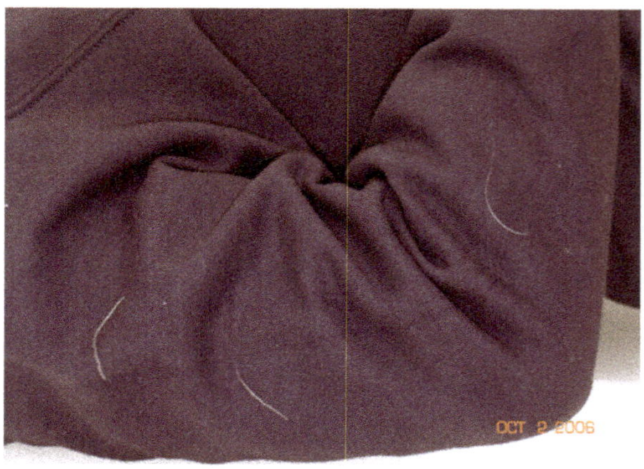

Figure 15.17 Our examination of the autopsy photographs disclosed unidentified white fibers or hairs on Luke Homan's right arm. They were never mentioned or discussed in any document, and no record existed of them ever being secured during the autopsy. This image is a recreation of the original autopsy photograph.

would mean that the body was contaminated in the controlled environment of the autopsy examination room. Or, the white fibers came from the body bag itself, which was not clean or was reused.

Hairs can be found on all sides of the clothing of pet owners since it permeates their home environment. The white fibers were only present on Luke's right side and not on his left. Therefore, they are not from a pet that was routinely within Luke's environment. We posited that Luke may have picked them up while laying on his right side in a location associated with a white-haired animal that was the pet of his murderer(s), and that he picked them up upon entering their environment (i.e., Locard's Exchange Principle). The vehicle that was searched with dogs and the alternate light source needs to be examined for similar hairs. Since the pet may no longer exist and the vehicle may have been cleaned after the police searched it, police should now check with friends, family, and neighbors (of both Luke and the owner's of the searched vehicle) to help determine whether the animal's existence was an historical fact.

Video Recordings

Closed circuit television (CCTV), also referred to as video surveillance, was nearly non-existent in La Crosse bars at the time Luke went missing and died. (Sadly, not much has changed to this day.) There was no functional video surveillance and recording in The Vibe that night. Even though the owners of The Library bar and Brothers Bar and Grill offered to pay for video surveillance along the riverfront, there was no video surveillance at their establishments on the evening that Luke went missing. In fact, according to police reports, video surveillance equipment was only functional and recording in 4 of the bars in downtown La Crosse on the evening that Luke went missing. Those bars were Cheap Shots, Dan's Bar, Top Shots, and Who's On Third. Of special note is the fact that no one has ever gone missing out of one of these four bars and then found drowned. Despite the fact that the drowning of young men in La Crosse had become a major local concern, Gannon and Duarte discovered that 85 percent of the bars in the downtown area actually did have video surveillance equipment that was sporadically functional. Not surprisingly, they were always oddly non-operational at the time of disappearances and drownings.

Cell Phone Records

Later in the morning after he went missing (September 30th), Luke's cell phone was recovered in his bedroom (halfway under his bed) by his next-door roommate. The roommate heard the phone's alarm go off at exactly 08:57 hours for a scheduled golf outing that Luke had planned with friends from out of town. We conducted further investigation which revealed that Luke's cell phone had outgoing calls and incoming text messages on it until 02:02 hours on September 30th. This told us that Luke had his phone with him throughout the night; or at the very least that someone had his phone and was using it that night. Either way, it should not have been under his bed the next morning.

The police never followed up on the fact that Luke's cell phone somehow made it home while he did not. They never obtained Luke's cell phone records. Patti Homan (the victim's mother) gave the phone records to the police on Wednesday, September 24, 2008 (almost two years after Luke's death). Patti had asked them to identify the persons associated with the incoming and outgoing calls on her son's cell phone. The police never did this. The police also never obtained GPS coordinates for any calls on Luke's cell phone to see where they might have originated from or whether it was even possible for Luke to have made the calls considering from where they may have originated. In December 2008, Patti asked them what they had accomplished relative to investigating Luke's cell phone. They commented that they could not find anything of significance, but they had acquired the phone records. They then literally handed her the same phone records that she had given to them 3 months earlier. Considering what we know about this group of killers, which likes to reintroduce victims' cell phones back into the scene where they should not be (like Luke's cell phone), we believe this was another taunting of the police by that group or a clue to the police that this case was also related to the Smiley Face homicides.

Computer

Luke's ex-girlfriend from a year ago stated that she had a number of "pop up" windows open while she was on her computer (on Friday, September 30, 2006, at 16:00 hours) and one window stated, "in the lime light as he is headed south." She later found out that Luke was reported missing. She believed someone hacked into her computer and left this message. She said the comments of an e-mail were generally up-beat, but the spelling/grammar was poor, and not apparently how Luke usually wrote. She offered her computer to Sergeant Blokhuis, who stated that he would confer with Special Agent Mathews, Wisconsin DCI to see whether they could do anything with retrieving the information from the computer. The police did not take the computer. No real interest was ever given to this piece of information except one of a cursory nature.

A report produced by the DCI showed that Luke's girlfriend thought that they should take the computer to see whether they could recover any information that may have proven useful in determining whether the person who sent the messages to her computer might be a person of interest in Luke's death. According to the report, her computer was attached to a common router in the rental property with six other computers; it would have been an easy trace for them. Instead, the agents discussed this and then said that unless there was significant reason to believe that the person who sent the e-mail to her was involved in Luke's death, then there really was no need to pursue this avenue of the investigation. Since when does an investigator conclude that potential information has nothing to do with anything before he or she even collects and analyzes the information? Standard Operating Procedure (SOP) suggests that an investigator collects and analyzes the information first to see whether it has anything to do with the investigation or any intrinsic value before summarily dismissing it as useless or unimportant information. Clearly, this information should have been followed-up.

Clothing

Our examination of Luke's autopsy pictures disclosed one final disturbing fact – someone may have removed his clothing, or at least his belt. This was consistent with what we knew about another aspect of the modus operandi of this group of offenders. We observed in the autopsy photographs that Luke's belt had 5 holes. The wear mark on the belt from routine daily wear was in the first hole, which allowed Luke to use the full

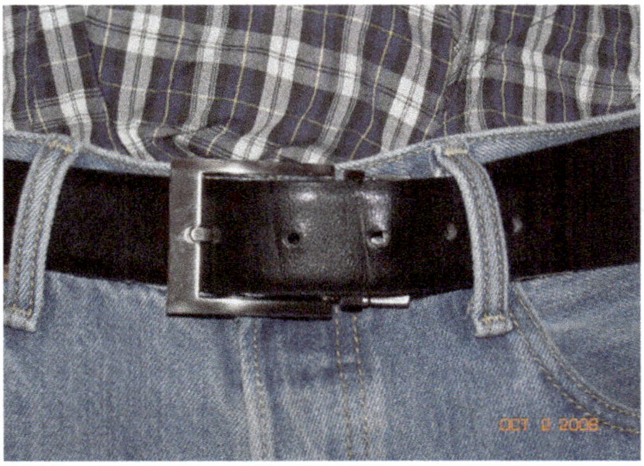

Figure 15.18 Wear marks on Luke Homan's belt indicated that it was not fastened in the hole in which it was routinely secured; it had been drawn more tightly. This fact was never reported in any autopsy or law enforcement document. This image is a recreation of the original autopsy photograph.

length of the belt. However, we could also clearly see that the belt was not fastened in that hole. Rather, Luke's belt was fastened in the last hole, which would restrict use of the belt to its shortest length. Someone had readjusted the belt to a much tighter position and several holes shorter (Figure 15.18). Faced with this empirical fact, we briefly entertained the idea that Luke may have done this to better secure his pants since they had been pulled down into a sag-and-bag position. We abandoned this idea quickly once we noticed that the belt had been passed through the first belt loop in front, but had missed the second belt loop on his left hip. We considered and discussed our own male behavior relative to putting on our belts over the years. We concluded that we have missed belt loops in the back on occasion, but we have never missed the belt loops on the left or right side—especially the second one on the left hip (Figure 15.19). This must have been done

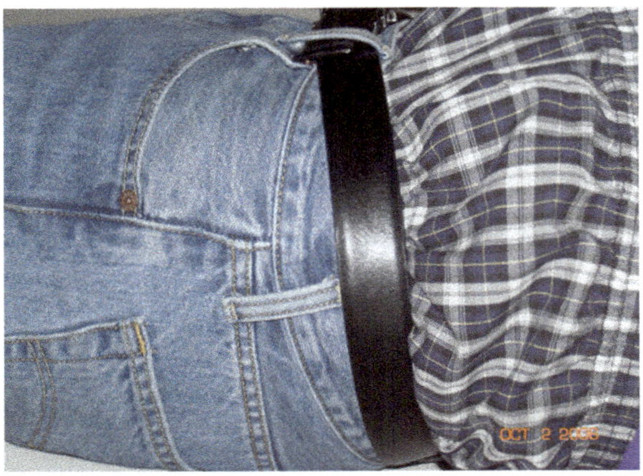

Figure 15.19 Somehow, the belt loop on Luke Homan's left hip (i.e., the second loop in the process) had been missed while putting on the belt. Again this fact was never reported in any autopsy or law enforcement document. This image is a recreation of the original autopsy photograph.

by someone who had hastily re-dressed him. Besides, if Luke had worn his pants in a sag-and-bag position often enough, then the loop on the belt in the photo would also have been more worn from this common practice. It was not! Also, the hems of his pants legs would have been worn and frayed. They were not!

Conclusion

In our professional opinion, we find the manner in which the investigation into Luke's death occurred to be egregious and appalling. Significant evidence was overlooked, ignored, or not sought, which caused us to ask several questions. Could it be that local stakeholders did not want to know the answer to important questions? It is like Duarte always tells us, "If you don't want to know the answers, then don't ask the questions."

1. FACT: The La Crosse Police Department investigators did not conduct initial and follow up interviews with all of those persons associated with the case.
   QUESTION: Why were the appropriate and routine interviews not done during this case?
2. FACT: The bloodhounds and cadaver dogs hit in identical places and were able to trace Luke's scent to the exact spot of his recovery, which demonstrated their proficiency in tracking both living and deceased humans. Luke's scent was confirmed to be in a vehicle by 2 of those same dogs, a tracking bloodhound and a cadaver dog.
   QUESTION: Why did the on-scene investigators from the La Crosse Police Department or the Wisconsin Division of Criminal Investigation not seize the vehicle and spend more time requestioning its occupants?
3. FACT: The La Crosse Police Department investigators used a black light and discovered human DNA material on the back of the right front passenger seat and on the right rear passenger seat in the vehicle.
   QUESTION: Why did this discovery not trigger seizure of the vehicle and collection of the DNA evidence in order to confirm or deny Luke's presence in the vehicle?
4. FACT: A blood trail was found on the Cameron Avenue Bridge. A vouchered sample was placed in Evidence Locker 9C.
   QUESTION: Why was it never tested for blood type or DNA?
5. FACT: Evidence indicated that Luke was in possession of his cell phone that night and that he used it. Yet, it was found back in his room under his bed.
   QUESTION: Why was this fact never explored or explained by investigators?
6. FACT: The Medical Examiner spotted and secured specimens from Luke's body of an orange fluorescent, unidentified material (i.e., the orange flecks).
   QUESTION: Why were these samples never tested or identified?
7. FACT: Although the orange flecks were noticed and recovered, the Medical Examiner and all others present during the autopsy (which included police investigators) did not notice the white fibers on Luke's body.
   QUESTION: How does one explain this disparity in attention to detail and autopsy protocol?
   QUESTION: Why was no attempt made to collect and identify the white fibers?

8. FACT: Descriptions of postmortem artifacts that are routinely included in an autopsy report were not recorded by this Medical Examiner.
   QUESTION: Were the descriptions omitted during transcription and compilation of the autopsy report, or were they never done in the first place?
9. FACT: Accurate descriptions of postmortem artifacts help investigators to determine the postmortem interval and time of death.
   QUESTION: Having received a less than descriptive autopsy report, why did investigators not insist on a better autopsy report?
10. FACT: Luke was recovered from the Mississippi River on October 2, 2006. His autopsy was performed that same day and transcribed the following day (October 3rd). The official autopsy report was not signed off by Dr. Lindsey Thomas until October 24th, who most likely waited for the final toxicology results. Her autopsy report was faxed to the La Crosse County Medical Examiner (John Steers) on October 26th at 08:39 hours.
    QUESTION: Why did the La Crosse County Medical Examiner issue a "News Release" on October 4th stating that the cause of death was cold water drowning before he had received the official and final report from Dr. Thomas?
11. FACT: Along with her faxed autopsy report (October 26th), Dr. Thomas included a short letter stating her final conclusions: the cause of death was drowning with alcohol intoxication as a contributing factor. No manner of death was stated.
    QUESTION: Why did Dr. Thomas not specify a manner of death?
    QUESTION: What evidence was available to John Steers that convinced him to issue a "News Release" on October 30th that proposed the manner of death as an accident?
12. FACT: Every minute of Allen's time from 22:00 to 03:00 hours and his associated whereabouts were accounted for; he was not with Luke.
    QUESTION: Since the La Crosse Police Department investigators suggested that Luke died shortly after bar closing at 02:00 hours as the result of an accidental fall into the Mississippi River, how can their theory concerning Allen's possible involvement in Luke's death, or even knowledge thereof, be explained?
13. FACT: By all professional assessments (i.e., the police officer who transported Allen to detox, and hospital staff), Allen was sufficiently intoxicated to support his claim that he could not clearly or accurately recall events from that evening.
    QUESTION: So, exactly what false information was it that he gave to La Crosse investigators to earn a court judgment for Obstructing (Wisconsin Statutes §946.41)?

Clearly, law enforcement realized that the dog alerts were suspicious and required further investigation, so they brought in an alternate light source which generated additional potential forensic evidence. Investigators interviewed associated persons of interest. Since they did not follow up by seizing the vehicle and testing the DNA material, then investigators must have believed that the answers which they received from the driver were sufficient enough to explain the presence of the DNA material.

Two very important points were demonstrated by the fact that both the bloodhound and cadaver dog traced Luke's scent to the vehicle and hit on Luke's scent in the vehicle. First, Luke was alive when he first entered the vehicle, which accounted for the bloodhound's hit for Luke's presence in the vehicle. Second, Luke was dead in the vehicle at a later time, which accounted for the cadaver dog's hit in the vehicle. This suggested to us that some unknown period of time had elapsed between the two times that Luke was in the vehicle. This information along with the lack of decomposition (putrefaction) and presence of rigidity (*rigor mortis*) suggested that he had been deceased for only a short period of time before entry into the water, and not for the entire period of time that he was missing. Furthermore, how could rigor going in be confused with rigor going out? Had the Medical Examiner said that Luke's body was just coming into rigor (as it clearly was in this situation), then a serious problem would have existed for this death investigation and this case clearly could not have been classified as an accident. Rather, police would have had to definitely call it a homicide.

The La Crosse Police Department's focus on Allen as a potential suspect was ludicrous. Allen apparently lost contact with Luke prior to 22:00 hours and did not re-establish contact the rest of the night. Allen had been seen roaming Riverside Park earlier that evening and had been picked up and delivered to detox by police. Luke was downtown drinking at 01:30 hours while Allen was in detox at Franciscan Skemp Hospital. Furthermore, Allen's purported BAC must have been incorrect given his time of release from detox. If it was correct, then something out of the norm or contrary to hospital protocol happened with Allen that night. The fact that Allen's scent was picked up by search dogs in several of the locations where Luke may have been can be attributed to the fact that Allen and others had personally searched on foot in most of those locations on September 30th, while police were doing nothing. The fact that Allen never denied being with Luke and only stated that he did not remember is a classic example of GHB (which was present in the 3 previous victims) which includes a lack of short term memory and is dispersed quickly from the body.

We concluded that Luke did not leave The Library bar at closing time and then proceed directly to Riverside Park, where he accidently tripped on loose cobblestones and fell into the Mississippi River, and drowned. We asserted that Luke had been abducted, and perhaps bound, for several hours prior to his murder. Based on our observation and assessment of antemortem wounds on Luke, we posited that he was involved in a fight for his life with multiple abductors. Autopsy evidence suggested to us that Luke was deceased upon being placed into the Mississippi River. Our findings relative to putrefaction, maceration, rigidity, and lividity, led us to conclude that Luke had not been dead for a period of 24 hours as originally thought. Rather, his time of death and entry into the water was even later than what was originally believed. Luke was most likely only dead for a period of 8 to 12 hours taking into account the affect of the water temperature (58 °Fahrenheit) and even the 2:1 ratio for water-to-land decomposition.

In our professional opinion, investigative protocols and policies – that are to some extent industry standards – were not followed in this case. A reluctance to move or act on evidence robbed Luke Homan and his parents of justice.

Epilogue 16

Differences

Assertions

A quest for justice began on February 20, 1997, for NYPD Detective Sergeant Kevin Gannon of the Missing Persons Squad in the Special Investigation Division of the Detective Bureau. The number of cases has grown steadily over the years. In the background, family members and a handful of close friends provided encouragement during the 17 year pursuit of the young men's killers. Duarte, Gilbertson, and Carlson joined Gannon's search for the truth. As our team learned more about the killers, we have reached out to law enforcement agencies from the city level to the federal level. Local police departments have contacted us in some cases and requested our advice and opinions. Yet, even in those cases, as in many others, no suspects were brought in for questioning or arrested. The manner of death in some of the cases was labeled "accidental." But, in most of the cases, it was declared to be "undetermined." The death investigations remained open and went cold, filed away, never to be seen or heard of again. That is until our team came along and actually listened to what the family members had to say. Having unsuccessfully captured the attention of law enforcement, we went to the American public via the media. As we took the cases to regional and national television, we naturally drew criticism. Our assertions concerning the killers have engendered controversy and debate.

For over a decade now, academically and athletically gifted young men (most of them in college) have been mysteriously found in bodies of water after a night of drinking with friends. The police and medical examiners have claimed that these deaths were nothing more than tragic drowning accidents fueled by alcohol that were unfortunately not witnessed by anyone time after time. Why was it that these accidents always happened when the victims were alone? Why was it that these usually happened during the coldest months of the year? Why was it that these victims were generally found in a body of water that was in the opposite direction that one would have expected the victim to travel? Why was it that their personal property was typically found in areas that had been previously searched? Unbeknownst to their friends, the young men would abruptly leave and unsuspectingly go for an unattended midnight walk. This was all done without ever informing their friends or anyone that they needed to get some air, wanted to go for a walk, or were going to walk home instead of driving or riding home (the way they initially came), and to do this alone. Does any of this seem logical?

Experts

As a generalization for 99 percent of the cases, the police and medical examiners reported there was no evidence that pointed to anything being suspicious, much less foul play being involved. In several of the cases, they publicly said that these cases were probably tragic accidents fueled by alcohol before the bodies were even recovered. There were also some criminology and criminal justice experts (e.g., university professors, former FBI profilers and police detectives, and investigative journalists) who stated that they looked at these cases and said there was no evidence that pointed to anything other than these cases just being tragic accidents. No mention was ever made as to which cases they had specifically looked at themselves. Their presentations in the media and on the Internet never identified – or even referred to – the actual documents or photographs that they had examined. To the best of our knowledge, no private or government individual, team, or agency has done what we have, that is, gone state to state, visited the sites, spoken with the parents, and read the associated documents.

A few of the experts reluctantly declared that although a few individual cases across the country may have actually been homicides, there was still no information that connected the cases to each other. This was exactly the situation in La Crosse, Wisconsin. The problem of young men drowning in waters near the city has drawn attention from local residents and concerned citizens across the United States. Early on, the public discourse involved the idea that a serial killer was on the loose. Not only was he active in the city of La Crosse, he traveled the midwest (i.e., Ohio, Indiana, Illinois, Michigan, Wisconsin, Minnesota, and Iowa) killing similar young men by means of drowning. An urban legend was born ("The I-80/90/94 Serial Killer").

The public conversation drew so much attention over the years that local officials asked the FBI to take a look at their cases. The FBI Behavioral Analysis Unit (BAU-2) at the National Center for the Analysis of Violent Crime reviewed eight cases: Richard Hlavaty, Charles Blatz, Anthony Skifton, Nathan Kapfer, Jeffrey Geesey, Patrick Runningen, Jared Dion and Lucas Homan. The BAU-2 released its final report in June 2007 and the results were discussed in the local newspaper by Chief Kondracki. He stated that two teams from the BAU-2 had worked independently and come to the same conclusions about the La Crosse Police Department's investigation. He proudly declared that the FBI profilers reported that no stone had been left unturned, and they had concluded that all of the eight cases were tragic and unfortunate accidents. The Chief expressed his hopes that the rumors of serial killer could now be put to rest once and for all time. He suggested that the real problem was binge and underage drinking.

We are not in total disagreement with the Chief's assertions or the BAU-2's findings. Although binge and underage drinking among college-age youth is a problem now, it has always been a problem to some extent across the United States. This holds true even for the city that is regionally famous for its Oktoberfest celebration. However, the recovery of deceased young men from local waters was not an issue until 1997. Furthermore, we cannot blame the FBI profiler(s) who conducted the review of the La Crosse cases and found no patterns or connections among the cases. We do not know what documents or photographs they saw. Did they see the same ones that we did and discussed in this book? Or, were some withheld from them? How will this book affect the overall discussion in the future? Will people's understanding and opinions of the deaths change as a result of reading this book? To what extent has our work impacted disagreement about the deaths?

Methodology

Patterns

In Chapter 1 (Introduction), we suggested that one must first demonstrate which cases are homicides before they can be linked. The next step would be to examine possible linkages. Since that analysis would require another whole book, we will only briefly identify and discuss some of the patterns that can be found among the information related to the cases presented herein. To what extent can patterns be identified? The answer is to a great extent. The analyses herein were not designed in order to prove the validity of a serial killer argument. Rather, the patterns emerged during routine modeling and incited critical questioning of the accident argument, which is premised upon randomness and probability of certain demographic and spatio-temporal variables.

There are a lot of people who question the existence of patterns among these cases. Some proclaim that patterns can only be seen when other related data is omitted. That is not how scientific research is done. Let us look at this in a context of studying tornadoes. A scientist starts by collecting data on all tornadoes. Then, the data is divided into groups based on the observed destruction and assigned a number (the Fujita Scale). Each tornado demonstrates specific characteristics that can be found within one of the F-Scale categories. A pattern exists across the F-Scale (a taxonomy) and patterns exist within each category of the scale (typologies).

Now, let us look at this in a context of studying drowning victims. A scientist starts by collecting data on all drowning victims. Then, the data is divided into groups based on the circumstances surrounding the deaths. Each group gets a name. Each drowning victim demonstrates specific characteristics that can be found within one of the named categories. A pattern exists within the overall grouping (a taxonomy) and patterns exist within each named category (typologies). A meteorologist does not examine an F2 tornado when he or she is studying F4s. Anything other than an F4 is excluded from the study because it does not qualify within the typology of an F4. Similarly, a victimologist would not include drownings that occurred as a result of boating accidents, swimming accidents, a witnessed suicide, and so forth.

As an investigative team, we did not examine all drownings and all the different circumstances surrounding them. In other words, we did not examine the whole taxonomy and all the typologies. We did, however, examine one of the typologies. We looked at college-age persons, who were out drinking with friends, became separated from them, were reported missing, and later found drown with no trace of foul play. We did not select only those along a certain corridor. We did not select only Caucasians. We did not purposively select only males. We did not select only high academic achievers or star athletes. We did not select only college-age students. Those are characteristics that came out in the data set all by themselves.

Profiling

It is not a matter of differences of professional opinion that engenders our disagreement with others regarding these deaths. Many of their statements are based on subjective interpretation and not on objective forensic facts. In this final chapter, we will not expound all of the intricate victimological details or disclose the criminological evidence that formed our understanding of the interconnectedness of these deaths. That information has been provided to law enforcement agencies over the years, and will be shared with them again upon request. In fact, law enforcement agencies already possessed most of the evidence used in this book because they produced it. We now present and discuss patterns among the information from this work. Our review focuses on La Crosse only because it serves as an excellent example of how these deaths link with each other and with cases in other cities.

Profiling, if done properly, can be a valid tool during the investigation of a crime. A robust crime profile should be exhaustive, incorporating as many concepts and variables as possible. It should include aspects of criminology, victimology, and criminalistics. A lot of different ideas have been proposed about what connects the victims to each other. Some people have suggested that a nexus can be found in the victims' physical traits, academic characteristics, religious beliefs or associated jewelry, as well as complex word or name associations and anagrams. A problem with this has been that the analysis tends to focus on only a handful of variables – a practice that can limit or bias an investigation. In this book, we disclose the extent of our analysis and database operationalization for the first time (Appendix E). Our profile included 7 concepts and 67 variables: *Personal Data* (16 variables), *Physical Data* (8 variables), *Health Data* (6 variables), *Scholastic Data* (6 variables), *Spatial Data* (5 variables), *Temporal Data* (6 variables), and *Event Data* (20 variables).

Analysis

Our analysis of the deaths of these young men involved three research methods. One was to gather as much victimological information as possible and to examine it for similarities (i.e., closeness or comparability). This was done both statistically (quantitatively) and textually (qualitatively). During the course of our investigation, we developed a profile of the victims in general. We employed geographic or map analysis to examine directions of travel and relationships between manmade features and locations. We also compiled a taxonomy based on the locations associated with the victims' residences, disappearances, and body recoveries (Appendix F, Taxonomy of Drowning Scenarios).

The most unique aspect of our analysis involved the development of two charts that display the postmortem artifacts in graphic form (Appendix D, Postmortem Artifacts – On Land). We started by reviewing the physical description of postmortem artifacts in 6 works written by authors who are considered to be the leading experts in forensic pathology and investigation (Armstrong & Erskine, 2011; DiMaio & DiMaio, 2001; Geberth, 2006; Hendrick, Zaferes, & Nelson, 2003; Shkrum & Ramsay, 2007; Spitz & Spitz, 2006). The time milestones and time periods that they presented were translated into colored bars (an example of this initial step can be seen in Figure 8.9). Since few were identical but all were similar, we then assessed the assembled material to form our time scale for the postmortem artifact of interest.

The two charts were used extensively throughout the investigation. We could place an "X" on the colored bars at positions that either matched the medical examiner's description as recorded in the autopsy report, or that matched our personal observations of recovery and autopsy photographs. If everything had progressed normally, then a vertical and reasonably straight line could be drawn through the marks. Use of these charts expanded into the development of additional unique analyses. Those approaches included timelines for the (a) assessment of postmortem artifact progression, (b) applied postmortem artifact progression models, (c) estimating "unaccounted for" time, (d) time of death approximation, and (e) estimation of the Postmortem Interval (PMI).

Similarities

Among Victims

One of the first things that catches most people's attention is the striking similarity among the victims. The victims were mostly white males between the ages of 17 and 27 years old. Most were athletes or in very good physical condition. Those who were athletes were typically a team captain or most valuable player. Many of them were wrestlers, or played basketball, soccer, baseball or lacrosse. Most were academic high achievers, with grade point averages (GPAs) often being over 3.25. Many of the victims were not in school on athletic scholarships, rather on academic scholarships. Many of them were majoring in areas that required knowledge of science and math; specifically, various fields of engineering. There were a few in the area of public safety and service, who studied criminal justice, insurance management, or risk assessment. Quite a few of them were about to celebrate a major milestone in their lives, like a birthday, graduation from college, a new job about to start, or a wedding.

One of the first things that caught Gilbertson's attention was the statistical indication that the victims' physical characteristics did not represent a random sample. If this was a naturally occurring social phenomenon and these cases truly were accidents, then randomization of the sample should be involved. When a random sample is drawn from a group of humans, then many variables associated with that group will present as a normal distribution. To scientists, this is known as Gauss' Law, but most people know it as the "Bell Curve" (Figure 16.1). When you go left and right 1 standard deviation, then you capture 68.26 percent of the data. When you go left and right 2 standard deviations, then you capture 95.46 percent of the data. When you go left and right 3 standard deviations, then you capture almost all of the data at 99.78 percent. A simple analogy is to view it like grades in a

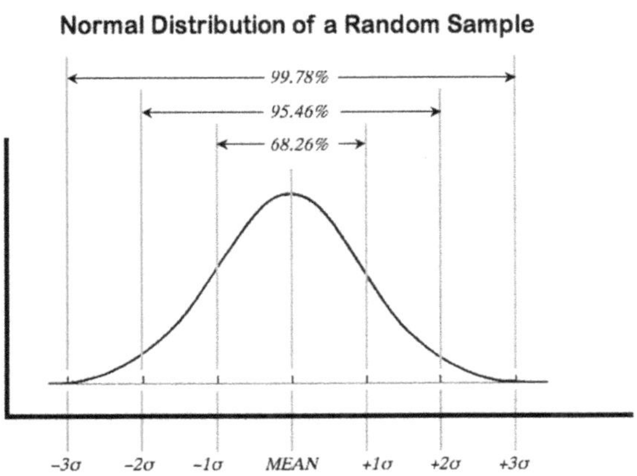

Figure 16.1 Normally, the distribution of data associated with a social phenomenon will form a "Bell Curve" with most of the data points for the variable of interest piling up around the average (statistical Mean).

classroom: a few "A"s (2.35%), some "B"s (13.5%), a bunch of "C"s (68%), some "D"s (13.5%), and a few "F"s (2.35%).

The assertion is that college-age men are drinking too much and drowning by accident in nearby waters. The Centers for Disease Control and Prevention verify on a regular basis that binge and excessive drinking behaviors are going up among college-age people. Government agency records also confirm the relationship between drinking and drowning. A close examination of such records discloses that drowning is most likely to occur during the summer months when mixed with outdoor recreation and water. Most drownings throughout the year are observed or witnessed. Additionally, the victims represent the diversity of U.S. society in age, race, biological sex, height and weight. On the other hand, the deaths that we investigated generally occurred during the Fall, Winter, and early Spring. They were not witnessed, and the victims are not diverse.

Some factors seem to support a killer argument in light of criminological theory, specifically, routine activities theory (Cohen & Felson, 1979). The authors of the theory posit that crime occurs as part of everyday routine activities. The paths of two people must cross somewhere in space at a certain time in order for them to meet and the criminal act to occur. One also needs a motivated offender and a suitable victim. Generally, the criminal act then occurs when there is no one around to defend or aid the victim (i.e., absence of a protector or guardian). It fits, right? We have a potential killer in search of the perfect victim. Their paths cross. The victim is alone without a protector and he snares him. The killer then takes him to the edge of water late at night and commits his evil act. But, what if the answer is as simple as some people propose? There are two killers – alcohol and water – in an accidental and deadly combination with no one around to hear the cries for help.

A major premise of the accident argument rests on the age of the victim. This thesis claims that the drinkers are young and inexperienced socially and with alcohol consumption abilities. Face it, college students do not start drinking when they turn 21; most started drinking in high school or the second day on campus. About 40 percent of the victims are 21 years old with about 24 percent each between 18 and 20, and between 22 and 23. This spread of the data makes sense to anyone who teaches college-age students and hears their stories the morning after in class. Relative to the victims in our database, some are minors (24%) and most are legal-age drinkers (76%). If the singular killer argument is correct, then one might expect the age range of the victims to be perhaps 2 to 4 years. And, the data do not demonstrate that. On the other hand, if the accidental death argument is correct, then the age range of drowning victims in these same cities should be quite broad and reflect the cities' demographics. The data do not support this premise either. This suggests that the deaths are not accidents and they are not the work of a singular killer.

It is necessary at this point to consider intervening or alternative variables that may be at work behind the scene. One of those variables may be the social acceptability of excessive drinking behaviors. According to survey data presented by the National Center for Chronic Disease Prevention and Health Promotion (NCCD, 2002), binge and chronic drinking is relatively high in the upper Midwest. The Center defines binge drinking as "all respondents 18 and older who report having five or more drinks on an occasion, one or more times in the past month;" and chronic drinking as "all male respondents 18 and older who report an average of more than two drinks per day and female respondents 18 and older who report an average of more than one drink per day." As can be seen in the table

Drinking Behaviors in the Midwest

STATE	PERCENT OF DRINKERS BINGE	CHRONIC
Wisconsin	24.8	7.8
Minnesota	21.1	5.5
Illinois	17.8	5.9
Michigan	16.9	5.9
Ohio	15.9	6.4
Indiana	15.9	5.4

Figure 16.2 In the Midwest, the percent of drinkers who self-reported binge drinking is about 2.5 to 3.8 times higher than the percent of self-reported chronic drinkers. (From National Center for Chronic Disease Prevention and Health Promotion (NCCD). 2002. *Behavioral Risk Factor Surveillance System Survey Data.* [Online.] Atlanta, Georgia: U.S. Department of Health and Human Services, Centers for Disease Control and Prevention. Available: http://apps.nccd.cdc.gov/brfss/Trends/TrendData.asp/.)

(Figure 16.2), a relationship generally exists between the percent of surveyed drinkers who reported binge drinking and those who reported chronic drinking.

If higher percentages of excessive drinking are evidence of greater social acceptance, then those states where excessive drinking may be more socially acceptable should also have the greatest number of the type of victims who are the focus of this book. Our database does seem to support this premise. Perhaps, then, U.S. society is encouraging certain drinking behaviors among college-age youth (particularly students) by allowing greater opportunities for excessive drinking within certain "college towns." The NCCD data seem to support the accident argument. The possible causal factors certainly fit well with the accident argument without much special consideration or explanation. Although the data may explain the number of victims in certain U.S. states, the data do not explain why there are victims in only certain cities and not in others.

Diversity in a population can be evidenced by two statistics, the mode and the standard deviation. The mode is the attribute of a variable that is the "most common" occurrence. For example, if the variable is *Race*, then the attributes include *White*, *Black*, and so forth. Whites (Caucasians) generally comprise the largest group in most cities in the United States. Thus, the mode for *Race* would be *White*. If there is diversity, then there may not be one mode. The distribution may present 2 modes (bimodal) or even more. When using profiling, it is extremely important to note whether the speaker is talking about the average offender (Mean) or the most common offender (Mode).

The standard deviation is another important statistic. It is the average distance of all data points from the Mean. The larger the standard deviation, then the more spread out the data are. The distribution curve will appear flatter, which reflects the greater diversity among the population. Conversely, the smaller the standard deviation, then the more spiked the distribution curve will appear and the less diverse the population. If these deaths are accidents, then they should be random and diverse to the extent that they reflect the demographics of the society from which they are drawn (i.e., random stratified sampling). The data points should be spread out across the graph.

Proponents of the accidental death hypothesis selectively ignore the fact that the variables that describe these victims and circumstances exist nationwide. The people, places, and situations that fit the profile for these deaths exist across the nation. If these deaths are

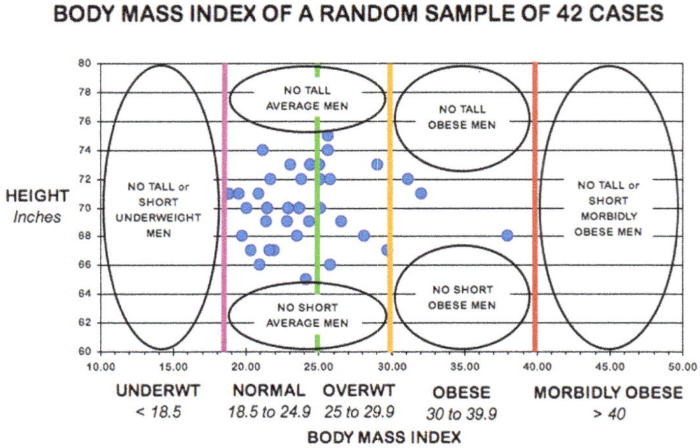

	HEIGHT	WEIGHT	BMI
MAXIMUM	75.00	250.00	38.01
MINIMUM	65.00	130.00	18.83
AVERAGE	70.26	170.57	24.25

	HEIGHT	WEIGHT	BMI
STD DEV	2.49	28.99	3.73
KURTOSIS	-0.79	0.32	3.58

(www.nhlbisupport.com/bmi/bmicalc.htm)

Figure 16.3 With the exception of a couple outliers, the majority of the victims were mostly within a range of 18.5 to about 26.0 for their Body Mass Index (BMI).

accidents, then they should exist nationwide. Yet, they do not! We have before us a very well-defined set of data. The data is delineated by very narrow victimological, geographic, and circumstantial attributes. If these are truly accidents, then where are the similarly situated victims nationwide? Why do we not read about a male, college-age victim in Daytona Beach or Cancun every year during Spring Break? There are plenty of young males, gallons of alcohol, lots of water, but no drowning victims.

Let us start again by accepting the assertion that college-age males might be more prone to demonstrate greater risk-taking behaviors. That is to say that they are more likely to act out youthful beliefs of invincibility and omnipotence. Even then, a set of truly representative and random victims should reflect a normal distribution (i.e., a Bell Curve). There should be short light-weight and heavy-weight victims, and there should be tall light-weight and heavy-weight victims. The population should not present any one personal demographic descriptor that dominates all the others (except male) and diversity in the population should exist. There should not be one distinct Mode.

However, a random sample of 42 cases demonstrates that the Body Mass Index (BMI) of the victims does not reflect all of the possible characteristics of college-age males who are self-reported binge or chronic drinkers and could become a victim of an accidental drowning (Figure 16.3). Are we to accept that short underweight or tall overweight college-age males do not binge drink? If we agree that they do binge drink, then are we to accept that they are somehow smarter and do not go near a river or lake while drinking? Certainly, to accept those remarks would be absolutely ludicrous from any perspective – scientific or otherwise.

Among Records

Not only are the victims quite similar to each other demographically, their official records are too. With the exception of Brinson, the official cause of death for all of the victims in this book was "drowning" (Figure 16.4). As we have shown, there were only a couple young men

Cause & Manner of Death as Officially Reported on the Autopsy Documents

NAME	CAUSE	MANNER	MEDICAL EXAMINER
Pat McNeil	*Drowning*	*Undetermined*	*Dr. Stephen de Roux*
Larry Andrews	*Drowning*	*Undetermined*	*Dr. Marie Macajoux*
Adam Falcon	*Drowning*	*Accident*	*Dr. Michael Sikirica*
Jerry Smith	*Drowning*	*Accident*	*Dr. Roland Kohr*
Brian Welzein	*Drowning*	*Undetermined*	*Dr. Young M. Kim*
Chris Jenkins	*Drowning †*	*Accident †*	*Dr. Raymond Rivera*
Jelani Brinson	*Undetermined*	*Undetermined*	*Dr. Janis Amatuzio*
Todd Geib	*Drowning*	*Undetermined*	*Dr. Brian Hunter*
Tommy Booth	*Drowning*	*Undetermined*	*Dr. Frederic Hellman*
Cullen Fortney	- - - - - - - - - - *Survivor - Not Applicable* - - - - - - - - - -		
Nate Kapfer	*Drowning*	*Undetermined ††*	*Dr. Lindsey Thomas*
Jeff Geesey	*Drowning*	*Undetermined ††*	*Dr. Lindsey Thomas*
Jared Dion	*Drowning*	*Undetermined ††*	*Dr. Lindsey Thomas*
Luke Homan	*Drowning*	*Accident ††*	*Dr. Lindsey Thomas*

† Dr. Raymond Rivera never specified a Cause or Manner of Death on his original Autopsy Report. The information presented here was found in other documents. The Manner of Death was officially changed to a Homicide in November 2006.

†† Dr. Lindsey Thomas only ever specified a Cause of Death and never specified a Manner of Death on any of these Autopsy Reports. The Manner of Death presented here was reported by John Steers, the La Crosse County Medical Examiner.

Figure 16.4 With the exception of Jelani Brinson, the medical examiners labeled these deaths as "drownings." It is surprising that some of the cases were labeled "undetermined."

who actually died as a result of asphyxia and subsequent hypoxia while being submerged in the water. Many of the victims were actually deceased before being placed into the water. Human intervention occurred when someone threw the young man's lifeless body into the water. In those cases, a person might propose that an "undetermined" manner of death could be assigned since the only known crime would be tampering with a corpse.

We found it odd that the deaths were all initially considered by police to be accidental drownings; with the exceptions of Jelani Brinson and Tommy Booth. Strangely, the Medical Examiners listed "undetermined" for a manner of death. If the young man drowned after a night of drinking and he did not accidentally fall into the water, then how did he get there? His entry into the water had to be an intentional homicide or suicide.

An examination of the time periods associated with the deaths disclosed another pattern within the official records. Throughout the previous chapters, we described the condition of the young men's bodies at autopsy and explained how to interpret them relative to the extent of progression of specific postmortem artifacts (e.g., rigidity, lividity, tepidity, putrefaction and maceration). Having identified the approximate point along the timeline that they had reached, we were able to estimate the *Time of Death to Autopsy*, which is also called the Postmortem Interval (PMI). The PMIs ranged from 1.25 days to 10.00 days, with an average time period of 3.79 days and a mode of about 3 days (Figure 16.5). This was an extremely important discovery and demonstrated that the cases were homicides.

First, if these deaths were accidental, then the time period of *Last Seen to Time of Death* should never exceed 1 day. In fact, it should actually be no more than a couple

Commonalities Among Case Study Time Periods

NAME	PRESUMED TIMES: Last Seen to Recovery	PRESUMED TIMES: Recovery to Autopsy	PRESUMED TIMES: Last Seen to Autopsy	ESTIMATED TIMES: Last Seen to Time of Death	ESTIMATED TIMES: Time of Death to Autopsy
Pat McNeil	*49.42 days* (1186 h 5 m)	*1.02 days* (24 h 25 m)	*50.44 days* (1210 h 30 m)	*46.44 days* (1114 h 30 m)	*4.00 days* (96 h 0 m)
Larry Andrews	*42.14 days* (1011 h 30 m)	*0.33 days* (8 h 0 m)	*42.47 days* (1019 h 30 m)	*39.47 days* (947 h 30 m)	*3.00 days* (72 h 0 m)
Adam Falcon	*5.55 days* (133 h 22 m)	*0.92 days* (22 h 15 m)	*6.47 days* (155 h 37 m)	*3.47 days* (83 h 37 m)	*3.00 days* (72 h 0 m)
Jerry Smith	*7.80 days* (188 h 0 m)	*0.46 days* (11 h 20 m)	*8.26 days* (199 h 20 m)	*6.26 days* (151 h 20 m)	*2.00 days* (48 h 0 m)
Brian Welzein	*76.59 days* (1838 h 23 m)	*0.68 days* (16 h 22 m)	*77.28 days* (1854 h 45 m)	*70.27 days* (1686 h 53 m)	*7.00 days* (168 h 0 m)
Chris Jenkins	*118.72 days* (2849 h 15 m)	*0.61 days* (14 h 45 m)	*119.33 days* (2864 h 0 m)	*109.33 days* (2624 h 0 m)	*10.00 days* (240 h 0 m) †
Jelani Brinson	*7.62 days* (182 h 59 m)	*1.94 days* (46 h 56 m)	*9.56 days* (229 h 55 m)	*6.27 days* (150 h 55 m)	*3.29 days* (79 h 0 m)
Todd Geib	*20.69 days* (496 h 50 m)	*0.82 days* (19 h 50 m)	*21.51 days* (516 h 40 m)	*18.53 days* (444 h 50 m)	*2.98 days* (71 h 50 m)
Tommy Booth	*14.61 days* (350 h 50 m)	*0.78 days* (18 h 50 m)	*15.39 days* (369 h 40 m)	*13.39 days* (321 h 40 m)	*2.00 days* (48 h 0 m)
Cullen Fortney	--------------- *Survivor - Not Applicable* ---------------				
Nate Kapfer	*41.63 days* (999 h 6 m)	*2.68 days* (64 h 24 m)	*44.31 days* (1063 h 30 m)	*38.63 days* (927 h 6 m)	*5.68 days* (136 h 24 m) ††
Jeff Geesey	*43.30 days* (1039 h 15 m)	*0.10 days* (2 h 30 m)	*43.40 days* (1041 h 45 m)	*40.30 days* (967 h 15 m)	*3.10 days* (74 h 30 m)
Jared Dion	*5.22 days* (125 h 30 m)	*0.21 days* (5 h 10 m)	*5.43 days* (130 h 40 m)	*3.43 days* (82 h 40 m)	*2.00 days* (48 h 0 m)
Luke Homan	*2.32 days* (55 h 51 m)	*0.23 days* (5 h 39 m)	*2.55 days* (61 h 30 m)	*1.30 days* (31 h 30 m)	*1.25 days* (30 h 0 m)

ESTIMATED TIME DECEASED: RANGE = 1 to 10, AVERAGE = 3.79, MODE = 3

† Christopher Jenkins was partially frozen at recovery and the extent of decomposition on his body reflected 5 to 7 days. However, 10 days elapsed from our estimated time of death to recovery.

†† Nathan Kapfer was frozen solid at recovery and the extent of decomposition on his body was minimal. After thawing out for 64 hours, postmortem artifacts reflected 72 hours at autopsy.

Figure 16.5 By using the Postmortem Artifacts chart (Appendix D), we were able to estimated time periods for the cases, from the time each young man was last seen to his autopsy.

hours. Second, the time period of *Last Seen to Autopsy* should be almost equal to the *Time of Death to Autopsy*. Third, by subtracting the *Time of Death to Autopsy* from the *Last Seen to Autopsy*, we were able to infer a startling characteristic of these deaths. This was revealed in the *Last Seen to Time of Death*. This temporal statistic told us that each of these young men was alive and missing for a period of time before his death. The cases could not be suicides, because that would mean that the men would have had to wandered around for days (1.30 to 109.33 days), found a food source and shelter, acquired some alcohol and gotten drunk, and then jumped into the water—all without anyone seeing them. Preposterous!

Fourth, *Last Seen to Time of Death* also provided us with some insight into the killers' modus operandi and minds. They were either holding the young men alive for days before they murdered them, or they killed them right away and somehow preserved their bodies. We believe that both methods were used. Clearly, Nate Kapfer is an example of preservation. A total of 59 hours 24 minutes passed between his body recovery and the first attempt to perform an autopsy. At that time, the Medical Examiner described him as frozen solid and left him out for an additional 25 hours to thaw. Given the outdoor air and water temperatures, Nate did not get that frozen due to environmental conditions. Human intervention had to have played a role. Furthermore, the extent of progression of postmortem artifacts on most of the men at the time of recovery and autopsy indicated that they had not been dead very long. These facts demonstrated to us that "criminal intent" (*mens rea*) was involved in the commission of these deaths.

Among Drugs

Another characteristic of the cases is the similarities among the toxicology tests for alcohol and drugs (Figure 16.6). Most of the cases that are considered to be a part of the "smiley face" phenomenon have been considered to be accidental drownings by officials. They propose that excessive drinking contributed to the victimization of these young men. Therefore, one would expect to see consistently high alcohol concentration numbers for blood (BAC), urine (UAC), and vitreous (VAC). The opposite is actually the truth.

Cullen Fortney survived his encounter with the Mississippi River in La Crosse during January 2006. He was not sober, but he could legally drive a car with his 0.043 BAC that was determined at 08:00 hours by the hospital. La Crosse Police Department investigators calculated that Cullen had to have consumed at least 8 drinks by the time he went missing (01:45 hours), which would have put him at a 0.163 BAC (twice the legal intoxication level of 0.08 mL). But, as we proved in Chapter 11, Cullen would have perished from hypothermia had he been in the water for nearly 6 hours. Since his true BAC probably was closer to the 0.043 when he entered the water, then some other substance must have had control of Cullen's memory. We will never know though. No additional drug testing and nothing

Results of Standard Alcohol/Drug Screens & Additional Testing

NAME	STANDARD TESTING	ADDITIONAL TESTING
Pat McNeil	ETOH 0.16 (Blood), 0.23 (Brain)	Never Performed
Larry Andrews	ETOH 0.19 (Blood), 0.21 (Brain), 0.30 (Urine) DIPHENHYDRAMINE (Urine)	Never Performed
Adam Falcon	ETOH 0.21 (Blood), 0.21 (Vitreous), 0.29 (Urine)	GHB present < 2 mcg (Urine)
Jerry Smith	ETOH 0.149 (Blood)	ETOH 0.162 & 0.163, NICOTINE 10 ng (Blood) COTININE < 10 ng, CAFFEINE unspecified (Blood) GHB/GBL 100 mcg (Liver)
Brian Welzien	ETOH 0.084 (Blood)	Never Performed
Chris Jenkins	ETOH 0.12 (Blood)	GHB 57 mcg (Unidentified)
Jelani Brinson	CAFFEINE 0.55 mcg (Blood) COTININE unspecified (Blood)	GHB 22 mcg (Urine) GHB 35.1 mcg (Blood)
Todd Geib	ETOH 0.12 (Blood) COTININE unspecified (Blood)	DESIPRAMINE 495 ng (Blood) AMITRIPTYLINE 51 ng (Blood)
Tommy Booth	ETOH 0.22 (Blood), 0.101 (Vitreous)	ALPRAZOLAM 0.01 mcg (Blood)
Cullen Fortney	ETOH 0.043 (Blood)	Never Performed
Nate Kapfer	ETOH 0.220 (Blood), N-PROPANOL present (Urine)	PEA present (Urine)
Jeff Geesey	ETOH 0.420 (Spleen), N-PROPANOL present (Spleen)	GHB 130 mcg (Liver)
Jared Dion	ETOH 0.289 (Blood), 0.270 (Vitreous), 0.400 (Urine)	GHB 11 mcg (unspecified)
Luke Homan	ETOH 0.32 (Vitreous), 0.39 (Urine)	GHB present ≥ 2 mcg, GHB/GBL < 5 mcg

ETOH: Ethyl Alcohol, GHB: Gamma Hydroxybutyrate, GBL: Gamma Butyrolactone, PEA: Phenethylamine (a GHB Analog).

Figure 16.6 When additional drug testing was done, then a debilitating substance was usually found in the victim's system. The most common was the date rape drug gamma-hydroxybutyrate (GHB) or another substance associated with it (e.g., GBL & PEA).

else was ever really done in the way of an investigation concerning his incident, probably because he survived.

Chris Jenkins was another example. He was assessed to have a 0.120 BAC at autopsy. He was also found to have GHB in his system (57 mcg). Officials tried to explain away the GHB as being the result of postmortem decomposition. But then, they did not account for the postmortem production of alcohols. So, either the presence of GHB was valid or the BAC was lower. You cannot have it any other way. A total of 119 days passed between when Chris was last seen to the time of his autopsy. As we demonstrated in Chapter 7, Chris' BAC would have increased by about 0.060 due to postmortem decomposition had he been deceased the entire 119 days. However, the absence of other alcohols that are also the result of postmortem decomposition (i.e., methanol, isopropanol, n-propanol, n-butanol, and acetone) proved that our assertion was correct. We concluded that Chris was not outdoors for nearly 4 months. He was only in the water for about 10 days, and therefore, the GHB was not the result of postmortem decomposition. Chris' case was changed from an accidental drowning to a homicide in November 2006 by the Minneapolis Police Department, and nothing more has really been done since then to find his killers.

With the exception of Jerry Smith, another interesting thing about these cases is that GHB is not a part of normal drug screening. The test has to be specially requested and is rather expensive. The families did not ask for the GHB test. The Medical Examiner ordered it along with the rest of the drug panels. This is in and of itself another similarity among the cases in this book. We were engaged by Robin Hill early on in her son's case. With her permission, we paid to preserve the autopsy specimens and ordered additional testing. In the other cases (i.e., Falcon, Brinson, Geib, Booth, Kapfer, Geesey, Dion, and Homan), the Medical Examiners ordered the extra tests right away. Why did they order it? Did they suspect something right away?

That is exactly what happened in the investigation of Jelani Brinson's death. His death remains a mystery since no definitive cause or manner of death could be determined by the Medical Examiner. While reviewing the autopsy report and photographs with Dr. Amatuzio in her office, Gilbertson discovered that she was suspicious from the start. She estimated the Postmortem Interval (PMI) and determined that Jelani had not been deceased the entire time he was missing. She knew that he should not have been in full rigor at the time of recovery. Since he had no alcohol or standard drugs in his system, she looked for other contributors. That is why she ordered the extra tests for GHB. The Anoka County Sheriff's Office has kept the case open.

Jelani's death is just one of the cases we have found where the young man was tested to be sober (relative to alcohol and typically used drugs), but clearly intoxicated as evidenced by witness statements and video recordings of his behavior. The whole issue of toxicological testing presents quite a challenge to law enforcement and medical examiners. Tests are expensive and budgets are limited. Which drugs do you test for as part of the "standard" drug scan? Certainly, autopsies for suspicious or unattended deaths should always test for the presence of any medication(s) that someone is supposed to be taking (e.g., Tommy Booth and Alprazolam). Knowing the dosage, the correlating serum concentration, and the drug's half-life can provide a lot of information about when the medication was last taken and how long it was until death.

Knowing which street drugs, prescription drugs, or over-the-counter drugs (OTCs) to test for requires a two-way conversation between the police department's drug task force and the medical examiner's office in order to identify local and national trends relative to drugs of abuse. People can become quite creative when it comes to the desire to alter their cognitive state by "catching a buzz." Some OTCs, when taken in large quantities, can act like street drugs and alter perceptions of reality, alertness, and reflexes. Some prescription drugs are sought after to such an extent that people will break into pharmacies after closing or people's homes in search of them (e.g., Oxycontin and Oxycodone, as well as other narcotics). A red flag should go up when a drug scan indicates the presence of tricyclic antidepressant drugs. Bells and whistles should be going off when those drugs are found at levels that would kill someone (e.g., Todd Geib and both desipramine and amitriptyline).

Lastly, given the staggering availability of date rape drugs on university and college campuses and in nearby towns, deceased bodies need to be tested for those drugs too. Standard drug scans include classes of drugs. But, in some of the toxicology reports that we have read, flunitrazepam was also included as a standard assay. This drug is more commonly known as Rohypnol, or on the street as "roofies." It falls within the class of drugs called benzodiazepines, which also includes alprazolam (Tommy Booth). Ketamine is also a commonly abused drug that produces dissociative anesthesia. It would facilitate an abduction or rape quite well. Depending on its availability on the street within a community, medical examiners may want to include it. Lastly, as we have seen during the course of our investigation (these case studies are only a handful of examples), medical examiners should always order tests for gamma-hydroxybutyrate (GHB) and gamma-butyrolactone (GBL). Relative to ease of street-level acquisition, they may also want to consider testing for phenethylamine (PEA), and other GHB analogs.

Among Cases

When drowning cases are cataloged, then it becomes apparent that most are observed and are related to boating or swimming activities during the summer months, and are often coupled with alcohol consumption. Some occur during winter months when people who are ice fishing or snowmobiling fall through thin ice. There exists a generally strong relationship between the various sites of importance: *Last Seen, Return To,* and *Recovery.* Individuals' bodies are normally recovered near the site where they were last seen, or along a path in the direction towards the place to which they were supposed to return to at that time. Accidents wherein an automobile leaves the roadway and enters a body of water would fit in this latter category. Whereon an individual was not observed entering the water, but was either tracked by scent dogs or physical evidence suggests that he took that path, then one finds that the path logically leads to a presumed point of entry into the body of water.

While analyzing the three primary directions of interest in the "smiley face" cases, Gilbertson noticed some patterns that could be organized according to their similarities. The subsequent taxonomy centered on cardinal directions related to specific locations rather than a standard analysis that would focus on travel along available roadways or footpaths. The analytical emphasis was not on determining the different characteristics of various routes taken to get to the water, rather, it centered on relationships among the endpoints of the two mathematical rays (i.e., *Last Seen* to *Return To*, and *Last Seen* to *Recovery*) and available evidence. Typologies represent categories or "pigeon holes" into which cases can be placed based on known characteristics of the victim, crime scene, and so forth. They can help to identifying similarities and differences relative to how the crimes were committed (*modus operandi*), and subsequently assist in determining the number of unique offenders or groups of offenders. A case may not fit perfectly into a typology, but it should be closer to one than another. Thus, typologies are referred to as ideal types and cases are plugged in relative to the best fit. Five typologies were identified (Figure 16.7; Appendix F, Taxonomy of Drowning Scenarios).

Typology 1. "At Residence and Drowned." Here, the *Last Seen*, *Return To*, and *Recovery* sites are co-located. Evidence may or may not exist that explains how and/or why the person entered the water and drowned. This could be an accident, a suicide, or a homicide. This is a typical accidental drowning. An example is a child who was last seen playing in the backyard and who was then discovered drowned in the swimming pool. Evidence suggests that he slipped and struck his head prior to entering the water. Another example is an adult who is found drowned in the backyard swimming pool, but there were no witnesses or physical evidence to suggest how he got into the pool or what may have contributed to his drowning.

Typology 2. "Disappeared from Residence and Drowned Elsewhere." In this scenario, the *Last Seen* and *Return To* sites are co-located, but the *Recovery* site is located elsewhere. Evidence may or may not exist that explains how and/or why the person left his home and entered the water and drowned. An example is a person who was last seen in a dorm room by a roommate, and evidence suggests that he left there moving along a certain path to the location where he was found drowned. Another example is where a student simply vanishes from his dorm room, leaving the television on and study books open, and no evidence exists explaining how he got from residence to the water.

Typology 3. "Away from Residence and Seen On or Near the Water in which Drowned." The *Last Seen* and *Recovery* sites are co-located, and the *Return To* site is located elsewhere. Evidence may or may not exist that explains how and/or why the person entered the water and drowned. An example is someone who lives in Town A and travels to Lake B, where he is observed by witnesses on shore to have fallen while waterskiing. Evidence suggests that he received a concussion upon striking the water and was rendered unconscious making him incapable of swimming. Another example is someone who lives in Town A and travels to Lake B to go fishing and is then found drowned. No evidence exists for how or why the boat capsized or why he did not survive.

Taxonomy of Drowning Scenarios

	TYPOLOGIES & DESCRIPTIONS
1	*At Residence and Drowned*
2	*Disappeared from Residence and Drowned Elsewhere*
3	*Away from Residence and Seen On or Near the Water in which Drowned*
4	*Drowned on the Way Back to Residence*
5	*Drowned in the Opposite Direction of Residence*

Figure 16.7 Typologies represent categories or "pigeon holes" into which cases can be placed based on known characteristics of the victim, crime scene, and so forth. Diagrams of the taxonomy can be seen in Appendix F.

Typology 4. "Drowned on the Way Back to Residence." The *Last Seen*, *Recovery*, and *Return To* sites are in different locations, but they are along a broad path from one to the other. Evidence may or may not exist that explains how and/or why the person entered the water and drowned. An example is someone who was last seen leaving a bar and was trying to get back to his residence. Evidence suggests that the route he was taking did lead in the general direction of his residence, but also led past the body of water in which he was found drowned. Another example is similar, but no evidence exists to explain why he veered off-course and ended up in the water. Only a handful of the 300 plus cases that we have examined fit this typology.

Typology 5. "Drowned in the Opposite Direction of Residence." As in Typology 4, the *Return To*, *Last Seen*, and *Recovery* sites are in different locations. However, in this typology, the *Return To* and *Recovery* sites are opposite directions from one another. Evidence may or may not exist that explains how and/or why the person entered the water and drowned. A key point is that the victim's residence and the location where he was found drowned are in opposite directions. Several examples exist: (1) where evidence suggests both routes may have been taken by a person – one leads in the direction of his residence and the other to where he was found drowned; (2) when evidence only leads in the direction of his body recovery site; (3) when evidence only leads in the direction of his residence; and lastly, (4) when no evidence exists to describe the route he took. This is the most common scenario that we have seen for these cases.

Among Evidence

There were similarities among additional, physical forensic evidence which substantiated our claim that these victims were murdered. Part of the similarity among the evidence was the evidence itself. For example, unidentified blue flecks and yellow fibers were visible on Pat McNeil at autopsy. Flourescent orange flecks and white fibers were visible on both Larry Andrews and Luke Homan. Fly larvae were found on Pat McNeil, while unidentified insects were discovered on Chris Jenkins, Tommy Booth, and Nate Kapfer. Mud or a slimy matter was reported to be on Adam Falcon, Chris Jenkins, and Nate Kapfer; but it was not found on the other young men who were in the same bodies of water. Shoe tracks were found in the mud of the river bottom near the bodies of Adam Falcon and Tommy Booth.

Another similarity was in what transpired regarding the evidence. This was related to whether or not the officials (law enforcement investigators and medical examiners) saw the evidence, whether or not they collected it, and then whether or not they did anything with it.

Saw It	Collected It	Acted on It
Yes	Yes	Yes
Yes	Yes	No
Yes	No	No
No	No	No

Yes-Yes-Yes. In one case, an official did go the extra mile with evidence by collecting it and analyzing it. Although the shoe tracks next to Booth's body had deteriorated and were indistinguishable, the Medical Examiner called in a scientist to determine how long the tracks would last in the water with that water current. That effort helped him to more accurately estimate the Postmortem Interval. In another case, forensics specialists at the Anoka County Sheriff's Office did try to recover data from Brinson's cell phone to no avail. Also, the hair found in Jenkins' hand was collected in February 2003 and sat in storage until December 2007, at which time is was finally tested after a lot of badgering by the family and us.

Yes-Yes-No. In some cases, officials saw the evidence and collected it, but then never did anything with it. One example of this happened in the Luke Homan case. The Minnesota Regional Medical Examiner's Office in Hastings (Minnesota) contracted with the City of La Crosse to perform autopsies. According to official records, the Medical Examiner inventoried small orange flecks of an unidentified material that she found on Luke's body. There was no indication where they were stored. Additionally, a trail of blood was found and samples were recovered from the Cameron Avenue Bridge during the investigation into Luke's death. It was placed into Evidence Locker 9C; perhaps the orange flecks went in there too. Since no official report could be found that discussed test results, we surmise that neither the orange flecks nor the blood samples were ever tested.

A few more examples of seeing evidence, collecting it, and then doing nothing with it were Geib, McNeil, Booth, and Smith. Nothing was ever done in Geib's case with a small piece of white plastic that was placed into a manila envelope labeled "Prop – 15." Additionally, supervisors would not let Gannon follow up on trying to identify a partial vehicle license plate number that he had received from a witness in McNeil's case. Other word-of-mouth evidence (i.e., witnesses' statements) was collected during interviews and not acted upon. Examples are the many incidents in Smith's case (e.g., assaults on the homeless man, the fake cop, and the possible abduction), as well as the statement made by Booth's uncle, an Army Major General, about gun-running. It was likely that none of this evidence was ever followed up since no reports indicating such were found.

Further examples of this handling of evidence was seen in Smith with the tracking dogs. Investigators discovered that the dog led them to the laundry room of an apartment complex at which Smith had no business being. The trail literally ended there. During the search for Falcon, shoe tracks were found by the spot where he was recovered. A total of 6 witnesses saw the tracks and a drawing of the sole pattern (almost to scale) was turned over to officials. The drawing disappeared never to be seen again. Also, using the data recovery provided by viaForensics, we were able to identify the location for a photograph that was taken while Smith and his cell phone should have been in the bar. That information, to our knowledge, was provided to attorneys and law enforcement who did nothing further with it.

Yes-No-No. There were some cases where officials even reported in writing that they saw the evidence, but then did not collect it. Examples of this are the fly larvae on McNeil. During the investigation into the deaths of Jenkins, Booth, and Kapfer, insects were reported, but no attempt was made to collect them, to identify their species, or to identify their stage of development. A forensic entomologist could have been consulted. A smokeless tobacco can was seen at the scene of Falcon's recovery. Perhaps, there were fingerprints on it. We will never know since it was not collected.

In a couple cases, sand and mud were potentially important pieces of evidence. Since the river bottom was muddy and not sandy, from where did the sand on Kapfer come? And, what about the sand found deep in the lumen of Welzien's trachea? In several of the cases, mud was reported on the body. It was always presumed to be from the river bottom. Case in point, we were recently asked to consult in a case wherein the victim's hands were covered with mud while his bare feet were clean. The mud could have been tested for pollutants and other naturally occurring chemicals and organisms. A forensic geologist or chemist might have been able to identify the site of origin for the sand and mud.

The most egregious example was in Homan. Herein, both a tracking dog and a cadaver dog hit on Homan's scent in the rear seat of a vehicle. Investigators recognized the significance of this and then used an alternate light source to identify blood on the seat. They saw the evidence, acknowledged its presence, and then chose not to collect the vehicle or a sample from the vehicle for further testing. They let the driver and the car go. This was not the only case where this kind of unprofessional behavior occurred. In a case not covered in this book, a K-9 indicated a hit inside a vehicle and officers let the car go. In that same case, they allowed the carpet and padding to be removed and hauled away from the apartment where the victim was last known to be, and then they ran a tracking dog through it the next day.

No-No-No. In a few cases, officials did not collect the evidence because they somehow did not see it – even though it was clearly visible to us in the autopsy or recovery photographs. They missed the blue flecks and yellow fibers on McNeil, the flourescent orange flecks and white fibers on Andrews, and the white fibers on Homan. The Anoka County Sheriff's Office did a pretty good job investigating Brinson's death, and they still are. We noticed in photographs a construction contractor's trailer parked in the driveway of the home where Brinson was last known to be. It was never searched. Phone records were often overlooked too. In Booth, it was apparent to us that the phone records should have been pulled for everyone who was with him that night. Since Homan was using his phone the night he vanished and then it was found under his bed in his apartment room, his phone records should have been examined for GPS data. In fact, his phone should have been given to an expert so data could be recovered from it like in Smith.

Commonalities

One Town

Having demonstrated the considerable extent of similarity among the cases, we now shift our attention to commonalities. In doing this, we shall use one town as the prime example (i.e., La Crosse, Wisconsin). There are several towns and cities that have multiple victims: Minneapolis, East Lansing, Eau Claire, Chicago, New York City, Boston, and Milwaukee. First, please note that none of the cities are in the U.S. South or West. Second, please note that La Crosse stands out, particularly in Wisconsin (Figure 16.8), from all other cities on account of the total number of victims in that city (9 young men in 13 years, from September 1997 to February 2010): Charles Blatz, Tony Skifton, Nate Kapfer, Jeff Geesey, Pat Runningen, Jared Dion, Luke Homan, Chris Melancon, and Craig Meyers.

La Crosse (Wisconsin) is an example of the disparate statistics that exist among these victims. According to U.S. Census Bureau data for La Crosse during the year 2000, 92.8% (47,454) was white, 47.1% (24,396) was male, and 43.2% (22,400) was under the age of 25. Assuming that those under age 15 would most likely not drink enough alcohol to end up in a local detoxification unit, then the population that would most likely become drunk and end up in detox would be within the age group 15–24 (14,417 or 27.8% of the total La Crosse population). According to Gundersen Lutheran Hospital in La Crosse, 15% of those individuals admitted as patients in their detoxification unit were identified as being

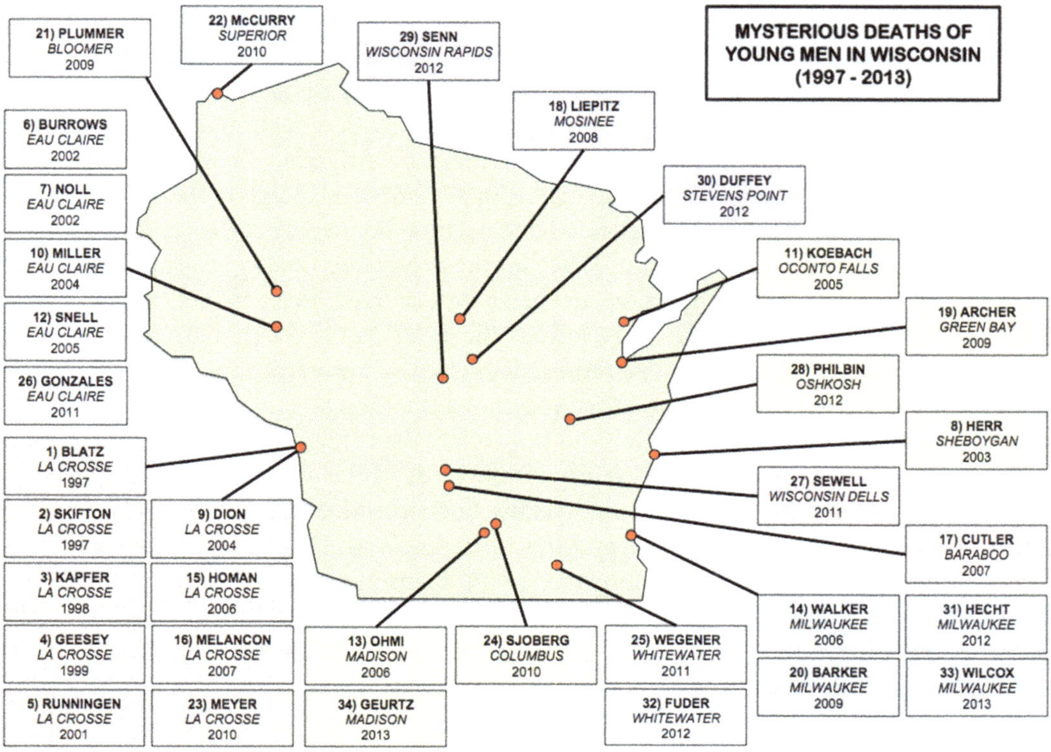

Figure 16.8 There are 34 mysterious deaths of young men in Wisconsin alone, with 9 of them having died in La Crosse, 5 in the area of Eau Claire and Bloomer, 3 near Stevens Point (including Wisconsin Rapids and Mosinee), 4 in the eastern part of the state (Oconto Fall, Green Bay, Oshkosh, and Sheboygan), 4 in Milwaukee, 3 in the Madison area, 2 in Whitewater, 2 in the Wisconsin Dells and Baraboo area, and 1 in Superior (who was from Duluth where possibly 3 other strange "drownings" occurred).

under the age of 25. The detox unit reported 4,562 admissions from 2000 through July 2004, of which 15% (684 persons) were under 25 years old. According to Franciscan Skemp Hospital, 15–20% of those individuals admitted as patients in their detoxification units were identified as being young people. The hospital reported 469 admissions for 2003, of which 15% (70 persons) to 20% (94 persons) were young people.

Although individuals ages 15–24 represent 27.8% of the La Crosse population of most likely drinkers, they only represent 15–20% of those admitted to local detoxification units. Therefore, the majority (80–85%) of those individuals admitted to La Crosse detoxification units are not college-age students. Thus, those individuals under the age 25 who were admitted to local detoxification units did not statistically represent their respective proportion of the total population of admissions. In other words, Gundersen Lutheran Hospital reported 4,562 admissions from 2000 through July 2004, of which 15% (684 persons) were under 25 years old. If those individuals who had access to alcohol and who were between ages 15–24 had been proportionately represented, then there would have been 1,268 (27.8% of 4,562) admissions for their age group alone. Franciscan Skemp Hospital reported 469 admissions for 2003, of which 15% (70 persons) to 20% (94 persons) were young people. If those individuals who had access to alcohol and who were ages 15–24 had been proportionately represented, then there would have been 130 (27.8% of 469) admissions for their age group alone.

14,417 = Number of 15–24 year olds in La Crosse.
(27.8% of the total La Crosse population)
684 = Actual number under age 25 admitted at Gundersen Lutheran.
(15% of their total admissions)
1,268 = Proportional number under age 25 that should have been admitted.
(27.8% of their total admissions)
70-90 = Actual number of Young People admitted at Franciscan Skemp.
(15–20% of their total admissions)
130 = Proportional number of Young People that should have been admitted.
(27.8% of their total admissions)

Therefore, the age group that contains the ages of the La Crosse drowning victims in question was under-represented at Gundersen Lutheran Hospital (1,268 – 684) by 584, and at Franciscan Skemp Hospital (130 – 70) by 60 to (130 – 94) 36. The demographics of these "drowning" victims in La Crosse were 100% white, 100% male, and 100% under the age of 25. Statistically, these victims over-represented their demographic group when compared to both the U.S. Census data and local hospital reporting. If these deaths in La Crosse were truly accidents, then the percentage of victims under age 25 should have been closer to 27.8% then it was to 100%. These statistics are so far apart that it becomes obvious to any eye (trained or untrained) that something is not right about these deaths. (*Source:* U.S. Census Bureau (2000). Table DP-1. Profile of General Demographic Characteristics: 2000. Geographic area: La Crosse, Wisconsin. Washington, DC: Author.)

The most striking commonality is that 5 young men were from the same county (Figure 16.9). We believe that they were targeted and stalked. Four (4) of them attended the same high school, that is, Arrowhead Union High School in Hartland, Wisconsin. Dion and Kruziki both wrestled on the same team at Arrowhead. Three of the victims drowned within 30 months of each other beginning with Dion (04/10/2004), then Kruziki (12/24/2005), and lastly Homan (9/30/2006). Dion and Homan were recovered at the south end of Riverside Park in La Crosse, while Kruziki drowned in East Dubuque, Illinois. Dion, Kruziki, and Wegener all lived near Hartland. La Crosse is about 180 miles west-northwest from Hartland. Hartland is west-northwest about 10 miles from Brookfield, which was Homan's hometown. Also, Hartland is about 15 miles from Milwaukee where Max Walker, Bryan Barker, Tom Hecht, and Nick Wilcox were "drowning" victims under similar circumstances. The statistical probability of this is staggering. A person would probably have better odds of being struck by lightening three times or winning the lottery twice.

Linkages to Waukesha County, Wisconsin

NAME	HOME	SCHOOL	COLLEGE	DIED IN	YEAR
Jared Dion	*Pewaukee*	*Arrowhead*	*UW-La Crosse*	*La Crosse*	*2004*
Matt Kruziki	*Hartland*	*Arrowhead*	*NA*	*East Dubuque*	*2005*
Luke Homan	*Brookfield*	*Central*	*UW-La Crosse*	*La Crosse*	*2006*
Mark Wegener	*Merton*	*Arrowhead*	*UW-Whitewater*	*Whitewater*	*2011*
"Bob Hanson"	*Confidential*	*Arrowhead*	*Confidential*	*N/A*	*2012*

NOTE: Dion and Kruziki wrestled on the same team at Arrowhead Union High School.

Figure 16.9 Skeptics claim there are no commonalities, patterns, or linkages among the cases. Yet, 5 individuals came from Waukesha County in Wisconsin, and 2 of them died in La Crosse.

Mark Wegener (05/28/2011) fits squarely into the pattern of commonalities. He did not drown. Rather, he was found at the bottom of a limestone quarry. Mark was attending the University of Wisconsin in Whitewater. Also attending UW-Whitewater was Benjamin Fuder, who went missing (07/29/2012) and was found in the same quarry. Mark was a classmate at Arrowhead Union High School with a young man whom we will call "Bob Hanson." Two men walked onto Bob's driveway near Hartland in 2012 and drew 2 horned smiley face graffitos (exactly like the one seen on the Internet). On the forehead of one of them, they wrote a date. Next to it, they wrote Bob's name. "Bob Hanson" did not become a victim. Instead, "Bob Hansen" several states away became a victim shortly thereafter.

Two Bars

There are 30 bars within about an 8 square block area in downtown La Crosse. There used to be more bars. But, as the popularity of huge bars grew, some of the smaller bars were bought up and consolidated into larger bars. For example, Ringside and Legends were sold and are now one bar called Whiskey River Saloon. There are approximately 23 bars along about 1050 feet that makes up the primary downtown drinking corridor. That means that there is another bar roughly every 50 feet along that corridor. College student drinking is a major contributor to the downtown economy.

Critics of our work purport that there are no patterns in La Crosse. There are 30 downtown bars, 9 victims, and no pattern – right? Correct! In fact, the FBI report on the La Crosse drownings said the same thing. Wrong answer! The last bar in which 4 of the 9 victims were drinking was The Library (Blatz, Kapfer, Geesey, and Homan). The last place where 2 of the 9 victims were seen drinking was John's bar (Dion and Fortney). This means that 44.4 percent of the victims were last drinking in 1 bar (The Library) and another 22.2 percent were last in another bar (John's). In total, 67 percent of the victims were last seen alive and drinking in only 2 of 30 downtown bars (Figures 11.1 and 16.10).

Furthermore, as shown earlier, 4 of the 9 victims (Kapfer, Geesey, Dion, and Homan) were known to have GHB in their systems. Based on Fortney's low BAC and failed memory, we may surmise that he was drugged as well. We will never know about the other 4 victims (Blatz, Skifton, Melancon, and Meyers) since they were not tested at autopsy like the others were. If they were, then those reports remain hidden somewhere; which is possible since we saw that in Dion's case. That means that 100 percent of the victims who were tested for GHB had the drug in them (Figure 16.10). It also means that 100 percent of the victims who were known to be drugged with GHB had come out of only 2 of 30 downtown bars (i.e., The Library or John's). But, keep in mind, there are not supposed to be any patterns among the La Crosse cases.

Closer examination of the dates reveals that the majority of the victims disappeared during three distinct time blocks: February 14th to 22nd, April 10th to 11th, and September 28th to 30th. This pattern is reinforced when some other Wisconsin "drowning" cases are included. For example, Craig Burrows in Eau Claire went missing on September 29th. Cullen Fortney (a survivor), as well as Mike Philbin in Oshkosh, disappeared on January 8th. Nathan Herr in Sheboygan vanished on January 10th.

Three Paths

Another set of commonalities among the La Crosse cases can be found in the tracking dog paths. The first commonality is that both Kapfer's and Dion's property was found in the

Commonalities Among the La Crosse Cases

NAME	DATE	LAST BAR	DRUGGED
Charles Blatz	9/28/1997	The Library	Unknown
Tony Skifton	10/10/1997	House Party	Unknown
Nate Kapfer	2/22/1998	The Library	YES
Jeff Geesey	4/11/1999	The Library	YES
Jared Dion	4/10/2004	John's	YES
Cullen Fortney	1/8/2006	John's	Likely
Luke Homan	9/30/2006	The Library	YES
Chris Melancon	9/30/2007	Brothers	Unknown
Craig Meyers	2/14/2010	Downtown Bar	Unknown

Figure 16.10 Once charted like this, commonalities emerge and form distinct patterns relative to the DATE a victim disappeared, the LAST BAR where he was seen drinking, and whether or not he was DRUGGED.

north end of Riverside Park. Kapfer's wallet, baseball cap, keys, and 4 municipal ordinance citations were found neatly placed on the west deck of the La Crosse Queen Gift Shop. This is reasonable since a tracking dog had followed his scent to that location (Figure 16.11, *Orange Line*). However, it is important to note that tracking dogs do not follow a person. They follow a person's scent, which could be left by another person who had previous contact with him or her (a.k.a., a transfer scent). This might help to explain how Dion's Boston Red Sox baseball cap was discovered hanging on a pole near the statue of Chief Hiawatha when no record of a tracking dog going to that area could be found. In other words, Dion probably did not walk to that end of the park and place his cap on the pole. Instead, someone else who had not touched him carried his cap up there and placed it in that location. Did the same thing happen with Kapfer's property?

In light of the assertion that these young men were supposed to be highly intoxicated (Kapfer 0.220 BAC, Geesey 0.420 Spleen, Dion 0.289 BAC, and Homan 0.320 VAC), it is understandable why the tracking dogs would wander around after leaving the bars. We

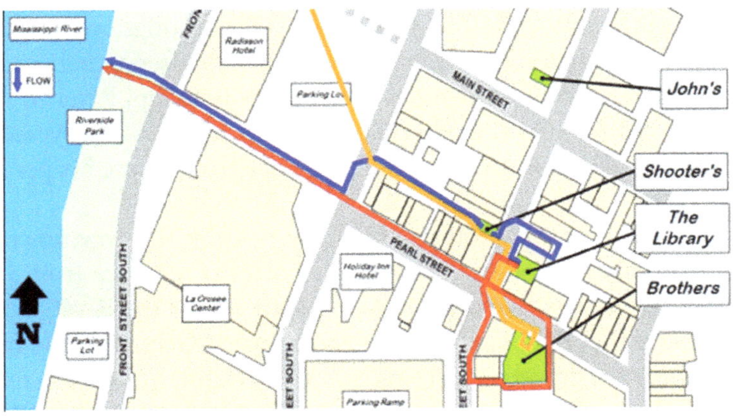

Figure 16.11 Commonalities exist among the K-9 search tracks for Nate Kapfer (*Orange Line*), Jeff Geesey (*Blue Line*), and Luke Homan (*Red Line*). Most significantly was that Kapfer's and Geesey's scent went through Shooter's bar and then straight to the river.

noticed that the tracking dog following Geesey's scent (*Blue Line*) was behind the Club Millennium and in the alley next to Big Al's pizzeria before heading to Riverside Park. The one following Homan's scent (*Red Line*) made a lap around Brothers Bar and Grill before going toward the river. This wandering does seem like the behavior of a really drunk young man. However, once all three scent tracks cleared the downtown bar area, they went straight to their end-points near the river's edge in the most direct paths possible. That does not correspond with the wandering tracks and indicates sober, focused, goal-oriented walking.

The most intriguing commonality is the fact that both Kapfer's (*Orange Line*) and Geesey's (*Blue Line*) scents went through Shooter's bar before going straight to their final point next to the river. The tracking dogs went in the front door, out the back door, down the alley through the middle of the block, and then directly to the river. Neither Kapfer nor Geesey were reported by anyone to have been in Shooter's. Kapfer was last seen at 02:30 hours walking north on 3rd Street South, which would have taken him right past Shooter's. Did he change his direction of travel halfway up the block and walk through the bar? No one stopped him from entering the bar 1/2 hour after closing, or from walking through the establishment? It is more likely that these two tracks were the result of transfer scents.

So, the prominent question is this: who left all these transfer scents for the dogs to track? We are not saying that any specific bar owner was involved in the deaths of the young men in any way. We are not saying that any specific bar employee was involved. In fact, it could have been a customer, who had the freedom to move about the downtown bars at will in order to stalk the victims. The extent of freedom of movement relative to leaving a bar at any time would have been impossible for an employee. That behavior would have resulted in not only getting the employee fired, it would have also likely identified the employee as being engaged in some sort of activity other than work. However, the fact that Kapfer's scent went through Shooter's bar suggests that whomever left these tracks was afforded greater access and freedom of movement in the bars than the average customer should have had after bar closing.

Four Locations

Patterns can also be seen in the locations of presumed water entry points and eventual body recovery locations (Figure 16.12). Personal property associated with Kapfer and Dion was found near the statue of Chief Hiawatha. Tracking dogs even picked up Kapfer's scent all along the north end of Riverside Park. We are supposed to believe that river currents somehow floated Kapfer's body miles down the Mississippi River to the spot where it ended up in Bluff Slough. On the other hand, Dion's body was recovered just north of the Cass Street Bridge, which was only a short distance from where his personal property had been found.

Likewise, both Geesey's and Homan's scents went from the downtown bar area into the park. Homan's body supposedly only traveled a short distance from its water entry point to the site where it was found at the very south end of the Riverside Park. We are again asked to believe that river currents somehow floated Geesey's body miles down the river to a location near the gravel pit just south of where Kapfer's body was recovered, while the river current only moved Homan's body several hundred yards.

So, we have personal property and dog tracks leading searchers to Riverside Park in all instances. But, we have the bodies ending up in two general clusters. One cluster (i.e., Dion and Homan) was near the presumed water entry points north of the Cass Street Bridge.

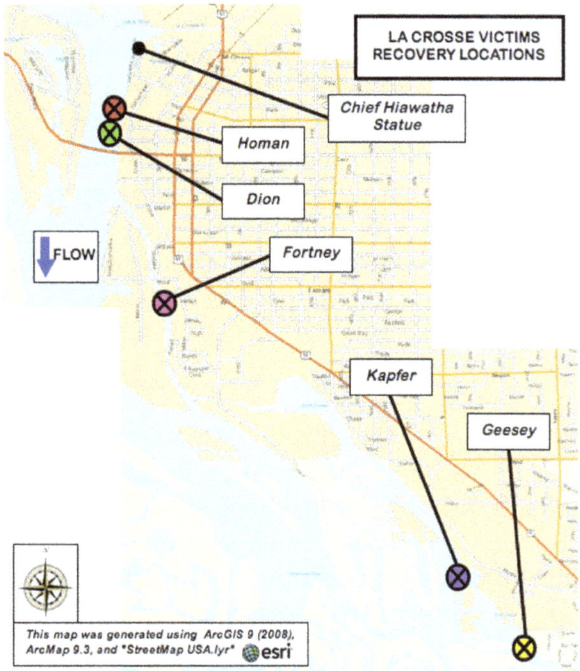

Figure 16.12 There are four common locations: (1) where the young men were drinking (i.e., The Library and John's), (2) where personal property was found in the park (i.e., near the statue of Chief Hiawatha); (3) where the victims presumably entered the water near Riverside Park, and (4) the 2 clusters where the bodies were recovered (i.e., Dion and Homan, and Kapfer and Geesey).

This was also the general area for Melancon and Meyers. The other cluster (Kapfer and Geesey) was miles away near the small town of Shelby. Kapfer's body impressively covered the great distance as a result of river current, while the miles between Geesey's dog tracks in the park and his body recovery was attributed to him having walked there. In order to believe that myth, one has to forget the fact that Geesey was the most intoxicated of all of the La Crosse victims with a 0.420 alcohol concentration.

There are four common locations. The first common location is where the young men were drinking (i.e., The Library and John's). The second location is where personal property was found in the park (i.e., near the statue of Chief Hiawatha). The third common location is the general area where the victims presumably entered the water near Riverside Park. And, the fourth common location is the 2 clusters where the bodies were recovered (i.e., Dion and Homan, and Kapfer and Geesey). A fifth somewhat common location is Niedbalski Bridge. Geesey's scent was tracked to that site and Fortney pulled himself from the river just south of the bridge. Also, Skifton's body was recovered here as well.

It seemed to us after examining and testing river currents in the La Crosse area, that bodies could not go in near Riverside Park and then end up in so many different areas. Specifically, they could not end up in Bluff Slough like Kapfer assuming that they entered the river near the statue of Chief Hiawatha. These body recovery locations were not common due to river currents. They were common to each other because they were secure and private sites where a killer or killers could dump a body late at night without being detected.

A final pattern exists for many of the cases in this book, but especially true for the La Crosse murders. This is a part of the overall pattern in the cases that we have examined.

The police would conduct a thorough search of the entire area surrounding the last known location using dogs, human searchers, and sometimes airborne infrared. They would find nothing. Then quite often, items of property belonging to a victim would be discovered the next day in those areas that had just been searched. Items of personal property were routinely recovered near the statue of Chief Hiawatha in the La Crosse cases. Another quality was that the property was usually found as though displayed, that is, neatly folded or arranged and placed in plain sight. This characteristic is typically associated with a sober person, and not someone who is intoxicated beyond a 0.08 BAC. It is also a trait that indicates an organized offender taunting authorities.

Conclusions

Our team has attempted to remain as scientifically objective as possible and to not let our judgment be influenced by the findings or opinions of others. It has been a difficult task to not get caught up in the mass hysteria of urban legend and our own emotions from having to work with the families of these tragic deaths. As investigators and social scientists, we opine that the following conclusions can be formed regarding the "smiley face" cases.

1. Several cases cannot be judged due to a lack of available information.
2. Some of the cases present evidence that suggests that they do not fit within the parameters of a serial phenomenon, but remain undetermined relative to actual events leading up to death; which means that some may be separate, unrelated accidents, suicides, or homicides.
3. Some of the cases are clearly, beyond a reasonable doubt, accidents or possible suicides.
4. Several cases exist, wherein, sufficient evidence suggests beyond a preponderance of the evidence that something is not right and that they are most likely homicides.
5. Many cases exist (such as those presented in this book), wherein, forensic evidence proves that they are abductions and homicides.

Therefore, we adamantly assert that the victims and their surviving family members have not received justice. These cases should be changed to reflect "homicide" as an official manner of death. Once switched, they require further investigation. They should not be changed and then left to linger and to die on the vine like Jenkins.

Closing Remarks

The Group

All of the naysayers have stated that there is no empirical evidence to link these cases to one killer. Even the FBI's BAU-2 report concerning the La Crosse cases stated that there was no evidence of a singular killer. On that point, we agree. The BAU-2 report also declared that there was no forensic evidence linking the cases to a serial offender (i.e., the BAU-2's area of expertise). We agree! During the course of our investigation, we have discovered that the cases are not the product of an individual or individuals who repeatedly commit murders (i.e. serial killers). Some individuals may have been present at most of the "drownings" in their city, which would make them serial killers. But, it is the group that repeated the offense of homicide. We found that these cases were the product of numerous small groups of 8 to 10 persons (i.e., cells).

In fairness to the BAU-2, its report was based on the case materials provided to it by the La Crosse Police Department's detective bureau. Since we do not know what they actually saw and the extent of their investigation, they may not have seen everything we saw. Did members of the BAU-2 physically travel to La Crosse to see the scenes for themselves (as we did several times), or did they sit in their offices and read reports? Knowing the thoroughness and highly technical capabilities of the FBI, we can only say that the BAU-2 either received inaccurate information from the La Crosse Police Department or it received incomplete files. There was also another confounding variable, that is, a generalizable inability to translate and interpret the messages in the reports given to them and to understand it. As our team member Adam Carlson always says, "local reports prepared for local consumption."

For the BAU-2 to state in its final report on the La Crosse cases that no patterns were found that associated the cases with a serial predator was correct. As we have pointed out and asserted repeatedly, these deaths are not the work of a roaming individual or individuals spreadout across the United States. They are the work of an organization that has repeatedly killed. To say that there are no patterns among any of the cases is absurd; case in point – La Crosse as presented above. Due to the totality of the evidence that we have uncovered, we suggest that the FBI take over the investigation into these deaths and this organization. Specifically, the FBI should go back in and take over the La Crosse cases and appoint a special prosecutor to reinvestigate those deaths. Even though an FBI investigation will never completely route out all those who are responsible for these murders, it will put a dent into what is currently becoming the most dangerous home-grown terrorist organization and threat to the security and sanctity of our homeland.

The Graffiti

Our detractors have rallied beneath the banner that there is no evidence linking these cases to an organized group. We disagree. Not only do we have informants who mentioned the names of persons in other states, we have the smiley face graffito (and 12 additional sets of graffiti). We have evidence that the smiley face (although admittedly a popular icon) is associated with the network of cells responsible for these deaths. Critics have commented on the fact that the graffiti in various locations were different sizes, colors, and stylizations (e.g., some with dots for eyes, some with Xs, and some with slashes). We agree. In fact, some were enclosed in a circle while most were not. Some had noses while most did not. And, only a few had horns. Most were white, while some were orange, blue, red, or pink. Handwriting is fairly unique to individuals and so is the artistic style of the persons throwing up the smiley faces. As any gang specialist can tell you, if you were to take 200 pictures of any specific gang-related graffito across the United States, then all of them will resemble each other and appear similar to the commonly portrayed icon of that "gang nation."

In the end, the smiley face graffito was the most important symbol relative to our identification of who was responsible for these murders. Using a digital camera, we found and recorded numerous symbols, words, and phrases at and near the last seen locations, residences, and body recovery sites. Gilbertson first determined which ones were clearly street gang related. He then sorted the remaining graffiti by similarity; for example, 4-pointed stars, 5-pointed, 6-pointed, 8-pointed, and asterisk would have gone into one category of "stars." That would be referred to as a "set." He then identified the unique symbols. Meaning that they were present only at specific locations within the target cities. The smiley face was not everywhere as some skeptics (who have not physically been out in the field themselves) would want the public to believe. That would be like saying that drawings of marijuana leaves were everywhere, and they were not. As we analyzed the 13 sets of graffiti, we discovered that they shifted. In Region 1 on the west side, we found graffiti A-B-C-D. In Region 2, we found A-B-C-E. Region 3 produced graffiti B-C-E-F, and so forth. Although not quite that simple, as it progressed easterly, we found that A and B were reintroduced into the mix. Once we got to Manhattan, we found L-M-A-B. That made perfect sense in light of the fact that one informant told us that he had traveled to New York early on to "straighten out a group that messed up and burned a guy." We heard that statement over a year before we saw the autopsy photographs of McNeil's burned body in Manhattan.

The sets of graffiti betray the underlying theosophy (religious and sociopolitical ideology) of the cells as an analyst moves from west to east. Not all cells use the smiley face. Not all cells are of the same theosophy. Many are, but not all. However, it is extremely important to note that although the theosophy held by cell members may reflect that of specific, larger, and more well-known organizations (e.g., gangs, organized crime families, secret societies, and cults), we do not claim that those more formal groups, as organizations, are responsible for these murders. In other words, the fact that a few extremely fundamentalist Muslims attacked the United States on September 11th does not mean that all Muslims want to kill us. The fact that a few extremely fundamentalist Christians shot abortion clinic doctors does not mean that all Christians want to kill abortion clinic doctors. We are saying that some members of the cells hold beliefs that are similar to those beliefs of larger, more well-known and formally established organizations. This was part of the reason that the graffiti confused so many people. Having informants to discuss this with helped us to find our way through the fog.

The Deaths

Everything that we originally mentioned in the press conference (April 28, 2008) with respect to these deaths is as true today as it was then. These young men were drugged, abducted, held for a period of time, murdered, and then placed into the water. This is still being done by an organized group of individuals. This is a form of domestic terrorism that is on the rise both here in the United States, and also in Canada as well as Europe. It has become more evident and grown in violence in the United States during the past three years. We believe that members of this movement will be associated with the next major domestic terror attack on our nation.

The United States should be embarrassed. We are technologically advanced when compared to many nations. Yet, we are handicapped when it comes to forensic investigation only because we have no real national standards for medical examiner qualifications or investigative protocols. You have now been presented with the forensic and anecdotal evidence, as well as our interpretations. In Chapter 1, you were instructed to take notes, to analyze the evidence for yourself, and to draw your own conclusions. What was the manner of death: undetermined, natural, accident, suicide, or homicide? Were these merely accidental drownings as authorities would proclaim, or were they homicides? Did law enforcement do all it could to investigate each case? Was there justice? Was evidence missed, or was it ignored? What did you decide?

References

Agency for Toxic Substances and Disease Registry (ATSDR). (2006, July). *Toxicological Profile for Hydrogen Sulfide*. Atlanta, GA: U.S. Department of Health and Human Services, Public Health Service.

Amatuzio, J. (2009, July 29). *Final Autopsy Report (Case # 02-09-0379)*. Ramsey, MN: Midwest Medical Examiner's Office.

Armstrong, E., & Erskine, K. (2011). *Water-Related Death Investigation: Practical Methods and Forensic Applications*. Boca Raton, FL: CRC Press.

Athanaselis, S., Stefanidou, M., & Koutselinis, A. (2005). Interpretation of postmortem alcohol concentrations. *Forensic Science International, 149*, 289–291.

Bauer, T., Moore, G., & Hutchins, G. (1980, December). The liver in sickle cell disease: A clinicopathologic study of 70 patients. *American Journal of Medicine, 69*(6), 833–837.

Becker, R. (2000, September). Myths of underwater recovery operations. *FBI Law Enforcement Bulletin, 69*(9), 1–5.

Benowitz, N., & Jacob, P. (1984). Daily intake of nicotine during cigarette smoking. *Clinical Pharmacology & Therapeutics, 35*(4), 499–504.

Benowitz, N., & Jacob, P. (1994). Metabolism of nicotine to cotinine studied by a dual stable isotope method. *Clinical Pharmacology & Therapeutics, 56*(5), 483–493.

Benowitz, N., & Jacob, P. (1997). Individual differences in nicotine kinetics and metabolism in humans. *National Institute on Drug Abuse Research Monograph, 173*, 48–64.

Bickel, M., Brochon, R., Friolet, B., Herrmann, B., & Stofer, A. (1967). Clinical and biochemical results of a fatal case of desipramine intoxication. *Psychopharmacology, 10*(5), 431–436.

Biological and Environmental Research Information System (BERIS) (2009, June 16). *DNA Forensics*. Washington, DC: Human Genome Program, Office of Biological and Environmental Research, U.S. Department of Energy Office of Science. [Online.] Available: http://www.ornl.gov/sci/techresources/Human_Genome/elsi/forensics.shtml.

Bohnert, M. (2004). Morphological findings in burned bodies. In M. Tsokos (Ed.), *Forensic Pathology Reviews, Vol. 1* (pp. 3–30). Totowa, NJ: Humana Press.

Bowen, R. (2005, August 28). *Control of Gastric Emptying*. [Online.] Fort Collins, CO: Department of Biomedical Sciences, Colorado State University. Available: http://www.vivo.colostate.edu/hbooks/pathphys/digestion/stomach/emptying.html.

Bowen, R. (2006, May 27). *Gastrointestinal Transit: How long does It Take?* [Online.] Fort Collins, CO: Department of Biomedical Sciences, Colorado State University. Available: http://www.vivo.colostate.edu/hbooks/pathphys/digestion/basics/transit.html.

Canfield, D. V., Kupiec, T., & Huffine, E. (1993, July). Postmortem alcohol production in fatal aircraft accidents. *Journal of Forensic Sciences, 38*(4), 914–917.

Canter-Lund, H., & Lund, J. W. G. (1995). *Freshwater Algae: Their Microscopic World Explored*. Champaign, IL: Biopress Limited (Balogh Scientific Books).

Centers for Disease Control and Prevention (2011). *Alcohol and Public Health*. Frequently Asked Questions. [Online.] Available: www.cdc.gov/alcohol/faqs.htm#howAlcoholAffect

Cohen, L. E., & Felson, Marcus (1979). Social change and crime rate trends: A routine activities approach. *American Sociological Review, 44*, 588–608.

Cooper, P. (2006). Burn injury. In G. Rutty (Ed.), *Essentials of Autopsy Practice: Current Methods and Modern Trends* (pp. 215–232). London, UK: Springer-Verlag.

Dahlin, K., Låstbom, L., Blomgren, B. & Ryrfeldt, A. (1997, October). Acute lung failure induced by tricyclic antidepressants. *Toxicology and Applied Pharmacology, 146*(2), 309–316.

Darley, J., & Latané, B. (1968). Bystander intervention in emergencies: diffusion of responsibility. *Journal of Personality and Social Psychology, 8*(4, Pt. 1), 377–383.

Delaware County Medical Examiner (DCME) (2008, February 3). *Investigator's Report* [Irene Lafore]. Lima, Pennsylvania: Office of the Medical Examiner, County of Delaware.

DiMaio, V. J. M., & DiMaio, D. (2001). *Forensic Pathology (2nd ed.).* New York: CRC Press.

Dix, J., & Graham, M. (1999). *Time of Death, Decomposition and Identification: An Atlas.* New York: CRC Press.

Einspruch, B. C., & Clark, S. M. (1992). Near fatality results from health food store sleeping potion. *Texas Medicine, 88*, 10.

FBI DNA Analysis Unit II (DNAAU-2) (2012). DNA-Mitochondrial. *Laboratory Services.* Washington, DC: Federal Bureau of Investigation, U.S. Department of Justice. [Online.] Available: http://www.fbi.gov/about-us/lab/mtdna.

Feyerabend, C., Bryant, A., Jarvis, M., & Russell, M. (1986, December). Determination of cotinine in biological fluids of nonsmokers by packed column gas-liquid chromatography. *Journal of Pharmacy and Pharmacology, 38*(12), 917–919.

Fourney, R. M. (1998). Mitochondrial DNA and forensic analysis: A primer for law enforcement. *Canadian Society of Forensic Science Journal, 31*(1), 45–53.

Gallo, V., Neasham, D., Airoldi, L., Ferrari, P., Jenab, M., Boffetta, P., Overvad, K., Tjønneland, A., Clavel-Chapelon, F., Boeing, H., Pala, V., Palli, D., Panico, S., Tumino, R., Arriola, L., Lund, E., Bueno-De-Mequita, B., Peeters, PH., Melander, O., Hallmans, G., Riboli, E., Saracci, R., & Vineis, P. (2010). Second-hand smoke, cotinine levels, and risk of circulatory mortality in a large cohort study of never-smokers. *Epidemiology, 21*(2), 207–214.

Garriott, J. C. (1996). Analysis for alcohol in postmortem specimens. In J. C. Garriott (Ed.), *Medicolegal Aspects of Alcohol* (3rd ed.) (151–169). Tuscon, AZ: Lawyers & Judges Publishing Company.

Geberth, V. J. (2006). *Practical Homicide Investigation: Tactics, Procedures, and Forensic Techniques (4th ed.).* New York: CRC Press.

Gilliland, M., & Bost, R. (1993, November). Alcohol in decomposed bodies: postmortem synthesis and distribution. *Journal of Forensic Science, 38*(6), 1266–1274.

Gori, G., & Lynch, C. (1985). Analytical cigarette yields as predictors of smoke bioavailability. *Regulatory Toxicology & Pharmacology, 5*(3), 314–326.

Hancock, P.A., & Weaver, J.L. (2005, March–April). On time distortion under stress. *Theoretical Issues in Ergonomics Science, 6*(2), 193–211.

Haupt, G. (2006, February). Drowning investigations. *FBI Law Enforcement Bulletin, 75*(2), 14–22.

Heatley, M., & Crane, J. (1990, April). The blood alcohol concentration at post-mortem in 175 fatal cases of alcohol intoxication. *Medicine, Science & the Law, 30*(2), 101–105.

Hendrick, W., Zaferes, A., & Nelson, C. (2003). *Homicidal Drowning Investigation.* Hurley, NY: Lifeguard Systems.

Howard, P., Murphy, G., & Dowling, R. (1991). Gallbladder emptying patterns in response to a normal meal in healthy subjects and patients with gall stones: ultrasound study. *Gut, 32*,1406–1411.

Hughes, P. L. & Rome, J. D. (1984, August). Cardiopulmonary collapse associated with an overdose of desipramine. *Mayo Clinic Proceedings, 59*(8), 574.

Hukkanen, J., Jacob, P., & Benowitz, N. (2005). Metabolism and disposition kinetics of nicotine. *Pharmacological Reviews, 57*(1), 79–115.

Huntington, T., Higley, L., & Baxendale, F. (2007, March). Maggot development during morgue storage and its effect on estimating the post-mortem interval. *Journal of Forensic Sciences, 52*(2), 453–458.

Ionescu, D., Janssen, J., & Omalu, B. (2005). *Final Diagnosis—Acute Combined Drug Overdose of Ethanol, Acetaminophen, Imipramine, Desipramine, Oxycodone and Diphenhydramine.*

[Online]. Pittsburgh, PA: Department of Pathology, School of Medicine, University of Pittsburgh. Available: http://path.upmc.edu/cases/case407/dx.html.

Isenberg, A. (2002, August). Forensic mitochondrial DNA analysis. *FBI Law Enforcement Bulletin, 71*(8), 16–22.

ISUPD (2009). Supplement Case Report, Page No. 3 of 63 (David Smith, May 2 at 04:57). *Case No. 09-1551*. Terre Haute, IN: Indiana State University Police Department.

ISUPD (2009). Supplement Case Report, Page No. 5 of 63 (Jacquelyn Smith, May 2 at 16:51). *Case No. 09-1551*. Terre Haute, IN: Indiana State University Police Department.

ISUPD (2009). Supplement Case Report, Page No. 6 of 63 (Brain Pierce, May 2 at 17:29). *Case No. 09-1551*. Terre Haute, IN: Indiana State University Police Department.

ISUPD (2009). Supplement Case Report, Page No. 7 of 63 (Chris Gresham, May 3 at 06:53). *Case No. 09-1551*. Terre Haute, IN: Indiana State University Police Department.

ISUPD (2009). Supplement Case Report, Page No. 8 of 63 (Joseph Newport, May 3 at 09:24). *Case No. 09-1551*. Terre Haute, IN: Indiana State University Police Department.

ISUPD (2009). Supplement Case Report, Page No. 9 of 63 (Joseph Newport, May 3 at 09:24). *Case No. 09-1551*. Terre Haute, IN: Indiana State University Police Department.

ISUPD (2009). Supplement Case Report, Page No. 10 of 63 (Joseph Newport, May 3 at 09:24). *Case No. 09-1551*. Terre Haute, IN: Indiana State University Police Department.

ISUPD (2009). Supplement Case Report, Page No. 11 of 63 (Joseph Newport, May 3 at 09:24). *Case No. 09-1551*. Terre Haute, IN: Indiana State University Police Department.

ISUPD (2009). Supplement Case Report, Page No. 12 of 63 (Joseph Newport, May 3 at 09:24). *Case No. 09-1551*. Terre Haute, IN: Indiana State University Police Department.

ISUPD (2009). Supplement Case Report, Page No. 13 of 63 (Heather Cummings, May 3 at 14:04). *Case No. 09-1551*. Terre Haute, IN: Indiana State University Police Department.

ISUPD (2009). Supplement Case Report, Page No. 14 of 63 (Jacquelyn Smith, May 3 at 14:21). *Case No. 09-1551*. Terre Haute, IN: Indiana State University Police Department.

ISUPD (2009). Supplement Case Report, Page No. 15 of 63 (Ian Loomis, May 3 at 16:33). *Case No. 09-1551*. Terre Haute, IN: Indiana State University Police Department.

ISUPD (2009). Supplement Case Report, Page No. 16 of 63 (Brenda Edington, May 3 at 19:06). *Case No. 09-1551*. Terre Haute, IN: Indiana State University Police Department.

ISUPD (2009). Supplement Case Report, Page No. 18 of 63 (Ian Loomis, May 4 at 17:10). *Case No. 09-1551*. Terre Haute, IN: Indiana State University Police Department.

ISUPD (2009). Supplement Case Report, Page No. 19 of 63 (Matthew Murray, May 4 at 17:21). *Case No. 09-1551*. Terre Haute, IN: Indiana State University Police Department.

ISUPD (2009). Supplement Case Report, Page No. 20 of 63 (Brent Denny, May 4 at 17:43). *Case No. 09-1551*. Terre Haute, IN: Indiana State University Police Department.

ISUPD (2009). Supplement Case Report, Page No. 21 of 63 (Joseph Newport, May 4 at 13:40). *Case No. 09-1551*. Terre Haute, IN: Indiana State University Police Department.

ISUPD (2009). Supplement Case Report, Page No. 23 of 63 (Joseph Newport, May 5 at 09:49). *Case No. 09-1551*. Terre Haute, IN: Indiana State University Police Department.

ISUPD (2009). Supplement Case Report, Page No. 25 of 63 (Ian Loomis, May 5 at 11:10). *Case No. 09-1551*. Terre Haute, IN: Indiana State University Police Department.

ISUPD (2009). Supplement Case Report, Page No. 26 of 63 (Brent Denny, May 5 at 15:12). *Case No. 09-1551*. Terre Haute, IN: Indiana State University Police Department.

ISUPD (2009). Supplement Case Report, Page No. 27 of 63 (Brenda Edington, May 5 at 21:22). *Case No. 09-1551*. Terre Haute, IN: Indiana State University Police Department.

ISUPD (2009). Supplement Case Report, Page No. 28 of 63 (Brenda Edington, May 5 at 23:20). *Case No. 09-1551*. Terre Haute, IN: Indiana State University Police Department.

ISUPD (2009). Supplement Case Report, Page No. 29 of 63 (Chris Gresham, May 6 at 01:05). *Case No. 09-1551*. Terre Haute, IN: Indiana State University Police Department.

ISUPD (2009). Supplement Case Report, Page No. 30 of 63 (Chris Gresham, May 6 at 03:54). *Case No. 09-1551*. Terre Haute, IN: Indiana State University Police Department.

ISUPD (2009). Supplement Case Report, Page No. 31 of 63 (Tamara Watts, May 6 at 06:23). *Case No. 09-1551.* Terre Haute, IN: Indiana State University Police Department.

ISUPD (2009). Supplement Case Report, Page No. 32 of 63 (Ian Loomis, May 6 at 09:58). *Case No. 09-1551.* Terre Haute, IN: Indiana State University Police Department.

ISUPD (2009). Supplement Case Report, Page No. 33 of 63 (Jeffrey Bellinger, May 6 at 11:08). *Case No. 09-1551.* Terre Haute, IN: Indiana State University Police Department.

ISUPD (2009). Supplement Case Report, Page No. 34 of 63 (Jacquelyn Smith, May 6 at 12:43). *Case No. 09-1551.* Terre Haute, IN: Indiana State University Police Department.

ISUPD (2009). Supplement Case Report, Page No. 35 of 63 (Brent Denny, May 6 at 12:59). *Case No. 09-1551.* Terre Haute, IN: Indiana State University Police Department.

Jarvis, M., Feyerabend, C., Bryant, A., Hedges, B., & Primatesta, P. (2001). Passive smoking in the home: plasma cotinine concentrations in nonsmokers with smoking partners. *Tobacco Control, 10*(4), 368–374.

Jarvis, M., Russell, M., & Feyerabend, C. (1983). Absorption of nicotine and carbon monoxide from passive smoking under natural conditions of exposure. *Thorax, 38*(11), 829–833.

Jarvis, M., Russell, M., Benowitz, N., & Feyerabend, C. (1988, June). Elimination of cotinine from body fluids" Implications for noninvasive measurement of tobacco smoke exposure. *American Journal of Public Health, 78*(6), 696–698.

Johnson, R., Lewis, R., Angier, M., & Vu, N. (2004, February). *The Formation of Ethanol in Postmortem Tissues.* Washington, DC: Office of Aerospace Medicine.

Kaiser, R. (2000, February 7). A New Year's mystery deepens. *Chicago Tribune.* [Online.] http://articles.chicagotribune.com/2000-02-07/news/0002070053_1_missing-persons-folder-fortunetellers.

Kakar, S., Kamath, P., & Burgart, L. (2004, August). Sinusoidal dilatation and congestion in liver biopsy: is it always due to venous outflow impairment? *Archives of Pathology & Laboratory Medicine, 128*(8), 901–904.

Kakizaki, E., Takahama, K., Seo, Y., Kozawa, S., Sakai, M., & Yukawa, N. (2008, April 7). Marine bacteria comprise a possible indicator of drowning in seawater. *Forensic Science International, 176*(2–3), 236–47.

Kreeger, L., & Weiss, D. (2003, November). Trial Issues: Admissibility. *Forensic DNA Fundamentals for the Prosecutor: Be Not Afraid.* Alexandria, VA: DNA Forensics Program, American Prosecutors Research Institute.

Kugelberg, F. C., & Jones, A. W. (2007). Interpreting results of ethanol analysis in postmortem specimens: A review of the literature. *Forensic Science International, 165*(1), 10–29.

La Crosse County Medical Examiner (2005, November 11), *River Drowning.ppt.* [Online.] Available: www.co.la-crosse.wi.us/departments/Medical%20Examiner/docs.

Levine, M., & Thompson, K. (2004). Identity, place, and bystander intervention: social categories and helping after natural disasters. *Journal of Social Psychology, 144*(3), 229–245.

Lin, D-L., Wang, S-M., Wu, C-H., Chen, B-G., & Liu, R. (2008). Chemical derivatization for analysis of drugs by GC-MS – a conceptual review. *Journal of Food and Drug Analysis, 16*(1), 1–10.

Linch, C., Whiting, D., & Holland, M. (2001, July). Human hair histogenesis for the mitochondrial DNA forensic scientist. *Journal of Forensic Sciences, 46*(4), 844–853.

Lucci, A., Campobasso, C.P., Cirnelli, A., & Lorenzini, G. (2008, November 20). A promising microbiological test for the diagnosis of drowning. *Forensic Science International 182*(1–3), 20–26.

Lunetta, P., Modell, J. H., & Sajantila, A. (2004). What is the incidence and significance of "dry lungs" in bodies found in water. *American Journal of Forensic Medicine and Pathology, 25*(4), 291–301.

Lunetta, P., Penttila, A., & Sajantila, A. (2002). Circumstances and macropathologic findings in 1,590 consecutive cases of bodies found in water. *American Journal of Forensic Medicine and Pathology, 23*(4), 371–376.

Manning, R., Levine, M., & Collins, A. (2007). The Kitty Genovese murder and the social psychology of helping: The parable of the 38 witnesses. *American Psychologist, 62*(6), 555–562.

Mesgarzadeh, M., Krishnamurthy, G. T., Bobba, V. A., & Langrell, K. (1983). Filling, postcholecystokinin emptying, and refilling of normal gallbladder: Effects of two different doses of CCK on refilling: Concise communication. *The Journal of Nuclear Medicine, 24*(8), 666–671.

Mills, L., Mwakyusa, D., & Milner, P. (1988, March). Histopathologic features of liver biopsy specimens in sickle cell disease. *Archives of Pathology & Laboratory Medicine, 112*(3), 290–294.

Moolchan, E., Cone, E., Wstadik, A., Huestis, M., & Preston, K. (2000, October). Cocaine and metabolite elimination patterns in chronic cocaine users during cessation: plasma and saliva analysis. *Journal of Analytical Toxicology, 24*(7), 458–466.

Morgan, B., & Vogt, K. (2004). We are 99.9% sure it is NOT a serial killer. *Campus Connection, April 26–May 2*, 1. Retrieved from the University of Wisconsin-La Crosse Web site: http://www.uwlax.edu/universityrelations/campusconnection/2004/spring/042604cc.pdf.

Morild, I. (1995, September). Pleural effusion in drowning. *The American Journal of Forensic Medicine and Pathology, 16*(3), 253–256.

Moritz, A., & Henriques, F. (1947a). Studies of thermal injury II. The relative importance of time and surface temperature in the causation of cutaneous burns. *American Journal of Pathology, 23*, 695–720.

Moritz, A., Henriques, F., Dutra, F., & Weisiger, J. (1947b). Studies of thermal injury IV. An exploration of the casualty-producing attributes of conflagrations; local and systemic effects of general cutaneous exposure to excessive circumambient (air) and circumradiant heat of varying duration and intensity. *American Journal of Pathology, 43*, 466–488.

Moriya, F., & Hashimoto, Y. (2004). Postmortem production of ethanol and n-propanol in the brain of drowned persons. *American Journal of Forensic Medicine & Pathology, 25*(2), 131–133.

Moriya, F., Nishimura, H., Furumiya, J., & Hashimoto, Y. (2006, July). Effects of drinking and smoking on endogenous levels of urinary g-hydroxybutyric acid, a preliminary study. *Legal Medicine, 8*(4), 231–234.

Murphy, S., Villalta, P., Ho, S-W., & von Weymarn, L. (2007). Analysis of [3',3'-d(2)]-nicotine and [3',3'-d(2)]-cotinine by capillary liquid chromatography-electrospray tandem mass spectrometry. *Journal of Chromatography B: Analytical Technologies in the Biomedical and Life Sciences, 857*(1), 1–8.

National Center for Chronic Disease Prevention and Health Promotion (NCCD). (2002). *Behavioral Risk Factor Surveillance System Survey Data.* [Online]. Atlanta, Georgia: U.S. Department of Health and Human Services, Centers for Disease Control and Prevention. Available: http://apps.nccd.cdc.gov/brfss/Trends/TrendData.asp/.

National Center for Injury Prevention and Control (NCIPC). (2005). *Web-based Injury Statistics Query and Reporting System (WISQARS) Injury Mortality Reports, 1999–2003.* [Online]. Atlanta, Georgia: U.S. Department of Health and Human Services, Centers for Disease Control and Prevention. Available: http://webappa.cdc.gov/sasweb/ncipc/mortrate10_sy.html/.

National Commission on the Future of DNA Evidence (2002, July). *Using DNA to Solve Cold Cases.* Washington, DC: Office of Justice Programs, National Institute of Justice, U.S. Department of Justice. (NCJ 194197). Available: https://www.ncjrs.gov/pdffiles1/nij/194197.pdf.

National Highway Traffic Safety Administration (2012). *Drugs and Human Performance Fact Sheets: Gamma-Hydroxybutyrate (Ghb, Gbl, And 1,4-Bd).* (NHTSA Fact Sheet) [Online]. Washington, DC: Author. Available http://www.nhtsa.gov/people/injury/research/job185drugs/gamma-hydroxybutyrate.htm

National Highway Traffic Safety Administration (NHTSA) (2012a). *Drugs and Human Performance Fact Sheets: Cannabis/Marijuana (D^9-Tetrahydrocannabinol, THC).* (NHTSA Fact Sheet) [Online]. Washington, DC: Author. Available: http://www.nhtsa.gov/people/injury/research/job185drugs/cannabis.htm.

National Highway Traffic Safety Administration (NHTSA) (2012b). *Drugs and Human Performance Fact Sheets: Gamma-Hydroxybutyrate (Ghb, Gbl, And 1,4-Bd).* (NHTSA Fact Sheet) [Online]. Washington, DC: Author. Available: http://www.nhtsa.gov/people/injury/research/job185drugs/gamma-hydroxybutyrate.htm.

National Human Genome Research Institute (2012a). *Deoxyribonucleic Acid (DNA).* Washington, DC: National Institutes of Health. [Online.] Available: http://www.genome.gov/Glossary/index.cfm?id=48.

National Human Genome Research Institute (2012b). *Mitochondrial DNA.* Washington, DC: National Institutes of Health. [Online.] Available: http://www.genome.gov/Glossary/index.cfm?id=129.

National Institute of Diabetes and Digestive and Kidney Diseases (NIDDK). (2008, April). *Your Digestive System and How It Works* (NIH Publication No. 08– 2681). National Institutes of Health.

National Library of Medicine (2011a, June 4). Mitochondrial DNA. *Genetics Home Reference.* Washington, DC: National Institutes of Health. [Online.] Available: http://ghr.nlm.nih.gov/chromosome/MT.

National Library of Medicine (2011b, June 4). What is DNA? *Genetics Home Reference.* Washington, DC: National Institutes of Health. [Online.] Available: http://ghr.nlm.nih.gov/handbook/basics/dna.

Nishimura, H., Moriya, F., & Hashimoto, Y. (2009, July). Mechnanisms of g-hydroxybutyric acid production during early postmortem period. *Forensic Toxicology, 27*(2), 55–60.

Ohio Department of Natural Resources (2011). *Surviving a Cold-water Accident.* [Online.] Available: www.dnr.state.oh.us/watercraft/safetytips/accident/tabid/2876/Default.aspx.

Pantanowitz, L., Warren, M., & Goulart, R. (2009, May–June). Anthracotic pigment in pleural fluid: a case report. *Acta Cytologica, 53*(3), 306–308.

Pavlov, I. P. (1927). *Conditioned Reflexes: An Investigation of the Physiological Activity of the Cerebral Cortex* (G.V. Anrep, Trans.). London, England: Oxford University Press.

Payutto, P. (1994). Dependent Origination: The Buddhist Law of Conditionality (B. Evans, Trans.). Bangkok, Thailand, Buddhadhamma Foundation.

Phillips, A., Tanner, J., & Cope, O. (1963, November). Burn therapy: IV. Respiratory tract damage (an account of the clinical, X-ray and postmortem findings) and the meaning of restlessness. *Annals of Surgery, 158*(5), 799–811.

Porrata, T. (2011). *Athletics & GHB: The Connection between GHB & Bodybuilding & Steroids.* [Online]. Mesa, AZ: Project GHB. Available: http://www.projectghb.org/athletics-ghb

Porrata, T. (2013). *Drug Rape.* [Online]. Mesa, AZ: Project GHB. Available: http://www.projectghb.org/drug-rape.

Reynolds, K. (2005, June 23). Missing Muskegon Co. Man becomes homicide investigation. *WZZM 13 News (abc).* Retrieved August 12, 2008, from http://www.wzzm13.com/news/news_article.aspx?storyid=41316.

Ridley Township Police Department (RTPD) (2008). *SUPPLEMENTAL* [Investigation Reports dated January 23, 2008 through February 6, 2008]. Woodlyn, Pennsylvania: Various Police Officers.

Round, F. E., Crawford, R. M., & Mann, G. (1990). *The Diatoms: Biology & Morphology of the Genera.* Cambridge, UK: Cambridge University Press.

Russell, M., Jarvis, M., Feyerabend, C., & Fernö, O. (1983). Nasal nicotine solution: a potential aid to giving up smoking? *British Medical Journal, 286*(6366), 683–684.

Search and Rescue Dogs of Pennsylvania (SARD-PA). (2008, January 26). *Daily Search Summary, Thomas J. Booth.* Malvern, Pennsylvania: SARD-PA.

Sepkovic, D., Haley, N., & Hoffman, D. (1986). Elimination from the body of tobacco products by smokers and passive smokers. *Journal of the American Medical Association, 256*(7), 863.

Shkrum, M., & Ramsay, D. (2007). *Forensic Pathology of Trauma: Common Problems for the Pathologist.* Totowa, NJ: Humana Press.

Shulgin, A. & Shulgin, A. (1991). *PiKHAL [Phenethylamines i Have Known and Loved]: A Chemical Love Story.* Berkeley, CA: Transform Press.

Sim, E., Muskawad, S., Lim, C., Yeo, J., Lim, K., Grignani, R., Durrani, A., Lau, G., & Duran, C. (2003, May). Comparison of human and porcine aortic valves. *Clinical Anatomy, 16*(3), 193–196.

Spitz, W., & Spitz, D. (Eds.) (2006). *Spitz and Fisher's Medicolegal Investigation of Death (4th ed.),* Table XXIII, p. 1222. Springfield, IL: Charles C. Thomas.

Springer, D. (2004, April 30). Dion autopsy doesn't answer all questions. *Winona Daily News.* [Online.] http://www.winonadailynews.com/news/article_58922c83-14d8-5f2c-82fd-3879508942b1.html.

Staff Writer (2000, January 16). Divers to search Lake Michigan for man missing since New Year's. *Chicago Tribune.* [Online.] http://articles.chicagotribune.com/2000-01-16/news/0001160284_1_lake-michigan-divers-search.

Statland, B., & Demas, T. (1980, March). Serum caffeine half-lives. Healthy subjects vs. patients having alcoholic hepatic disease. *American Journal of Clinical Pathology, 73*(3), 390–393.

Steers, J. (2004, April 25). *River Drowning – "Serial Killer or Urban Legend."* Retrieved August 8, 2008, from the La Crosse County Medical Examiner Web site: http://www.co.la-crosse.wi.us/departments/Medical%20Examiner/docs/River%20Drowning.ppt.

Stephany, J. (2008, March). *Report of Autopsy: Ereck Plancher.* Orlando, FL: Office of the Medical Examiner, District Nine.

Swift, B. 2006. The timing of death. In G. Rutty (Ed.), *Essentials of Autopsy Practice: Current Methods and Modern Trends* (pp. 189–214). London, UK: Springer-Verlag London Ltd.

U.S. Army Corps of Engineers (2011), Mississippi River Lock and Dam 7. [Online.] Available: http://www.mvp-wc.usace.army.mil/projects/Lock7.shtml.

Ursano, R., Fullerton, C., Epstein, R., Crowley, B., Vance, K., Kao, T., & Baum, A. (1999, November). Peritraumatic dissociation and posttraumatic stress disorder following motor vehicle accidents. *American Journal of Psychiatry, 156*, 1808–1810.

Usumoto, Y., Sameshima, N., Hikiji, W., Tsuji, A., Kudo, K., Inoue, H., & Ikeda, N. (2009, August 16). Electrolyte analysis of pleural effusion as an indicator of drowning in seawater and freshwater. *Journal of Forensic and Legal Medicine, 16*(6), 321–324.

Utah State University–Logan (2011). COOP Data, Station Name: LOWER ST ANTHONY FALLS, Station ID: 214884, Search Range: 10/31/2002 to 02/27/2003. *GIS Climate Search.* [Online.] Available: http://climate.usurf.usu.edu/products/data.php.

Virginia Polytechnic Institute and State University (2011). *Blood Alcohol Impairment Table for Men.* [Online.] Available: www.alcohol.vt.edu/Students/alcoholEffects/estimatingBAC/index.htm

Vree, T. B., Damsma, J., van den Bogert, A. G., & van der Kleijn, E. (1978). Pharmacokinetics of 4-hydroxybutyric acid in man, rhesus monkey and dog. In R. Frey (Ed.), *Neue Untersuchungen mit Gamma-hydroxibuttersaure* (21–39). Berlin, FRG: Springer.

Wall, M., Johnson, J., Jacob, P., & Benowitz, N. (1988). Cotinine in the serum, saliva, and urine of nonsmokers, passive smokers, and active smokers. *American Journal of Public Health, 78*(6), 699–701.

Wang, S-M., Giang, Y-S., Lu, M-J., & Kuo, T-L. (2006). Determination of gamma-hydroxybutyrate (GHB) in biological specimens by simultaneous extraction and chemical derivatization follwed by GC-MS. *Forensic Science Journal, 5*(1), 41–54.

Wigmore, J.G., & Chow, B.L.C. (2000). Case Report: Detection of Neo-Formation of Ethanol in a Postmortem Blood Sample Using N-Propanol and a Urine Sample. *Canadian Society of Forensic Science Journal*, 33(3), 145–149.

Williams, C., Eng, A., Botvin, G., Hill, P., & Wynder, E. (1979). Validation of students' self-reported cigarette smoking status with plasma cotinine levels. *American Journal of Public Health. 69*(12), 1272–1274.

Wilson, T., & Donato, M. (2000, January 12). Police fear foul play in disappearance. *Chicago Tribune.* [Online.] http://articles.chicagotribune.com/2000-01-12/news/0001120294_1_chicago-police-rush-street-block.

Witten, M., Quan, S., Sobonya. R., & Lemen, R. (1988, January). New developments in the pathogenesis of smoke inhalation-induced pulmonary edema. *The Western Journal of Medicine, 148*(1), 33–36.

Yorulmaz, C., Arican, N., Afacan, I., Dokgoz, H., & Asirdizer, M. (2003, September 9). Pleural effusion in bodies recovered from water. *Forensic Science International, 136*(1–3), 16–21.

Zhu, B., Quan, L., Li, D., Taniguchi, M., Kamikodai, Y., Tsuda, K., Fujita, M., Nishi, K., Tsuji, T., & Maeda, H. (2003, March). Postmortem lung weight in drownings: a comparison with acute asphyxiation and cardiac death. *Legal Medicine (Tokyo), 5*(1), 20–26.

Zuckerman, G. B. & Conway, E.E., Jr. (1993, May). Pulmonary complications following tricyclic antidepressant overdose in an adolescent. *The Annals of Pharmacotherapy, 27*(5), 572–574.

Bibliography

Official Documents Associated with the Case Studies

Chapter 2: McNeil

de Roux, S. (1997, April 8). *Report of Autopsy* (M.E. Case #K97-1668). New York, NY: Office of Chief Medical Examiner, City of New York.

de Roux, S. (1997, April 16). *Medical Certificate of Death*. New York, NY: Office of Chief Medical Examiner, City of New York.

Stajic, M. (1997, April 14). *Toxicology Laboratory* (Lab No. 1631/97, M.E. Case No. K97-1668). New York, NY: Office of Chief Medical Examiner, City of New York.

Chapter 3: Andrews

Macajoux, M. (1998, February 12). *Report of Autopsy* (M.E. Case #K98-777). New York, NY: Office of Chief Medical Examiner, City of New York.

McGee, M. (1998, February 12). *Toxicology Laboratory* (Lab No. 763/98, M.E. Case No. K98-777). New York, NY: Office of Chief Medical Examiner, City of New York.

Chapter 4: Falcon

National Medical Services (NMS). (2004, December 6). *Toxicology Report* (Workorder: 04296491, Patient ID: MS-04-548 10472-U-1). Willow Grove, PA: NMS.

Sikirica, M. (2005, February 28). *Final Autopsy Report* (Case #MS-04-548, OCA-04-222). Albany, NY: Forensic Medical Services.

Swift, T. (2004, December 9). *Forensic Toxicology Laboratory* (Laboratory Case Number 10472). Albany, NY: Albany Medical Center.

Chapter 5: Smith

American Institute of Toxicology Laboratories (AIT). (2009, May 27). *Toxicology Report* (Laboratory Case Number: 897834). Indianapolis, IN: AIT.

American Institute of Toxicology Laboratories (AIT). (2011, May 31). *Toxicology Report* (Laboratory Case Number: 897834). Indianapolis, IN: AIT.

American Institute of Toxicology Laboratories (AIT). (2012, June 4). *Toxicology Report* (Laboratory Case Number: 897834). Indianapolis, IN: AIT.

Hoog, A. (2010, June 8). *Forensics Media Analysis Preliminary Report: Analysis of iPhone* (Case Number: msth-001). Oak Park, IL: viaForensics.

Kohr, R. (2009, May 9). *Autopsy Report* (No. NC09-100). Terre Haute, IN: Department of Pathology, Terre Haute Regional Hospital.

Mast, J. (2009, May 12). *[Forensic Odontology Report.]* Terre Haute, IN: Mast Family Dentistry.

Chapter 6: Welzien

Kim, Y. (2000, March 18). *Autopsy Report* (Autopsy No. A-092-00). Crown Point, IN: Office of the Lake County Coroner.

Melyon, D. (2000, April 27). *Certificate of Death* (Brian R. Welzien). Crown Point, IN: Office of the Lake County Coroner.

Philpot, T. (2000, April 28). *Coroner's Verdict* (Autopsy #A-092-00). Crown Point, IN: Office of the Lake County Coroner.

Regional Laboratory Facility (2000, March 21). *Toxicology Final Report* (Patient ID: 092-2000). Wood Dale, IL: Quest Diagnostics.

Chapter 7: Jenkins

Jay, R. (2003, February 27). [Forensic Photographer's Report]. Minneapolis, MN: Crime Laboratory, Hennepin County Sheriff's Office.

Rivera, R. (2003, May 6). *Autopsy Report* (ME No. 03-0562). Minneapolis, MN: Hennepin County Medical Examiner's Office.

Chapter 8: Brinson

Abbott Northwestern Hospital Laboratory (2009, May 7). *Special Studies Technical Report – Final Report* (Case#:T09-729). Minneapolis, MN: Allina Medical Laboratories.

Amatuzio, J. (2009, August 13). *Medical Examiner's Final Summary* (Case # 02-09-0379). Ramsey, MN: Midwest Medical Examiner's Office.

Amatuzio, J. (2009, July 29). *Final Autopsy Report* (Case # 02-09-0379). Ramsey, MN: Midwest Medical Examiner's Office.

Clinical Laboratory P4 (2009, June 30). *Computer-Generated Facsimile Laboratory Report* (Patient ID No. T9676894). Minneapolis, MN: HCMC.

Department of Laboratory Medicine and Pathology (2009, June 1). [Toxicology Report] (HCMC MRN: X393789). Minneapolis, MN: Hennepin County Medical Center (HCMC).

Department of Laboratory Medicine and Pathology (2009, May 4). [Toxicology Report] (HCMC MRN: X393789). Minneapolis, MN: HCMC.

Department of Laboratory Medicine and Pathology (2009, May 9). [Toxicology Report] (HCMC MRN: X393789). Minneapolis, MN: HCMC.

Department of Laboratory Medicine and Pathology (2009, May 11). [Toxicology Report] (HCMC MRN: X393789). Minneapolis, MN: HCMC.

Department of Laboratory Medicine and Pathology (2009, May 13). [Toxicology Report] (HCMC MRN: X393789). Minneapolis, MN: HCMC.

Department of Laboratory Medicine and Pathology (2009, May 20). [Toxicology Report] (HCMC MRN: X393789). Minneapolis, MN: HCMC.

Department of Laboratory Medicine and Pathology (2009, June 30). [Toxicology Report] (HCMC MRN: X393789). Minneapolis, MN: HCMC.

National Medical Services (NMS). (2009, June 22). *Supplemental Report* (Workorder: 09113709, Patient ID: 02-09-0379 X3937789). Willow Grove, PA: NMS.

National Medical Services (NMS). (2009, May 29). *Toxicology Report* (Workorder: 09113709, Patient ID: 02-09-0379 X3937789). Willow Grove, PA: NMS.

Chapter 9: Geib

Gunaga, K. (2005, July 12). *Post-Mortem Drug Screen* (A-05-1374). Lansing, MI: Pathology Department, Sparrow Hospital.

Hunter, B. (2005, September 20). *Forensic Autopsy Report* (Case: SHA-05-01374). Lansing, MI: Sparrow Regional Laboratories, Sparrow Health System.

Chapter 10: Booth

Delaware County Medical Examiner (DCME) (2008, February 3). *Investigator's Report* [Irene Lafore]. Lima, Pennsylvania: Office of the Medical Examiner, County of Delaware.

Hellman, F. (2008, February 4). *Findings of the Medical Examiner* (OME No. 2008-0117). Lima, PA: Office of the Medical Examiner, County of Delaware.

Hellman, F. (2008, August 5). *Postmortem Report* (OME No. 2008-0117). Lima, PA: Office of the Medical Examiner, County of Delaware.

Kichtenwalner, M. (2008, March 10). *Toxicology Report* (Accession No: 08016965, Control No: 164255). Warminster, PA: DrugScan.

Chapter 11: Fortney

No autopsy report was generated since he survived, and no toxicology tests for drugs of abuse were performed.

Chapter 12: Kapfer

Clinical Laboratories (1998, April 8). [Toxicology Report] (Patient ID No: A98-1, Medical Record No: X282706). Minneapolis, MN: Hennepin County Medical Center (HCMC).

Clinical Laboratories (1998, April 9). [Toxicology Report] (Patient ID No: A98-1, Medical Record No: X282706). Minneapolis, MN: Hennepin County Medical Center (HCMC).

National Medical Services (NMS). (1998, May 9). *Analysis Report* (Control # 875977, Patient ID: X282706). Willow Grove, PA: NMS.

Poellinger, M. (1998, April 6). *Minnesota Regional Coroner's Office Investigative Report* (Case No. A98-001). Hastings, MN: Minnesota Regional Coroner's Office, Regina Medical Center.

Regina Medical Center Laboratory (1998, April 13). [Toxicology Report] (Patient ID No: A98-1). Hastings, MN: Regina Medical Center.

Regina Medical Center Laboratory (1998, June 2). [Toxicology Report] (Patient ID No: A98-1). Hastings, MN: Regina Medical Center.

Steers, J. (1998, June 12). *Final Ruling* (Nathan A. Kapfer). La Crosse, WI: Office of the Medical Examiner, County of La Crosse.

Thomas, L. (1998, April 7). *Pathology Report* (ACC NO: A98-1). Hastings, MN: Minnesota Regional Coroner's Office, Regina Medical Center.

Chapter 13: Geesey

Clinical Toxicology Laboratory (1999, July 14). [Toxicology Report] (Case No: A99-12). Minneapolis, MN: Hennepin County Medical Center (HCMC).

Department of Laboratory Medicine and Pathology (1999, July 7). [Toxicology Report] (HCMC MRN: X345792). Minneapolis, MN: Hennepin County Medical Center (HCMC).

National Medical Services (NMS). (1999, June 16). *Final Report* (Patient ID: A99-12 X282706). Willow Grove, PA: NMS.

Steers, J. (1999, July 20). *Final Ruling* (Jeffrey Geesey). La Crosse, WI: Office of the Medical Examiner, County of La Crosse.

Thomas, L. (1999, May 24). *Autopsy Report* (ACC NO: A99-12). Hastings, MN: Minnesota Regional Coroner's Office, Regina Medical Center.

Chapter 14: Dion

Regina Medical Center Laboratory (2004, April 15). [Toxicology Report] (Patient ID No: A04-9). Hastings, MN: Regina Medical Center.

Steers, J. (2004). *Final Ruling* (Jared Dion). La Crosse, WI: Office of the Medical Examiner, County of La Crosse. [Reprinted facsimile copy dated May 11, 2009].

Steers, J. (2004). [Investigative Report] (Case No: 04-073). La Crosse, WI: Office of the Medical Examiner, County of La Crosse. [Reprinted facsimile copy dated May 11, 2009].

Thomas, L. (2004, April 15). *Clothing/Property Form* (Case No: A04-9). Hastings, MN: Minnesota Regional Coroner's Office, Regina Medical Center.

Thomas, L. (2004, April 21). *Autopsy Report* (ACC NO: A04-09). Hastings, MN: Minnesota Regional Coroner's Office, Regina Medical Center.

Chapter 15: Homan

Regina Medical Center Laboratory (2006, October 2). [Toxicology Report] (Patient ID No: A06-24). Hastings, MN: Regina Medical Center.

Regina Medical Center Laboratory (2006, October 19). [Toxicology Report] (Patient ID No: A06-24). Hastings, MN: Regina Medical Center.

Regina Medical Center Laboratory (2006, October 23). [Toxicology Report] (Patient ID No: A06-24). Hastings, MN: Regina Medical Center.

Regional Laboratory Facility (2006, October 18). *Final Report* [Gamma Hydroxybutyric Acid] (Patient ID: Lucas Homan A06-24). Wood Dale, IL: Quest Diagnostics.

Regional Laboratory Facility (2006, October 19). *Final Report* [Chloroform] (Patient ID: Lucas Homan A06-24). Wood Dale, IL: Quest Diagnostics.

Steers, J. (2006, October 4). *News Release* (Lucas Homan). La Crosse, WI: Office of the Medical Examiner, County of La Crosse.

Steers, J. (2006, October 30). *News Release* (Lucas Homan). La Crosse, WI: Office of the Medical Examiner, County of La Crosse.

Steers, J. (2004). *Death Investigation Report* (Case No: 06-470087). La Crosse, WI: Office of the Medical Examiner, County of La Crosse.

Thomas, L. (2006, October 2). *Clothing/Property Form* (Case No: A06-24). Hastings, MN: Minnesota Regional Coroner's Office, Regina Medical Center.

Thomas, L. (2006, October 2). *Internal & Biological Evidence* (Case No: A06-24). Hastings, MN: Minnesota Regional Coroner's Office, Regina Medical Center.

Thomas, L. (2006, October 24). *Autopsy Report* (ACC NO: A06-24). Hastings, MN: Minnesota Regional Medical Examiner's Office, Regina Medical Center.

Thomas, L. (2004, October 24). [Letter to John Steers] (Lucas Homan). Hastings, MN: Minnesota Regional Medical Examiner's Office, Regina Medical Center.

Appendix A: Suggested Discussion Questions

Finding answers to these questions is an important step in understanding a crime (i.e., the victimization), the victim, and the potential offender.

Know the Victim

1. What were the physical characteristics of the victim: biological sex, age (date of birth), height, weight, body mass index, hair color, eye color, glasses, tattoos, and scars?
2. How would you describe the locations and associated behaviors of the victim (residence, place of employment and duties, locales of recreation, last seen or last known location, and the body recovery site)?
3. How do others describe the victim's thinking and acting on a regular basis: psychological makeup, social behavior, religious or spiritual beliefs?
4. How do others describe the victim's thinking and acting during the week prior to, and at the time of, the victimization: psychological makeup, social behavior, religious or spiritual beliefs?

Establish a Chronological Understanding of the Associated Events

5. What were the circumstances at the time of the victimization and who was involved: activities and events, dates and times, all associated locations and persons?
6. Was the victimization witnessed, by whom, and was a statement recorded?
7. If the victimization was not witnessed, then when did the victim go missing? This can be based on either (a) when someone saw the victim or he/she was recorded on a business' closed-circuit camera (LSEN, last seen), or (b) when someone personally spoke to the victim or received a voice mail (LHRD, last heard). Text messages and pings do not count since someone besides the victim may have sent them.
8. Who reported the victim missing and why did that person believe this to be strange?
9. What were the circumstances of any personal property that was found: dates and times, locations, who found it, how was it collected, and what happened to it?
10. Were any searches and interviews conducted: dates and times, all locations, associated persons or agencies, results and how they were used?

Important Points and Periods in Time

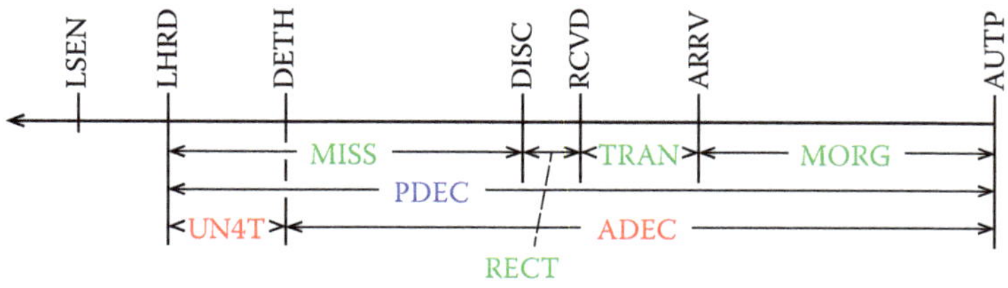

LSEN = Time the victim was last seen by another person or recorded on a camera.
LHRD = Time the victim's voice was last heard via personal phone call or voice mail.
DISC = Time the victim's body was first discovered.
RCVD = Time the victim's body was recovered and placed into a body bag.
ARRV = Time the victim's body arrived at the morgue.
AUTP = Time the autopsy started.
MISS = The amount of time since the victim was last seen or heard.
RECT = The amount of time between the body's discovery and recovery.
TRAN = The amount of time between recovery and the body's arrival at the morgue.
MORG = The amount of time between arrival at the morgue and start of the autopsy.
PDEC = The amount of time that the victim was presumed to be deceased.
DETH = Estimated time of death based on assessment of postmortem artifacts.
ADEC = The amount of time that the victim was estimated to be deceased.
UN4T = The amount of unaccounted-for time. (Where was the victim?)

11. What were the circumstances surrounding the body's discovery (DISC): who found it, location, associated persons or agencies, when was it first seen?
12. How much time (MISS) had elapsed from when the victim was LSEN or LHRD to DISC?
13. What were the circumstances surrounding the body's recovery (RCVD): who found it, location, associated persons or agencies, how and when it was recovered and placed into a body bag?
14. How much time (RECT) had elapsed from when the victim was DISC to RCVD?
15. How was the body transported, by whom, and under what environmental conditions?
16. When did the body arrive at the morgue (ARRV) and how long did it take to get from the recovery site to the morgue's cooler (TRAN)?
17. When was the autopsy conducted (AUTP) and how much time (MORG) has passed between when the victim's body arrived at the morgue and it was autopsied?
18. How long was the victim presumed to be deceased (PDEC); in other words, how much time had elapsed from when the victim was LSEN or LHRD to when the body was autopsied?

Identify Potentially Influential Environmental Factors

19. Were any environmental samples taken at the recovery site for possible use in later tests: water, grass, leaves, twigs, seeds or fruit, soil from the edge of the water as well as from the bottom, and insects?
20. What were the weather and environmental conditions during the time that the victim was missing: air and water temperatures, and precipitation?

Examine the Recovery and Autopsy Report and Photographs

21. Was a description of the body recorded at the time of recovery? If so, what was the condition of the postmortem artifacts at that time: rigor mortis, livor mortis, ocular changes, decomposition and maceration, trauma and injuries?
22. When was the autopsy (date and time) conducted, who performed it, and who was in attendance?
23. What bodily fluids, tissues, and other matter in or on the body were secured as specimens?
24. What tests were performed on bodily fluids, tissues, and other matter in or on the body; were those specimens compared to environmental samples taken at the body recovery site?
25. What were the results of those tests and how did investigators use them?

Critically Analyze All Variables

26. Was the overall extent of degradation of the body consistent with the weather and environmental conditions, as well as the length of time that the victim had been missing and presumed deceased (PDEC)?
27. Was a description of the body recorded at the time of recovery? If so, what was the condition of the postmortem artifacts at that time and then at autopsy? Did they change, how, and to what extent: rigor mortis, livor mortis, ocular changes, decomposition and maceration, trauma and injuries?
28. Does the condition of the postmortem artifacts suggest to you a later time of death (DETH)?
29. If you surmise a possible later time of death (DETH), then what is the estimated length of time that the victim has been missing and actually deceased (ADEC), as well as the period of unaccounted-for time (UN4T)?
30. What was the official cause of death?
31. What was the official manner of death: undetermined, natural, accident, suicide, or homicide?
32. Do you agree with the official cause and manner of death, and if not, what do you think they should be and why?

Assess and Recommend

33. What additional steps, if any, would you have taken then or now relative to investigating this young man's death?
34. What is your opinion of the quality and quantity of investigation into the victim's death?

Appendix B: Anatomical Descriptors – Body

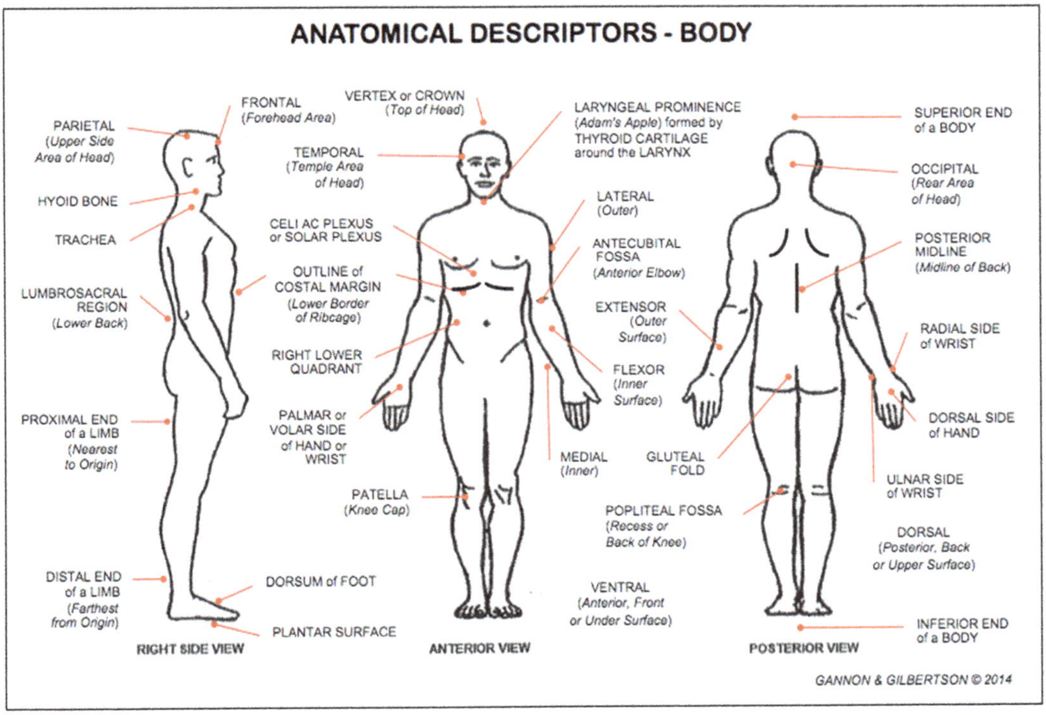

Appendix C: Anatomical Descriptors – Hand

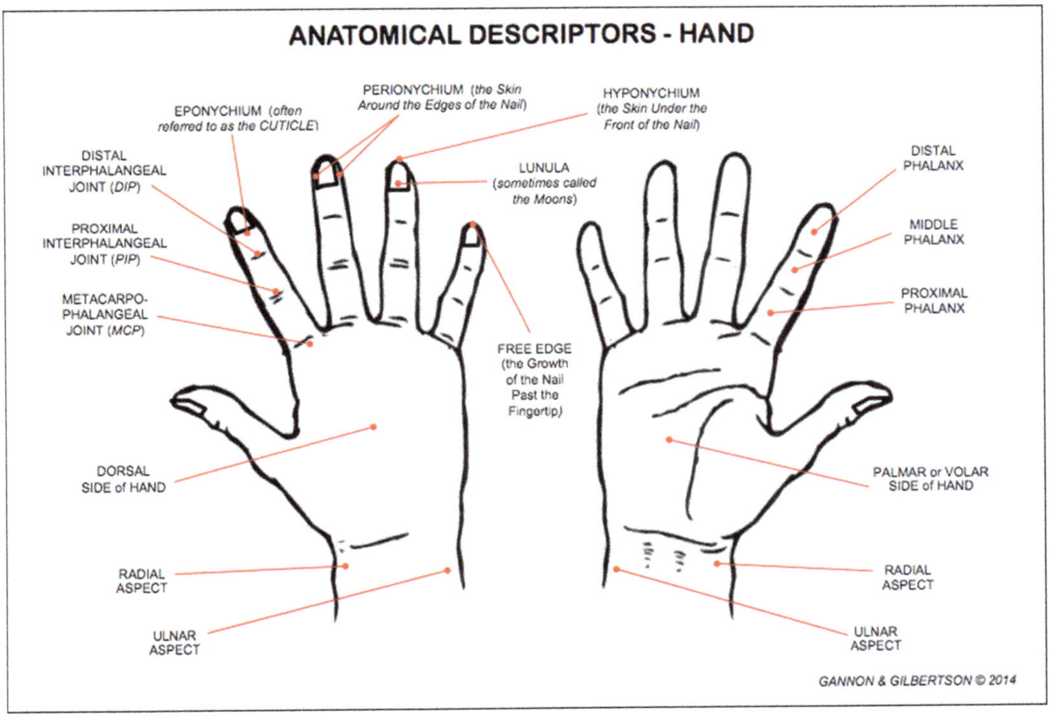

Appendix D: Postmortem Artifacts on Land

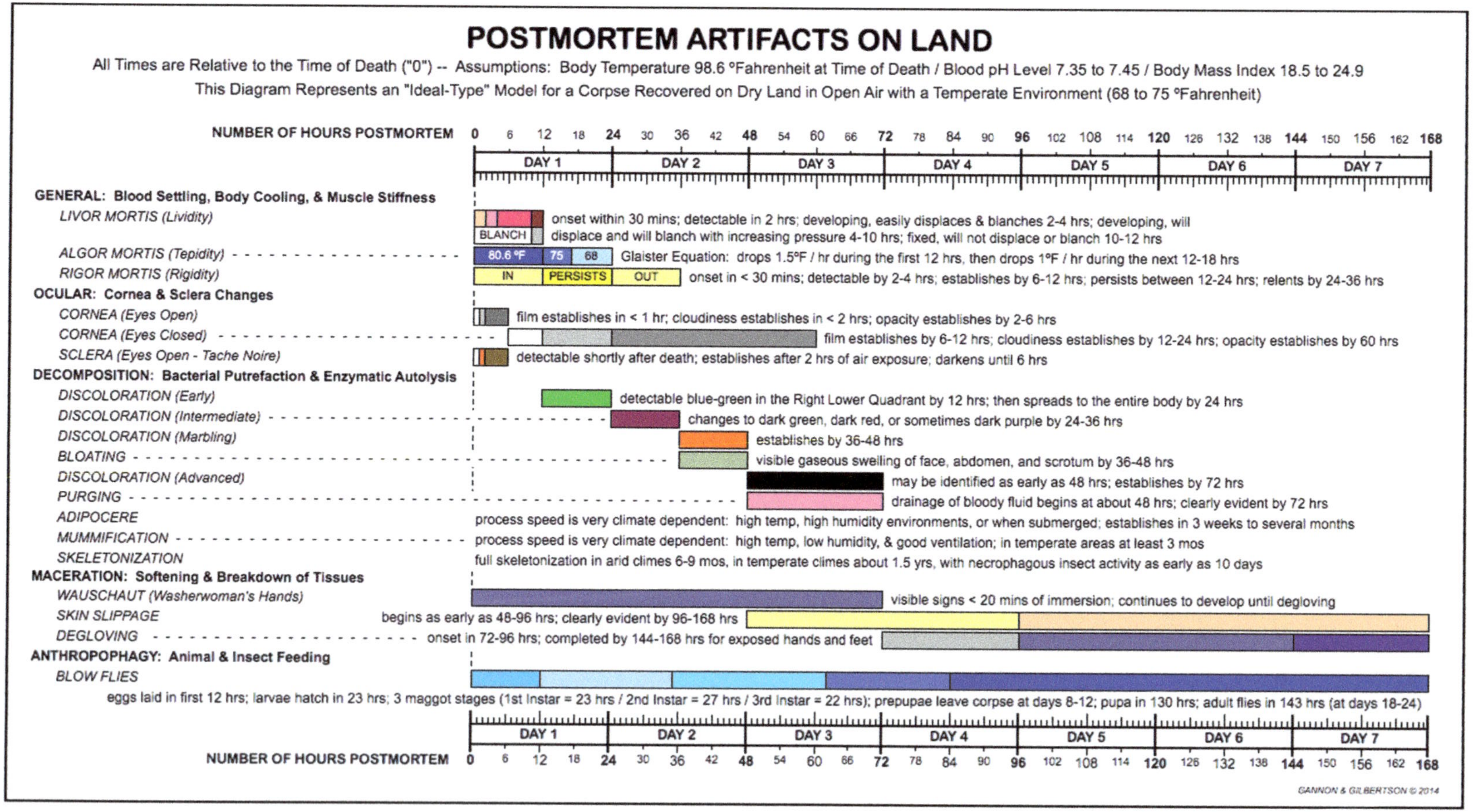
POSTMORTEM ARTIFACTS ON LAND
All Times are Relative to the Time of Death ("0") -- Assumptions: Body Temperature 98.6 °Fahrenheit at Time of Death / Blood pH Level 7.35 to 7.45 / Body Mass Index 18.5 to 24.9
This Diagram Represents an "Ideal-Type" Model for a Corpse Recovered on Dry Land in Open Air with a Temperate Environment (68 to 75 °Fahrenheit)
NUMBER OF HOURS POSTMORTEM
0 6 12 18 24 30 36 42 48 54 60 66 72 78 84 90 96 102 108 114 120 126 132 138 144 150 156 162 168
DAY 1 DAY 2 DAY 3 DAY 4 DAY 5 DAY 6 DAY 7
GENERAL: Blood Settling, Body Cooling, & Muscle Stiffness
LIVOR MORTIS (Lividity)
BLANCH
onset within 30 mins; detectable in 2 hrs; developing, easily displaces & blanches 2-4 hrs; developing, will displace and will blanch with increasing pressure 4-10 hrs; fixed, will not displace or blanch 10-12 hrs
ALGOR MORTIS (Tepidity)
80.6 °F 75 68
Glaister Equation: drops 1.5°F / hr during the first 12 hrs, then drops 1°F / hr during the next 12-18 hrs
RIGOR MORTIS (Rigidity)
IN PERSISTS OUT
onset in < 30 mins; detectable by 2-4 hrs; establishes by 6-12 hrs; persists between 12-24 hrs; relents by 24-36 hrs
OCULAR: Cornea & Sclera Changes
CORNEA (Eyes Open)
film establishes in < 1 hr; cloudiness establishes in < 2 hrs; opacity establishes by 2-6 hrs
CORNEA (Eyes Closed)
film establishes by 6-12 hrs; cloudiness establishes by 12-24 hrs; opacity establishes by 60 hrs
SCLERA (Eyes Open - Tache Noire)
detectable shortly after death; establishes after 2 hrs of air exposure; darkens until 6 hrs
DECOMPOSITION: Bacterial Putrefaction & Enzymatic Autolysis
DISCOLORATION (Early)
detectable blue-green in the Right Lower Quadrant by 12 hrs; then spreads to the entire body by 24 hrs
DISCOLORATION (Intermediate)
changes to dark green, dark red, or sometimes dark purple by 24-36 hrs
DISCOLORATION (Marbling)
establishes by 36-48 hrs
BLOATING
visible gaseous swelling of face, abdomen, and scrotum by 36-48 hrs
DISCOLORATION (Advanced)
may be identified as early as 48 hrs; establishes by 72 hrs
PURGING
drainage of bloody fluid begins at about 48 hrs; clearly evident by 72 hrs
ADIPOCERE
process speed is very climate dependent: high temp, high humidity environments, or when submerged; establishes in 3 weeks to several months
MUMMIFICATION
process speed is very climate dependent: high temp, low humidity, & good ventilation; in temperate areas at least 3 mos
SKELETONIZATION
full skeletonization in arid climes 6-9 mos, in temperate climes about 1.5 yrs, with necrophagous insect activity as early as 10 days
MACERATION: Softening & Breakdown of Tissues
WAUSCHAUT (Washerwoman's Hands)
visible signs < 20 mins of immersion; continues to develop until degloving
SKIN SLIPPAGE
begins as early as 48-96 hrs; clearly evident by 96-168 hrs
DEGLOVING
onset in 72-96 hrs; completed by 144-168 hrs for exposed hands and feet
ANTHROPOPHAGY: Animal & Insect Feeding
BLOW FLIES
eggs laid in first 12 hrs; larvae hatch in 23 hrs; 3 maggot stages (1st Instar = 23 hrs / 2nd Instar = 27 hrs / 3rd Instar = 22 hrs); prepupae leave corpse at days 8-12; pupa in 130 hrs; adult flies in 143 hrs (at days 18-24)
DAY 1 DAY 2 DAY 3 DAY 4 DAY 5 DAY 6 DAY 7
NUMBER OF HOURS POSTMORTEM
0 6 12 18 24 30 36 42 48 54 60 66 72 78 84 90 96 102 108 114 120 126 132 138 144 150 156 162 168
GANNON & GILBERTSON © 2014

Appendix E: Victim Profile Operationalization

Note: Blank cells in the database will indicate that an attribute is either unknown, unidentified, undetermined, not recovered, or has not been specified in either news articles, online links, law enforcement reports, search party reports, medical examiner reports, or other sources.

Presented below are the variables and their attributes. Listed in bold letters is the LABEL to be used as a column header in MS Excel or as the variable label in SPSS.

ENTER means there is a distinct set of attributes from which you must select.
LIST means you identify the attribute and enter it in a specified format.
DESCRIBE means you identify the attribute and enter it.

Personal Data

LASTNAME
LIST: Last
FIRSTNAME
LIST: First
FULLNAME
LIST: First Middle Last, Suffix
DOB (*Date of Birth*)
LIST: DAY mm/dd/yyyy (e.g., SUN 08/08/2008)
AGE
LIST: Age
ANCETH (*Ancestry or Ethnicity*)
DESCRIBE: Ancestry, National Origin, or Ethnic Group
LANGUAGE
DESCRIBE: Spoken or Primary Language
RELIGION
DESCRIBE: Identified Religion or Denomination
MARITAL
ENTER: Single, Engaged, Married, Separated, Divorced, or Widowed
JOB
DESCRIBE: Job or Position Title
FINAN (*Financial Status – Extent of Debt*)
ENTER: Severe, Moderate, None, Secure
EMPLOY (*Employment Status*)
ENTER: Unemployed, Sporadic (1-20 hours), Part-time (20-39 hours), Full-time (40 or more hours)

SES (*Socioeconomic Status*)
ENTER: Lower, Middle, or Upper
ACTY (*Activities*)
DESCRIBE: Activities at School, Church, or within the Community
ATTWATER (*Attitude Toward Water*)
ENTER: Fearful, Cautious, At Ease, Reckless
CRIMHIST (*Criminal History*)
DESCRIBE: Complaints, Charges, Convictions, and Sentences

Physical Data

HT (*Height*)
LIST: Inches
WT (*Weight*)
LIST: Pounds
BMI (*Body Mass Index*)
Automatically calculated with the spreadsheet
[(weight) divided by (height squared)] times 703
HAIR
ENTER: Bald, Shaved, Blonde, Red, Brown, or Black
FACIAL
ENTER: None, Stubble (unshaven), Mustache, Goatee, or Beard
EYES
ENTER: Blue, Green, Hazel, Brown, Black, or Mixed (specify)
MARKS (*Tattoos and Scars*)
DESCRIBE: Tattoos and Scars to include location on body
RACE
ENTER: White, Black, Asian, Middle Eastern, Native American

Health Data

TOBACCO
DESCRIBE: Extent of Use Reported by Others
CAFFEINE
DESCRIBE: Extent of Use Reported by Others
ALCOHOL
DESCRIBE: Extent of Use Reported by Others
DRUGUSE
Substance Use
DESCRIBE: Drug and Extent of Use Reported by Others (Recreational Drugs)
MEDHIST (*Physical Medical History*)
DESCRIBE: Reported Illnesses, Conditions, Diseases, Medications
PSYHIST (*Psychological Health History*)
DESCRIBE: Reported Illnesses, Conditions, Diseases, Medications

Scholastic Data

COLLEGE
DESCRIBE: Name of College or University Currently Attending
May be different than the college or university where the drowning took place; report year when graduated
MAJOR
DESCRIBE: Academic Major or Degree Program Area
GPA (*Grade Point Average*)
LIST: to 2 Decimal Places (4.00)
ATHLETICS
DESCRIBE: Primary Sports in which engaged
SCHOLARSHIP
DESCRIBE: Name of Financial Scholarship and purpose (sport, academic, other)
STUDORG
DESCRIBE: Name of Student Organizations in which held membership

Spatial Data

HOMETOWN
LIST: High School, City, ST Zip Code
RESLOC (*Residence Location*)
LIST: Name of Location, Number, Street, City, ST Zip Code
RETLOC (*Return to Location*)
LIST: Name of Location, Number, Street, City, ST Zip Code
LASLOC (*Last Seen Location*)
LIST: Name of Location, Number, Street, City, ST Zip Code
RECLOC (*Recovery Location*)
LIST: Name of Location, Number, Street, City, ST Zip Code

Temporal Data

LASNITE (*Last Seen on the "Night of" Date*)
LIST: DAY mm/dd/yyyy (e.g.,SAT 08/07/2008)
LASTIME (*Last Seen Date and Time*)
LIST: DAY mm/dd/yyyy tttt (e.g., SUN 08/08/2008 1425)
LSTYPE (*Source of Last Seen Time*)
ENTER: Witness or Camera
LASHEARD (*Last Heard Date and Time*)
LIST: DAY mm/dd/yyyy tttt (e.g., SUN 08/08/2008 1425)
LHTYPE (*Source of Last Heard Time*)
ENTER: Voice, Voice-mail, Text Msg, or E-mail
RECTIME (*Recovery Date and Time*)
LIST: DAY mm/dd/yyyy tttt (e.g., SUN 08/08/2008 1425)

Event Data

LASPROP (*Last Seen Property*)
  DESCRIBE: Clothing and Personal Effects at Time of Disappearance
RECPROP (*Recovery Property*)
  DESCRIBE: Clothing and Personal Effects at Time of Body Recovery
ASSOC (*Associates with Him that Night*)
  DESCRIBE: Names and Relationships to Each Other
CIRCUM (*Circumstances and Timeline for that Night*)
  DESCRIBE: Events leading up to disappearance
SUBSTAN (*Substances used that Night*)
  DESCRIBE: Reported Substance Consumed that Night by the Victim
WEATHER
  DESCRIBE: Precipitation and Ground Cover, Air and Water Temperature, Wind
MOON
  DESCRIBE: Phase Name, Percent of Illumination, Moonrise and Moonset
BODYPOS (*Body Position*)
  ENTER: Prone (face-down) or Supine (face-up)
BODTEMP (*Algor Mortis*)
  DESCRIBE: Quote the Medical Examiner's Report
RIGOR (*Rigor Mortis*)
  DESCRIBE: Quote the Medical Examiner's Report
LIVIDITY (*Livor Mortis*)
  DESCRIBE: Quote the Medical Examiner's Report
HANDS (*Washer-Woman's Hands*)
  DESCRIBE: Quote the Medical Examiner's Report
MACER (*Maceration - Skin Slippage)*
  DESCRIBE: Quote the Medical Examiner's Report
PUTRE (*Putrefaction - Decomposition and Marbling*)
  DESCRIBE: Quote the Medical Examiner's Report
TRAUMA (*Trauma to the Body*)
  DESCRIBE: Quote the Medical Examiner's Report
BAC (*Blood Alcohol Concentration*)
  LIST: in mcg/ml to 3 Decimal Places (0.000)
DRUGS
  DESCRIBE: Substances reported to have been found on the body or in the body during the autopsy or during the toxicology screening
MANNER (*Manner of Death*)
  DESCRIBE: Quote the Medical Examiner's Report
CAUSE (*Cause of Death*)
  DESCRIBE: Quote the Medical Examiner's Report
COMMENTS
  DESCRIBE: Write in any additional, complementary, or supplemental information that you may think is relevant; specific examples are: the grandparents' or parents' jobs or position titles; addresses of key people; and evidence of a victim's attitude regarding racial diversity.

Appendix F:
Taxonomy of Drowning Scenarios

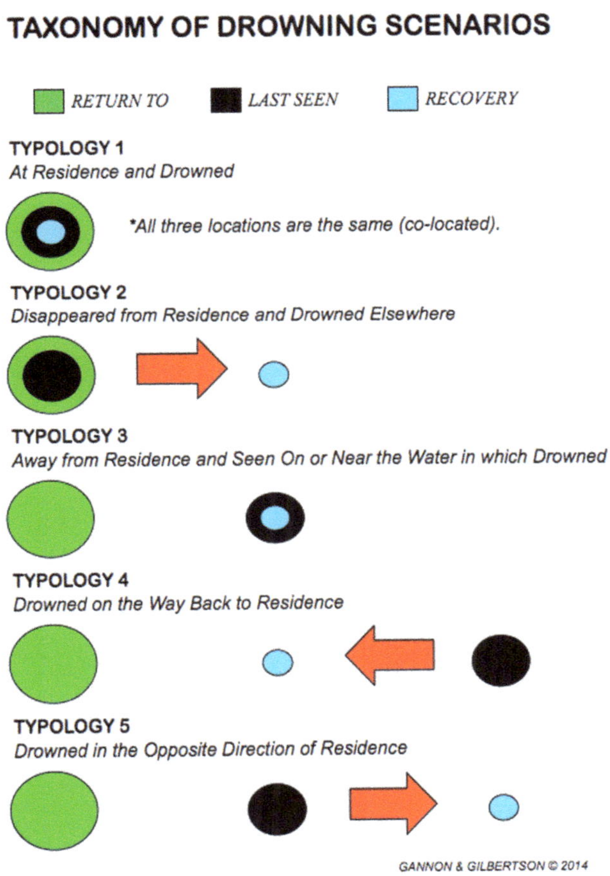

Appendix G: Investigating Linked Cases

Special note: Many people, including both law enforcement and the media, have referred to these crimes as "serial." Although some of the murders may have been committed by the same individuals within the same criminal cells, these crimes are neither serial, spree or mass homicides when one adheres to strict definitions established by the Federal Bureau of Investigation. They should, therefore, be referred to as "The Linked Smiley Face Homicides."

Step 1: Examine individual cases to determine which ones are actually the crime of interest.
Step 2: Using criminological and victimological variables, and not supposed commonalities, identify which cases are: (a) potentially linked crimes, or (b) separate crimes.

Step 1: Case Examination

1. HUMAN AND CANINE SEARCHES
   Locations, Equipment, and Results.
2. STATUS AND LOCATION OF PERSONAL PROPERTY
   Wallets, Hats, Clothing, Vehicles, and Cell Phones.
3. SCENARIO AND EVENTS TIMELINE
   Actors, Events, and Places Relative to Time.
4. LOCATION OF THE BODY
   Identified or Determined Point of Entry and Recovery.
5. CONDITION OF THE BODY
   Rigor Mortis, Masceration, Putrefaction and Marbling, Trauma, and Insects.
6. POSITION OF THE BODY
   Liver Mortis, Head Position, and Posing.
7. TOXICOLOGY
   Alcohol and Drug Screening.

Step 2: Case Linkage

1. VICTIMOLOGICAL
   Patterns within the victims' demographics.
2. SPATIAL
   Patterns of the events across the United States.
   Patterns of the events relative to manmade structures and geographic features.

3. TEMPORAL
   Patterns of the events relative to time.
4. EVIDENTIARY
   Patterns among the case examination evidence.
5. SYMBOLIC
   Patterns among the significant symbols left at or near the scene of the events.
6. TESTIMONIAL
   Patterns of corroboration among confidential informants' statements.

Appendix H: Recommended Protocols for Missing Person Investigations

While Still Missing

Establish Background

1. Personal Data: Full name, date of birth, height, weight, facial description (light skinned, beard, mustache, goatee), hair color and style, eye color, tattoos, birthmarks and scars, medical history, birth defects and physical disability, brain injury/trauma or cognitive disability.
2. Personal Property: Complete nomenclatures (e.g., sizes, colors, brand names, models, numbers) for clothing and shoes worn at the time, jewelry, cell phone, watch, glasses, iPod, iPad, wallet and money.
3. Social History: City of birth, birth order in family, race and ethnic background, marital status, close male and female friends, sexual orientation and level of activity, source and level of income, substance use (i.e., caffeine, tobacco, alcohol, and drugs), medications, any history of disappearing, wandering off, or attempted suicide, always with people or liked to be alone.
4. Metaphysical Qualities: Religious or spiritual beliefs (e.g., atheist, monotheist or polytheist, afterlife and consequences), distinct or unique philosophies and ideologies or other beliefs that may affect behavior.
5. Routine Activities: Normal daily events, dates, and times, all associated persons and addresses (e.g., personal, parents, significant other, friends, associates, and teachers), work addresses, places of entertainment and grocery shopping, all routes known or surmised to be used by the victim to and from these locations, normal modes of transportation used to and from locations.

Preliminary Investigation

1. Everyone the missing person was with that evening needs to be interviewed multiple times by a private investigator. Unfortunately, police will likely stop after one cursory interview. We have only ever seen a couple cases where a body was found in the water and police talked to everyone more than once. Sadly, it will be presumed to be an accidental drowning and handled as such – whether it is or not. Which, unfortunately, brings me to another point. From this time forward, always carry a digital recorder with you and record all conversations with police,

the Medical Examiner, and individuals with potential info on the case. They cost about $45–60.

2. Compile the names, addresses, and telephone numbers of all persons, agencies/businesses, and locations with whom the missing person had contact within the past 48 hours.
3. Catalog all events and actions of the missing person beginning 48 hours prior to, and following, disappearance.
4. Record the date, time, and address of where the missing person was last physically seen and known to be (by a human or a security camera) or where the missing person was assumed to be (said he was there or cell phone ping indicates possible presence).
5. Interview friends and witnesses to determine the missing person's plans (e.g., to go back to the dorm, or to go to an after-hours party).
6. Identify the address of the location to where the missing person was to return at that time or the location to which he/she was supposed to be headed.
7. Ask the police to contact the National Compliance Center for the cellular service provider and have them "ping" the phone, or tell you which towers the last 5 calls went through.
8. Discern the missing person's state of mind during the past 3 months: stable or variable, excited about life or depressed.
9. Assess the nature and extent of possible substance or chemical impairment and source.

Initial Search

1. Dogs can retrace a person's steps weeks and sometimes months later. Use both tracking dogs and cadaver dogs. Both should be used along the entire area where the missing person was last seen or suspected to have been. If the dogs lose the scent, then take them on a walk for several blocks – we have seen dogs re-acquire a scent.
2. Search locations where the missing person routinely went or should have been (e.g., dorm room, certain campus buildings and classrooms, workplace, hang-outs, and friends' residences)
3. Search locations where the missing person may have been within the previous 48 hours due to specific current activities that he/she was not routinely involved in, but had recently become involved in (e.g., rally for a political candidate, special committee meeting, or a date).
4. Search the immediate area out to 6 blocks (e.g., active and abandoned businesses and warehouses, residential structures and garages, public buildings, parks and over-grown areas, ditches and culverts, and storm drains).
5. Check all persons with whom the missing person communicated (e.g., family, significant others, friends, classmates, professors, and co-workers).
6. Check all means (e.g., cell phone, smart phone, iPad, netbook, laptop, or home personal computer) and forms (e.g. Twitter, texting, Skype, facebook, and MySpace) of social communication known to be used by the missing person.
7. Canvass the area looking personal property, that may or is known to belong to the missing person.

8. Canvass the area looking for foot, shoe, and tire prints or tracks, and for any type of ground disturbance (loose gravel, scattered rocks, or dirt).
9. Canvass the area noting what is supposed to be there and is missing, as well as what is there that is not normally there. Record the license plates of vehicles in the area and all activity. Specifically record anything that does not feel right or is clearly suspicious.
10. Look for a potential water entry spot (usually in the opposite direction of known or presumed travel, or discovered evidence), and then collect samples of water, plants and leaves, insects, and soil (in both directions for 300 yards at 100 yard intervals). In the event that the missing person is found deceased, these will be examined for chemical content/make-up, and for comparison with material found on and in the body during the autopsy.
11. Photograph all markings, taggings or graffiti, as well as anything that appears to more abnormal, altered, or out of place.
12. Immediately double check the entire area between where he was last seen and where he was recovered for videos at ATMs, banks, gas stations, convenience stores, businesses and so forth. He may have walked past an active security camera and left his image there telling you which way he went.

Subsequent Searches

1. Organize the searches (i.e., land, air, and water) for the victim using a grid system.
2. Keep a record for each search: map of searched area, date and start-end times, type of search assets used (e.g., bloodhound, cadaver dog, airborne or handheld FLIR), record the printed or typed names of search party personnel (photo ID when possible) and the areas where they participated, remarks about events.
3. Immediately bring in bloodhounds to scent the area before cross-contamination can occur.

   Attempt to keep those persons who recently had contact with the victim out of the area to prevent the possibility of a transfer scent.
4. If a scent is recovered, then bring in a second dog for independent corroboration.
5. Follow up with a cadaver dog in areas where the bloodhound indicted a significant hit.
6. Have investigator stay back and watch the scene.
7. Use human foot searches after K-9 searches, and photograph the search parties in action.
8. Inform the search party members of what to do when they find potential evidence (i.e., step back away from it, safe-guard it, do not touch it, and call for assistance from the person in charge of the search).
9. Specifically photograph nonparticipating onlookers, and ID acutely curious bystanders.
10. Photograph the area to be search before it is searched (establishing shot), then follow forensic photography protocols for evidence.
11. Contact the National Compliance Center for the cellular service provider and get the cell phone records: typical and recent calls, voicemail, text messages, emails, picture transmissions, address book, include tower and GPS data.

If Found Deceased

During The Body Recovery

1. Photograph and/or video-record the scene extensively, specifically the body, the recovery team, and the recovery process.
2. Keep a record of the recovery event: map of area, date and start-end times, type of search assets used (e.g., dive team, grappling hook, ropes, back boards or floatation devices, or boats), names of recovery party personnel (photo ID when necessary) and areas they were participated, remarks about events.
3. Photograph nonparticipating onlookers and ID acutely curious bystanders.
4. Ask them to place the body in the body bag where it is found (e.g., on the bottom or floating) and then recover it to a boat or shoreline. Case law demonstrates that evidence does not always wash away and will remain stuck to the clothing or body. Cases have been solved as a result of finding trace evidence on a body recovered from water.
5. Take samples around the body of water, plants and leaves, insects, and soil. These will be examined for chemical content/make-up, and for comparison with material found on and in the body during the autopsy.
   - If found on the bottom, then collect samples from under the body and along the nearest shoreline.
   - If found floating in a river but not bloated, then take samples back upstream for 300 yards at 100 yard intervals.
   - If found floating in a lake, then take samples along the nearest shoreline for 300 yards in both directions at 100 yard intervals.
6. Determine the path the body took to get to that location by immediately bringing in bloodhounds to scent the area before cross-contamination can occur. Attempt to keep those persons who had contact with the victim out of the area to prevent the formation of a transfer scent.
5. If a scent is recovered, then bring in a second dog for independent corroboration.
6. Follow up with a cadaver dog in areas where the bloodhound indicted a significant hit.
7. Have investigator stay back and watch the scene.
8. Use human foot searches after K-9 searches, and photograph the search parties in action.

Inform the search party members of what to do when they find potential evidence (i.e., step back away from it, safe-guard it, do not touch it, and call for assistance from the person in charge of the search).

Death Investigation

1. Re-interview everyone: friends, witnesses, bartenders, waitresses, bouncers, bar owners, other patrons, taxi and bus drivers, first responders, and police.
2. Make sure thorough autopsy is done on the victim by the Pathologist, Coroner, or Medical Examiner, to include all forensic autopsy photographs (i.e., a complete set of photos of the victim's hands, feet, legs, arms, neck, face, torso, back, scrotum,

abdomen, and so forth), look for needle marks on the victim, check for subcutaneous bruising.

3. Analyze all fluids found in the lungs and stomach. Medical Examiners seldom, if ever, preserve a sample and test the fluids from the lungs and stomach. If on the odd chance that they did, then have the samples tested to see whether they match the water samples you took earlier, as well as with water samples from where his body was recovered. The fluids samples from the lungs and stomach should not contain tap water chemicals (e.g., fluoride and chlorine).
4. Do additional toxicological testing. This item is perhaps the most important step that you can cause to happen right away as part of the autopsy. Did the Medical Examiner preserve any blood or tissue samples? They routinely do and keep them for a short time after the autopsy. These can be very valuable for gaining a deeper understanding of the victim's death and the circumstances of that evening. Standard "drug screen" tests that are done at autopsies only tell you whether or not a drug is present, and they often have a cut-off value. If the drug is present but it does not reach the cut-off, then its presence is reported as negative. That is why we always request the tests that determine "quantitation" (precise levels of substances). We always request quantitation tests for the following chemicals.
   - Test the blood and liver tissue sample for all alcohols (ethanol, methanol, isopropanol, n-propanol, n-butanol, and acetone) – which tells us a lot about the stage of the decomposition process, the extent of drinking, and any potential introduction of another drug.
   - Test the liver tissue sample for GHB, ketamine, and Rohypnol – which are the favorite date rape drugs used for abducting someone and walking him/her away from friends. Make sure the lab tests for GHB and its metabolites (Like GBL) in order to get a more accurate reading.
   - Test the blood for nicotine and cotinine (a nicotine metabolite) – if the person was a smoker, this will tell us how long it was since the last cigarette.
5. Even if the cell phone was underwater, do not neglect it as a piece of potential evidence. Cell phone signals and tower coverage can reach out as far as 10 miles in many cases. Each cell tower typically has three sides. A ping off a tower does not mean that the person was near that tower. A ping only means that that phone was closer to that tower than it was to another tower. Furthermore, it does not mean that the owner of the cell phone was near that tower either, since someone else may have been in possession of the phone. The owner could have been miles away. You can take the cell phone to a specialized company. They may be able to recover GPS data from it related to the last phone calls and text messages. This can be somewhat expensive, so call them first and discuss it with them. Several cell phone data recovery or repair companies can be found on the Internet. Many police departments and sheriff's offices have trained specialists as well.
6. The Medical Examiner should have taken a set of photos. We advise that you not personally look at the recovery or autopsy photos. These are not the images that you want in your memory. If you would like us – or anyone else – to look at any photos, then that is up to you. We would tactfully describe our findings to you. If the photos are not free from the Medical Examiner, then do not ask for all of them. That can be outrageously expensive (like $400). You only need a few photos and we can provide you with a short list of 20 or so.

7. Talk to the people who recovered the victim's body and find out which way he was laying: face-down or face-up. Ask them whether they could tell if the victim was still in rigor at recovery. Ask them whether they noticed anything unusual during the recovery relative to events and conditions, and so forth.

Index

A

B

H

For Product Safety Concerns and Information please contact our EU
representative GPSR@taylorandfrancis.com
Taylor & Francis Verlag GmbH, Kaufingerstraße 24, 80331 München, Germany

www.ingramcontent.com/pod-product-compliance
Ingram Content Group UK Ltd.
Pitfield, Milton Keynes, MK11 3LW, UK
UKHW050800180926
475701UK00008B/1154
* 9 7 8 0 3 6 7 6 5 5 9 3 8 *